Gonville & Caius College
The Statutes of the Founders

Frontispiece: John Caius, by an unknown artist, in the Panelled Combination Room.

Gonville & Caius College
The Statutes of the Founders

Michael Prichard

With assistance and contributions from

Christopher Brooke
and
Richard Duncan-Jones

THE BOYDELL PRESS

First published 2017
The Boydell Press, Woodbridge

ISBN 978 1 78327 268 6

The Boydell Press is an imprint of Boydell & Brewer Ltd
PO Box 9, Woodbridge, Suffolk IP12 3DF, UK
and of Boydell & Brewer Inc.
668 Mt Hope Avenue, Rochester, NY 14620–2731, USA
website: www.boydellandbrewer.com

A CIP catalogue record for this book is available
from the British Library

This publication is printed on acid-free paper

Typeset by BBR Design, Sheffield

In piam memoriam
collegii nostri
fundatorum

Contents

PART TWO: BACKGROUND AND AFTERMATH

V BACKGROUND

VI AFTERMATH

VII APPENDICES

Statutes

THE STATUTES OF EDMUND GONVILLE

[Gonville's text is continuous; numbers and titles have been added editorially.]

THE RE-ISSUED STATUTES OF WILLIAM BATEMAN 1355

THE STATUTES OF JOHN CAIUS

Plates

Preface

The present work arises from the desire of the Master and Fellows that the quincentenary in 2010 of Caius' birth should be marked by the preparation and publication of an edition and translation of the statutes that he made for his re-founded college in the years between 1558 and 1573. The Latin text of those statutes had been published in 1852 by the Royal Commissioners appointed to enquire into the university and colleges of Cambridge, and again by Venn in 1901, but in neither case had an English translation been supplied. As Caius' statutes supplemented but did not replace those made by William Bateman, any edition of the third founder's statutes would be incomplete without those of the second; and although there is not the same need to include the statutes which had been drafted in 1348 by the first founder, Edmund Gonville – since these were soon replaced in their entirety by Bateman, if indeed they had ever come formally into force – they have been included here for the sake of completeness and for the striking contrast which they present to the statutes of both the later founders.

The work falls into two Parts. The first contains four sections: Section I *Introduction*, Section II *The Statutes of Edmund Gonville*, Section III *The Statutes of William Bateman*, and Section IV *The Statutes of John Caius*. The second has three sections: Section V *Background*, Section VI *Aftermath*, and Section VII *Appendices*.

The first Part

Part I is principally devoted to editions and translations (in Sections II, III and IV) of the statutes given to the college by the three founders, and it also contains an introduction (in Section I) comparing the very different characteristics which are exhibited by the statutes of each of the founders. Editions and translations of two subsidiary works are also included in Sections III and IV. These are commentaries on the statutes of Bateman and Caius: first the "expositions" of Bateman's statutes that were written by Caius before he started to draft his

own statutes, and then the legally binding "interpretations" that were put upon Caius' statutes by Archbishop Parker two years after Caius' death and by his direction.

I am grateful to the late Professor Brooke for urging me to include Gonville's statutes; for they are more appealing, and more modern, both in character and in content, than those of either of the two succeeding founders, particularly those of Bateman, coming only four years after them. If we may judge from his statutes, Edmund Gonville was a most attractive person, more so than William Bateman and, arguably, than John Caius. Gonville's statutes are clear, succinct and confined to important constitutional issues; and, unlike Bateman's, Gonville's statutes do not attempt to stamp his personality upon his foundation and they do not dictate in minute detail the daily life of the community that they regulate. Furthermore they are designed specifically for a community of lay scholars and do not impose upon those scholars the quasi-monastic life that Bateman envisaged.

Bateman's statutes share one characteristic with those of Gonville: both were carefully drafted by – or at least with the help of – expert civilian lawyers, and as a result the meaning of both founders' statutes is almost always relatively straightforward to grasp. We have, however, a difficulty with Bateman's statutes which is not encountered in Gonville's. The difficulty is not that of understanding the wording or meaning of any of Bateman's provisions, but of knowing whether it was a provision which he intended *this* college to have; for Gonville Hall was his second foundation and he legislated for it somewhat cursorily by reference to the statutes which he had already formulated for his first foundation, Trinity Hall. As a result there has been great confusion from 1355 to the present day in the presentation and ordering of Bateman's statutes: no two versions have ever presented precisely the same text in the same order, and even the most recent version, by Venn in 1901, inadvertently omitted some provisions from its reproduction of the text of Bateman's statutes. Yet this discordance seems not to have provoked comment at any time, even when the text was relied upon in litigation.

Caius' statutes provide a striking contrast to those of Gonville and Bateman; for he drafted his statutes by himself, and even though he was a very good classical Latin scholar it is sometimes very difficult to understand what he really meant by a particular provision, even though we have the precise wording of what he wrote. Moreover, he revised and added to his statutes over a period of fifteen years and, working by himself, he was prone on occasion to overlook inconsistencies between what he was drafting at the time and what he had written earlier in another statute. His statutes are virtually unique in the number and detail of provisions regulating the management of the college's estates and manors and the anxious care for the maintenance of accurate and detailed accounts that they display. One might assume that these characteristics reflect the experience gained in the years during which he bore the responsibility for

these matters as Master and primary bursar, but all but one of the provisions on both subjects, the management of the college's estates and the maintenance of its accounts, had already appeared in the draft statutes which he drew up *before* he returned to the college. In contrast, what must clearly be attributed to the impact on him of his first seven troubled years as Master is the preoccupation with human failing and the consequently gloomy character of the provisions which appear for the first time in the final version of the statutes that he prepared in the final years of his life.

The second Part

Section V *Background* contains accounts of the circumstances in which the statutes of each of the three founders came into existence. The accounts of the backgrounds to Gonville's and Bateman's foundations and their statutes have been written by the late Christopher Brooke, who most generously made available his unrivalled knowledge and understanding of the life and work of the college's first two founders and the medieval period in which they lived. Needless to say, Christopher's contributions here, as well as his unstinted help with the rest of the work, have been invaluable: much of what he has written on the first two founders has not previously appeared in print. Far more has already been published about the life of the third founder and his re-foundation of the college, and for this reason the present writer's account of the background to Caius' statutes has concentrated upon those aspects which had most effect upon the contents and character of his statutes, and in particular upon his relations with individual fellows when he was Master. Those relations were admittedly fraught in the early years of his mastership – a period when he seems to have acted more as a founder than as a Master – but it is suggested here that relations with fellows of the college were far less unhappy in the later years of Caius' life than Venn may have led us to believe.

Section VI *Aftermath* consists of essays on five topics which were the subject of clear and emphatic instructions by Caius in his statutes but which, in later centuries, either were the subject of bitter dispute and litigation (the Master's negative vote and the Norfolk preference) or else were, by tacit agreement, construed in ways which ran counter to the clearly expressed intentions and wishes of the third founder (the restriction of the government of the college to the Master and the twelve senior fellows, the long rigidity that restricted stipends and the devious resort to dividends to supplement them).

The Master's negative vote had appeared in Bateman's statutes, but it was in the Tudor period when it became a contentious issue, not only in this college but in other colleges also, and was mirrored in the university in the struggle between the Caput and the Regents; it led in the early seventeenth century to a

Master's being formally charged before the Chancellor with unfitness for office, and it continued to fester in the college until the eighteenth century. The Norfolk preference was a subject of disagreement that gave rise to the dispute over the Master's negative vote, and it festered even longer and more bitterly. The story of the preference has been recounted in detail in earlier histories of the college, but those accounts tend to overlook two features in the story: the evasion of the preference by means of the practice of translating fellows between foundations, which was developed in the period preceding the Commonwealth, and the sharp resurgence of the dispute with the coming of the Restoration.

In contrast, relatively little has been written on the other three topics, and particularly the last two, stipends and dividends, for histories of the college have tended to shun any enquiry into the financial and economic history of the college. Both stipends and dividends were subjects on which Caius felt strongly and in his statutes he included detailed provisions on the former and emphatic prohibitions against the latter. His statutes on both subjects were set aside – very gradually in the case of stipends and almost immediately in the case of dividends – yet one searches in vain for either subject in the index to Venn's voluminous account of the history of the college (*Biographical History*, vol. III). An attempt has been made in the present work to remedy the neglect of those two topics. The result has been that the fourth and fifth chapters in Section VI, on stipends and dividends respectively, are disproportionately long and detailed, particularly that on dividends. In defence it may be argued that the chapter on dividends is largely devoted to two topics that are of general interest to economic and social historians: the management of corn rents in the three hundred years following Sir Thomas Smith's Act in 1576, and the practice of granting beneficial leases in return for entry fees that prevailed from the early sixteenth century to the last quarter of the nineteenth. The college is fortunate in having in its archives an extensive collection of rarely consulted records on both topics, but they appear to have escaped general attention since the First World War.

Section VII *Appendices* has nine appendices which contain transcripts and (where appropriate) translations of relevant documents to which frequent reference is made earlier in the work. Most of these documents are in the college's archives and some of them have appeared in Venn's edition of the *Annals* of the college, but since that work may not be readily available they have been reproduced here and supplemented with explanatory notes and cross-references.

Presentation has raised some questions that have troubled the writer far more than they warrant. One is the use of upper- and lower-case, particularly for the holders of offices and ranks such as fellows, scholars, bursars, deans, presidents and stewards: here the draftsman of the Commissioners' statutes for the college in the nineteenth and twentieth centuries would unhesitatingly have scattered capital letters, but capitals would have been an anachronism in the statutes of Gonville and of Bateman, and even in the time of Caius their use in the informal copying of such college documents seems still to have been

very much at the whim of the particular scribe, whether he was writing in Latin or in English.[1] To avoid a forest of capital letters, I have preferred lower-case both in the translation of Latin documents and in my own writing;[2] in the transcription of English documents, however, I have kept to the original choice of case, though I have substituted modern spelling in the transcription of longer passages in documents from the sixteenth and early seventeenth centuries. I have also tended to give the precise amount of sums of money specified in accounts in the archives, rather than round them to significant amounts, as the full figures are more quickly identifiable in those documents, most of which are not paginated or conveniently laid out.

No bibliography has been included as most of the sources cited are documents in the College Archives and do not yet have a firm title, class-list or other reference that could be given helpfully here. References to published works that have been cited frequently in more than one Section have been abbreviated and a list of the abbreviations has been appended to this Preface.

Work in archives tends to be a lonely business and I am all the more grateful to the College Archivist, James Cox, for the willing help he has given in tracking down and producing materials from an archive for which, through no fault of his, there is as yet no shelf-list and only a very elementary class-list; without his cheerful help and voluminous memory this work would not have been possible. In this task of tracking down archival material I am indebted also to two other archivists for their time and trouble in obtaining for me photographic copies of material in other archives which I was unable to visit: to Alexander Howell, James's assistant, and to Ruth Selman, a member of the college and Principal Early Modern Records Specialist at The National Archives.

I am grateful, too, to the many members of the Fellowship for the assistance and encouragement which they have given to me and for the kindly patience which they have shown during the long delay since they first welcomed the suggestion of an edition of the founders' statutes. Among them it is a pleasure to mention Dr Victoria Bateman for her guidance with the mathematical mysteries of economic history, Dr Annabel Brett for her assistance with some of Caius' more challenging Latin constructions, the Revd Dr Cally Hammond for her help in tracking down elusive references in Gonville's and Bateman's statutes, Professor Henry Parkes (now at the Institute of Sacred Music at Yale) for the light he shone on Caius' use of musical terms, Professor Malcolm Smith for the

1 Thus the scribe of Caius' statutes regularly wrote "*Custos*" in MS 711/756, but in his emendations Caius would write "*custos*" (cf. Statute 5). Lower-case would seem to have been widely used in the contemporary English translation of *custos* as "keeper". For an example of the indiscriminate use of upper- and lower-case, see the documents in *Gerrard's Case*, Appendix D below.

2 I have compromised in one very apparent instance and used upper-case for "Master", since that was the style invariably used in college documents after English replaced Latin in them from the Commonwealth onwards.

improvement of the text and the elimination of errors in the various chapters he read in typescript, and Professor Yao Liang, whose expert photography has greatly facilitated the reading of various manuscripts that I should otherwise have found virtually indecipherable and who has, in addition, provided the photographs of the documents in the College Archives and Library that are reproduced in the Plates. In addition to help from these and other members of the college it is a pleasure – in which I know Christopher Brooke would warmly have shared – to acknowledge the generous help that both he and I have received from Patrick Zutshi, of Corpus Christi College.

Above all, I am indebted to Christopher Brooke and to Richard Duncan-Jones for their invaluable assistance, particularly in the preparation of the texts and translations: without that assistance the first part of the work could not have been undertaken. In particular, I was always able to rely on Christopher's expert help with the correct reading of the original manuscripts of Gonville's and Bateman's statutes, while Richard's help has been invaluable with the translation and likely meaning of the many obscure passages which Caius' statutes contain and in tracking down the various classical references which Caius delighted in inserting into them. Their help has also been invaluable with the second Part, both in the spotting of errors and in the provision of references to many of the publications cited; in addition Christopher kindly contributed two chapters to Section V of this work, on Gonville's and Bateman's foundations, subjects on which his knowledge was unrivalled. Christopher's death on 27 December 2015 was a great loss to every student of the history of the College and it has been a particular loss to me in the final preparation of the present work: I much regret that he did not live to see the completion of a project to which he gave such enthusiastic support. Both he and Richard have saved me from innumerable errors. Merely to express my indebtedness to them in this Preface would be inadequate, and I am glad to have secured their consent to their names' appearing on the title page, though I must stress that their agreement to this does not make them responsible in any way for any of the errors and infelicities that remain despite their assistance.

Finally, there is John Venn. The present work could not have been contemplated, let alone undertaken, but for the immense treasure-house of information on the history of the College that he bequeathed to his successors in his *Biographical History* and numerous other works. I cannot do better than echo the tribute which Christopher paid to him in the Preface to his own *History* of the college: "every page of this book which is worth anything contains a tribute to his hobby and his learning".[3]

Michael Prichard
15 February 2017

[3] Brooke, *History*, pp. xiii–xiv.

Abbreviations

Admissions	*Admissions to Gonville & Caius College … March 1558/9 to June 1678/9*, ed. J. and S.C. Venn, London & Cambridge University Press (1887).
Annals	*The Annals of Gonville & Caius College*, by John Caius ed. J. Venn, Cambridge (1904).
B.H.	*Biographical History of Gonville & Caius College* vols. I–III ed. John Venn, Cambridge University Press (1897–1901). vol. IV(2), *Chronicle of the College Estates*, ed. E. Gross, Cambridge University Press (1912). vol. VII, ed. M.J. Prichard and J.B. Skemp, Cambridge University Press (1978).
Brooke, *History*	*A History of Gonville & Caius College*, by Christopher Brooke, The Boydell Press (1985, reprinted 1996).
C.O.	College Order.
Cooper, *Annals*	*Annals of Cambridge*, by C.H. Cooper, vols. I–V, Cambridge (1842).
Documents	*Documents relating to the University and Colleges of Cambridge*, vols. I–III, published by direction of the Royal Commissioners, London (1852).
Emmanuel College	*A History of Emmanuel College, Cambridge*, by Sarah Bendall, Christopher Brooke and Patrick Collinson, The Boydell Press (1999).
Historiae	*Historiae Cantebrigiensis Academiae …*, by John Caius, London (1574), reproduced in *Works* (see below).

H.U.C.	*A History of the University of Cambridge* vol. I, *The University to 1546*, by Damian Riehl Leader, Cambridge University Press (1988). vol. II, *1546–1750*, by Victor Morgan, Cambridge University Press (2004). vol. III, *1750–1870*, by Peter Searby, Cambridge University Press (1997). vol. IV, *1870–1900*, by Christopher Brooke, Cambridge University Press (1993).
Lamb, *Letters*	*A Collection of Letters, Statutes etc.*, ed. John Lamb, London (1838).
Lib. Rat.	*Liber Rationalis*, College Archives.
ODNB	*Oxford Dictionary of National Biography*, Oxford University Press (2004).
TH	Trinity Hall.
Riches & Responsibility	*Riches and Responsibility: A Financial History of Trinity College, Cambridge*, by Robert Nield, Cambridge (2008).
Works	*The Works of John Caius, M.D.*, ed. E.S. Roberts, Cambridge University Press (1912).

(MS references are to documents in the College Library unless otherwise stated. Where no MS or other reference is given, the work is to be found in the College Archives.)

Sigla

{...}	Scribal insertions, deletions and corrections in the original manuscript.
[...]	Text supplied editorially.
§	Denotes, in cross-references, a Section (I–VII) of the present work.

PART ONE

The Statutes

I

Introduction

I. 1

The Statutes of the Three Founders

Gonville and Caius College is exceptional in having had three separate founders, each of whom drew up statutes for their foundation: the rector Edmund Gonville, the bishop William Bateman and the doctor John Caius.[1] The statutes made by those founders are also exceptional, for they have two unique features: first, the statutes of the last founder did not supersede those of the second founder but took effect concurrently with them for over three hundred years; and second, the longest set of the three founders' statutes was formulated by someone – John Caius – who was not only a founder but had himself been a fellow of the college for which he was drawing up his statutes and was Master of that college during the years in which he was formulating the final draft of those statutes. The first feature gave rise to legal issues that continued to trouble the college until both the second and third founders' statutes were replaced in 1860, while the second feature gave to Caius' statutes the unique detail of their provisions and their exceptional character; for both these reasons John Caius' statutes in particular deserve greater attention than they have been given.

The three sets of statutes bear the stamp of their makers' very different personalities and the circumstances in which each of the sets of statutes came into existence.[2] In contrast to the short-lived statutes of the first founder, those of William Bateman continued in force for over five hundred years, and for the last three hundred of those years they were supplemented and largely supplanted by the much fuller statutes of the third founder, John Caius.

1 Perhaps more correctly, two founders, Edmund Gonville and John Caius, and a pretender to that title, William Bateman: see below. Robert Brady indignantly condemned Bateman for his "device in his pretended and fictitious deed of ffoundacion" (*Miscellanea*, MS 707/693, "Extracts", p. 1). It may be added that John Venn and E.S. Roberts continued late in their lives to regard Caius as the college's second founder: see the title-page to *The Works of John Caius* (1912).

2 On those circumstances see § V. 1–3 below.

The Statutes of Edmund Gonville

It is somewhat ironic that a modern lawyer who seeks to interpret the three sets of statutes is likely to find the short-lived statutes of the first founder more congenial than those of his successors. Whether those statutes ever came formally into existence is uncertain, since only an unsealed copy has survived. That copy was clearly produced for approval by the person already chosen by Gonville to be the first Master of his new foundation, John Colton, and the (still to be chosen) fellows thereof, and by the Chancellor and congregation of the University of Cambridge, as the second and third parties whose assent to the statutes was to be recorded in a deed sealed by all three parties. Gonville's statutes have therefore been termed "draft statutes" by Venn and others, but they were clearly in final form so far as Gonville was concerned and were as carefully preserved in the college's archives as its title-deeds: there is little reason to doubt that they would have been regarded as binding by Colton and his fellows during the four years before they received new statutes from the second founder in 1353.

From the little that we know of Edmund Gonville it is clear that he was an able and trusted administrator who gained the confidence of such powerful persons as Henry earl of Lancaster and his son Duke Henry, as well as that of the second founder, William Bateman, the bishop of Norwich, then the second city in the land and one of its most profitable dioceses.[3] We know too from his earlier actions in founding two other charitable institutions that he was a remarkably generous individual. He must also have been a very wealthy one, or at any rate a most persuasive fund-raiser, as he was in a position to contemplate the foundation in his lifetime of a hall in the university in Cambridge for a Master and up to twenty fellows or scholars[4] and to purchase three tenements and a garden in Lurteburghlane, now Free School Lane, for that purpose. Having obtained a licence in mortmain to do so in 1348, and taken steps in the following year to convey the intended site to his new foundation, he drew up statutes for it. From those statutes we are able to deduce that he was not only a competent and trusted administrator, but also a thoughtful and sensible legislator. Apart from the sole exception of the opening sentence of the preamble, which is uncharacteristically opaque, his statutes are succinct and precise, and their meaning is invariably clear. Moreover, they are modest and sensibly limited in their aim. Unlike the other founders, Gonville asked no

[3] For Gonville's involvement in the foundation of the college, see Professor Brooke's chapter on "*Edmund Gonville and his Foundation*", § V. 1 below.

[4] The broad term "*scolares*" is used in the licence in mortmain, but Gonville specifies "*socii*" in his statutes (Statute 25). When using the word "*socius*" he would not have had in mind the very particular meaning which "Fellow" later came to express, but simply the notion of a member of a scholarly community.

more for himself than that the hall should bear his name and he did not seek to impose a rigid daily routine upon the members of his hall. Instead he concentrated upon constitutional issues: the qualifications for a Master and for a fellow and the process for their election;[5] the grounds and process for expulsion;[6] the safe-guarding of the hall's funds;[7] entitlement to rooms and commons;[8] the obligation to reside full-time and to pursue a chosen course of study, which he assumed would normally lead to the study of theology, though he allowed to all fellows the freedom to study canon law and to a limited number the right to choose other faculties;[9] and the restriction of fellowships to those who were in need of financial support.[10] Like other founders, he required the regular audit of the hall's accounts, but he went further and, unlike most other founders, he required the society to budget in advance for foreseeable demands on the hall's funds.[11] His careful forethought for his new foundation is apparent also in the requirement in his statutes that those falling ill should always be provided with adequate food and drink and other necessities even if those expenses exceeded the normal budget – a humane touch not commonly found in the statutes of other founders and not in those of Bateman or Caius.[12]

Unlike the other founders, he avoided the temptation to specify unalterable requirements in minute detail, and he accepted the impossibility of a founder's foreseeing every possibility, recognising a consequent need to empower the society to make ordinances to meet those possibilities in the future.[13] A draftsman would automatically include such a power in college statutes today, but it is rare to find in the past any founder who made provision for subsequent legislation by the society: Edmund Gonville is an attractive exception. His statutes were rightly regarded later by a shrewd Master, Robert Brady, as "better and more rational" than those of his immediate successor,[14] and we may add, those of both his successors.

Two subjects are notably absent from his statutes: there is no provision for a library, and there is no mention of stipends. The omission of a provision for a library derives, we may assume, from a belief that the pressing need was to provide a hall of residence and that the university could best provide the facilities for study. The absence of any provision for stipends is perhaps less readily explained, but a clue may be found in Statute 22, which imposed a limit

5 Statutes 2 and 11.

6 Statutes 9, 10, 12 and 14.

7 Statutes 4, 5, 6, 23, 27 and 28.

8 Statutes 18, 22 and 23.

9 Statutes 3, 15, 16, 17 and 24.

10 Statutes 19–21.

11 Statute 5.

12 Statute 7.

13 Statute 14.

14 *Miscellanea*, MS 707/693, "*Extracts*", p. 2.

upon the total amount that might be expended by the house on the fellows' daily commons, not a cost per capita which might then be charged to the individual fellow (as later became the case until 1882):[15] it seems clear from that statute and from the two statutes immediately following that Gonville intended that the Master and fellows of his new house should be supported through the provision of board and lodging without charge, not through the payment of a stipend from which the recipient was required to meet the costs of that board and lodging.

By the time he died on 17 November 1351 Gonville had achieved nearly all that he had set himself to do three years earlier. He had obtained a royal licence to found and name a new college on a site which he had already acquired and to make statutes for it; he had appointed a Master and a small group of fellows – perhaps as many as four – and had vested in them the legal title to the site;[16] he had drafted a complete set of statutes for them in which he had named their college and under which they had lived for more than two years; and he had supported them financially during that period: but it seems that he had gone further, for he must have provided them with the funds which enabled them to enlarge the site by the purchase of adjoining land in the two months after his death.[17]

All but one of the tasks that he had set himself had thus been accomplished, and that one remaining task, the provision of a permanent fund which could provide a secure income from land for the new foundation, could be performed by a subsequent benefactor as readily as by a founder. According to Caius, Gonville had deferred the task during his lifetime, and had made Bateman his executor and entrusted to him a large amount of money (*grandem pecuniam*)

[15] It was not until 1882 that the statutes of the college provided that the expense of the fellows' dinner in the college hall should be paid out of the income of the college: Statute 40 (4).

[16] The property in Lurteburghlane appears to have been vested in Colton and the fellows as early as June 1349: for Gonville's deed of gift and the authority to his attorney to transfer seisin, see *B.H.* III, pp. 326–7. It was therefore Colton and the fellows who eventually executed the exchange of the original property for the present site in 1353. No fellows are identified by name in any document earlier than an abortive conveyance in 1354 of the manor of Triplow to John Colton of Terrington, Master, and four fellows, William of Rougham, the 'other' John of Terrington, William of Lee and Richard of Pulham; in his *Annals* Caius erroneously antedates the four names to Gonville's foundation deed of 4 June 1349.

[17] They acquired a small property to the north of the site from the University on 2 March 1352, and a larger property to the south from the Hospital of St. John on the following day: R. Willis and J.W. Clark, *The Architectural History of the University of Cambridge* (Cambridge University Press 1886), vol. I, p. 244; for a map of the site, see *B.H.* I, p. 4. Colton and his colleagues must have had from Gonville the funds needed for the purchase, for it is highly unlikely that Bateman contributed to it so soon after Gonville's death – he appears to have taken little or no interest in the foundation in Lurteburghlane while he was engaged in establishment of Trinity Hall. Gonville's generosity also seems to have supported them in the eighteen months or so before Bateman gave his first endowment to the college in 1354: see n. 22 below.

to provide that endowment and thus perfect what he, Gonville, had begun.[18] If Bateman was indeed appointed executor "he no waye discharged his trust according to Gonville's Intention":[19] instead he acted as if he were himself the founder.

The Statutes of William Bateman

A month after Gonville's death, and expressing the desire that his meritorious project should not fall into ruin, Bateman purported by deed to complete the project – but he did so by changing the name from Gonville Hall to the College of the Annunciation of the Blessed Mary and reserving to himself the free and unrestricted power to make such statutes and ordinances regulating the way of life of the community as seemed fit to him at the time.[20] In that deed he refrained from describing himself as founding the re-named college – in contrast to "our foundation" of Trinity Hall – and it was only a year later, in his first decree for the new college in November 1352 on the first anniversary of Gonville's death, that he formally styled himself as its founder (*fundator collegii annunciacionis beate Marie*), at the same time specifically denying that title to Gonville.[21] In the summer of the following year he arranged for Colton and the fellows to exchange the site in Lurteburghlane for its present site, and although the earlier site had been provided entirely by Gonville no mention of his name was made in the deed of arrangement which Bateman sealed in Colton's name.[22] From this

18 *Annals*, pp. 2–3. As Brady pointed out, Gonville had intended a foundation of a Master and twenty "scholars" and "without doubt left a sufficiency for that purpose": *Miscellanea*, MS 707/693, "*Extracts*", p. 1. As has been noted above, Gonville did not envisage the payment of stipends, simply board and lodging, and in his Statute 24 he provided that vacancies should be filled only if the resources of the house were sufficient to do so.

19 Brady, *Miscellanea*, MS 707/693, "*Extracts*", p. 1. Bateman's 'foundation' deed of 21 December 1351 (*B.H.* III, p. 327) refers to Gonville's intentions and states that death prevented him from completing his laudable purpose, but both Bateman's deed and his statutes carefully avoid imposing any obligation of executorship upon him.

20 Deed of 21 December 1351: *B.H.* III, p. 327. For Bateman's involvement in the foundation of the college, see Professor Brooke's chapter on "*William Bateman and his Foundation*", § V. 2 below. See too *B.H.* III, pp. 5–8.

21 *Sheriffe's Evidences*, MS 706/692, p. 26. It subsequently evoked from Caius the caustic marginal comment "*Batemannus Nomen fundatoris usurpat*". In his decree, in which he expressly described himself as *the* founder, Bateman described Gonville as the person who should be commemorated *next after* the founder (*post fundatorem*); see Professor Brooke' analysis of the decree in *The Caian* (1994), p. 67.

22 *B.H.* III, p. 329. The move was achieved by a straight exchange: it was therefore Gonville's money that provided for the acquisition of the present site. Bateman's first endowments (the rectorial tithes of Mutford, Foulden and Wilton) were not made until 1354. He may have made an abortive endowment of the manor of Triplow earlier that year, but it seems never to have

point onward Gonville's name disappears from all Bateman's documents for the re-named Hall of the Annunciation. The reason for the omission is revealed in the Treaty of Amity which was concluded three months later at his behest between Gonville's foundation and his own foundation, Trinity Hall, on 17 September 1353.[23] The purpose of the exchange was to establish and cement a bond between the two colleges as the fraternal offspring of a single foundation (*tanquam fratres amicissimi ex uno fundacionis stipite prodeuntes*), but at the same time to accord precedence to Trinity Hall on the unhistorical ground that it had been founded first – and that required the suppression of all reference to Edmund Gonville.

This explains the omission of any reference to Gonville in the statutes which Bateman had made for the 'younger sibling' ten days earlier on 7 September 1353. In those statutes he improperly and ungenerously air-brushed Gonville from the picture (though not from the memory of John Colton and the fellows of the erstwhile Gonville Hall, it would seem),[24] but apart from that criticism one may accept that the provisions in his statutes are written as clearly as those in Gonville's, although they differ greatly from them in their content, being drawn entirely from those that the bishop had made for Trinity Hall. Furthermore, whatever criticism one may make of Bateman's fulfilment of the trust Gonville had reposed in him, his statutes contained one very valuable clause which had been absent from Gonville's statutes: the provision of adequate safeguards for the preservation of its library, similar to those which he had earlier provided for Trinity Hall.[25]

The ready intelligibility of both Gonville's and Bateman's sets of statutes shows the influence of trained, professional civilian lawyers, but the two differ markedly in their character. In contrast to Gonville, who had not prescribed a detailed and rigid way of life for the members of his foundation, Bateman imposed a demanding daily rule upon those of his foundation not unlike that of a monastic order in its detailed rigidity,[26] even though he did not envisage his foundation to be a monastery any more than Gonville had done: in Venn's

been enjoyed by the college: see Professor Brooke in "*William Bateman and his Foundation*", § V. 2 below, and *B.H.* III, p. 7.

23 *B.H.* III, pp. 329–40.

24 See Professor Brooke's suggestion in his chapter on "*William Bateman and his Foundation*", § V. 2 below. By the fifteenth century Gonville's foundation had regained its name and precedence in the university, and the title "Gonville Hall" had been revived even in papal missives: see, *e.g.*, papal bull of 22 May 1481 (*B.H.* III, pp. 332–3); licence of 24 October 1501 and enclosed letter (*ibid.*, pp. 334–5).

25 Statute 11. For the college's library and its books, see Brooke, *History*, pp. 33–7.

26 For the repeated devotions required of the fellows, see the preamble to his statutes, notably requirement for the Angelic Salutation 50 times on bended knees daily and 150 times on Saturdays. For Professor Brooke's gentle comment ("His provision of prayers and masses indicates religious devotion of a very formal and conventional kind.") see below at p. 324. He imposed similar requirements upon the fellows of Trinity Hall (TH st. 14: *Documents*, II,

words, the fellows of both founders were "not supposed to contemplate a perpetual life in college, but rather to look forward to the highest departments of practical work in the world".[27] Gonville was content that their practical work in the world should be "made publicly available for the benefit of the commonwealth in full measure";[28] in contrast, Bateman was anxious that his own diocese should be first beneficiary, and he imposed an oath to that effect upon the keepers and fellows of his foundation, carefully providing that the bishop and chapter of Norwich should be kept fully informed of the names of those bound by that oath.[29]

Compared with the wording of some of Caius' statutes much later, we have little difficulty in comprehending what either Gonville or Bateman meant by their statutes. Bateman's legislation raises a different query: not what any given statute meant, but which statutes he intended to include. This uncertainty results from the way in which he indicated his intention. Having devoted much time and thought to the statutes he had drawn up for Trinity Hall, he merely listed the titles of twelve of those statutes and incorporated them into the statutes he was proposing to make for the Hall of the Annunciation by reference to that list of titles; however, he then set out the wording of five further statutes, and since these overlapped with some of the listed provisions taken from Trinity Hall, this left unclear precisely what should be incorporated. As a result there have been conflicting versions of his statutes for over six hundred years, despite the preservation in the college's archives of the original statutes which he made in 1353.[30]

The Statutes of John Caius

The statutes of John Caius differ in various ways both from those of Gonville and Bateman and also from those made by founders of other colleges, in that his statutes were made by someone who had earlier been a fellow of the very college he was re-founding and who had the personal experience, literary competence and self-confidence to be his own draftsman. In acting as such he appears to have sought no advice or assistance from others and his statutes contain philosophical reflections and moralising which are more suited to a personal diary than to a set of statutes. Furthermore, he was a founder who soon afterwards became Master of his re-founded college and thus had the opportunity to

pp. 427–8) and secured exequies even from the regent masters of the whole university (*B.H.* III, p. 330).

27 *B.H.* III, pp. 204–5.

28 Gonville's preamble to his statutes.

29 Statutes 16 (oath) and 12 (communication to Norwich).

30 See "*Bateman's Statutes: The Manuscript Confusion*", § I. 2.

revise, amend and add to the statutes in the light of his experience during the fourteen years in which he held the office of Master; as a consequence of those changes the final version of his statutes understandably contains inconsistencies and contradictions, some even within the same statute.[31] Being both founder and Master, he was open to the temptation to issue new statutes and changes of statutes too readily and peremptorily, and his tendency to do this helped to provoke the quarrels that beset his first seven years as Master and was the one issue on which Sir William Cecil imposed specific restrictions upon Caius' government of the college when those quarrels finally reached him as Chancellor in 1565.[32] In their final form Caius' statutes understandably contain passages in which the founder continued to express the very strong personal feelings which the bitter quarrels with some of the fellows had provoked in him in his early years as Master.[33]

Given that he acted as his own draftsman and sought no professional assistance it is not surprising that his statutes contain various characteristic features which distinguish them very clearly from the statutes of other founders: in particular, they contain (a) exceptionally detailed requirements for the keeping of accounts and other records,[34] (b) a unique attention to the management of the college's estates and to the technical drafting of the leases of its lands and manors,[35] (c) a very personal conception that serious misconduct constituted a breach (*periuria*) of the undertaking which every fellow gave in chapel on his admission and as such terminated the fellowship *ipso facto* without any formal process of deprivation,[36] (d) the express exclusion of appeal to any secular or ecclesiastical court against expulsion, and severe restrictions on appeals to the Visitors,[37] and (e) a gloomy preoccupation with the frailty of human nature and the need for the provision of due punishment, not merely as a prevention against evil consequences but also as a means of redeeming the frail offender, a theme which understandably has not been shared by other, more optimistic founders.[38]

[31] See, for example, Statutes 4, 8, 15 (Norfolk preference), 17 (student courses) and 28, 66 (room rents).

[32] See "*John Caius and his Foundation*", § V. 3, and Appendix C, at pp. 358–9 and 565ff below.

[33] For some examples see Statutes 32, 47, 49, 83, 104, 105.

[34] Statutes 45, 51, 73 (recording of fines and absences); 56, 57 (bursars' and stewards' accounts); 58 (chapel audit); 59, 62 (account books, annals, register of title-deeds, minute book of acts, matriculation book); 63 (admission fees audit); 64–67 (payment of bills); 71 (weekly commons accounts); 82 (silver audit); 84 (borrowings from chests and archives).

[35] Statutes 86 (duration of leases); 87, 80, 91 (rents and fines); 88 (landlord's rights); 90 (tenants' obligations); 92–94 (tenants' suitability); 96–103 (estate management).

[36] See Statute 105: "we rule that he who breaks his oath shall be expelled from the college and deprived of all benefit of it for ever". See too "*John Caius and his Foundation*", § V. 3 below.

[37] See Statutes 44 and 48.

[38] See in particular the second paragraph of Statute 105.

(a) At first sight one is tempted to attribute the insistence upon accounting and record-keeping in his statutes to the shocked anger which Caius expressed on his discovery of the parlous state of the college's finances and records that he found when he became Master. It would, however, be wrong to do so, as a requirement for all but one of the records specified in his final statutes is to be found in the surviving draft of the statutes that he presented to Thomas Bacon at the formal inauguration of the re-founded college on Lady Day, 25 March 1558: half-yearly accounts, interim accounts presented weekly each Saturday, annals of events occurring during the preceding year, volumes preserving title-deeds, minute-books recording corporate actions between audits (*pandectae*), an audited inventory of money and assets deposited in the chest and a register of items taken out of and returned to it.[39] The fact that all these requirements for accounting and record-keeping had already been carefully included in the statutes which he had provided for Bacon and his fellows helps to explain the very justifiable anger that he felt at the total disregard of those statutes which he found on his return as Master.

(b) Likewise, the remarkably minute attention given in the statutes to the technical requirements for the proper leasing and estate management of the college's lands should not be attributed to the difficulties and disputes which he experienced as Master with the holders of the long leases which the college had granted so improvidently in earlier years. All but one of those requirements are already to be found in the surviving draft of the statutes which were presented to Bacon in 1558:[40] the terms to be inserted in leases, the rights to be reserved to the college, the type of tenants to be preferred, the requirement for rentals and extents, the preservation of court rolls, the tight control of bailiffs and stewards, and the regular inspection of the college's properties by the Master and fellows.[41] These details are not to be found in statutes of other colleges at that time and they make his statutes unique. It is an intriguing question how and when he acquired such a detailed professional knowledge of estate management even before he became Master and before he had to face the task of wrestling with the

39 The one record that is not required in the draft statutes was the Matriculation Book, which appears to have been an idea which he conceived after he returned as Master. For the provisions of the draft statutes, see *Documents*, II, pp. 321–65.

40 The one exception was Statute 86, restricting the length of any lease to twenty years and prohibiting both reversionary leases and covenants to make such leases. This statute was made before the general prohibition imposed by Parliament in 1571 and was better drafted than the Act; it was clearly made in the light of the difficulties which Caius had experienced with the beneficial long leases granted by his predecessors: see the section on *Beneficial Leases* in "*Dividends*", § VI. 5 below.

41 *Documents*, II, pp. 321–65. The 1588 conveyance of his three manors to Bacon and the fellows expressly imposed upon them and their successors the obligation to "order, keep, rule and dispose the said issues manors lands tenements" in accordance with his statutes: *Annals*, pp. 74–5.

management of the college's manors and other lands. So far as we know, he had not invested any money in land until he purchased, in 1557, the three manors of Croxley and Snellshall, Runcton, and Burnham Thorpe as an endowment for his college shortly before its re-foundation; presumably it was not until then that he acquired his interest and knowledge in the technical aspects of the subject, and, if so, he absorbed the knowledge remarkably swiftly.[42]

(c) and (d) Caius' conception that serious misconduct constituted a breach (*periuria*) of the undertaking which every fellow gave in chapel on his admission, and as such terminated the fellowship *ipso facto* without any formal process of deprivation, coupled with his severe restriction upon appeals, runs counter to our modern-day concept of 'due process' and explains the criticism of the "overmuch rashness of the master for expelling fellows so suddenly" during his first seven years in that office which was expressed in 1565 by Archbishop Parker as well as by many in the university; and it was Warner's temerity in seeking redress in the Vice-Chancellor's court which brought about his expulsion and that of his two colleagues in 1565.[43]

(e) In their final version his statutes display a further feature which is not found in other statutes: the apparently gloomy preoccupation with the frailty of human nature and the need for the provision of due punishment, not merely as a protection against evil consequences but also as a means of redeeming the frail offender. He does seem to have been naturally reserved in his manner and severe in his judgments upon his fellow men, and the account which he gave in his *Historiae* of his impressions of university life on his return to Cambridge in 1559[44] has bolstered the belief that he had, by the time he returned as Master, become irritable, autocratic and increasingly ill at ease with the very different beliefs and liberal behaviour which had come to prevail in Cambridge since he had been a student there and that this depressive attitude explains the preoccupation with human frailty in his statutes.

This preoccupation with human frailty runs right through the final version of the statutes. The litany is long. All things were better in Bateman's day and the deterioration in standards in his own time called for a different regime (Statute 1). The unworthy must not be admitted to the college lest the seeds of all manner of evils should be sown, and those who are given to vice with no hope of coming to their senses should be expelled (Statute 15). Idleness is the breeding ground of insolence and ruin (Statutes 19, 21). The novel amusements of the time turn men into brutes (Statute 23). It is laudable that the arrogant should be put down as an example to others (Statute 43). The stirring up of strife is the most deadly of the seven deadly sins and would bring upon the college the

42 See *Caius' purchase of the Manors of Croxley, Runcton and Burnham Thorpe* in "*Supplementary Notes to Caius' Statutes*", § IV. 3, at pp. 302ff below.

43 See "*The Expulsion of Dethick, Warner and Spenser*", Appendix C below.

44 *Historiae*, p. 3.

fate of Troy (Statute 47). The keeper and the fellows would enjoy the benefits of the college more if they would only temper their greed (Statute 83). Caius was at pains to explain that all this condemnation was not because he took delight in imposing punishments but so that the prohibition of vice might warn a person against falling into it and teach him not to think that he could escape – "and thus he may become good or seek reluctantly to be so, which is the aim of all our statutes" (Statute 73) – for "I know it is in the nature of man to sin, and for a good man to correct his sins through chastisement" (Statute 105).

This preoccupation, however, does *not* appear in the draft statutes of 1558. Those earlier statutes naturally display an expectation of decorous behaviour and provisions for disciplinary proceedings and penalties in the same way that such provisions are to be found in the statutes of most founders, but the assumption running through Caius' final statutes that the frailty of human nature makes wrongdoing inevitable, and that the consequent need for punishment becomes a moral imperative, is not to be found anywhere in the draft of his original statutes. We find instead, in those draft statutes, that he provided that attendance at disputations was to be rewarded with the frugal provision of bread, cheese, drink and fruit (at the expense of the disputant), with the aim of fostering friendship and keeping fellows and scholars from wandering off into town:[45] the notion of fostering friendship, as opposed to correcting wrongdoing, is sadly absent from the final statutes.

We do not know when the disillusion which is so apparent in the final version of Caius' statutes first crept into them, for no chronological record of the intervening changes which he made between the first and the last draft of his statutes has survived. It is clear that the outrage of 13 December 1572 did *not* provoke the gloomy comments on the frailty of human nature in the final version of the statutes, for those statutes had already been completed before that outrage occurred.[46] It seems, rather, that the disillusion should be attributed to the bitter disputes which he had earlier had with particular fellows in his first seven years as Master, for his relations with the fellowship in his second seven years were very much better than Venn would have us believe and they would not have been responsible for the gloomy change of tone in the statutes.[47] In fact, most and perhaps all of the passionate outbursts in the statutes directly reflect Caius' angry response to the conduct of those particular fellows whom he expelled during his first seven years as Master,[48] and one suspects that the

45 *Documents*, II, p. 334.

46 The outrage occurred on 13 December and, apart from small clerical corrections, the only alteration that he seems to have made in the intervening few days before he appended his signature to the statutes on 1 January 1573 was to strike out the appointment of the Provost of King's as one of the superintendents of his scholars, and even that alteration was temporary. For the events of 13 December 1572, see "*John Caius and his Foundation*", § V. 3, at pp. 362ff below.

47 For Caius' relations with his fellows, see "*John Caius and his Foundation*", § V. 3 below.

48 See "*John Caius and his Foundation*", § V. 3, at pp. 347–59 below.

sententious pronouncements on the moral imperative for swift punishment and correction which we find in his statutes date from the time of those summary expulsions and were a subconscious response to the widespread criticism which they provoked,[49] not to a more deep-rooted pessimism.

When Caius died he left the college with statutes which were to endure for three hundred years, unaltered and unalterable. Those statutes were characteristically rigid and detailed to the point of fussiness – to the point of specifying amounts of money to the half-penny.[50] Inevitably, therefore, the degree of respect and compliance accorded to each individual statute during their long lives varied greatly. Some were obeyed scrupulously for as long as his statutes remained in force: for example, until the position was changed by Acts of Parliament in the nineteenth century the prohibition in Statute 100 against the alienation of land was scrupulously obeyed, even in those awkward and unprofitable instances in which, arguably, Caius had himself encouraged alienation.[51] In contrast, the equally peremptory restrictions in Statute 86 on the leasing of land were rapidly circumvented and totally frustrated with impressive ingenuity.[52] The provisions relating to the Norfolk Preference engendered bitter disputes throughout the lifetime of his statutes.[53] Some statutes instituted practices which have persisted to the present day, such as the maintenance of the Matriculation Book,[54] whereas the Annals which had been specified in the same statute did not survive beyond the middle of the seventeenth century. Other statutes demanded practices which were already becoming old-fashioned in Caius' own day and in due course were inevitably consigned to oblivion, such as the requirements to converse in Latin and to dress in a manner which Caius unrealistically deemed appropriate for all future time;[55] and almost immediately after his death other provisions, such as the requirement for prayers for the dead founder, were ruled not merely to be old-fashioned and out of favour but to contravene the law of the land and accordingly to be disregarded.[56]

While it is easy to decry the hopeless rigidity and detail of many of Caius' statutes – so very different from those of Edmund Gonville – there was one underlying theme that was notably in advance of its time. Fundamental to Caius and his statutes was the belief that the college was held by the Master and fellows not as beneficial owners but as fiduciaries of a charitable institution which they

49 *Ibid.*

50 Statute 91.

51 See the manor of Haglo and Pulton in the Forest of Dean, which was retained until 1859 (*B.H.* IV(2), p. 52), and Thornham and Titchwell in Norfolk, which "cost the College as much as they were worth" but were retained into the twentieth century (*ibid.*, pp. 89–90).

52 See the section on *Beneficial Leases* in "*Dividends*", § VI. 5 below.

53 See "*The Norfolk Preference*", § VI. 3 below.

54 Statute 59.

55 Statutes 9 and 27.

56 See Matthew Parker's interpretation of Statute 45.

held in trust for future generations as much as for themselves and their own generation: "When we say 'for the benefit of the College' in this and other places in the statutes, we do not mean for the benefit of the individual members of the College, but for the benefit of the College as a corporate entity … not so much for our benefit as that of our posterity."[57] That principle was greatly undermined in the course of the three hundred years during which Caius' statutes were in force,[58] yet it is now accepted as a self-evident truth. Caius would have approved.

57 Statute 63.

58 See "*Dividends*", § VI. 5 below.

I. 2

Bateman's Statutes: The Manuscript Confusion

Both the 1353 grant in which William Bateman originally specified his statutes for Gonville Hall[1] and the 1355 deed in which Walter of Elveden set out those statutes in full shortly after the bishop's death have always been carefully preserved in the archives of the college (BUR: DEEDS/ I 15, 16), and it is therefore surprising to the modern reader that the compilers who subsequently sought to produce a transcript of those statutes should have produced such variant versions. Two of those versions presented very different views of the statutes from the sixteenth century onward, and as a consequence they produced conflicting interpretations of the crucial provision on the Master's negative voice.

One version, MS 711/756, was formulated by Caius himself, and he included it with the copy of his own statutes that he completed in January 1573. He insisted that his version should be regarded as the 'authentic' version not only of his own statutes but of those of Bateman as well. He saw Bateman's listing of twelve of the statutes that he had already laid down for Trinity Hall as no more than a convenient, shorthand way of formulating briefly the text of his completely new statutes for Gonville Hall, and not as importing any interpretation that Bateman might already have expounded for the Master and the fellows of Trinity Hall: he was adamant that any such interpretation concerned Trinity Hall alone and was not to be adopted in his own college at any time.[2] In pursuance of this view, he drew his version exclusively from Walter of Elveden's 1355 re-issue and, like Elveden, he left out all reference to Trinity Hall; in particular, he omitted Bateman's direction that the fellows of Gonville Hall should observe fully and entirely each and every provision contained in the specified statutes of Trinity Hall.

The other view was expressed, almost certainly some forty years later, in the intriguing MS 760/424.[3] This version was also preserved in the archives, and, in

[1] More properly, for his new Hall of the Annunciation, but, since the name "Gonville Hall" was soon revived, it has been retained here.

[2] Caius' Statute 5.

[3] For MSS 711/756 and 760/424, see "*Caius Statutes: The Sources*", § I. 3, at pp. 30 and 32 below.

contrast to Caius' version, it reproduced the whole of the 1353 deed, including the references to Trinity Hall and the list of twelve of its statutes, before it set out the text of those statutes. It also included an important addition, namely, the *Interpretatio* which Bateman attached to his statutes for Trinity Hall; and, significantly, it contains a marginal mark[4] drawing attention to the crucial section in the *Interpretatio* which played an important part in the dispute over the Master's negative voice in *Allen's Case* in 1617.[5]

Bateman's original statutes[6]

The difficulties which faced the later compilers had their origin in three actions by Bateman when he produced the original version of his statutes for Gonville Hall in 1353.

First, at the end of his grant he set out in full five statutes which he desired to provide for Gonville Hall; in contrast, he had not set out in full the text of twelve preceding statutes, but merely directed that the new foundation should observe twelve of the statutes that he had earlier made for Trinity Hall and simply specified these by their rubrics or titles.[7] It seems clear that he did not anticipate a possible duplication or overlap in content between any of the listed statutes and those which he set out in full following them. The only one of those twelve statutes that presented an apparent overlap was Statute 3 (*de tempore eleccionis et forma*), since the corresponding Trinity Hall statute[8] had concluded with a provision reserving to Bateman personally a power to direct and effect the appointment and removal of both Master and fellows and this overlapped very considerably with a separate, but narrower, statute set out in full by Bateman for Gonville Hall at the end of his 1353 deed. As a consequence the Trinity Hall provision might have been thought to be out of place here; but its scope was more extensive[9] and although both forms of the provision had expired with the

4 MS 760, at p. 17; see Plate XV below.

5 See "*The Master's Negative Voice*", § VI. 2, and *Allen's Case* (1617), Appendix F below.

6 BUR: DEEDS/ I, 15. See Plate VIII below.

7 No numbers were attached to the statutes by Bateman or Elveden, or indeed by Sheriffe or Caius. The twelve listed statutes were first numbered in MS 760/424 in the early seventeenth century, but the final five statutes that Bateman set out in full have remained unnumbered until the present edition.

8 TH st. 4 in *Documents*, II, p. 420 (1852).

9 It was wider than the statute Bateman formulated in full for Gonville Hall; the Trinity Hall statute reserved to Bateman personally a power to direct and effect the appointment and removal of the Master as well as fellows, whereas the Gonville Hall statute reserved that power only in respect of the fellows.

death of Bateman on 6 January 1355, Elveden retained them both in his re-issue later that year, though in two widely separated statutes.[10]

Second, Bateman merely listed twelve of the Trinity Hall statutes by their titles, and he did not specify them more fully. As regards the first eleven listed statutes there was no uncertainty about their content, for the conclusion of each statute was clearly indicated in the statutes by the rubric of the following statute, and if any passage within a statute was to be omitted Bateman had been careful to specify this in his list. In contrast to the first eleven statutes, however, the end of the *twelfth* statute[11] was not clearly indicated by any following rubric: instead, it was followed in the Trinity Hall statutes by two further (untitled) provisions which related to quite distinct matters and which did not bear any title or rubric.[12] Furthermore, Bateman had similarly added in full in his 1353 grant of statutes for Gonville Hall *five* further untitled provisions to follow after the twelfth,[13] and the fifth of these overlapped with the first of the two untitled provisions for Trinity Hall.[14] This overlap and the absence of any paragraphing or punctuation in grants of the period, coupled with the absence of any rubric, meant that Bateman's 1353 grant left unclear what should be included in the twelfth statute. Was it merely the requirement that a certificate of names should be sent annually to the bishop of Norwich, or did it in addition include the provisions which followed directly after that requirement in the Trinity Hall statutes, particularly if those provisions overlapped with any of the five set out in full for Gonville Hall? All that was clear was that Statute 12 should be followed ultimately by the five provisions which Bateman had set out in full in 1353.

Third, Bateman prefaced his list of twelve of the statutes he had made for the fellows of Trinity Hall with a direction that each and every fellow of his new college should ensure fully and entirely the observance of each and every

[10] He included the more extensive formulation in Statute 3 *de tempore electionis et forma* (where it had been in the corresponding Trinity Hall statute), and he left Bateman's narrower 1353 formulation as Statute 18.

[11] The statute required the certification annually to Norwich of the names of the fellows of the college. It is TH st. 21 in *Documents*, II, pp. 423–4 (1852), and Statute 12 in the present edition of the 1355 re-issue below.

[12] First, the repeal of any earlier statutes for Trinity Hall and the reservation to Bateman personally of power to legislate further; and second, a requirement that the statutes should be read annually.

[13] The five provisions are: (a) the requirement to have graduated in arts and logic, (b) the restriction on the holding of benefices, (c) the terms of the oath, (d) clemency, (e) the powers reserved to Bateman to direct and effect the appointment and removal of fellows and to legislate further. As will be seen below, (a)–(d) became Statutes 14, 15, 16 and 17 in the 1355 re-issue below; (e) became Statute 18 but was also duplicated partly in Statute 3 and partly in Statute 13 in the re-issue.

[14] In Elveden's re-issue in 1355, the Trinity Hall statute (st. 21) reserving to Bateman the power to legislate further became Statute 13 and the statute for Gonville Hall that Bateman had set out in full became part of Statute 18.

provision contained in the listed statutes: this left open the question whether the twelve listed statutes should apply to Gonville Hall in precisely the same way and to the same extent as Bateman had already directed they should apply to Trinity Hall. As has been mentioned already, Caius fiercely maintained that Bateman's *Interpretatio* did not apply to Gonville Hall, and it was completely omitted from his own MS 711 and thus from the 'authentic' version. In contrast, it was included in the 'rival' version represented by MS 760.

Walter of Elveden's re-issue in 1355[15]

In 1355, very shortly after Bateman's death in Avignon on 6 January 1355, these questions faced his Vicar-General, the Official of Norwich, Walter of Elveden, when he was requested to provide Gonville Hall with a certified copy of its statutes, needed for transmission to the papal curia at Avignon.[16] In that certified copy he carefully omitted all reference to Trinity Hall and to the list of its statutes and he substituted in full the provisions of the statutes which Bateman had specified.[17] His decision to do this provided no problem as regards the first eleven statutes, but when he came to the *twelfth*, Elveden was faced with the question posed earlier: what provisions should be included in and after it?

His answer was to insert after Statute 12's requirement for annual certification to Norwich: (i) the first untitled provision that had immediately followed the requirement in the statutes for Trinity Hall;[18] (ii) the five untitled statutes that Bateman had written out in full in his 1353 grant of statutes to Gonville Hall;[19] and (iii) the second untitled provision for Trinity Hall, which required the reading of the statutes annually. This last provision, which had not featured anywhere in Bateman's 1353 statutes, became Statute 19.

15 BUR: DEEDS/ I, 16.

16 The excellent present state of the document might suggest that it was not itself transmitted to Avignon, even though it carries the requisite seals and notarial certification. If it was, then it was clearly transported with great care; the small wooden box in which it was housed for many centuries is still preserved in the archives.

17 He may have done this simply to avoid sending multiple documents to Avignon and to avoid causing confusion, but, as Professor Brooke has suggested, he may have done so deliberately in order to present Gonville Hall as a distinct legal entity: "*William Bateman and his Foundation*", § V. 2 below. Elveden did use the opportunity to make small alterations in the eleven statutes, notably in Statute 4.

18 *I.e.*, the repeal of any earlier statutes and the reservation to Bateman personally of power to legislate further; this became Statute 13 in Elveden's re-issue.

19 *I.e.*, the provisions (a)–(e) listed in n. 13 above; these became Statutes 14–18. Provision (e), now Statute 18, thus overlaps with Statutes 3 (preferring and removal of fellows) and 13 (further legislation) in Elveden's re-issue.

It is easy to understand the uncertainty which faced Elveden and to sympathise with his endeavour not to omit anything unjustifiably, but it remains baffling why he adopted the order in which he chose to include these final untitled provisions. In particular, annual reading of the statutes had not been required anywhere in the 1353 original and the inclusion of the requirement in the 1355 re-issue could only be justified if it was regarded as part of Statute 12 – yet it was isolated from that statute by Elveden. The fact that Elveden appended to the document the date of the original charter, 7 September 1353, immediately after this completely new statute must have caused some heart-searching to the notary, John of Winston, when he came to certify that he had seen, read and inspected every part of the original documents – not erased, effaced or falsified in any part – and that the 1355 re-issue accorded with those originals. It may be noted that the notary cautiously recorded that he had neither added nor omitted anything which "altered the sense or changed the meaning":[20] he carefully avoided any assertion that the notarised document reproduced the original word for word.

In short, the upshot was that the final five provisions which Bateman had set out in full in 1353 were faithfully reproduced by his Vicar-General in 1355: the requirement to have studied arts and logic (Statute 14), the restriction on the holding of a benefice (Statute 15), the terms of the oath (Statute 16), clemency (Statute 17) and, fifthly, the reservation to Bateman of the twin powers to override elections and to legislate in the future (Statute 18). Elveden included the fifth even though he had already inserted similar provisions (in Statutes 3 and 13) drawn from the statutes of Trinity Hall. Finally, Elveden had also introduced in conclusion two new provisions which had not featured anywhere in the 1353 charter: the repeal of earlier statutes (Statute 13)[21] and the annual reading of the statutes (Statute 19).

Sheriffe's Evidences

A century later the position was further complicated by the action of the author of the text known as *Sheriffe's Evidences*.[22] He started with a word-by-word transcription of Bateman's 1353 Statutes up to and including the requirement to observe the provisions in twelve statutes for Trinity Hall and the list of their titles. He then set out the contents of the twelve statutes. It is not clear whether he looked to Trinity Hall's originals for the text of those statutes or whether he

[20] "*nil addens vel minuens quod sensum mutet vel variet intellectum*".

[21] Bateman had not himself made any earlier statutes for Gonville Hall before 1353, though Elveden may have had in mind Gonville's draft statutes.

[22] MS 706/692.

simply drew upon Elveden's restatement of them, but when he reached Statute 3, *De Tempore et Eleccionis forma*, he parted company with Elveden's re-issue.[23]

He altered the rubric of Statute 3 significantly and widened it to cover "circumstances"[24] as well as procedure (time and form); and he omitted from the statute the reservation to Bateman of power over the appointment of the Master or a fellow that Elveden had imported from the corresponding Trinity Hall statute.[25] Instead he introduced three clauses qualifying eligibility for election. Two of these were brought forward from the later position which they had had in the 1353 and 1355 statutes, but one was an entirely novel provision which had not previously been included anywhere in those statutes.

He first brought forward one of the untitled provisions limiting eligibility for election which Bateman had set out in full in his 1353 charter and which Walter of Elveden had correctly left after Statute 12, namely, the requirement to have studied arts and logic.[26] He then introduced a novel clause giving preference to persons hailing from the diocese of Norwich in elections to the mastership and to fellowships: the celebrated 'Norfolk preference' clause. This clause appears to have been inserted around 1471–72 and a shrewd guess has now been made as to why it was included in the *Evidences*.[27] Finally, he brought forward a second provision limiting eligibility for election which Bateman had set out in full in his 1353 charter and which Walter of Elveden had also correctly placed after Statute 12, namely, the restriction on the holding of benefices.[28]

At first sight it might appear odd that the scribe of the *Evidences* not only inserted into Statute 3 the newly devised Norfolk preference clause but also placed on either side of it two of the untitled provisions that Bateman had set out in full in his 1353 charter and which Walter of Elveden had correctly left after Statute 12: namely, the requirement to have studied arts and logic, and the restriction on the holding of benefices.[29] The deliberate alteration of the rubric of Statute 3, however, suggests strongly that the purpose was to widen what had been a procedural statute to cover eligibility for election and thereby provide a natural home for the new Norfolk preference provision. That is certainly likely to have been the motive for the transfer of the arts requirement; but it is possible that the insertion here of the restriction on benefices was prompted merely by

23 *Ibid.*, at p. 18.

24 *Circumstanciis*. By this, he presumably meant eligibility, though such a meaning seems unusual.

25 He may have done so because it overlapped with Statute 19. It is however possible, as will be seen later, that he omitted it because his other changes had left no space and the provision had long expired upon Bateman's death.

26 Statute 14 in Elveden's 1355 re-issue.

27 For the suggested explanation, see Brooke, *History*, pp. 16–17. It is traditionally called the Norfolk preference, but it must be remembered that it was a preference for the diocese of Norwich.

28 Statute 15 in Elveden's 1355 re-issue.

29 Statutes 14 and 15 in Elveden's 1355 re-issue.

a mention in the new Norfolk preference clause of a direction to prefer those not beneficed to those who were beneficed, for the restriction on benefices was clearly inserted into Statute 3 as a belated afterthought *after* the scribe had finished writing out the new preference clause and had already moved on to writing out the next statute.[30]

Like Elveden, the scribe of the *Evidences* had no difficulty with the rest of the first eleven statutes, but at the end of the twelfth he again parted company with Elveden. He did not regard Statute 13 as being a part of Statute 12 and he omitted it completely.[31] He also omitted Statutes 14 and 15, since he had transferred their provisions (for the prior study of arts and logic restrictions on the holding of benefices) to Statute 3. Instead he proceeded straight to Statutes 16, 17 and 18, which he copied from the original 1353 grant. Finally, he returned to Elveden's re-issue of the statutes and included Statute 19's requirement for the annual reading of the statutes.

Sheriffe's Evidences thus introduced considerable confusion into the record and sequence of Bateman's statutes. It also made two significant and enduring changes to the character which Elveden had given to those statutes. First, it re-introduced Bateman's original linking of the college's statutes with those of Trinity Hall and his injunction that the fellows of his new college should ensure fully and entirely the observance of the provisions of twelve statutes of his earlier foundation;[32] secondly, it imported the entirely novel preference for natives of the diocese of Norwich. The Norfolk preference clause seems never to have been omitted thereafter and it was reproduced unchallenged in all subsequent versions of Bateman's statutes. From Sheriffe's time onward it stamped on the college its distinctive character as *the* Norfolk college until both Bateman's and Caius' statutes were repealed in 1860.

Caius and his 'authorised' version: MS 711/756

Although Caius always evinced a genuine respect for *Sheriffe's Evidences* and in general relied heavily upon that cartulary for the text of the college's medieval

30 The fact that the benefice restriction was added *after* the scribe had already passed to the next statute (Statute 4 *de inhabilibus personis dicti collegii*) meant that all but its first line had to be squeezed into the top margin – something not done anywhere else in this carefully measured cartulary: see Plate VII below. Perhaps it was lack of space or oversight that led him also to omit Bateman's reservation to himself of the power to override elections of a Master or a fellow.

31 He may have done so because it had expired on Bateman's death; but Statute 18 had also expired on the bishop's death, yet he kept that statute.

32 With the modification that the words of those statutes relating to civil and canon law should be extended to arts.

documents, he took from the work only one provision, the Norfolk preference, when he came to set down in MS 711 what he claimed to be the 'authentic' version of Bateman's statutes: in all other respects he returned to Elveden's version and, like Elveden, he omitted Bateman's references to Trinity Hall and its statutes.

When he came to Statute 3 he kept the Norfolk preference clause but reversed the two other changes which the *Evidences* had introduced into that statute. He omitted the two provisions flanking the new clause which the scribe of the *Evidences* had brought forward to Statute 3, and he returned them to the original position following Statute 12, where Elveden had placed them.[33] He also put back into Statute 3 the final sentence (reserving to Bateman personally a power to direct and effect the appointment and removal of both Master and fellows), which Elveden had imported from the corresponding Trinity Hall statute and which had been omitted by the scribe of the *Evidences*. It is therefore clear from the reversal of that scribe's changes and the return to Elveden's version that Caius must have been fully aware that the Norfolk preference clause had not featured anywhere in Bateman's original 1353 statutes or in Elveden's re-issue of them in 1355: it reveals a lack of candour which is uncharacteristic of Caius.[34]

The 'rival' version: MS 760/424

Unlike Caius, however, the author of MS 760 followed the *Evidences* in retaining the references to Trinity Hall and the list of its statutes which had been in the original 1353 grant; but he went much further, setting out the whole of the text of the 1353 original grant, including the five provisions which Bateman had set out there in full, and only then did he append the text of the twelve listed statutes. Like those before him, he had difficulty when he reached Statute 3. Again he followed the *Evidences* and included in it the same three provisions that had been introduced there: the requirement to have studied arts and logic, the Norfolk preference and the restriction on holding benefices. But he also put back into Statute 3 the power over appointment and dismissal of Master and fellows which Elveden had imported and the *Evidences* had omitted. It is clear from this that the author of MS 760 was, like Caius, alert to Elveden's version of Statute 3 and that he, like Caius, must also have been aware that the Norfolk preference had not featured anywhere in Bateman's original 1353 statutes or in Elveden's re-issue of them in 1355.

33 *I.e.*, as Statutes 14 and 15 (the requirement to have studied arts and logic and the restriction on the holding of benefices). His version therefore followed Statute 12 with the same seven statutes that Walter of Elveden had placed there in 1355.

34 Apart from this important difference in Statute 3 his version is a faithful reproduction of Elveden's 19 statutes.

When he had written out the rest of the twelve statutes the author of MS 760 was faced with a question which had not troubled the scribe of the *Evidences*: what else should follow Statute 12, given that he had already recited in full the five provisions set out by Bateman in the 1353 grant?[35] His answer was to omit all five statutes and to include only the two provisions imported from Trinity Hall by Elveden, *i.e.* Statutes 13 and 19. The result is that MS 760 presents the most complex of the various manuscript versions of Bateman's statutes, and for this reason it is tempting to disregard it as an amateurish exercise which has happened to survive and came late into the possession of the college. It would be wrong, however, to do so, for it is an intriguing manuscript. As explained elsewhere below, we now know that it has long been preserved in the archives of the college and that it contains thoughtful corrections and suggestions on Caius' own statutes.[36] It also contains various other documents relevant to the interpretation of the college's statutes, including the narrow interpretation given by Bateman himself to Trinity Hall on the Master's negative voice. That interpretation of the provision by Bateman had been deliberately omitted by Caius from MS 711 and he had specifically directed in his own statutes that Bateman's *Interpretatio* had no relevance for Gonville Hall. In contrast, a marginal mark in MS 760 not only includes the text of the *Interpretatio* but also highlights the passage on the Master's negative voice; and since that passage formed a crucial part in the fellows' case against Branthwaite in *Allen's Case* in 1617 it is possible that the manuscript was prepared at their instigation in the course of the case.[37]

The Commonwealth versions: MSS 727/754 and 728/755[38]

It is not surprising that the two editions produced during the Commonwealth also differed in their presentation of Bateman's statutes. The extreme Puritan version, MS 728/755, followed Caius' version (in MS 711) in its text of the specific statutes, but it eviscerated the preamble ruthlessly, excising from it completely the whole of the long section in which the bishop had lovingly set out in detail his requirements for prayers, and then numbered the rest of the preamble as Statute 1 (and consequently re-numbered all the subsequent statutes). In the more scholarly MS 727/754 towards the end of the Commonwealth, William Adamson restored the section in the preamble on prayers, but in other respects

[35] Statutes 14 (arts requirement), 15 (benefices restriction), 16 (oath), 17 (clemency) and 18 (reservation of powers).

[36] For MS 760/424 see "*The Statutes of John Caius: The Sources*", § I. 3, at p. 32 below.

[37] See Plate XV, "*The Master's Negative Voice*", § VI. 2, and *Allen's Case* (1617), Appendix F below.

[38] For these manuscripts, see "*The Statutes of John Caius: The Sources*", § I. 3, at pp. 33–4 below.

went back before Caius and returned to the *Evidences*.[39] On one feature, however, there was agreement: both versions included the Norfolk preference unquestioningly. Thereafter no further attempts to correct the text were made until the nineteenth century.

The printed versions

In the nineteenth century the divergence between the different versions of Bateman's statutes presented by the manuscripts was carried into print by the 1852 Commissioners. Having been refused access to the original grants of 1353 and 1355 and to the other manuscripts in the college's archives,[40] they turned to a manuscript in the University Library in order to print Bateman's statutes,[41] and appear to have started upon the printing of that version before they became aware that a copy of Caius' 'authentic' version of Bateman's statutes in MS 711 had been sent to Matthew Parker in 1575 and was preserved in Lambeth Palace Library.[42] At any rate, they chose to print the version which they found in the University Library and merely indicated how the Lambeth copy differed from it. The version they chose to print, however, had started life as a copy of the *Evidences*, and consequently, like the scribe of the *Evidences*, the Commissioners included the Norfolk preference but omitted Statutes 13, 14 and 15.[43]

Unfortunately that was not the final confusion. In 1901 Venn printed a carefully prepared transcript of William Bateman's statutes in his monumental *Biographical History* of the college.[44] To do so he returned to the original copy of the statutes which Walter of Elveden had provided for the college in 1355, and he strove meticulously to reproduce that version. To a great extent he succeeded admirably. However, as the pencilled notes which he made in his personal copy of the Commissioners' *Documents* show, he used the Commissioners' version as 'copy' for his own printer (as he also did for his edition of John Caius' statutes). He carefully compared Elveden's original with the version published by the Commissioners and made the necessary alterations for the printer. When doing so he correctly deleted from their version of Statute 3 both

39 Like the scribe of the *Evidences*, Adamson transferred the provisions on arts and logic and on benefices to Statute 3. He did, however, include Statute 13.

40 See "*Caius' Statutes: The Sources*", § I. 1, at p. 34 below.

41 CUL, Baker MSS xxix, p. 283.

42 Lambeth Library, MS 720.

43 *Documents*, II, 226, at pp. 232, 237–8. The Commissioners, like the scribe, had already included the text of Statutes 14 and 15 in Statute 3, and, like him, they omitted Statute 13 entirely.

44 *B.H.* III, pp. 345–52.

the Norfolk preference[45] and the two flanking provisions which the scribe of *Sheriffe's Evidences* had transposed there; but he later overlooked the need to restore those provisions to their original position following Statute 12 and to include the third statute (Statute 13) which the scribe and the Commissioners had omitted. As a result, Statutes 13, 14 and 15 do not appear anywhere in Venn's otherwise reliable transcript of Elveden's 1355 re-issue.[46]

Ironically, the emergence of differing versions of Bateman's statutes has produced difficulties over the centuries which are precisely the opposite of those presented by Caius' statutes. Caius made careful provision for the preservation of the text of his statutes and, apart from the occasional inevitable scribal errors, there has never been any difficulty in establishing what he dictated. The difficulty has been to work out what Caius meant by what he said, for he seems to have spurned legal assistance and acted as his own draftsman – with the result of great obscurity on numerous occasions. In contrast, Bateman had the assistance of experienced civil and canon lawyers and his statutes are markedly less obscure in their meaning: in the past the difficulty has not been to work out what he meant by what he said, but to ascertain just what he did say and in which statute he said it.

45 He carefully set it out in a postscript and noted that it had first appeared in *Sheriffe's Evidences*: *ibid.*, pp. 352–3.

46 The omission has come to light as a result of Professor Brooke's contribution to the redaction of the Bateman's statutes made for the purposes of this edition.

I. 3

Caius' Statutes: The Sources

Manuscript sources

Six manuscripts of Caius' statutes are listed in the catalogue of the college library.[1] They fall into three categories:

(i) Three manuscripts are of particular value in establishing the text and its meaning: these are the original copy signed by Caius (MS 711/756) and two further manuscripts in italic hand (MSS 755/370 and 760/424).[2] All three are cited very frequently in the notes to the present text, and they are identified there only by their (black) first number.[3] Of these three manuscripts, the first (MS 711) can be dated precisely to 1 January 1573, the second (MS 755) to the decade 1573–83, and the third (MS 760) almost certainly to the early seventeenth century.

(ii) A fourth (MS 636/462) appears also to date from Elizabeth's reign and, unlike the manuscripts already mentioned, it is in secretary hand.

(iii) The remaining two (MSS 727/754 and 728/755) date from the middle years of the seventeenth century and reveal an interesting aspect of the Puritan attitude to Caius' provisions for religious services in college.

Before these manuscripts are considered individually it may be helpful to note that Caius specifically gave the following instructions in his signed original: (i) two copies were to be deposited in Corpus Christi and King's

1 A seventh (MS 604/339) is also included incorrectly in the index to the catalogue but contains statutes of the university, not the college.

2 Curiously, Venn does not mention either the second or third in his *Biographical History*; as explained later, he may have been unaware that they had been temporarily moved into the library from the bursary, since they had only a second, red (shelf) number at the time he was writing.

3 This is the catalogue number and was used by M.R. James in his *A Descriptive Catalogue of MSS in the Library of Gonville & Caius College* (1907–8); the second (red) number is the shelf number. By a confusing co-incidence the catalogue number of MS 755/370 is the same as the shelf number of another of the copies of the statutes (MS 728/755).

Colleges (Statutes 25 and 107);[4] (ii) no more than one additional copy of the statutes should be transcribed (Statute 107); (iii) the additional copy should remain with the Master alone, or the president in his absence (Statute 107); and (iv) the additional copy should be transcribed on parchment which Caius had purchased personally for the purpose (Statute 108). He thus envisaged that there would be in the college only two copies, *i.e.*, the parchment copy and his own signed original from which the copy was to be transcribed. However, Archbishop Parker modified this restriction and directed that *three* copies of the statutes with his rulings incorporated into them should be preserved in the college, one in the archives of the college, a second in the possession of the Master and a third in the possession of the president "from which the other fellows may the more easily know them the better", making a total of five copies including those for King's and Corpus Christi Colleges which both he and Caius had required.[5]

Only two of those five manuscripts can be identified with certainty today. These are Caius' original copy (MS 711) and the parchment copy for which he made provision in Statute 108 (MS 755). The two copies intended for King's and Corpus have not been traced and may never have been made.[6] MS 760 appears to have been written considerably after Caius' and Parker's time, probably in the early seventeenth century for use in the litigation in *Allen's Case* in 1617.

The provenance of MSS 711, 755 and 760 requires explanation. There has never been any uncertainty as regards the location of MS 711: after Caius' death it was preserved in the treasury and was retained there so long as his statutes were in force. Those statutes were repealed in 1860, but the transitional provisions in the statute that replaced them meant that Caius' statutes remained legally relevant for some years afterward,[7] and until they ceased to do so MS 711 was retained in the treasury. At some time after 1860, and before 1900, it was permanently transferred to the library (almost certainly when the removal of the porter's lodge to the Gate of Humility in 1895 allowed for an enlargement of the bursary).[8] At the time of its transfer MS 711 was given a library catalogue number (*i.e.* its first, black number), and it was accordingly included in M.R. James's catalogue of the college's manuscripts in 1907–8. It did not, however, acquire a shelf number (*i.e.* its second, red number) until later.[9]

4 Neither of these manuscripts has been traced by the editor.

5 See Parker's *Interpretatio*, at p. 277 below.

6 See below for the possibility that MS 636/462 may have been the copy for King's College.

7 See "*The Fellowship and the Governing Body*", § VI. 1 below.

8 It had been transferred to the library by 1900 when Venn published his *Biographical History* vols. I–III: see *B.H.* III, p. 59, n. 1, where he mentions the transfer.

9 When M.R. James produced his catalogue of manuscripts in the college library (1907–8) he seems to have worked in King's and sent for manuscripts from the Caius library which were listed in its existing catalogue. He thus included only manuscripts that were listed in that catalogue, *i.e.*, had a first, black number. Ironically this meant that MS 711 was included in

Unlike MS 711, the provenance of MSS 755 and 760 has been something of a mystery. Neither manuscript was included in J.J. Smith's catalogue of the library in 1849; and neither seems to have been known to Venn at the time when he published his extensive researches into the college's archives in Volume III of his *Biographical History* in 1900. Furthermore, neither of them was included in James's catalogue when it was published in 1907–8, and they only appeared there in the supplement which he published in 1913. As a result one might conclude that they were acquired by the college at some time between 1908 and 1913. In fact, however, it is now clear that MSS 755 and 760 have been in the college all along and were kept in the treasury until 1853–54. (In the case of MS 755 it would appear to have remained largely unconsulted, as it is still in pristine condition.) In 1854 the college library was moved into more spacious accommodation following Salvin's alterations to Gonville Court, and, in order to relieve the much overcrowded treasury, MSS 755 and 760 were temporarily transferred to the new library from the treasury, together with a tranche of other bursary volumes. The transfer was intended to be temporary, and these bursary volumes were not entered into the library's catalogue and consequently were given only a shelf number, *i.e.* a red (second) number, without a catalogue number.[10] The removal of the porter's lodge from the Great Gate to the Gate of Humility in 1895 allowed the bursary to expand, and most of the transferred volumes were returned to it at that time. By then, however, Dr Caius' statutes had long been repealed and were merely of historical interest; unlike the other bursary volumes, therefore, MSS 755 and 760 were retained in the library, but they were not given catalogue numbers until after 1908.[11] The manuscripts therefore were not in the treasury at the time when Venn was working on his *Biographical History* and this fact, coupled with the fact that they did not then appear in the

James's catalogue, whereas the two manuscripts next discussed (MSS 755 and 760) were overlooked and omitted from his catalogue, even though they had been transferred to the library much earlier. (As explained below, they had acquired a red shelf number on their transfer, but not a catalogue number, and acquired a black number only after James had published his catalogue: cf. below.)

10 Their low shelf numbers (370 and 424, respectively) are significant, for they indicate that the two books were shelved in the library well before the twentieth century. (The writer is grateful to Mr Mark Statham, the College Librarian, for drawing his attention to the significance of the volumes' low shelf numbers.) The shelf numbers given to the tranche of books temporarily transferred from the bursary show that MS 755, the folio-sized parchment copy of the statutes, was shelved together with the rest of those books, while the small, quarto MS 760 was housed elsewhere in the library.

11 They had been given their black catalogue numbers in time to be included in the Supplement to M.R. James's Catalogue of MSS in 1913, but not in time to be included in the main catalogue (1907–8). For the return of the transferred volumes to the bursary in 1895, see the note by the Librarian (W.T. Lendrum) listing the volumes returned to the bursary on the end-papers of the library's copy of J.J. Smith's Catalogue. The returned volumes had been next to MS 755 on the shelves.

library catalogue, may explain why Venn appears to have been unaware of their existence in the college.

The various manuscripts may now be considered individually.

MS 711/756[12]

This has always been regarded by the college as the 'authoritative' copy, and it was kept in the treasury until it was transferred to the library late in the nineteenth century.[13] Its 'authority' derives from the fact that Caius subscribed his name at the bottom of various pages. A library note enclosed with the manuscript states that he signed at the end of each section, but this is misleading. He signed at the bottom of a number of right-hand pages,[14] but none of the signatures comes at the end of a section or other convenient break, such as the end of a statute: at the one section break where one might have expected him to sign, he did not do so.[15] It is clear that the signatures do not come at a natural break in the text, but simply at the end of a batch of pages that had been submitted to him by the scribe for scrutiny.

The manuscript contains a number of corrections, insertions and side-notes. Although the earlier pages of the manuscript contain more alterations than do the later pages,[16] there are some side-notes and alterations in the later pages, including one by Caius in the last statute.[17] In addition to corrections that appear to have been made by Caius himself, other corrections were clearly made by the scribe, and some of the side-notes have clearly been added later.[18] The manuscript has subsequently been bound up with two other documents also produced by Caius: a copy of Bateman's 1355 statutes (fols. 15–24) and Caius' Interpretations of the latter (fols. 24–25).[19]

The respect accorded to this copy of Caius' statutes is shown clearly by the college's practice of adding upon the blank sheets that follow the statutes a record of those decisions and documents that were considered of constitutional importance: (i) the decree on the Frankland fellows of 11 December 1592; (ii) the decision on the Frankland chaplain of 11 December 1595, both of which were signed by the then Master, Thomas Legge, and the participating fellows;

12 Pages are illustrated on Plates I–VI below.

13 See above.

14 *E.g.*, pp. 15, 39, 47 and 85. He also signed the postscript which he added at the end of the statutes, though the scribe supplied the signature at the end of the statutes themselves.

15 This was between Statutes 74 and 75, where the beginning of the second part of the statutes is marked as such not only in the text but also by a page-break in both MS 711 and MS 755. MS 711 goes so far as to leave a completely blank page between the two parts (p. 75).

16 *E.g.*, Statutes 6, 7, 12, 13, 17, 22, 23 and 25.

17 Statute 108.

18 *E.g.*, Statute 2 and (probably) Statute 86.

19 These precede and are separately paginated from Caius' statutes and the later additions to the volume.

(iii) copies of Mrs Frankland's will and the deed made between the college and Thomas Wendy's nephew re-establishing the Wendy fellowship in 1610; (iv) an extract from Dr Perse's will relating to the Perse fellows; (v) the alteration regarding the Frankland chaplain of 13 June 1628 and the negotiation with Martin Perse regarding Perse's property of 24 April 1639; (vi) the mandate from King Charles I concerning *Cooke's Case* (1636), together with the Commissioners' report; and, finally, (vii) a synopsis of (most of) Parker's *Interpretatio*. It is clear from the underlining of significant passages and marginal markings, and also from the dictionary notes of the meaning of obscure terms on the fly-leaf, that the volume was much consulted during the period before the Civil War. After the Commonwealth no further alterations or additions to the manuscript seem to have been made, and the emergence during the Commonwealth period of the series of volumes containing the *Gesta* meant that important decisions were recorded there, sometimes accompanied by the signatures of the participants.

MS 711 has provided the basis of the present edition of Caius' statutes. Alterations, corrections and marginal comments appearing in this manuscript have, as a general rule, been indicated in notes in the Latin text, and alternative readings presented in the printed editions and in other manuscripts have also been noted. As MS 711 was overseen by Caius himself the scribe's somewhat idiosyncratic punctuation and use of capital letters has been reproduced here without the alterations which were made in the Commissioners' printed edition in 1852 and adopted by Venn in 1901 in his *Biographical History*.

MS 755/370

This elegantly written manuscript in vellum is confined to Caius' statutes and still has its original boards and (the remains of) its strings. It is neatly and carefully written by a professional scribe within carefully ruled margins, and it is clearly the copy of his statutes which Caius directed the college to make after his death and for which he himself had purchased the necessary parchment at his own expense.[20] It was not written before Caius' death, but around the time when the college acquired various rulings on the interpretation of his statutes from Archbishop Parker in 1575; for the scribe included a marginal note against most (though not all) of the sections on which Parker gave a ruling. Apart from these references to Parker's *Interpretatio* nothing was added to Caius' text, and the pristine state of the manuscript shows that it must have remained virtually unused to the present day.

[20] Cf. Statute 108.

MS 760/424

This is the most intriguing of the various manuscripts that contain a copy of Caius' statutes. It was written on paper, but it was expensively bound in a vellum wrapper, with a rose and coronet impressed in the centre of each cover. In addition to Caius' statutes it also contains (i) a prolegomenon which reproduces Bateman's foundation deed and the confirmations of it by the Bishop of Ely and the chancellor of the University (which Caius had not included in MS 711); (ii) Bateman's statutes; (iii) the *Interpretatio* which Bateman gave to Trinity Hall in 1354 on the Master's negative voice (again, not included by Caius in MS 711), together with a note of Caius' ruling that Bateman's interpretation did not apply to Gonville's college;[21] (iv) Caius' *Expositiones* on Bateman's statutes; (v) Caius' own statutes; (vi) a synopsis of Matthew Parker's *Interpretatio* of the latter statutes; and finally (vii) an excerpt from the 1557 charter requiring that the Master and fellows conform with the statutes of both Bateman and Caius in their elections and other business and that the latter's statutes should not conflict with those of the former.

In contrast to the scribe who prepared MS 755 and was concerned simply to reproduce the text of MS 711 as neatly and accurately as he could, the writer of MS 760 was prepared to seek out additional documents such as Bateman's foundation deed and the deeds confirming it and, more significantly, the interpretation of the statute on the Master's negative voice which Bateman had given to Trinity Hall. Furthermore, he was attentive to the meaning and intention of the statutes he was copying, and the MS contains shrewd variations on suspect readings of the text, some of which had gone unchallenged in MS 755 and even in Caius' own copy, MS 711.[22] It also contains marginal highlighting of significant passages, especially that on the Master's negative voice.[23] For these reasons it seems likely that it was produced at the time of *Allen's Case* in 1617, perhaps at the behest of the fellows, for it incorporates the authorities which they put forward in their case against the Master, Branthwaite, with regard to the latter's negative voice.[24] Given the expensive binding and the impressed coronets and roses, it is not inconceivable that it was prepared for use by the chancellor, Thomas Howard Earl of Suffolk, in that case.

21 See Plate XV below.

22 See, *e.g.*, Statutes 8, 15, 25, 36, 41, 45, 73, 86, 88, 98 and postscript. The variant readings in MS 760, even when they have not been adopted here, display a critical faculty that is lacking in other copies.

23 See, *e.g.*, p. 17 (Plate XV below).

24 *Allen's Case* (1617), Appendix F below.

MS 636/462

This much-worn volume was given to the college library in 1838 from the papers of the late Dr Francis Barnes, who had been the Master of Peterhouse from 1788 to 1838. It contains Caius' statutes and his *Expositiones* of Bateman's statutes, but not the bishop's own statutes. There is no obvious reason which might explain why such a work should have come into his hands, for it is not a collector's piece; but it should be noted that Barnes had previously been a fellow and Vice-Provost of King's College before his appointment to the mastership of Peterhouse. Given that the manuscript appears to have been written in the reign of Elizabeth, it may possibly be the copy that was originally intended by Caius for King's College.[25]

It is written carefully in secretary hand and would seem to be a very early copy of the statutes; but it is on poor paper and is now much less easily read than the earlier three. A few sections are missing and it has been of little assistance editorially.

MS 728/755

In addition to incomplete lists of scholars to 1631, this manuscript contains a copy of Bateman's statutes, Caius' *Expositiones* and his own statutes and would appear to have been written late in the reign of Charles I or in the early Commonwealth. Editorially, it is noteworthy: the section in Statute 45 requiring a prayer to be said for the soul of John Caius is completely omitted for the first time.[26] Furthermore, it is the only surviving manuscript that contains a large and elaborate index and it would therefore appear to be the copy that was regarded in the nineteenth century as "the President's copy", *i.e.*, the working copy which Parker had required to be kept by the president for consultation by fellows.[27]

[25] Statutes 107, 108. Neither Corpus nor King's appears to possess a copy of Caius' statutes. The only other occasion during Legge's mastership which might explain its having been written would seem to be his dispute with Gerrard and other fellows in 1582 but there is nothing in the account of that dispute to suggest this. Although MS 636/462 has not been of great assistance editorially, it does contain an interesting note on the fly-leaf (made after its acquisition by the Library) that "There is a large and elaborate index of the matters in the Statutes – at the end of the President's copy." This would suggest that MS 728/755 was the president's copy, since it is the only manuscript which has such an index: see below.

[26] The Puritan influence is very marked: the manuscript eviscerates Bateman's statutes and omits entirely the long section containing Bateman's detailed requirements for prayers.

[27] For the description of it as the president's copy, see n. 25 above on MS 636/462. It can hardly have started life as the copy that Archbishop Parker had in mind, since it is combined with a list of later scholars and clearly came into existence long after his death.

MS 727/754

This copy was begun during the Commonwealth by William Adamson (*B.H.* I, pp. 352–3), who also helped to compile the *Registrum Magnum*, and it was completed by Thomas Gooch, later Master, in the eighteenth century. The fly-leaf contains the nice note that the statutes were transcribed by one of the senior fellows, "but it was in the late time of confusion, while they were not sworn to the statutes". Like MS 728/755, this manuscript also omits Caius' provision in Statute 45 for prayers for his soul after his death.[28]

LAMBETH MS 720

In addition to the manuscripts in the college library, mention should also be made of a manuscript in the library of Lambeth Palace: Lambeth MS 720. This was sent by the Master and the fellows to Archbishop Parker in 1574 when they sought his ruling on the interpretation of Caius' statutes. Lambeth MS 720 was transcribed by a notary, one Martinus Berye, and it is clear that Legge, a knowledgeable civilian, chose his scribe well; for Berye's transcription of Caius' MS 711 is faultless – he not only reproduced Caius' text accurately and certified each folio he wrote (Lambeth MS 720, fos. 36–72), but also added six pages of comments on his reading of the text he was copying. For the reason mentioned below, it was the copy which the Cambridge Commissioners were driven to use when they produced their printed copy of the college's statutes in 1852.[29] In fairness to Berye, it should be added that such (few) errors as there are in the Commissioners' printed text were not made by Berye, but result in each case from a misreading in 1852 of his transcript.

Printed texts

The Latin text of Caius' statutes has been printed in two publications easily accessible in Cambridge. The University Commissioners printed it in 1852 in the second of their three volumes of documents relating to the University and Colleges of Cambridge (*Documents*, vols. I–III); and Venn printed it in Volume III of his *Biographical History* in 1900.

Neither MS 711 nor any other manuscript in the college was consulted by the Commissioners – for they had been denied access to the college's statutes by the then Master, Benedict Chapman, as they were by several other colleges. Since the Commissioners could not make use of any manuscripts in the college's

28 Adamson did, however, include Bateman's detailed requirements for prayers which MS 728/755 excised (cf. n. 26 above).

29 *Documents*, II, pp. 226ff.

archives or library, they had to take their text from the notarised copy of MS 711 that had been sent by the Master and the fellows to Archbishop Parker in 1574, namely Lambeth MS 720 in Lambeth Palace library. As mentioned above, the 1852 printed text does contain a small number of errors which result from a misreading of the notary's writing.[30]

The copy of the Commissioners' *Documents* in the college library carries marginal annotations by Venn; these pencilled annotations indicate clearly that he used the 1852 printed text as a convenient proof for the printing of his own text in vol. III of his *Biographical History*. From the comparisons that have been made, it is clear that Venn made a few alterations or corrections to the 1852 text, though he modestly claimed no credit for them.[31] He did not spot all the mistaken readings in the 1852 text;[32] but he did pick up most of them.

The numbering of the Statutes

The scribe of the 'authoritative' MS 711 made three mistakes in his numbering of the statutes.

(i) The first mistake occurred in the middle of Statute 45 *De orationibus*, where the scribe mistakenly put the number "46" against a mere sub-paragraph of the statute.[33] As a result he gave to the next proper statute, *De adultis*, the number "47" instead of "46", which it should have had. The incorrect numbering in MS 711 continued for five statutes, *i.e.*, until it had reached the statute *De reis infamiae*, which was consequently wrongly numbered "51" instead of "50".

(ii) The second mistake then occurred when the scribe omitted to give any number to the statute (*De absentiis*) that followed immediately after his (wrongly numbered) "Statute 51", even though it dealt with an entirely new subject. The scribe's error of absorbing the statute *De absentiis* into Statute 51 had the unintended, though fortunate, consequence of

30 This was in secretary hand and, though neat and careful, is less easily read than MS 711's italic hand.

31 *E.g.*, Statutes 4, 15, 44, 45, 82 and 90.

32 *E.g.*, Statutes 88, 95, 96.

33 The first error in MS 711 can be explained. In that MS the bottom of the right-hand page 47 comes in the middle of Statute 45, just at the point preceding the word "*Scholastici*", which as a result comes at the top of the verso, *i.e.*, the left-hand page 48. That word is a sub-title and is therefore centred, even though it is not the title of a new statute. At the bottom of page 47, Caius has signed his name, which he appears to have done at the end of each bunch of pages produced by the scribe. This probably means that the scribe started a new batch of text on page 48 and, it would seem, he mistakenly inserted the number "46" against the centred entry "*Scholastici*" at the top of that page. See Plate VI below.

correcting the numbering of subsequent statutes: the statute following the unnumbered *De absentiis*, namely, *De absentia nocturna et portis claudendis*, was thus correctly given the number "52".[34]

(iii) The scribe's correct numbering of the statutes continued from Statute 52 as far as Statute 97, *De reparatione seu aedificatione*. At this point the scribe of MS 711 failed to give a new number to the next provision, *De declinatione sociorum ad Manera*: he simply absorbed the provision into Statute 97, even though it was clearly a new statute. As a result he numbered the remaining eight statutes as 98–107, whereas he should have given the number 98 to *De declinatione sociorum ad Manera* and numbered the remainder as 99–108.

All three mistakes were reproduced in the copy that was sent soon afterwards to Archbishop Parker at Lambeth Palace in 1574, and they were consequently adopted both by the Commissioners and by Venn in their printed texts.[35]

The mistakes made by the scribe of MS 711 must have been noticed very quickly in the college; for all three mistakes were corrected in the handsome vellum copy (MS 755) into which Caius' statutes were transcribed, as he had directed in Statute 108, soon after the Master and fellows had received Archbishop Parker's response in 1575. The scribe of MS 755 sensibly withheld the number "46" from the sub-paragraph of Statute 45 and correctly assigned it to the statute *De adultis* (in place of the "47" given to it in MS 711). When he reached the second mistake made in MS 711 he correctly gave the appropriate number "51" to the statute *De absentiis*, which MS 711 had left unnumbered. This restored the correspondence of numbering between the two manuscripts until he reached the third mistake in MS 711, *i.e.*, the failure to number the statute *De declinatione sociorum ad Manera*. Spotting the error, he correctly treated *De declinatione sociorum ad Manera* as a distinct statute and gave it the number "98". Thereafter the numbering continued to differ until the end, and as a result the final statute, *De contradictione Statutorum Rev. Patris et nostri* is correctly numbered "108" in MS 755, but is wrongly numbered "107" in MS 711 and the earlier printed texts.[36]

34 Whether the scribe of MS 711 simply made a second mistake and overlooked the need for a new number, or whether he realised his earlier error at that point and deliberately omitted any number in order to restore the correct sequence, we shall never know; but the result is that the subsequent numbering is correct until the third mistake is reached.

35 The 1852 Commissioners were restricted to reproducing the Lambeth copy of the statutes and Venn appears not to have been aware of MS 755, in which the mistakes were corrected.

36 This time the divergence is, of course, the other way round: for the last ten statutes MS 711 has the lower number, and MS 755 has the greater.

The present edition follows the numbering in MS 755, since two statutes would otherwise be left without a number and a third statute would be split between two numbers.[37] The result is as follows:

Statutes 1–45:	numbers correspond
Statute 45:	numbers diverge at this point
Statutes 46–51:	the numbers in MS 711 and the earlier printed texts are one greater than those in MS 755 and the present edition
Statute 52:	numbers re-converge
Statutes 52–96:	numbers correspond
Statute 97:	numbers diverge again
Statutes 98–108:	the numbers in MS 711 and the earlier printed texts are one less than those in MS 755 and the present edition.

37 The scribe of MS 760 also spotted and corrected the three mistakes in MS 711, but the third brought him to the bottom of a right-hand page and when he started a new statute at the top of the verso, *i.e.*, left-hand page, he overlooked Statute 99 (*De locandis possessionibus sine consensus fundatoris durante vita sua*) completely (or else omitted it because it had become obsolete by his time?) and passed straight to the statute *De possessionibus non vendendis*. His final statute was thus numbered 107 instead of 108.

II

The Statutes of Edmund Gonville, 1348

TEXT AND TRANSLATION

II

The Statutes of Edmund Gonville

[Cambridge, Gonville & Caius College, BUR: DEEDS/ I. 10.[a]]

[NOTE: In the manuscript the script is continuous; only the final two paragraphs are written separately.]

Omnibus ad quos presens scriptura pervenerit Edmundus de G. rector ecclesie de T. Norwicensis diocesis salutem et perpetuam memoriam rei geste.

Quoniam sapiencia moderatrix rerum omnium[b] super singula terrena preeminens cuius generosa possessio cum sparsa fuerit colligitur gratis errogata revertitur cum absconsa fuerit minuitur pupplicata suscipit incrementum hereditario iure cuiquam non descendit sed pocius inter studentes acquiritur litteris laboribus et doctrina. Cupiens universitatem Cantabriggie studencium huiusmodi numero decorari aulam seu domum scolarium in eadem erigere et de novo fundare ad honorem dei et sancte matris ecclesie et salutem anime mee necnon ad uberiorem sustentacionem pauperum scholarium et predictam aulam ex bonis meis temporalibus cum dei adiutorio duxi perpetuo sustentandam ut sic preciosa sciencie margarita suis vigiliis et studiis adquisita sub modio non lateat sed spargatur in universitate predicta et ad profectum rei pupplice minis[c] perfectis pupplicetur. Et ut scolarium huiusmodi societas sub firmioris pacis et concordie commodo dilatetur statuta quedam et ordinaciones utiles de peritorum concilio perpetuis temporibus feci duratura; que per

[a] It is unsealed and undated, and it identifies the parties by initials, but it is otherwise in final form for their approval.

[b] The phrase is drawn from Cicero, *de inventione* 1.5: "*moderatrix omnium rerum praesto est sapientia*". It is an intriguing question whether Gonville was acquainted with Cicero's works or whether the phrase was an unattributed aphorism in circulation at the time. (The writer is indebted to the Revd Cally Hammond for the reference.)

[c] As so often, it is difficult to distinguish 'm', 'n', 'i' and 'u'. It could be *nimis*.

II

The Statutes of Edmund Gonville

[NOTE: For convenience of reference numbered paragraphs and sub-paragraphs have been supplied editorially in both text and translation and various conjunctions have not been translated in consequence.]

To all persons to whom this present writing shall come: Edmund de Gonville rector of the church of Terrington in the diocese of Norwich [sends] greetings and an enduring record of the matter.

Since wisdom is the authoritative guide on all matters of an earthly nature and, being scarce, a worthy mastery of it is [to be] garnered and distributed freely, its value is diminished when it is kept secret and increased when it is made public, and it is no person's birthright but rather is acquired by students through study, work and teaching.[1] Desiring that the university of Cambridge should be embellished with a body of students of this kind [and wishing] to set up and found in it a new hall or house of scholars both for the honour of God and holy mother church and the salvation of my soul and also for the fuller support of poor scholars, I have made provision with God's help for the perpetual maintenance of the hall out of my worldly goods; so that the precious pearl of knowledge which is acquired by their eager attentiveness to study should not be hidden under a bushel but spread around in the university and made publicly available for the benefit of the commonwealth in full measure.[2] And so that a community of scholars of this sort may grow under [the shelter of] lasting peace and concord, I have, with the advice of experts, made certain statutes and practical ordinances to endure for all time, and I have arranged for

1 This first sentence differs greatly, in character and syntax, from Gonville's usual style; in it he labours to paraphrase and elaborate upon a concept derived from Cicero (see note to text). Elsewhere in the statutes his instructions are invariably clear, precise and succinct.

2 This assumes a reading as "*minis perfectis*" (see note to text).

cancellarium[a] et universitatem predictam coram eis primitus perlecta et plene discussa procuravi confirmari.[b]

[1.] In primis igitur volo ordino statuto quod dicta aula quam largiente domino erigere cupio et creare ex cognomine meo nomen capiat Aula de G. ex nunc pro perpetuo vocitetur.

[2.] Cedente vero vel decedente magistro domus mee predicte liberam habeant futuri magistri eleccionem socii dicte domus sub ea tamen que subsequitur forma ad eleccionem suam fore duxi procedendum.

i. Primo omnes socii dicte domus tunc presentes absentibus si qui fuerint per quindenam primitus expectatis dum tamen due partes ad minus presentes fuerint insimul conveniant coram seniore dicte domus tunc presente qui coram eo ad sancta dei evangelia corporale prestent iuramentum quod odio amore favore et alia quacumque affeccione inordinata positis post penitus illum de se ipsis vel aliis eligant in magistrum quem sciencia moribus industria conversacione et modestia magis credant necessarium utilem et idoneum pro administracione et regimine dicte domus. Qui senior duobus minoribus sociis pupplice coram omnibus consimile per omnia prestet iuramentum. Seniorem vero intelligo eum qui prius in dicta domo iuratus fuerat et admissus.

ii. Quo[c] facto dicti senior et iuniores qui tres scrutatores pariter existant seniori de residuis pupplice coram omnibus tunc presentibus ad sancta dei evangelia corporale prestent iuramentum quod dictum scrutinium fideliter et absque fraude facient scribent et referent et eciam pupplicabunt primo vota sua secundum ordinem et postea aliorum vota eciam secundum ordinem admissionis sue in dicta domo nisi alicui propter doctoratus statum aut magisterii sui in hoc duxerint differendum et postea vota infirmorum siqui tunc fuerint in dicta domo sigillatim examinent fideliter et secrete omniumque dicta in scriptis redigant et vota sic scripta mox pupplicent in communi.

a In references to the chancellor, as elsewhere, the scribe is inconsistent in his use of capitals (particularly 'c' and 's'). Lower case has been used in the translation throughout for such words as chancellor, university, fellow and scholar.

b MS has "*confirmavi*" in error.

c Lower case in MS but full stop indicates new sentence.

them to be confirmed by the chancellor and the university after they have first been read and discussed fully in a meeting.

[1.] I therefore will, order and decree first that the hall which I desire to erect and create with the Lord's bounty shall take its name from my surname [and] be called Gonville Hall from now in perpetuity.

[2.] On the resignation or death of the Master of my house the fellows of the house shall have unfettered choice of his successor provided [it is made] in accordance with the following procedure which I have laid down to be observed for his election.

i. First, after any absent fellows have been given fifteen days' notice [and] provided at least two-thirds are present, all the fellows of the house then present, shall assemble at the same time before the senior fellow of the house then present and take a bodily oath before him on God's holy gospels that they will put all dislike, favour and other improper consideration whatsoever utterly behind them and will choose as Master from among themselves or others the person whom they believe to be best qualified in learning, morals, application, behaviour and discretion, and most suitable and fitting for the management and government of the house. The fellow who is senior shall, with two more junior fellows, openly take an identical oath before everyone. I regard as senior the one who had been sworn and admitted to the house earlier.

ii. When this has been done the senior and the [two] more junior fellows shall serve as three scrutineers equally and they shall openly take a bodily oath on God's holy gospels before the senior of the remaining fellows and in front of all then present that they will conduct, record, return and announce the scrutiny[3] faithfully and without fraud, [taking] first their own votes in order and then the votes of the others also in order of their admission to the house, unless they have provided for a different order for any particular person on account of his degree of doctor or master; and afterwards they shall ascertain faithfully and privately[4] by sign the votes of any in the house who are sick and shall record in writing all that is said and without delay announce to the community the votes so written.

3 Unlike the term 'ballot', scrutiny did not imply a secret vote that was written by and known only to the voter.

4 "*Secrete*" would seem to indicate merely that the sick person's vote is taken at his bedside and not at the meeting; it does not imply a secret ballot, since that vote is then declared to the fellowship.

iii. Pupplicacione vero facta ille in quem maior pars consenserit sociorum cancellario vel eius vicem gerenti per scrutatores ipsos vel alias per alios socios per maiorem partem ad hoc deputatos illico presentetur qui absque sollempnitate vel difficultate quacumque informacione sola recepta de concordi numero eligencium eleccionem huiusmodi absque examinacione alia confirmare et ipsum electum ad magisterium curam et regimen dicte domus tam in temporalibus quam in spiritualibus admittere teneatur. Sicque admissus absque alia auctoritate aut induccione licite ministret et suum incontinenti officium exequatur.

iv. Poterit tamen dicta societas si absque domus ac eorum incommodo hoc senserit[d] faciendum presenciam absentis cancellarii pro confirmacione et admissione huiusmodi per tempus aliquod modicum expectare.

v. Volo tamen si tempore vacacionis magisterii due partes sociorum propter vacacionum tempora vel aliis de causis absentes fuerint quod expectacio quindena presentibus non sufficiat ad eleccionem huiusmodi celebrandam, sed presentes absentes eorundem absencium sumptibus faciant premuniri et eos per viginti dies a tempore diei cessacionis magisterii ad minus expectent.

vi. Iuret vero sic admissus in admissione sua domino cancellario[e] vel eius vicem-gerenti cuius {in}[f] iurisdictione in domum meam predictam et scolares dicte domus subicio quod officium sibi commissum tam in cura et administracione quam regimine dicte domus diligenter et fideliter exequetur quodque statuta et ordinationes presentes et eciam per cancellarium de consensu meo in posterum faciendas secundum eorum intellectum grammaticalem et communem pro viribus observabit nec contra ea conveniet in toto vel in parte per viam appellacionis aut querele aut alicuius iuris remedio seu colore sed ea faciet a sociis suis in quantum poterit observari.

vii. Si vero vota eligencium in parte equali numero sint divisa tunc cancellarius vel eius vicem-gerens cui contigerit eleccionem huiusmodi presentari gratificare poterit alteri nominato et quem utiliorem

d The scribe used the medieval form *sencerit*, and also wrote "*incommode*" as "*in comodo*".

e On this single occasion the chancellor is, for some reason, honoured with the virtually untranslatable title of "*dominus*".

f This first "*in*" is struck through and underlined with dots. Its original insertion left "*iurisdictione*" instead of "*iurisdictioni*". The second "*in*" is not deleted and attaches the words "*domum meam predictam et scolares dicte domus*" to "*iurisdictione*", thereby leaving "*subicio*" awkwardly without an object; however, Gonville's meaning is clear.

iii. After the result has been announced the person on whom the majority have agreed shall thereupon be presented to the chancellor or his deputy by the scrutineers themselves, or otherwise by other fellows assigned for the purpose by the majority;[5] and thereupon, without any formality or hurdle whatsoever [and] simply upon being informed of the number of electors in favour, he shall be obliged to confirm the election without any examination[6] and to admit the elected person to the mastership, care and government of the house in both temporalities and spiritualities. The person thus admitted shall lawfully undertake and execute his office forthwith without any authorisation or induction.

iv. However, if the chancellor is then absent and the community considers that it can be done without inconvenience to the house and to themselves, it may postpone this confirmation and admission for a reasonable time until he is present.

v. If two-thirds of the fellowship are absent during vacation or for other reasons on the occurrence of a vacancy in the mastership, it is my wish that fifteen days' delay shall not be sufficient for those present to make an election in the manner specified; but they shall give notice to the absentees [to attend] at their own expense and wait for them for at least twenty days from the date on which the mastership ended.

vi. At his admission by the chancellor or his deputy (to whose jurisdiction I submit my house and its scholars) the person so admitted shall swear that he will faithfully and diligently perform the office entrusted to him both in the care and management of the house and in its government, and that he will rigorously observe the statutes and the present ordinances, and those made subsequently by the chancellor with my consent, according to their grammatical and common sense; and that he will not proceed against them, in whole or in part, by way of appeal or complaint or by any process or colour of law, but will enforce their observance by his fellows to the best of his ability.

vii. If the votes of the electors are equally divided, then the chancellor or deputy to whom such an election falls to be submitted shall have power to select whichever nominee he judges to be more suitable to

5 The alternative allows for the election of the senior fellow or other scrutineer.

6 *I.e.*, without the civil law process of examination.

ipsorum viderit ad regendum ad magisterium huiusmodi admittere et ipsum sicut premittitur confirmare.

[3.] Magister vero sic prefectus residenciam ad minus pro tempore quo magistri universitatis legere teneantur in domo predicta continue faciat [...][a] personalem pro utilitate regiminis sui vel ex alia causa rationabili maiori eum expediat absentare.

[4.] Volo insuper quod semper magistro futuro acta [et] munimenta quamcunque administracionem predecessoris sui contingencia absque dilacione aliqua liberentur.

[5.] Faciat insuper magister noviter sic assumptus de consensu[b] duorum sociorum ad hoc a maiore parte deputatorum infra quindecim dies post admissionem suam proximos de bonorum mobilium et se moventium numero ac vera estimacione eorum et quantitate debitorum dicte domus nominibus creditorum specialiter expressis inventarium duplicatum cuius una parte penes se retenta alia pars penes societatem ipsam in archivis suis fideliter conservetur ut sic sciri poterit utrum sic admissus utiliter regat dictam domum qui eciam compotum reddat singulis annis post autumpnum ante resumpcionem magistrorum coram sociis suis presentibus dummodo maior pars sociorum tunc presens fuerit alioquin infra octo dies a tempore proxime resumpcionis magistrorum de bonis et expensis communibus in scriptis particulariter et distincte in quo status dicte domus tam in solucione debitorum illius anni quam bonorum omnium diminucione vel excessu specialiter exprimatur post quod tractetur communiter qualiter pro anno futuro sint maiores providencie faciende et alias in quadragesimali vacacione expense communes per socios videantur si notabilis suspicio vel administracio suspecta aut alia causa necessaria seu probabilis maiori parti sociorum dicte domus hoc suaserit faciendum.

[6.] Habeat insuper domus mea unam cistam communem bene ligatam in aliquo tuto loco reponendam cum tribus clausuris seu serruris distinctis et totidem clavibus dissimilibus quarum unam habeat magister et alias duas duo socii alii ad hoc singulis annis infra quindenam proximam post festum sancti Dionisii per maiorem partem sociorum preelecti in qua

[a] An indecipherable word (? *insuper*, but possibly *nisique*), which may have been crossed out, appears here.

[b] MS has "*concensu*"; cf. "*sencerit*" above.

govern, and to admit him to the mastership and confirm him in the manner stated above.

[3.] When he has been thus set in office the Master shall be continuously resident in person in the aforesaid house during the period when the university's masters are required to lecture, unless he needs to be absent on the business of its government or for any other reasonable cause.[7]

[4.] It is my wish that the deeds and muniments relating to any business whatsoever of his predecessor shall always be handed over to an incoming Master without delay.

[5.] With the consent of two fellows appointed by the majority for the purpose and within fifteen days immediately following his admission, an incoming Master shall make a duplicate inventory of the movable goods and livestock by their number and true valuation, together with the amount of the debts of the house with the names of the creditors being specifically recorded; one part of the inventory shall be retained in his possession [by the Master] and the other part by the community itself in its archives, so that it can thereby be known whether he has been governing the house properly since his admission. Following autumn each year, before the resumption of studies if the majority of the fellows are present, or otherwise within eight days after the start of the term, he shall render to the fellows who are then present a clear and detailed written account of assets and expenditure, in which the financial state of the house is fully set out as regards both the settlement of the year's debts and the reduction or increase in all [its] assets. After this the community shall discuss what provision should be made for major contingencies in the coming year, and the communal expenses shall be reviewed by the fellows subsequently in the Lent vacation, if grave suspicion or suspect administration, or other necessary or probable cause, persuades the majority of the fellows that this should be done.

[6.] My house shall have one well-bound common chest to be kept in some safe place with three separate locks or bars and the same number of differing keys.[8] The Master is to have one key and two fellows chosen annually by the majority of the fellows each year during the fortnight following the Feast of St Dennis[9] are to have the other two; and their common seal, all

7 The obscurity of the Latin text makes it uncertain whether the business of government (*pro utilitate regiminis sui*) is stated as the reason requiring continuous residence or as a reason allowing absence. The latter seems more likely.

8 Cf. Bateman's Statute 6, where he uses the more specific term *arca*.

9 9 October; it marked the beginning of Winter Term the following day: *H.U.C.*, I, p. 29.

sigillum eorum commune carte omnes et munimenta ac alie raciones et evidencie utiles dicte domui fideliter conserventur.

[7.] Item provideat magister quod infirmis sociis in cibis et potibus regimine et aliis necessariis secundum facultates domus competenter omni tempore ministretur etiam si expense huiusmodi communam excedere debeant dum tamen excessus huiusmodi ad modicum puta in septimana ad duos denarios vel tres se extendant.

[8.] Item ut dicte domus observetur honestas et studencium utilitas procuretur provideat magister dicte domus de consensu maioris partis sociorum suorum ad obsequia et servicia maiora seu principalia societatis dicte necessaria inter que barbitonsoris et lotricis officia computentur idoneos servientes quibus de communi sallario ministretur.

[9.] Item si magister casualiter fuerit criminosus vel de aliquo crimine notabili quod importat infamiam arguatur aut alias inutilis et hoc per maiorem partem societatis in aliqua congregatione regencium per socios debito iuramenti prestiti communiter reveletur ita quod cancellarius vel tunc presidens cum duobus ad minus regentibus per dictam congregationem ad hoc electis dicto magistro vocato veritatem inquirat summarie et de plano ipsumque a presidencia sua sine scriptura et ordine iudiciario de consensu eorum amoveat si iuxta compertam super delatis criminibus seu defectibus veritatem domus honestatem vel illius utilitatem rationabiliter fuerit amovendus; nulla contra hoc appellacione vel alio iuris communis seu specialis remedio quomodolibet valituro. Proviso quod nihilominus in societate remaneat atque domo tanquam socius et inposterum de ipso sicud de alio socio iudicetur. Si autem impotens fuerit ad regendum propter senectutem vel infirmitatem regat per substitutum ab eo nominatum si in eum consenserit maior pars sociorum.

[10.] Criminosi vero incorrigibiles vel propter suam culpam intollerabiles socii de domo totaliter expellantur sub ea tamen que subsequitur forma. Si vero aliquis de dicta societate seditiosus fuerit aut rixosus vel vagabundus studio non insistens neque proficiens vel alias criminosus in primo transgressu vel defectu notabili quo super hoc convictus fuerit per magistrum a percepcione comunarum suarum per certum tempus iuxta

charters and muniments and any accounts and title deeds that pertain to the house shall be kept securely in that chest.

[7.] The Master shall ensure that fellows who are ill are always adequately provided with food and drink and other necessities in keeping with what the house can afford, even if such expenses have to exceed the normal budget, provided however that such excess shall be kept within moderation, say, two or three pence a week.

[8.] In order to ensure that the propriety of the house should be maintained and the well-being of [its] students ensured, the Master of the house shall, with the consent of the majority of its fellows, make provision for the necessary offices and major or principal services of the community, among which the offices of a barber and a laundress[10] are to be reckoned suitable employees for whom he should make provision out of the common fund for servants' wages.

[9.] If the Master should by any chance be guilty of a crime, or charged with any blatant offence that imports infamy, or is otherwise injurious, and this is laid before a congregation of regents by the majority of the fellows upon oath duly taken by the fellows, the chancellor or the person then presiding shall thereupon summon the Master and enquire [into the charge] summarily in open court, together with at least two regents chosen for the purpose by the congregation, and shall with their consent remove him from his position of authority, without [the formality of] writing or judicial proceeding, if he ought reasonably to be removed in the light of the proven truth of the crimes or failings charged and the repute of the house or its well-being. There shall be no appeal against this and no remedy of general or local law shall be allowable in any way. He shall nevertheless remain in the community and house as a fellow and be treated like any other fellow. If he becomes incapable of governing as a result of senility or infirmity, he shall govern through a deputy nominated by him if the majority of the fellows agree to that.

[10.] Fellows who are incorrigible offenders or are through their own fault insufferable are to be expelled from the house completely, though [only] in the following manner. If any member of the society should be subversive, factious or a layabout[11] who neither devotes himself to study nor profits from it, or is seriously at fault in any other way, he shall, on the first transgression or conspicuous failing of which he has been found guilty by the Master, be excluded by sentence of the Master from receipt

[10] The two posts required by Gonville serve different needs from those specified by Bateman (baker and purveyor) or Caius (butler and purveyor).

[11] 'Vagabond' later acquired a statutory connotation.

arbitrium maioris partis sociorum secundum qualitatem et quantitatem delicti per magistri sentenciam excludatur. In secundo transgressu vel defectu pena duplicetur. In tercio pena quadruplicetur; et si incorrigibilis inveniatur tunc iudicio magistri et maioris partis sociorum a dicta domo finaliter expellatur et in loco illius alius idoneus subrogetur nullo appellacionis suplicacionis aut alicuius juris[a] communis seu specialis remedio in ea parte valituro qui sic amotus in virtute iuramenti prestiti absque difficultate aliqua sive spe redeundi statui suo quem ibidem tenuit illico pure et absolute cedere teneatur.

[**11.**] Item ut in domo mea nulla sit personarum accepcio socii dicte domus indistincte per scrutinium communiter faciendum sicut supra dicitur de magistro eligantur.

viii. Proviso quod idoneor moribus et sciencia qui libere fuerit condicionis et ad proficiendum aptior magisque videatur indigens omni favore odio timore familiaritate et amore et quovis alio exquisito colore penitus postpositis de dicta universitate eligatur.

ix. Illum voco rite electum in quem maior pars consenserit sociorum vel media eorumdem dum tamen magister concurrat.

x. Quando vero vota eligentium sociorum sint equalia tunc magister domus per gratificacionem assumere poterit quem sibi placuerit de equaliter sic electis.

xi. Volo eciam quod in dicta domo indifferenter sophiste generales bachilarii et magistri arcium abiliores tamen ad proficiendum in theologia sub forma superius annotata eligantur.

[**12.**] Socius eciam quilibet in suo ingressu verbaliter promittat obedienciam magistro in presencia sociorum qui virtute obediencie sic promisse nedum magistro sed eius vicemgerenti in eius absencia quicumque in canonicis mandatis monicionibus seu decretis licitis et honestis que tangunt utilitatem honestatem seu quietem eorum aut dicte domus teneatur prompcius obedire.

[**13.**] Caveat tamen magister ne in mandatis suis parcialis sit quibusdam nimis rigidus quibusdam nimis facilis et aliis onerosus.

[**14.**] Jurabit eciam quilibet socius in suo ingressu quod regulam dicte domus quo ad omnes eius particulas pro viribus observabit. Ad observacionem

[a] *Sic.*

of his commons for a period of time fixed by the majority of the fellows in the light of the nature and gravity of the offence. On his second transgression or failing the penalty shall be doubled. On his third, the penalty shall be quadrupled; and if he is then judged incorrigible by the Master and the majority of the fellows, he shall be expelled from the house for ever, with no appeal, petition for mercy, or any remedy of common or particular law being allowed; and another, more suitable person shall be elected in his place. On the strength of the oath he took [on admission], anyone so expelled shall be obliged forthwith to give up unconditionally and absolutely the status that he held at the time without any obstruction or hope of reinstatement.

[11.] To prevent favouritism in my house, the fellows of the house shall be elected impartially and by scrutiny conducted together in the manner specified above for the master:

viii. Provided that the person who is more suitable in morals and learning, is a free man, is more likely to make progress in his studies, and is deemed to be more in need, shall be selected from within the university, all favour, enmity, fear, acquaintance, affection and any other subtle specious pretext being put aside.

ix. I define as elected that person on whom the majority of the fellows, or half their number with the concurrence of the Master, have agreed.

x. When the votes of the electing fellows are indeed equally divided then the Master of the house shall be able to appoint at his discretion whichever he pleases of the candidates who have an equal number of votes.

xi. It is my wish that ordinary sophisters, bachelors and masters of arts of the house who are particularly suited to make progress in the study of theology shall be chosen impartially in the way stated above.

[12.] On his admission each fellow shall expressly promise obedience to the Master in the presence of the fellows, and by virtue of the obedience so promised he shall be bound promptly to obey not only the Master but also whoever is his deputy in his absence in [the observance of] the lawful and proper rules, instructions, warnings or orders which affect their well-being, good name or peace or that of the house.

[13.] The Master shall, however, take care not to be partial in his instructions, or too inflexible towards some, too easy-going towards some, and oppressive to others.

[14.] On his admission every fellow shall swear that he will strive to adhere to the rule of the house in all its particulars. The society shall have power

vero aliarum ordinacionum temporalium quas societas deliberacione previa communiter facere poterit quilibet socius compellatur per subtraccionem communarum vel aliis modis seu penis communiter statuendis quod extunc non prestabit consensum vel assensum alicui statuto vel ordinacioni per quod seu quam preiudicium[a] aliquod mihi seu universitati presenti ve ordinacioni secundum eius iudicium poterit iminere.

[15.] Item singuli sociorum artis dialectice priusquam se transferant ad aliam facultatem in eadem studeant legant et regant. Ita quod ultra quatuor annos ad maximum nullus legere presumat et in casu quo aliquis per idem tempus legere se disponat nullum librum logicalem vel naturalem iterato legat nisi in casu quo[b] dicta domus regente omnino careret in quo casu disponat magister domus qui pro tempore fuerit de consensu maioris partis sociorum de aliquo dicte domus qui continue regens existat ac pro voluntate sua legat quousque in eadem facultate aliquis dicte domus inceperit.

[16.] Volo insuper quod socius quilibet dicte domus postquam in artibus cessaverit ad teologiam duntaxat se transferat et in illa studeat et ad proficiendum diligenciam apponat et ad actus legendi et eciam opponendi se preparet nisi in casu quo de consensu magistri et sociorum omnium et singulorum unus vel duo de sociis ad aliam facultatem vel facultates se transferre disponatur seu disponantur et nisi in casu quo aliquis in iure canonico studere voluerit in quo quilibet socius qui illud affectaverit per biennium laborare et proficere libere poterit.

[17.] Socii etiam dicte domus ut abiliores reddantur disputaciones philosophie vel teologie semel faciant singulis septimanis in quarum qualibet omnes socii cessante causa legitima interesse teneantur.

[18.] Item habeat magister domus mee cameram principalem dicte domus pro voluntate sua et quoad alias cameras semper seniores pro voluntate eorum preferantur.

[19.] Item quilibet electus iuret in sua admissione quod ultra valorem viginti solidorum secundum communem estimacionem veri valoris ad terminum vite sue vel in perpetuum non poterit expendere.

[a] Venn reads "*preiudicium*", which would seem correct; but the MS appears to have "*preiudencium*". Both the Latin wording and the meaning of this passage are obscure. The injury to "me or the university" is presumably considered to arise from the disregard of the statutes made by Gonville and confirmed by the university: cf. the preamble and Statute 2(vi) (*statuta et ordinationes presentes et eciam per cancellarium de consensu meo in posterum faciendas*).

[b] MS dorse starts here.

to make temporary ordinances communally after earlier discussion; and each fellow shall be compelled to comply with any [such] ordinances by the withholding of commons or by other means or penalties to be decreed communally on the ground that he will not thereafter show agreement or assent to any statute or ordinance as a result of which some disregard could in its judgment impugn me or the university or a current ordinance.[12]

[**15.**] Each fellow shall study, lecture and teach on logic in the faculty of arts before he transfers to another faculty. Since no one may venture to lecture [on logic in the faculty of arts] for more than four years at most, and in the event that someone does plan to lecture for that long, he shall not lecture on any book on logic or natural philosophy a second time, unless it happens that the house does not have any regent; in that case the Master of the house may, with the agreement of the majority of the fellows, arrange for a member of the house to continue [to act] as regent and [that person] may lecture as he wishes until someone of the house incepts in that faculty.

[**16.**] It is also my wish that each fellow of the house shall, on finishing his studies in arts, transfer only to theology, study in it, strive to make progress [in it], and prepare himself for the act of proposing and responding. However, one or two of the fellows may choose to transfer to another faculty or faculties, with the unanimous consent of the Master and all the fellows; and if any fellow whatever wishes to study canon law, he is free to pursue that subject for a period of two years.

[**17.**] The fellows of the house shall conduct disputations in philosophy or theology once a week in order to improve their mastery of the subject, and all the fellows shall be bound to take part in each of these in the absence of a legitimate excuse.[13]

[**18.**] The Master of my house is to be entitled to the principal chamber in the house at his choice; and [fellows] are always to have the choice of the other chambers in order of seniority.

[**19.**] Whoever is elected shall swear on his admission that he will not have at his disposal property worth more than the amount of 20 shillings [a year] by common reckoning of its true value, either for a life interest or in perpetuity.[14]

12 See note to text.

13 The obligation to participate in 'commonplaces' (*loci communes*) is later found in Caius' Statute 18; see *Commonplaces* in "*Supplementary Notes to Caius' Statutes*", § IV. 3, at p. 286 below.

14 Taken literally, the Latin might seem to require that he promises not to spend more than 20s during his life-time or in perpetuity, even in the years after he has left the college; but the

[20.] Item nullus socius statum socii teneat in dicta domo a tempore quo acceptaverit beneficium ecclesiasticum et illud per unum annum quiete et pacifice possiderit aut alias habuerit ad terminum vite [sue] vel in perpetuum in temporalibus annui redditus seu …[a] ultra valorem XL solidorum secundum communem estimacionem veri valoris et dictum valorem proventus et illa percepit per unum annum pacifice et quiete et magistro domus dumtaxat excepto qui suo loco et gradibus nullatenus cedere teneatur donec in temporalibus annuatim expendere valeat C solidos secundum communem estimacionem veri valoris sicut premittitur tantum vel in spiritualibus centum [? solidos] secundum decimam tunc currente[m].[b] Idem vero volo observari si partem in temporalibus partem in spiritualibus magister usque ad summam habuerit pretaxatam.

[21.] Item nullum extraneum socium admittant ad moram in sua societate faciendam nisi ex causa evidenti utili et honesta et talis sit qui moribus vite regule ac studio dictorum scolarium se voluerit confirmare per quem regularis honestas dicte societatis nullatenus valeat impediri.

[22.] Item volo ordino et statuto quod communa dictorum sociorum decem denarios non excedat nisi in maioribus festis vel alias exigente necessaria causa honesta magistri et duorum custodum ciste iudicio decidend'.[c] Nec ultra communas suas dictorum sociorum magister seu quivis alius de domo percipiat. Cum vero dicta domus in facultatibus qualitercumque aucta fuerit et ad hoc sufficere valeat percipiat magister domus viginti solidos annuatim pro omnibus supportandis.

[23.] Item volo ordino et dispono quod nullus socius domus mee pro tempore pro quo ab Universitate se absentaverit pro communibus suis aliquid de dicta domo percipiat nisi in negociis collegii extra universitatem extiterit et hoc a maiori parte sociorum approbatum fuerit.

[24.] Volo eciam quod dicta domus ultra numerum viginti sociorum non gravetur; cedente vero vel decedente aliquo sociorum socii dicte domus non teneantur alium in loco illius eligere nisi ad hoc facultates dicte domus secundum formam pretaxatam sufficere dinoscantur.

[25.] Volo eciam quod dicta domus unum regentem in artibus continue habere teneatur.

[a] ? add "*proventus*".

[b] *I.e.*, the amount of tithe recorded for the property in the contemporary valuation of ecclesiastical property.

[c] Venn expands "*decidend*" in the MS as "*decidendum*", but the gerundive "*decidenda*" would seem more correct.

[20.] No fellow may hold the status of fellow in the house after he has accepted an ecclesiastical benefice and has held it unchallenged and undisturbed for one year, or may otherwise have an interest for life or in perpetuity in temporal property [producing] an annual rent or return of more than 40 shillings by the common reckoning of its true value and has collected the said amount of income for one year peaceably and quietly; with the sole exception of the Master, who shall not be required in any way to give up his office or rank until he has at his disposal secular property worth 100 shillings a year by the common reckoning of true value as set out immediately above, or 100 [shillings?] in spiritual property according to the tenth then current.[15] It is my wish that the same rule should apply if the Master has up to the total amount previously specified partly in secular property and partly in spiritual property.

[21.] They shall not admit an outsider[16] as a fellow to pass the time in their community except for clear, good and proper cause and [provided] he is someone who is willing to conform to the customary life, rule and study of the scholars and by whom the proper way of life for the community will not be disturbed in any way.

[22.] I wish, order and decree that the fellows' commons shall not exceed 10 pence except at major feasts and as required on other occasions for necessary and proper reasons to be decided by the judgement of the Master and the two keepers of the chest. Neither the Master nor anyone else from the house shall draw more than his fellows' commons. When the house has grown in resources for any reason and there is enough to support [the expense], the Master of the house may draw [a further] 20 shillings a year for provisioning all its members.

[23.] I wish, order and provide that no fellow of my house shall receive anything from the house for his commons in respect of time when he has been absent from the university, unless he was away from the university on college business and this has been approved by the majority of the fellows.

[24.] It is my wish that the house shall not be burdened with more than twenty fellows; indeed, on the departure or death of any fellow the fellows of the house shall not be bound to elect another in his place unless the resources of the house are reckoned to be sufficient to do so by the yardstick stated above.

[25.] It is my wish that the house shall always have one regent in arts.

requirement must mean that he should not, while a fellow, have a life interest or a fee simple in property worth more than 20s a year.

15 In his Statute 15, Bateman raised the maximum amount allowed to fellows to 100s.

16 One who is not already a member of Gonville Hall.

[**26.**] Item socii dicte domus honeste se habeant prevenientes invicem se honore et reverenciam precipue senioribus exhibeant iuniores.

[**27.**] Mee tamen intencionis non existit quod si per levem negligenciam socius aliquis vel magister contra predicta in aliquo evenerit quod propter hoc periurium incurrat sed duntaxat cum ex dolo fraude vel malicia[a] premissa contempserat observare et quatenus ipsum concernunt efficaciter adimplere.

In quorum omnium et singulorum testimonium sigillum meum ac sigillum magistri et sociorum domus mee predicte una cum sigillo communi reverendorum virorum cancellarii et universitatis Cantebrigie procuravi et feci hiis apponi. Dat' etc.

Et nos J. de T. magister dicte Aule et socii eiusdem tractatu super premissis inter nos habito diligenti premissas ordinaciones per nos cum diligencia recensitas et plene discussas tanquam nobis et prefate domui ac universitati predicte utiles et honestas sinceriter amplectentes quantum ad nos attinet approbamus specialiter et expresse et in signum approbacionis nostre et consensus huius sigillum nostrum de consensu nostro unanimi nullo socio penitus reclamante duximus apponendum. Dat' etc.

Nos insuper A. de (?)[b] cancellarius universitatis predicte et eius cetus unanimis propter hoc invicem specialiter congregati premissas ordinaciones coram nobis recitatas et discussas diligenter et distincte quas ad laudem dei et honorem universitatis predicte reputamus agnoscimus et dicimus esse factas tractatu super hiis habito diligenti de consensu nostro unanimi et assensu auctoritate nostra ex certa sciencia approbamus ratificamus et confirmamus per dictum dominum Edmundum de Goneville ac magistrum et scolares[c] Aule predicte super hiis specialiter requisita. In quarum approbacionis ratificacionis et confirmacionis testimonium sigillum nostrum commune fecimus hiis apponi. Dat' etc.

[a] The word comes at a much-worn fold and is now virtually unreadable; but Venn's rendering as "*malicia*" would appear correct.

[b] *Sheriffe's Evidences* (fol. 9) reads as "A. de G". In the margin of *Sheriffe* and in his own *Historiae* (II, p. 105), Caius expands this as "Antony of Grantchester", and in his turn Venn substitutes "Adam of Grantchester" (*B.H.* III, p. 345); both seem apocryphal. The second letter is not the form of 'G' used by the scribe everywhere else in the document. Professor Brooke has suggested that the letters "A" and "B" were being used *hypothetically*, as "X" and "Y" are commonly used today: Brooke, *History*, pp. 10–11.

[c] As in Bateman's statutes later, the term *scolares* is used: contrast the preceding paragraph.

[**26.**] The fellows of the house shall behave with propriety, outdoing each other in courtesy,[17] and in particular the more junior shall show respect to their seniors.

[**27.**] It is not, however, my intention that any fellow or the Master should incur [the consequences of] being foresworn if he should infringe any of the above [provisions] in any way through slight negligence, but only when, intentionally or dishonestly or with malice aforethought, he scorns to observe and give effect to them when they concern him.

In witness of all and singular of the above [provisions] I have arranged that my seal and the seal of the Master and fellows of my aforesaid house shall be appended to these [writings] together with the common seal of the chancellor and university of Cambridge. Given [this day], etc.

And we J. de T. [John Colton of Terrington] Master of the hall and the fellows thereof, after carefully discussing the above among ourselves, specifically and expressly give our assent to the ordinances set out above, which we have carefully examined and thoroughly discussed and which we welcome as helpful and befitting as much to us and the house as to the university, and as a sign of our assent and agreement to this we have directed that our seal shall be appended with our unanimous agreement [and] without any reservation by any fellow. Given [this day], etc.

After a clear and careful reading to us and discussion of the aforesaid ordinances, which we treat, acknowledge and declare to have been made to the glory of God and the honour of the university, we, A. de (?),[18] chancellor of the university and a unanimous congregation of the same, specially summoned for the purpose, do after full consideration approve ratify and confirm the aforesaid ordinances with our unanimous consent, assent and authority, based on the certain knowledge gained from Edmund de Gonville and the Master and scholars of the hall. In approval, ratification and confirmation of which we have caused our common seal to be appended. Given [this day], etc.

17 Cf. Romans 12:10: "in honour preferring one another".

18 See note to text.

III

The Statutes of William Bateman, 1353 and 1355

TEXT AND TRANSLATION

III. 1

The Original Statutes of William Bateman 1353

[Cambridge, Gonville & Caius College BUR: DEEDS/ I, 15.[a]]

Willelmus permissione divina Norwicensis episcopus dilectis filiis et alumpnis custodi et sociis collegii scolarium Aule Annunciacionis virginis et matris dei et hominis Iesu Cristi in Cantebriggia salutem et sciencie continuum incrementum cum benedictione dextere Salvatoris et nostra.

Filioli carisssimi, intencionem nostram et voluntatem circa statum et regimen collegii vestri et sociorum eiusdem qui pro tempore fuerint in uno statutorum tenore vobis presencium indicamus.

In primis quia ad honorem dei ac universitatis decorem universe literalis sciencie q …[b] fomentum fore credimus si facultas artium scientifica liberalium invalescat, statuimus et ordinamus quod omnes socii dicti vestri collegii qui pro tempore fuerint sint artiste et in ista facultate continuent quousque in illa magisterii gradum obtinuerint et per annum in eadem ordinarie legerint, ut est moris, quos statim post annum cessare volumus et ad iura civilia seu canonica, {*theologie*}[c] aut ad medicine scienciam iuxta eorum eleccionem liberam se transferre, proviso quod in sciencia quam elegerint audiendam continuet quilibet quousque deus sibi dederit in dicta sciencia doctoratum. Volumus

a See Plate VIII below.

b *Sic. que* or *quia*? Bateman's meaning is clear, but his words and syntax have perplexed copyists from Sheriffe onwards. His text is written as "… *universe l'ralis sci'e q' fomentum fore* …" and is reproduced in *Sheriffe's Evidences* with the same contractions. Caius expanded this as "… *universae{que} literalis scientiae ~~que~~ fomentum fore* …" (MS 711), interpreting the ambiguous *q'* as *que* and placing it after *scientiae* at first and then striking it through and appending it to *universae*. His emendations were copied into the Lambeth MS and reproduced by the Commissioners in 1852. Venn returned the *que* to its original position but appended it to *scientie*, thus giving: "… *universe literalis scientieque fomentum fore* …". The author of MS 760 adopted Caius' transposition of *que*, but also thoughtfully (as elsewhere) suggested *liberalis* in place of *literalis*. (For the unknown author of MS 760, see "*Caius' Statutes: Notes on Sources*", § I. 3 above.) The ambiguous *q'* has been disregarded in the present translation.

c *Sic* MS. Inserted in Bateman's own hand.

III. 1

The Original Statutes of William Bateman 1353

[References to Trinity Hall Statutes are given as TH st. 1 etc. (*Documents*, II, pp. 417–36).]

William by divine permission Bishop of Norwich to [his] beloved sons and wards the keeper and fellows of the college of scholars of the Hall of the Annunciation of the Virgin and Mother of Jesus Christ, god and man, in Cambridge, health and uninterrupted increase in learning, with the blessing of the Saviour's right hand and our [own].

Dearest children in God, we indicate to you by the tenor of [these] present statutes our intention and will concerning the constitution and rule of your college and its fellows.

First, because we believe that the fostering of unbounded learning and knowledge[1] will be to the honour of God and the adornment of the university if the ability to study the liberal arts becomes stronger, we decree and ordain that all fellows of your college shall be educated in arts, and shall continue in that faculty until they have obtained the degree of master in it and have been ordinary readers in it for a year, as is customary. It is our will that they cease immediately after [that] year and switch to civil or canon law, [or] the discipline of {*theology or*}[2] medicine at their free choice: provided that each one shall continue to pursue the discipline of his choice until God gives to him a doctorate in that discipline. It is our will, however, that there shall be only one or at most

1 See note to Latin text. The ambiguous *q'* has been disregarded in the present translation.

2 Bateman's own insertion – a belated recognition of Gonville's wishes, perhaps at John Colton's urging: see Professor Brooke in "*William Bateman and his Foundation*", § V. 2, at p. 326 below.

tamen qui in medicine sciencia in dicto collegio unicus tantum socius aut duo ad plus simul audire valeant et studere. Custodem vero collegii liberam electionem habere volumus ad insistendum literali sciencie quam duxerit preoptandum.

Ad hec cupientes vobis ac aliis sociis qui pro tempore fuerint subvenire de cistis nostris propriis si et cum nobis fuerit vita comes quousque cum auxilio Virginis benedicte habueritis per ministerium nostrum ad hoc sufficienciam facultatum, concedimus ex nunc cuilibet socio dicti collegii statum magisterii vel baccalariatus habenti duodecim denarios, cuilibet vero socio nullum gradum in scolis seu statum habenti decem denarios, septimanis singulis quibus in collegio presentes fuerint pro communis, et robas de una secta annis singulis competentes.

{*Cum autem per dei providentiam facultates proprias de redditibus perpetuis habuerint competentes et sufficientes plenarie ad subscripta volumus et ordinamus quod custos dicti collegii qui pro tempore fuerit singulis annis viij marcas; socius autem magister in quacunque facultate vj marcas; alius autem quiscunque socius v marcas pro omnibus eorum necessitatibus …,*[a] *et ulterius nomine prestimoniorum in festo Annunciacionis beate Marie quilibet tam custos quam socius dicti collegii ij solidos et in quocunque alio festo beate Marie xij denarios habeant annis singulis, qui tunc temporis presentes fuerint in collegio supradicto. Habeant insuper socii collegii ij officiarios, videlicet pistorem et dispensatorem, quorum utrumque pro stipendiis atque robis xx solidos recipere volumus de communi, et alios duos garciferos pro pistrina et coquina, quorum utrumque pro stipendiis atque robis unam marcam recipere volumus de communi. Ista sunt scripta et addita de propria manu nostra,*}[b] proponentes per graciam Salvatoris cum curis sollicitis[c] vos dotare, numerumque sociorum ac stipendia vestra iuxta dotacionis sufficienciam ampliare.[d]

Cupientes insuper vos ac alios socios qui pro tempore fuerint ad proprium meritum vestrumque ac aliorum spirituale suffragium excitare, volumus statuimus et ordinamus quod singulis diebus quilibet socius audiat unam missam aut eorum plures seu omnes unicam in communi. Et dum missam

[a] ?? *habeat* crossed out.

[b] The passage in italics is inserted in the margin, explicitly in Bateman's own hand.

[c] Bateman would have had in mind the appropriated rectories with which he was endowing the college.

[d] Cf. TH st. 15.

two fellows that are allowed to pursue and study the science of medicine at the same time; the keeper shall, however, have a free choice of pursuing the liberal science for which he cares to opt.[3]

To this end, desiring to maintain you and other fellows at any time out of our own funds if and while life attends us, until such time as, with the help of the Blessed Virgin, you shall have with our assistance sufficient means [of your own] to do this, we grant henceforth to each fellow of the college having the status of master or bachelor 12d., and to each fellow having no grade or standing in the schools 10d., for commons for each week in which they are present in college, and sufficient robes of one discipline[4] each year.

{*But when by the providence of God they have adequate and sufficient means of their own from perpetual rents to meet the costs fully, it is our will and we ordain that the keeper of the college shall have 8 marks each year; a fellow who is a master in any faculty 6 marks; and any other fellow 5 marks for all their necessary requirements. And further by way of prest-money*[5] *both the keeper and each of the fellows of the college shall each year have 2s. on the feast of the Annunciation of the Blessed Mary and 12d. on any other feast of the Blessed Mary, if they have been present in the college at that time. Furthermore the fellows of the college shall have two officials, viz., a baker and a purveyor,*[6] *each of whom we will shall receive 20s. for stipends and robes from the common chest,*[7] *and two other menial servants for bakehouse and kitchen, each of whom we will shall receive one mark for stipends and robes from the common chest – these words have been written and added in our own hand*}[8] – proposing with the grace of the Saviour to endow you with benefices with cure of souls and to increase the number of fellows and your stipends as the sufficiency of the endowment will allow.

Desiring to inspire you and other fellows at any time to earn your own rewards and the spiritual comfort of others, it is our will and we decree and ordain that every day each fellow shall hear one mass either in groups or all together in common at the one time. And while they hear mass, or at other

3 Cf. TH st. 1. *Scientia* imports learning and discipline as well as science in its modern sense.

4 *de una secta*; but possibly 'of one livery'.

5 In his *Expositiones aut Interpretationes*, Caius defined *prestimonia* as "*pecunia in hoc concessa, ut custos et socii sint presto et parati in collegio diebus praescriptis ex vulgari vocabulo* 'prestmony' *deducta voce*": MS 710. In the *liber rationalis* and other college accounts they are termed "distributions".

6 In Dr Caius' statutes the term *dispensator* was used as synonymous with *obsonator*, and the office was distinct from that of steward, a superior office held by a fellow: see Caius' Statute 2 and *The steward and his staff* in "*Supplementary Notes to Caius' Statutes*", § IV. 3, at pp. 297–8 below. In his Statute 8 Gonville had specified a baker and a laundress.

7 In the sense of the fund which is kept in the ark, the great and strong common chest required by Statute 6, *de sigillo et archa communi*.

8 The text of the passage in italics is written in the margin in the 1353 original, explicitly in Bateman's own hand: see Plate VIII below.

audierint, aut alia hora diei, si quis eorum misse tempore fuerit impeditus, dicat quilibet genibus flexis quinquagesies salutacionem angelicam cum illo fine, '*Et benedictus fructus ventris tui Iesu Deus et homo, amen*', cum oratione dominica post singulas denas salutaciones predictas, cum illa oratione in fine, '*Deus qui de Beate Marie*',[a] et pro nobis cum illa oratione, '*Rege quesumus Domine*',[b] dum fuerimus in humanis, et post mortem nostram cum illa oratione, '*Deus qui inter apostolicos sacerdotes*';[c] singulis etiam diebus sabbati omnes socii salvo iusto impedimento cuiuslibet unam missam de Annunciacione cum nota vel sine nota audiant in communibus et singulis dictis diebus dicant ter quinquagesies salutationes angelicas cum fine et orationibus ut prefertur. Singulis etiam diebus de mane cum de lectis surrexerint et de sero cum lectos iniverunt aut aliis horis diei et noctis si dictis horis fuerint impediti, dicat quilibet genibus flexis illam antiphonam de Annunciacione: '*Ingressus angelus ad Mariam dixit Ave Maria gratia plena Dominus tecum alleluia*' cum versiculo '*Rorate celi desuper*'[d] et cum oratione '*Deus qui de beate Marie*' et cum illa oratione dum fuerimus in hac vita '*Rege quesumus Domine*' et post mortem nostrum cum illa oratione '*Deus qui inter apostolicos sacerdotes*'. Et qualibet die hora qua placuerit dicat quilibet psalterium '*De profundis*'[e] cum oratione dominica et salutacione angelica pro animabus omnium collegii vestri benefactorum ac parentum nostreque et omnium fidelium defunctorum cum orationibus '*Miserere quesumus Domine*' et '*Inclina Domine*';[f] post mortem vero nostram cum illa etiam oratione '*Deus qui inter apostolicos sacerdotes*'.[g]

Volumus insuper quod omnes et singuli socii dicti collegii qui pro tempore fuerint plene et integraliter faciant observari omnia et singula que in duodecim statutis sociorum collegii sancti Trinitatis per eos iuratis et tam per archiepiscopum Cantuar(insem) quam per universitatem Cantebrigg(ie) confirmatis intitulatis inferius et descriptis plenius continentur extensis eorundem verbis facultates iuris civilis et canonum tangentibus ad facultatem seu scientiam artistorum.

[a] Collect for Vespers and Lauds for the Annunciation in the Roman Breviary.

[b] The reason for Bateman's choice of this prayer, unlike the others, is not apparent. He also required it in the corresponding provision in his statutes for Trinity Hall. The writer is grateful to the Dean, the Revd Cally Hammond, for the information that it appears in the Proper for Sexagesima in the Old Gelasian Sacramentary, but he has not been able to track it down in the Sarum or Roman Breviaries.

[c] Prayer for a deceased bishop in the Office for the Dead in the Roman Breviary.

[d] Isaiah xlv. 8; Introit of the Advent Mass of the Virgin Mary in the Roman Breviary.

[e] Psalm 129, Vulgate; 130 AV etc.

[f] Prayer for a deceased layman in the Office for the Dead in the Roman Breviary. Bateman omits (intentionally?) the requirement for the prayer *Rege quesumus Domine* during his lifetime: contrast TH st. 14.

[g] Cf. TH st. 14.

times of the day if any of them shall be prevented [from doing so] at the time of mass, each of them shall say fifty times on bended knees the Angelic Salutation with this ending *And blessed be the fruit of thy womb Jesus God and man, Amen*, with the Lord's Prayer after each ten of the aforesaid salutations, with the prayer *Deus qui de Beate Marie* at the end, [together] with the prayer, *Rege quesumus Domine* for us, while we are alive, and the prayer, *Deus qui inter apostolicos sacerdotes* after our death. Also on each Saturday all the fellows, except anyone [who is] prevented [from doing so] by good cause, shall hear one sung or spoken mass of the Annunciation in common, and on each of the said days shall say 150 Angelic Salutations with the ending and prayers as stated above. Also, each day at day-break when they arise from bed, and late in the evening when they retire to bed, or at other times of the day and night, if they are unable to so at these hours, each one shall say on bended knees the antiphon of the Annunciation *Ingressus angelus ad Mariam dixit, Ave Maria gracia plena, dominus tecum, alleluia*, with the versicle *Rorate celi desuper*, and with the prayer *Deus qui de Beate Marie*, [together] with the prayer *Rege quesumus domine* while we are alive and the prayer *Deus qui inter apostolicos sacerdotes* after our death. And each shall say at a time of day of his choosing the psalm *De profundis* with the Lord's Prayer and the Angelic Salutation for the souls of the benefactors of your college and of our parents and all the faithful departed, [together] with the prayers *Miserere quesumus Domine* and *Inclina Domine*; also the prayer *Deus qui inter apostolicos sacerdotes* after our death.

It is our will that each and every fellow of the college shall ensure fully and entirely the observance of each and every [provision] which is contained in the twelve statutes of the fellows of the College of the Holy Trinity,[9] sworn by them and confirmed by both the archbishop of Canterbury and the university of Cambridge, [that are] listed by title and detailed more fully below, their words relating to the faculties of civil and canon law being extended to the faculty or science of the arts.

[9] Trinity Hall. Cf. *Documents*, II, pp. 435–6.

Videlicet in statuto *de obediencia et gestu sociorum.*
Item in statuto *de habitu et condicione sociorum.*
Item in statuto *de tempore electionis et forma.*
Item in statuto *de inhabilibus personis dicti collegii* usque ad §[*sententiam*?]: [‘*exceptis presbyteris sociis canonistis* …’]
Item in statuto *de inhabili custode.*
Item in statuto *de sigillo et archa communi.*
Item in statuto *de compoto reddendo.*
Item in statuto *de residencia et absencia* exceptis verbis *que presbiteros comprehendunt.*
Item in statuto *de numero sociorum augendo* usque ad §[*sententiam*?]: *Et volumus.*[a]
Item in statuto *de bonis collegii non alienandis.*
Item in statuto *de libris collegii.*
Item in statuto *de sociorum nominibus episcopo Norwicen(si) et capitulo annis singulis intimandis.*

Volumus autem quod nullus alius quam artista eligat in socium dicte aule nec aliquis nisi prius per tres annos audiverit et studuerit in arte dialectica aut per duos ad minus annos excellenter proficerit in eadem.

Item ordinamus quod nullus curatum obtinens beneficium ecclesiasticum cuiuscumque valoris seu non curatum aut decanatum ruralem cuius redditus et proventus centum solidorum summam iuxta verum omnibus annis annuum valorem excedunt, eligi valeat in socium nec iam electus in dicto collegio ut socius ultra unius anni spacium et promocionis sue tempore remanere, excepto custode qui quodcumque beneficium obtinens ecclesiasticum, eciam si dignitas fuerit eligi valeat et iam electus in dicto officio remanere.[b]

Iuramentum autem quod vestrum quemlibet infra triduum ab hora recepcionis presencium, et alium quemlibet custodem et socium qui pro tempore fuerit, statim in cuiuslibet admissione tactis evangeliis subire et facere volumus, duximus ex habundanti presentibus inserendum.

Imprimis jurabit quilibet quod omnia statuta intitulata superius et descripta, fideliter quantum humana sinit fragilitas observabit. Item quod fidelis et diligens erit in quocumque officio quod eorum quemlibet in collegio habere contigerit in futurum. Item quod commodum et honorem collegii predicti et non contrarium quamdiu vixerit procurabit. Item quod quamdiu vixerit ad

[a] TH st. 17: “*Et volumus quod numerus augmentandus fiat de sociis legistis et canonistis alternatim* ….”

[b] Cf. TH st. 9.

Namely, in the statute [TH st. 2] *The obedience and behaviour of fellows.*
In the statute [TH st. 3] *The dress and deportment of fellows.*
In the statute [TH st. 4] *The time and form of elections.*
In the statute [TH st. 10] *Ineligibility for [membership of] the college*, as far as the words "*exceptis presbyteris sociis canonistis ...*".
In the statute [TH st. 11] *Ineligibility for the [office of] keeper.*
In the statute [TH st. 12] *The common seal and common chest.*
In the statute [TH st. 13] *Accounting.*
In the statute [TH st. 16] *Residence and absence*, except the words "*que presbiteros comprehendunt*".
In the statute [TH st. 17] *Increasing the number of fellows*, as far as the words "*Et volumus*".
In the statute [TH st. 18] *The requirement that the goods of the college shall not be alienated.*
In the statute [TH st. 19] *The books of the college.*
In the statute [TH st. 21] *The communication of the names of the fellows to the bishop and chapter of Norwich each year.*

It is our wish that no one other than a [graduate in] arts shall be elected a fellow of the Hall nor anyone unless he has heard [lectures] and studied in logic for three years or shown himself proficient in that subject for at least two years.[10]

We ordain that no one obtaining an ecclesiastical benefice with cure of souls of any value, or a benefice without cure of souls or rural deanery of which the true annual value of the income and return exceeds the sum of 100 shillings,[11] shall be eligible to be elected a fellow, nor if already elected [may he] remain as a fellow for longer than the duration of one year from the time of his appointment, with the exception of the keeper who, if he obtains an ecclesiastical benefice of any kind, shall be qualified to be elected if worthy and to remain in office if already elected.

We have directed that there shall be included in addition in these presents the oath which we wish to be put to and taken by each of you on the gospels within three days of the receipt of these presents and by every other keeper and fellow at any time immediately on their admission.

First, each person shall swear that he will observe all the statutes entitled and detailed above as faithfully as human frailty permits. Further, that he will be faithful and diligent in whatever office in college each of them may happen to have in the future. Further, that he will promote the advantage and honour of the college and not [work] against it so long as he shall live. Further, that he

[10] This clause and the four that follow it contain the five statutes that Bateman set out in full in 1353 in addition to the twelve statutes of Trinity Hall that he merely listed. For their chequered history in subsequent manuscripts, see "*Bateman's Statutes: The Manuscript Confusion*", § I. 2 above.

[11] Cf. the formulation in Statute 15 of the 1355 re-issue below. See also Gonville's Statute 20 above.

quemcumque statum ipsum contigerit pervenire, honorem et commodum ecclesie Norwicen(sis) et nunquam contrarium procurabit; et quod nunquam, quamdiu vixerit, erit in aliquo negocio causa vel lite contra aliquem episcopum Norwicens(em) qui pro tempore fuerit, nec contra ecclesiam, nec contra capitulum Norwicen(se); sed cum eis pro iusto et competenti salario cum extra exercicium scolasticum fuerit, quando et cum legitime fuerit requisitus.[a]

Volumus autem quod si quis ex facilitate aut subita mocione vel indeliberate absque deliberata condicta aut excogitata fraude vel dolo seu pertinacia, in aliquo premissorum offenderit vel peccaverit, paratus se corrigere et emendare, periurus propter hoc non senceatur,[b] nec pro periuro pro hoc ab aliis reputetur.[c]

Salva nobis semper potestate libera disponendi et ordinandi de sociis vestri collegii preficiendis et ammovendis ac de statutis predictis omnibus et singulis emendandis corrigendis suplendis, revocandis, et novis eciam faciendis, prout nostre consciencie videbitur, quamdiu fuerimus in hac luce.[d]

Datum apud Hoxne vij die mensis Septembris, Anno domini millesimo trescentesimo quinquagesimo tercio, et consecracionis nostre decimo.

[a] Cf. TH st. 20.

[b] *Sic* for *censeatur*.

[c] Cf. TH st. 20.

[d] Cf. TH st. 4 (applying to the keeper as well as the fellows) and st. 21. The final clause in the 1355 re-issue requiring annual readings of the statutes is not included in the 1353 original.

will promote the honour and advantage of the church of Norwich in whatever station to which he may happen to come and never [work] against it during his lifetime; and that he will never be a party at any time during his lifetime to any business or litigation against any bishop of Norwich, or against the church or chapter of Norwich, but will act on their behalf for a just and adequate stipend after completing his academic studies, whenever he is lawfully requested [to do so].[12]

It is our will that if anyone shall offend or sin in any of the above [provisions] by way of help or subtle suggestion or thoughtlessly without deliberate, collusive or premeditated fraud or deceit or contumacy, and is prepared to correct and mend his ways, he shall not be deemed forsworn nor shall he on that account be held by others to have broken his oath.

Reserving always to us the unrestricted power of ordering and effecting[13] the preferring and removing of fellows of your college and of amending, correcting, supplementing, and revoking each and every one of the aforesaid statutes, and also of making new ones as seems fit to [us and] our conscience, during our lifetime.

Dated at Hoxne the seventh day of September, A.D. 1353, and the tenth [year] of our consecration.

12 The final clause suggests that Bateman intended both his colleges to be recruiting grounds for his diocese – very like Walter Stapeldon in founding Exeter College, Oxford, in the 1310s: see Mark Buck, *Politics, Finance and the Church in the Reign of Edward II: Walter Stapeldon, Treasurer of England* (Cambridge, 1983), chap. 5.

13 In the context *disponendi* would seem to be correct, and not to be a mistake for *deponendi* (removing a person from office), since the word *ammovendis* is used seven words later for the removal of fellows.

III. 2

The Re-issued Statutes of Bishop Bateman 1355

[Cambridge, Gonville & Caius College, BUR: DEEDS/ I, 16.[a]]

Universis sancte matris ecclesie filiis ad quos presentes litere pervenerint, officialis Norwicensis,[b] salutem et rei geste memoriam perpetuo duraturam. Ad universitatis vestre noticiam volumus pervenire quod dilecti nobis in Cristo custos et scolares[c] collegii Annunciacionis Beate Marie Cantebrigg[ie] prout eorum assercio continebat, propter eciam eorum collegii negocia instrumenta nonnulla que eorum collegium concernunt eos oporteat in Romana curia exhibere ac propter viarum discrimina originalia non audent ad curiam destinare predictam propter quod nobis humiliter supplicarunt ut dicta eorum instrumenta transcribi ac eciam exemplari et in formam publicam redigi facere dignaremur, quorumdam vero dictorum instrumentorum tenor talis est.

…[d]

Willelmus permissione divina Norwicensis Episcopus dilectis filiis et alumpnis custodi et sociis collegii scolarium Aule Annunciacionis virginis et matris dei et hominis Iesu Cristi in Cantebrigg[ia], salutem et sciencie continuum incrementum cum benediccione dextere Salvatoris et nostra.

Filioli carissimi, intencionem nostram et voluntatem circa statum et regimen collegii vestri et sociorum ejusdem qui pro tempore fuerint, in vim statutorum tenore vobis presencium indicamus.

[a] For convenience of reference paragraphs and statute numbers have been supplied editorially in both text and translation and various conjunctions have not been translated in consequence.

[b] Walter of Elveden: see Brooke, *History*, p. 15.

[c] *I.e.*, *socii*. The term *scolares* is repeated at the end of the document. The ambiguity is to be found earlier in Edmund Gonville's draft statutes: cf. above. The concept of scholars who are pupils is not mentioned in the statutes, which concern themselves simply with the keeper and fellows. In the *Interpretatio* that Bateman added to his statutes for Trinity Hall he uses the term *scholares de minori forma* for students who are not fellows: *Documents*, II, pp. 438–9.

[d] Bishop Bateman's Foundation Deed follows, with confirmations. *Sheriffe's Evidences* (MS 706/692) and MSS 711, 760 start at the paragraph immediately thereafter.

III. 2

The Re-issued Statutes of Bishop Bateman 1355

The Official of Norwich to all the sons of Holy Mother Church to whom the present letters may come, greeting and everlasting memory of the event. We wish to bring to the notice of you all that our beloved in Christ the keeper and scholars of the College of the Annunciation of the Blessed Mary of Cambridge, as their statement sets forth, are, because of the business of their college, required to exhibit in the Roman curia[1] various documents which concern their college and do not dare send the originals to the curia because of the hazards of the journey, and for this reason they have humbly besought us that we will deign to have their documents transcribed and also exemplified and put into public form, and the tenor of these documents is as follows ….

William by divine permission bishop of Norwich to [his] beloved sons and wards the keeper and fellows of the college of scholars of the Hall of the Annunciation of the Virgin and Mother of Jesus Christ, God and man, in Cambridge, health and uninterrupted increase in learning, with the favourable blessing of the Saviour's right hand and our [own].

Dearest children in God, we indicate by the tenor of [these] presents to you with the force of statutes our intention and will concerning the constitution and rule of your college and its fellows.

1 The Master, John Colton, may well have been at Avignon already by this time (Brooke, *History*, p. 19), and, if so, that may underlie the need to send documents to the curia. See Christopher Brooke on "*William Bateman and his Foundation*", § V. 2 below.

In primis quod ad honorem dei ac universitatis decorem, universe literalis sciencieque fomentum fore credimus, si facultas arcium scientifica liberalium invalescat; statuimus et ordinamus quod omnes socii dicti vestri collegii qui pro tempore fueriut, sint arciste, et in illa facultate continuent quousque in illa magisterii gradum obtinuerint et in illa per annum ordinarie legerint, ut est moris. Quos statim post annum cessare volumus, et ad jura civilia seu canonica, theologie[a] aut medicine scienciam, juxta eorum eleccionem liberam se transferre. Proviso quod in sciencia quam elegerint audiendam continuet quilibet quousque deus sibi dederit in dicta sciencia doctoratum. Volumus tamen quod in medicine sciencia in dicto collegio unicus tantum socius aut duo ad plus simul audire valeant et studere. Custodem vero collegii liberam eleccionem habere volumus ad insistendum literali sciencie quam duxerit preoptandam.

Ad hec cupientes vobis ac aliis sociis qui pro tempore fuerint subvenire de cistis nostris propriis si et cum nobis fuerit vita comes quousque cum auxilio Virginis benedicte habueritis per ministerium nostrum ad hoc sufficienciam facultatum, concedimus ex nunc cuilibet socio dicti collegii statum magisterii vel bacalariatus habenti duodecim denarios, cuilibet vero socio nullum gradum in scolis seu statum habenti, decem denarios, septimanis singulis quibus in collegio presentes fuerint pro communis, et robas de una secta annis singulis competentes.

Cum autem per dei providenciam facultates proprias de redditibus perpetuis habuerint competentes et sufficientes plenarie ad subscripta, volumus et ordinamus quod custos dicti collegii qui pro tempore fuerit singulis annis octo marcas; socius autem magister in quacunque facultate sex marcas; alius autem quiscunque socius quinque marcas, pro omnibus eorum necessitatibus [habeat].[b] Et ulterius nomine prestimoniorum in festo Annunciacionis Beate Marie quilibet tam custos quam socius dicti collegii duos solidos, et in quocunque alio festo Beate Marie duodecim denarios habeant annis singulis qui tunc temporis presentes fuerint in collegio supradicto. Habeant insuper socii collegii duos officiarios, videlicet pistorem et dispensatorem, quorum utrumque pro stipendiis atque robis viginti solidos recipere volumus de communi, et alios duos garciferos pro

[a] In the original grant of 1353 this had been inserted by Bateman in his own hand.
[b] Omitted in the 1353 and 1355 MSS; likewise in MSS 711, 760.

First, because we believe that the fostering of unbounded learning and knowledge[2] will be to the honour of God and the adorning of the university if the ability to study the liberal arts becomes stronger, we decree and ordain that all fellows of your college shall be educated in arts, and shall continue in that faculty until they have obtained the degree of master in it and have been ordinary readers[3] in it for a year, as is customary. It is our will that they cease immediately after [that] year and switch to civil or canon law, [or] the discipline of theology or medicine at their free choice. Provided that each one shall continue in the discipline of his choice until God gives to him a doctorate in that discipline. It is our will, however, that there shall be only one or at most two fellows that are allowed to hear and study the science of medicine at the same time; the keeper shall, however, have a free choice of pursuing the liberal science for which he cares to opt.

To this end, desiring to maintain you and other fellows out of our own funds if and while life attends us, until such time as, with the help of the Blessed Virgin, you shall have with our assistance sufficient means [of your own] to do this, we grant henceforth to each fellow of the college having the status of master or bachelor 12d., and to each fellow having no grade or standing in the schools 10d., for commons for each week in which they are present in college, and sufficient robes of one discipline[4] each year.

But when by the providence of God they have adequate and sufficient means of their own from perpetual rents to meet the costs fully, it is our will and we ordain that the keeper of the college shall have 8 marks each year; a fellow who is a master in any faculty 6 marks; and any other fellow 5 marks for all their necessary requirements. And further both the keeper and each of the fellows of the college shall each year have 2s. by way of prest-money[5] on the feast of the Annunciation of the Blessed Mary and 12d. on any other feast of the Blessed Mary, if they have been present in the college at that time. Furthermore the fellows of the college shall have two officials, viz., a baker and a purveyor,[6] each of whom we will shall receive 20s. for stipends and robes from the common

2 For the perplexity caused by this phrase, see the note to the text and translation of the 1353 issue of Bateman's Statutes above.

3 For 'ordinary' lectures, see *H.U.C.*, I, pp. 30, 93–5. They were given by regent masters in the year or years following their inception.

4 *de una secta*; but possibly 'of one livery'.

5 In his *Expositiones aut Interpretationes*, Caius defined *prestimonia* as "*pecunia in hoc concessa, ut custos et socii sint presto et parati in collegio diebus praescriptis ex vulgari vocabulo* 'prestmony' *deducta voce*": MS 710. In the *liber rationalis* and other college accounts they are termed "distributions".

6 In Dr Caius' statutes the term *dispensator* is used as synonymous with *obsonator*, and the office is distinct from that of steward, a superior office held by a fellow: see Caius' Statute 2 and note. In his Statute 8 Gonville had specified a baker and a laundress.

pistrina et coquina, quorum utrumque pro stipendiis atque robis unam marcam recipere volumus de communi,[a] proponentes per graciam Salvatoris cum curis sollicitis[b] vos dotare, numerumque sociorum ac stipendia vestra juxta dotacionis sufficienciam ampliare.

Cupientes insuper vos ac alios socios qui pro tempore fuerint ad proprium meritum vestrumque ac aliorum spirituale suffragium excitare, volumus statuimus et ordinamus quod singulis diebus quilibet socius audiat unam missam aut eorum plures seu omnes unicam in communi. Et dum missam audierint, aut alia hora diei, si quis eorum misse tempore fuerit impeditus, dicat quilibet genibus flexis quinquagesies salutacionem angelicam cum illo fine, *Et benedictus fructus ventris tui Jesu Deus et homo, Amen,* cum oratione Dominica post singulas denas salutaciones predictas, cum illa oratione in fine, *Deus qui de Beate Marie,*[c] et pro nobis cum illa oratione, *Rege quesumus Domine,*[d] dum fuerimus in humanis, et post mortem nostram cum illa oratione, *Deus qui inter apostolicos sacerdotes.*[e] Singulis eciam diebus Sabbati omnes socii salvo justo impedimento cujuslibet, unam missam de Annunciacione cum nota vel sine nota audiant in communi, et singulis dictis diebus dicant ter quinquagesies salutaciones angelicas cum fine et oracionibus ut prefertur. Singulis eciam diebus de mane cum de lectis surrexerint, et de sero cum lectos intraverint, aut aliis horis diei et noctis, si dictis horis fuerint impediti, dicat quilibet genibus flexis illam antiphonam de Annunciacione, *Ingressus angelus ad Mariam dixit, Ave Maria gracia plena, Dominus tecum, Alleluia,* cum versiculo, *Rorate celi desuper,*[f] et cum oracione, *Deus qui de Beate Marie,* et cum illa oracione, dum fuerimus in hac vita, *Rege quesumus Domine,* et post mortem nostram cum illa oracione, *Deus qui inter apostolicos sacerdotes.* Et qualibet die hora qua placuerit dicat quilibet psalmum, *De profundis,*[g] cum Oracione dominica et Salutacione angelica pro animabus collegii vestri benefactorum ac parentum nostrorum et omnium fidelium defunctorum, cum oracionibus, *Miserere quesumus Domine,*

[a] The passage in heavy type (**Cum autem per Dei ... volumus de communi**) had been written in the margin in Bateman's original grant of the Statutes in 1353, explicitly in his own hand.

[b] Bateman would have had in mind the appropriated rectories with which he was endowing the college.

[c] Collect for Vespers and Lauds for the Annunciation in the Roman Breviary.

[d] The reason for Bateman's choice of this prayer, unlike the others, is not apparent. He also required it in the corresponding provision in his statutes for Trinity Hall. The writer is grateful to the Dean, the Revd Cally Hammond, for the information that it appears in the Proper for Sexagesima in the Old Gelasian Sacramentary, but he has not been able to track it down in the Sarum or Roman Breviaries.

[e] Prayer for a deceased bishop in the Office for the Dead in the Roman Breviary.

[f] Isaiah xlv. 8; Introit of the Advent Mass of the Virgin Mary in the Roman Breviary.

[g] Psalm 129, Vulgate; 130 AV etc.

chest,[7] and two other menial servants for bakehouse and kitchen, each of whom we will shall receive one mark for stipends and robes from the common chest – proposing with the grace of the Saviour to endow you with benefices with cure of souls and to increase the number of fellows and your stipends as the sufficiency of the endowment will allow.

Desiring to inspire you and other fellows to earn your own rewards and the spiritual comfort of others, it is our will and we decree and ordain that every day each fellow shall hear one mass either in groups or all together in common at the one time. And while they hear mass, or at other times of the day if any of them shall be prevented [from doing so] at the time of mass, each of them shall say fifty times on bended knees the Angelic Salutation with this ending *And blessed be the fruit of thy womb Jesus God and man, Amen*, with the Lord's Prayer after each ten of the salutations, with the prayer *Deus qui de Beate Marie* at the end, [together] with the prayer *Rege quesumus Domine* for us while we are alive and the prayer *Deus qui inter apostolicos sacerdotes* after our death. Also on each Saturday all the fellows, except anyone who is prevented [from doing so] by good cause, shall hear one sung or spoken mass of the Annunciation in common, and on each of the said days shall say 150 Angelic Salutations with the ending and prayers as stated above. Also, each day at day-break when they arise from bed, and late in the evening when they retire to bed, or at other times of the day and night, if they are unable to do so at these hours, each one shall say on bended knees the antiphon of the Annunciation *Ingressus angelus ad Mariam dixit, Ave Maria gracia plena, dominus tecum, alleluia*, with the versicle *Rorate celi desuper*, and with the prayer *Deus qui de Beate Marie*, [together] with the prayer *Rege quesumus domine* while we are in this life and the prayer *Deus qui inter apostolicos sacerdotes* after our death. And each shall say at a time of day of his choosing the psalm *De profundis* with the Lord's Prayer and the Angelic Salutation for the souls of the benefactors of your college and our parents and all the faithful departed, [together] with the prayers *Misere quesumus Domine*

[7] In the sense of the fund which is kept in the ark, the great and strong common chest required by Statute 6, *de sigillo et archa communi*: see *The arca, cistae, thesaurus and aerarium* in "*Supplementary Notes to Caius' Statutes*", § IV. 3, at p. 288 below.

et *Inclina Domine*;[a] post mortem vero nostram cum illa oracione, *Deus qui inter apostolicos sacerdotes*.[b]

[1][c] *De Obediencia et gestu sociorum, Rubrica.*

Item statuimus et ordinamus quod omnes socii dicti collegii presentes et futuri sint obedientes custodi dicti collegii qui pro tempore fuerit, et eo absente vel impedito alteri socio locum suum tenenti, quem ad hoc duxerit subrogandum, in licitis et honestis exercicium scolasticum et dicte aule regimen ac commodum tangentibus et honorem. Quodque omnes et singuli tam custos quam socii qui pro tempore fuerint, studio in facultatibus quibus institerint diligenter vacent, ac in collegio et extra honeste quiete et modeste se habeant, ac infra habitacionem eorum latino inter se communiter fruantur eloquio, singulisque septimanis ter, videlicet secundis quartis et sextis feriis de sero aliquod sophisma, problema, vel questionem theologie, philosophie, juris civilis vel canonici disputent in communi, nisi aliquo dictorum dierum legitime fuerint impediti, quo casu[d] hoc idem in crastino facere teneantur, nullusque sociorum collegii[e] a dictis disputacionibus seu earum aliqua absque causa racionabili se absentet. Socium insuper aut alium habeant cotidie in sacra scriptura lectorem in mensa, quem per notabile temporis spacium juxta arbitrium collegii presidentis cum silencio audiant in communi. Nullusque alius non socius collegii ad faciendum cum eis moram per aliquos dies continuam admittatur, absque omnium sociorum assensu concordi, nec cum eis ulterius moram faciat quam de omnium unanimi sociorum voluntate procedat.

[a] Prayer for a deceased layman in the Office for the Dead in the Roman Breviary. Bateman omits (intentionally?) the requirement for the prayer *Rege quesumus Domine* during his lifetime which he had included in the corresponding TH st. 14.

[b] At this point Caius' own copy, MS 711, follows the 1355 re-issue as presented in this transcript; in contrast, *Sheriffe's Evidences* (MS 706/692) and MS 760 both turn back to the 1353 grant and insert from it the reference to Trinity Hall and the list of titles of twelve of that college's statutes before returning to the 1355 re-issue. As a result MS 760 furnished a 'rival' version which emphasised the relevance of Trinity Hall's statutes and Bateman's own interpretation of them; this eventually became important in relation to the Norfolk preference. See "*Bateman's Statutes: The Manuscript Confusion*", § I. 2 above and "*The Norfolk Preference*", § VI. 3 below.

[c] For convenience of reference the statutes have been numbered editorially; MS 760 does likewise for some, but not all, statutes.

[d] *Sic* in the original and in *Sheriffe's Evidences* (MS 706/692). MSS 711, 760 have *quocirca*, as in the final paragraph (cf. below).

[e] MS: *collegio*. MSS 711 and 760 have *collegii*.

and *Inclina Domine*; also the prayer *Deus qui inter apostolicos sacerdotes* after our death.[8]

[**1**][9] *The obedience and behaviour of fellows.*

We decree and ordain that all fellows of the college both present and future shall be obedient to the keeper of the college, and in his absence or incapacity to another fellow acting in his stead whom he has chosen to be his deputy, in lawful and proper matters touching on academic performance and the honour and fitting governance of the hall. And that everyone, both the keeper and the fellows, shall have time for diligent study in their appointed faculties and shall bear themselves respectfully, quietly and modestly both within college and outside; and they shall employ Latin speech in their communal conversation within their place of residence and shall dispute in common some proposition, problem or question of theology, philosophy, civil or canon law three times each week, viz. on the second, fourth and sixth weekdays[10] in the evening, unless on any of the said days they shall be legitimately prevented [from doing so], in which case they shall be bound to do this on the morrow; and no fellow of the college shall absent himself from the disputations or any of them without good cause. Moreover they shall have a fellow or other person reading from Holy Scripture at table each day, and they shall listen in common and in silence to him for a meaningful period of time determined by the president of the college.[11] And no one who is not a fellow of the college shall be admitted to pass the time with them for the space of any day without the express agreement of all the fellows, nor to stay longer with them than it continues to be the unanimous wish of all the fellows.

8 At this point Bateman's original 1353 statutes required observance of twelve of Bateman's statutes for Trinity Hall, which were listed but not set out. In contrast the present copy re-issued by Walter of Elveden in 1355 sets out the text of the specified statutes and omits all reference to Trinity Hall. See "*Bateman's Statutes: The Manuscript Confusion*", § I. 2 above.

9 For convenience of reference numbers were added to the statutes editorially in MS 711 and in subsequent versions. The description of the title as a heading or 'rubric' (*rubrica*) is omitted editorially here from the translation of each statute; likewise "*item*", which merely performs the function of a bullet.

10 *I.e.*, Mondays, Wednesdays and Fridays (Sunday being liturgically the first day of the week, not the seventh as secular usage currently tends to count it).

11 *Collegii presidentis*. The reference to the "president" is drawn from the corresponding Trinity Hall statute (TH c. 2). An office of president is not mentioned anywhere else in Bateman's Statutes for Gonville Hall or until the sixteenth century, and the reference here is perhaps to the person presiding at table, *i.e.* the keeper or fellow presiding in his absence; but that would not explain the "*collegii*". The term in relation to Gonville Hall appears elsewhere only in the early years of the sixteenth century: see *The president* in "*Supplementary Notes to Caius' Statutes*", § IV. 3, at p. 291 below.

[2] *De Habitu et condicione sociorum, Rubrica.*

Item statuimus et ordinamus quod custos et omnes socii dicti collegii qui pro tempore fuerint, robis unius secte cum longis tabardis seu epitogiis[a] talaribus annis noviter singulis induantur; quodque custos et socii omnes et singuli tam diebus legibilibus in scolis, quam diebus festivis per vias publicas incedentes tabardis seu epitogiis talaribus communiter utantur, lecture communis presertim tempore magistrorum, nisi ex temporis qualitate aut alia causa rationabili aliud duxerint faciendum. Nullusque socius ad postulandum in advocatorum officio, nec eciam ad procurandum in procuratorum officio in causis communibus ut advocatus seu procurator communis se occupet quovismodo, nec eciam singulariter ex affeccione, si tali exercicio postulandi seu procurandi a lectura vel studio poterit notabiliter impediri. Volumus enim quod omnes socii studio intendant scolastico diligenter quousque habiles fuerint ad legendum et regendum in artibus. Et postquam in illa facultate per annum rexerint, ad alias facultates superius memoratas secundum modum et formam ibidem recitatas ad proficiendum ex tunc se convertant.

Si quis aut custos aut socius notabiliter in corpore dissolutus inhonestus aut inquietus rixosus inobediens seu rebellis, aut in studendo legendo seu proficiendo in scolis notabiliter negligens appareat in futurum, per custodem collegii cum assensu maioris partis sociorum collegii, si socius fuerit, vel per Cancellarium ad suggestionem duarum parcium sociorum collegii, si custos fuerit, corrigatur et puniatur. Quod si quis eorum rebellis protervus aut incorrigibilis notabiliter appareat in premissis, vel in aliquo premissorum, tunc nisi post terciam monicionem sibi per duas partes sociorum collegii, si custos fuerit, vel per custodem cum assensu majoris partis sociorum faciendam, si socius fuerit, trium ebdomadarum spacium continens,[b] a premissis destiterit, taliter quod judicio majoris partis sociorum manifeste appareat de omnibus et singulis premissis plene correctus et integraliter emendatus, a collegio et collegii commodo perpetuo excludatur. Custodes enim et socii dicti collegii qui pro tempore fuerint tamdiu in dicto collegio remaneant, quamdiu caste honeste obedienter pacifice et cum studendi diligencia se habebunt, et ulterius eos nullum jus habere volumus in dicto collegio remanendi, quin pro eorum defectibus in premissis possunt per modum superius descriptum a dicto collegio perpetuo ammoveri absque cujuscunque appellacionis remedio vel querele. Nos enim omnes et singulos sic correctos seu corrigendos, ammotos seu ammovendos, ab omni contradiccionis appellacionis et querele remedio statuimus penitus excludendos. Custodes tamen per solum cancellarium

[a] MS: *epitogii*.

[b] Original MS: MS 711 has *continentem*, in agreement with *monicionem*.

[2] *The dress and deportment of fellows.*

We decree and ordain that the keeper and all the fellows of the college shall be dressed in new robes of one livery[12] with long tabards or ankle-length gowns each year; and that the keeper and each and every fellow shall wear tabards or ankle-length gowns both in the schools on days appointed for lectures and when walking in the public streets on feast days, especially at ordinary lecture time, unless they think it fit to do otherwise on account of the weather or for other reasonable cause. And no fellow shall spend time in pleading in the office of advocate or soliciting in the office of proctor in public cases, as any public attorney or proctor would hold himself to do, or even in particular cases out of friendship, if such activity of pleading or soliciting could seriously impede him from attending lectures or studying; for it is our will that all fellows shall devote themselves diligently to academic study until they are qualified to read and lecture [as a regent] in arts. And when they have been a regent in their particular faculty for a year, they shall thereafter turn to qualifying in the other faculties listed above in the manner set out there.

If anyone who is either keeper or a fellow should in the future appear reprehensibly dissolute in body or dishonest, troublesome, contentious, disobedient or rebellious, or markedly neglectful in studying or making progress in the schools, he shall be corrected and punished by the keeper of the college with the agreement of the majority of the fellows of the college, if he is a fellow, or by the chancellor on the submission of two-thirds of the fellows of the college, if he is the keeper. But if any of them should appear wantonly rebellious or incorrigible in these matters or any of them, then, after he has been given three cautions over a period of three weeks by two-thirds of the fellows of the college if he is keeper, or by the keeper with the agreement of a majority of the fellows if he is a fellow, he shall be permanently excluded from the college and its benefits, unless it appears clearly in the judgment of the majority of the fellows that he has fully corrected his faults in each and every one of these matters and mended his ways. For the keeper and fellows of the college may remain in the college only so long as they are chaste[13] and behave worthily, obediently, peaceably and with diligence in study, and it is our will that they shall have no further right to remain in the college but may, for their faults in these matters, be removed from the college forever in the manner described above without any remedy of appeal or complaint; for we have determined that everyone who has thus been or is being corrected, or who has been or is being removed, should be entirely excluded from any remedy of appeal and plea. However, a keeper [may be

12 *unius secte*. Cf. n. 4 above.

13 In his statutes Caius very deliberately substituted 'celibate' for 'chaste'. The substitution was ruled invalid by Matthew Parker soon after Caius' death: see *Celibacy* in "*Supplementary Notes to Caius' Statutes*", § IV. 3, at p. 282 below.

universitatis Cantebriggie cum deliberacione duorum rectorum universitatis praedicte, et duorum doctorum regencium in dicta universitate, qui non fuerint de collegio predicto, quos idem cancellarius duxerit eligendos de facultatibus theologie, juris canonici vel civilis, et cum assensu duorum dictorum rectorum et doctorum, seu majoris partis eorum, et cum assensu concordi duarum parcium collegii supradicti. Socios vero per solum custodem cum assensu majoris partis sociorum dicti collegii ex premissis causis volumus ammoveri. Custodes autem collegii qui pro tempore fuerint, qui circa regimen collegii et negocia ejusdem oportebit sollicitis et intentis vigiliis occupari, a continuo scolastico exercicio haberi volumus excusatos.

Volumus insuper quod nullus de collegio nec custos nec alius ex quacunque causa contra collegium nec aliquem de collegio causam appellacionis nec querele, nec aliquam aliam litem, neque in ecclesiastico neque in seculari foro seu judicio prosequatur, sine expresso consensu majoris et sanioris partis collegii supradicti.[a]

[3] *De Tempore et eleccionis forma, Rubrica.*

Item statuimus et ordinamus quod vacante custode collegii supradicti, per mortem cessionem vel quovis alio modo, fiat eleccio de custode per socios dicte collegii infra mensem. Interim autem sanior vel senior socius collegii vices gerat custodis.[b] Eleccionem autem per viam scrutinii fieri volumus, et ille in quem major pars sociorum consenserit juris solempnitate submota, per universitatis

[a] *majoris et sanioris partis*. The phrase is reproduced from the relevant Trinity Hall statute [st. 3].

[b] *sanior vel senior*. In the selection of an individual Gonville had specified simple seniority in his draft statutes (*eum qui prius in dicta domo juratus fuerat et admissus*: Gonville's Statutes, Statute 2(i) above.); but Bateman imports the ecclesiastical practice of subordinating strict seniority to a discretion to prefer superior wisdom. That discretion might – arguably – be exercised by the keeper when there was a keeper; but it created an insoluble problem on the occasion of a vacancy in the mastership, and this was only solved by Matthew Parker in 1575 in his *Interpretatio*: see his interpretation of Caius' Statute 32 at p. 277 below.

removed] only by the chancellor of the university of Cambridge in consultation with two rectors[14] of the university and two regent doctors of the university who are not [members] of the college and have been chosen by the chancellor at his discretion from the faculties of theology, or canon or civil law, and with the assent of the two rectors and doctors, or a majority of them, and the assent of a two-thirds majority of the college. It is our will, however, that fellows [may] be removed on the above grounds by the keeper alone with the agreement of a majority of the fellows of the college. But it is our will that those who are keepers of the college and whose time must be taken up with the governance of the college and its affairs with anxious and attentive watchfulness shall be excused from undertaking uninterrupted academic duties in the schools.

It is our will that no member of the college – neither the keeper nor anyone else – shall on any ground pursue any cause of appeal or complaint against the college or any member of it, or any other legal proceeding, in either an ecclesiastical or secular forum or jurisdiction, without the express consent of the greater and wiser part of the college.[15]

[3] *The time and form of elections.*

We decree and ordain that when the [office of] keeper of the college becomes vacant, by death, resignation or in any other way, there shall be an election of a keeper by the fellows of the college within a month. In the meantime the wisest or most senior fellow of the college shall act in the place of the keeper. It is our will that the election shall be by way of scrutiny and that the person on whom the majority of the fellows are agreed shall forthwith, without any formality

14 *I.e.*, proctors. Until the later fourteenth century the proctors were called *rectores* (*H.U.C.*, I, p. 28); in the fifteenth century Henry VI would use the term *rector* for the Provost in the charter for his new King's College.

15 *majoris et sanioris partis*. The long-standing prejudice against mere numbers was enshrined in the Rule of St Benedict (sixth century) – always, of course, binding on most monastic houses – that an (abbot's) election should have the unanimous support of the community "*sive etiam pars quamvis parva congregationis saniore consilio*". This doctrine was even held by some in relation to papal elections in the schism of 1159. Alexander III was chosen by a majority of the cardinals, Victor IV claimed his supporters were older and wiser. The impasse in papal elections was solved in 1179 by the decree of the Third Lateran Council under which a two-thirds majority makes a man pope (the decree is still in force, though with the paraphernalia of the conclave added to it). For all other elections, the crucial statement was that of the Fourth Lateran Council of 1215 (c. 24 = Decretals of Gregory IX 1. 64. 2) – either all should agree, or "*maior et sanior pars*" (in some versions "*vel*", which is a little ambiguous but was commonly used at the time as the equivalent of *et*). Innocent III and the bishops in 1215 were doubtless not thinking of such tiny institutions as Trinity Hall and Gonville Hall in the 1350s would be – but the principle was naturally applied when their statutes were drawn up. (Note supplied by Christopher Brooke.)

Cantebrigg' Cancellarium absque cause cognicione protinus approbetur. Nullam autem potestatem habeat cancellarius predictus eleccionem predictam discutere vel eam approbare nec aliam jurisdiccionem propter hoc in electum nec eligentes exercere, sed solum electum sibi per majorem partem sociorum collegii presentatum illico extra-judicialiter approbare. Quod si vota in diversos divisa fuerint, ita quod nullus reperiatur vota majoris partis collegii habuisse, ad eligendum redeant iterato ac sepius, quousque per majoris partis eleccionem concordem eligatur aliquis in custodem, etiam eleccione facta primitus non cassata. Nullam enim juris solempnitatem sed solum majoris partis consensum per viam scrutinii in custodis et sociorum eleccione volumus observari. Quod si per eleccionem majoris partis sociorum concordem infra mensem provisum non fuerit collegio de custode, tunc provisio de custode pro illa vice ad cancellarium dicte universitatis, qui pro tempore fuerit, devolvatur; dum tamen cancellarius supradictus qui pro tempore fuerit aliquem socium dicti collegii doctorem aut bacalarium[a] in jure canonico vel civili, aut magistrum in artibus, si talis reperiatur ad hoc ydoneus in eodem; alioquin aliquem doctorem aut bacalareum juris canonici vel civilis extra collegium in dicta universitate studentem, vel magistrum in artibus in literatura famosum ad hoc ydoneum preficiat in custodem.

Sed si locus alicujus socii dicti collegii quovismodo vacaverit in futurum, volumus quod per custodis et majoris partis sociorum eleccionem concordem per viam scrutinii ut premittitur infra mensem alius subrogetur. Alioquin ad solum custodem provisio et ordinacio socii pertineat illa vice.[b]

[*Volumus insuper quod in omni electione prefectione et ordinatione custodis et sociorum imposterum faciend' omnis affectio singularis conspiratio et parcialitas excludatur, ut sic simpliciter melior et pro collegio utilior, quantum eis deus in conscientia ministraverit, elegatur. Proviso tamen semper quod in omnibus electionibus custodis collegii primo socius ejusdem collegii, si ad hoc reperiatur idoneus, aut alius nostre dioc[esis] famosus, et in electione sociorum scholares nostre dioc[esis] non beneficiati beneficiatis, ac pauperiores ditioribus ceteris paribus aliis omnibus preferantur.*][c]

[a] *Sheriffe's Evidences* (MS 706/692) and MS 760, but not Caius' MS 711, insert the words "*in theologia*" at this point and in the following clause.

[b] At this point *Sheriffe's Evidences* and MS 760 (but not Caius' MS 711) insert the requirement in Statute 14 to have read arts and logic (in place of the legal qualification required in the corresponding TH st. 4).

[c] The italicised words in square brackets containing the famous 'Norfolk preference' do not appear anywhere in either the 1353 or 1355 Statutes: see "*Bateman's Statutes: The Manuscript Confusion*", § I. 2 above. The passage seems to have originated in the fifteenth-century cartulary known as *Sheriffe's Evidences*: see Brooke, *History*, pp. 16–17 for the likely explanation of the insertion of this clause in the second half of the fifteenth century. It was later included in MSS 711 and 760, and it became the accepted tradition: see *B.H.* III, 352–3. The preference for those not beneficed led *Sheriffe's Evidences* and MS 760, but not Caius' MS 711, to include with this

of law, be approved by the chancellor without [the need for any] formal legal proceeding. The chancellor shall have no power to dispute the election or to give it his approval or to exercise [any] other jurisdiction in respect of the person elected or the electors, but only to approve forthwith without legal proceedings the person presented to him by the majority of the fellows of the college. But if the vote is divided between different [persons] so that no one is found to have the vote of a majority of the college[16] they shall reassemble a second time and as often as necessary until someone has been elected keeper by election agreed by the majority, the election once made being irreversible. For it is our will that no legal formality, but only the agreement of the majority by way of scrutiny, shall be observed in the election of a keeper or fellow. But if the college is not provided with a keeper by an election agreed by the majority within a month, the provision of a keeper on that occasion shall devolve upon the chancellor of the university at the time; provided, however, that the chancellor at the time shall give preference to some fellow of the college who is a doctor or bachelor of canon or civil law or master of arts, if such a one suitable for the [office] can be found; otherwise a doctor or bachelor of canon or civil law from outside the college who is studying in the university, or a master of arts distinguished in letters, who is suitable for the office.

But if the place of a fellow of the college becomes vacant in the future in any way, it is our will that it shall be filled by the election of another [person] chosen by the keeper and a majority of the fellows by way of scrutiny as specified above within a month. Otherwise the appointment and ordination of the fellow shall belong to the keeper alone on that occasion.

[*It is our wish that in every future election, choice or admission of a keeper and of fellows all personal affection, champerty and partiality shall be excluded, so that the person who is plainly better for, and more useful to, the college shall be chosen as God shall best guide [the electors] in [their] conscience: always provided however that in all elections of a keeper of the college a fellow of the college shall be [chosen] first, if one is found suitable for the office, or else another of distinction from our diocese, and in the election of fellows scholars from our diocese who are not beneficed shall be preferred to those who are beneficed and the poorer shall be preferred to those who are more wealthy, other things being equal.*][17]

[16] *majoris partis collegii*; treating the *collegium* as the community of fellows.

[17] See the note to the Latin text for the history of this clause.

Salva nobis libera potestate ordinandi et disponendi[a] de custode et sociis preficiendis et ammovendis dum fuerimus in hac vita.[b]

[4] *De inhabilibus personis dicti collegii, Rubrica.*

Item statuimus et ordinamus quod si socius dicti collegii cujuscunque status aut gradus fuerit, quandocunque seu quomodocunque inhabilis fuerit perpetua inhabilitate, aut tali quod judicio majoris partis sociorum non speratur in eo verisimiliter habilitas in futurum ad proficiendum ulterius in studio pro honore collegii supradicti, seu ad obtinendum gradum doctoratus *in aliqua facultate prius memorata,*[c] talis per custodem cum discrecione consilio et assensu majoris partis sociorum collegii protinus expellatur, et alius aptus et habilis ad proficiendum in sic ammoti locum per modum et formam superius descriptam eligatur.

[5] *De inhabili custode, Rubrica.*

Item statuimus et ordinamus quod si custos dicti collegii qui pro tempore fuerit per duas partes sociorum collegii inhabilis seu indignus ad dicti officii regimen ex causis justis et verisimilibus habeatur; tunc dictus custos ad cedendum voluntarie officio suo predicto per dicti collegii socios invitetur; quo si cedere spontanee noluerit, tunc Cancellarius universitatis predicte qui pro tempore fuerit, consulatur, qui recepta extrajudicialiter informacione a duabus partibus sociorum dicti collegii, dictum custodem remansurum decernat, vel ab officio removendum, cum deliberacione duorum rectorum universitatis et duorum doctorum regencium in eadem universitate, et assensu eorum, prout superius est expressum. Quem, si voluntarie cesserit invitatus, remanere volumus, si

insertion the restriction in Statute 15 on the holding of benefices: see "*Bateman's Statutes: The Manuscript Confusion*", § I. 2 above.

[a] *Sic* original MS (and TH c. 4 from which it was copied)); in the context *disponendi* does not seem to be a mistake for *deponendi* (removing a person from office), since the word *ammovendis* is used seven words later for the removal of fellows.

[b] This paragraph had been in the corresponding Trinity Hall statute (st. 4) and was therefore included here in Statute 3, even though a similar power in respect of the fellows (but not the keeper) was later reserved to Bateman in Statute 18 (as it had been in the original 1353 Statutes). *Sheriffe's Evidences* omitted it, no doubt because its force had expired with Bateman's death; but it was nevertheless included in MS 711 and (in brackets) in MS 760.

[c] The italicised words were substituted in the 1355 version for the restriction to the doctorate of Laws in the corresponding Trinity Hall statute (c. 10) that Bateman had specified (but not set out) in the 1353 version.

The power of ordering and effecting the preferring and removal of the keeper and of fellows is reserved to us while we are in this life.

[4] *Ineligibility for [membership of] the college.*

We decree and ordain that if a fellow of the college of whatever standing or degree shall at any time or in any way become incapable by reason of a permanent disability, or such that there is, in the judgment of the majority of the fellows, no likely prospect of his being fit to pursue study for the honour of the college in the future or to obtain the degree of doctor in any faculty specified above, then that person shall be expelled forthwith by the keeper with the wise counsel, advice and assent of the majority of the fellows of the college and another [person] suitable and able to make progress [in study] shall be elected in the manner and form described above in the place of the person so removed.

[5] *Ineligibility for [the office of] keeper.*

We decree and ordain that if a keeper of the college shall be adjudged by two-thirds of the fellows of the college for valid and convincing reasons to be unfit or unworthy to perform the office, then that keeper shall be invited by the fellows of the college to resign his office voluntarily; and if he is unwilling to resign voluntarily, then the chancellor of the university shall be consulted, and, after receiving an information extra-judicially from two-thirds of the fellows of the college, he shall (in consultation with two rectors[18] of the university and two regent doctors in that university and with their consent as specified above) decide [either] that the keeper shall remain or that he shall be removed from office. If he resigns voluntarily on request, it is our will that he shall remain as a

[18] *I.e.*, proctors: see note to Statute 3 above.

voluerit, ut socium de collegio, dum tamen habilis fuerit ad proficiendum in studio, et si beneficiatus non fuerit, aut beneficii sui condicio patiatur.

[**6**] *De sigillo communi et archa communi, Rubrica.*

Item statuimus et ordinamus quod dictum nostrum collegium habeat unum sigillum commune et unam archam communem magnam et fortem, in qua dictum sigillum, cartas, indenturas, munimenta, jocalia, et thesaurum dicti collegii volumus conservari, sub tribus clavibus diverse fabrice, quarum una penes unum, et altera penes alium, et tercia penes tercium remaneant socios, ad hoc per majorem partem sociorum annis singulis noviter eligendos. Et volumus quod singulis annis totum residuum remanens, ultra expensas necessarias collegii, in cista communi[a] pro thesauro collegii reponatur. Volumus insuper quod thesaurus collegii non expendatur nisi in edificacione vel reparacione domorum, murorum, vel clausure habitacionis seu rectoriarum[b] dicti collegii, seu in empcione reddituum perpetuorum pro collegio, aut in defensione jurium aut aliam utilitatem perpetuam ejusdem, non autem in commodum singularium personarum collegii supradicti; nec thesaurus pecunie cuiquam sub cujuscunque securitate ac alio colore seu titulo mutuetur.

[7] *De compoto reddendo.*

Item volumus et ordinamus quod custos collegii et custodes clavium ciste communis ejusdem, qui pro tempore fuerint, reddant fidelite compotum singulis annis de omnibus et singulis receptis, liberatis, expensis, gestis, et administratis per eos; et totum residuum quod super fuerit ultra expensas in thesaurum collegii convertatur. Et hoc volumus quod fiat quolibet anno bina vice, videlicet in septimanis proximis post resumpcionem magistrorum regencium in terminis

[a] By the word *cista* Bateman would have had in mind the same great and strong common chest or ark (*archa*) with three separate locks that he had just mentioned, but it came to denote a smaller chest or money-box that could be placed within the ark: see *The arca, cistae, thesaurus and aerarium* in "*Supplementary Notes to Caius' Statutes*", § IV. 3, at p. 288 below.

[b] *Sic* MS; likewise Trinity Hall c. 12, from which it was copied; but in the context it might be a scribal error for *tectoriarum* or *tecturarum*, *i.e.* "roofs".

fellow, if he wishes, so long, however, as he is qualified to pursue study and does not have a benefice or the nature of his benefice allows.[19]

[**6**] *The common seal and common chest.*

We decree and ordain that our college shall have one common seal and one great and strong common ark,[20] and it is our will that the seal, charters, indentures, muniments, precious objects and endowment of the college shall be kept in that chest, under three keys fashioned differently, of which one shall stay with one fellow, a second with another and the third with a third [fellow], each of whom is to be appointed afresh by a majority of the fellows annually. And it is our will that each year the whole balance remaining after the necessary expenses of the college [have been paid] shall be placed in the common chest for the endowment of the college. It is further our will that the endowment of the college shall not be spent except on the building or repair of houses, walls or curtilage[21] of the precincts[22] or rectories of the college, or in the purchase of perpetual rents for the college, or in the defence of the legal rights of the college but not for the benefit of any individual members of the college; and the money in the endowment is not to be lent to anyone on any security or any colour or title whatsoever.

[7] *Accounting.*

It is our will and we ordain that the keeper of the college and the keepers of the keys of its common chest at the time shall render a faithful account each year of each and every item received, allowed, expended, performed and managed by them, and the whole balance remaining after expenses shall be transferred to the endowment of the college. And it is our will that this shall be done twice every year, namely in the weeks next after the beginning of the terms following

19 *I.e.*, a benefice without cure of souls or one with cure of souls with a dispensation to be absent for study.

20 For the *arca*, see *The arca, cistae, thesaurus and aerarium* in "*Supplementary Notes to Caius' Statutes*", § IV. 3, at p. 288 below.

21 *Clausura* would seem to be used in the sense of a 'boundary wall', rather than the property ('close') it enclosed.

22 Being in the singular, *habitacio* presumably referred to the complex of buildings forming the college.

proximis post festa sancti Michaelis et Pasche, in presencia omnium sociorum dicti collegii tunc in universitate presencium, aut trium eorum ad minus, quos dictum collegium ad hoc duxerit eligendos. Volumus insuper quod in dictis compotorum diebus fiant due indenture de statu dicte Aule, et de toto residuo remanente, quarum una penes custodem remaneat, alia vero in archa communi reponatur.

[**8**] *De residencia et absencia, Rubrica.*

Item volentes dicti collegii personas ad continuum studii exercicium excitare, statuimus et ordinamus quod nullus socius, presertim sine licencia custodis aut ejus locum tenentis, nec custos presertim absque consilio et assensu duorum saniorum aut seniorum collegii extra Aulam seu hospicium pernoctet. Volumus tamen quod in licencia danda sociis per custodem et assensu per socios dando custodi non adhibeatur nimia difficultas, sed quod asserente se sub juramento collegio prestito, causam habere racionabilem absentandi, non denegetur absentandi facultas, presertim vacacionum temporibus. Sed tunc assignetur absentandi certum tempus juxta indigenciam ejusdem et qualitatem cause, infra quod cessante legitimo impedimento redire teneatur. Proviso quod medietas sociorum pro tutela Aule et bonorum ejusdem ad minus semper in collegio remaneant. Volumus insuper quod de porcione cujuslibet tam custodis quam alterius socii absencie sue tempore pro qualibet septimana qua absens fuerit, duodecim denarii subtrahantur, et illa pecunia in thesauro collegii reponatur. Salvo quod per unicum in quolibet anno mensem continuum vel discontinuum possit quilibet custos et socius absque subtraccionis alicujus pena se cum licencia ut premittitur absentare. Volumus insuper et ordinamus quod nec per custodem vel ejus locum tenentem socio licencia, nec custodi per duos seniores consilium et assensus dari possit se in[a] uno anno extra generalium vacacionum tempora, ultra unius mensis spacium continuum nec[b] discontinuum, semel nec diversis vicibus absentandi, nisi pro negociis collegii aut propriis causis necessariis, judicio et assensu custodis et majoris partis sociorum collegii concorditer approbandis.[c]

[a] The MS appears to have a single word that might be "*sed*" rather than the two words "*se in*"; but the latter makes better sense.

[b] Query why "*nec*" here, not "*vel*" as a few lines earlier? The writer of MS 760 was troubled by the question and substituted "*vel*" here, but not three words later. The MS just has an "n" or "v" with a superscript contraction (').

[c] The gist of this convoluted provision would seem to be (i) that 'extra-ordinary' leave, *i.e.* from the keeper and a majority of the fellows, is needed to be absent during term (*i.e.*, outside general vacations) for more than a month in total in any one year, and then only on college business or for personal reasons approved by them, and (ii) that 'ordinary' leave from the keeper or his

the feasts of St Michael and Easter,[23] in the presence of all the fellows of the college then present in the university, or at least three of them, whom the college shall see fit to elect for the purpose. It is our will further that during the days of accounting there shall be [executed] two indentures [recording] the [financial] position of the hall, and the total balance remaining, of which one shall stay with the keeper and the other be placed in the common chest.

[**8**] *Residence and absence.*

Wishing to encourage the members of the college to unbroken application to study, we decree and ordain that no fellow shall pass the night outside the hall or hospice, unless he has the especial leave of the keeper or his deputy, and no keeper [shall do so], except with the especial counsel and assent of two of the wiser or older [fellows] of the college. It is however our will that no great difficulty will hinder the giving of leave to fellows by the keeper or the giving of assent to the keeper by [the two] fellows, and that leave of absence will not be refused, particularly in vacation time, to anyone who states on his oath given to the college that he has good cause to be absent. But the period of absence shall be fixed at the time in the light of the need for it and the nature of its cause, and after that period [has elapsed] he shall be bound to return, barring any legitimate impediment. [The granting of leave is] subject to the proviso that at least half the fellowship remains in college for the safety of the hall and its property. During the time of anyone's absence, it is our will further that 12d. shall be deducted from the stipend of anyone (as much that of the keeper as of anyone else who is a fellow) for each week that he has been absent, and that the money shall be deposited in the college treasury;[24] save only that everyone, keeper and fellow, may, with the leave stated above, be absent without penalty of any deduction for [a period of] one month each year, either continuous or discontinuous. It is also our will and we ordain that a fellow shall not be given leave by the keeper or his deputy, and the keeper shall not be given counsel and agreement by two seniors, to be absent outside the time of general vacations in any one year for more than one month either continuously or discontinuously, and whether on one or on several occasions, except on college business or for necessary personal reasons approved by the judgment and agreement of the keeper and majority of the fellows of the college freely given.

23 In early university statutes Michaelmas Term ran from 10 October to 16 December, and Easter Term from the Wednesday after the First Sunday after Easter to 20 July: *H.U.C.*, I, pp. 29–30, citing M.B. Hackett, *Original Statutes of Cambridge University*, Cambridge, 1970, pp. 142–3.

24 The deductions from stipend for absence were regularly entered in the *liber rationalis*, but had ceased to be any deterrent by the eighteenth century, as a result of the fall in the value of money.

[9] *De numero sociorum augendo, Rubrica.*

Item statuimus et ordinamus quod quandocunque dictum collegium habuerit ex nostra, aut aliorum fidelium largicione, aut ex ejusdem collegii empcione, sufficientem seu habundantem ad hoc excrescenciam reddituum annuorum perpetuorum, teneatur sociorum pro tempore numerum juxta dictam reddituum annuorum perpetuorum excrescenciam ampliare; super quo custodis et sociorum qui pro tempore fuerint, sub juramento prestito coram deo conscienciam oneramus.

[10] *De bonis collegii non alienandis, Rubrica.*

Item statuimus et ordinamus quod bona immobilia dicti collegii sive sint temporalia sive spiritualia nullo modo nec aliquo unquam tempore alienentur. Et idem statuimus et ordinamus de perpetuis viribus incorporabilibus dicti collegii. Item idem statuimus de libris dicti collegii de presenti concessis seu datis ac futuris temporibus concedendis seu dandis collegio supradicto.

[11] *De libris collegii, Rubrica.*

Item statuimus et ordinamus quod in diebus compotorum superius descriptis, annis singulis coram custode et omnibus dicti collegii sociis tunc in universitate presentibus, ostendantur realiter visibiliter et distincte omnes libri dicti collegii, quos ex nostra liberalitate, seu aliorum fidelium pia largicione habent et eos habere contigerit in futurum, ut sic quolibet anno bis apparere poterit si aliquis liber dicti collegii perditus fuerit vel distractus. Volumus enim et statuimus quod nullus liber dicti collegii ullo unquam tempore vendatur, donetur, permutetur, vel alio quovis alienetur titulo vel colore, nec alicui alteri quam de collegio commodetur, nec alicui de collegio nec extra, nec in aula nec extra quaternatim tradatur pro copia describenda, nec per custodem nec aliquem alium ducatur vel portetur extra villam Cantebriggie, nec extra Aulam seu hospicium dicti collegii, neque integraliter neque particulariter quaternatim nisi ad scolas; ita tamen quod nullus liber pernoctet extra Aulam seu hospicium predictum, nisi aliquis liber fuerit religandus vel emendandus necessario; quo casu cum dictus liber religatus vel emendatus fuerit, ad Aulam predictam illico reportetur. Et volumus quod omnes libri dicti collegii ponantur in aliqua camera

deputy (if the absentee is a fellow) or from two senior fellows (if he is the keeper) is sufficient for leave in vacations (and even up to a month in term, it would seem).

[9] *Increasing the number of fellows.*

We decree and ordain that whenever the college has sufficiency or abundance of perpetual annual revenues to support an increase [in the number] of fellows – whether from our own generosity or that of others or from a purchase by the college itself – it shall be obliged to increase the number of fellows for the time being in line with the increased surplus of perpetual annual revenues; and to this end we lay the burden on the conscience of the keeper and fellows at the time on oath before God.

[10] *The requirement that the goods of the college shall not be alienated.*

We decree and ordain that the immovable property of the college, whether temporal or spiritual, shall never be alienated in any way or at any time; and we decree and ordain likewise as regards the perpetual incorporeal rights of the college. We decree likewise as regards the books of the college that have already been granted or given to it or that may be granted or given [to it] in the future.

[11] *The books of the college.*

We decree and ordain that all the books of the college which they have or may happen to have in the future as a result of our bounty or the pious generosity of others of the faithful shall be displayed every year physically, visibly and distinguishably in the presence of the keeper and all the fellows of the college then present in the university on the audit days described above, so that it may be apparent twice a year if any book has been lost or removed. For it is our will and we decree that no book of the college shall ever at any time be sold, given, exchanged or alienated on any colour or title; nor shall it be lent to anyone other than a member of the college; nor shall it be handed over in quires for copying to anyone, whether or not [he is] a member of the college and whether or not [it is done] within the hall or outside; nor shall it be taken or carried by the keeper or any other person outside the town of Cambridge, and not outside the hall or the hospice of the college, either in its entirety or in quires, except to the schools; even then, no book shall be outside the hall or the hospice overnight, unless a particular book needs to be re-bound or repaired, and in that case the book shall be brought back to the hall as soon as it has been re-bound or repaired. And it is our will that all the books of the college shall be placed in some secure

secura, pro libraria collegii deputanda, ut sic ad eos per omnes scolares collegii possit communis haberi recursus. Permittimus tamen quod libri textuum[a] utriusque juris scolaribus collegii indigentibus ad eorum peculiarem usum, dum tamen non portentur extra ut supra dicitur, usque ad certum tempus juxta discrecionem custodis et trium collegii seniorum poterunt commodari. Libros doctorum utriusque juris volumus in dicta librarie camera cum cathenis ferreis conligatos, ad sociorum communem usum continuo remanere.

[**12**] *De sociorum nominibus episcopo Norwicensi et capitulo annis singulis intimandis, Rubrica.*

Item ut episcopi Norwicenses qui pro tempore fuerint, et capitulum ejusdem ecclesie, de nominibus sociorum qui virtute juramenti superius ordinati dictorum episcoporum capitulo et ecclesie Norwicensis obsequiis astringuntur, plenius valeant informari, ut sic episcopi Norwicenses et capitulum ad eos et eorum singulos ad quemcumque statum vel gradum pervenerint recursum habere valeant in agendis; statuimus et ordinamus quod quilibet custos dicti collegii qui pro tempore fuerit, quolibet anno in synodo proxima post festum Sancti Michaelis in Norwic[ensi] ecclesia celebranda, certificet episcopum Norwic[ensem], qui pro tempore fuerit, si tunc presens fuerit, vel eo absente dicte synodo presidentem, necnon priorem et capitulum ejusdem ecclesie, de nominibus et cognominibus omnium tunc sociorum prefati collegii superstitium,[b] et eorum qui anno immediate precedente per mortem, cessionem, amocionem, seu alium quemcunque modum a collegio discesserint, per literas binas patentes sigillo communi collegii consignatas; quarum literarum una episcopo qui pro tempore fuerit et in ejus absencia dicte synodo presidenti, alia vero litera priori et capitulo dirigatur.

[NOTE: The statutes that follow are set out in the 1355 statutes, but without rubrics. As each of them has a distinct subject-matter, they have been editorially numbered here.][c]

[a] *Sheriffe's Evidences* and MS 760 insert "*Logicae, Philosophiae, Theologiae et*". MS 711 does not do so.

[b] *Sic* MS.

[c] Each was treated differently by later copyists from Sheriffe onwards. For their chequered history see "*Bateman's Statutes: The Manuscript Confusion*", § I. 2 above; as explained there, three of the statutes (Statutes 13, 14 and 15) were unintentionally omitted by Venn in his re-print of the 1355 statutes (*B.H.* III, p. 352).

room assigned as the library of the college, so that communal access may be had to them by all the scholars of the college. We allow, however, that the books of [*Logic, Philosophy, Theology and*][25] civil or canon law texts may be lent to poor scholars of the college for their personal use for such time as may be determined by the keeper and three seniors of the college, so long as they are not taken outside [the college] as stated above.[26] It is our will that books of doctors of civil or canon law [shall be] chained with iron shackles in the library-room [and] shall always stay there for the communal use of the fellows.

[**12**] *Communication of the names of the fellows to the bishop and chapter of Norwich each year.*

[It is our aim][27] that the bishop of Norwich at the time, and the chapter of that church, shall be fully informed of the names of fellows who are bound to serve the bishops chapter and church of Norwich by virtue of the oath ordained above[28] in order that the bishops of Norwich and chapter may in this way have recourse to one and all of them in legal business, whatever the standing or degree to which they have attained. [To this end] we decree and ordain that, each year at the synod next after the celebration of the feast of St Michael in Norwich cathedral, whoever is keeper of the college at the time shall certify to the then bishop of Norwich, if he is present, or to the president of the synod if he is absent, and also to the prior and chapter of that cathedral the names and surnames of all the fellows of the college who are living, and of those who have departed from the college in the year immediately preceding by reason of death, resignation, removal or any other cause whatsoever. [He shall do this] in two letters patent sealed with the common seal of the college, one of which letters [patent] shall be addressed to the bishop at the time and to the president of the synod if he is absent, and the other [letters patent] to the prior and chapter.[29]

25 Inserted in the fifteenth century in *Sheriffe's Evidences* (MS 706/692) and later in MS 760 but not MS 711.

26 This clause allowed the borrowings that are recorded in the remarkable borrowing register of the 1400s, on which see Catherine Hall's article in *Transactions of the Cambridge Bibliographical Society*; the register is edited by Peter Clarke in *Corpus of British Medieval Library Catalogues ... University of Cambridge*, ed. P. Clarke and R.W. Lovatt (London, 2002), p. 256.

27 For the convenience of the reader, Bateman's one, long and convoluted sentence has been divided into three separate sentences; hence the insertions introducing those sentences.

28 In fact it is below. It had been in the paragraph preceding the list of Trinity Hall statutes in the 1353 version (*i.e.* "above"), but that paragraph and the reference to Trinity Hall were omitted in the 1355 re-issue.

29 For the numbering of the subsequent statutes, see the editorial note which follows the Latin text of this statute.

[13][a]

Et premissa omnia et singula volumus observari, non obstantibus quibuscumque statutis et ordinacionibus alias per nos factis seu antea ordinatis, que omnia et singula in quantum sunt vel esse poterunt contraria statutis presentibus in toto vel in aliqua sui parte cassamus, irritamus et revocamus expresse. Presentia tamen statuta et eorum quodlibet augendi, duplicandi, mutandi, minuendi, interpretandi, corrigendi et super illis dispensandi aliaque nova statuta faciendi quociens et quando nobis videbitur oportunum quamdiu in hac vita fuerimus potestatem nobis liberam reservamus.

[14][b]

Volumus autem quod nullus alius quam artista eligatur in socium dicte aule nec aliquis nisi prius per tres annos audiverit et studuerit in arte dialectica aut per duos ad minus annos excellenter proficerit in eadem.

[15][c]

Item ordinamus quod nullus curatum obtinens beneficium cuiuscumque valoris seu non curatum aut decanatum ruralem cuius redditus et proventus centum solidorum summam iuxta verum omnibus annis annuum valorem excedunt, eligi valeat in socium, nec iam electus in dicto collegio ut socius ultra unius anni spacium a promocionis sue tempore remanere, excepto custode qui quodcumque beneficium obtinens ecclesiasticum, eciam si dignitas fuerit eligi valeat et iam electus in dicto officio remanere.

[a] The two sentences that here form Statute 13 were not included in the 1353 statutes; but they had followed immediately upon Statute 12 in the corresponding Trinity Hall statute (st. 21), and it was presumably for that reason that they were included here in the 1355 statutes. In MS 711 Caius confusingly ran on the first sentence as part of Statute 12 and then merged the second sentence with Statutes 14 and 15 and presented all three as a single paragraph at the end of Statute 12.

[b] Included here in the original and in MS 711, but omitted by Sheriffe and MS 760 (both having moved it to Statute 3).

[c] Included here in the original and in MS 711, but omitted by Sheriffe and MS 760 (both having moved it to Statute 3).

[13][30]

It is our wish that each and every one of the premises shall be observed, notwithstanding any statutes and ordinances whatsoever made otherwise or previously formulated by us, each and every one of which we annul, invalidate and expressly revoke insofar as they are or might be contrary to the present statutes in whole or in any part of them. We reserve to ourself, however, full power to enlarge, duplicate, alter, diminish, interpret, correct and dispense from those statutes and to make new statutes as often and whenever it seems fit to us so long as we are in this life.

[14]

It is our wish that no one other than a student in Arts shall be elected a fellow of the hall, and no one unless he has [first] heard [lectures on] and studied Logic for three years or has excelled therein for at least two years.

[15]

We ordain that no one obtaining a benefice with cure of souls of any value whatever, or a benefice without cure of souls or rural deanery of which the true annual value of the income and return exceeds the sum of 100 shillings,[31] shall be qualified to be elected a fellow, nor, if he is already a fellow, may he remain a fellow beyond the space of one year from the time of his preferment; with the exception of the keeper who, if he obtains an ecclesiastical benefice of any kind, shall be qualified to be elected if he is worthy and to remain in office if he is already elected.

30 See note to Latin text concerning the two sentences of this statute.

31 Cf. the formulation in the original 1353 issue of the statutes. See also Gonville's Statute 20 above.

[**16** *De iuramento*][a]

Juramentum autem quod vestrum quemlibet infra triduum ab hora recepcionis presencium, et alium quemlibet custodem et socium qui pro tempore fuerit, statim in cujuslibet admissione tactis evangeliis subire et facere volumus, duximus ex habundanti presentibus inserendum.

Imprimis jurabit quilibet quod omnia statuta intitulata superius et descripta, fideliter quatenus humana sinit fragilitas observabit. Item quod fidelis et diligens erit in quocumque officio quod eorum quemlibet in collegio habere contigerit in futurum. Item quod commodum et honorem collegii predicti et non contrarium quamdiu vixerit procurabit. Item quod quamdiu vixerit ad quemcumque statum ipsum contigerit pervenire, honorem et commodum ecclesie Norwicensis et nunquam contrarium procurabit; et quod nunquam, quamdiu vixerit, erit in aliquo negocio causa vel lite contra aliquem episcopum Norwicensem qui pro tempore fuerit, nec contra ecclesiam, nec contra capitulum Norwicense; sed cum eis pro justo et competenti salario cum extra exercicium scolasticum fuerit, quando et cum legitime fuerit requisitus.[b]

[**17** *Indulgentia*][c]

Volumus autem quod si quis ex facilitate aut subita mocione vel indeliberate absque deliberata condicta aut excogitata fraude vel dolo seu pertinacia, in aliquo praemissorum offenderit vel peccaverit, paratus se corrigere et emendare, perjurus propter hoo non censeatur, nec pro perjuro pro hoc ab aliis reputetur.

[**18**][d]

Salva nobis semper potestate libera disponendi et ordinandi de sociis vestri collegii preficiendis et ammovendis ac de statutis predictis omnibus et singulis

[a] MS 711 conveniently inserts this title, which is not in the original. *Sheriffe* gives the whole of the first paragraph as the title. MS 760 omits the statute here, having given it *before* Statutes 1–12.

[b] A marginal note in MS 711 (correctly) states that the rest of the oath is to be found in Caius' Statutes, fols. 7, 8.

[c] MSS 711 inserts this title. MS 760 omits the statute here, having given it (and the title) *before* Statutes 1–12.

[d] In content this paragraph forms a separate statute. It had been in the original 1353 statutes, but it had expired on Bateman's death in January 1355, and, although it was included in the 1355 re-issue and by subsequent copyists, it was never given a separate number or title. It overlaps in part with the last paragraph of Statute 3; that paragraph had been included in Statute 3 by Elveden and the overlap caused confusion later.

[16 *The Oath.*]

We have directed that there shall also be included in this document the oath which we wish to be put to and taken by each of you on the gospels within three days of the receipt of these presents and by every other keeper and fellow at the time immediately on their admission.

First, each person shall swear that he will observe all the statutes entitled and set out above as faithfully as human frailty permits. Further, that he will be faithful and diligent in whatever office in college each of them may have in the future. Further, that he will promote the advantage and honour of the college and not [work] against it so long as he shall live. Further, that he will promote the honour and advantage of the church of Norwich in whatever station to which he may happen to come during his lifetime and never [work] against it; and that he will never be a party at any time during his lifetime to any business or litigation against any bishop of Norwich, or against the church or the chapter of Norwich, but will act on their behalf for a just and adequate stipend when he has completed his academic studies, as and when he is lawfully required to do so.

[17 *Clemency.*]

It is our will that if anyone shall offend or sin against any of the above provisions by way of help or subtle suggestion, or thoughtlessly without deliberate, collusive or premeditated fraud or deceit or contumacy, and is prepared to correct and mend his ways, he shall not be deemed forsworn nor shall he on that account be held by others to be in breach of his oath.

[18]

Reserving always to us the unrestricted power of effecting[32] and of ordering the preferring and removing of fellows of your college and of amending, correcting,

[32] In the context *disponendi* would seem not to be a mistake for *deponendi* (removing a person from office), since the word *ammovendis* is used nine words later for the removal of fellows.

emendandis corrigendis supplendis, revocandis, et novis eciam faciendis, prout nostre consciencie videbitur, quamdiu fuerimus in hac luce.

[**19** *Statutorum lectio*][a]

Et ut ad observacionem statutorum predictorum omnes de collegio forcius et facilius excitentur, volumus et statuimus quod totus iste liber statutorum annis singulis in primis resumpcionum magistrorum diebus, post festa Sancti Michaelis et Pasche, coram omnibus dicti collegii custode et sociis in dicta universitate presentibus plenarie recitetur et integraliter perlegatur.

Datum apud Hoxne septimo die mensis Septembris, Anno domini millesimo ccc^{mo} quinquagesimo tercio, et consecracionis nostre decimo.

Nos igitur Officialis antedictus facta fide que requiritur in hac parte, dicta instrumenta originalia inspeximus diligenter et inspecta vidimus non rasa non cancellata non abolita nec in sui parte aliqua viciata sed eorum veris sigillis, de quibus in dictis instrumentis sit mencio consignata. Quocirca[b] originalia instrumenta per magistrum Johannem de Wynestone publicum auctoritate apostolica notarium precepimus[c] exemplari et postmodum per dictum notarium in nostra eciam presencia facta collacione dictorum transcriptorum in omnibus concordancium cum originalibus antedictis dicta transcripta vera esse exemplaria dictorum originalium et eandem auctoritatem cum originalibus obtinere judicialiter decrevimus et decernimus per presentes. In quorum omnium fidem et testimonium ad specialem requisicionem dictorum custodis et scolarium[d] sigillum officii nostri fecimus hiis apponi. Datum apud Norwicum in pleno loci consistorio, xix die mensis Maii, Anno domini millesimo ccc^{mo} quinquagesimo quinto.

Et ego Iohannes de Wynestone[e] *clericus Norwicen[sis] diocesis publicus auctoritate apostolica notarius exhibicioni presentacioni et ostensioni*

[a] MSS 711 and 760 insert this title. Bateman had not included this provision in his original 1353 statutes; it was copied into the 1355 re-issue from the Trinity Hall statutes where it had featured in the provisions following Statute 12 (TH st. 21).

[b] Cf. Statute 1 above, where MSS 711, 760 also have *quocirca*, but the original has *quo casu*.

[c] Reading *precepimus*, not *percepimus* as Venn did.

[d] *Sic.* Cf. the second sentence of the preamble (*custos et scolares Collegii Annunciationis …*).

[e] This would appear to be Winston, Suffolk, rather than Wyvestone, Suffolk.

supplementing, and revoking each and every one of the statutes, and also of making new ones as seems fit to [us and] our conscience, during our lifetime.

[19]

And in order that every member of the college may be spurred the more earnestly and readily to obedience to the statutes, it is our will and we decree that the whole of this book of statutes shall be recited in full and read out word for word every year on the first days of the terms following the feasts of St Michael and Easter in the presence of all those of the college, keeper and fellows, [then] present in the university.

Given at Hoxne on the seventh day of September in the year of the Lord 1353 and the tenth year of our consecration.

Accordingly we the aforesaid Official on our oath as required in that respect have dutifully inspected the original instruments and have seen that the inspected [instruments] have not been erased, cancelled, effaced or vitiated in any part but [are] sealed with their true seals, of which mention is made in the said instruments.[33] This being so, we have ordered the original instruments to be exemplified by Master John of Winston, notary public by papal authorisation, and, the said transcripts having afterwards and in our presence been collated in all [details] with the said originals by the said notary public, we decree and determine by these presents [that] the said transcripts be true exemplars of the said originals and are to enjoy the same authority as the originals. In trust and witness of all these [facts], at the special request of the said keeper and scholars,[34] we have had the official seal of our office appended to these [presents]. Given at Norwich in a full consistory there, the 19th day of May A.D. 1355.

> I, John of Winston, clerk of the diocese of Norwich and notary public by papal authorisation, was present in the cathedral church of Norwich on the nineteenth day of May in the year 1355 from the incarnation of our Lord according to the practice and reckoning of the English church, [being] the eighth year of the indiction[35] [and] the third year of the papacy

33 The official was Walter of Elveden, the vicar general of the diocese and keeper of the spiritualities. He seems to have exhibited a benevolent attitude to Gonville Hall in his inspection of the original documents: see Christopher Brooke's the chapter on "*William Bateman and his Foundation*", § V. 2 below, and his *History*, pp. 14–15. The formal language of the certificate has been retained in the translation.

34 *Sic*, as at the beginning of the preamble: see note to text.

35 The (69th) fifteen-year cycle of years or indiction then current began in 1347. For the use of indiction-years by notaries see C.R. Cheney, *Handbook of Dates for Students of British History*, ed. M. Jones (London, 2000), p. 3.

dictorum instrumentorum originalium ...(?) ac ... et decreti inquisitioni (?) cum omnibus aliis per ipsum dominum officialem Norwicen[sem] factis et habitis una cum discretis viris magistro Iohanne de Cove, Thoma de Shirforde, Iohanne de Thefford', Ada de Wykem'e,[a] *Willlelmo de Lee et Thoma de Hemenhale*[b] *clericis Norwicen[sis] et Lincoln[iensis] diocesum, testibus ad premissa vocatis specialiter et rogatis, die decima nona mensis Maii anno Domini ab incarnacione eiusdem secundum cursum et computacionem ecclesie Anglicane millesimo XXX° quinquagesimo quinto indictione octava pontificatus sanctissimi in Cristo patris et domini nostri domini Innocentii ... providencia pape sexti anno tertio in ecclesia cathedr[ali] Norwic[ensi] presens interfui, dictaque originalia omnia et singula non rasa non abolita nec in aliqua sui parte vitiata vidi legi et inspexi ea et ex mandato et auctoritate ipsius domini officialis Norwicens[is] ad rogatum dictorum custodis et collegii aliis occupatus*[c] *negociis feci fideliter exemplari, nil addens vel minuens quod sensum mutet vel variet' intellectum. Et facta diligenti collatione de presenti instrumento ad ipsa instrumenta originalia, quia ea concordare inveni, in hanc publicam formam redegi signoque meo consueto et inscriptione signavi in fidem et testimonium premissorum.*[d]

[a] Wickmere, Norfolk.

[b] Hempnall, Norfolk.

[c] If the correct reading is "*occupatus*", it is in the nominative and must therefore relate to the subject of the sentence, John of Winston, rather than to the keeper of the College (John of Colton). But query whether it refers to Colton's absence in Avignon.

[d] The notary's sign and signature are added at the foot of the document.

of our most holy father and lord in Christ the lord Innocent VI, at the production, presentation and showing of the original documents ... and ... inquiry together with everything else ordered by the Official of Norwich, in the presence of John of Cove, Thomas of Shirforde, John of Thetford, Adam of Wickmere, William of Lee and Thomas of Hempnall,[36] clerks of the dioceses of Norwich and Lincoln; and I saw, read and inspected every part of the said original [documents], which had not been erased, effaced or falsified in any part; and, on the instruction and authorisation of the official of Norwich and at the request of the said keeper and college, being [myself][37] engaged on other business, I have caused [the said originals] to be exemplified, neither adding nor omitting anything which altered the sense or changed the meaning. And because I find, after a careful comparison, that the present document accords with the originals, I have published it with my accustomed seal and signed it as a faithful witness of the premises.

36 For these highly respected men of substance and the significance of their involvement in the certification of the document, see Christopher Brooke's chapter on "*William Bateman and his Foundation*", § V. 2 below, and the works there cited. John de Cove was later archdeacon of Suffolk, Adam of Wickmere later Master of Trinity Hall and William of Lee a fellow of Gonville Hall.

37 See note to text.

III. 3

Expositiones seu interpretationes

[Cambridge, Gonville & Caius College Library, MS 711/756 and MS 760/424]

Expositiones seu interpretationes secundum sensum grammaticalem quorundam locorum in statutis Rev. Patris per nos Joannem Caium fundatorem, ad tollendas controversias et dissentiones inter socios per tempora futura, occasione nacta ex discordiis ortis ex sinistra interpretatione eorum nostris temporibus. Quae expositiones sive interpretationes ut pro statutis sint et habeantur, firmiter ordinamus et constituimus.

Cum praecipiat R. Pater in electione custodis ut sanior vel senior socius vices gerat custodis, potest oriri controversia uter gerat vices. Eam tollunt statuta universitatis per bonae memoriae Regem Edwardum Sextum edita,[a] viz. seniorem et saniorem socium communiter haberi qui praesidentis nomine appellatur. Quam sententiam et interpretationem nos admittimus et in vim statuti tenorem praesentium facimus.[b]

Alias senior socius esto qui prius in Collegio juratus fuit si non sit Bacchalaureus.[c]

Vacatio etiam officii Custodis[d] intelligatur ab ipso die mortis, cessionis, aut alterius modi legitimi.

Mensis spatium, viginti octo dierum.

Prestimonia, pecunia in hoc concessa, ut custos et socii sint presto et parati in Collegio diebus praescriptis, ex vulgari vocabulo *prestmony*, deducta voce.

[a] It is not clear which provision of Edward's Statutes of 1549 Caius had in his mind. A reference to the office of president was included in the Injunctions made soon after by Edward's Visitors; these refer to the "*singulorum collegiorum praesides*" and provide that he should be allowed to have 40 marks a year in certain cases, but they do not specify how the holder of the office was to be identified.

[b] A marginal reference to Matthew Parker's *Interpretatio* has been added later.

[c] Presumably a Bachelor of Arts, not a Bachelor of Theology; the latter, as now, ranked above Masters. In his draft statutes Edmund Gonville himself had specified as senior the one first sworn: *B.H.* III, 341.

[d] The scribe uses capital C for Custos from here on.

III. 3

The Exposition of Bateman's Statutes by John Caius

> Expositions or Interpretations according to their grammatical sense of certain passages in the Reverend Father's statutes by us John Caius founder in order to settle controversies and disagreements between fellows in the future arising out of disputes resulting from their incorrect interpretation in our time. We firmly direct and decree that these expositions or interpretations have, and are to be taken to have, the force of statutes.

When the Reverend Father directs that the senior or wiser fellow shall act in place of the keeper in the election of a [new] keeper the question which of the two shall act can give rise to controversy. The statutes of the university made by King Edward VI of blessed memory settle the question thus: the person holding the title of president is to be recognised as the senior or wiser fellow. We adopt this view and interpretation and give to the sense of these presents the force of a statute.[1]

Otherwise the senior fellow is to be the one who was first sworn in the college if he is not [simply] a Bachelor.

A vacancy in the office of keeper is to be understood to run from the day of death, retirement or other lawful termination.

The length of a month [is to be understood as] twenty-eight days.

"*Prestimonia*" is money granted in order that the keeper and fellows shall be on hand and ready in college on specific days, the word *prest-money* being taken from common parlance.[2]

1 In his statutes Caius subsequently frustrated this direction by providing that the president should be chosen by the keeper and as a consequence he only held office at that keeper's pleasure. As Parker pointed out in his *Interpretatio*, this meant that the office of president also fell vacant when the mastership fell vacant; and he ruled that the government of the college should rest with the senior fellow, notwithstanding Statute 32, until a new keeper had been elected and admitted, in accordance with the custom of other colleges. For the office of president, see *The president* in "*Supplementary Notes to Caius' Statutes*", § IV. 3, at p. 291 below.

2 Prest-money appears in the accounts (and in Caius' statutes) as "distributions": see the note to Statute 54.

Ne plures duobus medicinae studeant, de sociis suae fundationis intelligimus, non alienis, ut quibus licet Benefactoribus pro arbitratu suo quod velint studii genus constituere, et quot velint ejus studii personas.

Solum illud statutum de dissolutis in corpore, inhonestis, inquietis, rixosis, inobedientibus, negligentibus &c. subjicitur tribus admonitionibus, reliqua statuta jurisjurandis solis. Hinc in fine huius libri docet, qui perjuri censendi sunt et qui non sunt. Quod non faceret, si omnia statuta admonitionibus subjicerentur.

Quae per majorem partem sociorum fieri statuit Rev. Pater, per majorem partem sociorum omnium pro tempore existentium et praesentium in Collegio corpore et viva voce statuisse intelligimus: non absentium, et aut suo scripto aut aliena voce suffragantium: tum quod in hanc interpretationem accedit vetus consuetudo nostri collegii et statuta venerandi viri Edmundi Goneville: tum quod absens nescius causae est, et falsa praesentis persuasione (qui abuti velit aut potest ejus suffragio) seduci et corrumpi potest. Eam ob causam si sociorum major pars non adfuerit, volumus et statuimus ut per citationem communi Collegii sigillo obsignatam, et ostio presbiterii affixam,[a] intra dies octo interesse omnes admoneantur atque etiam teneantur, sub poena quadraginta solidorum cuique absenti imponenda.

De anno valedicendi.

Reverendus Pater ordinat in statutis: quod nullus curatum obtinens beneficium cujuscunque valoris, seu non curatum, aut decanatum ruralem, cujus redditus seu proventus centum solidorum summam, juxta verum communibus annis annuum valorem excedunt, eligi valeat in socium, nec jam electus in dicto collegio ut socius ultra unius anni spatium a promotionis suae tempore remanere excepto custode &c. Id sic interpretor: licere talibus remanere in collegio ut sociis uno anno et socii stipendium habere cum ceteris commoditatibus, sed non extra collegium, nec si discesserit a collegio et id reliquerit incumbens beneficio aut decanatui;[b] nec si vagetur in incertum per orbem, aut

[a] Although *Ostio presbiterii* ought to mean a door to an inner part of the chapel such as the chancel or sanctuary, Caius would have meant the main (and only?) chapel-door.

[b] Marginal reference added later to Parker's modification of this ruling in his *Interpretatio*.

We interpret [Bateman's] rule that there shall not be more than two fellows studying medicine [at any one time] to apply [only] to fellows on his own foundation not others; so that those who are benefactors are free to decide what course of study they wish [to be studied] and how many persons should study it.

Only in the case of one statute is there a [procedural] requirement for three warnings: namely that which applies to those who are lewd in body, dishonourable, troublesome, contentious, disobedient or rebellious, or neglectful [of their studies] etc. For [all] other statutes the one sanction is [for breach of] the [offender's] oath. This follows from [Bateman's] specifying at the end of his book which persons are to be deemed to have broken their oath and which are not;[3] for he would not have done this if all [his] statutes were subject to the requirement of three warnings.

Where the Reverend Father requires anything to be done by a majority of the fellows, we understand this as requiring a majority of all fellows at the time who are bodily present in college and vote in person, not those who are absent and vote either in writing or by proxy: for one thing, because the time-honoured custom of our college and the statutes of the venerable Edmund Gonville [both] point to this interpretation and, for another thing, because an absentee is not acquainted with the matter and is liable to be seduced and led astray by the false persuasion of someone present (who is anxious and able to misuse his vote). For this reason if a majority of the Fellowship is not on hand it is our will and we decree that everyone shall be summoned, by a notice given under the common seal of the college and affixed to the door of the chapel, to be present within eight days and they shall be bound to be so on pain of a penalty of 40s.

Of the year of departure.

The Reverend Father ordains in his statutes that no one who obtains a benefice with cure of souls of any value, or a benefice without cure or a rural deanery of which the income or return exceeds 100s. in its true annual value, may be elected a fellow; nor, if he is already a fellow, may he remain in the said college as a fellow for more than the space of one year from the time of his presentation, except the keeper etc. I interpret this as follows: that such persons are allowed to remain in college as fellows for one year and receive the fellowship stipend and other benefits, but not while they are away from college;[4] and not if he has left college and then relinquishes the benefice or deanery of which he

[3] Cf. Bateman's Statute 17.

[4] In his *Interpretatio* Matthew Parker modified this and allowed residence in the benefice: see his ruling on Statute 39 and this statute *de anno valedicendi*.

alia alibi tractet negotia, nec nisi diminutis in septimanas singulas duodecim denariis si abfuerit aliquando ultra unum mensem in anno integro: nec nisi fuerit socius fundatoris Batemanni, cui sua statuta posuit fundator, non bifundatorum sociis[a] quos nesciebat insecuturos, quique benefactorum suorum voluntate gubernantur.

[a] *Sic* MS 760, at p. 20 (and *semble* MS 711). This gives better sense than the 1852 printed version which has "*cui sua statuta possint, fundatoris non bifundatorum sociis,*".

is an incumbent; and not if he roams around the world or carries on business anywhere; and not without a weekly deduction of 12d. if he is away at any time for more than one month in the year; and only if he is a fellow on Bateman's foundation, i.e. is one to whom the founder has applied his statutes, not to fellows of co-founders of whose future existence he had no knowledge and who are subject to the will of their benefactors.[5]

[5] See note to Latin text. Notwithstanding this interpretation, valedictory years appear to have been allowed in later years to any of the twelve senior fellows, not merely to those on Bateman's foundation (*ex antiqua fundatione*).

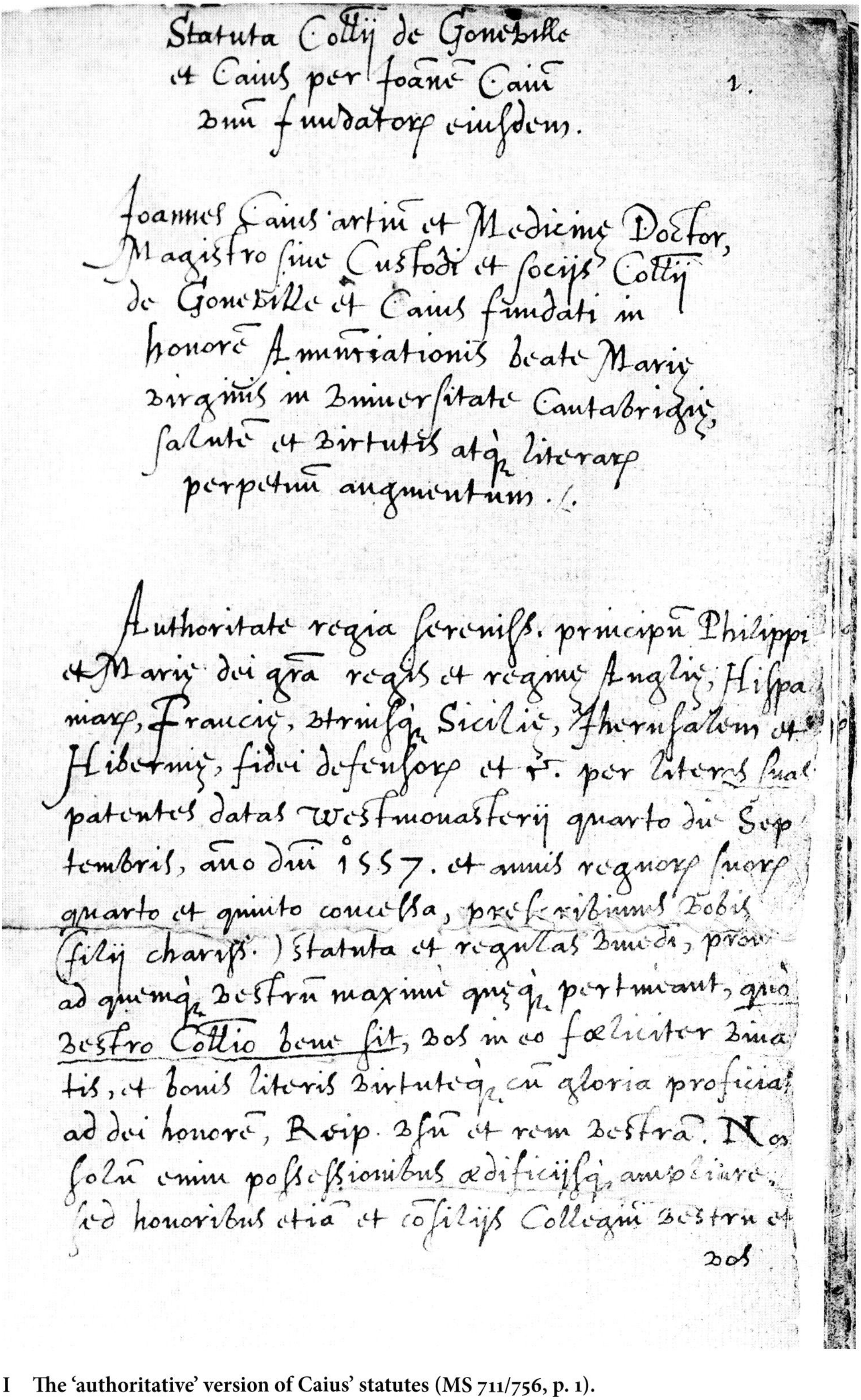

Statuta Collij de Gonevile
et Caius per Joanē Caiū 1.
dnū fundatorꝝ eiusdem.

Joannes Caius artiū et Medicinę Doctor,
Magistro siue Custodi et socijs Collij
de Gonevile et Caius fundati in
honorē Annuntiationis beatę Marię
virginis in Vniversitate Cantabrigię,
salutē et virtutis atq literarꝝ
perpetuum augmentum.

Authoritate regia serenissimorum principū Philippi
et Marię dei gra regis et reginę Anglię, Hispa
niarꝝ, Francię, vtriusq Sicilię, Jherusalem et
Hibernię, fidei defensorꝝ etc. per literas suas
patentes datas Westmonasterij quarto die Sep
tembris, ano dni 1557. et annis regnorꝝ suorꝝ
quarto et quinto concessa, praescribimus vobis
(filij chariss.) statuta et regulas vivendi, prout
ad quemq vestrū maximè quęq pertineant, quo
vestro Collio bene sit, vos in eo fœliciter viua
tis, et bonis literis virtuteq cū gloria proficiatis
ad dei honorē, Reip. vsū et rem vestra. Nos
solū enim possessionibus ædificijsq ampliare,
sed honoribus etiā et cōsilijs Collegiū vestrū et
vos

I The 'authoritative' version of Caius' statutes (MS 711/756, p. 1).
For MS 711/756 and other versions of Caius' statutes, see pp. 30ff above. The 'rival version', MS 760/424, is shown in Plate XV below.

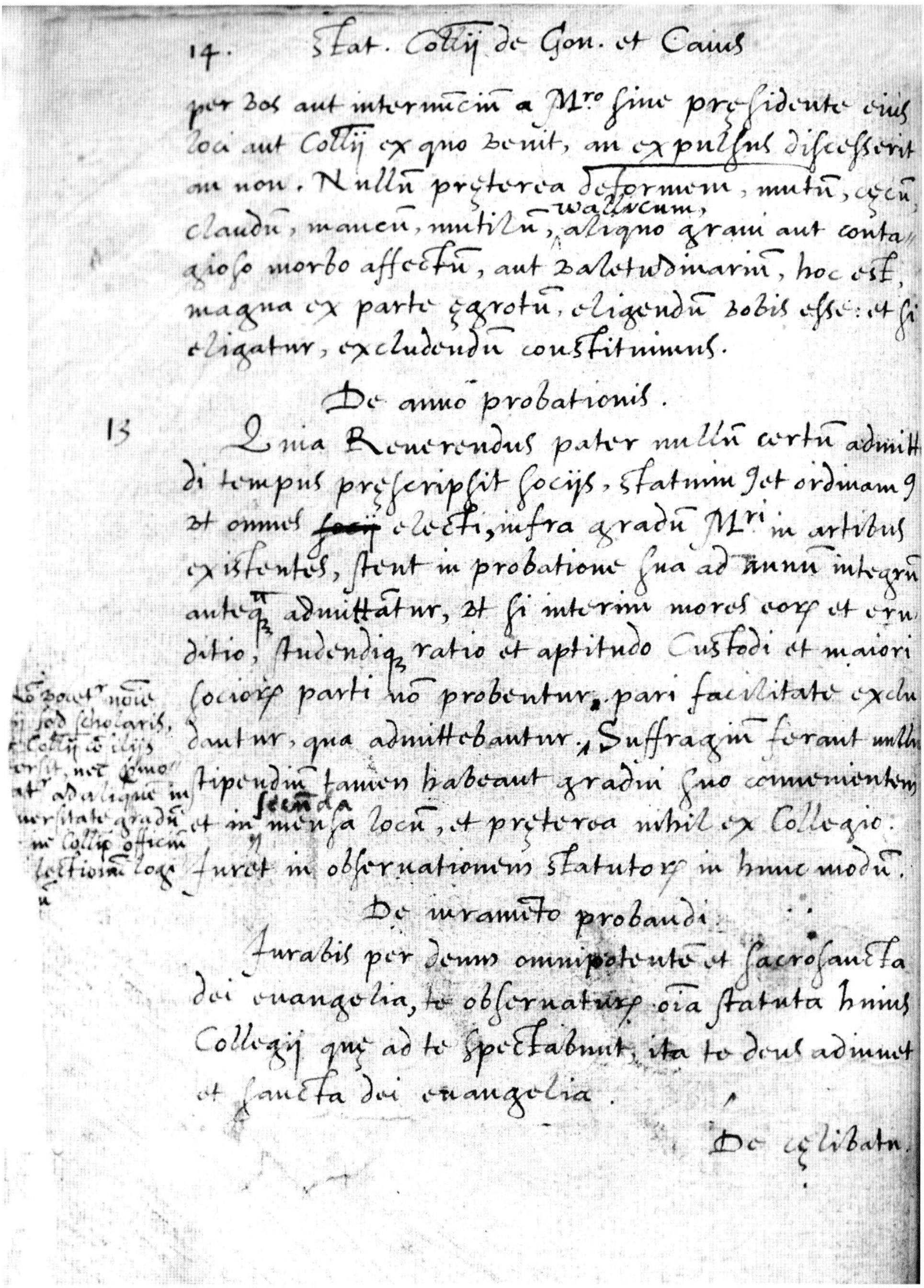

14. Stat. Collij de Gon. et Caius

per vos aut intermedium a M^ro sive praesidente eius
loci aut Collij ex quo venit, an expulsus discesserit
an non. Nullum praeterea deformem, mutum, caecum,
claudum, mancum, mutilum, Wallicum, aliquo gravi aut contagioso morbo affectum, aut valetudinarium, hoc est,
magna ex parte aegrotum, eligendum vobis esse: et si
eligatur, excludendum constituimus.

De anno probationis.

15 Quia Reverendus pater nullum certum admittendi tempus praescripsit socijs, statuimus et ordinamus
ut omnes electi, infra gradum M^ri in artibus
existentes, stent in probatione sua ad annum integrum
antequam admittatur, ut si interim mores eorum et eruditio, studendique ratio et aptitudo Custodi et maiori
sociorum parti non probentur, pari facilitate excludantur, qua admittebantur. Suffragium ferant nullum,
stipendium tamen habeant gradui suo convenientem
et in mensa secunda locum, et praeterea nihil ex Collegio.
Iuret in observationem statutorum in hunc modum.

De iuramento probandi.

Iurabis per deum omnipotentem et sacrosancta
dei evangelia, te observaturum omnia statuta huius
Collegij quae ad te spectabunt, ita te deus adiuvet
et sancta dei evangelia.

De caelibatu.

II Caius' apparent exclusion of Welshmen: Statute 12 (MS 711/756, p. 14).
For the interlinear insertion of "*Wallicum*" into Statute 12 (between lines 3 and 4), see pp. 280–2 below.

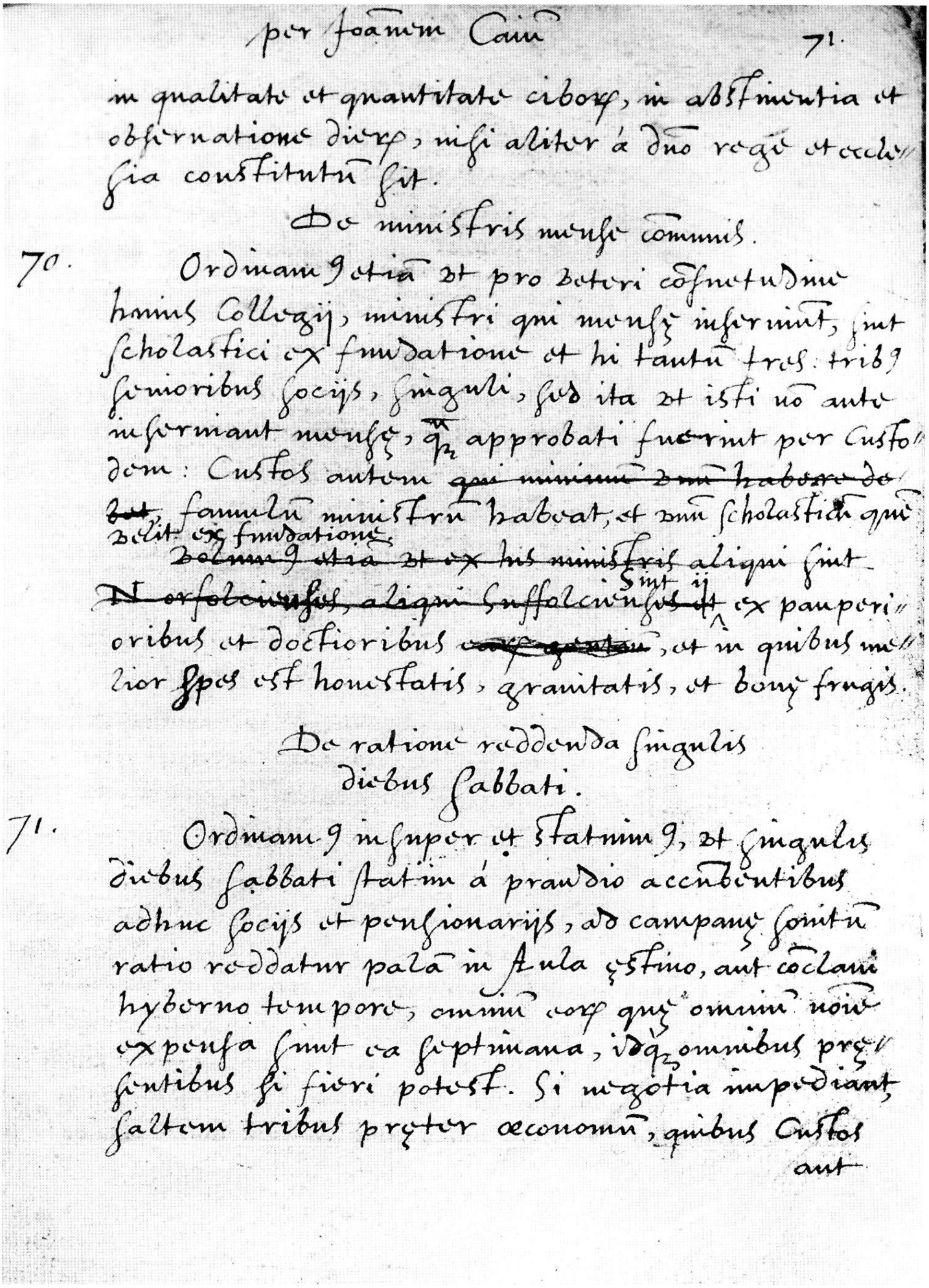

per Joannem Caium 71.
in qualitate et quantitate ciborum, in abstinentia et
observatione dierum, nisi aliter a dno rege et eccle//
sia constitutum sit.

De ministris mensae communis.

70. Ordinamus etiam ut pro veteri consuetudine
huius Collegij, ministri qui mensae inserviunt, sint
scholastici ex fundatione et hi tantum tres: tribus
senioribus socijs, singuli, sed ita ut isti non ante
inserviant mensae, quam approbati fuerint per Custo//
dem: Custos autem ~~qui minimum unum habere de~~
~~bet~~ famulum ministrum habeat, et unum scholasticum qui
velit ex fundatione
~~Volumus etiam ut ex his ministris aliqui sint~~
~~Norfolcienses, aliqui Suffolcienses et~~ sint ij ex pauperi//
oribus et doctioribus ~~[illegible]~~, et in quibus me//
lior spes est honestatis, gravitatis, et boni frugis.

De ratione reddenda singulis
diebus Sabbati.

71. Ordinamus insuper et statuimus, ut singulis
diebus sabbati statim a prandio accumbentibus
adhuc socijs et pensionarijs, ad campanae sonitum
ratio reddatur palam in Aula aestivo, aut coenaculo
hyberno tempore, omnium eorum quae omnium nomine
expensa sunt ea septimana, idque omnibus prae//
sentibus si fieri potest. Si negotia impediant,
saltem tribus praeter oeconomum, quibus Custos
aut

III Service at the common table: Statute 70 (MS 711/756, p. 71).
For this provision, see p. 213, nn. 168–9 below.

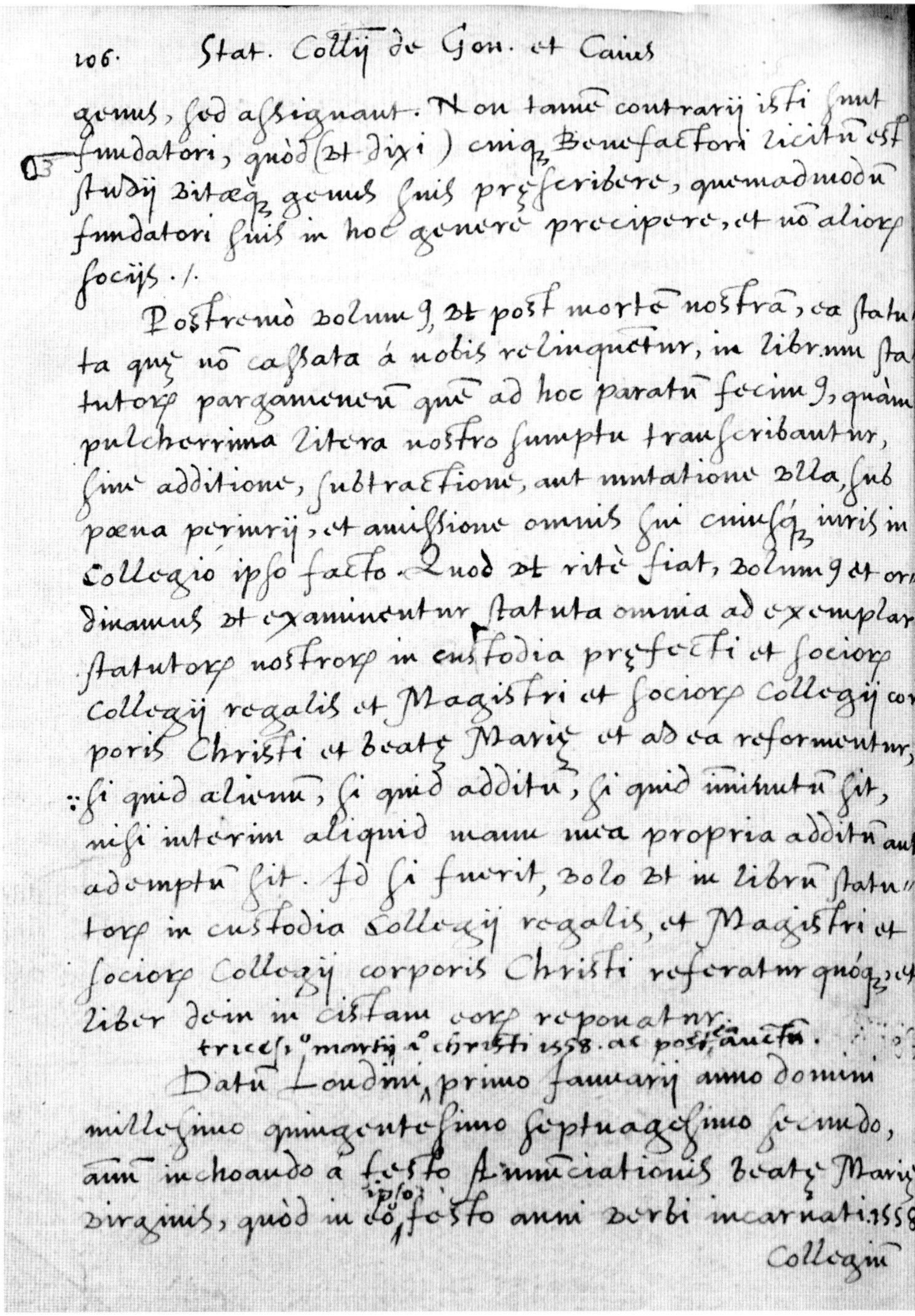
106. Stat. Collij de Gon. et Caius

genus, quod assignant. Non tamen contrarij isti sunt
fundatori, quod (ut dixi) cuique Benefactori licitum est
studij vitaeque genus suis praescribere, quemadmodum
fundatori suis in hoc genere praecipere, et non aliorum
socijs./

Postremo volumus, ut post mortem nostram, ea statuta quae non cassata a nobis relinquentur, in librum statutorum pargamenum quem ad hoc paratum fecimus, quam
pulcherrima litera nostro sumptu transcribantur,
sine additione, subtractione, aut mutatione ulla, sub
poena periurij, et amissione omnis sui cuiusque iuris in
Collegio ipso facto. Quod ut rite fiat, volumus et ordinamus ut examinentur statuta omnia ad exemplar
statutorum nostrorum in custodia praefecti et sociorum
Collegij regalis et Magistri et sociorum Collegij corporis Christi et beatae Mariae et ad ea reformentur,
si quid alienum, si quid additum, si quid imminutum sit,
nisi interim aliquid manu mea propria additum aut
ademptum sit. Id si fuerit, volo ut in librum statutorum in custodia Collegij regalis, et Magistri et
sociorum Collegij corporis Christi referatur quoque, et
liber dein in cistam eorum reponatur.
tricesimo martij anno Christi 1558. ac post aucta.

Datum Londini, primo Januarij anno domini
millesimo quingentesimo septuagesimo secundo,
anno inchoando a festo Annunciationis beatae Mariae
virginis, quod in eodem ipso festo anni verbi incarnati 1558
Collegium

IV and V The dating and authentication of Caius' statutes (MS 711/756, pp. 106, 107).
For the questions raised by Caius' amendment to the datum clause in Plate IV, see p. 263, n. 267 below. Despite the wording of the authentication, only the second signature in Plate V is Caius' autograph.

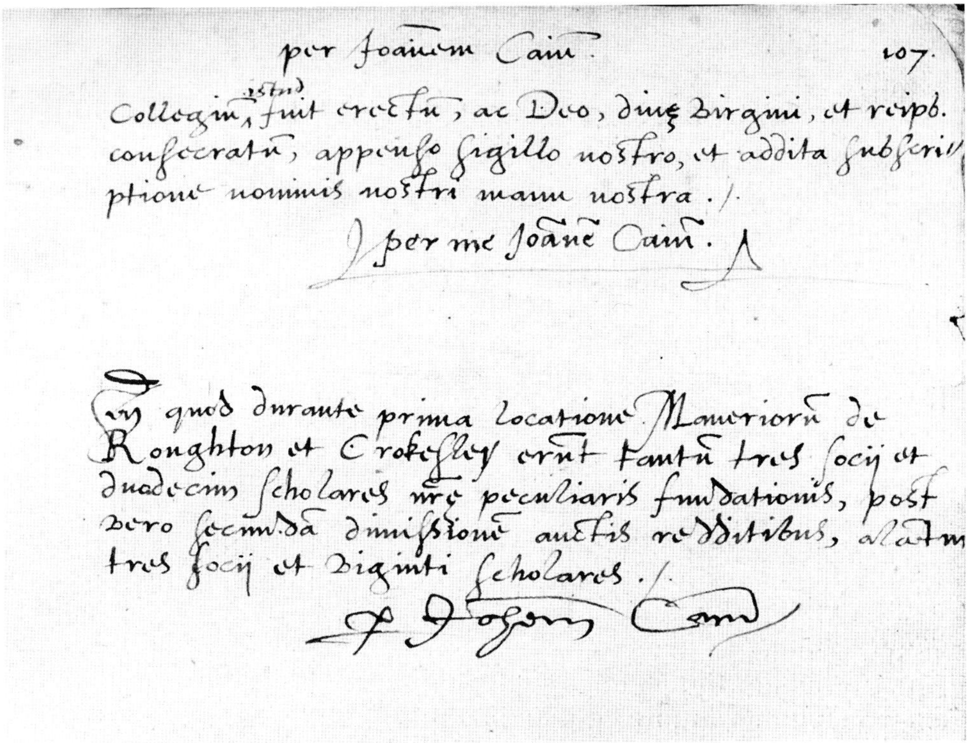
per Joannem Caium. 107.

Collegium istud fuit erectum, ac Deo, diuaeque Virgini, et reipub. consecratum, appenso sigillo nostro, et addita subscriptione nominis nostri manu nostra./

per me Joannem Caium.

Item quod durante prima locatione Maneriorum de Ronghton et Croxesley erant tantum tres socii et duodecim scholares nostrae peculiaris fundationis, post vero secunda dimissione auctis redditibus, alantur tres socii et viginti scholares./

Johannes Caius

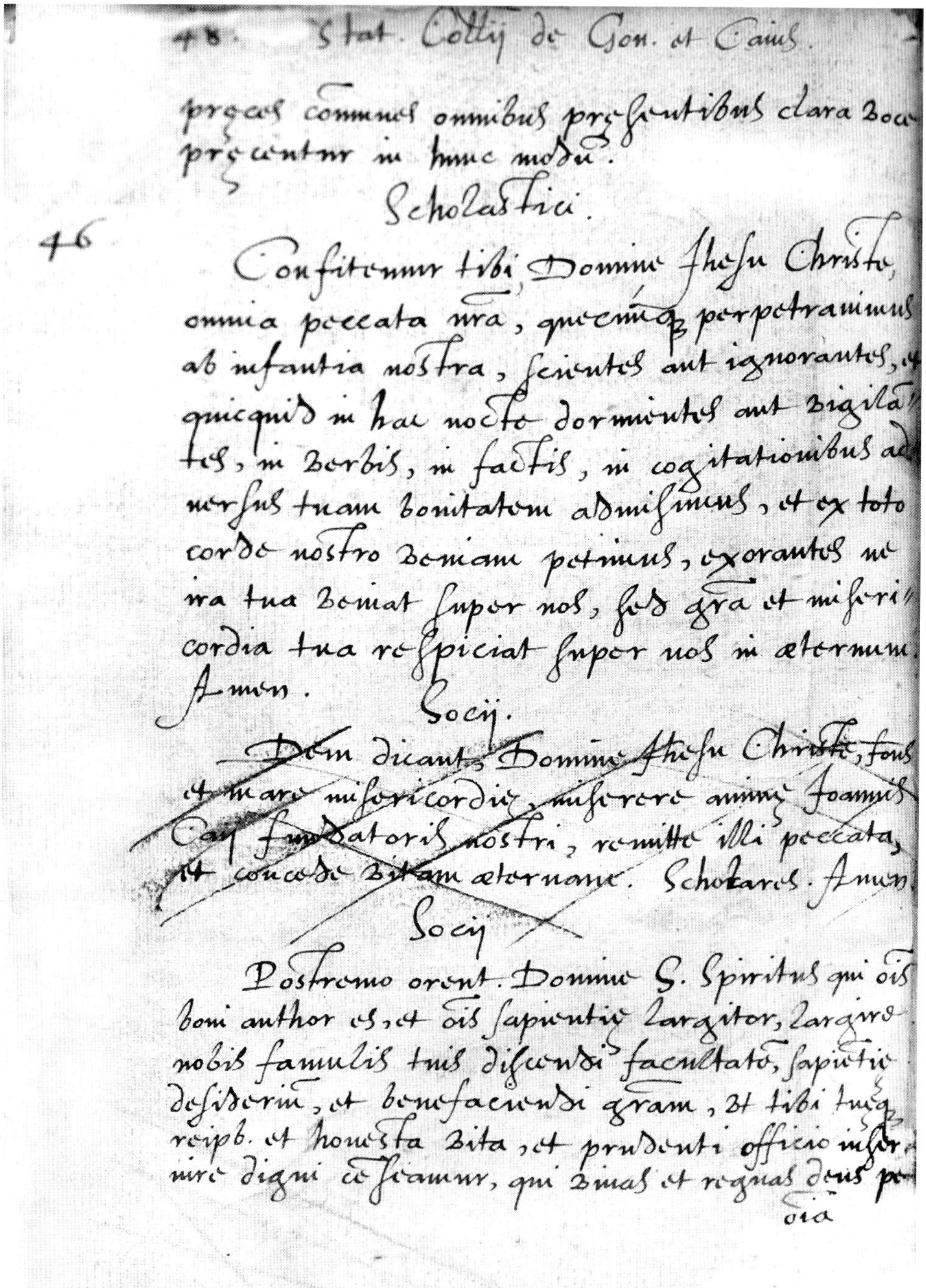

48. Stat. Collij de Gon. et Caius.

preces communes omnibus presentibus clara voce
precentur in hunc modu.

Scholastici.

46 Confitemur tibi Domine Jhesu Christe,
omnia peccata nra, quecunque perpetravimus
ab infantia nostra, scientes aut ignorantes, et
quicquid in hac nocte dormientes aut vigilantes, in verbis, in factis, in cogitationibus adversus tuam bonitatem admisimus, et ex toto
corde nostro veniam petimus, exorantes ne
ira tua veniat super nos, sed gra et misericordia tua respiciat super nos in aeternum.
Amen. Socij.

Dein dicant, Domine Jhesu Christe, fons
et mare misericordiae, miserere animae Joannis
Caij fundatoris nostri, remitte illi peccata,
et concede vitam aeternam. Scholares. Amen.

Socij

Postremo orent. Domine S. Spiritus qui ois
boni author es, et ois sapientiae largitor, largire
nobis famulis tuis discendi facultatem, sapientiae
desiderium, et benefaciendi gram, ut tibi tuaeque
reipub. et honesta vita, et prudenti officio inservire digni efficiamur, qui vivas et regnas deus per
oia

VI The Puritan deletion of the prayer for the dead John Caius (MS 711/756, p. 48).
Archbishop Parker had ruled the direction to be contrary to the law of the land and invalid, but it remained untouched in the versions of the statutes until the Commonwealth period: see p. 178, n. a below. For the scribe's mistaken insertion of "46" in the middle of Statute 45 and the consequent incorrect numbering of the statutes, see p. 35 above.

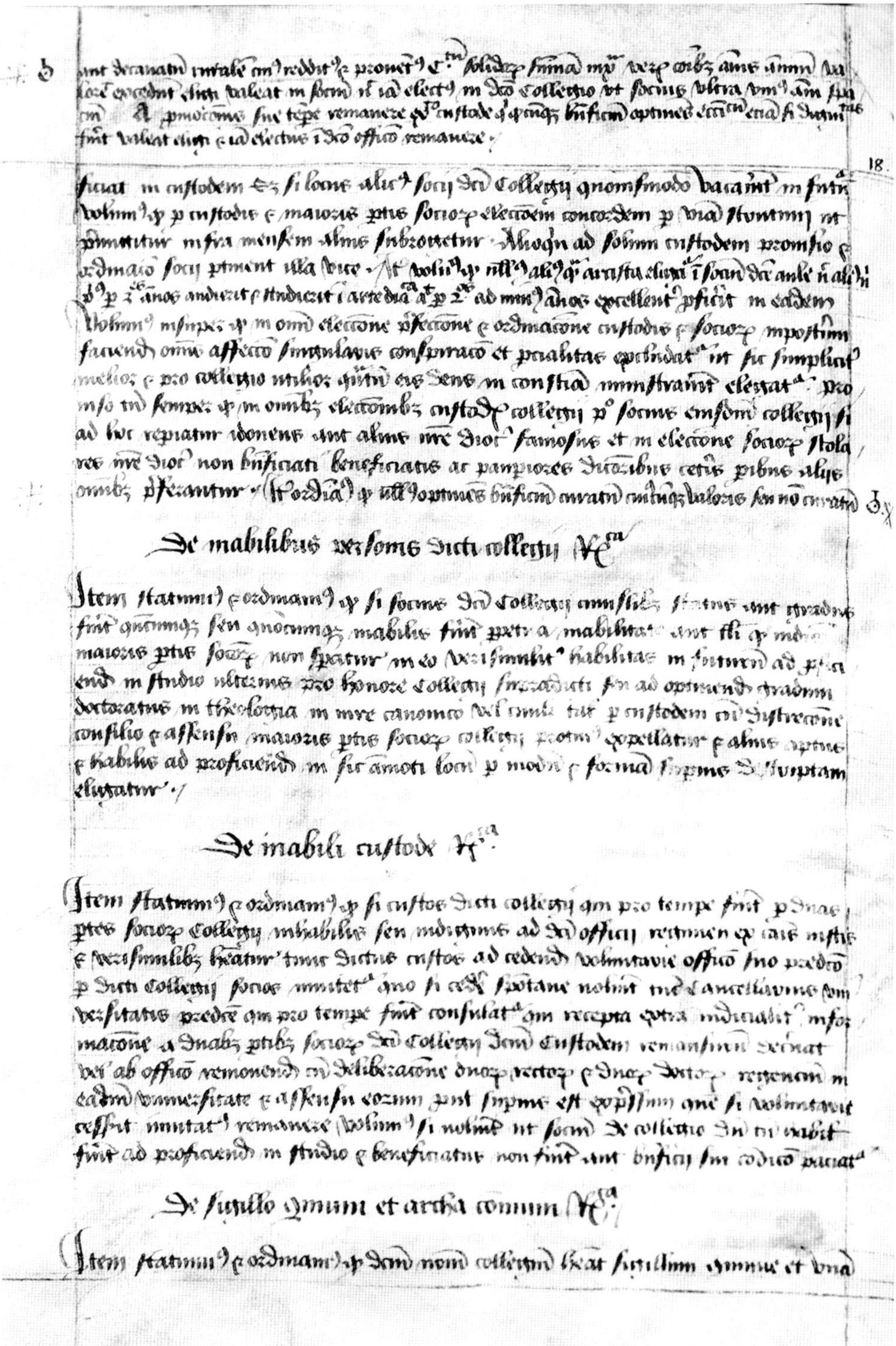

VII The insertion of the Norfolk Preference (Sheriffe's Evidences, MS 706/692, p. 18).
The hurried insertion into Bateman's third statute of the Norfolk preference and two other provisions is revealed by the scribe's need to complete that statute in the top margin *after* he had measured and marked out each page of his volume: see pp. 395–7 below.

VIII Bateman's initial grant of statutes, 1353 (BUR: DEEDS/ I. 15).
The insert filling the left-hand margin is expressly stated by Bateman to be in his own hand.

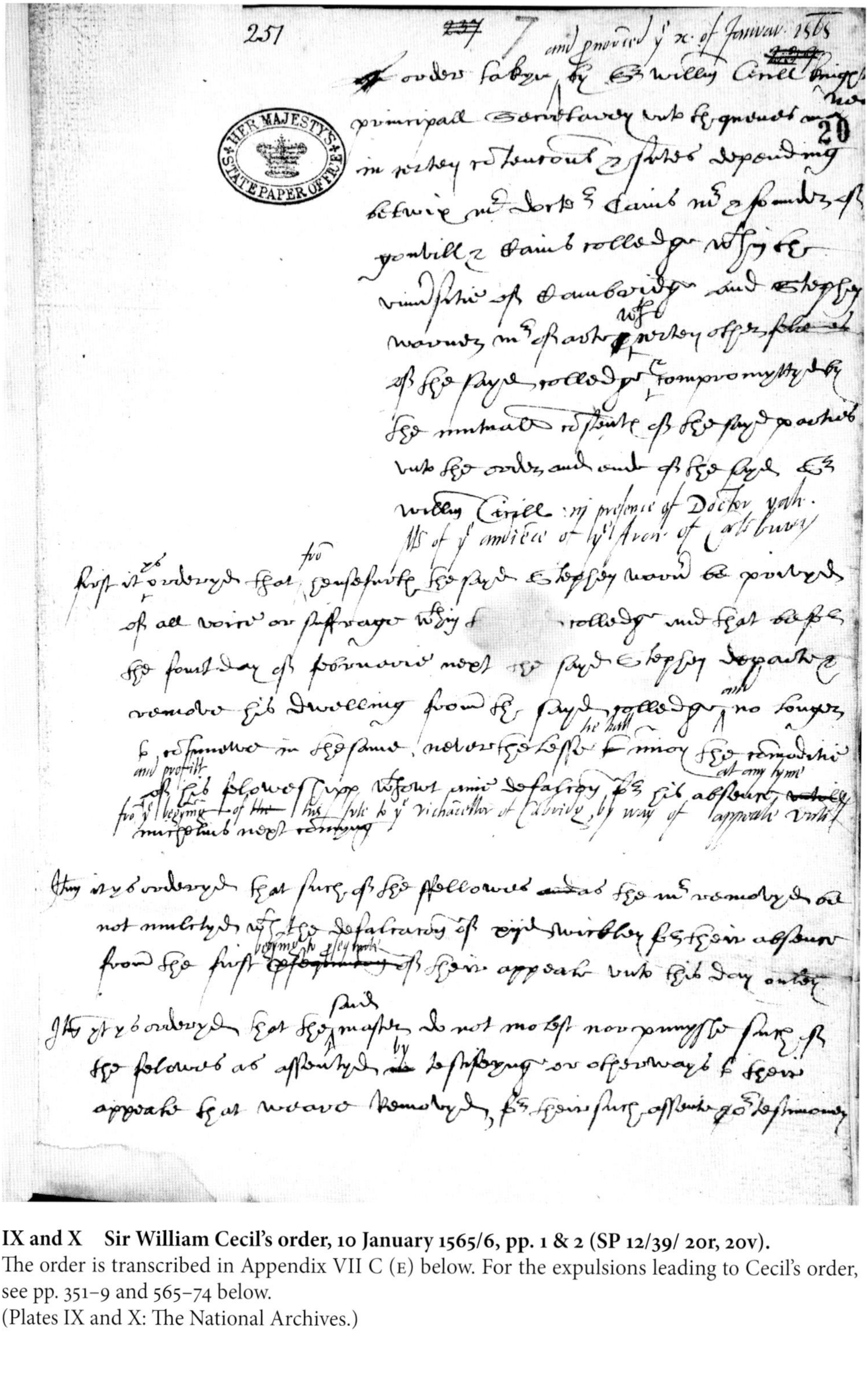

IX and X Sir William Cecil's order, 10 January 1565/6, pp. 1 & 2 (SP 12/39/ 20r, 20v).
The order is transcribed in Appendix VII C (E) below. For the expulsions leading to Cecil's order, see pp. 351–9 and 565–74 below.
(Plates IX and X: The National Archives.)

Yt ys further orderyd that mr Dervyk for that he hath hath soo [illegible] the space of one yere & more contrary to ye statute of ye colledge shall ~~do~~ after the 26 of marche next relinquysshe his felowshyp in the sayd colledge wth all the commodities therof or els to be [illegible] by ye [illegible] and the rest deprived therof

Yt ys also orderyd that such orders as ~~[illegible]~~ ye most Revd father ye Archbishop of Canterbury his grace ~~[illegible]~~ ye rev father ye B of London hath gyven & publisshed unto the sayd mr and companye and ~~after the sayd lordes~~ be not at this daye by the ~~[illegible]~~ [illegible] shall be observyd & performyd as they be not repugnant nor derogatorye to these orders nor anie of them

Concernyng mr Dethik and Mr Spenser it ys orderyd that after the 12 th day of January nether of them bothe shall anie wayse contende wth the sayd mr Dethik Garter for the title or possession of their felowshipp in the sayd colledge

It ys further orderyd that such statutes as the sayd Dethik Garter shall geve to the sayd colledge for the governement of the same or the members therof shalbe first ~~[illegible]~~ & publisshed by the sayd Dethik Garter wth ye sayd colledge in the presence of the greater part ~~[illegible]~~ of the hole companye of ye same at three severall days before they be had or accomplysshed ~~[illegible]~~ both statute and that at iiij^or severall tymes of ye yere durynge ye space of twoo whole yers ~~to begyn at ye 25 of March~~ ~~next~~ ~~[illegible]~~ all ye Statuts of ye house be redd distynctly & openly before ye [illegible] and ye Company. that is to saye ye 24 of March. ye 23 of June ye 28 of September and ye 24 of December

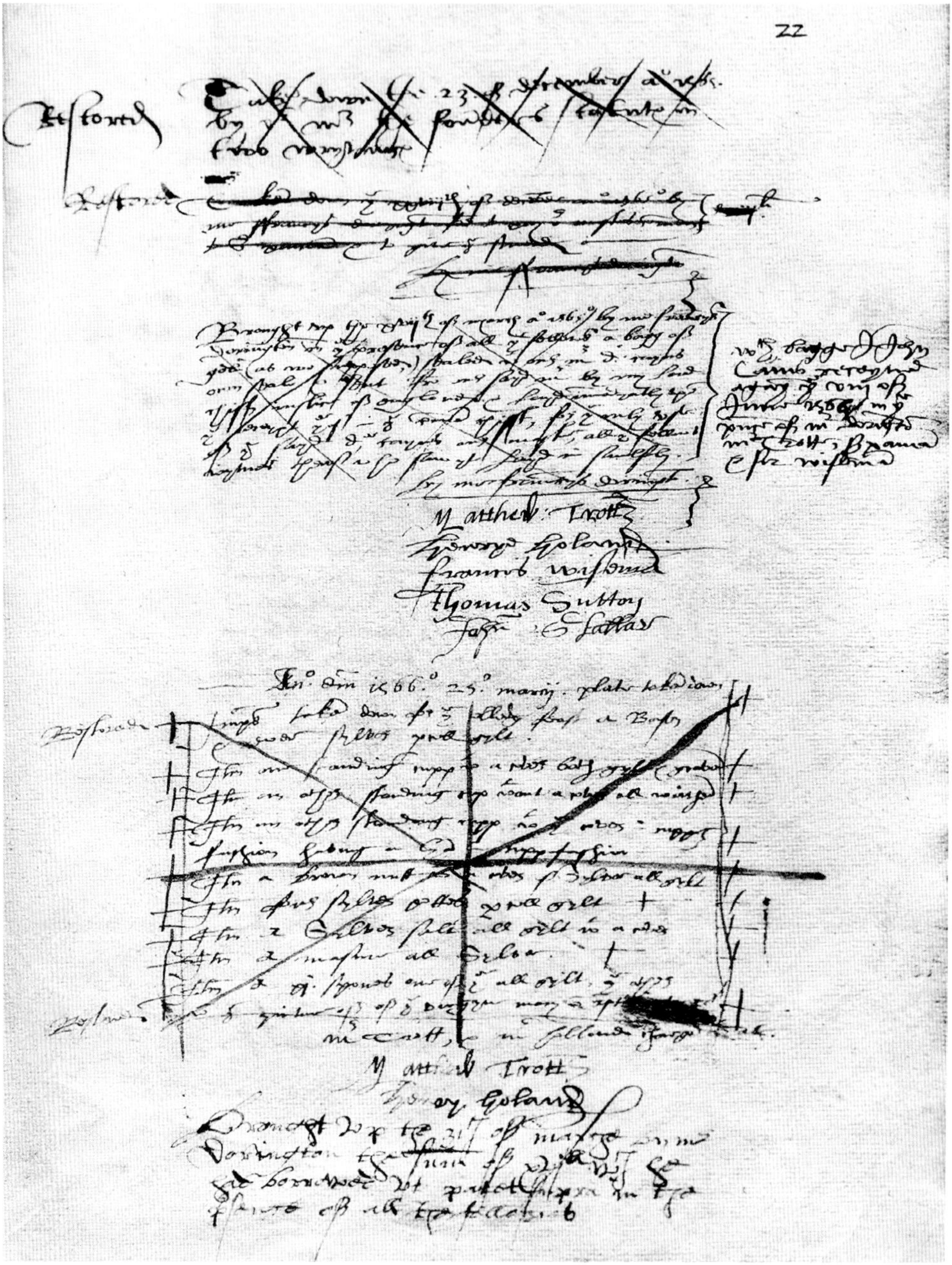

XI Caius' deposit of money with the Fellowship (*Pandectae*, fol. 22).
Until 1566 Caius had reimbursed the college *after* money had been expended on his projects from the chest, and his making deposits in advance in that year was clearly a novel practice; for his changed relations with the fellows after the expulsions of 1565, see p. 360, n. 129 below.
[*"Brought up the 17th of March 1565/6 by me Francis Dorington in the presence of all the fellows a bag of gold (as we supposed) sealed with our Master Dr Caius' own seal and sent for our said Master by the Lord Chief Justice of England and laid immediately upon receipt thereof in the common chest, for the only use of the said Dr Caius our Master, all the fellows witness thereof who saw it laid in surefully(?). By Mr Francis Dorington, Matthew Trott, Henry Hollond, Francis Wiseman, Thomas Sutton, John Stallar. Which bag I John Caius received again the 8th of June 1566 in the presence of Mr Dorington, Mr Trott, Ds(?) Paman. Ds(?) Wiseman"*]

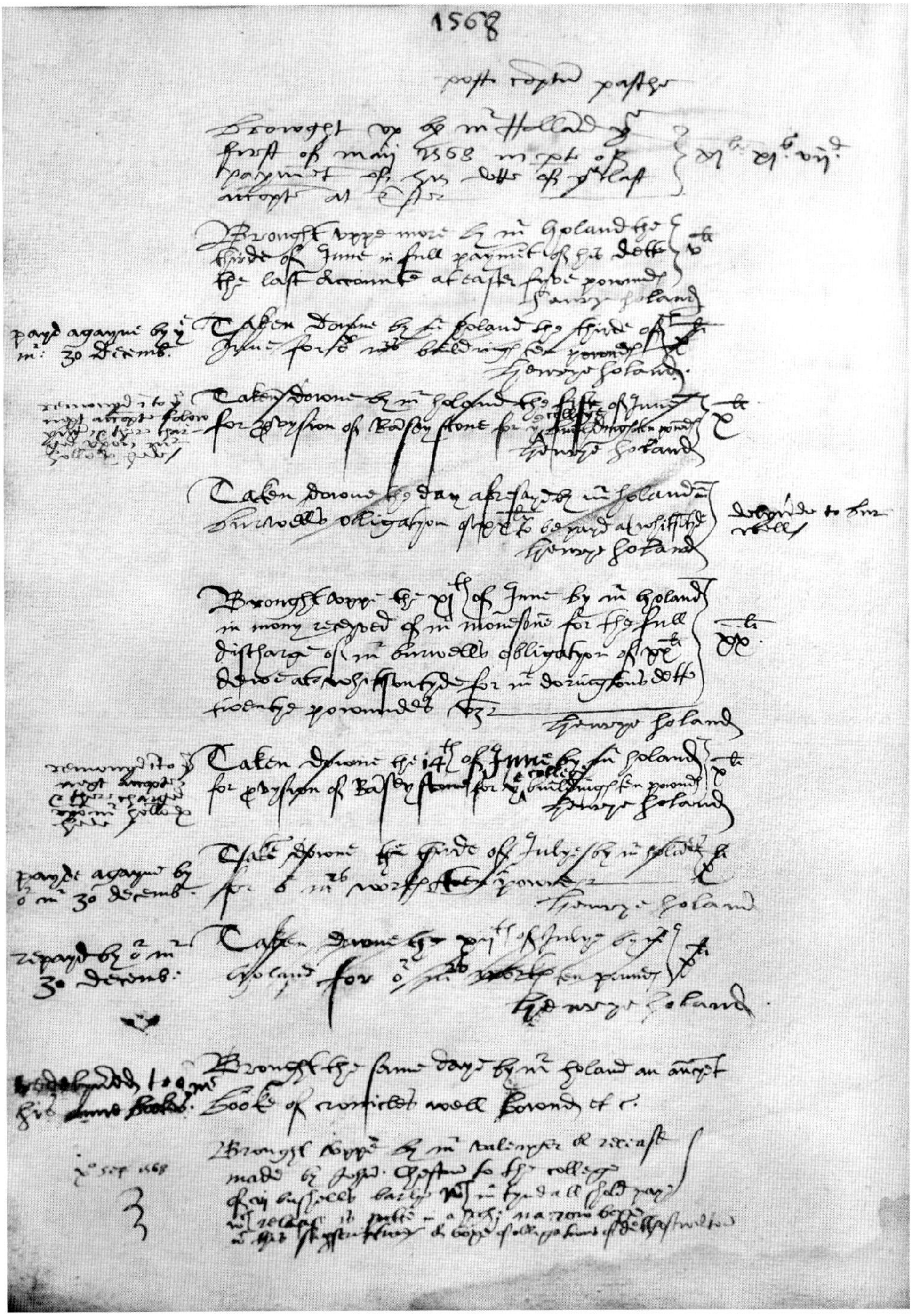

XII Henry Holland's management of the Chest, 1568 (*Pandectae*, fol. 28v).
For Holland's conscientious management of the chest, see pp. 360–2 below.

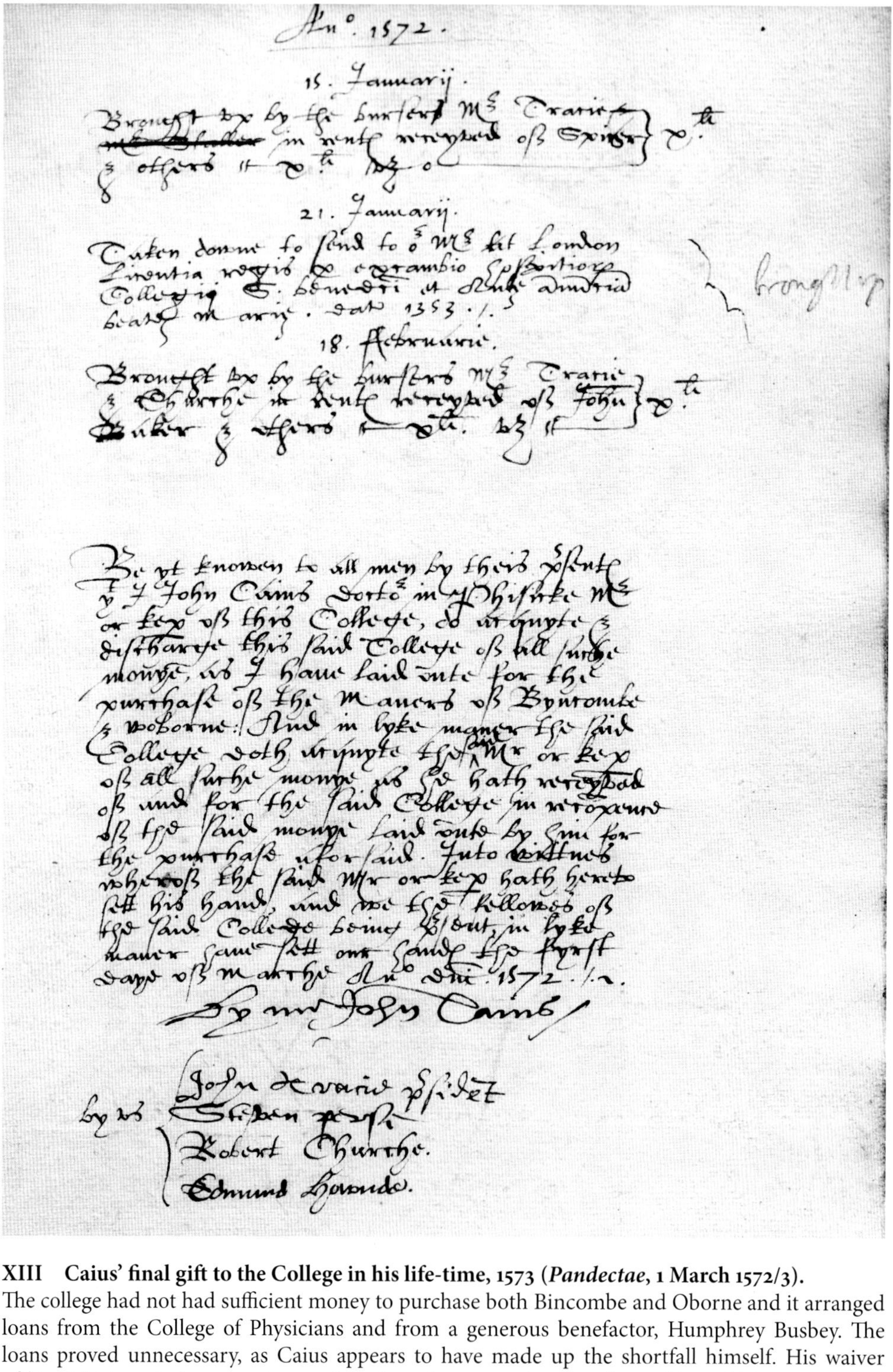
Ano. 1572.

15. Januarij.

21. Januarij.

Taken downe to send to our Mr at London Licentia regis de excambio possessionum Collegii S. Benedicti et Annunciationis beatae Mariae. Dat. 1353.

18. Februarii.

Be yt knowen to all men by theis presentes that I John Caius doctor in Phisicke Master or keper of this College, do acquyte & discharge this said College of all suche monye, as I have laid oute for the purchase of the Manors of Byncombe & Woborne: And in lyke maner the said College doth acquyte the said Mr or keper of all suche monye as he hath receyved of and for the said College in recompence of the said monye laid oute by him for the purchase aforsaid. In witnes whereof the said Mr or keper hath hereto sett his hand, and we the fellowes of the said College beinge present, in lyke maner have sett our handes the fyrst daye of Marche Ao dni. 1572.

by me John Caius

by us John Cravie president
Stephen Perse
Robert Churche.
Edmund Hownde.

XIII Caius' final gift to the College in his life-time, 1573 (*Pandectae*, 1 March 1572/3). The college had not had sufficient money to purchase both Bincombe and Oborne and it arranged loans from the College of Physicians and from a generous benefactor, Humphrey Busbey. The loans proved unnecessary, as Caius appears to have made up the shortfall himself. His waiver of his right to reimbursement came less than three months after the sacking of his rooms on 13 December 1572 and shows his continuing affection for the college and his friendly relations with the Fellowship despite that outrage. (Cf. the earlier entry for 21 January 1573 recording the sending to him *in London* of Edward III's licence to exchange sites with Corpus in 1353.) For an estimate of Caius' generosity to the college, see p. 368, n. 172 below.

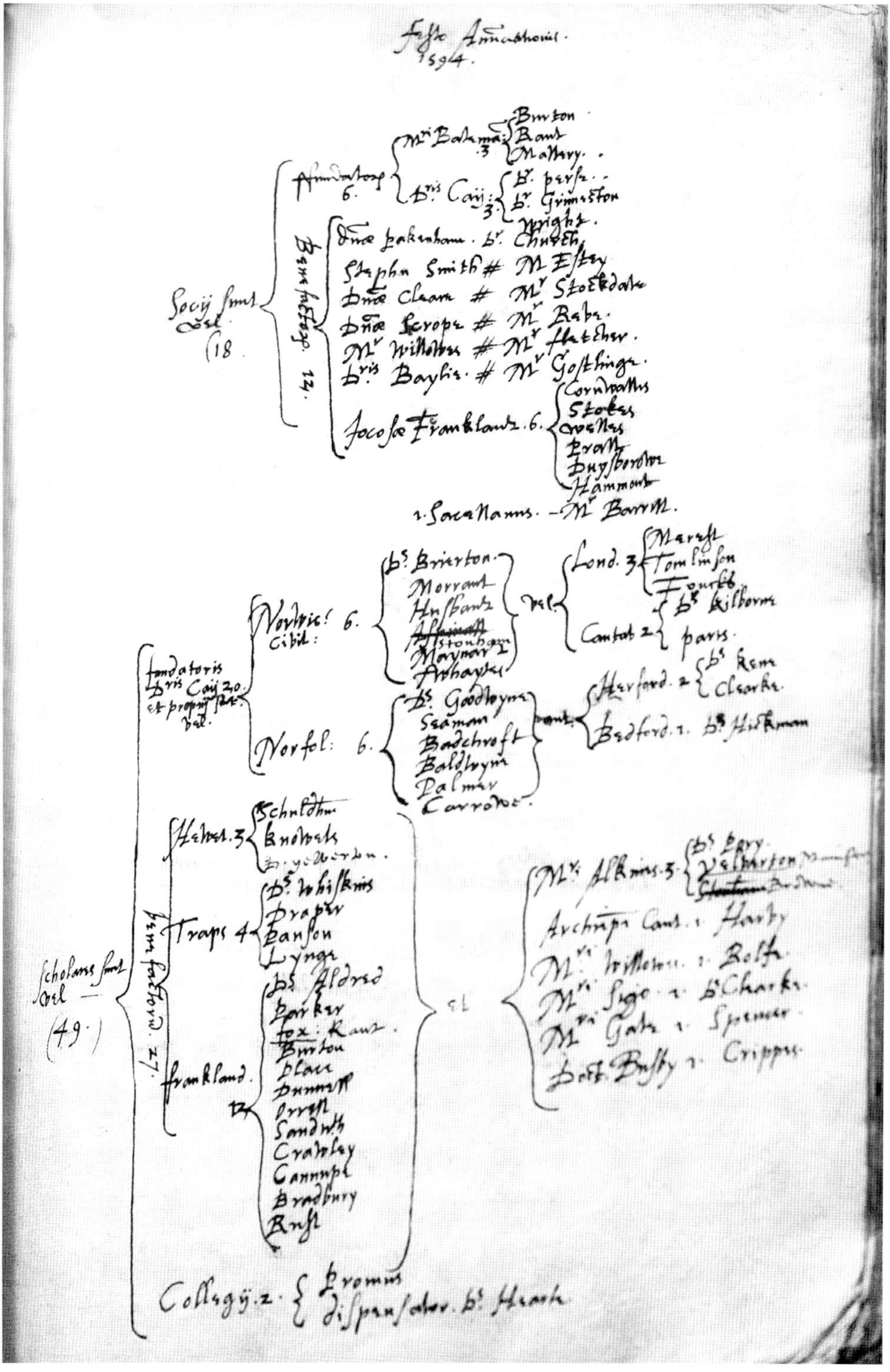

XIV Fellows and Scholars, Lady Day 1594 (*Exiit Book* (LD 1594)).
The list of fellows and scholars shows the great increase in their number as a result of the benefactions of John Caius and Joyce Frankland. Note the continued adherence to Caius' complex directions for the selection of his scholars (cf. Statute 15 at p. 131 below).

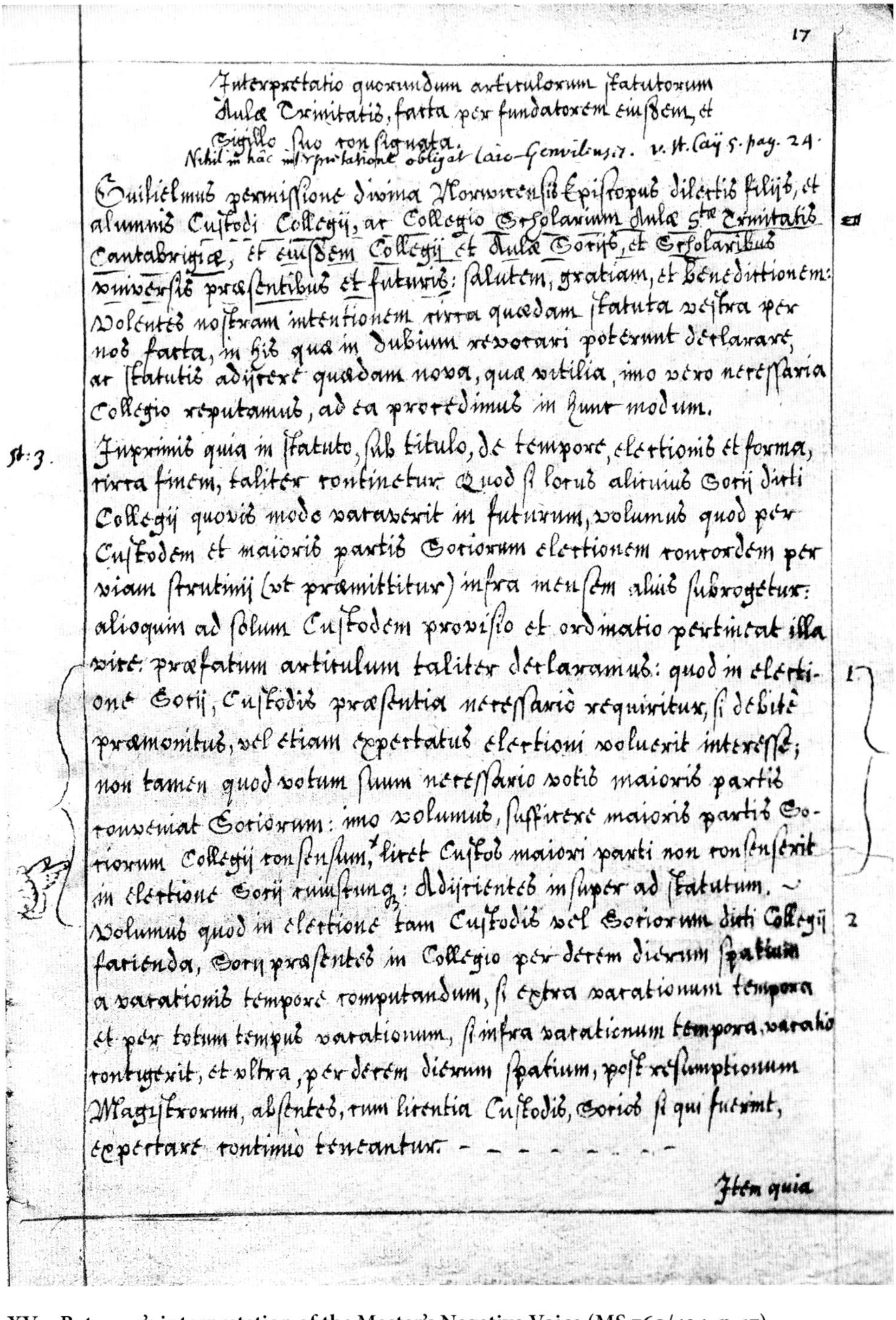

17

Interpretatio quorundam articulorum statutorum
Aulae Trinitatis, facta per fundatorem eiusdem, et
Sigillo suo consignata.
Nihil in hac interpretatione obligat Caio-Gonvilenses. v. St. Caij 5. pag. 24.

Guilielmus permissione divina Norwicensis Episcopus dilectis filijs, et
alumnis Custodi Collegij, ac Collegio Scholarium Aulae Sanctae Trinitatis
Cantabrigiae, et eiusdem Collegij et Aulae Socijs, et Scholaribus
universis praesentibus et futuris: salutem, gratiam, et benedictionem:
Volentes nostram intentionem circa quaedam statuta vestra per
nos facta, in his quae in dubium revocari poterunt declarare,
ac statutis adijcere quaedam nova, quae utilia, imo vero necessaria
Collegio reputamus, ad ea procedimus in hunc modum.

St. 3. Inprimis quia in statuto, sub titulo, de tempore, electionis et forma,
circa finem, taliter continetur Quod si locus alicuius Socij dicti
Collegij quovis modo vacaverit in futurum, volumus quod per
Custodem et maioris partis Sociorum electionem concordem per
viam scrutinij (ut praemittitur) infra mensem alius subrogetur:
alioquin ad solum Custodem provisio et ordinatio pertineat illa
vice: praefatum articulum taliter declaramus: quod in electione Socij, Custodis praesentia necessario requiritur, si debite 1
praemonitus, vel etiam expectatus electioni voluerit interesse;
non tamen quod votum suum necessario votis maioris partis
conveniat Sociorum: imo volumus, sufficere maioris partis Sociorum Collegij consensum, licet Custos maiori parti non consenserit
in electione Socij cuiuscunque: Adijcientes insuper ad statutum.
Volumus quod in electione tam Custodis vel Sociorum dicti Collegij 2
facienda, Socij praesentes in Collegio per decem dierum spatium
a vacationis tempore computandum, si extra vacationum tempora
et per totum tempus vacationum, si infra vacationum tempora, vacatio
contigerit, et ultra, per decem dierum spatium, post resumptionem
Magistrorum, absentes, cum licentia Custodis, Socios si qui fuerint,
expectare continuo teneantur.

Item quia

XV Bateman's interpretation of the Master's Negative Voice (MS 760/424, p. 17).
For the resort to Bateman's *Interpretatio* in *Allen's Case* (1617), see Appendix VII F below.

IV

The Statutes of John Caius, 1573

TEXT AND TRANSLATION

IV. 1

Iohannes Caius artium[a] et Medicinae Doctor, Magistro sive Custodi et sociis Collegii de Goneville et Caius fundati in honorem Annunciationis beatae Mariae virginis in Universitate Cantabrigiae, Salutem et virtutis atque literarum perpetuum augmentum.

[Cambridge, Gonville & Caius College Library. MSS 711/756, 755/370, 760/424[b]]

[NOTE: Interlinear and marginal insertions are italicised and marked with the sigla { }.]

1 Authoritate regia serenissimorum principum Philippi et Mariae dei gratia regis et reginae Angliae, Hispaniarum, Franciae, utriusque Siciliae, Iherusalem, et Hiberniae, fidei defensorum, &c., per literas suas patentes datas Westmonasterii quarto die Septembris, anno Domini 1557, et annis regnorum suorum quarto et quinto concessa, praescribimus vobis, (filii charissimi) statuta et regulas vivendi, prout ad quemque vestrum maxime quaeque pertineant, quo vestro Collegio bene sit, vos in eo faeliciter vivatis, et bonis literis virtuteque cum gloria proficiatis ad dei honorem, Reipublicae usum et rem vestram. Non solum enim possessionibus aedificiisque ampliare, sed honoribus etiam et consiliis Collegium vestrum et vos ornare et amplificare vehementer cupimus. Et quanquam statuta Reverendi patris Willelmi Bateman Norwicensis episcopi

[a] *Sic* MSS 711/756, 755/370 and Lambeth MS 720; similarly in Parker's *Interpretatio*. MS 760/424 alters to *Artium Magister*. The confusion may stem from Caius' original wording in his 1558 draft statutes, which had "*artis medicinae doctorem*" (*Documents*, II, p. 321).

[b] These three manuscripts are hereafter cited by their first number only. For them, see "*Caius' Statutes: The Sources*", § I. 3 above. As the version in MS 711 was supervised and authenticated by Caius himself, the present transcript follows that manuscript in its punctuation, spelling and use of capital letters. For pages from MS 711, see Plates I–VI, and for MS 760, Plate XV above.

IV. 1

John Caius [Master][1] of Arts and Doctor of Medicine to the Master or Keeper[2] and Fellows of the College of Gonville and Caius founded in honour of the Annunciation of Blessed Mary the Virgin in the University of Cambridge, Greeting and perpetual increase in excellence and learning.

[NOTE: Editorial additions are marked with square brackets.]

1. By the royal authority of the most serene Princes Philip and Mary, by the grace of God King and Queen of England, Spain,[3] France, both the Sicilies, Jerusalem and Ireland, defender of the faith etc., granted by their letters patent given at Westminster on the fourth day of September in the year of our Lord 1557 and the fourth and fifth years of their reign, we formulate for you, dear sons, statutes and rules of living, according as each of them shall particularly appertain to each of you, by reason of which your college may prosper, and you may live happily in it and prosper gloriously in learning and virtue to the honour of God, the benefit of the state and your own advantage. For we earnestly desire not only to enlarge your college with possessions and buildings, but also to adorn and enrich both you and it with honours and good counsels. And although the statutes of the Reverend Father William Bateman Bishop

1 See Plate I and note to Latin text. In English a Doctor of Medicine might be described as "Mr Doctor", as in *Status Collegii* (Mich. 1585): "Taken downe by Mr Doctor Perse Bursar for to pay the Steward".

2 The term 'keeper' was used in Caius' time and was well-known to him. It was employed in those parts of legal documents that were written in English at the time and it continued in use for many years after his death.

3 Literally, "the Spains"; many of Philip's kingdoms there were still constitutionally distinct.

(quae revereor et observo) satis multa et efficacia fuere suo saeculo, in quo omnia meliora, sedatiora, et moderatiora fuerunt, ratio tamen personarum atque rerum, morum et ingeniorum nostri temporis, vivendique licentia insolentior aliam dietam, alias leges postulat: etsi apud literarum studiosos conveniret ut bonum et honestum non legibus magis quam natura valeret. Ut id quoque adiiciam, habendam etiam rationem aliquam rerum et fundorum Collegii vestri, et eorum quae ad fundos pertinent, quibus prospectum minus est a Reverendo patre, quod ejus aetate omnino nulla praedia erant praeterquam appropriationes quaedam beneficiorum et eae paucae. Quare primo de personis: mox de rebus Collegii vestri statuemus.

De fundatione Collegii, et pertinentibus ad id ipsum.

2 Statuimus igitur et ordinamus in dei nomine et authoritate principum predictorum (quorum et aliorum futurorum honoribus et reipublicae hoc Collegium nostrum constituimus)[a] ut in hoc vestro Collegio (quod illi nomine de Goneville et Caius, &c. ut supra memoratum est, appellaverunt et stabiliverunt) sit unus Magister sive Custos, qui caeteris praesit in Collegio et tredecim socii sive plures, viri honesti, opinionis illaesae, devoti, casti, et literarum studio dediti, bonae existimationis atque famae, et probae vitae, in modo et forma inferiis descriptis eligendi. Ex his Magister sive Custos ex communi venerandi viri Edmundi Goneville, Reverendi patris Willelmi Bateman et nostra fundatione est: tres socii ex eorum fundatione sola: ex nostra item sola tres: ex Benefactorum septem. Super his in praesens fundamus hoc nostrum Collegium, ut et super aliis in futuro ubi fuerint. Ex hac quoque fundatione erunt ut pertinentes, viginti nostrae peculiaris fundationis scholares: Benefactorum praesentium novem, futurorum, quot sunt futuri: Collegii duo, promus videlicet et dispensator: praeter coquum et ejus ministrum, a Collegio isto fovendi pro ratione reddituum et fructuum annuorum Collegii vestri iam existentium aut futurorum, et voluntate Fundatorum ac Benefactorum suorum, ut de horum singulis suo loco statuemus.

[a] Caius speaks of Philip and Mary as still living: one of the few clear indications of a passage dating from 30 March 1558 or earlier.

of Norwich (which I revere and observe) were sufficient in number and effect in his day, when all things were better, more tranquil and more restrained, however, the standards of persons and things, habits and dispositions in our time, and the more arrogant licence in the way of living, call for a different regime, different laws, even though it would be appropriate for those seeking learning that goodness and integrity should prevail not so much from laws as naturally. For that reason too I shall set out in addition provisions that have regard to the goods and lands of your college and their appurtenances, a matter to which the Reverend Father did not give attention since in his day there were no lands at all other than some appropriations of benefices, and those but few. For that reason we make statutes first for the members and then for the property of your college.

The foundation of the college and the matters that pertain to it.

2. Accordingly we decree and direct in the name of God and by the authority of the aforementioned Princes (in whose honour and commonwealth and that of other future Princes we constitute this college of ours) that there shall be in this your college (which they have called and established under the name of Gonville and Caius etc. as set out above) a master or keeper who shall take precedence over others in the college, and thirteen or more fellows, worthy persons of unblemished beliefs, god-fearing, chaste and devoted to the pursuit of learning, of good standing and repute, and of irreproachable morals, to be elected in the way described below. Of these the master or keeper shall be a charge upon the common foundation of the venerable Edmund Gonville, the Revd Father William Bateman and ourself: three fellows upon their foundation alone: three upon our foundation alone: seven upon those of benefactors.[4] For the present we found this our college on these persons, allowing for the addition of such others as there may be in the future. There also shall be, as members appertaining to this foundation, twenty scholars on our own personal foundation: nine on those of present benefactors: and as many as may be upon those of future benefactors: two members of the college, namely the butler and the caterer; in addition to the cook and his assistant;[5] all to be maintained by the college itself in proportion to the present and future annual rents and profits of your college, and by the goodwill of their founders and benefactors, as we shall decree for each of them in their proper place.

[4] For these numbers see "*The Governing Body*", § VI. 1, at p. 371 below.

[5] For the steward's assistants, see *The steward and his staff: obsonator, promus, cook and under-cook* in "*Supplementary Notes to Caius' Statutes*", § IV. 3, at p. 297 below.

De legendis statutis ad res obeundas spectantibus.

3 Statuimus etiam et ordinamus ut ante omnes electiones et negotia, convocatis in sacellum (locum capitularem et consuetum) per Custodem aut eo absente sed iubente praesidentem, omnibus qui in universitate existunt sociis, et absentibus etiam, {*(excipio eum qui in partibus est transmarinis) ut intra dies quindecim adsint*,}[a] si id res gravis postulat, coram claraque voce recitentur omnia ea statuta, quae ad eas electiones et negotia de quibus agitur pertinent, ut ex his lectis scire liceat, quid in illis potissimum et quo modo sit agendum. {*Res graves voco emptiones aut locationes fundorum, custodis expulsionem, dissentiones, collegii defensiones et eius bonorum, hoc genus alia insignia mala aut bona.*}[b]

Qualis debet esse Custos.

4 Quemadmodum eligendus sit Custos, praescripsit Reverendus pater, ut non sit opus alium modum praefinire. Qualis autem esse debeat, quod non sociis (nisi paucis verbis in provisione) sed Cancellario idem descripsit, nos constituemus latius. Esto igitur Custos vir persona gravis, coelebs, Collegio frugi, aetate maturus, annorum minimum triginta, integer vitae, moribusque purus, bonae existimationis atque famae, scientia pollens, et rerum experientia prudens: cuius castitatis exemplum, vitae integritas, morum honestas et literarum splendor caeteris, studendi ac vivendi normam praebeat. Quod si experientia rerum seculari ad actiones obeundas, gerendaque Collegii negotia, tum frugi, prudens, exercitatus et providus, tum literarum literatorumque amator egregius extiterit, sola autem literatura excellenti non responderit, sed mediocri, modo ea loco, dignitati et officio conveniant, suficiens esto habilisque: quod Custodis officium magis in obeundis tractandisque prudenter Collegii negotiis positum sit, quam in versandis libris. Qui tamen egregiam literarum cognitionem cum singulari

a Marginal insertion in MS 711.

b Marginal insertion in MS 711. Unlike the scribe Caius does not use capitals for *custos* or *collegium*.

The reading of the statutes regarding the conduct of business.

3. We further decree and direct that before all elections and discharge of business, and after fellows who are present in the university have been summoned by the keeper, or by the president in his absence and at his direction, to meet in the chapel (the customary meeting-place), and absent fellows (excluding anyone who is overseas) have been given fifteen days' notice to attend if the importance of the business warrants it, all statutes relating to the elections and other business on the agenda shall be read aloud and in a clear voice at the meeting, so that it may be known from the reading of the statutes what is permissible and how it shall be done. I regard as important business the sale and leasing of land, the expulsion of the keeper, dissensions, protection of the college and its goods, and other such instances good or bad.[6]

The qualities required of the keeper.[7]

4. The Reverend Father has prescribed the procedure for the election of a keeper, and there is therefore no need to set out any other procedure. However, we set out the required qualifications more fully since he did not specify them for [an election by] the fellows (except briefly in a proviso), but only for the Chancellor. Accordingly, the keeper is to be a man who is sober in his person, celibate,[8] careful for the college, of mature years, at least thirty years of age, unblemished in morals, of good standing and repute, well-known for his learning and prudent in the conduct of business; and the example of his chastity, honest life, scrupulous morality and high scholarly achievement shall serve as a model to others of how to study and how to behave. But if he shall be outstanding in his worldly experience in discharging transactions and managing college business, and is both careful, prudent, energetic and foreseeing, and is at the same time a keen friend of learning and literature, he shall be deemed adequate and suitable, even though in learning alone he would not rank as outstanding, but only as moderate, provided those qualities are appropriate for the position, dignity and office; for the office of keeper lies more in implementing and conducting college business prudently than in book-learning. However, the person who does combine outstanding learning with exceptional

6 Caius added these concerns in the margin. They are very characteristic of him and reflect his views on the stewardship of his predecessor as Master, Thomas Bacon.

7 No requirements as regards degree and place of birth had been included in the 1558 draft statute: *Documents*, II, p. 324.

8 See *Celibacy* in "*Supplementary Notes to Caius' Statutes*", § IV. 3, at p. 282 below.

prudentia {*seculari*}[a] coniunxerit, omne ferat punctum, omne suffragium. Esto quoque Custos in Theologia Doctor aut Baccalaureus, aut in iure civili Doctor aut Baccalaureus, {*aut in Medicina Doctor aut Baccalaureus,*}[b] aut in artibus Magister ad hoc idoneus et fama celebris, modo coelibes fuerint,[c] et Diocesis Norwicensis, quod Reverendus pater concedit Custodi liberam electionem profitendi quam velit liberalem scientiam in principio statutorum suorum. Atque haec quidem de[d] socio in Custodem eligendo, qui in Collegio tum resederit cum Custodis electio per socios aut Cancellarium fuerit, dicta sunto. At si socius aliquando fuerit, nec iam est, in hoc commodior est Collegio, quo ditior, quod minus erit Collegio onerosus, et ad benefaciendum habilior, modo caetera talis fuerit, qualem supra definivimus, et qualitate et gradu, coelibatu et natione. Demum si socius non est vel fuit, Norfolcia tamen natus aut Suffolcia, et tali gradu insignitus, et qualitatibus praeditus, quales ante explicuimus, et sit praeterea unde vivat ad triginta libras aut amplius in annos, habilis esto, sive per socios sive per Cancellarium eligatur. Proviso, ut nullus qui fuit socius et expulsus est, aliquando in Custodem eligatur, sub poena periurii ipso facto. Et si per errorem aut imprudentiam, corruptionem aut perversitatem talis electus fuerit, (quod absit), sit electio pro nulla, et cuique socio vel infimo, vel sociis liberum erit in eum litem intendere et expellere.

De voce negativa Custodis.

5 Volumus etiam et statuimus ut Magister sive Custos Collegii vestri in rebus eiusdem quibuscunque suffragium seu vocem habeat negativam. Id quod et maiestas regia in statutis universitatis anno domini 1570 editis, confirmatis et sancitis praecepit, et Reverendus pater voluit, cum statuat, ut omnia fiant per

a Interlined in MS 711.
b Interlined in MS 711.
c *Sic* MSS.
d *Sic* MSS 711, 755, 760 and Lambeth MS 720; the 1852 text has "*do*", but corrected by Venn.

worldly wisdom will have everyone's approval and vote. Furthermore, the keeper is to be a Doctor or Bachelor of Theology, or a Doctor or Bachelor of Civil Law,[9] or a Doctor or Bachelor of Medicine, or a suitable and distinguished Master of Arts, provided that he is celibate and of the diocese of Norwich,[10] because the Reverend Father at the beginning of his statutes allowed to the keeper a free choice of pursuing whichever liberal field of knowledge he wished. These provisions apply to the election as master of a fellow who is resident in the college when the election is made either by the fellows or by the Chancellor; but if he has previously been but is not now a fellow, it is better for the college if he is wealthy, since he will be less of a burden on the college and better able to be of benefit to it, so long as he has in other respects the qualifications in attainment, rank, celibacy and place of birth which we have indicated above. If he is not and has not previously been a fellow, then, whether he is elected by the fellows or by the Chancellor, he shall be eligible provided he was born in Norfolk or Suffolk, holds the required degree and is gifted with the qualities that we have specified above, and has property of £30 or more where he lives: provided that no one who was a fellow and has been expelled shall at any time be elected keeper, on pain of being automatically [adjudged] false to his vows. And if by reason of any error or misjudgement, corruption or irregularity of procedure such a person shall have been elected (may it never happen), the election shall be deemed null and void, and it shall be open to any fellow or more junior person, or to the fellows as a body, to take proceedings against him and expel him.[11]

The negative voice of the keeper.[12]

5. We also wish and decree that the master or keeper of your college shall have a negative vote or voice in all its affairs whatsoever. This is what Her Royal Majesty directed in the university statutes that were made, confirmed and came into force in A.D. 1570[13] and what the Reverend Father intended when

9 The inclusion of canon law had ceased in 1535: *H.U.C.*, I, p. 332. Only later did the title of the degrees refer to two codes (LL.D. and LL.B., not D.C.L. and B.C.L).

10 Cf. Statute 8. On Caius' introduction of a restriction to the diocese of Norwich, see "*The Norfolk Preference*", § VI. 3 below.

11 Caius may have had Henry Dethick in mind. Dethick had been expelled and later allowed by Caius to return, and Archbishop Parker suspected him of having designs upon the mastership: see "*John Caius and his Foundation*", § V. 3, and Appendix C below.

12 No statute on the Master's negative voice was included in the statutes which Caius drafted in 1558, and its inclusion here may have been prompted by similar alterations in the statutes of other colleges. See "*The Master's Negative Voice*", § VI. 2 below.

13 Elizabeth's University Statutes 1570, c. 50 (§29). Caius was prominent in the dispute between the Heads of Houses on one side and the Proctors (and others) on the other side on this and other statutes: see "*The Master's Negative Voice*", § VI. 2 below.

Magistrum sive Custodem et maiorem sociorum partem coniunctive. Quod si aliter interpretatus is est Magistro et sociis aulae S. Trinitatis de Norwico, id ad vos nihil pertinet: quod de hoc vestro Collegio in eo scripto sermo non est, nec in eam interpretationem iurastis aliquando, sed de suo proprio S. Trinitatis videlicet. Qua authoritate concessa ne Custos insolescat, et diversum sentiente maiori sociorum parte, pro suo nutu et voluntate omnia gerat in iis quae nec ad honorem nec in rem Collegii faciunt, volumus ut res in controversia ad statuta nostra et Reverendi patris examinetur et rescindatur. Quod si ne id quidem potest fieri per sinistram aliquorum interpretationem, ordinamus ut res ad visitatores vestros referatur: quo discernant illi, rectius ne senserit aut egerit Custos an maior sociorum pars, et prout eorum visitatorum pars maior iudicaverit (modo statutis Reverendi patris et nostris consonet) sic esto, cedatque qui in errore fuit.

De iuramento Custodis et sociorum.

6 Iuramento a Reverendo patre Custodi et sociis praestituto, hoc etiam adiungimus: ut quilibet Custos atque socius, qui pro tempore fuerit, in haec verba iuret:

> Iurabis per Deum omnipotentem et sancta dei evangelia: quod omnia statuta superius et inferius in hoc libro per Iohannem Caium descripta et constituta, et durante vita sua naturali constituenda pro sensu grammaticali usu communi recepto, fideliter absque omni cavillatione, mala aut sinistra interpretatione, quantum sinit humana fragilitas, quantumque ad te pertinebunt, observabis.
>
> Iurabis item, quod non consenties ut Collegii huius nomen et incorporatio facta et constituta nomine de Goneville et Caius per regiam maiestatem alteretur aut dissolvatur: sed omnibus alteraturis, aut dissoluturis omnibus viribus adversaberis: quodque dicti Collegii Fundatores

he enacted that everything should be done by the master or keeper and the majority of the fellows jointly.[14] If this is interpreted differently for the Master and Fellows of the Hall of the Holy Trinity of Norwich,[15] that does not apply to you: because the import of that passage is not about your college but plainly concerns only his own Hall of the Holy Trinity, and you may not adopt that interpretation at any time. Since it is accepted by that authority that the keeper should not become overbearing and act entirely at his own will and pleasure and in conflict with the view of the majority of the fellowship in ways that are neither to the honour nor to the good of the college, it is our wish that anything done in conflict with our statutes and those of the Reverend Father shall be reviewed and rescinded. But if that cannot be achieved through a change of mind by any people,[16] we direct that the matter should be referred to your visitors and they shall settle whether the keeper or the majority of the fellowship has taken and acted upon the more correct view; and it shall be as the majority of the visitors decide (provided their decision conforms to the statutes of the Reverend Father and our own) and the party that was in the wrong shall give way.

The oath of the keeper and the fellows.

6. To the oath prescribed by the Reverend Father for the keeper and fellows we further add: that every keeper or fellow shall swear in these words:

> You shall swear by Almighty God and his Holy Gospels that you will observe, in accordance with the grammatical sense accepted by common usage, faithfully and without any quibbling, evil or flawed interpretation, all the statutes made and set out by John Caius above and below in this book, and any further statutes made by him during his life-time, so far as human frailty allows, and so far as they apply to you.
>
> You shall further swear that you will not consent that the name of this college and its incorporation in the name of Gonville & Caius as made and effected by the Crown should be altered or dissolved, but you will vigorously oppose every future alteration or dissolution;[17] and that you

14 Bateman's Statute 3, para. 2.

15 *I.e.*, Trinity Hall. The 'different interpretation' is that by Bateman himself in the *Interpretatio* he issued to Trinity Hall in respect of its corresponding statute: see Appendix A below.

16 The meaning of *sinistram aliquorum interpretationem* is obscure and the passage may perhaps mean "the strong disapproval of others".

17 Dissolution clearly remained a threat in Caius' mind, even after the colleges had been rescued from dissolution by Henry VIII's commission, of which his friend Matthew Parker had been an energetic member in the years following the dissolution of the monasteries and chantries.

plures quam constituit maiestas regia non admittes, Benefactores autem (quos Bifundatores vocant) quot possis recipies.

Insuper iurabis, quod dicti Collegii utilitatem, incrementum bonorum, terrarum, possessionum et reddituum, iurium, ac libertatum, bonorumque omnium conservationem ac defensionem, promotionem et expeditionem causarum et negotiorum sanis consiliis, beneficiis, favoribus et auxiliis, ad quemcunque statum, gradum, dignitatem aut officium in posterum perveneris, procurabis: Et si quem noveris seditiosum aut factiosum, aut seditionem aut factionem molientem, significabis Custodi aut Praesidenti quam primum, nec occultabis.

Iurabis item quod omnia ea observabis et praestabis, quae ex voluntate Fundatoris aut Benefactoris tui observanda et praestanda tibi sunt: ita te Deus adiuvet et sancta dei evangelia.

Custos item iurabit ulterius ad hunc modum.

Iurabis per deum omnipotentem et sancta dei evangelia te pro viribus curaturum, ut omnia statuta Collegii per Reverendum patrem et Iohannem Caium ordinata, et durante vita huius naturali ordinanda pro sensu grammaticali usu communi recepto, sine ullo fuco aut dolo observentur, etiam severius in licentiosos.[a]

Ad postremum iurabis, quod omnia et singula Collegii negotia in rem eiusdem fideliter diligenterque transiges, aut transigi procurabis, et ne Collegii bona dissipentur, neve in privatum tuum aut cuiusquam usum convertantur curiosius circumspicies et prohibebis, ita te deus adiuvet et sancta dei evangelia.

De creatione Custodis.

7 Dato iuramento Custodi, senior aut sanior socius, qui vacante Custode eius vices gessit, sine mora {*custodem creet et*}[b] in realem et corporalem possessionem eundem inducat, accumbereque dextro Sacelli sedile seu stallo summo

[a] In MS 711 six deleted lines follow; they include a mysterious reference to Bincombe rectory and a marginal note "*Caius delevit*".

[b] Marginal insertion in MS 711.

> will not accept more founders than the Crown has established, but will accept as many benefactors (who are called bi-founders) as you are able.
>
> Furthermore you shall swear that you will have a care for the welfare of the college, the increase of its goods, lands, possessions and rents, the preservation and defence of all its rights, liberties and goods, and the promotion and expediting of its lawsuits and affairs with wise counsels, services, favours and helps in whatsoever station, rank, dignity or office into which you may come hereafter; and if you should become aware of any seditious or disaffected person or anyone fostering sedition or discord, you will alert the keeper or president as soon as possible and will not conceal the matter.
>
> You shall further swear that you will observe and attend to all matters which are incumbent on you by the will of the founder or benefactor: so help you God and his Holy Gospels.

The keeper shall also swear further in this manner:

> You shall swear by Almighty God and his Holy Gospels that you will vigorously ensure that all the statutes of the college made by the Reverend Father and by John Caius or to be made by him during his natural life shall be observed in accordance with their grammatical sense as commonly understood without any deceit or fraud, and will do so the more rigorously against the licentious.
>
> Finally you shall swear that you will transact, or will arrange to be transacted, all college business faithfully and diligently, and that you will be assiduously on the alert for, and will prevent, both the squandering of the goods of the college and their conversion to your own private use or that of anyone else: so help you God and his Holy Gospels.

The institution of the keeper.

7. After the oath has been administered to the keeper, the senior or more weighty fellow who has acted in place of the keeper during the vacancy,[18] shall institute the keeper without delay and induct him into actual and corporeal possession and install him in the uppermost seat or stall on the right hand side

[18] For the phrase *senior aut senior*, see *The senior fellow* in "*Supplementary Notes to Caius' Statutes*", § IV. 3, at p. 291 below.

faciat seseque ex adverso constituat, et parata habens ante se virtutis insignia, praemissaque quam velit praefaciuncula, porrigendo seorsim singula ea, ad hunc modum Custodi dicet.

> Authoritate Fundatorum a principibus accepta creamus te, damusque tibi gubernandi authoritatem, tradimusque pulvinum reverentiae, librum cognitionis, et caduceum prudentis gubernationis, ut intelligamus omnes honore reverenti obedientiaque cognitione et prudenti gubernatione Collegium istud stare et permanere, staturum et permansurum. Quamobrem ne id memoria excidat tua, in solennioribus processionibus seu supplicationibus et festis principalibus cum ex more veteri, comitatus sociis, pensionariis et scholasticis omnibus tunc in universitate existentibus, indutis superpelliciis tantum, si nullo gradu insigniantur, superpelliciis atque etiam caputiis, suo cuiusque gradui accommodis (si graduati fuerint) deducendus es e cubiculo in sacellum, atque inde reducendus in cubiculum, aliisque temporibus opportunis gestari curabis ante te (sed intra domesticos parietes) librum et caduceum, et ante te in stallo tapete instrato pulvinum imponi, in reverentis obedientiae, et cognitionis studiosae signum nobis, et prudentis gubernationis tibi, ut quod virtus postulat, id usus confirmet.

Quo finito, congratulationeque habita, eum diem laete transigant omnes, et virtutis insignia quam mox in cistam publicam ornamentorum sacelli reponantur.

De electione {custodis et}[a] *sociorum, et qui in electionibus praeferendi.*

8 De sociorum electione, quod prudenter Reverendus pater constituit, non est cur velim de nostrorum electione plura addere, sed eos eo ablegare,[b] quos illius statutis ita hic subesse volumus, ut illius socii nostris, nisi in quibus aliter expresse providemus nostris et constituimus. Tantum hoc in praesentia ordinamus, ut in omni electione Custodis praeferantur qui ex comitatu

[a] Interlined in MS 711, probably by Caius. In his draft statutes (*Documents*, II, p. 327) he had originally applied Statute 8 only to the election of fellows; hence the inconsistency with Statute 4. See "*The Norfolk Preference*", VI. 3, at pp. 399–401 below.

[b] MSS 711, 755 and Lambeth MS 720 have *ablegare*; but MS 760 has *obligare*, which makes much better sense and is adopted in the translation.

of the chapel,[19] and place himself in front of him, and, having the insignia of virtue ready to hand before him and having made such short introduction as he sees fit, while proffering each of them separately, he shall address the keeper in the following manner:

> By the authority of the founders received from the princes we install you, and give to you the authority of government, and we hand to you the cushion of reverence, the book of learning and the rod of prudent government, so that we may all understand that this college abides and endures, and will abide and endure, in honour, respectful obedience, learning and prudent government. And so that this shall not escape your memory, in the more solemn processions and religious ceremonies and principal feasts, by ancient custom of the society, you shall be escorted from your chamber into the chapel and re-escorted from there back to your chamber, in the company of all fellows pensioners and scholars then residing in the university, wearing surplices alone if they have no degree, or surplices and hoods appropriate to their degree (if they are graduates) in accordance with the ancient custom of the society; and at other opportune times you shall ensure that the book and rod should be carried before you (but within the precincts only) and the cushion be placed before you in your curtained stall as a sign to us of respectful obedience and devoted learning, and of prudent government to you, so that what virtue requires is confirmed by practice.

When this has been done, and congratulations have been had, all shall pass the day joyfully, and the insignia of virtue shall immediately be replaced in the communal chest of the chapel valuables.

The election of the keeper and fellows and preference in elections.

8. As regards the election of fellows there is no reason why I should wish to add more about the election of our own fellows to the Reverend Father's wise provisions other than to require them to observe his statutes, in the same way that his fellows are to observe ours, with the exception of those statutes where we expressly stipulate differently for our own fellows. At this present time we only direct that in every election of a keeper preference shall be given to those

[19] In his draft statutes of 1558 Caius appears to direct that the ceremony of installation should take place in hall, not in the chapel (*accumbereque faciat mensae mediae in aula in banco*): *Documents*, II, p. 326.

Norfolciensi sunt nativi, in omni electione sociorum et scholarium,[a] itidem; post hos Suffolciae.

Itaque in Custodem primo socius Collegii qui est vel fuit (modo non erat expulsus) Norfolcia oriundus, si quis ex eis ad praescriptas Custodis qualitates, aliaque quae in eo requiruntur accedat, et nihil impediat, eligatur: quod omnes Fundatores, Norfolcienses, aut Norwicenses erant; et maxima pars Benefactorum item. Sin minus, alius eius nationis qui socius nec est nec fuit, eligatur, modo talis sit, qualem ante descripsimus. Sin horum nullus haberi potest, alius eiusdem Collegii socius qui aut est aut fuit, Suffolciensis: si quis idoneus ex praescriptis legibus et excellentis famae et prudentiae fuerit ac iudicii. In socios vero, eiusdem Collegii scholastici,[b] primo Norfolcienses, tum Suffolcienses praeferantur. Et si eius Collegii tales idonei non fuerint, ex aliis Collegiis tales assumantur, et quot sufficiant. Cum hoc tamen, ut nostrae peculiaris fundationis socii ex Norwico aut Norfolcia[c] nativi sint. Et in omni electione sociorum quorumcunque, ex Norfolcia et Suffolcia, ut pauperiores praeferantur, modo caetera respondeant et paria fuerint, iustissimum censemus. Nec excludimus indigorum generosorum filios natu minimos, quibus non est, quo vivant ex parentibus.

De sermone latino.

9 Statuimus etiam ut socii et pensionarii omnes et discipuli loquantur latine, et in mensa et in sacello, et alibi in Collegio, sub poena deprivationis comeatus sui communis eo die quo non utantur sermone latino maxima ex parte.

[a] Caius switches between *scholares* and *scholastici*, apparently without intending any difference: see the note following.

[b] *scholastici* here, but *scholares* in the preceding paragraph.

[c] Corrected from "*Suffolcia*".

who are born in the county of Norfolk, likewise in every election of fellows and scholars; and after those, natives of Suffolk.[20]

Accordingly one who is at the time a fellow of the college, or has been a fellow (provided he was not expelled), and who is Norfolk-born shall be chosen first as keeper if any of them satisfies the requirements for a keeper and there is no other impediment: because all the founders were from Norfolk or Norwich, and the majority of benefactors likewise. But if there is not such a person, anyone of that birth who is not a present or past fellow shall be chosen, provided he is such as we have described. But if no one of these can be had, anyone from Suffolk who is or was a fellow of this college may be chosen, if he is suitable under the rules stated above and is of excellent repute and prudence and judgement. In elections to fellowships scholars of this college, first from Norfolk, then from Suffolk, shall be preferred; and if there are none so qualified who are suitable, they shall be drawn from other colleges to fill any vacancies: with this proviso, however, that fellows of our own foundation shall be natives of Norwich or Norfolk. And in every election of any fellows whatsoever, from Norfolk and Suffolk, we judge it fairest that the poorer shall be preferred provided they satisfy other requirements and are of equal merit in other respects.[21] Nor do we exclude the younger sons of impoverished gentlemen, who have nothing from their parents to live on.

Speaking in Latin.

9. We decree that all fellows and pensioners and pupils shall speak in Latin, both at table and in chapel, and elsewhere in college, on pain of loss of commons on that day during which they do not for the most part use the Latin language.[22]

20 Note the introduction of a preference for Norfolk before Suffolk even though both were included in the diocese of Norwich: see "*The Norfolk Preference*", § VI. 3 below. As the next paragraph shows, Norwich is, for Caius, simply a town in Norfolk, not a diocese. The implication that those from other counties are excluded cannot apply to scholars: cf. Statute 15.

21 The preference for poverty was widespread in statutes at that time: see, *e.g.*, the Injunctions of Edward VI (1549), Mary (1557) and Elizabeth (1559): Lamb, *Letters*, pp. 144, 256, 304. See also Statute 15 below, and University Statutes 1570, s. 27.

22 See Parker's *Interpretatio* for his modification of this requirement, allowing speech in the vernacular with visitors and invoking the law of the land and the practice of the university as regards prayers in chapel.

De professione sociorum.

10 Volumus etiam et statuimus, ut unusquisque sociorum huius Collegii eius sit professionis ante electionem suam, cuius eum velit esse fundator aut benefactor suus, verum si non fuerit (prohibente necessitate aut aetate) volumus, ut ante vicessimum primum aetatis suae annum completum eius sit omnino professionis, ne voluntas fundatorum aut benefactorum defraudetur. Aetas, et aliis rationibus convenientibus et sacramento cuiusque suo intelligatur ante electionem aut post. Quod si professio nulla a benefactore constituta, aut praescripta sit, volumus ut finito primo cuiusque regentiae anno coram Custode et sociis profiteatur, cui se velit scientiae et vitae instituto addicere, et in librum actorum referatur, quo studia, exercitationes et caetera vita professioni respondeant.

De professione nostrorum sociorum.

11 Statuimus etiam, ut nostrae peculiaris fundationis socii duo Medicinae studiosi sint, tertius Theologiae, et in eis studiis perseverent, quousque Doctoratus gradum in ea facultate adepti fuerint. Eligantur autem hi statim finitis praesentibus locationibus, et auctis iam fundorum censibus annuis. Interim eligantur tantum viginti scholastici, et alantur ex praesentibus censibus huius locationis.

Qui non eligendi.

12 Nullus eligatur aut {*creetur*}[a] in Custodem, {*nullus eligatur aut admittatur in*}[b] socium aut scholarem huius Collegii, qui expulsus aut amotus prius aut

[a] Corrected from "*admittatur*".
[b] Interlined in MS 711.

The profession of a subject by fellows.

10. We wish and decree that, before he is elected, each one of the fellows of this college shall profess the subject prescribed by his founder or benefactor, but if he is prevented by age or necessity, we desire that he shall do so before the completion of his 21st year, so that the will of the founders or benefactors is not cheated. His age shall be ascertained both by his own oath and by other appropriate means either before or after his election. But if no subject has been laid down or specified by the benefactor, it is our wish that at the end of the first year as a regent [Master of Arts][23] he shall declare before the keeper and fellows to which branch of learning and academic path he wishes to apply himself, and it shall be recorded in the *Acta*[24] to which subject his studies, scholastic exercises and other activities pertain.

The profession of a subject by our own fellows.

11. We decree that two fellows of our own foundation shall study Medicine, a third Theology, and that they shall continue in their studies until they have attained the degree of Doctor in that Faculty; and they shall be elected as soon as the present leases have expired and the yearly rentals of the lands have been increased. In the meantime up to twenty scholars shall be elected and they shall be supported out of the present rentals of the current leases.[25]

Ineligibility.[26]

12. No one shall be elected or installed as keeper, or elected or admitted as fellow or scholar of this college, who has previously been expelled or removed

23 For regency, see *H.U.C.*, I, p. 105.

24 Caius originally envisaged the *Pandectae*, but that book was almost immediately confined to recording actions in the counting-house; eventually the *Acta* became the appropriate book: see *Caius and the college's accounts and records* in "*Supplementary Notes to Caius' Statutes*", § IV. 3, at p. 293 below.

25 He had originally intended to fund two fellowships and twelve scholarships, but he later aimed to increase the numbers to three and twenty, respectively, once the leases of Runcton and Croxley had been renewed after his death: see his postscript to the statutes, and "*The Governing Body*", § VI. 1 below. Here he directs that *up to* twenty scholars should be funded out of the existing rents without that delay (*interim*), but that became fully possible only in 1582 after his death.

26 Caius had originally been concerned only with the holding of benefices and physical defects when he first included it in his 1558 draft statutes: *Documents*, II, p. 328.

isto, aut alio Collegio est {*propter mores corruptos*}:[a] aut contentiosus homo per anteactam vitam fuerit. Si talis eligatur, vanam et irritam electionem volumus: sed neque cohabitandi potestatem tali concedimus. Eam ob causam, constituimus ut catalogus fiat expulsorum in libro rerum memorabilium, ne eo vitio aut alio rediens noceat, ob quod expulsus est. Ordinamus etiam ne quis expulsus alieno Collegio {*ob vitae iniquitatem aut studii negligentiam*}[b] in vestrum Collegium recipiatur. Utque eius rei certiores sitis, discite per vos aut internuntium a Magistro sive praesidente eius loci aut Collegio ex quo venit, an expulsus discesserit an non. Nullum praeterea deformem, mutum, caecum, claudum, mancum, mutilum, {*Wallicum,*}[c] aliquo gravi aut contagioso morbo affectum, aut valetudinarium, hoc est, magna ex parte aegrotum, eligendum vobis esse: et si eligatur, excludendum constituimus.

De anno probationis.

13 Quia Reverendus pater nullum certum admittendi tempus praescripsit sociis, statuimus et ordinamus ut omnes electi, infra gradum Magistri in artibus existentes, stent in probatione sua ad annum integrum antequam admittantur, ut si interim mores eorum et eruditio, studendique ratio et aptitudo Custodi et maiori sociorum parti non probentur, pari facilitate excludantur, qua admittebantur. {*Non vocetur nomine socii sed scholaris, nec Collegii consiliis intersit, nec promoveatur ad aliquem in universitate gradum aut in Collegio officium nisi lectionum logicalium.*}[d] Suffragium ferant nullum, stipendium tamen habeant gradui suo convenientem et in {*secunda*}[e] mensa locum, et praeterea nihil ex Collegio. Iuret in observationem statutorum in hunc modum.

De iuramento probandi.

Iurabis per deum omnipotentem et sacrosancta dei evangelia, te observaturum omnia statuta huius Collegii quae ad te spectabunt, ita te deus adiuvet et sancta dei evangelia.

[a] Marginal insertion in MS 711.

[b] Marginal insertion in MS 711.

[c] See Plate II above. The word *Wallicum* is inserted interlineally, either by the scribe or by Caius himself, more probably the scribe. The scribe of the original manuscript (MS 711) had a habit of using an initial capital letter for words he was not familiar with or did not understand: cf. Statute 96 (Latin text).

[d] Marginal insertion in MS 711.

[e] Interlined by Caius in MS 711.

from this or another college on grounds of immorality or has been a trouble-maker during his past life. If such a person should be elected, it is our wish that the election be null and void: and we do not grant the right of residence to such a person. For that reason we determine that a record of expulsions be kept in the book of notable events,[27] lest he should come back and commit the offence for which he was expelled or any other. We direct further that no one expelled from another college for moral turpitude or neglect of his studies shall be admitted to your college, and so that you may be the more sure of his guilt, you are to enquire, personally or by intermediary, from the master or president of the place or college from which he comes whether or not he left because he was expelled. Moreover, we decree that no person who is deformed, mute, blind, lame, crippled, maimed, infected with the French pox,[28] suffering from any serious or contagious disease, or sickly, that is, unwell for much of the time, shall be elected; and if he should be elected, he is to be excluded.

The year of probation.

13. As the Reverend Father did not provide any fixed moment of admission for fellows, we decree and direct that all who are elected when they are below the degree of Master of Arts, shall be on probation for a full year before they are admitted, so that if in the meantime their morals, erudition, aptitude and academic motivation are not proved to the keeper and the majority of the fellows they may be excluded as straightforwardly as they were admitted. Anyone in this category shall be called, not fellow, but scholar, and he shall not participate in college deliberations, nor be put forward for any degree in the university or office in college except giving lectures in logic. They shall have no vote, but they shall, however, have from the college the stipend appropriate to their degree and a place at the second table at meals and nothing beyond that from the college. They shall swear obedience to the statutes in the following manner:

Of the oath of probation.

> You shall swear by Almighty God and his Holy Gospels that you will observe all the statutes of this college so far as they apply to you: so help you God and his Holy Gospels.

27 See n. 24 above.

28 See *The apparent exclusion of Welshmen* in "*Supplementary Notes to Caius' Statutes*", § IV. 3, at p. 280 below.

De coelibatu.

14 Statuimus etiam, ut omnes vestri Collegii Custos, socii, scholares et pensionarii, coelibes sint, et perpetuo honestoque coelibatu tantisper vivant, dum in Collegio vestro permanserint, alioqui exulent et removeantur, tum ne sua quaerant commoda Collegii incommodo: tum ut sine solicitudine vivant, studiis quietius vacent, et prudentes sint. Coelibes vocamus, ante contractum matrimonium, non solennisatum tantum. Post alterum aut utrumque coniuges non coelibes iudicamus atque nuncupamus. Ut autem coelibes omnes sint, voluit etiam Reverendus pater, cum in statutis suis dicat Custodem et socios tamdiu in Collegio permansuros, quamdiu caste, honeste, obedienter, pacifice et cum studendi diligentia se habebunt, &c.

De electione nostrorum scholasticorum.

15 Volumus item[a] et ordinamus ut omnes scholastici nostrae peculiaris fundationis per Custodem et maiorem sociorum partem sine affectione aut corruptione eligantur, ex scholis Norwicensibus, sex Norwicenses: ex Norfolcia totidem: et si defectus fuerit in alterutro, suppleatur ex altero eorum Norfolcia aut Norwico, idque probe constet. Volo etiam ex Londino tres sed Organistas: ex comitatu Hertfordie duos: ex Cantabrigia aut ex eius comitatu duos: et ex comitatu Bedford unum. Sint annorum sedecim completorum antequam eligantur. Sint bonae staturae et ex parentibus prognati quos tenuis fortuna premit. Nam in paupertate virtutis Gymnasium constitutum est.[b] Secernantur omnes per Custodem ubi venerint, aut per praesidentem si absit Custos, sed consentiente prius eo, et proponantur eligendi sociis hi, quos Custos approbaverit, diligenter prius examinati ad tres dies in sacello publice, primo die per scholasticos, per insequentes duos dies per decanum et socios omnes praesentes, quam eligantur, an scribant scite, an canant musice, an grammaticen[c] calleant

[a] *Sic* MSS 711, 755 and Lambeth MS 720; but MS 760 has the better and more usual *etiam*.

[b] The phrase '*paupertas Gymnasium Virtutis*' appears to have been a commonplace (in German, French and Latin) at the time, not a literary borrowing.

[c] *Sic* MSS 711, 755 and Lambeth MS 720; Greek, but written in Roman characters. MS 760 has "*grammaticam*", no doubt because the scribe failed to note the Greek.

Celibacy.[29]

14. We decree that all members of your college, keeper, fellows, scholars and pensioners, shall be celibate, and live in perpetual and honest celibacy so long as they shall remain in your college; otherwise they shall leave and be struck off: first so that they do not seek from the college allowances to which they are not entitled, and second so that they may live without distraction, complete their studies more quietly and become the wiser. We define as celibate those for whom marriage has not yet been contracted, not simply those whose marriage has not [yet] been solemnised.[30] After either event we judge and deem them married, not celibate. Indeed, it was the will of the Reverend Father that all be celibate, when he states in his statutes that the keeper and fellows shall remain in college only so long as they bear themselves chastely, honestly, obediently, peacefully and with devotion to study, etc.

The election of our own scholars.[31]

15. We wish and direct that all scholars of our own foundation shall be elected by the keeper and majority of the fellows without favour or bribery: six Norwich boys from Norwich schools, and the same number from Norfolk; and if there is a shortfall from either it may be supplied from the other, Norfolk or Norwich, and that shall be clearly understood. It is also my wish that there shall be three from London, provided they are polyphonists:[32] two from Hertfordshire: two from Cambridge or Cambridgeshire: and one from Bedfordshire.[33] They shall be fully sixteen years of age before they are elected. They shall be of a good height and born of parents whom fortune has not favoured: for poverty is the training-school of virtue. A check on where they have come from shall be made by the keeper, or by the president if the keeper is absent, but with his prior consent, and those whom the keeper has approved shall be put forward to the fellows for election, after they have been rigorously examined for three days publicly in the chapel, on the first day by the scholars, on the following two days by the dean and all the resident fellows before they are elected, as to whether they write legibly, sing musically, construe Latin properly, are polyphonists,

[29] See *Celibacy* in "*Supplementary Notes to Caius' Statutes*", § IV. 3, at p. 282 below.

[30] The definition of 'celibacy' did not appear in Caius' draft statutes in 1558: *Documents*, II p. 335.

[31] For the application of this statute in 1594, see the list of fellows and scholars in Plate XIV above.

[32] See the note on *organistae* kindly provided by Dr Roger Bowers of Jesus College in "*Supplementary Notes to Caius' Statutes*", § IV. 3, at p. 285 below.

[33] Caius had provided only for the twelve scholars from Norwich and Norfolk in his draft statutes of 1558, not for any from other counties: *Documents*, II p. 341.

perfecte, an organistae sint, an graece sciant, et an carmen componant, observatione etiam habita, an sint proborum morum, an bonae indolis et spei, an ingeniosi, an dociles, an diligentes. Qui his qualitatibus praediti sunt habiles sunto: caeteri inhabiles. Cuius rei iudicium esto penes Custodem et maiorem sociorum partem sine affectione aut largitione, aut corruptione aliqua, quas maxime damnamus in electionibus, ne improbi, contentiosi et inepti assumantur, et omnis mali semina iactentur et probi reiiciantur, et si qui ambiant (ut fere fit) literis et virtutibus ambiant, non favoribus. {*Ad haec cum fundatores gratis dant sua sociis et scholasticis, quam est turpe et ignominiosum Custodi et sociis ex sociis et scholaribus eligendis aut admittendis lucrum facere et de recipiendis aut palam aut tacite pacisci, ut si tantam pecuniam largiantur, eligetur*[a] *aut admittetur socius aut scholaris. Verum cuique sic affecto aut agenti sive sit Custos Collegii sive socius, anathema sit, et expellatur talis pestis Collegio in aeternum.*}[b] Ex nostris autem Norfolciensibus et Norwicensibus scholasticis, minimum duos peritos organistas volumus. Sin ex Norfolcia aut ex Norwico haberi non possunt, saltem ex Suffolcia, Londino et Cantabrigia. Si ne ex his quidem, unde libet ex Anglia. Quod si quando Custodi et maiorum sociorum parti scholastici videbuntur vitiis dediti sine spe recipiscendi, aut negligentia vel natura indociles, inobedientes, protervi, aut rebelles, excludantur, et alii habiles sufficiantur. Ubi scholasticorum nostrorum loca quoquo modo vacaverint, volumus ut intra sex septimanas alii sufficiantur ex Norfolcia, Norwico et aliis locis iam assignatis: quorum tres septimanas assignamus sociis admonendi senatores et cives Norwicenses, aut aliarum scholarum Norfolciae praefectos, ut scholasticos[c] secernant: alias tres senatoribus et civibus iisdem et praefectis, ut eosdem Cantabrigiam mittant. Idem tempus concedimus etiam Hertfordiensibus et Cantabrigiensibus, si ex Academia et aliis Collegiis haberi non possint hi omnes.[d] Id enim satius fuerit; erunt enim eruditiores.

a "*eligentur aut admittetur*" acc. MSS 711, 755 and Lambeth MS 720, but the plural *eligentur* was no doubt suggested by the immediately preceding (and correct) plural "*largiantur*"; Venn corrects to *eligetur*. The scribe of MS 760 makes all three verbs plural: "*largiantur, eligantur aut admittantur*".

b Marginal insertion in MS 711. It is in different ink – another example of Caius' later preoccupation with wrongdoing? Pole's *Ordinances for the Colleges 1557* (Ord. 3) contained a similar provision against bribery: Lamb, *Letters*, p. 256.

c Interestingly, Caius uses *scolasticos*, whereas he used *scholarum* four words earlier. It is almost as if he intends *scolasticos* to denote potential scholars, and *scholarum* to denote them after they have been formally elected; but this nuance does not always appear elsewhere.

d See the note to the translation. Significantly there is a line-break immediately before "*si*" in Caius' own MS 711 (and in MS 760).

know Greek, and can write verse;[34] and after scrutiny as to whether they are of commendable morals, of good character and promise, clever, teachable and diligent. Those who are possessed of these qualities are suitable: the others are not. The judgement of this shall lie with the keeper and majority of the fellows without favour, generosity or bribery, which we greatly deplore in elections, lest the unworthy, the trouble-makers and the inept are chosen, and the seeds of all manner of evil are sown and the worthy rejected, and so that if any solicit election (as commonly happens) they do so on their learning and merit, not through favours. Considering that founders freely give their own property to fellows and scholars, how wicked and ignominious it is for the keeper and fellows to make a profit out of electing or admitting fellows and scholars and to bargain openly or secretly with applicants that if they give so much money in bribes, a particular person will be elected or admitted as fellow or scholar; truly anyone swayed or acting in this way, whether he be keeper or fellow, shall be anathema and such a bane shall be expelled from the college for ever. It is our wish that at least two of our scholars from Norfolk and Norwich shall be polyphonists. If they cannot be had from Norfolk or Norwich, then at any rate from Suffolk, London and Cambridge. And if not even from there, then at will from anywhere in England. But if when the scholars seem to the keeper and the majority of the fellows to be given to vice with no hope of coming to their senses, or are unteachable either by reason of neglect or the disposition of their nature, disobedient, impudent or rebellious, they are to be excluded and others who are suitable chosen in their place. Where the places of our scholars become vacant in any way, it is our wish that within six weeks the numbers shall be made up from Norfolk, Norwich and the other places already specified; we assign three of those weeks for the fellows to warn the aldermen and citizens of Norwich and the headmasters of the other scholars of Norfolk that they should pick out scholars; and the three further weeks for those aldermen and citizens and headmasters to send the same to Cambridge. We allow the same time also for those of Hertford and Cambridge. But only if all these replacements cannot be had from within the university and the other colleges;[35] for that will be preferable, since those will be more erudite.

[34] In a draft which he wrote in English, Caius had required "That every scholar shall sing at the least his plain song, and know his grammar, both Greek & Latin; and those only shall be eligible, except great scarcity of apt scholars there be, in which case it shall be sufficient if he know his grammar only": MS 714/570, cited *B.H.* III, p. 60.

[35] As punctuated by the scribe, the direction to resort first to the university and other colleges is limited to the case of Hertfordshire and Cambridgeshire. However, it makes more sense if the "*hi omnes*" is read as meaning that the direction to look first for replacements in the university and colleges before going back to the requisite county or town is intended to apply to *all* the localities previously mentioned, not just Cambridgeshire and Hertfordshire, and that the direction became narrowed to those two counties by a scribal error.

Ad hunc modum etiam caeteri omnes Collegii vestri scholastici secernantur, habiles et aetate et persona censeantur, examinentur, eligantur, probentur, retineantur et reiiciantur, nisi aliter a Benefactoribus constitutum sit.

De obedientia, moribus et studio scholasticorum.

16 Obediant scholastici omnes Custodi et praesidenti: obediant etiam decanis, qui eorum moribus formandis et eruditioni augendae, cum disciplina aut secus intendant.

Volumus etiam ut omnes scholastici atque in universum omnes qui in aliquo gradu honoris literarii fuerint, modeste et reverenter erga superiores se gerant, tum domi, tum foris ubicunque in Academia eos convenerint, aut eis obviam fuerint. Dent operam linguae graecae et latinae, scientiis liberalibus ea lingua qua quaeque scripta sunt, praecipue logicae et rhetoricae, dein utrique philosophiae naturali et morali, in eis se exerceant causas dubias contravertendo, solito more in Aula a tertia ad quartam, latine semper et ubique per Collegium loquendo. Volumus etiam ut teneant artem numerorum et modorum, hoc est Arithmeticam et Musicam.

De exercitio scholastico Medicinae studiosorum, scholasticorum et pensionariorum.

17 Quod sit futurum exercitium scholasticum sociorum, et quibus diebus, praescripsit Reverendus pater. Quod autem Medicorum, scholarium et pensionariorum fuerit, de quibus ille tacuit, nos iam dicemus.

Statuimus igitur ut socii Medicinae studiosi, Medicinae quaestionem disputent, hoc est opponent et respondeant per vices, per se suo loco, hoc est sacello, tempore atque ordine: pensionarii maiores Baccalaurei, per se, si non

All the other scholars of your college shall be selected, judged suitable in age and person, examined, elected, tested, retained and rejected in this manner, unless it is directed otherwise by their benefactors.

The obedience, morals and study of scholars.

16. All scholars shall be obedient to the keeper and the president, and also to the deans who shall attend to the fashioning of their morals and the increase of their learning with discipline or in other ways.

It is also our wish that all scholars and, more generally, all who are at any stage in a degree course shall behave discreetly and respectfully towards their superiors wherever they are at meetings with them or encounter them either in college or elsewhere in the university. They shall devote their work to the Greek and Latin languages, to the liberal sciences in the language in which each of them is written, especially logic and rhetoric, and thereafter to both natural and moral philosophy; in these they shall do exercises by arguing moot cases in the traditional manner in hall from three to four o'clock, always in Latin, which they are to speak everywhere in college.[36] It is our further wish that they shall pursue the art of numbers and modes, that is, arithmetic and music.

The academic course of students of medicine, [and] scholars and pensioners.

17. The Reverend Father has set out what should be the academic course of fellows and on what days it should be undertaken. We speak now about that of medical [students], scholars and pensioners, of which he said nothing.[37]

Accordingly, we decree that fellows studying medicine shall dispute a medical question, that is, they shall present and reply to it, each one in his proper place, that is, in the chapel at the due time and in the correct order. Major pensioners shall [dispute] in person if they are Bachelors, and, if they are not, either in

[36] Cf. Statute 9 and the modification made by Archbishop Parker in his *Interpretatio*, § IV. 2, at p. 271 below.

[37] The paragraphing is misleading. In the second paragraph only the first sentence relates to students of medicine: the rest of the paragraph is not so restricted. In his statutes Bateman had not provided any course of study for scholars and pensioners, and, as Caius had noticed in his draft statutes in 1558, the course which Bateman provided for fellows (Statute 1) was not suitable for those fellows studying medicine. Medicine was a postgraduate Faculty and all scholars and pensioners would be in the Faculty of Arts until graduation. See Parker's *Interpretatio* requiring adherence to this statute despite the college's assertion that Caius relaxed it.

Baccalaurei, per se vel per alium {*sub poena quinque solidorum totiens quotiens*},[a] probarent tamen magis,[b] si per se, discendi causa. At scholares et pensionarii minores per se suo loco, tempore atque ordine, quisque in ea facultate quam profitetur. Et ne ulla intermittatur quaestio seu problema scholasticorum et pensionariorum minorum hora tertia ad quartam in Aula singulis diebus (in qua lectiones quoque sint suis horis) nec sociorum et pensionariorum maiorum in sacello ter in septimana a sexta ad septimam, pro voluntate Reverendi patris et nostra, ne in vacationibus quidem ante festum S. Bartholomei, ut nec in terminis, omnino constituimus, tum quod multitudo sociorum maior iam est quam olim fuit Reverendi patris aetate, et scholares et pensionarii multi, qui per ea tempora pauci erant aut nulli; tum quod nihil aeque confirmat studia atque exercitium; nec quicquam perinde stimulat accenditque ad studia, atque rei male gerendae verecundia, aut bene actae gloria. Et quia quaevis disputatio et lectio, unius tantum est horae integrae, pellendae omnes morae in initiis sunt.

De commemorationibus Fundatorum, communibus locis et declamationibus.

18 Idem statuimus de commemorationibus Fundatorum in fine cuiusque termini, et in vacationibus etiam: de locis communibus singulis diebus veneris mane a sociis in sacello: et declamationibus singulis diebus sabbati sub vespere a iuventute in aula pertractandis. Qui socius aut pensionarius maior in Academia existens abest a disputationibus in sacello, locis communibus et commemorationibus, solvat singulis vicibus tres solidos et quatuor denarios, nisi venia Custodis aut eo absente praesidentis, propter aliquam gravem causam abfuerit: sin autem tardius venerit duodecim denarios. Positiones item recitentur in utroque loco ex memoria, non ex libro, sub pari poena: ne qui recitent scriptis confisi, minus memoriae studeant, et praesidio literarum diligentiam in perdiscendo ac memoriam remittant. Itidem si quis scholasticus abfuerit a suisa disputationibus, lectionibus et aliis exercitiis scholasticis, aut si ibi fuerit, nec

[a] Marginal insertion in MS 711 in a different hand, probably Caius'.
[b] Written as "*magis tamen*" with a superscript reversal of order by the scribe.

person or else through another on pain of a fine of 5 shillings on each occasion, though they will gain more credit if they act in person; but the scholars and minor pensioners shall do so in person in their proper place at the due time and in their due order, each one in the Faculty to which he belongs. And we particularly lay down that there shall be no interruption in the question or problem undertaken by the scholars and minor pensioners from three to four o'clock each day in hall (where the lectures are also to be held at their own times), nor in that of the fellows and major pensioners in chapel three times a week from six to seven, as desired by the Reverend Father and ourself; and no interruption in vacation before the Feast of St Bartholomew,[38] any more than in term. This is, on the one hand, because the number of fellows is now greater than it was in the time of the Reverend Father, and the scholars and pensioners are now many, whereas there were few if any then;[39] and on the other because nothing improves one's studies as much as practice, and nothing stimulates and spurs one to study more than the shame of performing badly or the distinction of doing well. And because every disputation and lecture is only of one unbroken hour's duration, all delays in starting are to be strictly avoided.

The commemorations of founders, commonplaces and the practice of public speaking.

18. We make the same decree for commemorations of founders[40] [held] at the end of each term and also those in vacations, for commonplaces by the fellows in the chapel every Friday in the morning,[41] and for practice in public speaking by the young in hall every Saturday in the evening. Any resident fellow or major pensioner who is absent from disputations in chapel, commonplaces and commemorations shall pay 3s. 4d. on each occasion, unless for some serious reason he had leave from the keeper or, in his absence, the president; and 12d. if he arrives at all late. Theses shall be expounded in each one's place from memory, not from a book, on pain of the same penalty, lest readers who rely on what is written pay scant attention to memory and abandon memory and diligence in learning by heart to reliance on the written word. In the same way, if any scholar is absent from his disputations, lectures and other scholastic exercises, or if, having been present, he does not remain for the full hour or longer, or arrives

38 24 August.

39 At the foundation in September 1557 there may have been as many as 33 pensioners, compared with 29 other members of the college (1 Master, 10 fellows, 10 scholars, 3 *pauperes* and 5 *ministri*: Caius, *Historiae*, p. 52, reprinted in *Works*).

40 Caius frequently uses *fundatores* to include benefactors as well as founders, and he may have envisaged both here.

41 See *Commonplaces* in "*Supplementary Notes to Caius' Statutes*", § IV. 3, at p. 286 below.

tamen permanserit ad horam unam integram aut amplius, aut si tardus venerit, pro discretione decanorum, per eos aut eorum alterum mulctetur aut castigetur.

De lectionibus et reverentia Baccalaureorum.

19 Statuimus etiam et ordinamus, ut artium Baccalaurei sive socii fuerint sive pensionarii, {*sub poena quinque solidorum*},[a] audiant lectiones ordinarias utriusque philosophiae praelegente decanorum altero in aula mane singulis terminis, et extra terminos {*in feriis quas vacationes nominant*}[b] ea diligentia et maiori ad tuendam existimationem, qua cum adhuc sophistae essent, usque dum Magistri artium fuerint, ne otio torpescant, licentia insolescant, neve sibi alioqui persuadeant omnia sibi licere, nullis legibus aut literarum aut civilitatis obligari, suo arbitratu posse male feriari, et bonas horas in suam perniciem male collocare.

Volumus etiam ut Baccalaurei, socii et pensionarii ea utantur reverentia, et domi et foris, in Custodem, Doctores, Decanos, Bacealaureos Theologiae et Magistros artium, qua usi sunt antequam in societatem et gradum asciti sunt. In mensa item seorsum sedeant ab illis, interposito spatio, in discrimen.

Statuimus etiam et ordinamus, ut si sors tulerit ut socius artium Magister iunior sit Baccalaureo socio, Baccalaureus cedat in omnibus Magistro usque dum sit plene consecutus gradum Magisterii et perfunctus omnibus sit, quae ad eum gradum pertinent. Aequum enim est ut contribulis factus serves ordinem, idque non in hoc tantum, sed in aliis omnibus etiam.

De mimia familiaritate.

20 Statuimus item ne consuetudinem nimium familiarem Magistri cum Doctoribus habeant, aut Baccalaurei cum Magistris aut scholares cum

[a] Interlined correction in MS 711 replacing "*et scholastici omnes*"; it is in a different hand, probably Caius'.

[b] Interlined correction in MS 711 replacing "*singulis diebus quibus ordinarie legitur*"; it is also in a different hand, probably Caius'. It is not entirely clear whether final inserted word is "*nominant*" or "*vocant*", but it was read as *nominant* in Lambeth MS 720 and in the vellum copy produced soon after Caius' death (MS 755) and subsequently in the 1852 printed version (*Documents*, II, p. 253) and *B.H.* III, p. 359. Caius' normal phrase was "*ut vulgus vocant*" and one may perhaps detect a slight air of disapproval of the period outside term being officially termed a 'vacation': cf. Statute 21 (*quas vacationes dicunt*).

late, he shall at the discretion of the deans be fined or chastised[42] by them or one of them.

[Attendance at] lectures and respectful conduct by Bachelors.

19. We decree and direct that Bachelors of Arts, whether they are fellows or pensioners, shall on pain of 5s. attend regular lectures in each subject given by one of the deans in hall in the morning each term, and out of term on weekdays which are termed vacations, with the same industry and more, in order to maintain the ranking which they previously had as sophisters[43] until they become Masters of Arts, lest they grow sluggish from idleness, become accustomed to licence, and persuade themselves that they are free to do whatever they like, are bound by no rules of learning or civility, may behave badly when they will, and waste valuable time to their ruin.

It is our wish that Bachelors, whether they are fellows or pensioners, shall behave as respectfully towards the keeper, Doctors, deans, Bachelors of Theology and Masters of Arts, both in college and outside it, as they did before they were called to their fellowship and degree. At table they shall sit separately by themselves with an intervening space dividing them from those persons.

We further decree and direct that if it should chance to happen that a fellow who is a Master of Arts is junior to a fellow who is a Bachelor, the Bachelor should give place in all things to the Master of Arts until he has proceeded fully to the degree of Master and fulfilled all the requirements for that degree. For it is only fair that you should keep your rank not only in this, but in all other things, when you become a member of a society.

Excessive familiarity.[44]

20. We decree that masters should not have undue familiarity with Doctors, or Bachelors with Masters, or scholars with Bachelors: so that there should be no

42 *I.e.*, by corporal punishment; query flogging. The deans shared the fines: see *Allen's Case* (1617) Appendix F below.

43 *I.e.*, in their third and fourth years immediately before graduating B.A. For *sophista generalis*, see *H.U.C.*, I, pp. 96–8. The terms junior and senior sophister were still used in the college's gate-lists after the Second World War to denote undergraduates other than freshmen and only dropped into disuse with those gate-lists.

44 See Parker's *Interpretatio*, § IV. 2, at p. 271 below, for his reconciliation of this statute with the preceding Statute 19 in respect of fines for non-attendance at lectures.

Baccalaureis: ut absit contemptus, et servetur gravitas. Qui diligenter ad lectiones non venerint, aut praescripta civilitate usi non fuerint, mulcta esto prima vice sex denarii; secunda, octo; tertia, duodecim denarii, et sic deinceps duplicando. Disputent etiam inter se exercitii causa, sed moderante Decanorum altero, horis et loco consuetis. Cupio enim ut omnibus modis omnes docti sint et civiles, decorumque observent, ad reipublicae usum et sui commodum et honorem, seu ut vulgo dicimus, honestatem.

De professore[a] *graecae et latinae linguae et pronuntiatione earundem.*

21 Statuimus insuper ut humaniorum literarum graece et latine lector, {*per omnes terminos et*}[b] {*per*}[c] ascholias[d] seu intermissiones scholarum {*etiam*},[e] quas vacationes dicunt, praelegat lectionem aliquam humaniorum literarum iuventuti vestrae, ne otio corrumpantur, deterioresque licentia fiant: utque et ille et decani, Custos et omnes socii, et scholastici quicunque in studiis, lectionibus, sermonibus, et familiari colloquio utantur veteri et recepta publicaque omnium regionum graecae et latinae linguae pronuntiatione, quae neque obsoleta est, neque privati alicuius hominis opinione nuper nata et suscepta est, sed quae iam olim sapientum et literatorum hominum iudicio recepta publice et omnibus regionibus usitata est.

De impedimentis studiorum.

22 Ordinamus etiam ne quis animalia ulla ad usum venationis, aut aucupii, deliciasve alat aut utatur in Collegio, ne studentium animi a studiis avocentur: neve intra Collegii limites sagittandi metas erigat, spheristerium constituat, aut

[a] Caius' use of the term *professor* is not a scribal error, for he uses it also in Statute 79. Here he would seem to have in mind an activity rather than a person. In his *Interpretatio* Parker substituted the more appropriate *praelectore* for *professore*.

[b] Marginal insertion in MS 711 in a different hand, probably Caius'; it is also interlined in Lambeth MS 720.

[c] Interlined in MS 711.

[d] Greek, but written in Roman characters; a rather esoteric, but characteristic, appeal to a term as defined by Aristotle. For Caius the term would mean 'a period for business instead of study', *i.e.* times when the Schools are closed.

[e] Interlined in MS 711.

contempt, and dignity should be preserved. Those who do not attend lectures, or do not behave with the required civility, shall be fined 6d. for the first offence; 8d. for the second; 12d. for the third, and so on doubling the increase.[45] They shall also dispute among themselves to gain the benefit of practice, but under the direction of one or other of the deans, at the customary hours and place. For I desire that all shall be skilled and courteous, and behave decorously, for the benefit of the common weal and their own advantage and distinction, or what we call integrity in common parlance.

Use of the Greek and Latin language[s] and their pronunciation.

21. We decree that the lecturer on the humanities in Greek and Latin shall give some lecture on the humanities to your young men throughout every term and also during closure of the Schools[46] or intermissions in teaching known as vacations, lest they are corrupted through idleness and become degenerate from licence; and we decree further that both he and the deans, keeper and all the fellows, and all the scholars whatsoever shall adopt in their studies, lectures, sermons and ordinary conversation the pronunciation of the Greek and Latin languages publicly accepted everywhere, which is neither obsolete nor derived from and adopted by the opinion of any private person, but which for a very long time now has been accepted in the judgement of wise and learned men and is in public use everywhere.[47]

Distractions from study.

22. We direct that no one shall keep or use in college any animals for hunting or fowling or as pets lest the minds of the students are distracted from their studies;[48] nor, for the same reason, shall anyone put up archery targets, lay out tennis-courts, or toss an axe within the boundaries of the college; the latter

[45] It is only the increase that doubles, though this is not spelled out very clearly.

[46] See note to Latin text.

[47] In his *Historiae* (p. 100) Caius lamented that the new-style pronunciation had taken hold late in Henry VIII's reign and he wrote a pamphlet on the pronunciation of Greek, which was published in 1574 after his death (reprinted in E.S. Roberts, *The Works of John Caius* (1912)): see *B.H.* III, p. 62. See Parker's *Interpretatio*, at p. 271 below, for his tactful direction that university usage should prevail, notwithstanding Statute 21.

[48] In Statute 75 the prohibition is extended to rabbits and dogs – on account of their burrowing tendencies.

axim[a] iaciat, eadem de causa: haec sub poena expulsionis; illa sex solidorum et octo denariorum totiens quotiens. {*Exercere se tamen arcu in campis, aut pilae reciprocatione in Collegio licet, modo id fiat sine nocumento Collegii et locis aptis.*}[b]

De tabernis alariis, lusibus et cubitu.

23 Statuimus item ne quis Collegii vestri frequentet tabernas alarias, aut oenopolia, nisi advensae parentis aut hospitis causa, semel tantum aut bis in anno, nec ulla de causa loca infamia aut suspecta: nec cubent alienis cubiculis sed suis, nec extra Collegium pernoctent sed intra; neve lusus illicitos exerceant aut frequentent {*sub poena singulorum* vi^{s} viii^{d} *totiens quotiens.*[c]

Statuimus etiam ne}[d] vagos mimos (qui lucri causa stultos lusus stulto popello representant) in diversoriis invisant: neve taurorum, ursorum et canum certaminibus intersint. Nam ut haec stultae vagaeque multitudini sunt aptiora, ita liberalium studiorum hominibus parum sunt accommoda: tum quod solutis tauris atque ursis sunt periculosa: tum quod nova haec oblectamenta rei suae nesciae iuventuti, literarum desideria extinguunt, rem diminuunt, bonas horas consumunt, et ex hominibus brutos faciunt. {*Qui aliter fecerit, si adultus fuerit, mulcta esto* ii^{s} vi^{d}*: si non adultus, gravis correctio.*}[e] Sint scholastici in cubiculis hora octava post meridiem, neque egrediantur nisi cogente natura, aut gravi causa per Custodem aut eo absente praesidentem approbanda. Qui secus fecerit, mulcta esto seu correctio, prout alterutra cuique conveniat, pro iudicio Custodis aut eo absente praesidentis: et eo gravior, si, quod interdiu posset transigi, in {*nocturnum*}[f] tempus sit dilatum, ut egrediendi sit excusatio.

a *Sic* MSS 711, 755 and 760. Greek, but written in Roman characters. Caius' scribe varied in his practice in this matter; cf. *grammaticen* earlier.

b A later addition, probably by Caius. The words to "*modo id fiat*" are inserted in the space before the rubric to Statute 23 and the insertion is completed in the margin.

c It is clear from a deleted passage at the foot of MS 711 (p. 25) that Caius at one time intended a separate statute ("*Cubandum suis quibusque cubiculis*") requiring fellows and pensioners to sleep in their own rooms on pain of 6s. 8d.: "*Statuimus etiam ne quis sociorum aut pensionariorum alieno quam sue cubat cubiculo suo sub pena 6s. 8d.*" Scholars would not have had a room of their own.

d Marginal insertion in MS 711, probably by Caius.

e Marginal insertion in MS 711.

f Marginal insertion in MS 711, probably by Caius.

offences on pain of expulsion: the former on pain of 6s. 8d. on each and every occasion. It shall be permissible, however, to practise with bows in the fields, or play with balls in college, provided that it is done in suitable places and without causing a nuisance to the college.

Backstreet taverns, plays and sleeping quarters.

23. We decree that no member of your college shall frequent backstreet taverns, or wine-shops, except on the occasion of a visit by a parent or guest, and then only once or twice a year at most, and on no account frequent places of ill repute or suspicion; and that they shall not sleep in any other rooms than their own, or pass the night outside the college but only within it; and that they shall not take part in or frequent illegal games on pain of 6s. 8d. on each and every occasion.

We also decree that they shall not go to inns to see travelling players (who for the sake of gain perform foolish plays for the foolish rabble); nor shall they attend bullfights, bear-fights or dog-fights. For the more suitable these are for the foolish and shiftless multitude, so the less suitable they are for men of liberal studies; for one thing, there is the danger from unleashed bulls and bears, and for another these novel amusements for young folk careless of their resources smother the desire for learning, use up their money, take the best hours of the day and turn men into brutes. Any adult who breaks this rule shall be fined 2s. 6d., and anyone who is not an adult shall be severely chastised. Scholars shall be in their rooms by 8 p.m., and they shall not leave them, except for a call of nature or on other serious grounds approved by the keeper or the president in his absence.[49] Anyone who does otherwise shall be fined or chastised as the one or other punishment seems fitting to the keeper or the president in his absence; and the offence is all the greater if what could be done during daytime is deliberately postponed till night-time in order to furnish an excuse for leaving one's room.

[49] In his *Interpretatio* Parker modified the requirement, ruling that it was sufficient for them to be within college by 8 p.m. and that they did not have to confine themselves strictly to their rooms.

De Decanis.

24 Decanorum officium esto iuventutem doctrina instruere, mores omni in loco componere, ut ad preces veniant diligentes esse, ne anglice sed latine loquantur curare, corrupte loquentes docere, disputationibus praeesse, disputantes dirigere et docere, maleficos castigare, studiosos laudare et praeferre: ne absint a cubiculis hora octava sub noctem circumspicere, sub poena quinque solidorum totiens quotiens, caeteraque peragere, quae principales solebant nostro tempore, de quibus in annalibus huius Collegii et in historia Cantabrigiensis Academiae copiosius diximus. Eligantur per Custodem et maiorem sociorum partem in computo S. Michaelis. Salarium esto in singulos terminos in quibus sine omissione legerint, ex unoquoque scholasticorum {*ex fundatione et ex unoquoque scholasticorum*}[a] pensionariorum sedecim denarii, Baccalaureorum pensionariorum viginti denarii: quibus priventur nisi praelegendi officio diligentiores fuerint, officioque removeantur. Dividatur autem salarium, ut olim, inter duos principales, quod parem oportet esse laborem. Sint Decani homines docti, graves atque probi. Et ex his legat unus Aristotelis logicam et naturalem philosophiam et quae ad eas pertinent: alter eius moralem et aliquem Platonis librum ordinarie, extraordinarie vero quem probaverit Custos ex veteribus scriptoribus.

De superintendentibus nostrorum[b] *sociorum et scholasticorum.*

25 Statuimus etiam et ordinamus ut {*Praepositus Collegii regalis beatae Mariae et S. Nicholai de Cantabrigia et*}[c] Magister sive Custos Collegii Corporis Christi et beatae Mariae in {*eadem*},[d] qui pro tempore fuerint, quotannis die nostro emortuali, et sexto die Octobris die nostro natali, prandeant apud vos,

[a] The scribe originally omitted the "*et*" when writing "*ex unoquoque scholasticorum* [*et*] *pensionariorum sedecim denarii*" and corrected his error by inserting "*et*" in the margin. When he checked the manuscript, Caius added into the margin an instruction that the scholar's fee should be met by the foundation ("*ex fundatione*"), but had to squeeze it in next to the "*et*" and he then mistakenly added *unoquoque scholasticorum* a second time. It is clear from the manuscript that the correct reading should be "*ex unoquoque scholasticorum ex fundatione et ex pensionariorum sedecim denarii*".

[b] The "*n'rorum*" in Lambeth MS 720 is misread as "*morum*" in *Documents*, II, p. 256 and in *B.H.* III, p. 360.

[c] For deletions and restorations of the references to King's in this statute, see *Caius and the Provost of King's* in "*Supplementary Notes to Caius' statutes*", § IV. 3, at p. 290 below.

[d] Caius also replaced *eadem* with *Cantabrigia* until he restored the reference to King's.

The deans.[50]

24. It is to be the office of the deans to impart learning to the young, to fashion their habits in every particular, so that they come to be diligent at prayer, to take care that they do not speak in English but in Latin, to teach those speaking badly, to preside at disputations, to direct and teach the disputants, to chastise wrongdoers, to encourage and advance the studious, to ensure that they are not absent from their chambers during the night from 8 p.m., on pain of 5s. on each and every occasion,[51] and to perform those other tasks which used to be prominent in our time and of which we have written more fully in the Annals of this college and in the History of Cambridge University.[52] They shall be elected by the keeper and the majority of the fellows at the Michaelmas audit. For each term in which they lecture for the full course the salary shall be 16d. from each scholar (to be paid out of the foundation) and each pensioner, and 20d. from each Bachelor-pensioner;[53] these payments shall be withheld if they have not been diligent enough in discharging the office of lecturing, and they shall be removed from the office. The salary shall be divided as customarily between the two as principals because the work ought to be shared equally.[54] The deans shall be men who are learned, weighty and morally upright. One of them shall lecture on Aristotelian logic and natural philosophy and the matters that pertain to them; the other on moral philosophy, ordinarily some book of Plato, but exceptionally a book which the keeper has chosen from other ancient writers.[55]

The superintendents of our fellows and scholars.

25. We decree and direct that whoever shall be the Provost of the King's College of the Blessed Mary and St Nicholas of Cambridge[56] and the master or keeper of the College of Corpus Christi and the Blessed Mary in the same place on the anniversary of our mortuary day[57] and of our birthday on the 6th October

50 For the deans' emoluments, see "*Stipends*", § VI. 4 below.

51 The deans kept the fines: see *Allen's Case* (1617) Appendix F below.

52 It is not clear which passages in the *Annals* and the *History* Caius had specifically in mind.

53 *I.e.*, Bachelors who were not scholars. Scholars were allowed to keep their scholarships after graduation until they obtained their Master's degree.

54 See "*Stipends*", § VI. 4, at p. 458 below. The deans also kept and shared the fines for non-attendance: *ibid.* at pp. 461–2, and see *Allen's Case* (1617) Appendix F below.

55 The meaning of an "extraordinary reading" was raised with Parker, who simply applied the statute literally and without comment in his *Interpretatio*.

56 See note to Latin text.

57 29 July.

et finito utriusque diei prandio, praesententur illis palam in aula aut conclavi per Custodem aut eius locum tenentem, omnes nostri tres socii et omnes nostri viginti scholares ex Norfolcia, Norwico et aliunde (ut iam ante dixi in electione scholasticorum) oriundi, per quos, si qui defuerint, admonendi Custos et socii sunt, ut intra sex septimanas integer numerus ex Norfolcia, Norwico, caeterisque iam ante commemoratis locis suppleantur[a] sub poena quadraginta solidorum ex suo cuiusque stipendio Collegio {*Regali et*}[b] corporis Christi impendendorum, aut pluris pro discretione superintendentis, usque dum numerum ex praedictis comitatu, civitate et locis aliis impleverint.

Proviso ut non praesententur aliorum socii aut scholares loco aut nomine nostrorum, dolo malo: in quod attentos volumus et rogamus hos nostros superintendentes. Quamobrem in diligentiorem executionem voluntatis nostrae et certiorem cognitionem officii et obedientiae vestrae (filii charissimi) volumus et ordinamus ut {*idem Praepositus et scholares Regalis Collegii et*}[c] Magister et socii Collegii corporis Christi et beatae Mariae, in archivis suis tuto salvoque in perpetuum asservent Statuta nostra. Chartam autem donationis nostrae, indenturam inter me et vos, et obligationem, qua vos mihi tenemini in mille quingentis libris legalis monetae Angliae ad observanda omnia, quae in indenturis praedictis continentur, volumus in archivis Magistri et sociorum Collegii corporis Christi conservari: ut si conditiones omnes et singulas non praestiteritis, liceat superintendentibus praedictis iure exigere a vobis eam pecuniam virtute obligationis, et cogere vos aliis rationibus ad eas conditiones, in quas obligati estis, praestandas. Quod ut faciant, omnem nostri authoritatem concedimus, sic tamen ut non utantur in vos rigore iuris, sed omni humanitate, saepius admonendo officii, nisi si vos nullo humanitatis officio adduci poteritis, ut haec praestetis ad quae obligati estis, in quo casu volo extremo iure utantur contra vos Collegii vestri sumptibus, et eam pecuniam in usos pios aedificiorum sacrorum et publicarum Scholarum Cantabrigiensis Academiae convertant. Demum volumus praedictum Magistrum et socios Collegii corporis Christi et beatae Mariae chartam donationis nostrae, indenturam inter me et Collegium vestrum et obligationem supradictam Praeposito supradicto, qui pro tempore fuerit, ostendere, nec usum praesentem denegare, si id Collegii nostri causa exigat.

[a] The singular *integer numerus* does not agree with the plural *suppleantur*: *sic* MSS 711, 755. MS 760 has *suppleatur*.

[b] Similarly deleted and restored by Caius.

[c] Similarly deleted and restored by Caius. Here Caius refers correctly to the "Provost and scholars"; cf. Statute 108 where he uses the more colloquial title of "Provost and Fellows".

each year[58] shall dine with you, and that at the conclusion of dinner on each day there shall be presented to them by the keeper or his deputy, openly in hall or in the parlour,[59] each of our three fellows and each of our twenty scholars coming from Norfolk, Norwich or elsewhere (as I have stated above [in the statute] on the election of scholars); and if any are missing the keeper and fellows are to be warned by them that the full number is to be made good within six weeks from Norfolk, Norwich and other places already specified above, on pain of 40s. to be paid to King's and Corpus Christi Colleges out of the stipend of each missing fellow or scholar or more at the discretion of the superintendent[s][60] until they have made up the number from the specified county, city and other places.

Fellows or scholars on other foundations must not be substituted fraudulently for our own: we wish and request that our superintendents are attentive to this. With a view to ensuring the more diligent execution of our wishes and the more certain recognition of your duty and obedience, dear sons, we wish and direct that the same Provost and Scholars of King's College and the Master and Fellows of the College of Corpus Christi and the Blessed Mary shall preserve our statutes in their archives safely and securely in perpetuity. It is our wish also that our deed of gift, the indenture between me and you, and the bond by which you were bound to me in the sum of £1,500 of lawful English money for the due observance of everything contained in the said indentures shall be kept together in the archives of the Master and Fellows of Corpus Christi College: so that if you shall not observe each and every one of the conditions it shall be permissible for the aforesaid superintendents to exact that money at law and to compel you by other means to observe those conditions which you are obliged to perform. In order that they may do this, we confer on them all our authority, not, however, so that they should use this power against you with the full vigour of the law, but instead amicably, by frequently reminding you of your duty, except in the event that you cannot be brought by any friendly means to do your duty and perform your obligations; in which case it is my wish that they proceed against you with the full vigour of the law at the expense of your college, and devote that money to the charitable uses of religious buildings and the public Schools of Cambridge University. In that event it is our wish that the said Master and Fellows of the College of Corpus Christi and the Blessed Mary produce our deed of gift, the indenture between me and your college and the aforesaid bond to the aforesaid provost at the time and do not refrain from prompt action if the good of our college demands it.

58 See Parker's *Interpretatio*, allowing superintendents to substitute their presidents or senior fellows in case of illness, absence or inability to act.

59 The room used for meetings after dinner in winter (*B.H.* III, p. 197): see *The Parlour* in "*Supplementary Notes to Caius' Statutes*", § IV. 3, at p. 287 below.

60 Written in the singular even before Caius excluded the Provost of King's.

Volumus etiam, ut superintendentes cum libeat aut occasio dabitur, omnia statuta nostra in Collegii sui cuiusque custodia perlegant, et cum eisdem in custodia vestri conferant, ut si quid immutatum tempore aut truncatum sit, si quid incendio aut alia ratione pereat (quod deus avertat) ad ea reponatur. Facta collatione et restitutis omnibus, in cistula[a] cuiusque Collegii reponantur, quae singulae tribus clavibus reserentur. Ex quibus unam habeat regale Collegium; secundam Collegium corporis Christi et beatae Mariae: tertiam Collegium vestrum in communi cista vestra conservandam.

Proviso quod Custos atque socii Collegii vestri non detrectent aliquando aut cistulam aperire, aut statuta porrigere, cum superintendentes istis de causis aut aliis necessariis ea postulaverint, sic tamen ut reponantur intra octiduum, et cista Collegii vestri, clavibus praedictis reseretur. Habeant autem singuli superintendentes utroque die ex nostro tres solidos et quatuor denarios. Habeant etiam in commeatum communem singulorum istorum dierum, ut in eis gaudeant et laetentur[b] Custos socii et scholastici omnes ex fundatione praesentes, viginti solidos ultra impensas communium mensarum ordinarias. Prandeant quoque eisdem diebus apud vos {*Superintendentes et*}[c] Bedelli armigeri universitatis.

De anniversario nostro.

26 Volumus etiam ut die nostro anniversario hora nona ante prandium conveniant solenniter in sacellum Custos, socii et scholastici omnes ex fundatione cum superpelliciis et caputiis, prout cuique convenit et cantu prius habita commemoratione vel exequiis, prout leges regni patientur, habeat Custos ex nostro duodecim denarios: socii Magistri sex denarios, singuli Baccalaurei quatuor denarios, et singuli scholastici duos denarios, qui praesentes fuerint. In eo die volumus etiam ut concio fiat, cuius capita haec sunto.

De mortalitate corporis nostri; de contemptu mundi: de bona vita traducenda: de virtutibus studio conquirendis: de humilitatis et

[a] *Cistula* would seem to be an archaic form of *cistella*.

[b] In his use of the phrase "*gaudeant et laetentur*" here and in Statute 41, Caius perhaps harks back to Gaudete and Laetare Sundays in Advent and Lent respectively; cf., too, the note to Statute 92 below.

[c] Interlined insertion in MS 711.

It is our wish that the superintendents shall, when they wish or occasion requires, read through the copy of all our statutes in the custody of each college and compare them with those in your custody, so that if anything has been altered over time or excised or anything has perished through fire or for another reason (which God forbid) it can be made good. After they have been collated and everything made good they shall be put back in the chests of each college, which shall each be secured with three keys. King's College shall have one of these keys; the College of Corpus Christi and the Blessed Mary the second; and your college the third, which shall be kept in your common chest.[61]

Provided that the keeper and fellows of your college shall not at any time refuse to open the chest or produce the statutes when the superintendents have requested them to do so for these or any other necessary reasons, so long as they are put back within eight days and the chest of your college is secured with the aforesaid keys. The superintendents shall each have 3s. 4d. a day from our foundation. The keeper, fellows and all the scholars on the foundation in residence shall have 20s. towards the common meal on each of those days over and above the ordinary expenses of the common meal, so that they may rejoice and be merry. The superintendents and the esquires bedell of the university shall also dine with you on those days.

Our anniversary.

26. It is our wish that at nine o'clock on the day of our anniversary[62] the keeper and fellows and all the scholars on our foundation shall gather solemnly in the chapel before their meal,[63] wearing surplices and appropriate hoods, and after a commemoration, or such exequies as the law of the land permits, has been sung, the keeper shall receive 12d. from our foundation: and, if they have been present, fellows who are Masters 6d., each of the fellows who are Bachelors 4d. and each of the scholars 2d. On that day it is our further wish that a sermon shall be delivered on the following topics:

> On the mortality of our body: on scorning the world: on the leading of a good life: on the virtues of pursuing study: on the fruits of humility

[61] For the common chest, see *The arca, cistae, thesaurus and aerarium* in "*Supplementary Notes to Caius' Statutes*", § IV. 3. at p. 288 below. The three keys specified in this statute are not, of course, the three keys to the *arca* specified by Bateman and envisaged in Statute 80 below.

[62] See Parker's *Interpretatio* for his restriction of this to the anniversary of Caius' death and excluding a commemoration on his birthday. Parker also required that the form of the commemoration should comply with the statutes of the Crown.

[63] Venn believed the main meal (*prandium*) was about 10 a.m. and supper (*cena*) about 5 p.m. at that time: *B.H.* III, pp. 181, 184. *Prandium* appears again in Statute 52. For 'breakfast' see the note to Statute 74.

obedientiae fructu: de laude tranquillae vitae: de seditionibus vitiisque debellandis: de modestia et gravitate: de morte ultima rerum linea, quae bonos facit felices, malos autem prorsus miseros.

De vestitu.

27 Statuimus etiam et ordinamus ut omnes vestri Collegii Custos, socii et scholares utantur veste longa ad talos usque dimissa, manicis latis, collari sacerdotali antiquo, colore nigro, violaceo, aut inter utrumque medio, sic tamen ut omnes eodem colore vestiantur. Eam ob rem ordinamus, ne quis in Custodem, socium aut scholarem vestri Collegii ante admittatur quam talem togam solennem atque propriam habeat, et exomidem quoque eiusdem panni et coloris, si graduatus fuerit gradui suo convenientem humeris iniiciendam. Quod si admissus vestis eius colorem aut formam deponat aut mutet, aut eius generis togam propriam vel non habeat vel non utatur, aut tunicam, exomidem, habitum, caputium, aut superpellicium non habeat vel non utatur et publice et privatim, volumus ut excludatur omni Collegii beneficio et iure usque dum habuerit et usus fuerit quotidiano usu eius formae et coloris veste.

Volumus etiam ut sub togis utantur omnes tunicis aut sagis (quae cassaccas vocant) ne his exuti, aut non induti, saltatores, non scholastici videantur sub pari poena.

Statuimus etiam, ut superpellicium proprium unusquisque habeat, tam pensionariorum, quam Custodum, sociorum et scholarium omnium: habitum quoque et caputium, qui graduati sunt, ad usus suos in scholis omnibus diebus, et sacello vestro festivis. Sintque caputia pelle littuanica (quam miniveram dicunt) subducta, si regentes sint: agnina, si Baccalaurei: serico, si non regentes, sub poena viginti solidorum.

Ad postremum, constituimus ut commemorati omnes utantur pileis quadratis, et caeteris omnibus, de quibus prius, quam diu fuerint in Collegio

and obedience: on the praiseworthiness of a peaceful life: on the need to suppress dissensions and vices: on modesty and dignity: on death as the final end of all things, which makes the good joyful and the wrongdoers utterly miserable.

Dress.

27. We decree and direct that all members of your college, keeper, fellows and scholars, shall wear a long ankle-length garment, with open sleeves, traditional clerical collar, black or violet or in between the two in colour, but so that all wear the same colour.[64] For this reason we direct that no one shall be admitted as keeper, fellow or scholar of your college before he has such a formal and proper gown and also, set on his shoulders, an exomis[65] of the same cloth and colour and appropriate to his degree if he is a graduate. But if he discards or changes the colour or shape of his garment or does not use it after he has been admitted, or does not have or use, both in private and in public, either tunic, exomis, habit, hood or surplice, it is our wish that he be excluded from all benefit and right in the college until he has and uses each day a garment of that form and colour.

It is our further wish that, on pain of the same penalty, all shall wear tunics or close-fitting sleeved garments (which are called cassocks) under their gowns, lest having taken them off or not put them on they are taken to be tumblers rather than students.

We decree that everyone shall have his own surplice, pensioners as well as keeper and all fellows and scholars; also graduates are to have habit and hood for use in the Schools on all days and in your chapel on feast days: and the hoods should be lined with Lithuanian fur (which is called miniver) if they are Regents, lambs-fur if they are Bachelors, silk if they are non-Regent Masters, on pain of a fine of 20s.

Finally, we lay down that, so long as they are members of your college, all should be mindful to wear, not only in the college but also outside it, square

64 See Parker's *Interpretatio* tactfully substituting the dress required by university statutes and the laws of the realm. Laud's local investigators in 1636 were to mention Caius as a place which varied in its attention to dress. "The Clericall Habit appointed for Students here is generally neglected unless it be in King's College only … At Trinitie and otherwhiles at Caius, they keep their order for their wide Sleeve Gowns and for their Caps too when they list to put any on, but for the rest of their garments they are as light and fond as others.": Cooper, *Annals*, III, p. 280.

65 *Exomis* was the latinised form of a Greek word which was in turn anglicised in the nineteenth century. It should mean a sleeveless vest with straps which leave the shoulders bare, or at any rate the shoulder of the working arm; but it is highly doubtful if this was what Caius meant, since he later requires that it should not be worn below the gown or tucked in its sleeves. It is more likely that he meant some form of badge or emblem hung over the shoulders.

vestro, non solum intra Collegium sed extra, et eis decentibus, hoc est, non detritis, non laceris, non depilibus, non minimis, non maximis, sed capitis magnitudini aptis et accommodis. Nemo in vestimento quocunque utatur serico, praeterquam Custos, doctores cuiuscunque facultatis et Baccalaurei in Theologia beneficiati. Nemo caligis manticatis, sed cruri conformibus, nemo camisiis crispatis, nisi simplici, rara et humili crispa, et ea in collo tantum: nec galero acuminato, nec in Collegio nec extra. Qui in istis omnibus aut singulis aliter fecerit, si is socius – – –[a] aut scholasticus ex fundatione sit, poena esto privatio ab omni Collegii beneficio, usque dum praescripta omnia praestiterit: si pensionarius maior, mulcta esto sex solidi et octo denarii commeatui communi impendendi, maxime si in publicum prodeat indecenter, hoc est sine veste longa et scholastica supra memorata, sineque exomide humero iniecta et pileo quadrato capiti apto. Quam etiam mulctam socio indecenter prodeunti constituimus: scholastico autem ex fundatione mulcta indicatur trium solidorum et quatuor denariorum toties quoties non ita prodierit.

Volumus etiam ut cum rus proficiscendum sit, omnes socii et scholastici ex fundatione togam etiam curtam habeant et utantur, coloris et formae supradictae, et se in eadem Custodi aut eo absente praesidenti ostendant cum prodeundum sit, sub poena suprascripta. Esto quoque eadem mulcta utenti cum rus proficiscatur capello seu galero turbinato aut acuminato.

Providemus ne quis dicatur aut habeatur uti exomide atque pileo, qui postquam e Collegio excesserit, gestet ea sub toga aut in manicis.

De cubiculis.

28 Statuimus insuper ut Custos habeat in proprium usum id cubiculum, a quo prospectus est in sacellum inter utrumque Collegium medium, una cum

[a] *Sic* MS 711.

caps and all other items which I have mentioned above; and that these items should be in a decent state, that is, not worn out, not torn, not moth-eaten, not too small or too big but of the right size to fit the wearer.[66] No one shall wear silken dress, except the keeper, Doctors of any Faculty and beneficed Bachelors in Theology. No one shall wear boots with hoops, but only those that fit tight to the leg; no one frilly shirts, but plain, loose-textured ones with an inconspicuous ruffle and that ruffle only at the neck; and not a pointed hat, either in the college or outside.[67] If he is a fellow or a scholar on the foundation who does otherwise in all or any of these matters, the penalty shall be loss of all benefit of the college until he has fulfilled all that is required; if he is a major pensioner the fine shall be 6s. 8d. to be expended on communal provisions, especially if he appears improperly dressed in public, that is, without the long scholastic garment specified above and without exomis set on the shoulder and without a square cap on his head. We fix the same fine for a fellow appearing improperly dressed; while the fine for a scholar on the foundation shall be specified as 3s. 4d. each time he goes forth not properly dressed.

It is our wish that when they journey to the country, all fellows and scholars on the foundation shall have and wear a short gown of the form and colour stated above, and they shall show themselves to the keeper or the president in his absence when they set out, on pain of the punishment stated above. The fine shall be the same for anyone wearing a conical or pointed cap or hat when he journeys to the country.

We rule that no one can be described or accepted as wearing exomis and cap if he wears them under his cloak or in his sleeves when he goes out of the college

Rooms.[68]

28. We decree that the keeper shall have for his own use that room in the middle between each of the two Colleges[69] from which there is a view into the chapel,[70] together with the ground-floor room and another next to it in

66 Thinking only of the cap, Caius speaks absentmindedly of "the wearer's head".

67 See the final section of statute 46 of Elizabeth's Statutes of 1570 for similar prohibitions. Cf. the contemporary protest against the Proctors and their friends "who do not only go very disorderly in Cambridge wearing the most part their hats and continually very unseemly ruffs at their hands and great Galligaskens and Barrelled hose stuffed with horse Tails with skabilonions and knit netherstocks to fine for scholars …": Lamb, *Letters*, p. 402.

68 For Caius' confusing directions as to the payment of room rent and for the dividend *pro cubiculis*, see the section on *Room Rents* in "*Dividends*", § VI. 5, at pp. 482ff below.

69 *I.e.*, between Gonville and Caius Courts.

70 The Master had his own (upstairs) entrance into the chapel, and the room above the ante-chapel which had been an oratory before it became the Treasury.

subiecto cubiculo et altero illi proximo ad austrum ex nostra sedificatione. Sed illud quoque, quod inter aulam et bibliothecam est, suis et {*Collegii*}[a] amicis excipiendis illi elargimur, usque dum Magistro atque sociis conclave hybernum ex eo, aut aulae incrementum, communibus usibus facere visum fuerit. Reliqua cubicula disponat Custos cui velit, numero sociorum, scholasticorum aut pensionariorum, pro discretione sua et temporum personarumque ratione, sic tamen ut socii pensionariis: seniores iunioribus: Magistri Baccalaureis, suo quisque ordine graduque praeferantur, nisi inobedientia, contumacia, inutilitas vel sua vel in Collegium, negligentia studiorum, aut aliud vitium suaserit in correctionem faciendum: sic etiam ut ratio munditiei numerique personarum propter valetudinem habeatur. Scholares vero dominae Ioannae Traps solvant cubiculi sui pensionem, ut alii pensionarii solent. In summa ordinamus ut omnes illi scholastici, qui ex aliqua fundatione sunt, quorum Benefactores ieiunas poss[ess]iones[b] elargiti sunt, aut largientur, sic ut praeter stipendium scholasticorum nihil aut parum Collegio superfuerit ad usus extraordinarios, solvant pensiones cubiculorum, ut ii qui non sunt ex aliqua fundatione, quos pensionarios vocamus. Excipio unum scholasticum ex fundatione indigum cuique socio assignandum, ad usus suos in cubiculo, modo cubet in eodem, et

[a] Interlined insertion in MS 711.

[b] *Possiones* in MS 711; corrected to *possessiones* in MSS 755, 760 and Lambeth MS 720.

the court we have built to the south.[71] But we also make available to him that room which is between the hall and the library for receiving his and the college's friends, until such time as the master and fellows see fit to put it to communal use as a parlour in winter or an overflow from the hall.[72] The keeper shall, at his discretion and in the light of personal circumstances at the time, allocate the remaining rooms to such number of fellows, scholars and pensioners as he pleases, but in such a way that fellows are preferred to pensioners,[73] seniors to juniors, and Masters to Bachelors, each according to his own rank and degree, unless disobedience, contumacy,[74] inattention either to his own affairs or those of the college, neglect of studies or other shortcoming argues for something different by way of punishment. For reasons of health the allocation of rooms shall also take account of hygiene, and of the number being accommodated. Mistress Joan Trapps' scholars have to pay the rent of their room, as others who are pensioners do. As a general rule we lay down that all scholars on any foundation[75] whose benefactors have provided or may in the future provide barely sufficient funds – with the result that nothing or very little beyond the stipends of the scholars is available to the college for extraordinary uses – are to pay the rents of their rooms, in the same way as those who are not on any foundation and whom we call pensioners. I make an exception for one needy scholar on a foundation to be assigned to each fellow for assistance in his

71 As has been pointed out (Watkins, Brooke and Richmond, "The Master's Lodge" in *The Caian* (1999), p. 110), Caius provided much more accommodation in the Lodge, and his mention of just three rooms has therefore been regarded as possibly disingenuous. This seems a little harsh; for he was not given to ostentatious living personally and was doubtless content with three rooms *for his personal use*. He attached great importance to attracting major pensioners to the college, as he rightly realised that only they were likely to be able to provide funds for maintaining the buildings, since benefactions founding scholarships would leave nothing over for the buildings; it was these major pensioners for whom he intended the use of the other rooms.

72 Or possibly, "whenever it is not needed by the keeper and fellows for communal use as a parlour in winter or an overflow from the hall". It is not entirely clear from the wording of the statute (*usque dum*) whether Caius is referring to the seasonal use of the room for a parlour in winter or an overflow from the hall as an existing practice or is merely envisaging its communal use as a future possibility: see *The Parlour* in "*Supplementary Notes to Caius' Statutes*", § IV. 3, at p. 287 below.

73 Scholars are not mentioned as they would not have had individual rooms of their own.

74 The offence of stubborn refusal to submit to lawful authority.

75 Hereafter in this paragraph Caius applies the term 'foundation' to the funding of a benefaction or trust.

eos scholasticos, quorum fundationes erant ante annum Domini miliesimum quingentesimum et quadragesimum.

Proviso ut omnia cubicula Collegii per nos extructa ad decennium a festo nativitatis domini 1570 pensionariis tantum elocentur. Quod si quis sociorum Collegii Gonvilli, quod velit cubiculorum nostri Collegii, solvat pensionem pro singulo quoque inferiori cubiculo viginti solidos, et pro superiori viginti sex solidos et octo denarios in arca nostra reponendos, ad sarcienda, tecta aliasque reparationes eiusdem faciendas. Ornetque ea cubicula quivis habiturus, et omnia in eis necessaria suo sumptu faciat, et corrupta reficiat, discedensque in eo ea omnia Collegio relinquat, sive ferreum opus sit, sive ligneum, sive vitreum, sive plumbeum, sive cementitium, sive lapideum, sive alterius materiei. Hocque non solum de Collegio nostrae fabricae sed universo Collegio constitutum volumus. Qui aliter fecerint, mulctentur in duplo, nec tamen sinantur amoveri quae facta sunt. Volumus tamen ut post mortem nostram

room,[76] provided he resides there, and also for those scholars whose foundations were established before 1540 A.D.[77]

Provided that all rooms of the college built by us shall be allocated only to pensioners during the ten years from Christmas 1570.[78] Accordingly, if any of the fellows of Gonville College[79] wishes to have one of the rooms of our College,[80] he must pay a rent of 20s. for any single ground-floor room, or 26s. 8d. for an upstairs room, into our ark[81] for the maintenance of its roofs and repairs. And everyone who occupies one of those rooms shall decorate it, and maintain it at his own expense, and make good any damage, and on his departure he shall leave everything in it to the college, whether the work is of iron, or wood, or glass, or lead, or mortar, or stone, or other material.[82] It is our wish that this rule shall be applied not only in respect of the fabric of our own College but in respect of the college as a whole. Any who do otherwise shall pay double the usual fine, but they shall not on that ground be permitted to remove what has been done. It is our wish, however, that after our death the fellows and scholars

76 This is one of the rare references by Dr Caius in his statutes to a class of scholars who were later called 'sizars', a term that had appeared in this college by 1586: *Lib. Rat.* Mich. 1586 (where the *oeconomus* is described as "*pro com' socior', scol' et sizar' Collegii*" in those years in which there were any sizars, though not in other years). They were excused charges in return for serving as waiters in Hall and acting as servants to the Master and to fellows in their rooms, and were later viewed as pensioners rather than scholars: cf. *B.H.* III, p. 273.

77 The date of the death of Thomas Alkyn, who had created scholarships by deed the previous year. He was the last of the four benefactors who had endowed scholarships at Gonville Hall. A fifth, Peter Hewet, later endowed scholarships in the months preceding the re-foundation, but Caius, in effect, exempted from rent the holders of all scholarships which had been endowed at Gonville Hall.

78 This direction clashes with the provision lower down that his fellows and scholars may occupy those rooms rent-free for ten years after his death: see "*Dividends*", § VI. 5 below. It appears to be a late change of mind in December 1570, possibly prompted by a temporary shortage of money caused by the purchase of the manor of Oborne in the previous month: see *Pandectae*, 30 November 1570 (loans from the College of Physicians and Caius' friend William Barker negotiated but ultimately not taken).

79 Fellows who are (or will in the future be) on the earlier foundations and entitled to accommodation in Gonville Court.

80 *I.e.*, Caius Court.

81 By "*our* ark" Caius must mean the funds of his own foundation, but his use of the word *arca* in this restricted sense is unique: contrast his more usual "our chest" at the end of this statute. For the *arca* and *cista*, and the English terms 'ark' and 'hutch', see *The arca, cistae, thesaurus and aerarium* in "*Supplementary Notes to Caius' Statutes*", § IV. 3, at p. 288 below.

82 In 1562–63 Edward Parker, the future Lord Morley, paid £7 for the decoration of his room: *B.H.* I, p. 50. In 1564 Humphrey Busby, major pensioner, built a stone window in his room for £5: *ibid.*, p. 53. Those events occurred in Caius' lifetime, no doubt with his consent: his prohibition on any alteration was intended to apply *after* his death. In 1575 a supplementary query whether the provision extended to all ornaments or only to firm fixtures was formulated by Legge and the fellows for submission to Archbishop Parker, but apparently was not considered by him before his death in May that year: Lambeth MS 720, fols. 10, 11.

liceat sociis et scholasticis nostrae peculiaris fundationis in eis sine pensione intra decennium habitare, arctius iniungentes, sub poena expulsionis, ne qua fiat alteratio aut mutatio formae fabricae nostri Collegii ab ea quam nos vivi reliquimus: neve aliae fenestrae aut ostia museave,[a] aut alia mutatio quaecunque in ea fiat: utque minimum septem pensionariis maioribus in perpetuum septem cubicula reserventur in nostro Collegio per nos extructo, in reparationes eiusdem, quas fieri volumus ex pensionibus eorum et aliorum pensionariorum Collegii nostrae fundationis in cista nostra ad eum usum reservandis. Nolumus enim ut pensiones nostri Collegii dividantur inter socios iniuria Collegii nostri.

De tecto plumbeo portae virtutis.

29 Prohibemus etiam ne quid in tecto plumbeo, quo nostri Collegii virtutis porta contegitur, insoletur solive exponatur, ne qua ambulatio fiat: neve quis ingressus nisi cum resarciendum quid sit.

De non claudendo latere Collegii nostri meridionali.

30 Praeterea statuimus ne quod aedificium construatur, quod universum latus Collegii nostrae fundationis meridionale claudat, ne prohibita libera perspiratione aer conclusus vitietur, et valetudinem nostrorum et maxime Collegii Gonevilli, offendat ac utrisque morbos accelerat atque mortem.

[a] For *musea* see *Annals*, p. 192, and *B.H.* III, pp. 69, 189.

of our own foundation shall be allowed for ten years to occupy them rent-free; but we strictly enjoin, on pain of expulsion, that there shall be no alteration or change in the appearance of the buildings of our College from the way we leave it when we are alive, that no other windows, entrances or studies, or other alteration whatsoever, shall be made in them, and that at least seven rooms built by us in our College shall be reserved for seven major pensioners[83] in perpetuity to meet its repairs, which we wish to be paid for out of their room-rents and those of other pensioners of the college of our foundation, which are to be kept in our chest for that purpose.[84] For we wish that the rents of our College shall not be shared out among the fellows to the detriment of our College.[85]

The lead roof of the Gate of Virtue.

29. We prohibit the laying out or exposing to the sun of anything on the lead roof which covers the Gate of Virtue of our College or any means of walking on it; or that anyone shall go on it except when some repair is needed.

The obligation not to shut in the south side of our College.[86]

30. Furthermore, we decree that no building shall be constructed which encloses the whole of the south side of the college of our foundation, lest the stagnant air become infected through the failure to allow it to flow freely and does harm to the health of our members and particularly those of Gonville College, bringing illnesses and death to both Colleges.

[83] For Caius' deliberate policy of encouraging the admission of major pensioners see "*John Caius and his Foundation*", § V. 3, at p. 344 below.

[84] For "our" chest see n. 81 above.

[85] For the payment of room rent and for the dividend *pro cubiculis*, see *Room Rents* in "*Dividends*", § VI. 5 below.

[86] *I.e.*, Caius Court. Throughout this and the preceding two statutes Caius has the two Courts in mind when he speaks of "our College" and "Gonville College". Caius fails to explain why the enclosing of Caius Court should pose a special threat to the health of residents of Gonville Court.

De potestate Praesidentis.[a]

31 Praesidens per Custodem electus, superiorem locum habeat post Custodem in omnibus locis Collegii, in omnibus concessionibus, non solum absente Custode ruri aut in universitate Cantabrigiae, sed etiam praesente in Collegio, et in eodem aliter impedito. Id quod non solum congruum iudicamus, sed et sententia statutorum Reverendi patris et nostra comprobamus et constituimus. Proviso ut si Praesidens contentiosus aut factiosus homo fuerit, liceat Custodi eum ab officio amovere. Iuret Praesidens se observaturum, absente Custode, in quae Custos observanda iuravit.

De potestate nulla senioris socii.

32 Quoniam Reverendus pater nullam authoritatem concedit seniori socio, nisi disiunctivam vacante Custode per mortem, &c. volumus et constituimus ut senior socius absente Custode et Praesidente nec sit Praesidens, nec habeatur, nec aliam potestatem exerceat, quam a Custode aut Praesidente acceperit. Accepturum autem eum nullam nisi bonus vir sit et pacificus, nullisque factionibus deditus, sed alium quemvis bonum virum speramus et statuimus. Non prohibemus tamen quin senior socius possit esse praesidens, si Custos voluerit, et si Custodi prudens, probus, pacificus, diligens, et idoneus visus fuerit. Volumus tamen ut quisquis in absentia Custodis aut praesidentis substitutus fuerit per eorum alterum postremo discedentem, is tantum agat quantum eius fidei commissum est, et non aliud nec amplius. Quod si aliquando senior socius absente Custode aut praesidente sibi aliquam authoritatem arrogaverit aliud agendi, quam a Custode aut Praesidente illi est commissum, si quicquam illis absentibus innovaverit, mutaverit, obligaverit, locaverit aut quemquam admiserit, elegerit aut cuiquam licentiam dederit, gratiam cuiusquam proposuerit, aut aliud quid egerit, quod ad Custodis aut Praesidentis officium pertinebit, eis vivis et in officio permanentibus, statuimus ut illud irritum sit et inane, et ille expellatur, et consentientes atque suffragantes, omni salario, communi mensa, cubiculo et omni iure beneficioque Collegii ad sex menses deprivetur: quod usu comperimus seniorem socium non existentem

[a] It is only in this statute that *Praesidens* is ever given an initial capital letter.

The power of the president.[87]

31. The president chosen by the keeper shall have seniority after the keeper everywhere in college and in all privileges, not only when the keeper is absent in the country or in the university of Cambridge but also when he is present in college and is otherwise engaged. We approve and enact this, which we judge to accord not only with our own sense but with that of the Reverend Father's statutes: provided that the keeper may remove the president from office if he is quarrelsome or disaffected. The president shall swear that he will, during the absence of the keeper, observe those [rules] which the keeper has sworn to observe.

The denial of any power to the senior fellow.

32. Since the Reverend Father gave no power to the senior fellow, except in the particular event of a vacancy in the office of keeper through death etc., it is our wish and ruling that the senior fellow shall not be president or regarded as such in the absence of the keeper and president, nor shall he exercise any power which he has not received from the keeper or president.[88] But we hope and decree that he shall not receive such power unless he is a worthy and peaceable person, and not given to disaffection, but that some other person who is worthy shall do so. However, we do not prohibit the senior fellow from being president, if that is the wish of the keeper and he is deemed by the keeper to be prudent, upright, peaceable, industrious and suitable. Furthermore it is our wish that, in the absence of the keeper or president, whoever is appointed deputy by the last of the two to depart shall only act to the extent of his trust, and not otherwise or more widely. But if on any occasion when the keeper or president is absent, the senior fellow shall arrogate to himself any authority to do anything other than what he has been entrusted to do by the keeper or president, or if he renews a deed, makes a loan, enters into a bond, grants a lease or admits anyone as a tenant, elects or gives a licence to anyone, proposes a grace [in the university] for anyone, or does anything else which pertains to the office of keeper or president during their lives and continuance in office, we declare that his action shall be null and void, and that he shall be expelled and aiders and abettors shall be deprived of all stipend, commons, room and all right and benefit in the college for six months; because we have found by experience that a senior fellow

[87] See *The president* in "*Supplementary Notes to Caius' Statutes*", § IV. 3, at p. 291 below.

[88] See Parker's *Interpretatio* for his preservation of the powers of the senior fellow during a vacancy in the mastership (since the president held office only during the tenure of the Master who appointed him).

Praesidentem, si vir malus sit, imprudens et factiosus, instrumentum esse omnis dissentionis, omnis mali et iniquitatis. Ne autem suffragantes et consentientes expellantur, per indulgentiam concedimus, scientes alioqui agentes et consentientes pari poena esse puniendos.

De gradibus sumendis.

33 Si per Custodem aut praesidentem admonitus socius aut scholaris gradum suscipere recusaverit, distulerit aut contempserit, cum per statuta universitatis et Collegii nostri licebit, nulla existente causa legitima iudicio Custodis et maioris sociorum partis, per quam stat quo minus procedat, statuimus ut a Collegio removeatur.

Statuimus etiam ne quis Magister regens nostri Collegii necessariam suam regentiam deponat ante quinquennium, si per universitatis statuta licebit. Volumus etiam et ordinamus ne quis sophista promoveatur ad gradum Baccalaureatus antequam ad quatuor annos completos diligenter studuerit Logicae et Philosophiae: nec Baccalaureus ad gradum Magisterii, ante annos quatuor post determinationem suam in artibus: nec Theologiae Baccalaureus ante annos septem a gradu Magisterii suscepto: nec Doctor in aliqua facultate ad pileum vocetur aut accedat, ante annos decem post Magisterium suum, quod paucioribus annis maturi ad hos gradus esse non possunt. Si quis tamen ex his omnibus egregie doctus et moribus atque gravitate idoneus et maturus ad gradum suscipiendum minori tempore, Custodi et maiori sociorum parti videatur, (quod rarum est, si virtutem aestimes et non affectum) suscipiat bonis avibus.

De approbandis qui in gradibus initiandi sunt.

34 Sed ut neminem recusare volumus gradum debito modo in Collegio concessum, ita volumus et statuimus, ne quis praesumat per se vel per interpositam personam gratiam suam ad gradum aliquem obtinendum universitati

who is not president will (if he is a bad man, rash and quarrelsome) be the instrument of all discord, all wrong and iniquity.[89] But in clemency we allow that his aiders and abettors shall not be expelled, even though we know that aiders and abettors in general receive the same punishment as the principal.[90]

The obligation to graduate.

33. If a fellow or scholar refuses, delays or scorns to take a degree after he has been admonished [to do so] by the keeper, when he is qualified by the statutes of the university and our college, and in the judgement of the keeper and majority of the fellows no valid reason exists why he should not do so, we decree that he shall be removed from the college.

We also decree that no one who is a regent master of our college shall resign his regency earlier than five years if that period is allowed by university statutes. We further wish and direct that no one who is a sophister shall proceed to the degree of Bachelor before he has studied logic and philosophy diligently for four complete years: nor a Bachelor to the degree of Master less than four years after his determination in Arts:[91] nor [shall a person become] a Bachelor of Divinity earlier than seven years after taking the degree of Master: nor shall a Doctor in any Faculty be called or take the doctor's cap earlier than ten years after his Master's degree, for they cannot be ready for those degrees in fewer years. However, if anyone of all these is judged by the keeper and majority of the fellows to be outstanding in learning, suitable in conduct and consequence, and of sufficient maturity to take the degree in a shorter time, (which is rare, if you judge by worth rather than influence) he is most welcome to do so.

The requirement of approval to graduate.

34. But just as it is our wish that no one shall refuse a degree awarded in due manner in college, we wish and decree that no one shall presume, either in person or by proxy, to propose or support a proposal to the university for a grace for him to proceed to any degree, unless his morals and erudition have

[89] Caius clearly had William Clarke in mind. For his expulsion see "*John Caius and his Foundation*", § V. 3, at pp. 348–51 below.

[90] At common law accessories before or at the fact to a felony received the same sentence as the principals; only accessories after the fact were treated more leniently. Caius' "clemency" to those aiding such a senior fellow may be an allusion to the case of Henry Dethick: see the preceding note.

[91] For the 'act of determination' by which a sophister became a B.A. ('responding to the question') see *H.U.C.*, I, pp. 98–102. For sophister, see n. 43 to Statute 19 above.

proponere aut propositum acceptare, nisi prius per Custodem aut eo absente praesidentem et maiorem sociorum partem in Collegio capitulari loco approbati fuerint eius mores et eruditio, et nisi compleverit omnia quae ad eum gradum requisita sunt per statuta universitatis et Collegii nostri, Custode, vel eo absente, praesidente et non alio, gratiam proponente, si homo illis dignus videbitur, qui gratiam habeat: alioqui mulcta esto praesumenti vel acceptanti, privatio omnis iuris beneficiique Collegii in aeternum.

De approbatis non reiiciendis.

35 Sic ut ante dixi approbato, statuimus ut nemo regentium aut non regentium nostri Collegii, aut alius quivis eiusdem vel ambitione vel suffragio suo aut alieno, in scholis aut extra contravenire audeat, sed omni conatu promovere contendat, sub poena deprivationis, adactis etiam eis ad confessionem adversationis suae iuramento, qui adversati esse creduntur.

De Collegio non onerando et abundantiori praedio.

36 Ne autem oneretur Collegium alendo cuiusquam socium aut scholarem, augendove eius salarium, victum aut vestitum, aut cubiculum gratis concedendo, supra redditum ex fundatoris aut benefactoris sui fundo praediove natum, omnino constituimus. Non solum autem, ut non oneretur Collegium statuendum duximus, sed ex omnium fundationibus, ut aliquid annui redditus supersit Collegio ultra stipendium socii aut scholaris, sociorum aut scholarium, in usus extraordinarios, velut in reparationes et iuris actiones pro defensione fundorum aut ad ea pertinentium, et in[a] id genus alia incidentia, necessario ordinamus.

[a] *Sic* MS 711; in MS 755 the "*in*" appears to have been scratched out; MS 760 and Lambeth MS 720 have "*et id genus*", as in the printed texts. But MS 711 seems to give the better sense and grammar.

been approved by the keeper, or the president in his absence, and the majority of the fellows in college in the principal meeting-place,[92] and unless he has completed all the requirements of the statutes of both the university and our college for that degree, and the keeper, or the president in his absence, but no one else, has proposed the grace, if he is considered by them to be a person worthy to have the grace. The punishment for anyone presuming or agreeing to proceed in any other way shall be deprivation of all right and benefit in the college for ever.

The duty not to oppose graduation after approval.

35. After anyone has been approved in the manner I have stated, we decree that no regent or non-regent of our college or any other member of it shall presume to oppose the grace by canvassing or by his or another's voting in the Schools or elsewhere, but shall strive to promote it on pain of deprivation, after those who are believed to be opponents have been put on oath to declare their opposition.

The protection of the college and the surplus income from estates.

36. We lay down categorically that the college shall not be burdened with maintaining any fellow or scholar, or with supplementing his stipend through the grant of free victuals, clothing and accommodation, beyond what is provided by the income of the property or estate provided by his founder or benefactor. We are not only moved to make this rule so that the college may not be burdened, but in addition we direct that any surplus income from all foundations[93] over and above the stipend of the fellow or scholar, fellows or scholars, shall accrue to the college for extraordinary uses such as for repairs and any litigation in the necessary defence of the estates or their appurtenances, and for other incidentals of that kind.[94]

92 Probably still the chapel normally.

93 *Fundationes* is again used to cover benefactions as well as foundations *stricti sensu*.

94 Caius had carefully included this last direction in his original statutes in 1558 (*Documents*, II, p. 345), and it was doubtless in the forefront of the minds of the Master (Thomas Legge) and fellows when they adopted the decree of 11 December 1592 on the Frankland fellows. For this and the introduction of dividends, see "*The Decree on the Frankland Fellows, 11 December 1592*", Appendix E below, and "*Dividends*", § VI. 5 below.

De incremento stipendii Custodis.

37 Volumus etiam ut post mortem nostram Custos habeat in incrementum stipendii sui, in splendorem officii et diligentiam suam in promovendis bonis literis, conservandis Collegii bonis, perlustrandis Collegii possessionibus, observandis exequendisque statutis, quatuor libras tredecim solidos et quatuor denarios ex perquisitis curiarum Maneriorum nostrorum de Crokesley et Snelleshall, Ronghton et Burnham Thorpe in secundis locationibus, quae huic nostro Collegio dedimus in perpetuam elemosinam: sic ut totum stipendium a prioribus fundatoribus et nobis concessum decem librarum sit. Si quid autem ex perquisitis ultra quatuor libras tredecim solidos et quatuor denarios superfuerit, id totum in usus Collegii cedat. Hoc incrementum stipendii cum praedictis conditionibus tum hac potissimum concedimus, ut plurima sit in Collegio Custodis praesentia, rara absentia, nisi in causis Collegii, quod usu comperimus Custodis praesentiam prodesse multum, absentiam obesse plurimum. Quod si interesse et residere in Collegio nostro noluerit (legibus regni non obstantibus) volumus et statuimus, ut privetur augmento ex perquisitis stipendii, sic ut augmentum ex perquisitis cedat in usus Collegii usque dum permanere in Collegio et residere Custos voluerit. Quo tempore, volumus, ut in eum referatur augmentum ex perquisitis.[a]

De stipendiis sociorum et scholasticorum nostrae peculiaris fundationis.

38 Volumus item et statuimus, ut unusquisque nostrorum sociorum in artibus Magister, habeat in stipendium octo marcas: in artibus Baccalaureus quinque marcas: et singuli scholares quatuor marcas.

[a] At this point in MS 711 Caius' scribe starts a new page with some discarded draft provisions before realising and correcting his mistake.

An increase in stipend for the keeper.

37. It is our further wish that the keeper shall receive £4. 13s. 4d. after our death as an increase in his stipend towards the enhancement of his office and his industry in the promotion of learning, the preservation of the college's goods, the overseeing of the college's possessions and the observance and execution of the statutes. The additional money is to come, on the second letting, out of the perquisites of the courts of our manors of Croxley and Snellshall, Runcton and Burnham Thorpe, which we have given to this our college in perpetual alms: so that the whole stipend granted by the earlier founders and ourself shall be £10.[95] But if anything remains from these perquisites beyond the £4. 13s. 4d., then the whole of the excess is to go to the use of the college.[96] We grant this increase in stipend, with the aforesaid conditions, but especially this one, namely, that the keeper shall be in college for most of the time and rarely absent except on college business. For we know from experience that the presence of the keeper is of great benefit to the college and his absence greatly to its prejudice. But if he is unwilling to take an interest in and reside in our college (when the laws of the realm are not an obstacle [to his doing so]),[97] we wish and decree that he shall be deprived of the increment to his stipend from the perquisites, so that the increase from the perquisites shall go to the use of the college until such time as the keeper is willing to stay in college and reside there. It is our wish that the increase from the perquisites shall be restored to him when he does so.

The stipends of the fellows and scholars of our own foundation.

38. It is our wish and decree that each one of our fellows shall have a stipend of 8 marks if he is a Master of Arts: 5 marks if he is a Bachelor of Arts: and each scholar shall have 4 marks.[98]

95 As the arithmetic implies, £5. 6s. 8d. had been the Master's core stipend at Gonville Hall, as reported to Henry VIII by his Commissioners in 1545–46 (*B.H.* III, p. 338). Caius not only forbore to change this in his own favour, but gave up the stipend altogether for seven years to help the financing of one of his building projects: *Annals*, p. 122.

96 For the interaction of this statute and Statute 95 see n. 244 to Statute 95.

97 Caius here appears to use the *non obstante* clause in the sense of "provided the law of the realm is not an obstacle" rather than in the sense of "notwithstanding the law of the realm": contrast its use in royal grants of dispensing and suspending powers.

98 £5. 6s. 8d., £3. 6s. 8d. and £2. 13s. 4d., respectively. In this statute and in Statutes 37 and 40 Caius switched between marks and pounds sterling and by doing so renders the picture more complicated to modern eyes. For the three different levels in the stipends that senior fellows received

Subsidium nostrorum sociorum.

39 Quia omnia triplo cariora hodie sunt, quam anteactis temporibus, sic ut non sit ex stipendio nostro unde nostrorum sociorum necessitas ad plenum sublevetur, idcirco statuimus et ordinamus in huberiorem studiorum materiem, ut omnes nostrae peculiaris fundationis socii Doctores in Theologia et Medicina, Baccalaurei in eisdem, et artium Magistri, possint ultra stipendium nostrum, percipere et retinere singuli in subsidium studiorum suorum, pensionem aliquam, portionem, annuitatem, liberam capellam aut praebendam, ad clarum annuum valorem decem librarum sex solidorum et octo denariorum et infra, sed non ultra, sive in una praebenda, sive in duabus: modo animarum curam, impedimentum studiorum, aut absentiam a Collegio non requirant ea;[a] et modo ad luxum et saginam non abutantur eis, qui habeant et percipiant. Haec si fecerint, volumus et statuimus, ut intra unius anni spatium a subsidio accepto { }[b] societatem suam deponant {*et relinquant*}. Hanc lubentius et ea conditione largior subsidii facultatem, ut mei socii gratis et sine mercede doceant, erudiant, bonis moribus instruant et tueantur scholasticos meos, hoc est, tutores eorum sint, usque dum socii fuerint aut artium Magistri aut alio modo illis provisum sit.

De veste solenni et liberatura.

40 At ubi fructus seu proventus annui praediorum nostrorum increverint, seu maiores fuerint, finitis videlicet prasentibus locationibus, elargimur

[a] *Sic* MSS 711, 755, 760 and Lambeth MS 720. Query "*ea*"? ("*requirant*" presupposes a plural, but each of the possible subjects is feminine.)

[b] Caius here deletes "*aut subsidium reliquant, qui habent, aut*" and adds "*et relinquant*" at the end of the sentence in place of some deleted words.

The maintenance of our fellows.

39. Because the cost of everything is three times what it was in past times,[99] so it is that the needs of our fellows cannot be met entirely out of the stipend we provide; therefore we decree and direct for the greater support of their studies that all the fellows of our own foundation who are Doctors in Theology and Medicine, Bachelors in these subjects and Masters of Arts shall each be allowed, in addition to our stipend, to receive and retain in support of their studies some other pension, portion, annuity, free chapel[100] or prebend to the clear annual value of £10. 6s. 8d. or less, but not more, whether in one prebend or two: provided they do not require cure of souls, interference with study or absence from college: and provided that those who receive and enjoy them do not squander them in excess and feasting. If they do so, it is our wish and decree that within the space of one year from accepting the supplementary payment they shall surrender and relinquish their fellowship.[101] I bestow the assistance of this supplementary payment very willingly and on condition that my fellows freely and without payment teach, inform, instil with good morals, and have a care for my scholars, that is, that they are to be their tutors until they become fellows or M.A.s or provision is made for them in some other way.[102]

Formal dress and livery.[103]

40. However, when the fruits or annual produce of our lands increase, or become more considerable, namely, at the expiry of the present leases, we grant

as a consequence until 1860, see *The tripartite pattern of the establishment* in "*Stipends*", § VI. 4, at p. 427 below.

99 Caius does not specify what time span he has in mind. He would have been thinking of the price of wheat and malt, which varied greatly with the state of the harvest: see *B.H.* IV(2), p. iv, citing Thorold Rogers, *Prices*, for average prices for wheat and malt in 1575 (15s. 11d. and 10s. 10d. a quarter, compared with 4s. for wheat in 1547 and 4s. 8d. for malt in 1543). Caius extols the cheapness of a time long ago in his *History of the University*, p. 101 (reprinted in *Works*).

100 *liberam capellam*: the term 'free chapel' was used in legal documents in Caius' time: cf. 14 & 15 Hen. VIII c.9 (1523) and 37 Hen. VIII c.4 (1547). It means a chapel free from episcopal control: see J.H. Denton, *English Royal Free Chapels 1100–1300* (Manchester, 1970), ch. 1.

101 See Parker's *Interpretatio* for his (deliberately?) opaque ruling on the question whether a fellow who was absent from college and enjoying a benefice might keep the stipend and other benefits of his fellowship – on the ground that it was allowable by the laws of the land. See too *Cooke's Case* (1636) Appendix G below.

102 See Parker's *Interpretatio* allowing payment not exceeding 10s. for tuition, at the keeper's discretion, in cases where a fellow has not yet received the prebend allowed to him by the statute.

103 For this statute see "*Stipends*", § VI. 4 below.

unicuique nostrorum sociorum in artibus Magistrorum viginti sex solidos et octo denarios: Baccalaureorum unicuique viginti solidos: et unicuique scholasticorum tredecim solidos et quatuor denarios ad vestem solennem emendam et utendam, quam vulgus scholasticorum liberaturam vocat.

De commemoratione Benefactorum.

41 Statuimus item ut quotannis quatuor commemorationes fiant pro fundatoribus et benefactoribus in fine cuiusque termini sive trimestris spatii, uno aliquo die profesto, in quorum singulis volumus ut Custos, socii et scholares ex fundatione habeant ex nostro[a] coniunctim tredecim solidos et quatuor denarios, singulis diebus commemorationum, ut musae honeste gaudeant et laetentur:[b] sic ut Custos atque socii habeant sex solidos et octo denarios: scholares item sex solidos et octo denarios, quia duplo maior numerus horum est quam illorum.

Anatomia.

42 Praeterea expendi volumus in Anatomiam singulis annis brumali tempore a studiosis Medicinae nostri Collegii, vel ab eorum aliquo conficiendam, et in sepulturam honestam dissecti corporis apud S. Michaelem viginti sex solidos et octo denarios, observato ut praesidens,[c] socii, scholares omnes et pensionarii praesentes in Collegio comitentur ad sepulturam emortuum et dissectum corpus tanta reverentia et ordine, quanta si esset corpus dignioris personae, propter commoditatem inde perceptam. Proviso, quod si plura corpora velint eodem tempore (possunt autem quot velint licentia principis in archivis reservata) eisdem sumptibus dissecentur et inhumentur. Ne autem irreverenter

[a] *Sic* MSS 711 and 755 and printed texts. MS 760 has "*custos, socii et scholares ex fundatione coniunctim* 13^s *et* 4^d *habeant ex nostro diebus singulis*". See note to the translation.

[b] For Caius' use of the phrase "*gaudeant et laetentur*", see Statute 25, at p. 148, n. b, and Statute 92, at p. 240, n. a.

[c] *Sic* MSS 711, 755, 760.

to each of our fellows who are M.A.s 26s. 8d.: to each of those who are B.A.s 20s.: and to each of the scholars 13s. 4d., to purchase and use formal attire, which is commonly called academic dress.

The commemoration of benefactors.

41. We decree that there shall be four commemorations of founders and benefactors each year, one at the end of each term or period of three months on a day which is the eve of a feast-day. In order that the muses may properly rejoice and be merry, at each of these it is our wish that the keeper, fellows and scholars on the foundation shall collectively have 13s. 4d. from our endowment for each commemoration day; and in such a way that the keeper and fellows shall have 6s. 8d. between them, and the scholars likewise also 6s. 8d. between them, since there are twice as many of the latter as there are of the former.[104]

Anatomy.

42. It is our wish that 26s. 8d. shall be spent in winter-time every year on the practice of anatomy by the medical students of our college or any of them, and on the respectful burial of the dissected body in St Michael's grave-yard, provided that the president,[105] fellows and all the scholars and pensioners in residence in the college shall commit the dissected corpse to the grave with as much reverence and ceremony as though it were the body of a respectable person,[106] in recognition of the benefit received from it: provided that if more bodies are wanted at that time (and by royal licence preserved in the archives the students may have as many as they want) they shall be dissected and buried with the same outlay.[107] But the keeper or the president in his absence shall have

[104] Unlike Statute 45 (*nostrae peculiaris fundationis*) and Statute 66 (*pensionarii … nostri collegii*), where Caius singles out those on his own foundation, this gift appears not to have been so restricted. It was clearly intended to enhance the communal meal and not to be payments to individuals; moreover, Caius' statement that there are twice as many scholars as there are Master and fellows was only reasonably correct if he was counting *all* scholars and *all* fellows.

[105] For once the president is given a task otherwise than as the mere deputy of the keeper in his absence; but the keeper himself is required to ensure that due respect to the corpse is shown by the medical students.

[106] The dissected body would be that of a felon.

[107] See Parker's *Interpretatio* restricting the outlay to a total of 26s. 8d. for the whole year, not for each dissection and burial.

et inhumaniter tractent humanum corpus Medicinae studiosi, curabit Custos aut eo absente praesidens.

De Expulsis.

43 Volumus insuper et statuimus, ut si quis sociorum pronunciatus fuerit non socius per Custodem aut, eo absente, praesidentem cum consensu maioris partis sociorum, et tamen contendat de iure suo violenter contra Custodem aut praesidentem: sic ut ad mensam communem venire praesumat, etsi prohibitus, aut cibaria, quo minus ad mensam preferantur, intercipiat aut apposita de mensa tollat aut deturbet, sit ipso facto non socius, quod pacifice non egerit, etsi de expulsione sua prius aliqua fuerat dubitatio. Oramusque dominum Cancellarium et Procancellarium, ut Custodi et maiori sociorum parti adsit, et hominem rebellem in carcerem propter contumaciam detrudat, ne quas turbas et tragedias in Collegio excitet. Id si Procancellarius facere recusaverit, volumus et statuimus authoritate principum nobis concessa, ut Custos et omnes socii sub poena periurii, admotis manibus eum rebellem in cippos coniiciant, ut ibi remaneat quousque poenituerit facti,[a] tantisper dum visum fuerit Custodi et maiori sociorum parti: quod condignum iudicamus, ut parcere subiectis, sic debellare superbos, in exemplum aliorum.[b] Siquidem acrioribus suppliciis perniciosus civis, quam acerbissimus hostis coercendus.

De visitatore et appellationibus.

44 Quod si Custodis et maioris sociorum partis sententiae stare noluerit, sed causam appellationis aut querelae velit prosequi, assensu habito ad id maioris et sanioris partis Collegii, volumus et statuimus ut causam prosequatur suis sumptibus coram visitatoribus vestri Collegii, quos oramus et obsecramus ut post mortem nostram omnes causas appellationis audiant et determinent, sed non eas in quibus sine consensu maioris et sanioris partis Collegii sit appellatio,

[a] It is written in the variant form *poenituerit*, which might suggest punishment (*poena*); but Caius had in mind repentance for the wrongdoing (*paenituerit facti*).

[b] Cf. Virgil, *Aeneid* VI, 853. (The writer is indebted to Dr Duncan-Jones for this reference.)

a care that the medical students do not treat the human body with any lack of respect or humanity.

Expulsion.

43. We wish and decree that if one of the fellows shall have been adjudged not to have the status of a fellow by the keeper, or the president in his absence, with the agreement of the majority of the fellows, and he nevertheless asserts his entitlement violently against the keeper or president, as by presuming to come to the common table even though forbidden, or he intercepts the food when it is being brought to the table or takes it from the table or causes a disturbance, then, because he does not act peaceably, he shall automatically cease to be a fellow even if there had been some doubt about his earlier expulsion. And we request the Chancellor and Vice-Chancellor to assist the keeper and majority of the fellows and commit the rebellious person to prison for contempt, lest he provoke disturbances and make scenes in college. If the Vice-Chancellor refuses to do this, we wish and decree with the authority conferred on us by their Majesties that the keeper and all the fellows shall, on pain of breaking their oaths, lay hands on that rebel and place him in the stocks,[108] so that he stays there until he has repented of his deed sufficiently in the judgement of the keeper and the majority of the fellows:[109] for we judge it laudable that just as the submissive should be treated with forbearance, so must the arrogant be put down as an example to others. Indeed, if a citizen makes a pest of himself with acrimonious protests, then he must be coerced as a most grievous enemy.

The visitor and appeals.

44. In the event that [a member of the society] is unwilling to accept the decision of the keeper and majority of the fellows, but wishes to pursue a suit of appeal or complaint, after obtaining the assent to this of the greater and wiser part of the college, we wish and decree that he should prosecute his case before the visitors of your college at his own expense. We entreat and beseech the visitors to hear and determine all causes of appeal after our death, but not those in which the appeal is made without the consent of the greater and wiser

[108] For a petition against their use, see Brooke, *History*, pp. 70–1. The 1571 university decree against public bathing implies that stocks were a standard item in college halls, and that placing errant fellows in the stocks for a day was an appropriate way of punishing them: Cooper, *Annals*, II, p. 277.

[109] See note to the text for *paenituerit*.

nec eas in quibus appellatio fit propter aliquas punitiones aut expulsiones post tres admonitiones: nam utramque appellationem excludit Reverendus pater. Obsecramusque visitatores ut benigniores sint Custodi in omnibus causis amovendi, corrigendi et puniendi socios et scholares pro delictis suis, aut defectibus, ut fiant obedientes, boni atque docti, et eum defendant contra insolentiam eorum potius quam impugnent, ne ferocient illi. Praesumimus enim Custodem, bonum esse virum, et Custodem ac maiorem sociorum partem recte omnia facere. Severiores autem sunto visitatores in Custodem si Collegio inutilis is sit, si bona Collegii, pecuniam, evidentias, terras aut possessiones dissipet aut vendat, dissipari aut divendi sinat, si ea locet sibi aut sociis, aut etiam aliis, idque aliis rationibus quam a nobis praescriptum est, si redditus diminuat, si fructus eorum aliter distribuerit, quam pro voluntate fundatorum et benefactorum constitutum sit: si statuta Reverendi patris et nostra exequi neglexerit, et si aliis in causis deliquerit, in quibus severitas est exigenda pro salute Collegii et tranquillitate eorum, qui in eo boni, docti, obedientes, et literarum studiosi sunt et futuri. De quibus omnibus aliisque causis licebit visitatoribus dato iureiurando inquirere cum requisiti fuerint, noxas offensasque secundum vim, formam et effectum statutorum Reverendi patris et nostri aut alterius nostrum, et non aliter corrigere et emendare.[a] Quorum omnium aut duorum consentientium visitatorum sententiae, volumus et statuimus, Custodem omnes et singulos socios omnino stare et obedire sub poena periurii. Oramusque dominos visitatores, ne aliam authoritatem aut iurisdictionem sibi arrogent in Custodem, socios et scholares, aut in bona et terras Collegii exerceant, quam per Reverendi patris statuta et nostra aut alterius nostrum ordinatum est. Visitatores autem constituimus venerandos viros Magistrum Collegii corporis Christi et beatae Mariae in Cantabrigia, et Magistrum sive Custodem Aulae S. Trinitatis in eadem, amicos nostros, et loco aut fundatione fratres, et seniorem in Medicina Doctorem totius universitatis, aequa potestate omnes, quibus commendamus hoc nostrum Collegium, oramusque ut componant omnes lites ac controversias, pacem in eo stabiliant de tempore in tempus, et

[a] *Sic* MSS 711, 755, 760, Lambeth MS 720 and Venn; misread as *etemen dare* in 1852 text.

part of the college, nor those in which the appeal is against any punishments or expulsion imposed after three formal warnings; for the Reverend Father excludes any appeal in either of these two cases. We beseech the visitors that they should be sympathetic towards the keeper in all cases of the removal, correction and punishment of fellows and scholars for their wrongdoings and defaults, so that they may become obedient, good and well-mannered, and that the visitors should protect him against their insolence rather than oppose him, lest they become aggressively arrogant. For we presume that the keeper will be a good person, and that the keeper and the majority of the fellows will act correctly in all matters. But the visitors are to be very severe upon the keeper if he should be a hindrance to the college; or if he should waste or sell the goods, money, title-deeds, lands or possessions of the college, or allow them to be wasted or sold away; or if he should lease them to himself or to fellows, or indeed to others if he does so for reasons not specified by us; or if he should reduce the rents or distribute the income from them in a way other than that laid down by the will of the founders and benefactors; or if he should fail to have regard for the statutes of the Reverend Father and ourself; and if he should fail in other matters in which strictness is required for the good of the college and the tranquillity of those of its present and future members who are good, well-mannered, obedient and assiduous in their studies. In respect of all these and other matters it shall be lawful for the visitors to inquire by oath when they are requested to do so, and to correct and put right any wrongs and offences in accordance with the force, form and effect of the statutes of the Reverend Father and ourself or either of us and not otherwise. We wish and decree that the keeper and each and every fellow shall accept and obey the decision of the visitors or any two of them unreservedly on pain of breaking their oaths. And we beg our respected visitors[110] not to take upon themselves any authority and jurisdiction over the keeper, fellows and scholars, or take any action in respect of the goods and lands of the college, other than is directed by the statutes of the Reverend Father and ourself or either of us. We appoint as visitors those venerable persons the Master of the College of Corpus Christi and the Blessed Mary in Cambridge and the Master or Keeper of Trinity Hall in the same place, our friends, and [our] brothers in rank and foundation,[111] and the senior Doctor of Medicine in the whole university, each with equal power, to whom we commend our college and pray that they will settle all law-suits and controversies, establish peace in it from time to time and compel the fellows

[110] The term "*dominus*" was used as a polite title in circumstances in which the literal translation "lord" today is inappropriate; hence the rather free translation adopted here. In the university's class-lists and degree-lists the practice of prefixing Ds or *Dominus* to the names of Bachelors has survived to the present day.

[111] In his 1558 draft statutes Caius had appointed the Vice-Chancellor as Visitor (*Documents*, II, pp. 350–2).

socios ac scholares ad obedientiam, studia et oivilitatem (si aliter nequeant honestis persuasionibus) cogant, et ad exequenda decreta sua secundum statuta nostra ordinata, etiam Procancellarii opem, si opus sit, implorent, ut rebelles carcere aut alio supplicio puniantur, et a maleficio, discordia et inobedientia coerceantur. Haec agant visitatores nostri in omnibus causis, nisi in quibus Reverendus pater Willelmus Bateman ad Cancellarium universitatis, rectores et Doctores eiusdem iudicium refert: inter quos, ut visitatores nostri, aut eorum aliqui esse possunt, Cancellarium et Procancellarium oramus et obsecramus. Sit merces singulis visitatoribus pro integra visitatione, ubi requisiti fuerint, sex solidi et octo denarii, et singulis diebus visitationis pro commeatu suo in prandio in mensa privata, sex solidi et octo denarii.

De Orationibus.

45 Ordinamus etiam, ut in gratiarum actionibus in mensa communi, in exequiis, in commemorationibus privatis, in concionibus publicis, et aliis orationibus publicis et privatis Custos socii et pensionarii, qui pro tempore fuerint, nominatim facient mentionem Edmundi Goneville, Gulielmi Bateman et Iohannis Caii fundatorum.

Item volumus ut omnes socii et scholares nostrae peculiaris fundationis qui pro tempore fuerint in Sacello singulis diebus mane hora quinta, consueta praecum hora, socii genibus inclinati in stallis seu sedilibus aeditioribus, scholastici in humilioribus, in orientem conversi, et in genua procumbentes deni et deni, duobus ordinibus, suo quisque gradu et senioritate, ante praeces communes omnibus praesentibus clara voce praecentur in hunc modum.

Scholastici.

[–/46][a] Confitemur tibi, Domine Ihesu Christe, omnia peccata nostra, quaecunque perpetravimus ab infantia nostra, scientes aut ignorantes, et quicquid in hac nocte dormientes aut vigilantes, in verbis, in factis,

[a] Number wrongly inserted in MS 711 and Lambeth 720; but the error was spotted and corrected in MS 755 and MS 760, both of which omit any number. The wrong numbering in MS 711, Lambeth 720 and the printed texts continues until Statute 51. See Plate VI and "*Caius' Statutes: The Sources*", § I. 3 above.

and scholars to obedience, study and good manners by force (if they cannot otherwise do so by honest persuasion) and that if need be they will seek the assistance of the Vice-Chancellor in the enforcement of their decrees made in accordance with our statutes by punishing the rebels with prison or other punishment and turning them away from wrongdoing, discord and disobedience. Our visitors shall have power to do these things in all cases, except those which the Reverend Father William Bateman refers to the Chancellor of the university, Rectors[112] and Doctors thereof: amongst whom we entreat and beseech the Chancellor and Vice-Chancellor that our visitors or some of them may be included. The payment to each of the visitors, when they are summoned, shall be 6s. 8d. for the complete visitation and 6s. 8d. each day of the visitation towards their commons at dinner in a private room.

Prayers.[113]

45. We direct that when thanks are given at the common table, at exequies,[114] private commemorations, public meetings and other public and private prayers, the keeper, fellows and pensioners shall include mention of the founders Edmund Gonville, William Bateman and John Caius.

We also wish that all the fellows and scholars of our own foundation shall clearly say the following prayer aloud in chapel each day at 5 a.m.,[115] the accustomed hour for prayers, before the common prayers and in the presence of all, the fellows kneeling in the higher stalls or seats, the scholars in the lower, and turned to the east and kneeling ten and ten in two rows,[116] each according to his degree and seniority.

Scholars.

–/46. We confess to you Lord Jesus Christ all our sins whatsoever which we have committed since our infancy, knowing or unknowing, and everything which we have permitted against thy goodness in this

[112] Copied from Bateman, in whose time *rectores* was the term used to denote the proctors.

[113] For Caius' proposed order of service in the reign of Philip and Mary in his draft statutes of 1558, see *Documents*, II, pp. 330–3.

[114] See Parker's *Interpretatio* prohibiting exequies and excluding prayers (for the dead) at commemorations. See also note to Latin text at p. 178, n. a.

[115] Cardinal Pole in his University Ordinances 1557, Ord. 22, had provided for daily mass in every college where there were three priests. Although Elizabeth's statutes and ordinances had progressively reduced the number of times a week that the exercises of commonplaces should follow morning prayers in colleges, they did not affect college statutes for daily prayers themselves: see notes to Statute 18.

[116] Caius envisaged twenty scholars on his foundation.

in cogitationibus adversus tuam bonitatem admisimus, et ex toto corde nostro veniam petimus, exorantes ne ira tua veniat super nos, sed gratia et misericordia tua respiciat super nos in aeternum. Amen.

Socii.

{~~*Dein dicant: Domine Ihesu Christe, fons et mare misericordiae, miserere animae Iohannis Caii fundatoris nostri, remitte illi peccata et concede vitam aeternam. Scholares.– Amen.*~~

~~*Socii*~~}[a]

Postremo orent Domine S. Spiritus qui omnis boni author es, et omnis sapientiae largitor, largire nobis famulis tuis discendi facultatem, sapientiae desiderium, et benefaciendi gratiam, ut tibi tuaeque reipublicae et honesta vita et prudenti officio inservire digni censeamur, qui vivis et regnas deus per omnia saecula saeculorum. Scholares. – Amen.

Socii.

Deus pacis et dilectionis maneat semper nobiscum.
Scholares. – Amen.

Quibus peractis, summissa voce recitata oratione dominica,{ },[b] reverentia divinorum[c] sacrique loci habita, se recipiant ad praeces communes et usitatas.

Constituimus etiam, ut qui ex nostris has praeces nostras aut omiserit, aut his non interfuerit, nisi subsit gravis causa aegritudinis aut alterius negotii, per Custodem aut eo absente praesidentem approbanda, solvat primo, in usus Custodis, aut eo absente praesidentis, socius duos denarios, scholasticus unum denarium; secundo, socius quatuor denarios, scholasticus duos denarios: tertio,

a In MS 711 the italicised words in braces have been crossed out in a manner that suggests it was not done by Caius himself: see Plate VI above. The words also appear in all three of the other early copies of the statutes: in Lambeth MS 720 in 1574, in MS 755 (the vellum copy that was written shortly thereafter, and in MS 760 (which was probably written in the early seventeenth century). It being a prayer for the dead, the words were no doubt struck through at a later date by an overzealous reformer in pursuance of Archbishop Parker's ruling in his *Interpretatio* in January 1575 that exequies and prayers for the dead should be omitted. It was probably deleted in the time of the Commonwealth, as it is omitted completely from the two copies of the statutes produced in that period: MS 727/754 (started by William Adamson [*B.H.* I, p. 352] and completed by Thomas Gooch, later Master [*B.H.* I, p. 489]) and MS 728/755. (For MSS 727/754 and 728/755, see "*Caius' Statutes: The Sources*", § I. 3, at pp. 33–4 above.)

b In MS 711 a passage here specifying in addition the Hail Mary and the Apostles' Creed (*salutatione angelica, et symbolo Apostolico*) has been struck through and a note inserted in the margin appearing to say that Caius deleted it (? *Caius delevit*). The passage is omitted in MSS 755 and 760 and later copies.

c *Sic* MSS 711, 755, 760; wrongly printed as *reverenti adivinorum* in 1852 text, but corrected by Venn.

past night, sleeping or waking, in word, deed or thought, and we beg forgiveness with all our heart, beseeching that your wrath may not fall upon us, but your grace and mercy shine upon us for ever. Amen.

The fellows shall then say:

Lord Jesus Christ, the fountain and sea of mercy, have mercy on the soul of our founder John Caius, and forgive him his sins and grant to him life everlasting.

Scholars. – Amen.[117]

The fellows finally say:

Lord Holy Spirit who art the author of all good and the giver of all wisdom, grant to us your servants the ability to teach, the desire to learn and the grace to do good, so that, by an honest life and prudent service, we may be deemed worthy to serve you and your heavenly kingdom, who lives and reigns for ever and ever.

Scholars. – Amen.

Fellows.

May the God of peace and joy remain with us for ever.

Scholars. – Amen.

After this has been done and the Lord's Prayer recited in a humble voice, with the reverence due to the divine service and the sanctity of the place, they shall turn to the customary common prayers.

We further lay down that, unless he is excused for serious reasons of health or other business approved by the keeper or the president in his absence, any of the members of our foundation who either omits these prayers of ours or is not present at them, shall pay a fine, to be used by the keeper or the president in his absence, of 2d. on the first occasion if a fellow, and 1d. if a scholar: on the second, a fellow 4d., scholars 2d.: on the third, a fellow 6d., a scholar 3d., and

[117] On the italicised words, see note to Latin text and Plate VI.

socius sex denarios, scholasticus tres denarios, et sic deinceps duplicando totiens quotiens. Atque ut in absentiis, sic in tarditatibus par mulcta aut correctio esto.

Ad postremum ordinamus, ut publicis seu communibus praecibus (quas hora quinta mane fieri ac celebrari volumus, et in termino et extra) et aliis divinis officiis festivis diebus seu matutinis seu vespertinis omnes socii, pensionarii et scholares intersint; alioqui mulcta esto cuique socio aut pensionario maiori absenti aut tardanti, prima vice quatuor denarii; {*minori aut scholari adulto, duo denarii:*}[a] non adulto correctio: secunda vice socio et pensionario maiori sex denarii, minori et scholari adulto tres denarii, non adulto geminata correctio: tertia octo denarii: at quarta et sic deinceps maior mulcta esto aut correctio pro discretione Custodis, aut, eo absente, praesidentis. Mulctae sociorum cedant in usus Collegii in libro rerum actarum memorabilium notandae, et in rationibus seu computis ordinariis solvendae, de offendentis salario tanto dempto, quanta mulcta est. Usque adeo grave iudicamus homini sapientiae studioso non fudisse praeces, aut non egisse gratias authori omnis sapientiae. Excipimus grandaevos a precibus hora quinta, si velint, quorum aetas annum sexagesimum vel attigit vel excessit, sed ita ut aliis diei temporibus eas alacrius exequantur. Volumus etiam ut divinis officiis festivis diebus omnes socii, scholares, et pensionarii cantu, lectione canora et organis (qui hoc possunt) laudent deum.

[a] In MS 711, interlined insertion.

increasing proportionately thereafter on each occasion.[118] And the penalties for late attendance shall be the same as those for absence.

Finally we direct that all fellows, pensioners and scholars shall attend public or communal prayers (which we wish to be celebrated at 5 o'clock in the morning both in and out of term) and at other divine offices on feast days either in the morning or evening;[119] otherwise the fine for each fellow or major pensioner who is absent or late shall be 4d. on the first occasion; for an adult minor pensioner or scholar 2d. and corporal punishment if he is not an adult: on the second occasion 6d. for a fellow or major pensioner, 3d. for an adult minor pensioner or scholar and double the corporal punishment if he is not an adult: on the third 8d.; but on the fourth the fine shall be successively greater or else corporal punishment at the discretion of the keeper or the president in his absence. The fines of the fellows[120] shall be used for the benefit of the college and shall be recorded in the memorandum book[121] and charged in the ordinary accounts by deducting the amount of the fine from the stipend of the offender: so serious do we judge it for a man seeking wisdom not to have offered up prayers or given thanks to the author of all wisdom. We exempt the very elderly who have reached 60 years of age or more from 5 o'clock prayers if they wish, but on the understanding that they perform them the more eagerly at other times of the day.[122] It is our further wish that at divine offices on feast days all fellows, scholars and pensioners shall praise God with singing, chanting and the playing of organs (by those who are able to play them).[123]

118 The arithmetic is clear, if the Latin is not: it is not double the amount of the penalty each time, but double the increase; this produces an amount double the number of times the offence has been committed, *i.e.* in the case of a fellow the next amount in the series will be 8d., not 12d.

119 This fourth paragraph repeats, in substance, for all members of the college what Caius has just prescribed in the second and third paragraphs for fellows and scholars on his own foundation (apart from the special confession required of the latter). It does, however, prescribe heavier penalties for non-attendance; yet there was only one chapel and all were to be there at 5 a.m. Did he intend his fellows and scholars to pay both fines?

120 The fines of the scholars and pensioners for non-attendance were allowed to the deans: see *Allen's Case* (1617) Appendix F below.

121 Caius probably envisaged the *Pandectae* initially; but that book quickly became confined to acts done in the counting-house, and fines came to be recorded in the *Acta*: see *Caius and the college's accounts and records* in "*Supplementary Notes to Caius' Statutes*", § IV. 3, at p. 293 below.

122 Edward VI's Visitors in 1549 had excused those aged over 60 from early morning academic exercises: Lamb, *Letters*, p. 148.

123 Despite the growing Puritanical objection to church music, organs still existed in college chapels, including that of Caius. King's organs survived until the bishop of Ely peremptorily demanded their sale in *c.* 1576: Heywood and Wright, *Ancient Laws … for King's College, Cambridge* (London 1850), p. 233. Archbishop Laud's investigators in 1636 say of Caius: "Their Statutes require that there shall be an Organ in the Chapell and that Schollers be skilful in singing. This singing they neglect and that the organ they have long since sold away.": Cooper, *Annals*, III, p. 282. See the note on *Organista* in "*Supplementary Notes to Caius' Statutes*", § IV. 3, at p. 285 below, kindly provided by Dr Roger Bowers of Jesus College.

De adultis.

46/47 Adultos vocamus qui annum exegerint decimum octavum. Etenim ante eam aetatem et antiquitas[a] et nostra memoria quoque braccas inducere adolescentia non solebat, contenta tibialibus ad genua tantum productis, et longis tunicis ad talos usque dimissis: {*volumus item ut non anni solum faciant adultum, sed cum annis morum gravitas atque probitas etiam.*}[b]

De contentionibus evitandis.

47/48 Quia usus docet contentiones esse Collegiorum pestes, statuimus et ordinamus, ne quisquam sociorum, scholarium aut pensionariorum vestri Collegii contentiones, lites aut discordias per se vel per alium excitet, aut excitatas quovis modo nutriat, neque quicquam actum aut agendum in Collegio reprehendat, aut ad alium quemcunque deferat, sed omnem rem quae ipsum offendit et Collegio nocere potest, ter privatim ad Custodem, aut eo absente praesidentem, honeste et quiete referat, sic ut inter singulas relationes sex dies interponantur, ut possit considerari iustane sit an iniusta querela: ut si offensa aliqua sit, per Custodem et maiorem sociorum partem secundum statuta Reverendi patris et nostra transigatur ac finiatur. Nolumus enim iure civili aut externo iudicio ali lites vestras, sed transigi et finiri statutis Reverendi patris et nostris, hoc est, privatis legibus vestrae tranquillitati et utilitati accommodis, et regia authoritate per nos sancitis, intra limites Collegii vestri per Custodem et maiorem sociorum partem secundum sensum grammaticalem, et usu communi receptum: aut si id non potest fieri, iudicio visitatorum et superintendentium. Qui vero secus fecerit, aut Custodis et maioris sociorum partis sententiae non paruerit, ipso facto expellatur sine alicuius querelae aut appellationis remedio. και *γαρ νοχ οσιη κακα ραπτειν αλληλοισιν*, ut Homerus Odyss. II. de domestico dissidio proverbio dixit.[c] Impium enim est mala inter vos accumulare aggravando. Quamobrem constituimus et ordinamus, ut qui contra sensum

[a] *Sic* MSS 711, 755, 760 and Lambeth MS 720; 1852 text gives *antiquitus*, which would seem more correct.

[b] In MS 711, this is an interlined correction of a quite different passage.

[c] *The Odyssey*, Book 16, line 423 (ed. A.T. Murray, rev. G.E. Dimock: Harvard University Press, 1995). (The writer is indebted to Dr Duncan-Jones for this reference.)

Adults.

46/47. We call adults those who have completed their eighteenth year. For before that age, both in older times and also within our memory, youths have not been accustomed to wear breeches, and have been content with leggings taken only to the knees and with long tunics down to the ankles; it is our further wish that years alone shall not make an adult but seriousness and probity of conduct coupled with years.

The avoidance of strife.

47/48. Because experience teaches us that disputes are the bane of colleges, we decree and direct that no fellow, scholar or pensioner of your college shall stir up disputes, lawsuits[124] or controversies, either personally or through another, or foster them in any way when they have been stirred up, and that he shall not find fault with anything done or about to be done in college or complain to anyone whatsoever.[125] Instead he should privately refer whatever troubles him and may hurt the college to the keeper or to the president in his absence three times frankly and peaceably, allowing an interval of six days to elapse between each reference, so that it can be considered whether the complaint is justified or unjustified, and so that, if any wrong has been done, it may be settled and disposed of by the keeper and the majority of the fellows in accordance with the statutes of the Reverend Father and ourself. For it is our wish that your disputes shall not be settled and disposed of by the civil law or any external judgment, but by the statutes of the Reverend Father and ourself, that is, by private laws devised for your tranquillity and benefit and enacted by us with royal authority, and applied within the bounds of the college by the keeper and majority of the fellows according to their grammatical sense and as commonly understood; or if this is not possible, then by the judgment of the visitors and superintendents. Truly, whoever acts otherwise or does not submit to the decision of the keeper and majority of the fellows, shall be expelled *ipso facto* without the remedy of any suit or appeal. As Homer has said in Odyssey II in an adage about domestic strife "it is an impious thing to plot evil one against another". For it is impious to compound evils by aggravating them. For this reason we determine and direct

124 *Lites* could mean quarrels; but, given the lawsuits brought by Clarke and other expelled fellows, the more specific meaning seems intended: cf. the following note.

125 Caius probably had in mind the cases of Dethick, Warner and Spenser: see "*John Caius and his Foundation*", § V. 3, and Appendix C below.

statutorum et voluntatem nostram velit litigare iureve contendere, primo expellatur, tum suo sumptu et commeatu litiget si volet, non Collegii aut benefactoris sui: tam odiosa res est nobis contentio et deo execrabilis. Nam cum alia vitia sex tantum odit Deus, septimum, hoc est eum qui seminat inter fratres discordias, detestatur anima eius, ut ait Salomon proverbiorum sexto.[a] Etenim discordiae ruinae sunt Collegiorum, quae eis artibus facile conservantur, quibus in initio constituta sunt, {*nempe*}[b] pace, sedulitate atque studio: verum ubi pro labore dissidia, pro pace discordia, pro continentia et aequitate animi, libido atque superbia invasere, fortuna simul immutatur cum moribus. Itaque animis dissentientibus, omnia in peius prolabuntur, studia negliguntur, res et publica et privata exhauritur, demum Ilias malorum consequitur.[c]

De non appellando.

48/49 Itidem, si quis per Custodem et maiorem sociorum partem amotus seu eiectus Collegio pro inhabilitate, culpa vel demerito suo quocunque, per se vel per alium apud principes, nobiles, proceres, praelatos aut alios quoscunque de restitutione sua contra statuta agat, aut actionem contra Collegium, Custodem, praesidentem aut aliquem socium, ea de causa intendat conquerendo, litigando, aut appellando in seculari seu ecclesiastico foro quocunque, nisi cum consensu maioris et sanioris partis sociorum Collegii praesentium, in causis tantum per Reverendum patrem assignatis et intra viginti quatuor horas ab expulsione appellationem prosequatur, et intra decem dies finiat statuimus ut is ipso facto censeatur inhabilis ut recipiatur.

Proviso ut expellendorum aut expulsorum suffragia nulla sint in expellendo, aut in appellatione concedenda: neque absentium sociorum: neque sociorum post appellationem aut ante expulsionem ad appellationem suffragantium, sive praesentes tum fuerint, sive postea redierint, prius absentes: quod conspirantium et dissidium molientium haec videantur potius, quam suppliciter culpam deprecantium, et iustam causam honestis rationibus defendentium.

a Proverbs, 6, 16–19.

b Interlined insertion in MS 711.

c Cf. Cicero, *Ad Atticum* 161.3 (Shackleton Bailey), 8, 11, 3 (traditional). (The writer is indebted to Dr Duncan-Jones for this reference.) Caius was a person for whom classical literature came readily to mind and he had a weakness for displaying his erudition.

that a person who wishes, in defiance of the purpose of the statutes and our will, to dispute or sue at law, shall first be expelled, and then he may litigate at his own expense and maintenance if he wishes, and not at that of the college or his benefactor: so hateful to us and execrable to God is strife. For while God hates all six other vices, the seventh is an utter abomination to him, that is, a man who sows discords among brothers, as Solomon says in the sixth chapter of the Book of Proverbs. For discords are the ruin of colleges which may easily be kept safe by those practices for which they have first been created, namely, by peace, application and study: truly, where dissensions are wont to drive out work, discords to drive out peace, licence and arrogance to drive out self-control and fair-mindedness, fortune changes in step with morality. Accordingly where there are quarrelling minds everything goes to ruin, studies are neglected, both public and private good is at an end, and finally the result is a Trojan war of evils.

Restrictions on appeals.

48/49. Similarly, if anyone who has been removed or ejected from the college by the keeper and majority of the fellows for any lack of aptitude, fault or demerit of his whatsoever, either personally or through a third party, raises the question of his restoration before princes, nobles, prominent citizens, prelates or anyone else whatsoever in contravention of our statutes or brings legal proceedings against the college, keeper, president or any fellow in that matter by complaining, litigating or appealing in any secular or ecclesiastical court whatsoever, [then] unless he prosecutes an appeal with the consent of the greater and wiser part of the fellows of the college in residence (and only in those cases which are specified by the Reverend Father and within twenty-four hours of his expulsion) and completes his appeal within ten days, we decree that he shall automatically be adjudged disqualified from being heard.

Provided that no votes in relation to an expulsion or appeal shall be allowed to those who have themselves been expelled or are in the process of being expelled:[126] or to absent fellows: and neither shall there be voting on an appeal by fellows who seek to vote after the appeal or before the expulsion, whether they were present at the time or came back later after being absent, because such votes may seem like votes of persons conspiring and stirring things up rather than of persons addressing the wrong calmly and upholding the right side in a proper manner.

[126] Caius probably had in mind the cases of Dethick and Spenser, who appear to have supported Warner in his suit before the Vice-Chancellor: see the preceding note.

De verbis indecoris, armis non gestandis et pugna.

49/50 Statuimus praeterea ne quis vestri Collegii utatur in Collegio aut extra verbis indecentibus, contumeliosis, opprobriosis, aut quibus inest aliquid scommatis, irrisionis, aut convitii in Custodem aut eius locum tenentem, aut in socium vestri Collegii aliquem, sed contra, ut omnem debitam ac decentem reverentiam in verbis et actionibus Custodi et praesidenti exhibeat, et fraterno amore, sermone et actione socios omnes complectatur: sub poena imponenda pro ratione delicti, et iudicio Custodis aut eo absente praesidentis, et duorum sociorum, quos alteruter duxerit sibi assumendos. Quod si quis arma gestaverit intra Collegii praecinctum ultra cultellum ad ciborum usum, aut violentas manus cuiquam iniecerit vellicando, aut percusserit male tractando, aut quoquo modo pugnando, mulcta esto quadraginta solidi. {*At si Custodem aut praesidentem vel leviter percusserit, expellatur.*}[a] Si vero sanguinem detraxerit, aut abutatur cultello cibario, aut non deponat iussus, expellatur Collegio et omni Collegii beneficio ipso facto, et solvat libras tres.

De reis infamiae.

50/51 Idem de reis infamiae propter aliquod grave crimen per Custodem et maiorem sociorum partem iudicatis statuimus.

De absentia.

51/–[b] Constituimus etiam ut unusquisque data venia quoquam profecturus, in libro rerum memorabilium apud Custodem aut eo absente praesidentem

[a] Interlined insertion in MS 711.

[b] This statute is not numbered in MS 711, Lambeth MS 720 and the modern printed versions. The scribes of MS 755 and MS 760 did number it, and thereby took advantage of the omission to re-equate their numbering with that of MS 711. See Statute 45 and "*Caius' Statutes: The Sources*", § I. 3, at pp. 35–7 above.

Unbecoming words, the duty not to carry arms, and fighting.[127]

49/50. We decree that a member of your college shall not use, either in or out of college, any words that are indecent, insolent or offensive, or in which there is anything scoffing, mocking or contentious towards the keeper or his deputy or any fellow of your college, but that he shall, on the contrary, show all due and becoming respect in words and actions towards the keeper and the president and shall embrace all fellows with fraternal love in word and deed, on pain of punishment befitting the offence and at the discretion of the keeper or the president in his absence, and two fellows, whom the one or the other has called upon to join them. But if anyone bears arms within the precincts of the college other than his knife for use at table, or lays violent hands on anyone spitefully,[128] or strikes him in rough treatment or any sort of fighting, he shall be fined 40s. But if he strikes the keeper or president even lightly, he shall be expelled. If indeed he draws blood or misuses his table knife or does not put it down when ordered to do so, he shall be expelled forthwith from the college and all its benefits and shall pay £3.[129]

Infamy.

50/51. We decree the same for those adjudged guilty of infamy by the keeper and the majority of the fellows on account of any grave offence.

Absence.

51/– We lay down that anyone given leave of absence shall write in the memorandum book,[130] in the presence of the keeper or the president in his

[127] In his 1558 draft statutes Caius had limited the prohibition to the carrying of arms: *Documents*, II, p. 348.

[128] The classical sense of *vellicando* was relatively mild ('tauntingly'), but the medieval sense was more sinister ('with intent to rob'). "Spitefully" would seem to lie conveniently between the two meanings.

[129] In their appeal against their expulsion Warner and Spenser charged one Dorrington, the president, with causing bloodshed: see Appendix C, at p. 572 below.

[130] It is not clear which of the sets of records mentioned in Statute 59 Caius had in mind here: see *Caius and the college's accounts and records* in "*Supplementary Notes to Caius' Statutes*", § IV. 3, at p. 293 below. The *Exiit Books*, which also contained the early *Acta*, came to serve the purpose.

sua manu et diem quo profecturus est, et quo rediturus est scribat: et suae profectionis causam veram dicat sub iuramento Collegio praestito.

Statuimus item ne quis quocunque nomine, praetextu aut colore Collegii negotiorum, sua aut aliorum agat negotia Collegii sumptibus.

De absentia nocturna et portis claudendis.

52 Statuimus etiam et ordinamus ut portae humilitatis, virtutis et honoris nostri Collegii, et earum festrae[a] seu valvulae, aliaeque omnes utriusque Collegii portae, omnibus totius hyemis noctibus, concludantur cum primis tenebris seu crepusculo, non reserandae ante lucem sequentis diei, praeter portam Collegii Gonevilli maiorem aut eius festram, quam occludi quidem volumus cum primis tenebris, sed ad ingressum et egressum obserari et reserari per ianitorem usque ad horam octavam hybernis noctibus et non ultra, ad nonam vero aestivis noctibus et non ulterius. Qui autem ante has suo quoque tempore horas ingressus non est, excludatur, et excluso socio aut pensionario maiori pernoctanti extra Collegium mulcta esto, primo quinque solidi: secundo, decem solidi: tertio, expulsio: scholastico aut pensionario minori duo solidi et sex denarii primo: secundo, quinque solidi, et tertio expulsio. At post clausas portas atque festras, qui aliunde ingressus aut egressus fuerit, expellatur Collegio in aeternum. Ut haec rite gerantur atque observentur, praesidens singulis noctibus vigilanter circumspiciat, ut omnes portae atque valvulae, suis quibus dixi temporibus claudantur et obserentur, et obditis pessulis, claves in Custodis aut suum cubiculum si Custos absit referantur. Hybernas noctes voco, tenebras cuiusque diei naturalis, a primo die Augusti ad festum Annunciationis beatae Mariae. Sed ne inter ea festa ante multam lucem mane aperiantur portae aut festrae, nisi gravi de causa, omnino constituimus. Verum ut porta seu valvae Collegii Gonevilli postremo occlusae noctu sunt, ita primas reserari mane volumus, et toto die (nisi in prandio et coena) patere. Humilitatis quoque portae atque festrae interim dum prandetur et coenatur, clausae sunto. Si quis

[a] Presumably an accepted contraction of *fenestrae*. (It cannot have been accidental, for *festra* is repeated five lines later.)

absence, in his own hand both the day of his departure and the day on which he will be returning; and he shall state the true reason for his departure on his oath furnished to the college.

We also decree that no one shall on any ground or pretext, or under colour of college business of any kind conduct his own business or that of any other person at college expense.

Absence at night and the shutting of the gates.

52. We decree and direct that the Gates of Humility, Virtue and Honour of our College and all their wickets or small gates, and all other gates of both Colleges shall be shut nightly throughout winter-time at the onset of nightfall or dusk, and not re-opened till light the following day, other than the large gate of Gonville College[131] or its wicket, which we indeed wish to be closed at nightfall, but to be locked and opened by the porter to allow entrance and exit until 8 p.m. on winter nights and not after, and until 9 p.m. in summer nights and not later.[132] But anyone who has not come in by the respective time shall be excluded, and the fine for a fellow or major pensioner who is excluded and passes the night outside college shall be 5s. on the first occasion: 10s. on the second occasion: and expulsion on the third: for a scholar or minor pensioner 2s. 6d. on the first occasion: 5s. on the second: and expulsion on the third. But anyone who enters or leaves in any other way after the gates and wickets have been shut shall be expelled from the college for ever. In order that these rules shall be properly carried out and observed, the president shall go round vigilantly each night and check that all gates and their wickets are shut at the times we have specified and that after the bolts have been fastened the keys are taken to the keeper's room or to his own room if the keeper is absent. I class as winter nights the hours of darkness between the first of August and the Feast of the Annunciation of the Blessed Virgin Mary.[133] We lay down firmly that between those dates the gates or wickets shall not be opened before full light in the morning, except for grave cause. It is our clear wish that just as the gates or wickets of Gonville College are the last to be shut at night, so they are to be opened first in the morning and kept open all day (except at lunch and dinner times). Also, the doors and wickets of the Gate of Humility shall be shut during lunch and dinner time. If

[131] As elsewhere, Caius has in mind the physical court, not the legal foundation or corporation. The original gate in Gonville Court opening to Trinity Lane was still the main entrance to the college; it is visible in Loggan's print of 1690.

[132] The gate-hours of closure at 8 p.m. in the winter and 9 p.m. in the summer were already standard in the university: cf. Pole's University Ordinances 1557, Ord. 32; and Elizabeth's Statutes 1570, stat. 50, ord. 34.

[133] 25 March, the start of the English calendar year.

autem horis prandii aut coenae velit ingredi aut egredi, per festram portae Collegii Gonevilli ingrediatur aut egrediatur.

Statuimus etiam, ut porta honoris Collegii nostri una cum festra occludatur interdiu, idque toto die, si id commode potest fieri: at horis quibus legitur aut disputatur in scholis vel maxime: ne transeuntes perrumpant studentium solitudinem, studia inquietent, atria inordinato gressu corrumpant, et lutosa reddant: aedificia violent: neglecta sustollant, et ex privata via, publicam longo usu praescribendo faciant. Proinde cum itum est ad scholas, Ianitor praesto sit qui eam aperiat et recludat.

Statuimus etiam ne quis sociorum, scholarium aut pensionariorum, ullarum huius Collegii portarum aut valvularum claves habeat privatas, imo neque publicas praeter Custodem, aut eo absente praesidentem, ne occultus et furtivus sit egressus aliquando ad maleficia.

De custodia Collegii.

53 Constituimus etiam ut in omnibus concionibus, omnibus tragediis et comoediis extra Collegium habitis atque recitatis, omnibus nundinis, tres minimum socii domi sint, et sex scholastici ex fundatione ad Collegii custodiam: et ut sociorum unus cum scholasticis duobus divagetur per omnes Collegii partes usque dum caeteri redierint, et excubias diligenter agat propter furta, incendia, aut iniurias externas, omnino constituimus. Diligentiores autem fieri volumus, ubi quid in nostro Collegio geratur, ob quod magna scholasticorum aut aliorum confluentia fuerit, ut in concionibus, comoediis aut tragediis, quas privatas esse volumus, si quae fuerint, propter turbas, et interdiu seu meridie propter infortunia.

anyone wishes to enter or leave during the hours of lunch or dinner, he shall do so through the wicket of the gate of Gonville College.

We decree that the Gate of Honour of our College and its wicket shall be shut during the day, and for the whole day, if this can be done conveniently: especially at the hours at which there are lectures and disputations in the Schools; so that people passing through may not disturb the quiet of the students, interrupt their studies, spoil the courts[134] by excessive passage and make them dirty, invade the buildings, cause wear and tear, and turn a private right of way into a public one by prescription through long use. Accordingly, when members of the college go to the Schools, the porter shall be on hand to open and shut that gate.[135]

We decree that no fellow, scholar or pensioner shall have private keys to any of the gates or doors of this college, and even less the public keys, other than the keeper or the president in his absence, lest there should be secret and furtive departures for wrongdoing at any time.

The security of the college.

53. We decree that on the occasion of all public addresses, tragedies and comedies staged and played outside college, and on all market-days, at least three fellows and six scholars on the foundation shall remain in the college for its security;[136] and we firmly decree that one of the fellows with two scholars shall patrol all areas of the college until the others return, and shall keep a diligent watch for thefts, fires or harm from outside. And it is our wish that they shall be even more diligent when anything is taking place in college, because of the large gathering of students[137] and others, as there are at public addresses, comedies or tragedies. These we wish to be private if they do take place, on account of the commotions, and held in the daytime and preferably at mid-day in case of possible accidents.

[134] *Atria*: possibly stair-wells or reception areas, but used elsewhere for courts; see the 1558 draft statute *De Atrio*, prohibiting the bringing of horses and carts into the *atrium*: *Documents*, II, p. 358.

[135] When Caius was writing the Statutes in 1570–72, the Gate of Honour had not yet been built and he had in mind that the porter would open and shut the gate itself. When it was finally constructed it had a wicket, and in his *Interpretatio* in 1575 Parker allowed fellows a key to the wicket during the day. This was the first time that fellows were given their own key to the college. The surviving metal-work indicates that the wicket could be barred at night.

[136] See Parker's *Interpretatio* reducing to two fellows and three scholars the numbers required to remain in college.

[137] *Scholasticorum* would seem to be used here in the sense of students generally rather than scholars on the foundation.

De absentia in regionibus ultramarinis.

54 Statuimus insuper ne cui detur aut absentandi aut studendi copia in transmarinis regionibus, nisi concordi consensu Custodis et omnium Collegii sociorum, idque sub sigillo communi, atque ad annos tantum tres in toto, et non nisi Medicinae studioso, quod Theologia et ius civile pari diligentia et professione hic atque ibi condiscuntur, nec nisi singulis suceessivis vicibus migraturis, et una aliqua universitate studiis suis accommodatissima, ut Patavii, Bononiae, montis pessulani aut Parisiis commoraturis. Sit is ante profectionem Magister artium trium annorum, diligenterque in Aristotile, Platone et Galeno, etiam graece ante versatus. Sit gravis et studiosus. Habeat stipendium integrum detractis in septimanas singulas duodecim denariis, ex statuto Reverendi patris et nostro consensu, uno tantum mense annuatim excepto, detractisque distributionibus, exequiarum nummis et dividendis, ut vocant, sic ut his Collegium fruatur interim. Iurabit ante discessum quicunque profecturus, se studio tantum Medicinae alienas regiones velle invisere, reipublicae Britannicae ac Collegii nostri honori consulere et consulturum.

De absentia scholasticorum.

55 Ordinamus insuper ut stipendiis omnium scholasticorum fundationis huius Collegii, qui abfuerint, ultra mensem continuum vel discontinuum in toto anno, subtrahantur in septimanas singulas, sex denarii, usque dum redierint. Quod si intra menses tres non redierint, priventur omni suo stipendio in aeternum. {*Sociis et pensionariis maioribus in festis nataliciis, pascalibus, beatae Mariae, pentecostes et aliis festis principalibus et maioribus absentibus mulcta esto iii^{s} iiii^{d}.*}[a]

[a] In MS 711, footnote insertion.

Absence abroad.

54. We decree that no financial assistance shall be given to anyone to reside or study overseas except with the common consent of the keeper and all the fellows of the college, given under the college seal, and then for a maximum of three years and only for medical studies, because theology and civil law may be studied here with the same effectiveness and expertise as they are in foreign universities. On the condition moreover that only one goes at a time and then to a single named university most appropriate to his studies, such as Padua, Bologna, Montpellier or Paris. He shall also be a Master of Arts of three years' standing before he goes and well-versed in Greek and in Aristotle, Plato and Galen. He must be sober and studious. He shall have his full stipend minus 12d. a week as allowed by the statute of the Reverend Father and ourself, except for one whole month a year,[138] and minus distributions,[139] exequy money and dividends, as people call them, so that the college enjoys these benefits in the meantime. Before he departs, anyone who is about to go abroad shall swear that he wishes to go to foreign parts solely to study medicine and that he is mindful of the honour of the British state and our college and will continue to be so.

Absence [on the part] of scholars.

55. We direct that, until they return, 6d. a week shall be deducted from the stipends of all scholars on the foundation of this college[140] who shall have been absent for more than one month continuously or at intervals during the year. But if they have not returned within three months they shall be deprived of their whole stipend for ever. For fellows and major pensioners who are absent on the feast-days of Christmas, Easter, the Blessed Mary, Pentecost and other principal and major feast-days the fine shall be 3s. 4d.[141]

[138] Caius fails to make clear whether the month is taken off the stipend or merely off the deduction, but the latter seems more probable.

[139] *Distributiones* regularly appear in the accounts until the reforms of the nineteenth century: 5s at Lady Day and 3s at Michaelmas. The term is nowhere defined in the statutes, but the extra 2s at Lady Day indicates that it refers to Bateman's *prestimonium*, a payment for being resident and available in college, since he had directed that the Master and fellows should have 1s for each of Our Lady's feast days and an extra 2s at Lady Day. See "*Dividends*", § VI. 5, at p. 481, n. 11 below.

[140] *I.e.*, both foundations; cf. Statutes 41 and 66.

[141] See Parker's *Interpretatio* declaring that fine to be just and lawful.

Volumus etiam et ordinamus, ut socii Musici et organistae, ut et scholares Musici et organistae, non absint festis maioribus et solennioribus per omnem annum, imo neque aliis diebus festis, nisi gravi de causa, per Custodem, aut eo absente praesidentem, approbanda.

Statuimus etiam ne scholastici quoquam divagentur sine licentia Custodis, aut eo absente praesidentis, sub poena trium solidorum et quatuor denariorum aut correctionis, prout haec cuique conveniunt, ut si mora in Collegio opus sit, non absint, sed semper praesto sint.

De bursariis, oeconomo, et debitis omnium post rationes seu computa solvendis.

56 Custos et alius socius nostri Collegii notae diligentiae, frugalitatis atque fidei, bursarii seu receptores proventuum annuorum et debitorum Collegii sunto, per Custodem et maiorem sociorum partem quotannis aut in computo S. Michaelis aut Annuntiationis beatae Mariae eligendus; vel duo socii dictarum qualitatum, qui neque prodigi sunt neque aere alieno obstricti, si Custos per negotia nequeat. Hi pecuniam acceptam et expensam in librum accepti et expensi referant, additis singulis summis, suis utriusque nominibus, sua manu scriptis. Volumus etiam ut tertius sit, qui expendat, eisdem, quibus illi conditionibus: et in discrimen, illi bursarii, iste oeconomus appelletur, et si quem sub se habuerit, obsonator seu dispensator nominetur. Primi in annum, tertius in tres menses eligatur: obsonator, qui subest oeconomo, longius aut brevius pro rebus ab eo bene aut male gestis. Sit autem is scholasticus ex fundatione Collegii. Oeconomi cura sit, ut promus, coquusque atque obsonator quoque sua faciant officia, suae fidei commissa conservent, munditiem curent, et perdita restituant. Quod ni fecerint, ipse damnum praestet. Bursarii quam acceperint pecuniam,

We wish and direct that fellows who are musicians and polyphonists,[142] and the scholars who are musicians and polyphonists, shall not be absent on major and solemn feast-days throughout the year, and not even on other feast-days except for grave cause approved by the keeper or the president in his absence.

We decree that scholars shall not wander off without the permission of the keeper or the president in his absence on pain of 3s. 4d. or chastisement, as seems appropriate in each case, so that if there is a need for their presence in college they shall not be absent but always be on hand.

The bursars, steward and the settlement of all debts after accounting.[143]

56. The keeper and another fellow of our college known for his industry, frugality and trustworthiness, who is to be elected by the keeper and the majority of the fellows yearly either at the Michaelmas audit or at the audit on the Annunciation of the Blessed Mary, shall be the bursars or receivers of the annual produce and debts due to the college; or else two fellows with the same qualities who are neither spendthrift nor financially in debt to anyone, if the keeper is unable to transact business. These persons shall record money received and paid out in the book of receipts and expenditure, with the individual amounts entered, written in the name and hand of each of them. It is our further wish that there shall be a third person who shall pay out with the same requirement of record-keeping as the first two; and to distinguish them the first two shall be called bursars and the third steward, and if he should have anyone under him, that person shall be called caterer or purveyor.[144] The first two shall be elected for a year, the third for three months;[145] the caterer, who is under the steward, for longer or shorter periods depending on how well or badly he performs his office. He shall be a scholar on the foundation of the college. It shall be the responsibility of the steward that the butler, the cook, and also the caterer, perform their duties, preserve what is entrusted to their care, maintain cleanliness and make good any losses. If they do not do this, he shall be personally liable for the loss. The bursars shall carry into the counting-house

[142] Cf. Statute 15, and the note on *organistae* by Dr Roger Bowers of Jesus College in "*Supplementary Notes to Caius' Statutes*", § IV. 3, at p. 285 below.

[143] For the emoluments of the bursar and the steward, see "*Stipends*", § VI. 4 below.

[144] For the *oeconomus*, *obsonator* and *dispensator*, see *The steward and his staff* in "*Supplementary Notes to Caius' Statutes*", § IV. 3, at p. 297 below.

[145] In his draft 1558 statutes Caius had provided that the fellow-bursar should be elected, but he had not specified a specific term; and he had directed that the function of steward should be discharged for a period of three months by fellows in order of seniority unless they were profligate or in debt: *Documents*, II, p. 348.

statim in aerarium puro auro aut argento referant, et in cista communi reponant: nec in custodia sua amplius quinque libris unquam habeant: nec in usus suos convertant, aut aliis mutuo dent. Recipiant autem pecuniam in Aula praesenti altero socio. Reddat uterque rationem singulis computis semestribus ordinariis, sed oeconomus singulis tribus mensibus, cum Custos diem dixerit, obsonator oeconomo singulis diebus. Omnes etiam citius et quando Custodi visum est, si eorum aut negligentia, aut inutilitas, aut alia iusta causa subesse visa est, et ad rationes invitet atque etiam cogat, ut malo venienti mature occurrat. Omnes quod debent aut suo aut pupillorum nomine, Collegio persolvant ante dies quindecim, rationes proxime insequentes, exactos, etiam si eius pecuniae alios habeant debitores. Alioqui cogantur iure et occupatione bonorum suorum ad solutionem, et omni fructu iureque sodalitii sui priventur ipso facto usque dum persolverint: neque locum, neque lautiam,[a] hoc est, neque cubiculum neque victum vel suo vel alieno nomine iureve habeant in Collegio usque dum persolverint: quod usu comperimus extrema damna debitorum non persolutorum causa Collegium pertulisse, et magnas turbas et tragoedias[b] in ea excitatas esse. Quod si intra triginta dies non persolverint, ipso facto sint non socii. Quae autem bursariis et oeconomo constituta pcena est pro non solutione debitorum, eandem etiam omnibus aliis sociis et scholaribus debitoribus constituimus. Custodi autem duos menses assignamus, cupimus tamen ut exempli gratia primus solvat, neque quicquam debeat, neque offendatur, si quis ad solutionem provocet. Omnes etiam sive socii sive pensionarii, quod debent suo aut pupillorum nomine, Collegio, oeconomo aut bursariis persolvant, etiam aliis temporibus quam computorum aut diebus quindecim insequentibus. Conquirant autem omnes sua sibi debita, quibus possunt modis legitimis. Nam quibus ante dixi, ut illi persolvant, necessarium et constitutum est.

[a] '*Locus et lauti*' would appear to have been a common phrase for 'board and lodging', not a quotation.

[b] *Sic* here, but elsewhere in MS 711 *tragedias*.

immediately and in pure gold or silver any money that they receive and place it in the common chest;[146] and they shall never have in their custody more than five pounds;[147] nor shall they convert that money to their own use or lend it to anyone else. They shall receive any money in hall in the presence of another fellow;[148] each of them shall render an account at each ordinary six-monthly audit, but the steward shall do so every three months on a day appointed by the keeper, and the caterer to the steward every day. Furthermore, all of them shall render their accounts sooner and when the keeper decides, if there appears to be neglect or incompetence on their part or any other good reason, and he may call for accounts and also insist on them, so that he may forestall any impending crisis. All shall pay to the college what they owe on their own account or that of their pupils within fifteen days next following the accounting, and do so in full, even if they are owed that money by other debtors. Otherwise they shall be compelled to make payment by process of law and distraint of their goods, and they will automatically lose all benefit and entitlement in the society until they have discharged their indebtedness; and they shall have neither board nor lodging, that is, they shall have neither room nor victuals in college in their own or anyone else's name and right until they have paid; because we have learned from experience that the college bears very heavy losses on account of the failure of debtors to pay their debts and that this brings great distress and suffering. But if they do not pay within 30 days they shall *ipso facto* cease to be fellows.[149] And we lay down these penalties for the bursars and steward for the non-payment of debts as well as for all other fellows and scholars who are debtors. But we allow two months' grace to the keeper, though we should like him to be the first to pay as a good example, so that he neither owes anything nor is affronted if anyone should call upon him to settle. Furthermore, all persons, whether fellows or pensioners, shall pay to the steward or the bursars what they owe to the college on their own or their pupils' account, even at other times than the accounting or fifteen days following it; and all should collect debts owed to them by whatever legal means they can, for, as we have said above about them, it is necessary and requisite that they themselves pay.

146 For the *aerarium* and the *cista communis*, see *The arca, cistae, thesaurus and aerarium* in "*Supplementary Notes to Caius' Statutes*", § IV. 3, at p. 288 below.

147 In his draft 1558 statutes Caius had allowed the bursars to hold £10 in copper coinage. The Injunctions of Edward VI (1559) and the statutes of Elizabeth (1559 and 1570) prohibited stewards, bursars and similar officers from having in their custody money for more than one month's provision: Lamb, *Letters* (1838), pp. 142–3, 303; *Documents*, I, p. 493.

148 In his draft 1558 statutes Caius had required the presence of two fellows, but in those statutes there had been only one bursar.

149 *I.e.*, without the need for formal expulsion. See "*John Caius and his Foundation*", § V. 3 below.

Iuramentum Bursariorum.

57[a] Iurabitis per deum omnipotentem et sancta dei evangelia, vos fideliter acturos cum Collegio in officio vestro Bursariorum, et omnem pecuniam Collegii nomine acceptam eidem bona fide restituetis, expensaeque veram et fidelem rationem, sine ulla fraude aut dolo, reddetis; nec utimini Collegii pecunia, aut in usus vestros convertimini, nec aliis eam mutuo dabitis: librosque rationales accepti et expensi scite scriptos Collegio relinquetis, cum officio defuncti fueritis, caeteraque facietis, quae ad officia vestra et vos ex statutis pertinent, ita vos deus adiuvet et sancta dei evangelia.

De Sacellano.

58 Iunior socius nostri Collegii, modo frugi homo et nulli obaeratus sit sacellanus esto pro veteri more, habeatque curam omnium bonorum Sacelli, et in eisdem e cista eximendis et reponendis, ornandoque Sacello, praesto semper praesensque sit, cultumque in eo et munditiem[b] per sacristas, hoc est, per eos qui Bibliam legunt et Sacelli curam habent, curet. Sit inter Collegium et eum bipartitus index omnium Sacelli bonorum de quibus rationem reddet coram Custode et sociis officium relicturus.

De secretario seu registro.

59 Volumus etiam et statuimus, ut ex sociis aliquis qui quam scitissime scribat, et optimi stili sit, eligatur per Custodem et maiorem sociorum partem, qui pro tempore fuerint, in Collegii secretarium seu registrum, in annum, biennium aut triennium, prout spes melioris aut metus deterioris fuerit: ut sine

[a] This is given a separate number in the MSS and in modern printed editions; but it would seem more properly to be part of Statute 56.

[b] *Munditiem* is also used in Statute 56 and is therefore presumably not a clerical error for *munditiam* but a medieval form. [MSS 711, 755, 760 and Lambeth MS 720 have *munditiem*.]

The oath of bursars.

57. You shall swear by Almighty God and His Holy Gospels that you will deal faithfully with the college in your office of bursars, and you will deliver up to the college all money received on its behalf, and render a true and faithful account of expenditure without any fraud or deceit; and that you will not make personal use of the money of the college or convert it to your own uses; nor will you lend it to any others; and that you will hand over to the college properly written account books of income and expenditure when you lay down your office, and do such other things as pertain to your office and are required of you by the statutes, so help you God and His Holy Gospels.

The chaplain.

58. A junior fellow of our college,[150] provided he is a frugal man and is not encumbered with debt, shall be chaplain in accordance with ancient custom and he shall have the care of all the chapel belongings and shall always be present when these are taken out from and returned to the chest[151] and when the chapel is being prepared, and he shall oversee the maintaining and cleaning of it by the sacristans, that is, by those who do the bible readings and have the care of the chapel. He and the college shall have duplicate lists of all the chapel belongings for which he shall account to the keeper and the fellows when he leaves office.[152]

The secretary or registrary.

59. It is our wish and we decree that one of the fellows who writes particularly skilfully and has a good penmanship shall be elected to the office of college secretary or registrary by the keeper and the majority of the fellows at the time, for one, two or three years according as there is hope of better or fear of

[150] Since Caius frequently tended to use the comparative broadly rather than to make precise comparisons, *iunior* is probably used here to mean 'one of the younger' fellows, not *the* junior fellow. The ambiguity is not easily resolved, but it would be surprising if the office were held for an entirely indefinite period until a more junior fellow was elected and then passed immediately to him. Caius also refers to "our college", but presumably in the sense of the whole college (as in Statutes 53 and 82), not in the narrow sense in which the words are used in Statutes 28, 29, 30, 52, and especially 66.

[151] Presumably a quite separate chest, not the "great hutch" or the money-chest which were in the counting-room: see *The arca, cistae, thesaurus and aerarium* in "*Supplementary Notes to Caius' Statutes*", § IV. 3, at p. 288 below.

[152] *Bipartus* would suggest an indenture.

foedatione librorum et varietate literarum, omnia referantur in libros quaeque suos quam pulcherrime, videlicet in rationalem, rationes accepti et expensi: in annales, res gestae singulo quoque anno: in evidentiarum volumen, evidentiae: et in commentarium rerum gestarum seu pandectas, omnia promiscue usque ad tempus computorum. Quo tempore omnia memorabilia secernantur, et in suos cuiusque argumenti libros, ordinis et circumstantiarum habita ratione digerantur. Tot enim libros habeatis volumus in conservationem rerum omnium: rationum videlicet, annalium, evidentiarum et pandectarum, quae commentarium rerum gestarum latino nomine dicimus, praeter librum matriculationis.[a] Quod si quando secretarius absit, et res urgeat, ita scribere alius incipiat, ut utraeque literae uno intuitu sub aspectum non cadant, sed discretae sint vel pagina versa, vel interposito folio. Habeat viginti solidos in subsidium.

Ad extremum[b] illud in universum de omnibus officiariis constitutum volumus, ut si quis in officio ineptus, dormitans aut inutilis Collegio, sociis aut utrisque usu deprehenditur aut dolo malo, fraudeve cum eis egerit, sibi tantum non publicae rei studens ac prospiciens, Custodi et maiori sociorum parti liceat eum quando velint ab officio removere, et alium aptum, vigilantem, bonae frugis atque fidei, ad eum modum, quo iam ante constitutum est, substituere.

De distributione officiorum.

60 Statuimus etiam et ordinamus, ne quis socius plura habeat officia uno, eodem tempore, quo distributio officiorum per omnes socios fiat, pro cuiusque qualitate: nisi duo officia necessario cadant in unum propter duas in eo qualitates eximias praeter caeteros: ut qui idem utilior Collegio et egregius orator est et scite scribit, sit ille et Bursarius et secretarius. At si alter illi par sit alterutra qualitate, singuli singula habeant officia. Subsidia vero duo Galfridi

[a] The inclusion of the Matriculation Book is oddly put, almost as an afterthought, and may suggest that it was added to an earlier list after Caius started that Book in 1559.

[b] The subject matter of this paragraph would suggest that it should be a new statute, and its opening words support that suggestion; but it was not numbered as one.

worse;[153] so that everything can be recorded in his books as neatly as possible without disfiguring the books or in a variety of handwriting, namely, items of income and expenditure in the Account Book: things done in each particular year in the Annals: copies of leases in the Evidences Book: and, in the record book of things done or Pandects, all that has been done corporately up to the time of the audit.[154] By that time everything which is worthy of record shall be separated and arranged in the appropriate books, in its right order and position. For it is our wish that you should have that number of books for preserving a record of all things: namely, Accounts, Annals, Evidences and Pandects, which is the Latin name we give to the record of transactions, in addition to the Matriculation Book.[155] If at any time the secretary is absent and the matter is pressing, someone else shall take over writing, but in such a way that what each person has written shall not appear together at one glance but as separate entries on the back of the page or on an interleaved sheet. He shall have a salary of 20s.[156]

Finally, it is our wish that it be laid down as a universal rule for all officers, that if anyone is found in practice to be incompetent in office, slothful or of no use to the college, to the fellowship or to either of the two, or he acts with bad faith or fraud in his dealings with them, seeking and having in mind only his own advantage and not that of the common good, it shall be lawful for the keeper and the majority of the fellows to remove him from office whenever they wish and substitute another who is suited to the post, vigilant, frugal and faithful, for the remainder of the term for which he had been appointed.

The allocation of offices.

60. We decree and direct that a fellow shall not have more than one office at any one time, so that they can be allocated among all fellows according to the fitness of each; unless two offices necessarily fall upon one person because he has outstanding qualities for both offices above the others. Thus someone who is particularly useful to the college and a distinguished speaker and writes skilfully may be both bursar and secretary. But if there is another who is his equal in either capacity, each shall have a single office. In particular, those on

153 In the 1558 draft statutes the secretary was elected "*in perpetuum*": *Documents*, II, p. 349.

154 For these books, see *Caius and the college's accounts and records* in "*Notes to Caius' Statutes*", § IV. 3, at p. 293 below.

155 The substance of this paragraph must have been written early, because the book referred to as the Pandects was almost immediately confined to acts done in the counting-house; furthermore, the Matriculation Book seems to have been added to the list later: see preceding footnote.

156 See "*Stipends*", § VI. 4 below.

Knight Theologiae Doctoris et unum Magistri Ioannis Whiteacres Clerici apud S. Mariam maiorem quibus collata sunt, alia officia non habeant: nisi officiis magis idonei caeteris sociis fuerint aut necessitas rei atque temporis cogat ut cum subsidio officium etiam eisdem conferatur.

Proviso quod nec subsidium nec officium conferatur inobedienti, rebelli aut contumaci in Custodem aut praesidentem, aut inutili vel sibi vel Collegio, aut hominibus parum studiosis literarum, idque in eorum disciplinam et correctionem: etsi collata iam sunt, per Custodem sustollantur, aut eo absente, praesidentem Custodis mandato.

De concionatoribus.

61 Constituimus praeterea et ordinamus, ut quibus collata sunt subsidia Galfridi Knight et Ioannis Whiteacres iubente Custode, sine praemio concionentur in rectoriis huius Collegii appropriatis per se et apud S. Mariam quoque maiorem Cantabrigiae per se, (quod honoratius est) vel per alium (quod indecentius est), suo sumptu, quoties ad id tenetur Collegium vestrum vel legibus universitatis, vel privatis Collegii: atque etiam apud Barningham in aegritudine aut alio rationali defectu vel impedimento socii Magistri Smythe, per Custodem aut eo absente praesidentem approbando. Constituimus etiam ut socii sacerdotes huius Collegii, consuetis temporibus commemorationum seu commendationum fundatorum et benefactorum, iubente Custode latine concionentur in sacello, et caetera peragant, quae ad id officii pertinent.

De catalogo ingredientium seu de matriculatione.

62 Insuper statuimus ut singuli socii et pensionarii maiores, qui pro tempore fuerint, in tutelam suam scholasticos admissuri, in primo eorum ingressu in Collegium, ante exactas horas viginti quatuor, rem (adductis discipulis) referant Custodi, aut eo absente, praesidenti, et relatis eorum nominibus in catalogum per secretarium examinatoque per Custodem aut, eo absente, praesidentem

whom are bestowed the two salaries of Geoffrey Knight Doctor of Theology and the one salary of Master John Whitacre, clerk, of Great St Mary's, shall not have other offices, unless they are more suited to the offices than the other fellows or the necessity or pressure of time requires that the office is conferred on them in addition to the salary.[157]

Provided that no salary or office is conferred on anyone who is disobedient, rebellious or disrespectful towards the keeper or president, or is of no use to himself or to the college, or is a man too little devoted to learning, and this is intended as a lesson to them to mend their ways; and if such things have already been conferred, they shall be taken away by the keeper or, in his absence, by the president with his authority.

Preachers.[158]

61. We determine and direct that those to whom the salaries of Geoffrey Knight and John Whitacre are allocated shall preach in person in the rectories appropriated to this college without payment as instructed by the keeper, and also at Great St Mary's Cambridge in person (which is fitting) or by deputy (which is unbecoming) at his own expense, whenever your college is obliged to provide a preacher by the laws of the university or its own private ones: and also to preach at Barningham in the event of the sickness or other reasonable inability or impediment of Master Smith's fellow approved by the keeper or the president in his absence.

We further determine that fellows of this college who are priests shall, when directed by the keeper, preach in Latin in the chapel on the traditional occasions of the commemorations or commendations of founders and benefactors and perform those other duties which pertain to their office.

The enrolment of freshmen and matriculation.

62. We decree that all those who are fellows and major pensioners at the time and will be taking scholars into their care shall, on the first arrival of the latter in college, report the fact within twenty-four hours to the keeper or the president in his absence, bringing their pupils with them. And after the pupils' names have been recorded in the matriculation book by the secretary and they

[157] See the note to Statute 61 following.

[158] For the posts established by Geoffrey Knight and John Whitacre, see "*Supplementary Notes to Caius' Statutes*", § IV. 3, at p. 299 below. For the fellowship established by Stephen Smith in 1478 and the holder's obligation to preach at Barningham, Suffolk: see *B.H.* III, p. 214.

unoquoque, sintne grammatici an non, detur commorandi venia locusque aut secus.[a] Non enim volumus, ut quis recipiatur in Collegium qui grammaticus non est, ne ex universitate fiat schola grammaticorum, quo nomine hodie male audit Academia. Horum atque adeo omnium vestro hoc Collegio inhabitaturorum nomina, tum personae, tum patriae, tum parentis atque scholae in catalogum referantur: habita etiam ratione conditionis et aetatis, ut annum decimum quartum habeat unusquisque pensionarius, scholaris ex fundatione sedecim, solvatque pensionarius maior, octo denarios: scholaris seu pensionarius minor, quatuor denarios secretario, praemium libri emendi[b] et in catalogum referendi nomina. Quod si intra horas viginti quatuor nulla fiat significatio, ut supra comprehensum est, singuli tutores, quorum interest, solvant in singulos dies ante significationem in usus Collegii duodecim denarios. Sit autem liber matriculationis in custodia Custodis, aut eo absente, praesidentis. Volumus etiam ut diligens observatio sit, ad quem statum, gradum aut dignitatem quisque ascenderit, qui in matriculationis catalogum sit relatus, ut ea dignitas, status aut gradus eius nomini suo tempore ascribatur, ut si quando opus sit, vobis esse possit in adversis refugio, in secundis ornamento.

De ingredientium nummo.

63 Ordinamus etiam, ut unusquisque primo suo ingressu in Collegium solvat Custodi aut eius locum tenenti, si pensionarius maior sit, sex solidos et octo denarios in usus mensae communis et aliarum rerum necessarios: sin minor, tres solidos et quatuor denarios in usus mensae suae communis et aliarum rerum necessarios. Et si quis matriculatus discesserit, et post redierit, iterum solvat pro ingressu. Quibus acceptis, Custos aut in eius absentia praesidens emat omnia quae ad sacellum, mensam, promptuarium, fontem, fenestras

[a] *Secus*: *i.e.*, he is required to leave if he fails to satisfy the keeper or president as to his competence in Latin and is not given permission to stay.

[b] Presumably "*emendi*" ("to be purchased") as written, not "*emendandi*" ("to be revised").

have each been examined by the keeper or the president in his absence on their knowledge of Latin, they shall be permitted to stay and given a room but not otherwise. For we do not want anyone admitted to the college without a command of Latin, in case the university turns into a grammar-school, as it is already reproached with being.[159] The details of these and indeed of all residents of your college shall be entered in the matriculation book, first their own name, then their native county, then the details of their parent and school; and a note shall be made of their circumstances and age, [to ensure] that every pensioner shall have completed his fourteenth year and scholars on the foundation their sixteenth year, and that each major pensioner shall pay 8d., and a scholar or minor pensioner 4d., to the secretary as a fee for the cost of the book and entering their names in the list. But if within twenty-four hours no entry has been made as is specified above, each tutor concerned shall pay 12d. daily to the use of the college until the entry has been made. The matriculation book shall be in the safe-keeping of the keeper or the president in his absence. It is our further wish that a careful note shall be taken of any position, degree or dignity attained by each person entered in the matriculation book, and that the dignity, position or degree attained shall be entered against his name at the time, so that, if need ever arises, he can provide you with a haven in tempest and be an ornament in fair weather.

The admission fee.

63. We direct that each person on his first admission to the college shall pay to the keeper or his deputy, to be put towards the common meal and other necessaries, 6s. 8d. if he is a major pensioner and 3s. 4d. if he is a minor pensioner.[160] And if anyone who has matriculated leaves and then returns, he shall pay for admission again. The keeper or the president in his absence shall buy out of the proceeds whatever is needed for the chapel, the common table, the store-room,

[159] University statutes forbade the teaching of grammar, *i.e.* Latin, in colleges. An exception was made by Edward VI's Visitors in 1549 in the case of Jesus College as regards its choristers, and this was extended to King's and Trinity (which also had choristers) by Elizabeth's Visitors in 1559: Lamb, *Letters*, pp. 142, 303. The Statutes of Elizabeth 1570, ch. 50, ord. 21, restricted the exception to King's and Trinity. (The reduction in choir music in services under Edward VI had by then led to the discontinuance of boy choristers at Jesus: Bevan and Glazebrook, *Jesus College, The Statutes of 1549/59*, p. 21.)

[160] In the draft 1558 statutes minor pensioners had to pay only 12d.: *Documents*, II, p. 340. At the re-foundation there were 33 pensioners compared with 29 other members in college (*Historiae*, p. 52); Caius deliberately encouraged the admission of major pensioners, who paid larger fees, and there were as many as 11 in 1564 (*B.H.* III, p. 63); see "*John Caius and his foundation*", § V. 3, at p. 344 below. Pensioners' rents accrued to the college and were not included in the dividend *pro cubiculis*; see the section on *Room Rents* in "*Dividends*", § VI. 5 below.

Aulae, et culinam necessaria sunt, et tam accepti quam expensi rationem reddat semestribus rationibus seu computis ordinariis, ut addendo deducendoque videatur quae reliqui summa fiat, ut si quid superfuerit, in aerarium referatur in usus Collegii. Cum in usus Collegii et hoc et aliis statutorum locis dicimus, non in usus personarum Collegii intelligimus, sed in publicum usum publici et realis Collegii (cuius thesauri custos est aerarium): non tam nostrum quam posteritatis nostrae habita ratione. Nam praeter suum cuique stipendium, liberaturam, servitia, distributiones, et officia, nihil ad singulas personas, neque ad easdem iunctas pertinet. Caetera communia sunto, ad communes Collegii usus reservata, ad publicas Collegii nostrorum temporum et posterorum necessitates, incidentes calamitates, fortunae graves adversitates, odiosas lites, decora ornamenta, necessarias aedificationes, utilium fundorum emptiones, et hoc genus alias res communes. Quo magis prohibemus sub poena periurii, expulsionis, et restitutionis rei ablatae, ne quis propria sibi dicat, quae sunt Collegio communia, neve qui inter se distribuant ea, iniquo sensu dicentes se Collegium esse, suaque esse omnia, licereque ea inter se dividere, et ut propria possidere, nullam habentes rationem posteritatis suae. Quasi vero quae Collegii essent, non perinde essent communia posteris atque praesentibus in eosdem usus communes, quos iam ante exposuimus.

De obedientia pensionariorum et solutionibus.

64 Observent omnes pensionarii omnia statuta Collegii se concernentia, obediant Custodi et eo absente eius locum tenenti, nec se intromittant Collegii aut collegarum negotiis aut discordiis, nec damnum faciant aut procurent. Cum discedendum est, debita persolvant, discessus sui per tres dies aut minimum

the well,[161] the kitchen and the windows of the hall, and he shall make a return of income and expenditure in the ordinary six-monthly accounts or audits, so that it can be calculated what balance remains and any surplus may be transferred to the counting-house for the use of the college. When we say "for the use of the college" in this and other places in the statutes, we do not mean for the benefit of the individual members of the college, but for the benefit of the college as a corporate entity (of whose wealth the counting-house is the guardian)[162] to be held not so much for our benefit as that of our posterity.[163] For nothing belongs to any member personally either individually or collectively, apart from his stipend, livery, payments for services, distributions[164] and offices. Everything else shall be kept in common for the corporate uses of the college, for the collective needs of our own and future times, as a provision against possible calamities, heavy misfortunes, vexatious lawsuits, becoming ornamentation, essential building repairs, purchases of income-producing properties, and other communal exigencies of this kind. We forbid emphatically that anyone should claim as his private property those things that are common to the college, on pain of breaking his oath, expulsion and restoration of the object taken; nor shall they distribute them among themselves on the false pretext that they are the college and that all the property is theirs, and that it is lawful to divide it up amongst themselves and thereby enjoy it as their own property without regard for posterity – just as if the property of the college were not the common property of future as well as present generations for those collective uses which we have just expounded above.[165]

Obedience by pensioners and the payment of [their] bills.

64. All pensioners shall observe each of the statutes of the college which apply to them, shall be obedient to the keeper and his deputy in his absence, and shall not involve themselves in the affairs of the college by meddling in its business or its disputes; nor shall they do or cause damage to the college. When it is time to go down, they shall pay their bills, and give three or at least two days' notice

[161] The *fons ille culinarius* in the kitchen quarters, which was closed in 1578 when a fountain was erected in Gonville Court: *Annals*, p. 190.

[162] See *The arca, cistae, thesaurus and aerarium* in "*Supplementary Notes to Caius' Statutes*", § IV. 3, at p. 288 below.

[163] The term 'use' had a technical legal meaning of the beneficial interest enjoyed under a trust or use, devices that were particularly popular for protecting future beneficiaries.

[164] The prest-money allowed half-yearly by Bateman to fellows who made themselves available in college on specific days: see note to Statute 54; also "*John Caius' Exposition of the Statutes of William Bateman*", § III. 3, at p. 103 above, and "*Dividends*", § VI. 5, at p. 481 below.

[165] A condemnation of the management of Gonville Hall under Bacon?

duos Custodem aut eo absente praesidentem ante admoneant, quam discedant. Haec omnia nisi fecerint, statuimus, ut eorum fideiussores, quos unumquemque habere volumus in primo ingressu suo in Collegium, idem praestent et persolvant: et illi mulctentur pro arbitrio Custodis, aut eo absente, praesidentis.

De tutore et fideiussore pupillorum et pensionariorwm et solutionibus.

65 Statuimus insuper et ordinamus ut omnes scholastici et pensionarii, habeant socios Collegii tutores et praedes, ne quid damni aut desperati debiti Collegio accidat, utque[a] si quod damnum accidat aut debitum, tutores et praedes seu fideiussores praestent. Sed ne tutoribus quidem aut fideiussoribus parcendum, si quid nomine suo, pupillorum, aut eorum pro quibus fidem fecerint debeant ultra mensem: quod his suo vitio magna ex parte indigis, non est saepissime quod solvant ultra tempus menstruum. Si tutores et praedes fallant, priventur ipsi omni Collegii beneficio usque dum persolverint,[b] et aliis rationibus supra memoratis cogantur ad solutionem seu pecuniae pensionem.

De pensionariis debitoribus.

66 Constituimus etiam ut pensionarii tam maiores quam minores nostri Collegii singulis septimanis, singulis summum quindecim diebus pro arbitrio oeconomi persolvant eidem oeconomo quod eorum nominibus expensi aut mulctae nomine ascriptum est, alioqui omni victu excludantur usque dum persolverint: utque etiam pensiones cubiculorum utriusque Collegii tertio quoque mense persolvantur, praeterea constituimus.

Volumus etiam et statuimus, ut pensionarius optimi cuiusque cubiculi Collegii Gonevilli pensionem solvat annuatim eidem Collegio in reparationes eiusdem, prout decretum est communi consensu Custodis et sociorum duodecimo decembris 1569.

Ubi in statutis nostris scribo utrumque Collegium seu utriusque Collegii, non intelligo diversa esse ratione et incorporatione Collegia, sed aedificio tantum et authore, in distinctionem rerum utriusque Collegii, inque proprium in loquendo usum, et ne usus peccet in memoriam.

[a] *Sic* MSS 711, 755 and Lambeth MS 720; printed as *atque* by Commissioners and Venn. MS 760 has "*ut si quod*".

[b] Sic MSS 711, 755, 760 and Lambeth MS 720; printed as *usque eo dum persolverit* by Commissioners and Venn.

of their departure to the keeper or the president in his absence before they go. Unless they have done all these things, we decree that their sureties, whom we require each one to have on their first admission to the college, shall be liable for and pay their debts; and they themselves shall be fined at the discretion of the keeper or the president in his absence.

The tutor and surety of pupils and pensioners and payment of [their] bills.

65. We decree and direct that all scholars and pensioners shall have fellows of the college as tutors and sureties, lest any loss or bad debt falls upon the college, and so that, if any loss or debt does occur, the tutors and sureties or guarantors shall be liable for it. But tutors or guarantors shall in no way be spared if they owe for more than a month anything on their own behalf or that of those who are their pupils or for whom they have gone surety: because it rarely happens that those who largely have themselves to blame for being in debt pay up after a month. If tutors and sureties default, they shall themselves be deprived of all benefit from the college until they have paid, and they shall be compelled by the other means mentioned [in Stat. 56] above to make payment in full or by instalments.

Indebted pensioners.

66. We determine that both major and minor pensioners of our college shall each pay weekly or at most fortnightly to the steward as he decides whatever is debited to their names as expenses or fines on pain of exclusion from all meals until they have paid; and we further determine that the rents of the rooms in each College shall be paid quarterly.

We wish and decree that each pensioner shall make the repair-payment for his chosen room in Gonville College annually to that College, as decreed by the common consent of the keeper and fellows on 12 December 1569.

Where I write in our statutes "each College" or "of each College" I do not mean that the Colleges are different in purpose or incorporation, but only in respect of buildings and founder, in the context of which I use particular language to distinguish the property of each. [I clarify] this lest [my] usage should be misunderstood in the future.

De ratione discedentium et solutione.

67 Statuimus insuper, ut ineatur ratio debiti cum quocunque discessuro a Collegio, et morte vel aliter Collegium relicturo, ut si quid Collegio debeat, ante discessum aut mortem persolvat. Quod si facere recusaverit, aut idoneos fideiussores non dederit, retineantur eius bona Collegii nomine usque dum persolverit. Quae bona si non redemerit intra mensem, venalia proscribantur. Et si debitis non aequentur et solvendo non suffecerint, intendatur actio debiti de reliquo aut universo in eum qui discesserit, aut in executores aut fideiussores eius qui obierit, et prosequendum ad solutionem extremi debiti.

De mensa communi.

68 Ad haec, statuimus et ordinamus ut omnes et singuli socii et pensionarii maiores vestri Collegii in universitate existentes, in mensa communi vivant suis ipsorum omnium sumptibus, sub poena pretii commeatus communis singularum septimanarum, in quibus a mensa vel semel uno die abfuerint, persolvendi in usus Collegii, nisi gravi aliquo morbo, per Custodem aut eius locum tenentem approbando, in cubiculis detineantur ut egredi non possint sine valetudinis dispendio. Idem etiam observandum statuimus scholasticis in sua mensa communi, sub poena duodecim denariorum in commeatum communem reliquorum commensalium singulis septimanis quibus sine licentia abfuerint vel {*semel*}[a] uno die persolvendorum.

De observandis consuetudinibus antiquis in mensa.

69 Sit eadem vivendi ratio in mensa {*et alibi in Collegio*}[b] quae olim in qualitate et quantitate ciborum, in abstinentia et observatione dierum, nisi aliter a domino rege[c] et ecclesia constitutum sit.

[a] Interlined insertion in MS 711.
[b] Interlined insertion in MS 711.
[c] *a domino rege*: Cf. the use of the term "Court of King's Bench", even though the 'King' was Elizabeth.

The settlement of accounts on departure.

67. We decree that a statement of account shall be produced for anyone about to depart from the college through death or any other reason, so that if he owes anything to the college he can pay it before departure or death. But if he refuses to do this, or does not produce suitable sureties, his goods shall be retained in the name of the college until he has made payment, and if he has not redeemed them within a month they shall be put up for sale. If he is not good for his debts and cannot settle them, an action of debt for the whole or for the balance shall be brought against the person who has departed, or against the executors or sureties of anyone who has died, and it shall be pursued until the debt has been paid in full.

The common table.

68. As to this we decree and direct that each and every fellow and major pensioner of your college while at the university shall take all meals at their common table entirely at their own expense, on pain of paying to the use of the college the charge for commons for each week in which they have been absent from table for even one day, unless they are detained in their rooms by some grave illness recognised by the keeper or his deputy which prevents their going out without danger to health.[166] We further decree the same rule for scholars at their common table on pain of 12d. towards the commons of the rest of the diners[167] for each week in which they shall have been absent without permission even for one day.

Observance of ancient customs at table.

69. The standard of meals at table and elsewhere in college shall be that which has been customary in respect of the quality and quantity of food, abstinence [from meat] and observance of the [liturgical] calendar, unless laid down otherwise by the Sovereign and the Church.

166 The danger might be to the health of other diners, not just that of the excused person. See Parker's *Interpretatio* allowing anyone to be absent with the keeper's agreement, even if they are not ill, provided that they do not partake of a meal in the college.

167 Diners at *that* table, presumably, not all diners in Hall. Minor pensioners and sizars were recorded in the Matriculation Book as being admitted to the Scholars' Table.

De ministris mensae communis.[a]

70 Ordinamus etiam ut pro veteri consuetudine huius Collegii, ministri qui mensae inserviunt, sint scholastici ex fundatione et hi tantum tres: tribus senioribus sociis, singuli, sed ita ut isti non ante inserviant mensae, quam approbati fuerint per Custodem: Custos autem {~~*qui minimum unum habere debet*~~}[b] famulum ministrum habeat {*et unum scholasticum quem velit ex fundatione.*}[c]

{~~*Volumus etiam ut ex his ministris aliqui sint Norfolcienses, aliqui Suffolcienses et*~~}[d] Sint ii ex pauperioribus et doctioribus { },[e] et in quibus melior spes est honestatis, gravitatis et bonae frugis.

De ratione reddenda singulis diebus sabbati.

71 Ordinamus insuper et statuimus, ut singulis diebus sabbati statim a prandio accumbentibus adhuc sociis et pensionariis, ad campanae sonitum, ratio reddatur palam in Aula aestivo, aut conclavi hyberno tempore, omnium eorum quae omnium nomine expensa sunt ea septimana, idque omnibus praesentibus si fieri potest. Si negotia impediant, saltem tribus praeter oeconomum,[f] quibus Custos aut praesidens moram indixerit, variatis vicibus singulis septimanis pro ratione et ordine cubiculorum. Qui iubente Custode aut praesidente interesse noluerint, mulcta esto duodecim denarii, communi sumptui mensae impendendi.

a For this statute see Plate III above.

b MS 711 here includes and deletes the words "*qui minimum unum habere debet*". Other MSS omit them.

c Interlined insertion in MS 711.

d MS 711 here includes and deletes the words "*Volumus etiam ut ex his ministris aliqui sint Norfolcienses, aliqui Suffolcienses et*" and replaces them with "*Sint ii*".

e MS 711 here includes and deletes two indecipherable words.

f The punctuation incorrectly inserted in the 1852 text and by Venn is misleading and has been corrected.

Waiters at the common table.

70. We direct, in accordance with the long-established custom of this college, that the waiters who serve at table shall be scholars on the foundation and as many as[168] three of these, one for each of the three senior fellows,[169] but on condition that they shall not wait at table until they have been approved by the keeper; the keeper may have one scholar of his choice on the foundation as his personal waiter.

They are to be chosen from the poorer and more learned [scholars] who show promise of honesty, sobriety and good achievement.[170]

The rendering of account each Saturday.

71. We further direct and decree that each Saturday, immediately after lunch while the fellows and pensioners are still seated at table, at the ringing of the bell an account shall be given openly, in hall in summer or in the parlour in winter, of all those expenses which have been incurred in the name of everyone and paid during the week, and that shall be done in the presence of everybody if this is possible;[171] if business prevents this, then in the presence of at least three persons (in addition to the steward),[172] whom the keeper or president shall select to stay, taken in turn each week according to room number and order. The fine for those who refuse to stay when required by the keeper or president shall be 12d., to be put towards the expenses of the common table.

168 But possibly "at least" three of these – depending on the meaning of *tantum*.

169 Although the proper classical interpretation should perhaps be that the three most senior fellows had one waiter each and the other fellows had to fend for themselves, Caius' use of the distributive leaves some doubt whether he did not mean that each group of three fellows by seniority had one waiter, *i.e.*, that the three waiters served nine fellows, particularly since he seems to have regarded the privilege of having a waiter to oneself as being confined to the Master (cf. the deleted phrase). For this statute see Plate III above.

170 Waiting at the fellows' table apparently conferred the advantage of eating up the left-overs (*B.H.* III, p. 182).

171 In his draft statutes in 1558 Caius had made attendance optional, apart from a requirement for two plus the steward: *Documents*, II, p. 346. For the term *conclave* see the note to Statute 28 above.

172 Only two (in addition to the steward) had been required in the draft 1558 statutes: see preceding note.

De publicis ei privatis conviviis.

72 Ordinamus etiam et constituimus ne solennes epulae in festo Annuntiationis beatae Mariae virginis, et in festo conceptionis beatae Mariae, Collegii nomine celebratae, excedant una vice quadraginta solidos, quod velimus eas moderatas esse. Quod si ultra expensum sit, id communi Custodis et sociorum sumptui pro more veteri, non privato Collegii nomini ascribatur.

Praeterea statuimus ne oeconomus, obsonator seu dispensator, expendant ipsi, aut tradant alteri Collegii pecuniam in privata convivia cuiusquam sociorum, scholarium vel pensionariorum, aut in alias {*res*}[a] privatas eorum emendas, sub poena restituendae pecuniae, et praeterea mulctae viginti solidorum aut pluris, pro iudicio Custodis, aut eo absente, praesidentis indicendae.

Proviso ut liceat singulis sociis ex promptuario duodecim tantum denariorum panem atque potum singulis septimanis in usus proprios suo sumptu assumere, modo id non faciant ad alendos malefactores aut criminosos, quos statuta aut in aeternum excludunt, aut ad tempus amovent aut commeatu mulctant. Qui autem istos aluerit, aut eis aliquo modo subsidio fuerit, nisi destiterit prima admonitione, pro inimico Collegii habeatur, et Collegio et omni eius beneficio excludatur in aeternum: usque adeo alienos cupimus omnes a seditione, abominanda illa corruptela morum, calamitate et peste tranquillitatis et literarum.

[a] Interlined insertion in MS 711.

Public and private entertaining.

72. We direct and determine that the solemn banquets on the feast of the Annunciation of the Blessed Virgin Mary and the feast of the Conception of the Blessed Mary[173] celebrated in the name of the college shall not exceed 40s. on any one occasion, for we wish them to be moderate. But if more is spent, this shall be charged to the keeper and fellows on their commons accounts in accordance with ancient custom, and not charged to the college itself.

In addition we decree that the steward and the caterer or purveyor shall not themselves spend or pay out to another person any college money for private entertaining by any of the fellows, scholars or pensioners, or on other private purchases for them, on pain of restoring the money and paying in addition a fine of 20s. or more to be fixed at the discretion of the keeper or the president in his absence.

Provided that fellows individually shall be allowed to draw bread and drink from the buttery[174] for their own use and at their own expense to the value of not more than 12d. each week,[175] provided they do not do this to feed wrongdoers and guilty men whom the statutes have either excluded for ever or suspended for a time or fined by way of forfeiture of commons. Anyone who feeds those persons, or gives support to them in any way, shall be deemed an enemy of the college, if he does not desist from doing so at the first warning, and he shall be excluded from it and from all benefit from it for ever: so great is our desire to keep everyone from sedition, that abominable corrupter of morals, and from calamity and ruin of peace and learning.[176]

173 25 March and 8 December. See Parker's *Interpretatio* prohibiting the celebration of the Feast of the Conception.

174 *Ex promptuario*: presumably from the buttery. This was re-sited and rebuilt a few years later in 1578: *Annals*, p. 190.

175 'Beevers'; cf. the Ordinances of 16 October 1516 for the practice in Peterhouse (*Documents*, II, 51) and the statutes of Jesus College 1516, ch. xx for the rules of that college (Bowen and Glazebrook, *Statutes of Jesus College 1549/1559*, p. 34). Venn, however, thought that the statute refers here to "breakfast" and that 'beever' was a monastic term that applied to a similar evening event: *B.H.* III, pp. 181, 184.

176 Contrast Caius' more mellow view of warming drinks after winter disputations in his draft statutes of 1558: *Documents*, II, 334. The change in attitude may possibly reflect the disputes which led to the expulsion of Dethick, Warner and Spenser in 1565: see "*John Caius and his Foundation*", § V. 3 below.

De mulcta solvenda.

73 Statuimus insuper ut nemo mulctam sibi pro offensa secundum statuta inflictam solvere recuset cum requisita fuerit, sub poena deprivationis ab omni Collegii beneficio usque dum persolverit.

Volumus etiam ut in singulis rationibus seu computis ordinariis semestribus, praesidens reddat rationem mulctarum acceptarum, ut eorum nominibus qui deliquerint ascribantur in rationum libris.

Volumus item ut omnes mulctae cedant Collegio, nisi aliter expresse ordinatum sit per nos. Quia usu comperimus, si in usus mensae communis conferantur, in rationes accepti et expensi cuiusque septimanae socios non libenter relaturos, si Custos absit: quod se mutuo in delictis parcant, in quae saepissime incidunt, et operas mutuas tradere desiderant. Quae cautio ideo a nobis posita est, non quod suppliciis delectamur, sed ut vitia prohibeamus, ut ne quis in ea incidat praemoneamus: ac si incidat, ne qua se evasurum putet doceamus, atque ita bonus[a] fiat vel invitus studeat, quo omnia statuta nostra referuntur.

De secretis non revelandis.[b]

74 Volumus etiam et ordinamus, ne quis secreta Collegii cuiquam revelet, sub poena periurii aut quadraginta solidorum, pro arbitrio Custodis, aut, eo absente, praesidentis.

Statuimus etiam, ut si quis, a Custode aut praesidente iussus ut e cubiculo {*aut mensa*}[c] discedat, cum quid perpetraverit ob quod nec usum cubiculi aut mensae habere poterit ex statuto vel ad tempus vel in aeternum, vi restiterit nec obedierit, vis vi repellatur sine personarum nocumento, et foris eiiciatur a cubiculo {*aut mensa*}[d] et excludatur Collegio et omni eius beneficio in aeternum.

Ad postremum, si provisum sufficienter non sit omnibus incidentibus, (est enim difficile) volumus et statuimus, ut offensarum punitio atque mulcta penes iudicium et discretionem Custodis aut, eo absente, praesidentis sit, sed cum consilio Custodis.

a MS 755 has "*ita ut bonus*", which seems to make better sense. MS 760 has *ita vel bonus.*
b The second and third paragraphs of this statute should, properly, be distinct statutes.
c Interlined insertion in MS 711.
d Interlined insertion in MS 711.

Payment of fines.

73. We decree that no one shall refuse to pay any fine for offences imposed on him in accordance with the statutes when he is called upon to do so, on pain of deprivation of all benefit from the college until he does so.

We further will that the president shall present an account of fines received at each regular half-yearly account or audit, so that the names of those who have been at fault may be entered in the account books.

It is our wish also that all fines shall go to the college unless we have expressly directed otherwise. The reason is that we have learned by experience that if they are put to the benefit of the common table, the fellows do not readily record them in the weekly accounts of its income and expenditure, if the keeper is absent: because they let each other off in respect of the sort of offences in which they are themselves frequently involved, and are willing to do each other a good turn.[177] We put in this caveat not because we take delight in imposing punishments but so that by forbidding vices we may warn anyone against falling into them; and so that, should anyone do so, we may teach him that he should not think he can escape; and thus he may become good or seek reluctantly to be so, which is the aim of all our statutes.

Confidentiality.

74. We wish and direct that no one shall reveal the secrets of the college to anyone on pain of breaking his oath or [being fined] 40s., as decided by the keeper or the president in his absence.

We decree that if anyone has been ordered by the keeper or president to leave his room or the common table when he has done something for which a statute deprives him of the use of room or common table temporarily or permanently and he stays put and refuses to obey, force shall be met with force without harm to any person and he shall be ejected from his room or the common table and excluded from college and deprived of all benefit of it for ever.

Finally, if any provision does not sufficiently meet all situations (for it is difficult to do so), we wish and decree that punishment and fine for offences shall lie in the jurisdiction and discretion of the keeper or the president in his absence but with his knowledge.

[177] The reference to fellows was later used as an excuse to limit the whole paragraph to fines on fellows, thus allowing the deans to receive the junior members' fines in lieu of a stipend: see Branthwaite's accusation and the fellows' answer in *Allen's Case* (1617) Appendix F, discussed in "*Stipends*", § VI. 4, at pp. 405–7 below.

Hactenus de personis Collegii diximus, deinceps de rebus eiusdem et possessionibus statuemus.[a]

De aedificiis, atrio, aliisque locis atque rebus Collegii conservandis.

75 Statuimus insuper et ordinamus, ut aedificia resque Collegii illesae conserventur et ne quis (etiam si Custos fuerit) addat aut detrahat eisdem, diruat, aedificet mutet ve[b] quicquam sine consilio et assensu Custodis et trium seniorum aut saniorum, graviorum et experientium virorum Collegii, ne per imprudentiam aedes aut debilitentur aut collabantur. Quod si de fundamento, trabe, tigno, muro parte ve[c] alia principaliori res agetur, non sine consilio architecti, fabri materiarii aut cementarii negotium transigatur.

Ad haec, ne suffodiantur muri aut aedes, statuimus et arctius iniungimus, ne quis cuniculos aut canes in nostro Collegio alat.

De incendio.

76 Praeterea ordinamus, ut unusquisque foco suo et lucernis prospiciat, et ne quis candelas columnis, parietibus aliis ve[d] ligneis materiebus affigat, sub poena expulsionis, damni praestandi (si quid fuerit) et mulctae gravioris.

[a] This is, in effect, the start of Part II and is treated as such in MSS 711, 755 and 760. MS 711 leaves a page (p. 75) blank before Part II; the layout here mirrors that of MSS 755 and 760.

[b] *Sic* MS 711.

[c] *Sic* MS 711.

[d] *Sic* MS 711.

So far we have spoken of the members of the college. Hereafter we shall make statutes about its property and possessions.[178]

The buildings, court[179] *and other places and property of the college.*

75. We decree and direct that the buildings and property of the college shall be kept undamaged and that no one (even if he should be the keeper) shall add to or take anything away from them, demolish, build or change anything without the advice and agreement of the keeper and three senior or more weighty fellows,[180] sober and experienced men of the college, lest by imprudence the buildings become weakened and collapse. But if anything needs to be done to a foundation, beam, woodwork, wall or other part of the main structures, no work shall be commissioned without the advice of an architect, carpenter or mason.

To ensure that the walls and dwellings shall not be undermined we decree and strenuously enjoin that no one shall keep rabbits or dogs in our college.[181]

Fire.[182]

76. We direct that each and every one shall take care of his hearth and lights, and that no one shall attach candles to columns, walls or other woodwork, on pain of expulsion, making good the damage (if any) and paying a very heavy fine.

[178] See note to Latin text. Caius had already made the same division into two Parts in his draft statutes in 1558: *Documents*, II, p. 352. The fact that many of the provisions relating to the college's estates had already been drafted before Caius became Master was perhaps due to the difficulties that were concealed in the grant to him of the manors of Croxley, Runcton and Burnham Thorpe: see *Caius' purchase of the Manors of Croxley, Runcton and Burnham Thorpe* in "*Supplementary Notes to Caius' Statutes*", § IV. 3, at pp. 302–8 below.

[179] For "*atrium*" see note to Latin text of Statute 52. Caius speaks of only one court and failed to alter his rubric to the plural; he did likewise in Statute 78.

[180] Caius had not included *saniorum* ("more weighty") when he first drafted the statute in 1558: *Documents*, II, p. 357.

[181] For livestock see also Statute 22.

[182] Fire was a hazard much in Caius' mind; there had been a serious fire in college in 1564, and again in 1566, which he carefully recorded in his Annals: *Annals*, pp. 111, 122.

De damnis non faciendis.

77 Item ne quis damnum inferat ostiis, proostiis[a] foribus, portis, fenestris, seris, vitris, mensis, domibus, muris, hortis, arboribus, aut aliis rebus nostri Collegii secando, sculpendo, rumpendo aut aliis modis vitiando aut corrumpendo constituimus, sub poena damni praestandi et mulctae ulterius persolvendae pro discretione Custodis aut eius locum tenentis.

De atrii munditie.

78 Volumus etiam et ordinamus ne quis Collegii muros eiusdem aut portas permingat, atrium aut hortos aqua aut urina defoedet, aut currus equosve introducat, nisi aedificationis causa, aut lignis, ossibus, aliisve quibuscunque rebus occupet aut conspergat, aut lectos, stragula peristromatave soli exponat, sub poena trium solidorum et quatuor denariorum, totiens quotiens.

De libris Collegii.

79 Statuimus et ordinamus, ne quis nostri Collegii libros bibliothecae publicae laceret, male tractet, apertos relinquat aut abstrahat, signacula tollat, sub poena imponenda pro discretione Custodis, aut eius locum tenentis. Qua de causa volumes, ut quotannis professor graecae et latinae linguae curam habeat bibliothecae communis, prospiciatque ne surripiantur libri, aut aperte relinquantur, aut damnum nocumentumve patiantur, sibique coniunctum habeat scholasticum aliquem ex fundatione gravem et studiosum per Custodem eligendum in maiorem curam et diligentiam, et in bibliothecae munditiem. Quod officium nisi rite exequantur, mulcta esto professori singulis vicibus duodecim denarii, scholastico sex denarii.

[a] In his draft statutes in 1558, Caius had written "*postibus*" (gate-frames) not "*proostiis*". It is unclear what difference he had in mind between *ostiis*, *proostiis foribus*, and *portis*, or whether "*proostiis foribus*" is to be read together as a single concept.

Avoidance of damage.

77. We determine that no one shall do damage to the outer or inner gate-ways,[183] gates, doors, windows, locks and bolts,[184] glass, tables, dwellings, walls, gardens, trees or other things of our college by cutting, carving, breaking or by damaging or ruining in other ways, on pain of making good the damage and paying a fine in addition at the discretion of the keeper or his deputy.

Cleanliness of the court.[185]

78. We wish and direct that no member of the college shall relieve himself upon its walls or doors, or foul the court or gardens with water or urine, or bring in carts or horses, otherwise than for building purposes, or fill them with, or scatter in them, firewood or bones or any other things, or lay out beds, blankets or carpets in the sun, on pain of paying 3s. 4d. whenever it happens.[186]

The books of the college.

79. We decree and direct that no one of our college shall tear the books of the communal library of our college, maltreat them, leave them open or off their shelves, make any marks in them on pain of a penalty to be imposed at the discretion of the keeper or his deputy. For this reason it is our wish that each year the person teaching Greek and Latin shall have charge of the communal library and take care that books are not surreptitiously removed or left about open or suffer loss or harm, and he shall have the assistance of a sober and studious scholar on the foundation selected by the keeper for the better care, management and cleanliness of the library. If the task is not performed properly, the teacher shall be fined 12d. on each occasion and the scholar 6d.

[183] See note to Latin text.

[184] Or perhaps "bars".

[185] Caius originally drafted his statute before Caius Court was built; hence the fact that he confines his injunction to one court (as he did in Statute 75), in contrast to the "gardens". Cf. the 1558 draft statute *de Atrio*: *Documents*, II, p. 358.

[186] In 1558 the fine for scholars had been less severe, 12d. for adults and corporal punishment for younger scholars: *Documents*, II, p. 358.

De clavibus aerarii non denegandis Custodi et maiori sociorum parti.

80 Statuimus etiam et ordinamus, ne quis clavium custos, Custodi Collegii et maiori sociorum parti claves aerarii et cistae communis deneget, aut factioso, inobedienti, prodigo, aut alieno a nostro Collegio tradat, sub poena expulsionis ipso facto.

De obsignandis scriptis.

81 Statuimus insuper, ne qua charta aut quod pargamenum mundum et non scriptum, signo publico obsignetur, neve aliud scriptum, nisi id publice in aerario distincte et clara voce coram Custode et sociis omnibus in universitate existentibus perlegatur, nec nisi Custos et maior sociorum omnium pro tempore existentium et praesentium pars (si res magni momenti sit) in obsignationem eiusdem expresse consenserit, nec nisi in commentarium rerum gestarum prius referatur. Atque ut lubentius socii intersint, volumus ut omnes socii praesentes coniunctim habeant pro unoquoque sigillo, quod non Collegii tantum causa concedendum sit, decem solidos ex eo, cui sigillum conceditur. Habeat etiam Collegium ex eodem pro cera duodecim denarios.

De vasis argenteis.

82 Ordinamus insuper, ut vasa argentea nostri Collegii, quae aut nostra aut aliorum donatione, aut aliis rationibus possidetis, non vendantur, non donentur, non quoquo modo alienentur, aut de loco in locum extra Collegium transferantur, neque cuiquam accommodentur aut oppignorentur, neve inter Custodem et socios dividantur ut propria, sed concludantur in arca communi, et conserventur in usus Collegii, et in casus adversos incendii aut ruinae

The obligation not to withhold the keys of the counting-house from the keeper and majority of the fellows.[187]

80. We decree and direct that no key-keeper shall withhold the keys of the counting-house and common chest from the keeper and the majority of the fellows; nor shall he hand them over to anyone who is disaffected, disobedient, thriftless or is not a member of our college, on pain of automatic expulsion.

Sealing of documents.

81. We decree that no charter or parchment of any kind which is blank and not written on shall be sealed with the common seal, nor shall anything be written unless it has first been read out publicly aloud and distinctly in the counting-house in the presence of the keeper and all the fellows resident in the university and then, if it is a matter of great importance, only if the keeper and the majority of the fellows at the time, being present, expressly consent to its being sealed, and only if it is first recorded in the *Gesta*.[188] And so that the fellows may be more ready to participate, we wish all fellows present to have jointly for each sealing (other than sealings done solely for collegiate purposes) the sum of 10s. from the person for whose benefit the sealing is done. The college shall also receive from that person 12d. for the wax.

Silver vessels.

82. We direct that the silver vessels of our college[189] which you possess from our own or another's gift or in any other ways shall not be sold, given or parted with in any way, or moved from place to place outside the college, nor lent or pledged to anyone, nor divided between the keeper and fellows as their own property. But instead they shall be locked away in the common ark[190] and kept as corporate property for college use and against the risk of fire or collapse of

[187] See *The arca, cistae, thesaurus and aerarium* in "*Supplementary Notes to Caius' Statutes*", § IV. 3, at p. 288 below.

[188] In the *Pandectae*, not the (later) *Acta*: see *Caius and the college's accounts and records* in "*Supplementary Notes to Caius' Statutes*", § IV. 3, at p. 293 below. In 1558 Caius had written "*in librum actorum*" (*Documents*, II, p. 354).

[189] The words "our college" are used here in the wider sense, as in Statute 58; see the note to that statute.

[190] For the *arca*, see *The arca, cistae, thesaurus and aerarium* in "*Supplementary Notes to Caius' Statutes*", § IV. 3, at p. 288 below.

aedificiorum (quod tamen Deus avertat) ut communia. In quibus casibus volumes, ut vendantur, si aliter non sit, unde reficiantur ac reparentur, quae adversa fortuna inciderunt: et ne in usus publicos veniant, nisi cum solennitas festi, loci, hoc est, Annuntiationis beatae Mariae, aut in commemorationibus aut exequiis fundatorum, et temporibus visitationum, et superintendentium et ea pauca, aut magnatum aut summorum Collegii amicorum adventibus, non autem in comitiis Magistrorum, et determinationibus Baccalaureorum, constituimus: quod usu observavimus peiora omnia, sordidiora, contusa et rasa magis redire ad aerarium quam cum exempta fuerant. Excipio Custodis aut praesidentis comitia, nec iis quidem nisi laventur aqua munda atque calida et sapone, purissimisque linamentis undique exsiccentur prius, quam reponantur vasa. Idem de iis linamentis Collegii quae ad solenniores usus asservantur, ordinamus. Excipio ea etiam quae quotidianis usibus mensae communis Custodis et sociorum necessaria sunt, ut salinaria duo aut tria, et cochlearia quot sunt in mensa personae: excipio etiam poculum[a] unum et crateres duos in usus Custodis, aut eo absente praesidentis, ad excipiendos Collegii amicos. Horum omnium ratio reddatur annis singulis a Custode aut praesidente, coram sociis: illorum a promo quidem coram oeconomo, ab oeconomo vero coram Custode atque sociis pro tempore et quoties caeterarum rerum Collegii ratio reddenda est ex statuto.

Fiat etiam inter Custodem et Collegium et inter oeconomum et Custodem bipartitus index communi cista reponendus, ut si quid pereat aut corruptum sit, per eum restituatur, cuius vitio peribat aut corrumpebatur.

[a] *pocula unum et crateres duos* according to the 1852 text; but Venn and MSS 711, 755, 760 and Lambeth MS 720 have the undoubtedly correct *poculum unum et crateres duos*.

buildings (which God forbid). In those cases it is our wish that they be sold, if there is no alternative, so that the damage caused by the disaster may be repaired and made good. And we determine that the vessels shall not be brought out for public use except when the solemnities of the feast of this place are being celebrated, that is, the Feast of the Annunciation of the Blessed Virgin Mary, or at commemorations or exequies for founders or at times of visitations and visits by the superintendents,[191] which times are rare, or visits by magnates or distinguished friends of the college; but not at assemblies of Masters or examinations of Bachelors,[192] because we know from experience that everything returns to the counting-house in a worse state, dented and scratched, than when it was taken out. I make an exception for meetings of the keeper or president, and not even then unless the vessels are washed with hot clean water and soap, and they are thoroughly dried with completely clean linen before they are put away. We direct the same for those linens of the college which are kept for solemn use. I further except those vessels which are needed for the daily use of the common table of the keeper and fellows, namely two or three salt-cellars and as many spoons as there are persons at table;[193] I also except one cup and two bowls for the use of the keeper or the president in his absence when entertaining friends of the college. An account shall be rendered of all these last-mentioned items annually by the keeper or president in the presence of the fellows; and, most certainly, an account of those items mentioned earlier [shall be made] by the butler to the steward,[194] and indeed by the steward to the keeper and fellows at such times and as often as an audit of other college possessions is required by statute.

A duplicate record between the keeper and the college and between the steward and the keeper shall be kept in the common chest, so that if anything is lost or is damaged, it shall be made good by the person by whose fault it was lost or damaged.[195]

191 Cf. Statute 25.

192 See Parker's *Interpretatio* lifting this restriction.

193 In 1558 Caius had allowed twelve spoons and one salt-cellar: *Documents*, II, p. 356.

194 For the *promus*, see *The steward and his staff* in "*Supplementary Notes to Caius' Statutes*", § IV. 3, at p. 297 below.

195 The description "*bipartus*" suggests that it took the form of an indenture. Contrast Caius' use of *cista* here with *arca* earlier in the statute: see *The arca, cistae, thesaurus and aerarium* in "*Supplementary Notes to Caius' Statutes*", § IV. 3, at p. 288 below.

Ne sit commune proprium.

83 Statuimus etiam et ordinamus, ne quis Custos, socius aut alius nostri Collegii ex communi faciat proprium sub poena periurii et deprivationis ab omni Collegii beneficio ipso facto: et restituendi in integrum quibus licet modis quod abstulerit. Non faciet autem ex communi proprium, qui suo contentus vivit sine cupiditate alieni. Etenim cum vita hominum sine cupiditate agebatur, sua cuique satis placebant. Postea vero quum superbia et libido in Collegia irrepserant, ipsa libido causam tollendi habuit, et maximam licentiam in maxima iniquitate posuit. Quod si Custos atque socii moderari sibi, atque cupiditati temperare potuissent, aequabilius et constantius sese Collegiorum res haberent, neque aliud alio ferri, aut ut proprium occupari, iniuste divendi aut dimitti, neque mutari ac misceri omnia cerneretis: quod non futurum spero progrediente aetate, et incommodum docente experientia atque usu.

De indice exemptorum e cistis et archivis.

84 Cum pecunia, vasa argentea, scripta seu evidentiae ex cistis seu archivis desumuntur, statuimus et ordinamus, ut in libros pandectarum referatur, quid, quantum, cui, ad quod tempus, quando, et quamobrem id desumptum sit, addito suscipientis nomine, et subscriptione, ut constituto tempore restituantur, ne incuria aut oblivione pereant. Sintque cum eximantur Custos aut praesidens et socii minimum quatuor praesentes: plures aut omnes si commode fieri potest. Eximi autem evidentias ex archivis, et alio transferri prohibemus, nisi in causa litium et actione iuris.

The preservation of corporate property from appropriation as private property.

83. We decree and direct that no one, whether he be keeper, fellow or other member of our college, shall appropriate corporate property as his own, on pain of breaking his oath and automatic deprivation of all benefit from the college, and of restoring what he took in its entirety by all permissible means. He who lives content and without envy of another does not make common property his own. For when life is lived without envy, one is satisfied with what is one's own. Truly, after pride and self-indulgence had crept into colleges, that very self-indulgence was the cause of ruin and turned unbounded licence into unbounded injustice. But if the keeper and the fellows had been able to restrain themselves and temper their greed[196] they would have enjoyed the things of the college more equably and more surely, and you would accept that nothing should be taken away from another or treated as private property, or unjustly sold or given away, or lent or exchanged; which I hope will not happen in future when, with the passage of time, experience and practice have shown how self-defeating these things are.

The listing of things taken out of the chests or the archives.

84. When money, silver vessels, writings or title-deeds are taken out of the chests or archives,[197] we decree and direct that it shall be noted in the Pandects, what, how much, to whom, for how long, when and why they were taken out, together with the name and signature of the person taking them out, so that they shall be restored at the agreed time and not be lost as a result of inattention or forgetfulness. When they are taken out, the keeper or president and at least four fellows shall be present; more or all if that can be done conveniently. But we prohibit title-deeds being taken out of the archives or transferred elsewhere, except in a legal dispute and an action at law.[198]

[196] A very pointed reflection upon the mastership of his predecessor, Thomas Bacon, and the state in which Caius found the college on Bacon's death in January 1559; see "*John Caius and his Foundation*", § V. 3 below. Cf. *Annals*, p. 42, and Brooke, *History*, p. 51.

[197] For chests and archives, see *The arca, cistae, thesaurus and aerarium* in "*Supplementary Notes to Caius' Statutes*", § IV. 3, at p. 288 below.

[198] The Pandects show that Caius frequently had title deeds sent to him in London; most of his work on legal transactions and disputes for the college seems to have been conducted there, but he also had such documents sent to him there for historical purposes.

De non obligando Collegio aliorum causa quam sua.

85 Statuimus insuper et firmiter observandum ordinamus, ne quis Custos aut socii Collegii vestri, qui pro tempore fuerint, aut eorum pars aliqua obliget aut obligent Collegium, possessiones eiusdem, aut seipsos sub Collegii nomine pro quoquam eiusdem, aut alieno ab eo Collegio, sub quacunque securitate, obligatione aut pignore: tum quia alienam fidem praestare in nemine situm est, et spondentibus semper praesto noxa est: tum quod pignora saepissime aliena sunt, quae iure a possessoribus repeti possunt; et obligationes charta tantum et pargamena sunt.

De locationibus terrarum et earum terminis.

86 Volumus etiam et statuimus, ut in locandis ad firmam terris, tenementis et hereditamentis Collegii vestri, diligenter provideatis, ne locentur unquam sine consensu expresso Custodis et maioris partis sociorum omnium pro tempore existentium et praesentium, neve integra et universa praedia seu maneria vestra cuiquam ad firmam concedatis, sed situm tantum manerii et terras dominicales sine devastatione, neve terras vestras in parte vel in toto per reversionem aut reversionis promissionem,[a] quocunque pretio dimittatis antequam prior earum dimissio seu locatio ad plenum finita et terminata sit, nisi in manus vestras reddant priorem indenturam. Quod si reversio facta fuerit sine consensu Custodis aut[b] maioris sociorum partis, pro nulla habeatur. Demum ne locentur terrae vestrae cuiquam ad feodi firmam, neve ultra annos viginti,

[a] At this point MS 711, at p. 82, has a marginal reference to the statute of 13 Elizabeth [ch. 10, s. 2] restricting the length of leases made by a college. It is a later comment: MSS 755, 760 and Lambeth MS 720 have no marginal note.

[b] *aut* is probably a scribal error for *et*: MSS 711, 755 and Lambeth MS 720 have *aut*; MS 760 has *et*.

The duty not to impose legal obligations on the college on behalf of others.

85. We decree and direct that it shall be a firm rule that none who are keeper or fellows of our college, or any of them, shall subject the college, any of its possessions or themselves in the name of the college to any security, bond or pledge whatsoever on behalf of any member of the college or any stranger to it: for one thing, because no one has the right to pledge another person's credit, and harm always comes to pledgors; and for another, because the things that are most commonly in the hands of non-owners as pledges can be taken from the possessor by process of law,[199] and obligations under seal, charters and parchments particularly so.

Leases of lands and the length of the term.

86. We wish and decree that you shall diligently ensure when leasing the lands, tenements and hereditaments of your college to farm[200] that they are never let without the express agreement of the keeper and the majority of all the fellows and in their presence; and that you will not rent out your estates or a manor in its entirety to anyone, but only the site of the manor[201] and the demesne lands[202] without the right to commit waste; and that you will not demise your lands, in part or in whole, in reversion or promise of reversion at any price whatsoever before the prior demise or lease of them has been completed, unless the tenants have surrendered the prior lease into your hands.[203] If a reversionary lease is made without the consent of the keeper and majority of the fellows, it shall be held null and void. In particular, we lay down categorically that your lands shall not be leased to anyone

[199] *I.e.*, by distraint. Bailiffs could seize property found in the possession of a debtor, whether or not owned by him.

[200] See *Caius' use of the terms firma and firmarius* in "*Supplementary Notes to Caius' Statutes*", § IV. 3, at p. 300 below.

[201] For the 'site' of the manor see *Caius' purchase of Croxley, Runcton and Burnham Thorpe* in "*Supplementary Notes to Caius' Statutes*", § IV. 3, at pp. 303–4 and n. 110 below.

[202] The term 'demesne lands' had become usual in the vernacular: in 1558 Caius had referred to *terras dominicales* as "lands commonly called 'demayne lands'" (*quas demayne lands vulgus nominat*): *Documents*, II, p. 358.

[203] Parliament also banned reversionary leases. Unlike Caius, however, it overlooked the loophole of contracts for a future renewal of a lease, and a further Act was required in 1576: see "*Dividends*", § VI. 5 at pp. 524–5 below.

si tamdiu vixerint: ne aut oblivione deleantur, aut firmarii vestri vos defraudent aut contemnant, aut ne per temporum vicissitudines huberiori redditu aut alio commodo permisso successores vestri iniuria vestra depriventur, omnino constituimus. Appropriationes autem beneficiorum ne ultra quinquennium elocentur, in literis appropriationum ecclesiarum de Mutford et Foulden Reverendus pater ordinavit. Alioqui si ad decennium elocentur (modo non ultra) grave non fuisset. Atque ut certior expeditiorque annorum supputatio sit, volumus ut in omnibus indenturis annus domini primo, diligenter ascribatur post regis. Et quia saepius usu comperimus, inutiles malosque Custodes atque socios, sibi et cognationi suae magis studere, quam rei publicae Collegiorum, tum minuendis fundorum redditibus, tum largiendis fundis pluribus annis et aliis personis quam par est aut permissum sit per statuta vestra, statuimus et ordinamus, ut huiusmodi scriptum locationis seu indentura, et quodcunque aliud quod non consentiet statutis Reverendi patris et nostris, non omnino obsignetur sigillo communi Collegii: volumusque ut omnes et singuli socii, si culpa fuerit in Custode, et Custos, si culpa in sociis, quoad possunt impediant, ne huiusmodi scriptum seu indentura, aut aliud quodcunque non consentiens statutis Reverendi patris et nostris, sub sigillum veniat, et ante futurae iniquitatis visitatores nostros admoneant, quam sigillo communi perniciosum scriptum obsignetur, in hoc ut illi quoque prohibeant et a facinore sua authoritate cohibeant. Hoc qui fecerit, benedictio domini super eum. Qui contra, maledictio et dira execratio. At aliquem futurum in Collegio in omni aetate, quem dominus benedicet, speramus et optamus.

Tempora solutionis reddituum.

87 Tempora autem solutionis seu pensionis reddituum vestrorum per aequales portiones, sunto festum Annuntiationis beatae Mariae et festum S. Michaelis

in fee farm[204] or for more than twenty years if the tenants shall live so long,[205] lest they should disappear into oblivion, or your farmers defraud and disregard you, or your successors be prevented by your wrongdoing from obtaining a better rent or other benefit which takes account of changes in the times. The Reverend Father directed in the letters of appropriation of the churches of Mutford and Foulden[206] that lands appropriated to church livings should not be let out for more than five years. However, in the case of other churches it will acceptable if they are let out for ten years (but not for longer). In order that the calculation of years may be more certain and quicker, it is our wish that in all indentures the year of the Lord shall be written first and the regnal year after it. And because we have found by experience that ineffectual and ill-intentioned keepers and fellows[207] have more regard for themselves and their kindred than for the common good of their colleges, in one way, by reducing the rents of lands, and in another, by granting lands for more years and to persons other than is appropriate or permitted by your statutes, we decree and direct that written leases or indentures of this sort or anything else that is not consonant with the statutes of the Reverend Father and ourself shall in no circumstances be sealed with the common seal of the college; and it is our wish that each and every fellow (if the keeper is the one at fault) and the keeper (if the fault lies in the fellows) shall, so far as they are able, prevent this sort of writing or indenture, or anything else that is not consonant with the statutes of the Reverend Father and ourself, from coming under the seal and shall alert our visitors to the impending illegality before the wrongful writing is sealed with the common seal, with the aim that they too will prohibit it and by an exercise of their authority constrain [the wrongdoers] from the misdeed. May the blessing of the Lord be on him who does this. Curses and dire execration be on those who do the opposite. But we hope and desire that every future member of the college will always be one whom the Lord blesses.

The due dates for the payment of rents.

87. The due dates for the payment of your rents in full or payment by instalments in equal parts are the feast of the Annunciation of the Blessed Mary and

[204] The medieval fee-farm conferred a freehold interest on the tenant, whose rights of action were thereby greatly strengthened; hence Caius' prohibition against letting in fee-farm and the well-known preference of Tudor landlords for leasing by terms of years.

[205] Parliament imposed a restriction to 21 years, but preserved the validity of any shorter restriction imposed by the private statutes of a college. In his 1558 statutes Caius had restricted the term to 12 years: *Documents*, II, p. 359.

[206] For these letters see *B.H.* III, p. 7. For Mutford, see *B.H.* IV(2), pp. 66ff; for Foulden, *ibid.*, pp. 44ff.

[207] No doubt Caius had his predecessor (Bacon) in mind here as in Statute 83 above, but Bacon's own predecessor, Styrmin, was in fact far more to blame: see "*Dividends*", § VI. 5 below.

Archangeli, in illo prima, in hoc secunda pecuniae pensio esto. Nec ultra octo aut summum quindecim dies fiat pensionis dilatio, sub poena forisfactionis iuris sui quod habuit ratione dimissionis aut indenturae suae, ut solutiones et pecuniae pensiones respondeant rationibus seu computis vestris ordinariis. Locus solutionis esto Aula Collegii vestri: materia aurum et argentum probum et legitimum. Voco hoc loco pensionem, solutionem, latinorum more.

Quae reservanda.

88 Reservabitis vobis, curias, letas, dies iuridicas, quas vocant Lawdayes, redditus liberorum et custumariorum tenentium, et eorum servitia, redditus operum autumnalium, redditus firmae, redditus siccos et quoscunque alios, averagium, libertates, warda, maritagia, relevia, bona caduca, hoc est, res damnatorum, aut quae possessione vacua fortuitis dominorum mortibus occupantur, ut interpretatur Iustinianus lib. 19°,[a] escaeta haec vocant iurisconsulti: wayfiata (id est bona furto in vestrum dominium translata), extrahuras (hoc est errantia animalia quae non norunt possessorem), harietas (id est animalia aut aliae res quae a morte aut mutatione tenentium dominis persolvuntur): advocationes ecclesiarum, perquisita curiarum, recognitionis pecuniam,[b] caeterasque omnes regalitates, consuetudines et commoditates: sylvas etiam grandiorum arborum, roboraque omnia et materiem, maxime in Ronghton et aliis maneriis vestris Cantabrigiae vicinis reservabitis, ut si aedificandum quid sit, minoribus impensis robora habeatis. Liberum ingressum quoque in omnes partes Manerii vestri[c] ad eadem aliaque quaecunque vestra, et egressum transferendo, transvehendo seu traducendo omnia retinebitis.

[a] Caius' reference to Book 19 would seem to be an error as there is nothing in the Digest or Institutes that is apposite. He must be citing Codex Iustinianus, Bk 10, ch. 10. "X.X" in his Latin has apparently been corrupted to "XIX", *i.e.*, 19.

[b] Although MS 755, Lambeth MS 720, the 1852 text and Venn read *recognitiones* and *pecuniam* as two distinct items, it is clear that the correct text should be *recognitionis pecuniam*, *i.e.* recognition money, as given in MS 760 and almost certainly in MS 711 (which has "*recognitioni*" truncated by the cutting of the edge of the page and "*pecuniam*" on the next line); otherwise *pecuniam* would be left isolated as a meaningless item: cf. Statute 91, para. 4.

[c] As it is in the singular (and written with a capital 'M') Caius may be referring only to the Manor of Runcton. If it is only this one manor, "*ad eadem*" may well refer to the oaks just mentioned.

the feast of St Michael the Archangel;[208] the first instalment at the former, the second instalment at the latter. Payment of an instalment shall not be delayed for more than eight or at most fifteen days[209] on pain of forfeiture of the title which the tenant has under his demise or indenture, so that payments and instalments of money may be reflected in your normal accounts or audits. The place of payment is to be the hall of your college: its form genuine and lawful gold and silver. I use the term 'instalment' here for a payment following the Latin usage.

The reservation of rights.

88. You shall reserve to yourselves courts, leets, those court days which are called law-days, the rents of freehold and customary tenants and their services, the renting of harvest works, leasehold rents, dry rents and all other rents, average,[210] liberties, wards, marriages, reliefs, goods no longer owned, that is the property of condemned felons or which has become ownerless by the chance death of owners as Justinian interprets in Book 19, called escheats by lawyers,[211] waifs (that is, stolen goods carried into your lordship),[212] strays (that is, animals which do not recognise the possessor),[213] heriots (that is, animals or other things which are payable to the lords on the death or change of tenants), advowsons of churches, perquisites of courts, recognition money,[214] and all other royalties customs and profits: and also you shall reserve woods of great trees, and all oak-trees and oak-wood, especially in Runcton and your other manors close to Cambridge, so that if any building is needed you will have oaks available at less expense. In addition you shall retain the right of free entrance and egress in all parts of your manor to these oaks and all other property of yours for the purposes of removing, carrying or leading everything away.

208 25 March and 29 September, respectively.

209 Twenty-eight days had been allowed in the 1558 draft statutes: *Documents*, II, p. 359.

210 A tenurial obligation to provide horse-drawn transport for the lord; cf. Statutes 90 and 91.

211 In common law terms, escheats *propter delictum tenentis* and *propter defectum tenentis*.

212 Caius restricts the term *waif* to its most common instance, goods abandoned by a thief, but it could apply to abandonment (waiver of title) by an owner as well as by a thief.

213 A curious definition, but clearly strays are meant by the word *extrahuras*.

214 Not 'recognisances' (which were acknowledgements of indebtedness), but fees paid by tenants on their 'recognition' by incoming lords in a court of recognition. See note to Latin text.

De redditibus non minuendis.

89 Non diminuetis veterem redditum (quem ex universalibus Collegii rentalibus et veteribus locationis indenturis discetis) ullarum possessionum vestrarum, sed eum etiam augebitis pro ratione hubertatis et bonitatis rei dimissae aut locatae, et necessitate Collegii. Quem nos auximus redditum, non amplius augebitis, sed eo censu retinebitis.

Conditiones firmariorum.

90 Volumus insuper et ordinamus, ut firmarii omnes Collegii vestri teneantur suis impensis reficere, reaedificare, reparare, sustinere et repurgare domos, aedificia, fossas, ripas atque littora, vicos atque pavimenta, aquarum cursus atque caetera omnia: exonerare vos contra dominum regem et dominum feudi seu feodi, et alios omnes in omnibus, et defendere omnia illis locata iure et aliis modis rationi consentaneis suis sumptibus, seseque obligent grandiori pecunia ad ea praestanda omnia, quae in indenturis continentur, et ne ante annorum terminum locationi renuntient, remve locatam in manus vestras ante praefinitum tempus restituant, obligentur. Teneantur etiam aedificare, si quid aedificandum sit, intra dies viginti octo ex quo admoniti eius fuerint, aut coget necessitas, si intra viginti octo dies absolvi possit.

Maintenance of rents.

89. You shall not reduce the old rent[215] (which you may ascertain from all the rent-books of the college and the old indentures of lease) of any of your possessions, but you are to increase it in the light of the fruitfulness and value of the property demised or leased and the needs of the college. You may not further increase any rent which we have ourself increased, but you shall keep it at that figure.[216]

The obligations of lessees.[217]

90. We wish and direct that all lessees of your college shall be bound at their own expense to renew, rebuild, repair, maintain and clean houses, buildings, ditches, banks and shores, roads and paved ways, watercourses and other things, to indemnify you in all things against the lord king and the lord of the feud or fee[218] and all others, and to defend everything leased to them both at law and in other reasonable ways at their own expense; and that they bind themselves in substantial sums of money to honour all those undertakings that are contained in the indentures; and not to renounce the lease before the expiry of the term or to surrender the property leased before the due date. If any building should be necessary, they are also to be bound to carry it out within 28 days from the time when they were advised of the need or from the moment when the need arises, if it can be achieved within 28 days.

215 The term "old rent" had a specialised meaning: it excluded any increase made in the second half of the sixteenth century. It was called "th'accustomed rent" in the Act of 1571 restraining Cambridge colleges from granting leases for terms longer than 21 years, and "the old rent" in Sir Thomas Smith's Corn Act of 1576. See *B.H.* IV(2), p. iii.

216 Taken literally this appears to prohibit the college from *ever* raising any rent which Caius had himself increased, but he was very conscious of the effects of inflation (cf. Statute 39) and it seems more likely that the prohibition was directed to the *first renewal* of the college's existing leases, all of which, without exception, greatly needed raising as soon as the first opportunity arose. In the case of the three manors of Croxley, Runcton and Burnham, Caius had calculated in advance (in Statute 91) what that increase should be and his direction here was intended simply to avoid any re-calculation in those cases when the first renewal came up, not to freeze any rents for ever.

217 See *Caius' use of the terms firma and firmarius* in "*Supplementary Notes to Caius' Statutes*", § IV. 3, at p. 300 below.

218 The feudal overlord from whom the freehold tenant (here, the college) held the freehold which was being leased out to a leasehold tenant; like lawyers, Caius could not resist using two words, *feudum* and *feodum*, where one would suffice.

Adferant vobis sexto quoque anno in Collegium rentalia nova omnium tenentium et reddituum, operum autumnalium, averagii, gallorum, gallinarum, et caponum, ovorum, panium et caeterorum omnium ad maneria vestra pertinentium, et octavo quoque anno terrarium[a] omnium terrarum vestrarum et earum limitum.

Ad haec obligentur firmarii vestri omnes vobis, famulis, seneschallo curiarum vestrarum, supervisori, et equis vestris, locum lautiamque praebere, cum aut Curiae aut Letae tenendae sunt, aut supervisiones faciendae, tantisper dum ibi necessario manendum sit: annisque singulis arbores (maxime quercus) minimum quinquaginta, locis aptis et accommodis, temporibus opportunis et spatiis aeque distantibus inserere et plantare, non fundos vestros cum alienis permutare, non sinere alios tenentes aut inhabitantes Manerii vestri (praeter eos ad quos iure pacti licet) oves suas in agro compascuo seu in faldagio (ut vocant) vestro compascere, ne permissione vestra in consuetudinem vertant tolerantiam vestram cum diminutione aut sublatione iuris vestri. Quamobrem faldagium vestrum non nisi firmariis vestris locandum constituimus: non alienos aut suos agros stercoratione animalium vestro agro nutritorum laetos facere, sed vestros obligate: non laetamen vendere, aut donare in fraudem fundi vestri: redditus terrarum, tenementorum et servitiorum vestrorum conservare, libertates defendere,[b] et ne sua culpa aut defectu pereant, procurare, et suo damno si quid pereat restituere, nec ius suum aut integrum aut particulare in quenquam aut donatione aut alienatione quacunque transferre, ne derivatio[c] iuris sui in alios, vobis veri tenentis aut firmarii vestri cognitionem adimant, neve aliis concedant, quorum aut potentia vobis obesse potest, aut improbitas, inopia vel vicinitas nocere: neve vendendo quae non emerant, rerum pretia intendant atque augeant incommodo publico. Cautio item fiat, ut si alienaverit uxori moriens, ne fruatur uxor, nisi secundus maritus approbetur Magistro sive Custodi et sociis Collegii vestri. Proinde talibus locate,[d] qui inhabitare et residere volunt, et vobis honestate sua placuerint, alioqui non habituri: recusantes omnino consentire ut firmarius det, vendat, concedat, alienet aut oppignoret alteri interesse suum seu titulum vel terminum annorum rei locatae, aut alicuius eius partis: qui ideo conducit ut alteri locet, commodo suo non vestro, mercandi gratia locationes quaerens, non usus causa. Imo ne inhabitantibus

a *Sic* MSS 711, 755, 760, Lambeth MS 720 and Venn; in the 1852 text it is wrongly given as *terrarum*.

b In MS 711 the words *libertates defendere* are deleted and then rewritten (apparently in Caius' hand) and the rest of the page is left blank.

c *Sic* MSS 711, 755, 760 and Lambeth MS 720; printed as *derivatione* by the Commissioners and by Venn.

d *Sic* MSS 711, 755, 760 and Lambeth MS 720. The direct imperative is unusual for Caius.

They shall also bring to you in college every five years new rental-books of all tenants and rents, of harvest works, of average,[219] of cocks, hens and capons, sheep, loaves and all other things appertaining to your manor, and every seven years a terrier[220] of all your lands and their boundaries.

All your lessees shall be bound as follows: to provide board and lodging for you, your servants, the steward of your courts, your surveyor and your horses, for as long as it is necessary for them to remain there, when a court or leet is to be held or surveys are to be made: and every year to sow and plant at least fifty trees (principally oaks) in suitable places and at favourable times and equally spaced: not to exchange your lands with those of others: not to allow other tenants or inhabitants of your manor (other than those rightfully entitled by contract) to graze their sheep on your common pasture or your foldage (as they call it),[221] lest through your tolerating this they convert your licence into a prescriptive right to the consequent diminution and undermining of your right (for this reason we determine that your foldage shall not be let to any but your lessees):[222] not to manure their own lands or those of others with the dung of animals nourished on your land, but to do so for your land: not to sell or give it away to the detriment of your land: to reserve the rents of your lands, tenements and services: to defend your liberties and to ensure that nothing perishes through their fault or neglect, and to make good any loss at their own expense: and not to alienate their interest in whole or in part to any person by gift or in any other way, lest by transfer of their title you should lose track of your true tenant or lessee, and lest they alienate to others whose power may hurt you or whose dishonesty, indigence or proximity may harm you: and lest, by selling what they have not bought, they distort or increase the price of things to the public detriment. Care shall also be taken so that, if [a lessee] alienates to his wife when he is dying, the wife shall not enjoy the tenancy unless her second husband is approved by the master or keeper and fellows of your college. Accordingly lease to those who wish to live and reside on the property, and who satisfy you of their honesty, otherwise they are not to be accepted; and adamantly refuse to allow a clause that a lessee may give, sell, pass, alienate or pledge to any other his interest title or term of years in the property leased or any part of it: for he who thus takes a lease in order to sub-let it and seeks leases in order to sell them, not in order to work them, is pursuing his own benefit, not yours. Least of all may you let your lands and tenements even to resident lessees

[219] A tenurial obligation to provide horse-drawn transport for the lord; cf. Statutes 88 and 91.

[220] A list of land-holdings, principally by location and particularly of manorial holdings. See Blount, *Law Dictionary* (1670): "Terrar … is a Book, Survey, or Land-Roll, wherein the several lands are described; containing the quantity of Acres, boundaries, Tenants names, and such like." In his draft statutes Caius had specified third year and fifth year for the new rentals and terriers, respectively: *Documents*, II, p. 359.

[221] Sheep-walks with movable folds.

[222] Brackets added editorially to prevent the sentence interrupting the list of obligations.

quidem et residentibus firmariis sic locabitis terras aut tenementa vestra, ut ius locatum, interesse, titulum, vel terminum annorum, aut aliquam eius partem aut indenturam ipsam dare, vendere, concedere, aut alienare liceat sine licentia vestra expressa in scriptis: quod necessarium frenum id est inutilibus, rebellibus et licentiosis firmariis: et hoc sub poena amittendi omne ius suum in re locata, si aliter faciant. Sed firmariis vestris ne committatis curam grandiorum arborum, ne decutiant suo commodo, sed alium substituetis in eum usum.

Has omnes et singulas locationum conditiones qui non praestiterint, mulcta ex pacto esto omnis sui iuris in rebus locatis omissio seu forisfactio ipso facto.

De censu extento maneriorum nostrorum de Ronghton, Crokesley et BurnhamThorpe.

91 Situm igitur tantum manerii vestri de Rongeton seu Ronghton Holme, cum terris dominicalibus, cuniculis, diebus precariis (quos Bendayes seu Bondayes vocant), panibus, ovis, gallis, gallinis, caponibus et faldagio locabitis per indenturam ad annos tantum viginti, pro annuo redditu quadraginta librarum, sic ut non faciant vastum: tantum enim oblatum est: reservabitis vobis quae iam antea reservanda constituimus.

Itidem manerii vestri de Crokesley et Snelleshal terras tantum vestras dominicales cum situ manerii absque sylvis, cum eo ut non faciant vastum, locabitis libris viginti quinque. At cum sylvis ceduis et subcrescentibus (quas subboscos iurisconsulti nominant) roboribus seu materia (quam meremium iurisperiti vocant) exceptis, non minoris dimittetis quadraginta libris, quomodo nos iam locavimus: reservabitis quae iam prius reservanda ordinavimus.

Situm etiam manerii vestri de Burnham Thorpe seu Burnham Wimondham, terras dominicales et faldagium, cum decimis de Burnham Overey de decima

living on the land[223] with a term that the right of letting, the ownership, the leasehold term or some part of it or the deed of indenture itself may be given, sold, made over or alienated without your express written consent;[224] for this is a necessary bridle on useless, rebellious and dishonest lessees; and the penalty for breach of this is to be loss of all their right in the leased property. But you are not to commit the care of fully-grown trees to your lessees, lest they cut them down for their own benefit; instead, you shall appoint another to have that care.

The penalty for those who do not observe each and every one of these conditions of their leases shall be the automatic loss or forfeiture of all their right in the property leased.[225]

The assessed annual value of our Manors of Runcton, Croxley and Burnham Thorpe.[226]

91. You shall therefore lease only the site of your manor of Runcton or Runcton Holme with its demesne lands, rabbit-warrens, boon-days (commonly called bendays or bond-days),[227] loaves, eggs, cocks, hens, capons and foldage by indenture for not more than 20 years, and with liability for waste, at an annual rent of £40, for that much has been offered for it. You shall reserve to yourselves all that we have just now determined should be reserved.

In the same way you shall lease, with liability for waste, only the demesne lands of your manor of Croxley and Snellshall with the site of the manor for £25 without the woods; but with the inclusion of woods, coppices and the undergrowth (which the lawyers call sub-boscage) other than the oaks or wood for working (which the lawyers call timber), you shall demise it for not less than £40, in the way we have now leased it. You shall reserve to yourselves all that we have just now directed should be reserved.

You shall lease also the site of your manor of Burnham Thorpe or Burnham Wymondham, its demesne lands and foldage with the tithes of Burnham Overy

223 *Inhabitantibus*: Caius clearly has in mind (both here and in the preceding sentence) the medieval and modern sense of an 'inhabitant' rather than the original Latin sense of a 'non-resident'.

224 *I.e.*, the lease must contain a covenant against assignment or sub-letting without the landlord's consent.

225 In 1575 a supplementary query on this paragraph was formulated by Legge and the fellows for submission to Archbishop Parker, but apparently not considered by him before his death in May that year: Lambeth MS 720, fols. 10, 11.

226 See *Caius' purchase of Croxley, Runcton and Burnham Thorpe* in "*Supplementary Notes to Caius' Statutes*", § IV. 3, at p. 302 below.

227 Days of service on which an unfree tenant might be required by the custom of the manor to do unpaid work for his lord.

Garba seu fasce frugum, de pensione et portione de Peterston, non minoris locabitis tredecim libris sex solidis et octo denariis: quia faldagium pluris est ipsis terris reliquis. Reservatis caeteris quae reservanda diximus.

Iam vero cum redditus reservatus liberorum et custumariorum tenentium manerii de Ronghton &c. extenditur ad libras duodecim et amplius, et redditus firmae ad libras quadraginta, universus fructus certus, erunt librae quinquaginta duae, ultra perquisita curiarum et pecuniam recognitionis, &c.

Itidem cum redditus liberorum et custumariorum tenentium manerii de Crokesley et Snelleshal reservatus, existit octo librarum, &c. et averagii communibus annis sex solidorum et octo denariorum et operum autumnalium quatuor librarum, si his iungas libras quadraginta redditus firmae, tota firma ad libras quinquaginta duas sex solidos et octo denarios extenditur.

Ad postremum, redditu firmae praedii de Burnham Thorpe existente duodecim libris et liberorum ac custumariorum tenentium circiter quinque libras, septem solidos sex denarios et obolum, integra summa est, decem et septem librae, septem solidi, sex denarii et obolus. Quorum omnium summae collectae, in universum faciunt centum et viginti unam libras, quatuordecim solidos, duos denarios et obolum: qui est census trium illorum praediorum extentus.

De affectione secludenda in locationibus.

92 Statuimus insuper et ordinamus ita in locationibus ut in gravioribus aliis Collegii negotiis atque rebus, ne Custos aut eius locum tenens, qui pro tempore fuerit, aliquid solus tentet citra caeterorum aut saltem maioris partis sociorum omnium pro tempore existentium et praesentium expressum consensum: neve locationes aut dimissiones fiant unquam in favorem cuiusquam privati, amicitiae, praemii aut cognationis causa, sed in favorem Collegii communis amici et parentis. Quare in locationibus absit omnis affectio et corruptio, omnis privata utilitas, tantum honestum et commune Collegii commodum spectetur. Ex eius enim uberibus alimini, ex eo omnes vivitis.[a] Atque ob id addendum aliquid, non adimendum; indulgendum ut liberi, non utendum pro arbitratu ut domini. Quamobrem statuimus etiam ne locetis quicquam cognatis vestris

[a] This well-known biblical and classical depiction of an institution as an *alma mater* would have been familiar to Caius, particularly from the Introit for *Laetare* Sunday (Isaiah lxvi. 10, 11): cf. the possible reference to *Gaudete* and *Laetare* Sundays in Statutes 25 and 41. Characteristically, he maintains the digression for a further sentence before returning to the subject of the statute.

that arise from the corn tithe or bundle of crops and from the entitlement and share of Peterston for not less than £13. 6s. 8d.: because the foldage is worth more than the rest of the lands.[228] You shall reserve to yourselves all that we have just now specified should be reserved.

Now truly since the reserved rent of the free and customary tenants of the Manor of Runcton etc. amounts to £12 and more, and the rent from the leasing to £40, the whole fixed income will be £52 in addition to the perquisites of court and recognition money etc.

In the same way since the present rent of the free and customary tenants of the manor of Croxley and Snellshall is reserved at £8 etc., and the average[229] in normal years amounts to 6s. 8d. and the harvest works £4, if you join to these the rent from the leasing of £40 the total farm comes to £52. 6s. 8d.

Finally, the present rent from the leasing of the estate of Burnham Thorpe being £12 and that of the free and customary tenants around £5. 7s. 6½d., the total sum is £17. 7s. 6½d. The sums collected from all these sources amount to £121. 14s. 2½d.: which is the valuation of the extent of the three estates.[230]

The avoidance of partiality in leasing.

92. We decree and direct that, in leasing as in other very weighty college affairs or business, the keeper or his deputy shall not attempt to act by himself without the express consent of the rest of the fellows, or at any rate a majority of the total number, and in their presence: nor shall leases or demises ever be made for the benefit of any personal acquaintance for the sake of friendship, reward or relationship but only for the benefit of the college as the common friend and parent. For that reason leasing shall be free from all partiality and corruption, all private advantage, and only the honest and common benefit of the college shall be considered. For from its breasts you will be nourished, from it you will all derive life. Accordingly, it is something to be augmented not diminished, treated considerately [by you] as its children not used capriciously [by you] as its owners. For that reason too we decree that you shall not

[228] For the tithes of Burnham Overy and Peterston and the foldage, see *Caius' purchase of Croxley, Runcton and Burnham Thorpe* in "*Supplementary Notes to Caius' Statutes*", § IV. 3, at pp. 306–8 below.

[229] See Statutes 88 and 90 above: the tenurial obligation to provide horse-drawn transport for the lord.

[230] The arithmetic adds up only if the rent from Burnham Thorpe excludes the share of the tithe of Burnham Overy, *i.e.* is £12, not £13. 6s. 8d. In fact the rent of Burnham Thorpe was much less than £12 at that time (or at any time later): see *Caius' purchase of Croxley, Runcton and Burnham Thorpe* in "*Supplementary Notes to Caius' Statutes*", § IV. 3, at pp. 306–8 below.

aut vobis ipsis aut vestrum cuiquam directe aut indirecte, per interpositam personam aut secus, fraude, aut dolo ullo, quod usus docet id fore exitio Collegio vestro, quemadmodum et aliis est Collegiis.

De firmariis.

93 Volumus etiam et statuimus, ne terras, tenementa, beneficia appropriata, aut alia hereditamenta Collegii vestri aliis locetis aut dimittatis, quam honestis ex plebe colonis, qui ad utendum et occupandum, redditusque persolvendum sufficientes fuerint, et dicti Collegii utilitatem in huiusmodi locationibus consulere velint et possint: tum ne populares priventur suo vivendi genere, tum ne (si aliis locetis) hi suo supercilio, potentia et imperio vos premant, vestra per iniuriam vobis surripiant, quae nisi iure ac lite contra eos recuperare vobis erit perdifficile.

Utilitatem quam dixi Collegii, honestate metior, ut pretia rerum intra modum fiant, et paulo minora quam vicinorum praediorum eius bonitatis. Utilitatem voco, incrementum redditus, et firmarum quos vocant fines: quos utrosque in commodum Collegii, non Custodis et sociorum volumus conservari. Permittimus tamen Custodi atque sociis, ut ultra redditus atque fines Collegio acquisitos, oves aliquot castratos, pingues, atque porcos, aliaque altilia in commendationem atque augmentum mensae suae communis solennioribus festis et commemorationibus fundatorum, ex pacto sibi et successoribus suis a firmariis exigant.

Ad haec ordinamus ne terras vestras aut maneria vestra iis locetis, qui aut in eisdem villis in quibus vestra sunt, aut in proximis terras possideant, ne iure occupationis, vestra suis coniungant, et finito dimissionis termino vestra

lease anything to your relations, or to yourselves, or to any of you,[231] directly or indirectly through an intermediary or otherwise, fraudulently or deceitfully, for experience shows that to be the ruin of your college[232] in the way it is for other colleges.

Lessees.[233]

93. We wish and decree that you shall not lease or demise any lands, tenements, appropriated benefices or other hereditaments of your college to any but respectable farming folk from the neighbourhood[234] who would be of sufficient means to work and occupy and pay the rent and who would both wish and be able to respect the said college's interest in such leases. This should be done, for one thing lest common folk should lose their means of livelihood, and for another, lest by leasing to persons of a different class they should become a burden to you by their arrogance, might and lordliness, and unlawfully deprive you of your property, which it will be very difficult for you to recover except by [recourse to] law and litigation.

I judge the interest of the college to which I have referred properly to mean that prices should remain within moderation and a little lower than those of nearby estates of the same quality. I include in the term interest the increase of rents and farms[235] which are called fines, both of which we wish to be kept for the benefit of the college, not that of the keeper and fellows.[236] However, we allow to the keeper and the fellows that, apart from the rents and fines accruing to the college, they may require from the lessees, as a term of the contract made with them and their successors, a few sheep, fattened wethers and pigs and other fatted fowls towards the embellishment and increase of their common table at the more important feasts and commemorations of the founders.

To these ends we direct that you shall not lease your lands or manors to those who possess land in those vills[237] in which your land is situated, or in the neighbourhood, lest they join your land to their own and at the expiry of the term they retain your land and claim it as their own. And we determine that this is

[231] See Parker's *Interpretatio* allowing such leases with the unanimous consent of the Master and *all* the fellows.

[232] A further reflection on Bacon's mastership. Cf. Statutes 83 and 86 above.

[233] For the term *firmarius*, see *Caius' use of the terms firma and firmarius* in "*Supplementary Notes to Caius' Statutes*", § IV. 3, at pp. 300–2 below.

[234] In mediaeval usage the term *plebs* had acquired an association with the parish.

[235] Used in the sense of a 'hiring-fee' or entry fine; see *Caius' use of the terms firma and firmarius* in "*Supplementary Notes to Caius' Statutes*", § IV. 3, at p. 300 below.

[236] His direction proved to be in vain: see "*Dividends*", § VI. 5 below.

[237] Originally a feudal institution, but by Caius' time a civil parish.

retineant et sibi vendicent. Atque hoc in locatione situs manerii de Ronghton vel maxime observandum constituimus, propter dominum de Thorpland et terrae tenentes eiusdem. Quibus tantum abest ut locatum volumus, ut etiam ex pacto cum his quibus locabitis cautum grandi pecunia volumus, ne et illi supradictis dominis et tenentibus manerii de Thorpland ullis conditionibus locent, aut alii cuipiam, per quem ad eorum manus pervenire possint.

Qui in firmis praeferendi.

94 Statuimus etiam ut hi praeferantur in firmis, qui prius erant firmarii, modo fuerint honesti ex plebe coloni, et anteactis temporibus se bene et in rem Collegii gesserint in eisdem, et nec in eisdem villis, nec in proximis possessiones habeant, et terras colere ac redditus augere et persolvere aeque ut alii, aliasque quas ante commemoravimus locationis conditiones praestare possint et velint.

De finibus terrarum[a] *per copiam aut firmam concedendarum.*

95 Sint etiam fines terrarum vestrarum per copiam curiae concedendarum,[b] non iidem semper, sed diversi, quo vobis liceat eos augere quando volueritis. Volumus item ut in copiis rotularum curiae, terrarum acrae seu iugera, et loca seu tenementa suis nominibus numerentur, censeantur et suis limitibus circumscribantur. Constituimus itidem, ut harietarum, operum autumnalium, redditus, et ne vastum tenentes faciant, aut terrarum permutationem, mentio in copiis fiat. Fines autem firmarum pro ratione fertilitatis et foecunditatis terrarum fiant: sed non antequam ad iustum censum aucti redditus fuerint: ne

[a] The 1852 text and Venn wrongly print *firmarum*. MSS 711, 755, 760 and Lambeth MS 720 correctly give "*terrarum*".

[b] Copyhold land was transferred by surrender and re-grant recorded on the court rolls, copies of which served as title-deeds. Hence the *concedendarum* (surrender).

most particularly to be observed when leasing the site of the manor of Runcton because of the owner of Thorpeland and the tenants of his land. It is quite out of the question that we should wish that it be leased to those persons, and for this reason it is our further wish that a guarantee is to be taken in a large sum of money by contract with those to whom you lease it, that they do not let to the aforesaid lords and tenants of the manor of Thorpeland on any conditions, or to anyone else through whom it could come into their hands.[238]

Preferred lessees.

94. We decree that existing lessees should be preferred in lettings, as long as they are respectable farming folk from the neighbourhood,[239] have conducted themselves well and in the interest of the college in those farms in the past, do not have holdings of their own in the same localities or nearby, and are able and willing to till the lands, increase the return, pay [a fair rent] and fulfil all the other terms which we have detailed above in like manner as others.

Fines of lands transferable by copy or farm.[240]

95. The fines on transfers of your copyhold lands are not to be fixed permanently, but are to be variable, so that it shall be lawful for you to increase them when you wish.[241] It is our further wish that the acres or *jugera*[242] of the lands and the sites or holdings shall be listed and rated under their names on the copies of the court rolls and their boundaries delimited. We lay down that mention shall likewise be made in the copies of heriots, harvest works, rent and the obligation not to commit waste or exchange lands. The fines for farms[243] shall be levied in proportion to the fertility and fruitfulness of the lands, but not before the rents

[238] Thorpeland is south of and adjacent to Runcton Holme, about five miles north of Downham Market. For this fierce injunction, see *Caius' purchase of Croxley, Runcton and Burnham Thorpe* in "*Supplementary Notes to Caius' Statutes*", § IV. 3, at p. 306 below.

[239] Cf. Statute 93 and note.

[240] In Statute 95 Caius combines provisions for entry fines on copyhold lands with entry fines on "farms", *i.e.* leasehold lands at a rent or 'farm' (*firma*) for the purpose of working it. The two entry fines were very different in nature: see "*Dividends*", § VI. 5, at pp. 515ff below

[241] Such entry fines were 'arbitrary', but by law they had to be reasonable.

[242] Caius is using a Roman term which was so little used in England that it remained untranslated as 'juger' until the nineteenth century. The Roman *iugerum* was about two-thirds of an acre, but here and in Statute 102 the word is used as interchangeable with the acre.

[243] *I.e.*, leases: see *Caius' use of the terms firma and firmarius* in "*Supplementary Notes to Caius' Statutes*", § IV. 3, at p. 300 below.

fines consumant redditus. Fines autem Collegii esse volumus, non Magistri[a] et sociorum, praeterquam fines et amerciamenta maneriorum nostrorum de Ronghton, Crokesley et Snelleshall, quae Custodi dedimus in augmentum salarii sui sub ea conditione, ut in Collegio resideat.

De Senescallo et Ballivo.[b]

96 Officium Seneschalli curiarum vestrarum et Ballivorum vestrorum perpetuum esse nolumus, nec durante vita, sed annuum, et durante bene placito vestro, tantisper videlicet dum se bene et fideliter gesserit in eisdem, nec ullus tenentium vestrorum sit seneschallus, ne faveat magis partibus tenentium quam vestrum. Ballivus autem[c] si frugi homo fuerit atque fidus, diligenter et in rem vestram colligat, positis vadibus, omnes redditus liberorum et custumariorum tenentium, redditus firmae, perquisita curiarum, recognitionis pecuniam, et caetera incidentia, annuatimque durante officio suo, fidelem rationem eorum reddat, nisi consuetudine maneriorum tenentes debeant colligere (ut in manerio vestro de Ronghton) et Refes ac Reperefes (ut curiarum vestrarum rotulae vocant)[d] ad hoc constituere.

Merces Seneschalli esto pro ratione laboris, nec illi persolvatur a firmario, priusquam singularum curiarum et extentarum rotulas scite pargameno scriptas, et eadem longitudine latitudineque cum prioribus rotulis coaptatas, ad Collegium vestrum vel attulerit vel tuto obsignatas miserit. Quo facto per litteras vestras firmario significabitis ut mercedem persolvat.

a Caius uses the term *Magister* for the Masters of other colleges, but it is unusual for him not to use *Custos* for his own college.

b The use of capital letters in this statute for such officers as *Seneschallus* and *Ballivus* is uncharacteristic of the scribe.

c If *autem* suggests any contrast here between stewards and bailiffs, it probably relates to the fact that stewards could not be tenants, whereas bailiffs might be, rather than to any difference in length of tenure.

d MSS 711, 755, 760 all have *rotulae vocant*, not *vocantur*, as given in the 1852 text and Venn. *Reperefes* is an idiosyncratic spelling of *riperevus* ('reap-reeve') and *refes* for 'reeve'. The use of an 'f' in place of the more common 'v' is to be found in statute 88 ('*wayfiata*') and may be either a personal idiosyncracy or an East Anglian one. *Rotulus* was almost always masculine in the Middle Ages, not feminine as here.

have been raised to the appropriate level, lest the fines eat up the rents. It is our wish that the fines shall accrue to the college, and not to the master and fellows personally, other than the fines and amercements of our manors of Runcton, Croxley and Snellshall, which we have given to the keeper in augmentation of his stipend on the condition that he resides in the college.[244]

The steward and the bailiff.[245]

96. It is our wish that the office of steward of your courts and of your bailiffs shall not be perpetual or for life but annual and at your good pleasure, that is, for such time as the holder shall perform the office well and faithfully; nor shall any of your tenants be steward, lest he take the side of the tenants instead of yours. The bailiff, however, if he is an honest and faithful man shall, after sureties have been given, collect diligently and on your behalf the rent of freehold and copyhold tenants, leasehold rents, perquisites of court, recognition-money[246] and other incidentals and shall annually render a faithful account of them during his period of office, unless the tenants of the manors are obliged by custom to collect them (as in your manor of Runcton) and to appoint reeves and reap-reeves (as the rolls of your courts call them) to do this.

The fee of the steward shall be in proportion to the work, and it shall not be paid to him by the [college's] lessee before he has brought or sent safely sealed to your college the rolls of each one of the courts and extents neatly written on parchment and formatted like earlier rolls in length and width. When this has been done you shall signify by your letters to the lessee that he should pay the fee.

[244] The omission of Burnham Thorpe was presumably an oversight: cf. Statute 37. Here Caius appears to grant to the Master the whole of the fines arising from both copyholds and leaseholds in the two manors, thereby reversing his direction in Statute 37. Subsequent generations correctly understood that he did not intend to do so and was merely referring to the provision he had made in Statute 37 for augmenting the Master's stipend by a specific amount and was not granting to him personally the whole amount of the fines from both the leaseholds and copyholds. The fines from the *copyholds* were not paid to the Master but entered in the Bursar's Book as *recepta extraordinaria* like other occasional income of the college, and the Master received just the augmented stipend (*e.g.*, *Bursar's Book*, Lady Day 1610). The fines on the *leases* were also not paid to the Master but were divided between the Master and senior fellows like the fines on other leases (*e.g.*, *Gostlin's Note Book*, Fines for Mich. 1677, Croxley and Runcton).

[245] See *Manorial Stewards and Bailiffs* in "*Supplementary Notes to Caius' Statutes*", § IV. 3, at p. 308 below.

[246] See Statute 88 above for recognition-money.

Prohibemus etiam, ne quando penes Senescallum sit custodia evidentiarum vestrarum, nec diutius habeat, quam vos praesentes fueritis.

Curias autem minimum duas esse volumus quotannis in singulis maneriis, propter sylvarum conservationem, et unam particularem supervisionem singulis temporibus quibus curiarum gratia interfueritis.

De reparatione seu aedificatione.

97 Ordinamus etiam, ut sedulo curetis, cum aedificia vestra locetis redemptoribus (quos firmarios vocant) praecipua inter caeteras conditio apponatur, curent ut sarta tectaque sint omnia, corrupta omnia reficiant, adempta restituant, collapsa vel diruta reaedificent suo tempore, hoc est, si novorum aedificiorum structurae, aut magnae reparationes fiant, inter principium Martii et primum Octobris: reparationibus et reaedificationibus, quae commode absque dispendio differri non possunt, duntaxat exceptis. Eas enim quam citissime fieri volumus.

Volumus etiam, ut aedificia diligenter invisatis, circumspiciatisque intus et foris, an sarta tectaque sint, an aliqua reparatione indigeant.

De declinatione sociorum ad maneria.

98/–[a] Constituimus praeterea, ut si Custos aut sociorum aliquis in proximo fuerit quacunque de causa maneriis, terris, aut tenementis vestris, ad ea declinet, et cognita conditione rerum omnium, Custodi, aut eo absente praesidenti referat, ut si quid damni aut incommodi incidat, admoniti quorum interest, damnum praestent et resarciant.

[a] MS 711 and Lambeth MS 720 set out *De declinatione sociorum ad maneria* as a separate statute with its title, but fail to number it; they are followed in this by the printed texts. The need for a number was quickly noticed, however, and the number "98" inserted in MSS 755 and 760. See "*Caius' Statutes: The Sources*", § I. 3, at p. 36 above.

We further direct that the steward should never at any time have custody of your title-deeds, and that he shall only have them in his hand when you are present.

It is our wish also that there shall be at least two courts a year in each and every manor to ensure the conservation of the woods and one specially commissioned survey at each of the times when you will be present to hold a court.

Repair [and] building.

97. We direct that you should take particular care when you let out your buildings on contract to hirers (who are called 'lessees') that a very specific condition is inserted, with others, that they should have a care that everything is in sound order and roofed, that they make good everything damaged, restore everything removed, rebuild everything that has collapsed or been demolished [and do so] at the proper time, that is, so that the construction of any new buildings or major repairs are done between the beginning of March and October 1st.[247] Only repairs and re-buildings which cannot be deferred conveniently and without loss are excepted. It is our wish that these last tasks should be completed as quickly as possible.

It is also our wish that you shall diligently visit buildings, inspect inside and outside to check that they are in sound order and roofed and whether any repairs are needed.

Visits of fellows to manors.

98/– If for any reason the keeper or any fellow should be in the neighbourhood of your manors, lands or tenements, we determine that, he should visit them and having noted the state of everything he should make a report to the keeper or the president in his absence so that, if any damage or loss has occurred, those concerned may, having being warned, be liable for the loss and obliged to make it good.

[247] In his draft statutes in 1558 Caius had specified the feast of SS. Simon and Jude (28 October) instead of 1 October: *Documents*, II, p. 363.

De non locandis possessionibus sine consensu fundatoris durante vita sua.

99/98 Et quo commodiores Collegio locationes fiant, statuimus et ordinamus, ne terras, tenementa aut alia Collegii hereditamenta cuiquam locetis, aut alia ematis, durante vita nostra naturali, sine expresso consensu nostro. Decrevimus enim quantum possumus nostro consilio et experientia vos iuvare, et omnibus modis Collegio prodesse, in incrementum virtutis et literarum.

De possessionibus non vendendis.

100/99 Statuimus etiam et ordinamus, ne vendatis terras vestras in Ronghton, Burnham Thorpe in comitatu Norfolciae, Crokesley et Snelleshall in Ricmersworthe in comitatu Hertfordiae, Byncombe et Woborne in comitatu Dorcestriae, Mortimers in Newnham iuxta Cantabrigiam, Aynells in Westoning in comitatu Bedford, nec alias terras vestras in Teversham, Stowequi, Barton, Cantabrigia, Chesterton, Grancester, et aliis locis Cantabrigiae vicinis: nec alias terras aut possessiones vestras: sed eas si potestis, augebitis: nisi ad comparandum integrum, fructuosum et utile manerium velitis tenementa pusilla et minutas parcellas terrarum vestrarum in longinquo et nullo manerio positarum iusto pretio vendere: ut sunt ea quae sunt in Thornham et Tichewel in comitatu Norfolciae.

De evidentiis conservandis et acquirendis.

101/100 Statuimus etiam, ut omnes et singuli Custodes atque socii, qui pro tempore fuerint, Collegii evidentias in archivis conservent, ne in cubicula aut alia loca iuris causa distrahant: studeantque omnibus honestis modis per se suosque amicos omnia scripta, evidentias, terraria, custumaria, rotulas

The requirement of the consent of the founder to leasing during his lifetime.

99/98. So that leases shall be the more advantageous to the college, we decree and direct that you shall not, during our natural lifetime, lease the lands, tenements or other hereditaments of the college to anyone, or purchase other lands, without our express consent. For we have resolved to aid you to our utmost with our advice and experience, and to be of assistance to the college in every way, in pursuit of the increase of virtue and learning.

Possessions which are not to be sold.[248]

100/99. We decree and direct that you shall not sell your lands in Runcton and Burnham Thorpe in the county of Norfolk, Croxley and Snellshall in Rickmansworth in the county of Hertford,[249] Bincombe and Oborne in the county of Dorset, Mortimer's in Newnham adjoining Cambridge, Aynells in Westoning in the county of Bedford; nor your other lands in Teversham, Stowe-cum-Quy, Barton, Cambridge, Chesterton, Grantchester and other places in the vicinity of Cambridge; nor your other lands or possessions; but you may enlarge them if you are able. If however you should wish to sell at a fair price [any] insignificant tenements and small parcels of your lands that are situated remotely and outside any manor in order to unite a manor as a single, fruitful and useful whole, you may do so: such as those properties which are in Thornham and Titchwell in the county of Norfolk.[250]

The safe-keeping and acquisition of title-deeds.

101/100. We decree that each and every keeper and the fellows at the time shall keep the title-deeds of the property of the college safely in the archives lest they be taken by way of lawful distraint while they are in their [personal] rooms or in other places; and they shall strive by all lawful means, whether personally or through their friends, to acquire for the college all documents, title-deeds,

248 For these possessions, see E. Gross, "*Chronicle of the Estates*", in *B.H.* IV(2).

249 For Runcton, Burnham Thorpe, Croxley and Snellshall, see *Caius' purchase of Croxley, Runcton and Burnham Thorpe* in "*Supplementary Notes to Caius' Statutes*", § IV. 3, at p. 302 below.

250 Despite this strong hint they were still in the college's hands centuries later. In 1753 Thornham was found to contain 57 separate parcels, and Titchwell 28 parcels: *B.H.* IV(2), p. 89.

curiarum, computorum, extentarum et rentalium maneriorum, terrarum, tenementorum, beneficiorum et possessionum Collegii vestri quarumcunque deperdita aut nondum acquisita, Collegio acquirere, et suis locis in eodem reponere, nec ullam occasionem ad id praetermittere, non solum dum fuerint in societate, sed cum defuncti ea recesserint a Collegio.

De supervisione maneriorum.

102/101 Ne quid vestrum firmariorum aut tenentium vitio corrumpatur aut adimatur, statuimus et ordinamus ut quarto quoque anno invisatis omnia praedia vestra, et sexto anno etiam lustretis omnia et singula maneria, terras, tenementa et beneficia vestra peragrando omnia, intelligendoque in cuius sunt quaeque possessione, quotque acras sive iugera, quot loca[a] et tenementa quisque tenet, et an assignentur ea per cardines et decumanos, an secus, libere ne an custumarie, an in villanageo, per indenturam an per rotulam curiae, ad firmam an aliter, in agris, clausuris,[b] sylvis an in pratis positas: quibus nominibus censeantur, quibus finibus seu limitibus circumscribantur, qua quantitate et acrarum numero aestimentur. Quae omnia commendabitis suo anno atque ordine libro evidentiarum, in archivis asservato. Sumptus faciant commeatus firmarii, dum fueritis apud eos, ut est ante constitutum.

Iugera vocamus, acras: cardines, agrorum limites a meridie ad septentrionem: decumanos, ab oriente in occidentem, secundum mundi cardines atque plagas quas iugera respiciunt. Sic ut cardines respiciant latitudinem: decumani longitudinem. Nam decumanus significat longum et maximum, ut decumanus fluctus, decumana porta, decumanum ovum, quia decimum quodque maius aestimatur. Plinius lib. 18°. cap. 33°. et 34°. Politianus etiam epist. 2ª. lib. epist. primo.[c]

[a] It is possible that *loca* is the use of a (permissible) neuter plural of *locus* (to mean places in a particular region); but it would seem more likely that it connotes a building of some sort, and that the singular of the medieval feminine *loca* or *logia* (meaning 'lodge, shed, hut') has been used mistakenly instead of the plural *locae*.

[b] While *clausurae* might be enclosures in the technical sense, the nature of the list suggests that Caius has in mind their physical nature rather than their legal status, *i.e.* closes.

[c] Pliny, *Natural History*, Book 18, ss. 76 and 77, ed. H. Rackham; Poliziano, *Letters*, 2006 Bk 1, letter 2, ch. 2, ed. S. Butler. (The writer is indebted to Dr Duncan-Jones for the modern references.)

terriers,[251] custumals, court rolls, accounts, extents[252] and rentals of manors, lands, tenements, benefices, and possessions whatsoever belonging to your college which have been lost or not yet acquired by it, and to return them to their places in it, and not to overlook any opportunity to do this, not only while they are members of the society, but when they have ceased to be so and left the college.

The inspection of manors.

102/101. Lest anything should be spoiled or taken away through the fault of your lessees or tenants, we decree and direct that every three years you shall also visit all your lands, and every five years you shall survey all and every one of your manors, lands, tenements and benefices, by going round all of them, and ascertaining in whose possession each one of them is, how many acres or *jugera*,[253] how many barns and tenements each one holds, and whether they are assigned by cardinals and decumans[254] or otherwise, are freehold or copyhold, or held in villeinage, by indenture or by court roll, leased to farm or otherwise, located in fields, closes, woods or in meadows: under what names they are assessed, by what borders or markings their boundaries are delimited, in what quantity and number of acres they are assessed. You shall enter all these matters in the book of title deeds kept in the archives in their correct year and order. The tenants shall meet the cost of provisions during the time you are with them, as has been laid down above.

We call *jugera* acres: cardinals the limits of fields from south to north: decumans those from east to west, according to the poles of the earth and zones to which the *jugera* relate. Just as cardinals have regard to latitude, so decumans [have regard to] longitude.[255] For 'decuman' signifies that something is long and large; as a "decuman (or immense) wave", a "decuman (or main) gate",[256] a "decuman (or enormous) egg"; because anything at all large is measured in multiples of tens: Pliny, Book 18, chs. 33 and 34; also Poliziano, Letters, Volume 2, Book 1.

251 See n. 220 to Statute 90, at p. 237 above.

252 Manorial surveys.

253 See n. 242 to Statute 95, at p. 245 above.

254 In Caius' day, the terms were simply transliterated and used in English in the form given here.

255 Caius' explanation confuses rather than clarifies. 'Cardinals' are measured at a point along a decuman, but they indicate longitude; in a similar way 'decumans' indicate latitude. It is possible that Caius was using "*respiciant*" in a technical, astronomical sense; but one suspects that he was confused in his attempt to combine classical learning with estate management. In the list of baffling terms on the fly-leaf of MS 711, cardinals and decumans were defined more simply and succinctly as lines running from south to north and from east to west, respectively: "*limites a meridie ad septentrionem*" and "*limites ab orienti in occidentem*".

256 The *porta decumana* had been the main gate of a Roman army camp, placed furthest from the enemy and guarded by the tenth cohort of the garrison legion.

De supervisoribus terrarum.[a]

103/102 Ad supervisionem istam faciendam, volumus et ordinamus, ut Custos et alius socius (quem Custos et maior sociorum pars propter rerum usum et experientiam, frugalitatem et prudentiam bonumque erga Collegium affectum duxerint eligendum) in supervisores praeficiantur. His in redditu suo, reddita vera et particulari ratione omnium et singulorum quae ea de causa necessario expensa sunt, et iuramento suo confirmata, viatici sumptus faciat Collegium, tantisper dum alibi fuerint quam apud firmarios aut amicos. Proviso non futuros plures Custode, socio uno, uno Custodis famulo, et tribus equis Collegii sumptibus. Nam si Custos indigus sit, unus famulus sufficiat: si abundans, et plures voluerit, ipse reliquorum sumptus faciat. Custos enim honorem ex officio magis spectet quam commodum, prodesse magis Collegio ut bene audiat, quam ex eo ditescere ut male audiat, charitatis officio fungi potius quam domini. Qui huiusce animi non est, indignus est ut sit Custos. Nam qui Collegii custodiam desiderat, charitatis opus desiderat. Proinde prodesse literis et reipublicae debet et paupertati studere omnibus modis et conservando res Collegii praesentes, et acquirendo futuras.

De observatione statutorum.

104/103 Ista omnia statuta a Reverendo patre seorsum, et a nobis in praesenti libro praescripta atque durante vita nostra naturali praescribenda, ad honorem dei, utilitatem patriae et Collegii spectantia, eiusdem singulas personas atque res ad honestatem, ordinem, literarum et virtutis incrementum, atque reipub. et universitatis decus dirigentia, ut singuli Custodes atque socii nostri Collegii et scholastici, qui pro tempore fuerint, prout ad eorum singulos pertineant, diligenter observent, per honorem et utilitatem Collegii, honestatem et virtutem suam, reipub. et universitatis decus obtestamur, et per salutem animarum suarum, quas fidei et iuramenti sui sacri et spontanei religio astrinxit, ac per viscera et misericordias Ihesu Christi Salvatoris nostri et tremendi iudicis

[a] Wrongly read as *supervisionibus* in *Documents*, II, p. 301 and *B.H.* III, p. 386.

Inspectors of lands.

103/102. We wish and direct that this inspection shall be undertaken by the keeper and one other, a fellow whom the keeper and the majority of the fellows judge suitable on account of his acquaintance with and experience of business, frugality and good prudence in relation to the college. On their return the college shall recompense them for their travelling costs on the submission of a true and detailed account of each and every necessary expense incurred in the matter and confirmed on their oath, for such time as they were lodged elsewhere than with lessees or friends; provided that the college is not charged for more than the expenses of the keeper, one fellow, one manservant for the keeper and three horses. For if the keeper is not well off, one manservant will suffice: if he is affluent and wants more, he is to pay for the rest himself. The keeper should look for honour from his office rather than profit, act towards the college so that he is well-regarded, rather than enriching himself so that he is regarded ill, and should perform his office in a spirit of generosity rather than possessiveness. Whoever is not of this mind is unworthy to be keeper. For whoever seeks the care of the college seeks a work of charity.[257] Accordingly, he should promote learning and the common good, and practise frugality in every way, both by conserving the college's existing property and by making future additions to it.

Observance of the statutes.[258]

104/103. For the honour and benefit of the college, for their own integrity and virtue and for the good name of the state and university, we entreat each and every keeper, fellow and scholar to observe scrupulously, so far as they apply to each of them, all those statutes which have been prescribed by the Reverend Father himself and by ourself in the present book, and any which may in the future be prescribed by us during our lifetime, and which have as their goal the honour of God the benefit of the country and the college and steer its members and affairs to integrity, orderliness and an increase in learning and virtue and the good name of the state and university; and we beseech this for the salvation of their souls which conscience has bound by their sacred and voluntary pledge and oath, and through the bowels of compassion and mercy of Jesus Christ our Saviour and awesome judge. For the whole well-being of your college is founded

[257] In Statute 4 Caius had set £30 as a minimum property-qualification for any Master from outside the fellowship.

[258] The complexity of the syntax of this statute is exceptional even for Caius. It is reflected in the translation.

obsecramus.[a] In observatione enim statutorum omnis salus Collegii vestri sita est, quae nihil praecipiunt quod non est honestum et utile.

Eidem autem et iuramentum suum qui neglexerit aut contempserit, honestatis, literarum et virtutis finibus qui contineri nolit, quem nec honor dei, utilitas sua et Collegii, nec reipub. et academiae decus movent, sed quaerit et procurat, quaeret aut procurabit aliquando per se vel per alium appellando, querendo aut supplicando (nisi in ea supplicatione simplex sit submissio, quod sub nomine supplicationis iuris contentio saepissime alitur, et tacita appellationis et querelae prosecutio continetur) aliter vivere, aliterque sibi caeterisque prospectum, consultum aut dispensatum iri in parte vel in toto, per alios, aut per alias rationes quam per ista statuta Reverendi patris et nostra authoritate principum sancita constitutum et decretum est, istisque nostris statutis conabitur contraire, aliquid addere, diminuere, aut aliter quam pro sensu grammatico eadem interpretari, vel cum eis dispensare, execrabilis esto, priveturque is sive Custos sive socius aut scholasticus sit, omni Collegii beneficio, et excludatur in aeternum. Constituimus praeterea, ne quae consuetudo praevaleat adversus statutum aliquod aut Rev. patris aut nostrum.

De indulgentia.

105/104 Ut autem observari haec statuta nostra maxime cupimus in rem cuiusque, ita si quis parum considerate ex praecipiti passione et humana fragilitate, eorum aliquod quae ad mores pertinent, violaverit, promptus ad correctionem facti, et emendationem vitae, volumus ut ob id non habeatur periurus. Contra qui fecerit, periurus esto, nisi offenderit in ea statuta quibus poenae seu mulctas propositae sunt, aut admonitiones. Ea autem statuta subiici volumus admonitionibus, quae aut moram trium septimanarum patiuntur sine praesenti aut futuro damno et periculo Collegii aut personarum eiusdem, aut non nimis urgent. Caetera periuriis. At qui periurus est, constituimus ut expellatur Collegio et privetur omni eius beneficio in aeternum.

[a] Cf. "*per viscera misericordae Dei nostri*": Luke 1:78.

on the observance of its statutes, which require nothing that is not proper and beneficial.

But he who neglects or spurns his oath, who is unwilling to be constrained by the bounds of integrity, learning and virtue, and who is moved neither by the honour of God, his own well-being and that of the college, nor by the good name of the state and the university, but seeks and procures, or may seek and procure at any time in the future, by the making, either personally or through a third party, of an appeal, complaint or supplication (unless there is an unconditional submission in that supplication, since a lawsuit is very often pursued in the guise of a supplication, and the prosecution of an appeal or complaint is tacitly contained in it),[259] to behave differently and to contrive that some interpretation, ruling or dispensation[260] should be applied differently to him than to others, wholly or in part, through other persons or on other grounds than is determined and decreed by those statutes of the Reverend Father and ourself made with royal authority, and strives to flout those statutes of ours, or to add anything to them, or take anything away from them, or interpret them otherwise than in their grammatical sense, or dispense with them, shall be accursed; and, whether he be keeper, fellow or scholar, he shall be deprived of all benefit of the college and excluded from it for ever. We determine furthermore that no custom shall prevail against a statute of either the Reverend Father or ourself.

Clemency.

105/104. Just as we desire greatly that our statutes are observed for the good of each person, so, if anyone has breached any of those which pertain to behaviour unthinkingly, out of sudden passion and human frailty, and is spurred to correct the deed and improve his life, it is our wish that he shall not be held to have broken his oath on that account. He who has acted in a different manner shall be judged to have broken his oath, unless his offence is against those statutes which provide specifically for a penalty or a fine or admonitions. It is our wish that statutes shall [only] be subject to admonitions if they allow for a delay of three weeks when there is no present or future loss and risk to the college or its members or else the matter is not pressing. Breach of [all] other statutes [shall amount to] oath-breaking; and we rule that he who breaks his oath shall be expelled from the college and deprived of all benefit of it for ever.

259 Caius probably had in mind the cases of Clarke, Dethick, Warner and Spenser: see "*John Caius and his Foundation*", § V. 3 below.

260 *Dispensatum*: here Caius could be using the verb *dispensare* in the sense of 'apply to' rather than 'waive'; but its second use five lines later indicates that he is referring to the legal notion of a power to waive or 'dispense with'; cf. Statute 106 following.

Periurium autem ut grave crimen est, ita cuiusque est providere ne in id sua culpa et voluntate incidat, ut cui postea nisi expellendi correctione mederi non licet, propter exemplum aliorum. Neque enim animus noster movetur ad correctionem, quia ipsi laesi sumus, sed quia alii, sed ut disciplina servetur, mores corrigantur, licentia comprimatur. Etenim vitiosa est in peccatis irae suae cohibitio. Siquidem iusta ira non est ira, sed mater disciplinae: quae utique cupiditas ultionis non est, cum non praecessit iniuria. Neque enim in homines aliter commoveri, si deliquerint, cum Demonace censeo,[a] vitia tamen corrigenda statuo. Siquidem medicus non indignatur aegrotis, sed morbis medetur. Nam scio hominis esse peccare, boni vero hominis emendare per disciplinam peccata. Neque indignandum si quis ob malefacta det poenas. Etenim longe miserius est meruisse poenas quam dedisse: et facile supplicium perpetietur, qui se honesta vita a supplicio liberare noverit. Itaque etsi non ira, at certe disciplina necessaria est, cum multi hodie sint οισιν ουτε βῶμος, ουτε πιστις, ουθ' ορκος μενει, hoc est, quibus nec religio, nec fides, nec iusiurandum curae sunt, uti in Lacones Aristophanes solebat dicere.[b] A quibus hominum morumque generibus, nostros omnes longe abesse cupimus, oramusque patrem, filium et spiritum sanctum, ut vos omnes in decenti ordine, honestate morum et sanctitate vitae conservent in aeternum: quod certe fiet, si vicissim Deo patri, filio et spiritui sancto vosmetipsos dederitis et devoveritis supplices, bonasque literas et virtutes illis ducibus et Magistris amplectamini atque excolatis, alioqui frustra divinam imploraturi opem.

De potestate fundatori reservata.

106/105 Praescripta haec omnia et singula diligenter observari statuimus, aliaque omnia et singula statuta ante per nos ordinata et a primo Ianuarii anni domini 1557 ad hunc usque diem primum eiusdem mensis anni salutis 1572 per nos edita, et hic non comprehensa, irrita facimus et expresse revocamus. Reservata tamen nobis semper potestate, haec quoque statuta omnia et singula mutandi, minuendi, augendi, supplendi, corrigendi, interpretandi, delendi, et alia nova faciendi, et super his et illis omnibus atque singulis dispensandi,

[a] Lucian, *Demonax*, chap. 7. (The writer is indebted to Dr Duncan-Jones for both this and the following reference.)

[b] *Acharnians*, l. 308, ed. J. Henderson, Harvard University Press, 1998.

Since breaking one's oath is a grave sin, so it is the responsibility of each person to ensure that he does not incur it through his fault or desire, lest it cannot later be corrected except through the penalty of expulsion as an example to others. For we are not moved to punish because we are ourself harmed, but because others are, and so that discipline may be preserved, habits corrected and licence restrained. For suppressing one's anger in the face of wrongdoing is [itself] wrong. Just as rightful anger is not anger, but the mother of discipline: in the same way anger is in no way a desire for revenge, when injury has not prompted it. Like Demonax, I judge that we are not to act differently towards those who transgress with evil in their hearts, and in that belief I decree that crimes must be punished: in the same way a doctor is not offended by the sick but cures the sickness. For I know it is in the nature of man to sin, and for a good man to make amends for his sins through penance. And it is not unbecoming if one imposes penalties for wrongdoing. For it is far worse to have deserved punishment than to inflict it: and he who turns over a new leaf through punishment bears that punishment easily. Therefore, though there is no anger, penance is certainly necessary when many today are people who abide by no altar, no agreement, no oath, that is, persons to whom neither religion, nor good faith, nor an oath mean anything, as Aristophanes was accustomed to say about the Spartans. We desire all our people to be very far removed from those types of men and morals, and we pray to the Father, Son and Holy Spirit that you may all be kept safe in your proper station, integrity of morals and sanctity of life for ever: which will assuredly happen if you in turn give yourselves and devote your entreaties to God the Father, Son and Holy Spirit, and embrace and cultivate good learning and virtues with those counsellors and teachers to guide you, otherwise you will crave divine bounty in vain.[261]

Reservation of powers to the founder.

106/105. We decree that each and every one of these rules shall be scrupulously observed, and we render null and void and expressly revoke each and every statute previously made and issued by ourself between the 1st January A.D. 1557/8[262] to this first day of the same month in the year of Grace 1572/3 that is not incorporated here: always reserving to ourself, however, power to amend, modify, add to, supplement, correct, interpret or delete all and every one of these statutes, and make other new provisions, and to dispense from all

[261] This second paragraph of the statute was not contained in Caius' draft statutes in 1558 and its inclusion here is a striking illustration of his later tendency to moralise at length on human frailty and the need for correction, and thereby justify his earlier expulsions; cf. Statutes 43, 47, 72, 104.

[262] *I.e.*, 1 January 1558 (NS). Contrast the final date clause below, where Caius refers to 30 March 1558 as the date on which his first statutes were issued.

quando et quoties nobis videbitur durante vita nostra naturali: Reservata etiam nobis potestate libera eligendi et amovendi socios et scholares nostros, et de eis disponendi, ordinandi et determinandi, prout nobis videbitur, quamdiu fuerimus in hac vita.

De lectione statutorum bis singulis annis.

107/106 Statuimus etiam et ordinamus, ut statuta ista nostra omnia diligenter, clare et sine omissione perlegantur bis annis singulis eisdem temporibus quibus statuta Reverendi patris perleguntur, ne quis causetur ignorantiam. Illud etiam statuentes, ne plura statutorum exemplaria uno (praeter ea quae in Collegio corporis Christi et beatae Mariae, et in archivis Collegii regalis reponuntur) transcribantur, et eo apud solum Custodem, aut eo absente praesidentem, in usus quotidianos remanente. Non negamus tamen cuiquam in certiorem cognitionem officii sui et vivendi regulam, non ad contentionem, quin ad Custodem, aut eo absente praesidentem, statuta videndi et legendi, non autem transcribendi causa, cum velit recurrat, nec id denegatum volumus.

{*De contradictione statutorum Reverendi patris et nostri.*}[a]

108/107 Volumus etiam, ut si qua in re contradicunt aut repugnant statuta nostra statutis Reverendi Patris, (quod potest evenire, non sponte mea, sed vel oblivione, vel incuria, vel sinistra interpretatione volentium abuti eis vel repellere in malum aliquod) sic ut ex eo controversia oriatur inter Custodem et socios, aut inter socios ipsos, per visitatores nostros definiatur et determinetur, utra statuta salubrius aut commodius praecipiant in rem praesentem, usum, commodum aut necessitatem Collegii, Custodis et sociorum, et ea praevaleant. Proviso ut si quae statuta nostra diversa fuerint a statutis Reverendi patris, aut eorum vim intendant atque augeant, aut ad nostros fundos, nostram donationem, fundationem, peculiares nostros socios aut scholasticos pertineant, non ob id censeantur contradicere et repugnare.[b] Verbi gratia,

[a] In MS 711 this rubric has been added interlineally, perhaps by Caius himself.
[b] Here MS 711 has a marginal reference "*ex. gr.1*".

and every one of both the former and the latter statutes when and as often as we think fit during our natural life; reserving also to ourself unrestricted power to elect and remove our fellows and scholars and to make arrangements, rules and adjudications concerning them as we see fit for so long as we are in this life.

Reading of the statutes twice annually.

107/106. We decree and direct that all these statutes of ours shall be read aloud scrupulously, clearly and without any omission twice each year at those times at which the statutes of the Reverend Father are read, so that no one can plead ignorance: and we decree further that no more than one copy of the statutes (other than those which are deposited in the College of Corpus Christi and the Blessed Mary and in the archives of King's College)[263] shall be transcribed, and that that copy shall remain with the keeper alone or the president in his absence for daily use.[264] We do not, however, deny to anyone the right to have recourse at will to the keeper or the president in his absence in order to see and read the statutes for the clearer ascertainment of his office and rules of conduct, but not in order to stir up strife or to transcribe them; and it is our wish that this be not denied.

Contradictions between our own statutes and those of the Reverend Father.

108/107. It is our wish that if our statutes contradict or conflict with those of the Reverend Father in any matter (which can happen, not deliberately but from forgetfulness or oversight or perverse interpretation by those wishing to misuse them or reject them for some improper purpose) so that a dispute arises between the keeper and the fellows or among the fellows themselves from this, it shall be settled and decided by our visitors which body of statutes meets the matter in question [and serves] the purposes, convenience or needs of the college, keeper and fellows better and more conveniently, and they shall prevail: provided that if those of our statutes which are different from those of the Reverend Father either reinforce or augment them, or simply apply to our own funds, our own gift and foundation, or to our own fellows or scholars, they shall not on that account be deemed to contradict or be in conflict. For example, the

263 Cf. Statute 25. No reference to the two colleges was included in the draft version of this statute in 1558.

264 This is the parchment copy prescribed by Caius in the final paragraph of the next statute, *i.e.* MS 755.

Reverendus pater statuit ut plures medici uno non sint, aut summum duobus: ego autem volo duos meos aut tres. Haec non repugnant nec contradicunt, quia non sunt in eodem genere. Ille enim intelligit non futuros plures ex sua vel in sua fundatione, non in mea, quam nescivit futuram. Et ego intelligo futuros duos {*meos aut tres*}[a] in mea, non in sua. Mihi enim licet in omnes quos libet honestos usus mea impendere sine adversatione aliqua. Ad haec, Reverendus pater praecipit, ut post annum regentiae unusquisque eligat quam velit studii sui rationem in vitam: Benefactores qui {*post illum et*}[b] ante nos fuerunt, contra, non sociorum suorum arbitrio relinquunt studii et vitae genus, sed assignant. Non tamen contrarii isti sunt fundatori, quod (ut dixi) cuique Benefactori licitum est studii vitaeque genus suis praescribere, quemadmodum fundatori suis in hoc genere praecipere, et non aliorum sociis.

Postremo volumes, ut post mortem nostram, ea statuta, quae non cassata a nobis relinquentur, in librum statutorum pargameneum quem ad hoc paratum fecimus, quam pulcherrima litera nostro sumptu transcribantur sine additione, subtractione, aut mutatione ulla sub poena periurii et amissionis omnis sui cuiusque iuris in Collegio ipso facto. Quod ut rite fiat, volumus et ordinamus ut examinentur statuta omnia ad exemplar statutorum nostrorum in custodia praefecti et sociorum Collegii regalis[c] et Magistri et sociorum Collegii corporis Christi et beatae Mariae et ad ea reformentur, si quid alienum, si quid additum, si quid imminutum sit, nisi interim aliquid manu mea propria additum aut ademptum sit. Id si fuerit, volo ut in librum statutorum in custodia Collegii regalis, et Magistri et sociorum Collegii corporis Christi referatur quoque et liber dein in cistam eorum reponatur.

Datum Londini {*tricesimo martii an^o^ christi 1558 ac postea auctum*}[d] primo Ianuarii anno domini millesimo quingentesimo septuagesimo secundo,

[a] In MS 711, an interlined insertion, perhaps by Caius. It suggests that the statute was originally written before Caius changed his mind and increased to three the number of fellowships he proposed to endow.

[b] In MS 711, interlined insertion.

[c] Oddly, Caius refers here to the *praefectus*, not the *praepositus*. He also uses the more colloquial form "Provost and Fellows": contrast Statute 25 ("Provost and scholars").

[d] In MS 711, interlined insertion by Caius himself: see Plate IV above. In the text as originally written by the scribe, Caius was stated to be in London on 1 January 1573; if so, he must have returned to London even earlier than has generally been supposed after the sacking of his room on 13 December 1572. Caius' insertion may have been intended to correct that statement, though it would have been simpler to substitute "Cambridge" for "London", if that had been his purpose. For the puzzling "30 March 1558", see the note to the translation.

Reverend Father decrees that there should not be more than one medical fellow or at most two; but it is my wish that there should be two or three of mine. These are not in conflict or contradictory, because they do not apply to the same case. For he means that there should not be more of his or on his foundation, not on my foundation, a future event which he could not foresee; and I mean that there shall be two or three on my foundation, not on his.[265] For it is permissible for me to impose on my foundation any proper uses whatever without any conflict. To take another example, the Reverend Father decrees that after the year of regency each person should choose the field of lifetime study he wishes [to pursue]; whereas benefactors who came after him and before ourself, took a different line and did not leave the field of study and life to the decision of their fellows, but specified it. They are not, however, thereby in conflict with the founder, because (as I have said) it is open to each benefactor to prescribe the type of study and life for his fellows, just as it is for the founder to prescribe for his fellows and not for those of others.

Finally it is our wish that after our death those statutes which have not been repealed by ourself shall be transcribed as handsomely as possible, at our expense, into the parchment statute book which we have had made ready,[266] without any addition, subtraction or alteration on pain of oath-breaking and automatic deprivation of all entitlement in the college. In order that this be done correctly, we wish and direct that all the statutes shall be compared with the copy of our statutes in the custody of the Provost and Fellows of King's College and that of the Master and Fellows of the College of Corpus Christi and the Blessed Mary and corrected against them if anything is different, anything added, or anything modified, unless something has been added or removed in my own hand in the meantime. If that happens, it is my wish that it be noted also in [each of] the book[s] of statutes in the custody of King's College and the Master and Fellows of Corpus Christi College and the book then replaced in their chest.

Given at London {*on the 30th March*[267] *in the year of Christ 1558 and afterwards enlarged*} on the 1st January A.D. 1572/3, the year running from

[265] These generous provisions soon bore fruit, and less than a century later Thomas Fuller listed 27 medical men of great note from Caius (William Harvey among them) saying "such a little Montpel[l]ier is this College alone for eminent physicians": *History of the University of Cambridge* (1665), 1840 ed., p. 191 Cf. Statute 54 above.

[266] The vellum copy, MS 755 in the college library; see "*Caius' Statutes: The Sources*", § I. 3, at p. 31 above.

[267] The italicised words in braces were inserted by Caius and they raise two queries: (i) Caius' whereabouts on 1 January 1572/3; for this, see the note to the text; (ii) the precise date of the first statutes he issued in 1558. His insertion here gives 30 March 1558 as the date of his first statutes, but the day of the month must be a slip, as he had given a copy of the statutes to Bacon at the re-founding ceremony on 25 March 1558: *Annals*, p. 57. He gave yet a third date two pages earlier in the manuscript, where he referred (in Statute 106) to 1 January 1557/8 as the date of his

anno inchoando a festo Annuntiationis beatae Mariae virginis, quod in eo {*ipso*}[a] festo anni verbi incarnati 1558 Collegium {*istud*}[b] fuit erectum, ac Deo, divae virgini, et reipub. consecratum, appenso sigillo nostro, et addita subscriptione nominis nostri manu nostra.

Per me Ioannem Caium[c]

Memorandum[d] quod durante prima locatione Maneriorum de Ronghton et Crokesley erunt tantum tres socii et duodecim scholares nostrae peculiaris fundationis, post vero secundam dimissionem auctis redditbus, alantur tres socii et viginti scholares.

Per Ióhannem Caium[e]

a In MS 711, interlined insertion.

b In MS 711, interlined insertion.

c Depite the statement that Caius has signed his name with his own hand (*subscriptione nominis nostri manu nostra*), the signature is made with the scribe's pen and would seem to be in his hand, not Caius' autograph. Contrast the signature to the postscript which follows immediately and is made with a different pen. See Plate V above.

d MS 760 and Venn interpret the symbol thus; MSS 711, 755 and Lambeth MS 720 have a symbol that might be "M" or "Viz.". The 1852 text opts for "St.".

e Caius' autograph and own pen; hence the difference in spelling of "*Iohannem*"?

the feast of the Annunciation of Blessed Mary the Virgin, because on that very feast of the year of the Word Incarnate 1558,[268] this college was established and dedicated to God, the Holy Virgin and the State, with our seal attached and the addition of our name subscribed in our hand.

By me John Caius.

Note. As to the direction that there shall be up to three fellows and twelve scholars on our own foundation during the period of the first leasing of the manors of Runcton and Croxley, after the commencement of the second demise three fellows and twenty scholars shall be supported out of the increased rents.[269]

By me John Caius.

first statutes. (There is a similar confusion over the date of his earlier draft statutes which refer to the grant of the Charter in September 1557 and must have been drafted after it; they carry the very late date of 20 April 1558 and this was subsequently wrongly corrected to 7 May 1557, thereby predating the Charter: see *B.H.* III, p. 59.)

268 The Anglican calendar year started on 25 March.

269 Caius had originally provided for two fellows and twelve scholars in his draft statutes of 1557 and in the Charter, and he had in fact already increased the provision to three and twenty, respectively, in Statute 2 of the present statutes. It would seem, however, that neither the number of fellows nor that of scholars was to be increased until the second leasing: see Statute 11 and "*The Governing Body*", § VI. 1 below.

IV. 2

Interpretatio Statutorum Johannis Caii

[Cambridge, Gonville & Caius College BUR: DEEDS/ I, 48]

Ad perpetuam rei memoriam.

Johannes Caius artium et medicine doctor[a] nuper custos sive magister Collegii Gonevill et Caius in Academia Cantabrigiensi, summo in bonas literas amore et solicitudine tactus et ut posteris de Repub. bene merendi exemplum proponeret, sociosque et amicos suos ad consimilem gratitudinem excitaret, sumptus non mediocres in propagando collegium literatorum in eadem Academia insumpsit, cujus processus felices ex animo optans tanquam quidem gubernator statuta varia suis observanda promulgavit. Que ut speratum sortirentur effectum verbis quibusdam testamenti et ultime voluntatis suas obnixe rogavit nos **Matthaeum** providentia divina Cantuariensem Archiepiscopum totius Anglie Primatem et Metropolitanum ut duranti vita nostra naturali curam ejusdem fundacionis haberemus, quam per litteras patentes **Philippi** et **Mariae**[b] regis et regine Anglie datas Westmonasterii quarto die Septembris anno Domini 1557 et annis regnorum eorundem regis et regine quarto et quinto impetravit potestate et auctoritate plena condendi et decernendi quedam decreta, ordinaciones et statuta quantum ad collegium antedictum per illum fundatum attinet dummodo decretis ordinacionibus et statutis per reverendum patrem **Willielmum** quondam Norwicensem Episcopum primum ejusdem collegii cum venerando viro Edmundo Gonevill fundatorem antehac editis non repugnent, vel contraria sint neque regali prerogative eorundem regis et regine et successorum suorum adversentur.

[a] The phrase "*artium et medicinae doctor*" repeats the words of Caius' statutes themselves as given in MS 711, a copy of which had been sent to Parker at his request.

[b] In the case of the name of the two Queens, Mary and Elizabeth, and Matthew Parker's own Christian name the diphthong '*ae*' is used, but not generally – even "*in beate Marie Virginis*".

IV. 2

The Interpretation by Matthew Parker of the Statutes of John Caius

[NOTE: Editorial additions are marked with square brackets.]

To be a permanent record of the matter.

John Caius, doctor of arts and medicine lately keeper or master of Gonville and Caius College in the University of Cambridge, took upon himself the not inconsiderable expense of founding a college of scholars in that university. In this he was prompted both by a very great love of and solicitude for learning and by the desire to furnish an example of meritorious conduct to later generations of the realm and to spur his friends and associates to similar [acts of] generosity. Because he was personally eager for the happy progress [of his college] and was its governor[1] he issued various statutes to be observed by his fellow-members. In order that these should have the desired effect he earnestly and expressly requested in his last will and testament that we Matthew by divine providence Archbishop of All England and Metropolitan[2] should during our natural life have that charge of his foundation which he had himself obtained by the letters patent of Philip and Mary king and queen of England given at Westminster 4 September 1557 and in the 4th and 5th years of the reigns of that King and Queen with full power and authority to formulate and enact decrees, ordinances and statutes applicable to the aforesaid college founded by him, provided always that they should not conflict with, or contradict, the decrees, ordinances and statutes earlier issued by the reverend father William [Bateman] sometime Bishop of Norwich first founder of that college with the venerable Edmund Gonville and provided also that they should not run counter to the royal prerogative of the same king and queen and her successors.[3]

1 *Gubernator* had acquired this sense in relation to schools by the sixteenth century.

2 Parker would have known that the title of Metropolitan was of doubtful origin.

3 The translation breaks up what would otherwise be a somewhat indigestible preamble.

Cumque idem Johannes per ultimam voluntatem et testamentum suum nobis dicto Matthaeo (ut antea retulimus) hanc curam commendaverit ut[a] omnia dicta statuta per eundem de dicto suo collegio edita chirographo et sigillo suo consignata supervideremus: et si quod ambiguum vel dubium in eis vel eorum aliquo oriatur id per nos dictum Archiepiscopum explicari et declarari decreverit; nam in dicto suo testamento sic habetur Volo et jubeo ut ejusdem domini Archiepiscopi censuram et interpretacionem magister et socii ejusdem collegii ita fideliter exequantur ac si meum ipsius fuisset scriptum.

Cum igitur Thomas Legge artium magister prefati collegii magister sive custos et socii ejusdem ardua quedam et difficilia in ejusdem statutis examinari et definiri per litteras suas nos prefatum Matthaeum interpellarint necnon in litteris et epistulis suis ad nos missis sic scribant: Quod per auctoritatem dignitati tue concessam poteris pro arbitratu tuo vel acumine dubitandi vel decernendi judicio uti, quo omnis in posterum contentionis et turbarum ansa precidatur, hanc censuram tuam in his etiam imploramus que tam facile inventionem nostram latere poterant quam acrimoniae et sagacitati tue patere: ut latius in dictis litteris communi suo sigillo communitis continetur dat. Cantabrigie in Collegio Gonevill et Caii Quarti Calendas Quintilis anno domini 1574.

Hinc est quod nos predictus Matthaeus potestati auctoritati et peticioni predicti innitentes ambigua et dubia tam per nos previsa quam per magistrum et socios predictos oblata, proposita et a nobis in hunc modum definita exposuimus et declaravimus viz.

Primo exponimus et declaramus: Cum reverendus pater Willielmus Bateman Norwicensis quondam episcopus magistrum et socios quosdam in dicto collegio constituerit, ac inter alia decreta magistrum sive custodem et socios ejusdem castos esse debere &c. necnon predicus Johannes Caius ultimus post dictum reverendum patrem fundator statuto 14 de coelibatu decreverit quod neque magister nec socius eligatur qui quoquo modo matrimonium contraxerit mutata voce *castum* in *coelibem* atque ita contra prerogativam regiam et primi fundatoris verba vocem hanc *coelibem* duriter admodum exposuerit: Nos Matthaeus antedictus idem Johannis Caii statutum quoad illum articulum reverendi patris statuto repugnare declaramus nec ita juxta litteram exponi ut verba ejusdem prae se ferunt.

[a] The 1852 transcript (but not Lambeth MS 720) prints "*et*", thereby creating an abrupt and awkward switch from the indicative (*commendaverit*) to the subjunctive (*supervideremus*).

And whereas the same John by his last will and testament commended this care to us the said Matthew (as we have earlier stated) so that we might oversee all the said statutes promulgated for his said college in his hand and countersigned with his seal; and if any ambiguity or doubt should arise on them, or any of them, he stipulated that it should be explained and expounded by us the said Archbishop, for it is stated in his said will: "I will and direct that the master and fellows of the same college shall faithfully observe the ruling and interpretation of the same lord Archbishop just as if I had written it myself."

Accordingly, whereas Thomas Legge master of arts master or keeper of the said college and the fellows thereof have appealed to us the said Matthew by letter to consider and clarify difficulties and perplexities in these statutes, writing in their letters and missives addressed to us: "Since by the authority vested in you by your position you are able reach a judgement through your authority and skill in identifying and evaluating doubts, whereby all occasion for contention and quarrels in the future may be summarily cut short, we implore your ruling in these matters which are as opaque to us as they are clear to your acuity and wisdom": as is more fully contained in the said letters with their common seal given at Cambridge in Gonville and Caius College on the 28th of June A.D. 1574.[4]

It is for this reason that we the aforesaid Matthew in pursuance of the aforesaid power, authority and petition do expound and explain the ambiguities and uncertainties noticed by us or submitted by the master and fellows aforesaid: viz.

FIRST,[5] we rule and make known that, whereas the reverend father William Bateman sometime bishop of Norwich established a master and fellows in the said college, and among other decrees [laid down] that its master or keeper and fellows should be chaste etc., and the said John Caius the subsequent founder after the said reverend father decreed in **Statute 14** *Of celibacy* that neither the master nor a fellow should be elected who had in any way contracted marriage, having changed the word 'chaste' to 'celibate' and so, contrary to the royal prerogative and the words of the first founder, expounded the word 'celibate' exceedingly harshly: we the aforesaid Matthew declare that that statute of John Caius conflicts with the statute of the reverend father, so far as that provision is concerned, and is not to be expounded beyond the literal meaning that its words bear.[6]

4 Lambeth MS 720, fol. 13. Parker does no more than reproduce a phraseology by the Master and fellows that Uriah Heep would have been hard pressed to equal.

5 The first two rulings, *i.e.* on celibacy and the use of Latin, had not been sought by the Master and fellows (Lambeth MS 720, fols. 23–7), but Parker was aware of the Queen's strong views on both subjects.

6 See *Celibacy* in "*Supplementary Note to Caius' Statutes*", § IV. 3, at p. 282 below.

Item cum statuto 9 tit. de Sermone Latino decretum sit, Quod socii, pensionarii omnes et discipuli latine loquantur sub poena deprivacionis &c. Declaramus quod inter se latine loquentur aut grece, cum advenis vero cuique liberum erit sermone patrio uti, ut res postulat, tam in mensa quam alibi infra collegium, et quod preces quotidianas eodem modo et forma qua princeps in suis statutis publice editis decrevit peragent, vel qua Cancellarius aut Procancellarius ordinaverit vel qua maxima pars Collegiorum infra Academiam de facto usa fuerit.

Item ubi queritur an sophiste possint supplere vicem unam singulis septimanis in problematibus observandis (quod a Domino Caio permissum fuisse affirmatis), quia hec res tam per statuta reverendi patris quam Johannis Caii utrobique decernitur, ad illorum statuta recurrendum censemus.

Quod ad mulctam attinet eorum qui a communibus locis abfuerint in statuto 18 tit. de commemorationibus fundatorum communibus locis &c. statuta regia in hac re sequenda esse pronunciamus et mulcte moderacionem penes custodis arbitrium futuram.

Item locos illos nempe in statuto 19 tit. de lectionibus et reverentia Baccalaureorum ac etiam in statuto 20 tit. de nimia familiaritate, quos repugnare putatis, ita conciliandos arbitramur ut prior ad Baccalaureos, posterior ad scholasticos non graduatos referatur.

Item questionem e statuto 21 tit. de prelectore[a] grece linguae, motam de modo pronunciandi grecam linguam, sic declaramus, optantes ut modestia vestra in hac re id quod in Academia publice preceptum est preponere privato velit, ne soli sapere videamini.

Queritis preterea moti statuto 23 tit. de tabernis, lusibus et cubitu, an scholastici teneantur esse in cubiculis tam [a]estate quam hyeme hora octava post meridiem: sic respondemus: Cum regia Maiestas in statutis suis constituerit

[a] It should be noted that Parker substitutes "*praelectore*" for the awkward "*professore*" in Caius' statute.

Whereas it is decreed in **Statute 9**, *Of Latin Speech*, that all fellows pensioners and students shall speak in Latin on pain of deprivation etc., we declare that they shall speak Latin or Greek among themselves, [but] anyone shall be free to converse with visitors in the vernacular, as circumstances may require, both at table and elsewhere in college and that they shall recite daily prayers in the manner and form which the sovereign has decreed in the statutes publicly issued or which the Chancellor or Vice-Chancellor has ordained or which the majority of colleges in the University have adopted.[7]

Where it is asked [in respect of **Statute 17**] whether sophisters can substitute one deputy each week in problem classes (which you state had been allowed by Master Caius): because this matter is laid down both in the statutes of the reverend father and in those of John Caius, we rule that there must be a return to their statutes.

As regards the fine in **Statute 18** entitled *Of Commemorations of founders, commonplaces* etc. for those who absent themselves from commonplaces: we declare that the royal statutes should be followed in this matter and that the assessment of the fine shall in future lie with the keeper.[8]

As regards those passages in **Statute 19** entitled *Of lectures and respectful behaviour of bachelors* and those in **Statute 20** entitled *Of excessive familiarity*, which you believe to be in conflict: we rule that they are assuredly to be reconciled on the basis that the first refers to Bachelors and the second to scholars who are not graduates.[9]

As regards the question arising from **Statute 21** entitled *Of the praelector of the Greek language*, concerning the pronunciation of the Greek language: we rule in the following way, namely, we desire that your sense of propriety in this matter should lead you to put the public University rule before [your own] private beliefs, lest you should appear [to think yourselves] the only ones in the right.[10]

Arising from **Statute 23** entitled *Of taverns, games and rooms* you ask moreover whether scholars are required to be in their rooms by 8 p.m. in summer as well as in winter: we reply as follows, namely, given that the Queen's

7 Parker does not specify clearly whether he has in mind Elizabeth's University Statutes of 1570 or general Acts of Parliament. Chapter 50 § 38 of the 1570 Statutes only required certain prayers in colleges to be *sung* in English and the final prayer to be *said* in English. In 1565 Parker had been obliged to charge the Master of his own college, Corpus Christi, of the need to keep the Queen's "late order … for Latin prayers to be said in the Colleges, for the better accustoming of the scholars to the learned language" for which she had devised a Latin book of prayers; and he had "counselled" the Master of Gonvill Hall (*sic*) in the matter.

8 See *Commonplaces* in "*Supplementary Notes to Caius' Statutes*", § IV. 3, at p. 286 below.

9 Scholars retained their award until they became M.A.s.

10 Parker tactfully hints that the college should adopt the humanist pronunciation that Caius had set his face against while he was alive.

tempus occludendi collegiorum portas, si scholastici domi in collegio illis horis fuerint, satis esse interpretamur.

Ubi questio est etiam de statuto 24 tit. de decanis Quid sit legere extraordinarie, hoc interpretamur e[ss]e extraordinarie legere, cum et librum et authorem legendum custos pro arbitratu suo nominaverit.

Quantum ad statutum 26 titulo de Anniversario attinet: nullam fore commemoracionem in sacello die ejus natalitio statuit; quamobrem ejus commemorationem tantum in die suo emortuali eo modo fieri decernimus qui in regiis statutis in comemoracionibus pro benefactoribus prescribitur observandus.

Et ad questionem de vestitu in statuto 27 tit. de vestitu terminandam, decentissimum judicamus ut id teneatur quod statuta Academie et leges regni in hac causa fieri jubent.

Quoad statutum 39 tit. subsidium nostrorum sociorum in quo Dominus Caius fundacionis sue sociis scholasticos gratis docere precipit, quia dictis suis sociis licentiam prebenda vel alia exhibicione ad certum valorem gaudendi concessit, et incertum sit utrum ante prebendam vel exhibicionem obtentam iidem socii a scholaribus aliquid pro institucione exigant, optamus ut socii eos gratis instruant, verum si quid scholares dare cogentur, id penes Magistrum erit, tam numerum scholarium sociis assignare, quam annuam mercedem ante hujusmodi prebendam obtentam, modo idem stipendium annuum valorem decem solidorum non excedat.

Quod attinet ad vestem solennem statuto 40 tit. de veste solenni, quam liberaturum ille vocat, &c. Si census annuus collegio per Dominum Caium acquisitus tantis oneribus sufficiat, custos et bursarii hanc illis beneficentiam prestare posse declaramus.

Statutum 42 tit. de anatomia sic declaramus. Quod si unum aut plura corpora dissecentur et aperiantur sumptus funeris et aliorum onerum 26^{s} 8^{d} [a] pro una vice in illo anno non excedet.[b]

Statutum 45 de orat. sic exponimus. Quoniam exequie et orationes pro mortuis hoc seculo sine suspicione peragi nequeant, ideo pretermitti censemus. Cumque D. Caius nullius solemnis commemoracionis nominum fundatorum

a Written thus in numerals in the original.

b *Pro una vice in illo anno*: *Pro una vice* is somewhat ambiguous and could be read as "on any one occasion". However, MS 760 suggests that it was not understood in that way: it omits the words *pro una vice*, making it clear that Parker was understood to limit the total expenditure to 26s. 8d. in a year and that the limit could not be avoided by having dissections on more than one day.

Majesty in her statutes fixed the time for closing the gates of colleges, we interpret it as being sufficient if scholars are inside the college by those hours.[11]

On **Statute 24**, *Of the deans*, where there is also a question as to the meaning of an extra-ordinary reading, we interpret this to mean that a reading is extra-ordinary when the keeper selects the book and author at his discretion.

As to the ambit of **Statute 26** entitled *Of the anniversary* and the fact that he did not provide that there should be a commemoration in chapel on his birthday: we decree for this reason that his commemoration should only be on his mortuary day [and should be] in the form that is prescribed for use in the Crown's statutes on the commemoration of benefactors.[12]

And as to the question of dress which has to be settled in **Statute 27** entitled *Of dress*: we adjudge that it is most fitting that the relevant requirements of University statutes and the laws of the realm should be observed.[13]

As regards **Statute 39** entitled *Subsidy of our fellows* in which Master Caius ordered the fellows of his foundation to teach scholars free of charge: since he allowed those fellows freedom to enjoy a prebend or other emolument [up] to a certain value, and it is uncertain whether those same fellows may demand anything from the scholars for instruction before a prebend or emolument is obtained, we prefer that the fellows shall instruct them without charge, [but] if indeed the scholars are required to pay anything, it shall be for the master to decide both the number of scholars to assign to fellows and the annual fee payable [during the period] before a prebend of this kind is obtained, provided that the supplementary payment shall not exceed the value of 10s. a year.

As regards the meaning of formal attire in **Statute 40** entitled *Of formal attire*, which he calls livery etc.: if the annual income acquired for the College by Master Caius is sufficient to bear such costs, we declare that the keeper and bursars may meet the cost of this benefit for [the members of his foundation].[14]

[As regards] **Statute 42** entitled *Of Anatomy* we declare thus: if one or more bodies are dissected and interred the cost of the funeral and other expenses shall not exceed 26s. 8d. once in that year.

We expound **Statute 45** *Of Prayers* thus: since exequies and prayers for the dead may not be performed in this age without suspicion, we rule that they should be omitted. And since Master Caius mentioned nothing about a solemn

11 Statutes of Elizabeth 1570, chap. 50, § 34 (*Documents*, I, p. 493). Parker sensibly relaxes Caius' injunction that scholars had to be in their own rooms after the specified hour, ruling that it is sufficient that they be within the college.

12 See the Statutes of Elizabeth 1570, chap. 50, § 38.

13 See the Statutes of Elizabeth 1570, chap. 46.

14 In Statute 40 Caius had provided for the payments only to be made when the current leases were renewed; Parker allows payments to be made earlier if the income is sufficient. The college immediately took advantage of Parker's ruling and paid to the Caius fellows the same livery as other fellows received, but full payments were not made until the leases of Croxley and Runcton had been renewed in 1582: see "*Stipends*", § VI. 4, at pp. 428–9 below.

pro publicis concionibus meminerit, volumus statutum in eo articulo observari ut ne quid addatur.

Statuti 52 de absentia nocturna hec est nostra interpretatio: si festra in porta honoris duabus seris claudatur, quarum altera noctu, altera interdiu clauditur, cuilibet sociorum clave ejus sere que diei inservit gaudere licebit.

Statutum 53 de custodia collegii approbamus cum hac moderacione quod duo socii et tres scholares tantum in collegio remanere possint ad meliorem eius tutelam.

Statutum 55 tit. de absentia scholasticorum quoad mulctam absentium in festo Nativitatis et similibus festis, justum et legitimum pronuntiamus.

Statutum 68 de mensa communi exponimus quod concedente magistro a communi mensa cuivis abesse licebit, modo in suo aut alterius cubiculo privata mensa non utatur.

Quoad dubium statuti 83[a] tit. de vasis argenteis &c. licebit in comitiis et determinacionibus vasis argenteis et linteis uti, modo damnum vasorum et linteorum detrimenta per inauguratos et convivia celebrantes resarciantur.

Statutum 93[b] tit. de affectione secludenda in locationibus arbitramur legitimum, nisi magister et socii omnes contrarium senserint, cum hac provisione quod collegium per hujusmodi locationem nihil detrimenti capiat.

Quoad questionem quam ultimo loco movetis de anno valedicendi, exponimus quod socius absens a collegio et in beneficio residens ac omnia onera collegii cum ceteris ferens eo fruatur: nam in his et aliis hujusmodi casibus privata statuta publicis Regni legibus cedere debent.

[a] The statute in question is in fact Statute 82, not 83; likewise Statute 92, not 93, in the paragraph that follows.

[b] Statute 92; see above.

commemoration of the names of founders as a form of public sermon, it is our wish that the statute should be observed strictly in this matter in order that nothing might be added.

Our interpretation of **Statute 52** *Of Absence Overnight* is this: if the door of the Gate of Honour has two leaves, one of which is kept shut at night and the other throughout the day as well, it shall be permissible for each of the fellows to enjoy the use of a key to that leaf which is in use during the day.[15]

We approve **Statute 53** *Of the custody of the college* with this qualification, namely, that at least two fellows and three scholars are able to remain in college for its better protection.

We declare **Statute 55** *Of the absence of scholars* to be just and lawful as regards the fine on those absent at Christmas and similar feasts.

We interpret **Statute 68** *Of the common table* [as meaning] that anyone may be absent from the common table with the agreement of the master, provided that he does not partake of a private meal in his own or anyone else's room.

As regards the doubt on **Statute [82]** entitled *Of silver vessels* etc., it shall be permissible to use the silver vessels and the linens at celebrations for the conferring of M.A.s and B.A.s, provided any damage to the vessels and spoiling of the linens is made good by those graduating and those taking part in the festivities.

We judge **Statute [92]** entitled *Of the avoidance of partiality in leasing* to be right and proper, unless the master and all the fellows are agreed otherwise, [and] with the proviso that the college shall incur no detriment as a result of a lease of this kind.[16]

As regards the question which you raise at the end about the statute *Of the year of departure*, we rule that a fellow absent from college and resident in a benefice and bearing all the burdens of the college with others shall enjoy [the benefit of his fellowship] during that time: for in these and other such cases private statutes should give way to the public laws of the realm.[17]

15 The ironwork on the Gate still shows that the wicket could be used during the day and barred during the night.

16 Parker allows a lease to be made to the Master or a fellow, or to a relation of theirs, but only if it is made with the unanimous consent of all fellows, not merely a majority.

17 Parker is here referring, not so much to Statute 39, but more specifically to the statute *De anno valedicendi* which Caius had expounded in his *Expositiones seu Interpretationes* of Bateman's Statutes (§ III. 3 above). In that statute Caius had only allowed a fellow to keep his fellowship for a valedictory year after obtaining a disqualifying benefice if he was not absent from the college (in the same way in which, in Statute 39, he only allowed a fellow to keep even a permissible benefice provided he continued to be resident in college). Parker overrules the requirement of residence in college and allows that a fellow may, during his valedictory year, keep his fellowship stipend even though he is resident in the benefice. He presumably has 21 Henry VIII, c. 13, ss. 15, 17 in mind when he suggests that the law of the land requires residence in the benefice; see also Elizabeth's University Statutes (1570), chap. 50 § 26 (*Documents*, I, pp. 492–3).

Item cum in statuto 32 omnis regendi potestas absenti magistro seniori socio adempta sit et presidi per magistrum solum statuto data, que electio presidis vivente magistro solum valet, in hoc casu collegii regimen ad seniorem socium presentem spectabit {iuxta gradum et senioritatem in Academia}[a] donec novus magister eligatur et admittatur juxta aliorum collegiorum consuetudinem.

Ad hec cum in statuto 25 tit. de superintendentibus nulla substituti mentio facta sit, alterutro superintendentium morbo laborante aut absente vel aliter impedito, equissimum putamus licere dictis superintendibus sic impeditis, chirographo suo vel testibus idoneis presidem suum assignare vel seniorem socium ut locos suos suppleant.

{*Preterea quantum ad statutum 72 attinet viz. de publicis et privatis conviviis, equum putamus ut semel in anno scilicet in festo Annunciacionis beate Marie Virginis expendantur illae quatuor lib. in recepcione amicorum vestrorum ita ut non necesse fuerit epulari in festo Concepcionis ejusdem, cum illud festum legibus hujus regni Anglie juste aboleatur. Quod autem ad reliquum statuti pertinet, observetur fundatoris voluntas.*}[b]

Postremo omnia et singula statuta composiciones et consuetudines que sacris scripturis vel regiis statutis repugnant auctoritate regia abrogantur et annihilantur.

Volumus denique has interpretaciones singulis statutorum collegii antedicti libris conjungi ne e memoria excidant ac quinque libros cum hujusmodi interpretacionibus preparari quorum unum in Archivis antedicti Collegii Gonevill et Caius, alium in Collegio {*regali, tertium in Collegio*}[c] Corporis Christi et beate Marie Virginis Cantabrigie, quartum in manibus custodis sive magistri Collegii Gonevill et Caius predicti, quintum vero et ultimum in manibus presidentis antedicti collegii qui pro tempore fuerit, quo ceteri socii facilius de eisdem certiores fiant, servari precipimus.

Proviso semper quod si nos dictus Mattheus Cantuariensis Archiepiscopus latiorem exposicionem dederimus quam aut predicta concessio et voluntas testimentaria permittunt: vel petitio Magistri et sociorum (de ambiguis propositis dissolvendis) valuerit:[d] tamen nos Mattheus per presentes notum facimus

a Interlined insertion.

b The italicised paragraph in brackets is inserted in the margin.

c Interlined insertion in a different hand. Caius had been dead for more than a year before Parker's deed was written, but the initial omission of King's College here is reminiscent of Caius' own temporary deletion of the references to that college in his Statute 25: see note to that statute. However, the references to King's College in Caius' statute had already been restored by the time a copy was sent to Lambeth (Lambeth MS 720) and the initial omission here may have been due simply to the fact that the restored words had been underlined in the copy of Caius' statutes sent to Lambeth.

d Reading *valuerit* as given in the 1852 text, but MSS 711, 760 give *voluerit*: if that reading is correct, "warrants" should be replaced by "seeks".

Given [the fact] that **Statute 32** takes away from the senior fellow all power of government in the absence of the master and confers it solely on a president appointed by the master, and since the election of a president is valid only while the master is alive, the government of the college will, in the event [of a vacancy in the mastership], rest with the fellow present who is senior {in degree and standing in the University} until a new master is elected and admitted, in accordance with the custom of other colleges.[18]

As to the fact that **Statute 25** entitled *Of Superintendents* makes no mention of a substitute if either superintendent should be ill or absent or otherwise unable to act, we believe it is best to allow superintendents who are prevented thus from acting to appoint, [in writing] under their own hand or suitably witnessed, their president or senior fellow to take their place.

{Furthermore, as far as **Statute 72**, viz. *Of Public and Private Feasts* is concerned, we believe it is right that the £4 should be spent on a single occasion each year, namely on the feast of the Annunciation of blessed Mary the Virgin, on the entertainment of your friends, making it unnecessary to have a dinner on the feast of her Conception, since that feast has duly been abolished by the laws of this realm of England. However, the will of the Founder is to be observed as regards the rest of this statute.}[19]

Finally, all statutes, arrangements and customs which are contrary to Holy Scripture or the statutes of the realm are abolished and rendered null and void by royal authority.[20]

It is our wish that hereafter these rulings shall bound up with each of the books of statutes of the aforesaid college lest they be forgotten; and we order that five books with the rulings incorporated in them in this way be prepared, one of which is to be preserved in the archives of the said Gonville and Caius College, *another in King's College*,[21] a third in the College of Corpus Christi and blessed Mary the Virgin of Cambridge, a fourth in the hands of the keeper or master of the aforesaid Gonville and Caius College, and a fifth and last one in the hands of the president of the aforesaid college at the time, from which the other fellows may the more easily come to know them better.[22]

Always provided that if we the said Matthew Archbishop of Canterbury have ruled more widely than either the aforesaid grant and testamentary will allows or than the petition of the master and fellows (for the resolution of ambiguous provisions) warrants, then we Matthew hereby make known through these

18 The last three rulings, *i.e.* on Statutes 32, 25 and 72, had not been sought by the College: Lambeth MS 720, fols. 23–7.

19 See note to Latin text. Parker leaves unchanged the statute's prohibition against any college subsidy of private entertaining and its limitation to 12d. a week of a fellow's buttery allowance.

20 In his final proviso Parker is careful to invoke his overriding powers as archbishop.

21 See note to Latin text.

22 A striking modification of Caius' restrictions as to the occasions on which a fellow might ask to see the statutes.

quod auctoritate nobis data per statutum parliamenti anno xxv[to] illustrissimi principis Henrici octavi, quondam regis Anglie et nuper potestate legitima iterum confirmata cum statutis ejusdem Johannis Caii secundum has *nostras*[a] exposiciones quantum in nobis est et jura regni patiuntur tenore presentium dispensamus.

In cujus rei testimonium tam sigillum ad facultates quo in hac parte utimur quam sigillum nostrum magnum presentibus apposuimus.

Dat apud Lambithe in manerio nostro ibidem[b] primo die mensis Januarii Anno Domini secundum cursum et computacionem Ecclesie Anglicane 1574[c] et anno regni Domine nostre Domine Elizabethae Dei gratia Anglie Francie et Hibernie regine fidei defensoris &c. decimo septimo nostreque consecrationis anno decimo sexto.

[The following acceptance by the college is attached to Parker's deed.]

Et nos Magister sive Custos Collegii Gonville et Caius in Academia Cantebrigensi, et Socii sive Scholares eiusdem Collegii hoc publicum instrumentum omniaque et singula in eodem contenta et specificata pro nobis et Succesoribus nostris quantum in nobis est ratificamus, approbamus, et confirmamus per presentes. **In cuius rei** testimonium sigillum nostrum communem presentibus apposuimus. **Dat** in Collegio nostro predicto vicesimo quarto die Januaris anno domini 1574. Et in Regni Domine nostre Elizabethae dei gratia Anglie, Francie et Hibernie Regine fidei defensoris etc. decimo septimo. [sigla]

Thomas Legge.

Edmundus Hownde Robertus Churche Stephanus Perse Joannes Depup Joannes Paman Johannes Trace

Simon Cannon et Thomas Temple[d]

a The italicised word is virtually illegible. MSS 711, 760 read as "*nostras*"; the 1852 text gives "*litteras*"and supplies "*et*".

b The archbishopric had acquired the whole Manor of Lambeth, not merely the buildings now known as Lambeth Palace.

c Written thus in numerals in the original.

d The original submission on 28 June 1574 had been signed by Legge and the first six of the fellows signing here. Cannon and Temple had been elected subsequently in the period before 24 January 1575, when Parker's rulings were received and accepted by the Master and the fellows. A further list of queries (on Statutes 28 and 90 and the question whether the Charter empowered Caius to make statutes contravening ancient customs having the force of law) appears to have been formulated and sent to Lambeth by Legge and the eight fellows, but Parker died in May 1575 without having made a ruling: Lambeth MS 720, fols. 10–11.

presents that, by the authority given to us by the Act of Parliament of the 25th year of the most illustrious prince Henry VIII, sometime king of England, and lately re-confirmed by lawful authority, we dispense with the statutes of the same John Caius by these presents, through these our rulings, so far as it lies in our power to do so and the laws of the realm permit.[23]

In witness whereof we attach to [these] presents both the seal which we use in this field for granting a faculty and also our great seal.

Given at Lambeth in our manor there on the first day of January in the year of the Lord according to the course and reckoning of the Church of England 1574 [*i.e.* 1575] and in the 17th year of the reign of our Lady the Lady Elizabeth by the grace of God Queen of England, France and Ireland, defender of the faith etc. and in the 16th year of our consecration.

[The following acceptance by the college is attached to Parker's deed.]

And we, the Master or Keeper of Gonville & Caius College in the University of Cambridge, and Fellows or Scholars of that College, by [these] presents ratify, approve and confirm this public instrument and all and singular contained and specified in it for ourselves and our successors so far as it lies in us. In witness whereof we attach our seal to [these] presents. Given in our aforesaid College on the 24th day of January A.D. 1574/5 and in the seventeenth year of the reign of our [Sovereign] Lady Elizabeth by the grace of God Queen of England, France and Ireland, defender of the faith etc.

Thomas Legge.

Edmund Hownd [President 1573–6, *B.H.* I, 62] Robert Churche [*B.H.* I, 58] Stephen Perse [*B.H.* I, 57] John Depup [*B.H.* I, 61] John Paman [*B.H.* I, 79] John Tracie [*B.H.* I, 65]

Simon Cannon [*B.H.* I, 72] and Thomas Temple [*B.H.* I, 73]

23 Having ruled certain of John Caius' statutes to be invalid as against the doctrines of the Church of England (cf. the marginal ruling on Statute 72), Parker carefully invokes the overriding powers vested in him as archbishop by Act of Parliament.

IV. 3

Supplementary Notes to Caius' Statutes

The apparent exclusion of Welshmen. [Statute 12]

The most widely known provision in Caius' statutes today is the apparent inclusion of Welshmen among those whom his college was forbidden to admit. This appeared, in Statute 12, in a list which was otherwise restricted to persons suffering from a medical condition or disability: those who were deformed, mute, blind, lame, crippled, maimed, "*Wallicum*", suffering from any serious or contagious disease, or sickly, that is, unwell for much of the time.[1] Before any attempt is made to explain what Caius had in mind by the word *Wallicum*, three points must be borne in mind.

(i) In the original manuscript (MS 711) the word *Wallicum* was inserted above the line and appears to have been added by the scribe at the time of writing rather than by Caius himself later: whether the scribe was making an addition at Caius' direction or was merely correcting his own mistaken transcription of a draft written earlier is not clear.[2]

(ii) The word *Wallicum* had not been included in the list of disqualifying medical conditions which Caius had drawn up in the draft statutes he prepared in 1558: "anyone deformed, suffering from any serious or contagious illness, or sickly".[3]

(iii) The 1558 draft statute had been restricted to the election of a fellow or scholar, and the initial thrust of Statute 12 was likewise directed to the election of a Master, fellow or scholar. Its later wording (*recipiatur*),

[1] *Nullum praeterea deformem, mutum caecum, claudum, mancum, mutilum, Wallicum, aliquot gravi aut contagio morbo affectum, aut valetudinarium, hoc est, magna ex parte aegrotum.* See Plate II above.

[2] From the uniformity of the script the latter would seem more likely, though it is surprising that a professional scribe should have overlooked such an unexpected word written with an initial capital letter, if it had appeared in a draft from which he was copying. It should be noted that the scribe of MS 711 had a habit of using an initial capital letter for words he was not familiar with or did not understand: cf. Statute 96 (Latin text).

[3] *deformis, aliquot gravi aut contagioso morbo affectus aut valetudinarius*: *Documents*, II, p. 328.

however, was wide enough to extend to the admission of all members of the college, including pensioners, and it would have been odd if Caius, a physician, had intended that a list of disqualifications which included contagious diseases should apply to scholars but not to pensioners: the disqualifications, including "*Wallicum*", whatever it meant, must have been intended to apply to all classes of members of the college.

In the original manuscript MS 711 the word is clearly written as "*Wallicum*" and, as so written, it would necessarily seem to mean 'Welsh', however out-of-place or offensive its inclusion in a list of medical disabilities and diseases might be. The belief in the college that Caius had indeed intended to exclude Welshmen goes back a long way. Dr Gooch, the Master, wrote in the eighteenth century that:

> There is a traditional story that Dr Caius had been affronted and beaten by a Welshman, but whatever was the occasion of his prejudice to that country ... it appears (Annales Coll.) that out of all, or almost all the English counties Fellows have been chosen, but not one out of Wales. This likewise shews, that the opinion of the College has always been, that *Wallicus* in the Statute is not a fictitious term, for habit, constitution, or Distemper of a particular person, but signifys a Welchman.[4]

If such an assault by a Welshman did ever take place one might have expected that it would had occurred when Caius' early professional journeys took him to the West Country,[5] but it is clear from his draft statutes that Caius had not been nursing any grudge in 1558, and in his first year as Master he may have admitted a Welshman from Glamorgan.[6] If he had subsequently been assaulted in college while he was Master, it is difficult to believe that it would not have been mentioned in the *Annales* or that the offender's dismissal from the college would not have been recorded in the *Pandectae*; and, given the single-minded attention to the well-being of the college which runs through Caius' statutes, it would have been uncharacteristic of him to have inserted the exclusion so casually merely to satisfy a personal grievance, if the assault had been unconnected with the college.[7] Furthermore, if Statute 12 was understood

4 MS 621/457, pp. 75, 77.

5 We know that his travels took him to Shrewsbury: *B.H.* III, p. 34.

6 John Stradlyng (*B.H.* I, p. 44).

7 Caius was capable of acting impetuously, as his temporary excision of the Provost of King's from Statute 25 shows; but his action on that occasion was very directly the result of an event in college, and he soon restored his original provision. See Brooke, *History*, pp. 69–70, for the difficulty of finding a possible culprit within the college who might have been a Welshman. Hugh Glyn (*B.H.* I, p. 42) has been suggested, but although he may have been a Welshman he seems to have been blameless. He was one of the fellows named in the Charter and Caius made him president when he became Master in January 1559; Glyn soon ceased to reside and departed from the college finally in October that same year. His absence from college was not

by his colleagues at the time as prohibiting the admission of Welshmen, it is curious that it did not prevent them from admitting an undoubted Welshman, John Price of Merionthshire, as a major pensioner less than a year after Caius' death.[8]

Since the word *Wallicum* cannot sensibly bear any other meaning than 'Welsh' in the context, that leaves only the possibility that the word was a scribal error for *Gallicum* and that Caius had in mind the *morbus Gallicus*, venereal disease. The term *morbus Gallicus* for "the French pox" was well established in Caius' day, and he had referred to the disease in his Annals of the College of Physicians only months before he completed his statutes for the college.[9] It is difficult to envisage how such a scribal error could have arisen, either by the scribe's misreading of a draft or mishearing of a word dictated by Caius,[10] and it presupposes a serious oversight in Caius' correction of the text;[11] furthermore, the word *Gallicus* was not commonly used to denote a person infected with the illness. Despite these difficulties, the suggestion that the word was intended to indicate infection with a venereal disease is distinctly more acceptable than reliance upon a bizarre tale for which there appears to be no contemporary evidence.[12]

Celibacy. [Statute 14]

In his statutes Bateman had required that the keeper and the fellows should remain in college only so long as they behaved chastely, worthily, obediently, peaceably and with diligence in study.[13] In the draft statutes which Caius wrote in 1558 before he became Master and before Queen Mary had died, he substituted the adjective 'celibate' for the adverb 'chastely' and widened the

attributed to any fault, however, and in a residence report to the university he was stated to be away "on the business of settling law-suits" (*absens, in componendis litibus*), unlike another fellow, John Cowell, who was described in the same report to the university as "suspended indefinitely" (*suspensus, quousque*): *B.H.* I, p. 42.

8 *B.H.* I, p. 77. Price was admitted from Clare as an M.A. It is conceivable, of course, that the statute was read as restricted to the election of a fellow or scholar; however, that would have meant attributing to Caius a desire to exclude students with a serious or contagious disease if they were fellows or scholars, but not if they were major pensioners who took their meals at the fellows' table.

9 Brooke, *History*, p. 69, citing *Annales Coll. Med.*, p. 70.

10 The scribe may have misheard or mistaken '*Gallicus*' as '*Guallicus*', a version of *Wallicus*. For examples of phonetic spelling by the scribe, see Statutes 88 (*wayfiata*) and 96 (*reperefes*).

11 There are similar oversights elsewhere in MS 711: *e.g.*, the incorrect numbering of Statutes 46 to 51 and failure to number Statute 98.

12 See the balanced assessment in Brooke, *History*, at pp. 69–70.

13 Statute 2.

prohibition to all members of the college, but he did not include a definition of 'celibacy'.[14] In the final version of his statutes he reformulated the prohibition much more peremptorily in Statute 14: it was applied expressly to scholars and pensioners as well as Master and fellows, and the term 'celibate' was defined to exclude those who had contracted to marry as well as those whose marriage had been solemnised. By the time that the final version of his statutes was completed in January 1573, a markedly more limited rule omitting Masters had been reaffirmed for colleges in Elizabeth's statutes for the university in 1570.[15] This expressly prohibited fellows from being married and made marriage an automatic and immediate disqualification for them, but it said nothing, one way or the other, about Masters or scholars and pensioners; consequently, it was not directly incompatible with Caius' statute, which could be regarded as merely widening the scope of the royal rule for his own college.

When Caius died at the end of July 1573 there were therefore three distinct statutory rules bearing on the question of celibacy, each differently worded but none directly contradicting the others: Bateman's, Caius' and the university's. That fact, however, provoked no query in the college, for Caius had already resigned the mastership to a confirmed bachelor, Thomas Legge, and the question was not among those which the college sent to Archbishop Parker the following year seeking his ruling upon the meaning and effect of various provisions in Caius' statutes. In his response, however, Parker chose to raise two questions of his own, before he turned to the questions which the college had asked: celibacy first, and then the use of Latin.[16] As Parker knew, the Queen had strong views on both these subjects, and he was equally aware that very clear rules on celibacy had been formulated for the university in the royal statutes which had been issued in her name in 1570, less than five years earlier.[17] Caius' ban on marriage did not directly conflict with Elizabeth's statutes but it went further in one respect, for it applied the ban to Masters of colleges, whereas they had clearly been omitted from the ban in the royal statutes.[18] Furthermore, his ban on Masters' marrying brought back painful memories of the summary

[14] *Documents*, II, p. 335.

[15] Statutes of Queen Elizabeth 1570, chap. 50, § 33 (*Documents*, I, p. 493). The prohibition had been included in Edward VI's statutes of 1549 and Elizabeth's re-issue of the statutes of 1559: Lamb, *Letters*, pp. 138, 293.

[16] It is interesting that he chose to start his rulings with questions which the college had not asked, but on which Elizabeth had strong views, and his rulings on both subjects were equally opaque.

[17] For Elizabeth's views, see Brooke, *History*, p. 68. Parker had initially been the principal commissioner responsible for her first statutes in 1559.

[18] In 1584 Sir Walter Mildmay chose a married man, Laurence Chaderton, to be Master of his new college, Emmanuel.

dismissal of married Masters in the first days of Mary's reign,[19] and his sweeping requirement of celibacy might be adjudged suspiciously reminiscent of an earlier Catholic age and reign.

Against this background, Parker chose to tread cautiously. A happily married man himself, he was well aware of the Queen's views on clerical marriage and his unrequested ruling was carefully opaque: insofar as Caius had substituted the word 'celibate' for 'chaste' and had interpreted that word to exclude persons who had simply contracted to marry, his statute was judged to conflict with that of Bateman and was not to be understood beyond the literal meaning that its words would bear. The archbishop did not elaborate further: in particular he did not mention the royal statute and he did not hint that a college's statutes might make a separate rule for Masters different from that for fellows. As a result the only clear conclusion that emerged from his ruling was that a contract to marry did not disqualify a person from membership of the college, but whether a solemnised marriage was *ipso facto* a bar to membership under its statutes, and whether it was a bar to the mastership as well as to a fellowship, or whether the college's statutes merely required Masters and fellows to conduct themselves "chastely" as Bateman had specified was left unanswered. So, too, was the constitutional question whether Caius could apply to his own college a ban that was more extensive than the one which had been expressly prescribed for colleges by Elizabeth's statutes for the university.[20]

Despite the uncertainty left by Parker's ruling, it was always taken for granted thereafter that marriage was an absolute and immediate disqualification for any fellowship in Caius' college, though the question whether the disqualification flowed from his statute for the college or from Elizabeth's statute for the university was never addressed. If it flowed from Caius' statute, then, on any reading of that statute, the bar should have applied as much to a Master as to a fellow, yet there was a complete absence of comment or argument on any of the five occasions when the office of Master was held by a married man before 1860. The silence on the first two occasions is easily explained: William Dell was appointed by a vote of the House of Commons during the Interregnum, when scant regard was shown for Caius' statutes, and Robert Brady was admitted to the office at the Restoration by virtue of a royal mandate which would have been regarded as sufficient authority to disregard those statutes.[21] In neither case did the fact of their marriage make any impact on the life of the college, for, so far as

[19] The masters of Peterhouse (Ainsworth) and St Catharine's (Sandys) had been summarily dismissed, and at Corpus Parker himself had avoided the same fate only by resignation: Mullinger, *The University of Cambridge from the Royal Injunctions of 1535 to the Accession of Charles the First* (1884), pp. 150–1.

[20] Edward VI's statutes for Trinity College in 1552 had allowed a Regius professor to marry: Statute 25 (J.B. Mullinger, *op. cit.*, p. 626 (1884)). The provision was omitted when Elizabeth revived the college's pre-Marian statutes in 1560.

[21] For the appointments of Dell in 1649 and Brady in 1660 see *B.H.* III, pp. 94–5, 105.

is known, Mrs Dell never entered the college and although Mrs Brady did reside in Cambridge on occasions and presumably was living in the college when she died,[22] she appears to have been childless. By the eighteenth century the fact that the college had already had two married Masters whose tenures of the office had stretched over more than half a century appears to have accustomed the college to the notion that its Masters were no more restricted from marrying than those of other colleges. At any rate, when Thomas Gooch became Master in 1716 his marriage soon afterwards to the first of his three wives was accepted without the slightest comment, and the college raised no objection to the considerable expense of enlarging the lodge to accommodate his new family and the necessary staff. After his death in 1754 the college reverted to choosing celibate Masters, but in 1811 Caius' statute was equally silently disregarded on the occasion of the brief marriage of the then Master, Martin Davy, and, finally, again on the marriage of the Master, Edwin Guest, in September 1859. By the time Guest married the repeal of the founders' statutes awaited only the formal approval of the Queen in Council; furthermore, Elizabeth's statutes for the university had only three more months to run before they would cease to have effect, and it was those royal statutes which provided the sole justification for exempting Masters from Caius' requirement of celibacy. The fellows did not have to wait much longer. The repeal of Elizabeth's statutes took effect on 1 January 1860,[23] and the founders' statutes for the college finally ceased to have effect on 1 July in the same year; six months later, on 1 January 1861, the first fellow took advantage of their repeal to marry.[24]

Caius' use of the terms 'Organa' and 'Organista'. [Statutes 15 and 46]

The following notes on the term *organista* in Statutes 15 and 46 have kindly been provided by Dr Roger Bowers of Jesus College:

"Statute 15

It is a tribute to the conservatism of Dr Caius that in the 1572 revision of the statutes he preserved unchanged provisions which plainly related specifically to the conduct of the Catholic Latin liturgy in force at the time of their original drafting in 1558.

22 Her death in 1680 is recorded in the parish register of St Michael's: *B.H.* III, p. 106.

23 Cambridge University Act 1856, s.41.

24 Anthony Steel; cf. *B.H.* II, p. 323, Brooke, *History*, pp. 223–4.

It is pretty plain that the term *organista* was being used in one of its senses commoner at the time, of 'singer of polyphonic music'. By the mid-1550s the Latin service was adorned with two styles of music: plainsong and polyphony. Anyone with a reasonable ear and a modest intelligence could be taught how to sing the plainsong of the liturgy. It was one-dimensional music, having pitch but no rhythm, and melody but no harmony, and every Catholic priest and parish clerk in the land could sing it. But there was also the polyphonic music composed by the likes of Robert Fayrfax and John Taverner, Nicholas Ludford and Thomas Tallis, Christopher Tye and John Sheppard. This was music of great complexity and elaboration, composed in four, five or six independent parts (or even more), sung from a form of musical notation similar to but more complex and difficult than that of today, and requiring technical mastery of phrasing, intonation, breath control, rhythmic accuracy, and sheer vocal stamina. Largely, these were skills possessed only by youths and men who in boyhood had been professionally trained as singing-boys at one or other of the great cathedral or collegiate churches, or household chapels of the secular and episcopal aristocracy. (As Dr Caius evidently knew, such institutions were thickest on the ground in London; Norwich and Norfolk also were well provided.) Dr Caius in 1558 evidently wanted a high standard of singing in his college chapel, extending to elaborate polyphony as well as to the routine plainsong; and to get it, he wanted a proportion of his scholars to be recruited from those who in boyhood had been taught the necessary skills as church singing-boys and choristers. In the context of Statute 15, therefore, no single modern word adequately conveys the meaning of *organista*; it means 'singer trained in polyphonic music'.

Statute 46

Organa, despite its plural form, normally denoted the single instrument. *Cantus* here refers to singing in both styles, plainsong and polyphony; *lectio canora* refers to the remaining style of singing, the chanted monotone used for the lessons and prayers. *In organis* refers to playing the organ. Thus in a few words, Dr Caius summed up all the styles of music-making germane to the Latin church service."

Commonplaces. [Statute 18]

Commonplaces were brief moral discourses given in turn by each fellow, whether he was in Holy Orders or not.[25] Edward VI's Visitors in 1549 required the academic exercise of commonplaces immediately after Prayers at 5 a.m.,

[25] *B.H.* III, p. 167.

daily in King's, Trinity and St John's and three times a week in other colleges; this requirement was reduced by Elizabeth's Visitors in 1559 to three times a week in the three royal colleges and twice a week in others.[26] The reduction was confirmed in her Statutes of 1570 (c. 50, ord. 4). Since Caius required them only once a week in Statute 18, the conflict was referred to Parker, who ruled that Elizabeth's statutes should be followed in this matter; he did, however, moderate Caius' heavy penalty and substitute the keeper's discretion for the fixed amount of any fine.[27]

The Parlour. [Statutes 25, 28 and 71]

In the sixteenth and early seventeenth centuries the Latin terms *parlora* and *conclave* were used synonymously,[28] and the standard word in use in English was 'parlour'. So far as any discussion of the buildings of this college before 1653 is concerned, the term *conclave* is ambiguous: it may indicate (i) the ground-floor room where the Undercroft now is, or (ii) the first-floor room above it between the Hall and the Library where the Senior Combination Room now is. The ground-floor room, though low and narrow and somewhat gloomy, seems to have been used as a parlour for the fellows in (and before) Caius' time, and since it had the inestimable attraction of a brazier or a fire-place it could serve as a substitute for the Hall in winter; for, as Caius remarked, the Hall had no heating until 1565.[29] In contrast, the first-floor room appears to have been a bedchamber (*cubiculum*), and Caius slept in it when he came to Cambridge to inaugurate his new college in 1558.[30] It was this upper room which Caius allocated in Statute 28 for use by the Master's or college's guests until (or perhaps unless) it should be needed for communal use as a parlour (*conclave*) or as an overflow from Hall – the wording of the statute leaves it unclear precisely when the room started to be used for communal use as opposed to a bedchamber.[31]

26 Lamb, *Letters*, pp. 145, 305.

27 See Parker's *Interpretatio*, § IV. 2, at p. 271 above.

28 R. Willis and J.W. Clark, *The Architectural History of the University of Cambridge* (1886), II, pp. 48–9.

29 In that year, as a result of the combined generosity of a former fellow (Bishop Shaxton) and a current major pensioner (Humphrey Busbye), a large new movable iron brazier was installed in the Hall and a sufficient fund provided to meet the cost of fuel for it (*ignis gratuitus*) in winter on Sundays, feast-days, the twelve days of Christmas and days of exceptional cold: *Annals*, p. 121. Before that date the Master and fellows had to provide fuel for the fire in the parlour out of their own pockets: *ibid.*

30 *Annals*, p. 58.

31 Statute 28. It is not entirely clear from the wording of the statute (*usque dum*) whether Caius is referring to the seasonal use of the room for a parlour in winter or an overflow from Hall as

It is therefore uncertain until the middle of the seventeenth century which of the two rooms was used, in winter, as a parlour (*conclave*) for the Master and fellows and for the steward's weekly rendering of accounts on Saturdays.[32] Whichever it was, the room was also used as an overflow from Hall and, on the anniversary days of Caius' death and birth (29 July and 6 October), for the presentation of Caius' fellows and scholars to the superintendents if for any reason that was not done in Hall.[33] In 1653 the first-floor room was converted into "a publicke entertaining roome for College ffeastes and other publicke occasions of the College".[34] It soon became the Combination Room, while the lower room ceased to be a fellows' parlour and became a fuel store.[35]

The arca, cistae, thesaurus *and* aerarium. *[Statutes 25, 28, 56, 58, 63, 80, 81, 82 and 84]*

In his statutes Bateman used the term "*arca*" to identify the great and strong chest with three keys fashioned differently in which he directed the college to keep its seal, muniments, precious objects and treasure.[36] By the sixteenth century, and doubtless earlier, the English term used colloquially within the college for that chest was "the hutch",[37] but in the formal context of the statutes of both Bateman and Caius the sense of the Latin term with its nuance of solemnity, security and solidity is conveyed better by the word "ark", and for that reason it is used in the translation of those statutes here.

The two founders also use the more general term "*cista*" (chest) without making any clear distinction between that and the *arca*, but whereas "*arca*" is invariably used in the singular by both founders, the term "*cista*" was on occasion used by Caius in the plural.[38] It is clear, as might be expected, that a smaller container fashioned to fit within the ark, in the form of a coffer or a drawer, would have been needed to keep coins conveniently separate from the other objects even in Bateman's time, and such a container, termed the "tyll", was in use by Caius' time.[39] In addition, containers would be needed to protect the increasing number of charters and other fragile title deeds from damaging

a practice which already existed or is merely envisaging its communal use as a future possible alteration in the allocation of the room.

32 Statutes 28 and 71.

33 Statute 25.

34 *B.H.* III, p. 197, citing the *Gesta*, 25 April 1656.

35 *Ibid.*

36 Statute 6.

37 *Pandectae*, fol. 19v.

38 Statute 84.

39 *Pandectae*, fol. 21.

contact with objects such as plate that had frequently to be taken in and out from the ark. Caius did on occasion use the term *cista* or *citula* (*cistella*) for containers for holding documents,[40] but in general, however, it seems to be money-chest or till that Caius principally had in mind when he used the word *cista*, particularly when he referred to it as the *communis cista*.

Reference is also made in Caius' time to the putting of documents into "the Master's chest",[41] and he directed in his statutes that rents from the rooms which he had built in Caius court should be kept separate "in our chest" (*in cistra nostra*) exclusively for the maintenance of its roofs and repairs.[42] Access to this chest, it would seem, was not restricted to Caius personally, and it is therefore likely that it was placed with the college's other chests rather than in Caius' own chamber. The fact that he had a separate chest does not mean that he kept much of his own money there: most of that money came to him in London either from his medical practice or from the rents of the three manors which he had purchased from the Crown and to which he was still entitled as the immediate reversioner,[43] and in his earlier years as Master he adopted the practice of reimbursing the college in tranches for money that it had expended on his behalf on his building projects; it was only in his last seven years as Master that he transmitted money to the college in advance, in sealed bags or purses, for use at his future direction.[44]

In the absence of any banks or safe-deposits the chests contained in effect the total movable wealth (*thesaurus*) of the college. For Bateman the safety of that wealth had to depend solely upon the security provided by the one great and strong chest or ark (*unam archam communem magnam et fortem*) which he required the college to have. For Caius, however, that was insufficient without the additional security of a strong-room in which the hutch could be kept permanently and its contents audited and he converted the oratory above the chapel ante-chamber to serve as such a room: it was this specific room, the "counting-house", that he invariably had in mind when he referred to the

40 See Statute 25, where he uses the term *cista* and *cistula* for two separate containers, (i) the container in which a collated copy of his statutes was to be kept and to which King's, Corpus and Caius Colleges had keys and (ii) the common chest (*communis cista*) in which his own college's key to that other chest was to be kept.

41 *Pandectae*, fol. 19v.

42 Statute 28. Earlier in that statute he had, quite exceptionally, used the phrase "our ark" (*in arca nostra*) as if the container envisaged was a second hutch.

43 The three manors were subject to long leases when he transferred them to the college, and he had arranged for the college's freehold reversion to be leased back to him for seventy years. The rents from the tenants were therefore payable to him, and he reimbursed the college for the stipends it paid to those on his foundation, such as Spenser: *Pandectae*, fol. 18v.

44 *Pandectae*, fols. 18v and 21v (reimbursement), fols. 22 and 30 (deposit of sealed bags); and see "*John Caius and his Foundation*", § V. 3, at p. 353, n. 91 and p. 360, n. 129 below. His change of practice clearly came as a novelty to the fellows and the receipt of the sealed bags was carefully attested by all the resident fellows: see Plate XI above.

aerarium and when he declared it to be the essential guardian of the college's wealth – "*cuius thesauri custos est aerarium*".[45]

Caius and the Provost of King's. [Statute 25]

A marginal note in MS 711 states that Caius deleted the (editorially) italicised words and the references to the Provost of King's in Statute 25 and then restored them (*Caius delevit et restituit*) with "*stet*".[46] It is intriguing why and when Caius made the deletion and then changed his mind. It is not clear either why he had chosen the Provost of King's as one of the superintendents to oversee the progress of his fellows and scholars in the first place.[47] He had not included any provision for superintendents in his draft statutes in 1558, and although he had two close friends and correspondents in King's, Thomas Hatcher and Abraham Hartwell, neither of them was provost; at the time when he must have first thought of Statute 25, that office was held by Philip Baker, who was widely suspected of Romish tendencies and, like Caius, was said to have an attachment to vestments.[48] In the course of the upsurge of strident Puritanism in Cambridge in the late 1560s Baker was unseated from his office and forced to flee the country to Catholic Louvain in 1570, and, by the time Caius' scribe completed MS 711 at the end of 1572, the provost of King's was Roger Goade, who had helped in the ransacking of Caius' rooms on 13 December 1572. That episode may have caused Caius to make the deletion before he signed off MS 711 on 1 January 1573; if so, he seems to have relented in his last few remaining months, for he did not delete his reference to King's in the final paragraph of his statutes[49] and the references to that college in Statute 25 had been restored in the copy of the statutes sent to Matthew Parker in June 1574 (Lambeth MS 720, fol. 44). Although the references to King's had already been restored in the copy sent to Parker, a reference to that college was, by a remarkable co-incidence, also omitted from his *Interpretatio* by the archbishop's scribe at Lambeth and had to be inserted interlineally before his deed was sent to the college in January 1575.[50]

45 Statute 63.

46 The note appears to be in Caius' own hand. See pp. 144 and 146 above.

47 The choice of Corpus is explained by the long-standing association between Gonville Hall and Corpus and the friendship between Parker and Caius. The Master of Corpus was made one of the Visitors of Caius' new college and the safe-keeping of the £1,500 penal bond between Caius and the fellows was entrusted to him. It is surprising that Caius did not choose the Master of Trinity Hall, one of his other Visitors, to be the second superintendent.

48 Cf. Cooper, *Annals*, II, pp. 244–7.

49 Oddly, he referred there to the *praefectus*, not the *praepositus*.

50 See the note to Parker's final direction (for the making of copies of the statutes) in his *Interpretatio*, § IV. 2, at p. 276, n. c above.

The president. [Statute 31]

In his statutes Bateman made one reference to a "president of the College", but he did so in a statute which he drew without amendment from his statutes for Trinity Hall, and since he did not mention the office elsewhere in his statutes for Gonville Hall, it is clear that his failure to delete the reference when he borrowed the statute was an unintentional oversight. In contrast Caius did very deliberately devote a provision in his statutes to the office of president and this has led to a mistaken belief that he created the office and that various references to a president earlier in the sixteenth century refer to the principals of Fishwick Hostel. However, Caius' rubric to Statute 31 is carefully worded to refer to the power of the president, not to create a new office;[51] and in his *Expositio* of Bateman's Statutes Caius appears to assume that the office of president preceded his re-foundation of Gonville Hall, for he cited there the statutes of Edward VI as defining the *senior et sanior socius* as the person holding the title of president in each college.[52] The office of president had in fact existed *de facto* in Gonville Hall before the re-foundation of the college in 1557 and it had been held by many well-respected fellows, such as Shaxton, Skipp, Wendy and Mapted.[53] Venn believed that they were simply the principals of Fishwick Hostel, but, even if the office of president had originated in that way, it had grown greatly in both importance and seniority by the beginning of the sixteenth century and the president was by then regarded not simply as principal of Fishwick Hostel, but as being the president of Gonville Hall and the Master's deputy in the same way that he was in other colleges. This explains why the office continued to exist after the loss of Fishwick Hostel to Trinity College in 1546.[54]

The senior fellow. [Statute 32]

Having entrusted the choice of a new Master to the fellows of the college, each of the three founders recognised the need to identify in his statutes who should take charge of the process of electing a new Master in the event of a vacancy and who should act in his place in the meantime. Edmund Gonville's answer to the first question (and by implication the second) was characteristically clear and succinct: the senior fellow present at a meeting of the fellows, and that fellow

[51] In the same way, his next statute refers to the absence of any power in the senior fellow.

[52] The provision was in the Injunctions made by Edward's Visitors, and it survived in Elizabeth's 1570 statutes (ch. 50, § 26: *Documents*, I, pp. 492–3).

[53] *B.H.* III, pp. 19, 20, 24 and 29.

[54] The office was specifically mentioned when Peter Hewet endowed three scholarships in 1556, one to be awarded by the Master, the second by the president and the third by the senior fellow: *Annals*, p. 24; *B.H.* III, p. 226.

was the one who had been sworn and admitted before the others present.[55] Bateman answered the second question (and by implication the first) less precisely: the weightier or more senior (*sanior vel senior*) fellow of the college.[56] He had already imported into his statutes from monastic tradition and canon law (via the statutes he had earlier drafted for Trinity Hall) the imprecise concept of a wiser or more weighty part of the fellowship[57] as distinct from a numerical majority and he now extended the concept to the invidious choice of an individual fellow. Bateman thus introduced the ecclesiastical practice of subordinating strict seniority to a discretion to prefer superior wisdom, but he furnished no guidance on how it was to be exercised or who was to exercise it.

Two centuries later, in his draft statutes of 1558,[58] Caius sought to explain the term *sanior* as the one who is guided by a right conscience, who follows the meaning of the statutes impartially and who is supported by the greater reason and equity: "*Saniorem vero qui conscientia recti duciter, qui sensum statutorum sine affectione sequitur, et qui maiori rationi et aequitati nititur.*" He recognised, however, in those draft statutes that Gonville had specified only the senior fellow, and in an attempt to reconcile the views of the two earlier founders he gave to the majority of the fellows the power for eight days to replace the senior fellow with the "*sanior*" in the event of impropriety. By the time that he completed the final version of the statutes in 1572, he had discarded Gonville's choice of the senior fellow in favour of Bateman's choice of the weightier or more senior fellow, as he was bound to do by the terms of Philip and Mary's charter;[59] however, like Bateman, he did not indicate who was to select the weightier of the fellows.[60] That question was subtly addressed by Archbishop Parker in 1575, two years after Caius' death. The proper construction of Statute 32 had not been included among the questions submitted by the college to Parker for his interpretation, but he did, nevertheless, take the opportunity to rule upon the statute in his *Interpretatio*:[61] in his view, although Caius had taken away all power from the senior fellow and conferred it upon a president, since a Master's appointment of a president lapsed with his death, the government of the college during a

55 Gonville's Statute 2(i): *Seniorem vero intelligo eum qui prius in dicta domo iuratus fuerat et admissus.*

56 Bateman's Statute 3.

57 See Bateman's Statute 2 and Professor Brooke's note thereto.

58 *Documents*, II, p. 324.

59 Statute 7. In writing "*senior aut sanior*", Caius reversed Bateman's wording.

60 Presumably the task of choosing would have fallen to the greater or weightier part of the fellows. The question was made unnecessary in 1575 by Matthew Parker's ruling in his *Interpretatio* that the senior fellow should act in the event of a vacancy in the mastership: see his interpretation of Caius' Statute 32.

61 See Parker's *Interpretatio*, § IV. 2, at p. 277 above; note the interlined insertion. He also ruled on Statutes 25 and 27, which had also not been raised with him, as well as on the delicate subjects of celibacy and the use of Latin, which he had addressed urgently before any others.

vacancy in the mastership necessarily must fall to the senior fellow present – *and that fellow should be the one who was senior in degree and standing in the university*. Parker justified this neat compromise between seniority and superior wisdom as being in accordance with the custom of other colleges. His ruling was never challenged and Gonville's original choice of seniority according to the time of election as a fellow was not restored until 1882.[62]

In addition to the position during a vacancy in the mastership, Caius also considered in Statute 32 the status of the (most) senior fellow when there was a Master in office. When he became Master he initially continued for a few months the tradition of appointing the most senior fellow, Hugh Glyn, as president.[63] Glyn soon returned to North Wales, and, by now confronted with the parlous state in which the college had been left by Bacon and the fellows of Gonville Hall, Caius very pointedly broke with tradition and omitted to appoint as president the most senior of those fellows still surviving. This was William Clarke, whom he later expelled and who is clearly the person whom Caius had in mind as "a bad, rash and quarrelsome" senior fellow who should not be appointed president.[64] His troubled relations with Clarke explain why Caius took great trouble to insist that the senior fellow should not take the place of the president when the Master and his president were absent, and to strip him so emphatically of any power whatsoever during a Master's tenure of his office unless it had been expressly deputed to him by the Master or the president.[65]

Caius and the college's accounts and records. [Statutes 56 and 59]

Caius' dismay at the state in which he found the college's finances on becoming Master and his innate affection for the past and its records led him to make two separate provisions in his statutes for the keeping of (a) the college's half-yearly accounts and (b) its permanent records.[66]

(a) In Statute 56 he required the two bursars to maintain a record of all the individual amounts of money received and paid out by them and to render an account at the half-yearly audits required by Bateman's statutes of all receipts and payments made during the six months since the previous audit, while the steward should do likewise at an audit every three months.[67] He further

62 College Statutes (1882), Statute 12(1).
63 *Pandectae*, fol. 2 (24 January 1559).
64 See Statute 32.
65 See "*John Caius and his Foundation*", § V. 3, at p. 350 below.
66 For a fuller account of these records, see *B.H.* III, pp. 264–6.
67 He also directed that a further account of expenditure on provisions should be rendered weekly in Hall by the steward: Statute 71.

directed that the bursars' half-yearly accounts should be recorded in a book; but, while some half-yearly accounts survive from the time of Gonville Hall and were (much) later bound up in a book,[68] no such book has survived for Caius' or Legge's time as Master and one has to wonder whether the half-yearly accounts were systematically preserved in a permanent book until 1609, when the long-running series of Bursar's Books was begun following Legge's death.[69] Although we do not have the bursars' accounts of their time it is clear from Statute 56 that they were, like the later Bursar's Books, intended simply to be records of the receipts and payments made by the bursar or bursars during the relevant half-year and did not serve as a record of (i) balances carried over from the preceding accounting period in the form of money in the treasury or (ii) unpaid debts owed to the college, any more than the later Bursar's Books did. While Caius was Master the first of these two vital functions appears to have been served by the *Pandectae*, which included a statement of the balance in the chest following an audit, and the second function by the indentures between the Master and the college which Bateman had required,[70] but in Legge's time these functions came to be performed by two different series of records, each of which has survived from the 1580s. A record of the balances held in the chest at the end of each accounting period was maintained in the series of audits of the chest known as the "*Status Collegii*", while a cumulative list of outstanding debts owed to the college was preserved in the "*Libri Rationales*" each half-year after the record of commons accounts of the members of the college.[71] Neither of the two series of records has been accorded the importance which they deserve.[72]

68 They run, with substantial gaps from 1422 to 1523: BUR: F/ *Gonville Hall Accounts Bk*; cf. *B.H.* III, p. 265. Indentures between the keeper and the fellowship have also survived for the years 1491–1563 and 1567–89, as required by Bateman (Statute 7); however, they are not accounts of payments and receipts, but simply records of such outstanding debts as remained unpaid at the time of the audit. Furthermore, the indentures do not record any balance remaining in the chest, as Bateman had directed. *Pace B.H.* III (p. 266) the indentures cease in 1589, shortly after their function had been taken over by the *Libri Rationales* and the *Status Collegii*.

69 It is clear from the recording in its opening folios of key papers from earlier years that the first Bursar's Book (1609–34) started a new series and is not simply the earliest surviving volume of a series already running. Its introduction coincides with the change in bursarial practice which occurred in the last years of Legge's mastership and first year of Branthwaite's: until that time fellows had regularly held the office of bursar for only one year at a time, but the college's most senior and experienced fellow, Stephen Perse, was called upon to act as bursar in all but one of the five years from 1603 to 1608, and he may well have been responsible for the improved record-keeping which apparently occurred then.

70 See n. 68 above for the indentures, and pp. 295–6 below for the *Pandectae*.

71 The *Status Collegii* runs from 1584, and the *Libri Rationales* from 1581. Between them, they took over the function of the Indentures, which ceased in 1589.

72 In their accounts of the college records, neither Venn nor Gross anywhere mentions the *Status Collegii*, though they still existed in their time, and both regard the *Libri Rationales* as a subsidiary bursarial account limited to the commons accounts of members of the foundation, *i.e.* the Master, fellows and scholars: *B.H.* III, pp. 262–9 (Venn), IV(2), pp. i–ii (Gross).

The *Status Collegii* recorded the audit of the chest which took place separately from, and several weeks after, the half-yearly audit of the accounts, and, as such, served one of the purposes of the duplicate indentures recording the financial status of the college and the balance remaining in the chest which Bateman had required in his statutes;[73] that series of indentures appears to have petered out by 1589,[74] soon after the *Status Collegii* began in 1584.[75] Although the *Libri Rationales* later became simply a bursarial record of the commons accounts of members of the foundation, they had had a wider purpose in the sixteenth century. Like Bateman's indentures, they included not only the members' commons accounts but also a statement of the college's tenants and the rents they paid, together with a (unique) record of outstanding debts owed to the college. It was compiled by the *registrary*, not by the bursar or the steward, after he had personally inspected the relevant accounts, and it was clearly the record of accounts that the registrary was directed to compile along with the other permanent records entrusted to him in Statute 59.[76]

(b) As well as this record of accounts Caius laid upon the registrary in this statute the obligation to record the year's events in the Annals and the college's corporate actions in the Pandects; in addition he was to transcribe copies of leases granted by the college into the Book of Evidences and to enrol the details of all freshmen in the Matriculation Book. The Annals and the Matriculation Book have been extensively described (and transcribed) by Venn and no further comment is needed here.[77] The title "Book of Evidences" (*Liber evidentiarum*) might suggest that it contained a record of the college's title deeds, but it contained instead copies of the leases granted by the college and although the first volume was properly inscribed as the Book of Leases (*Liber demissionum*) it was bound as the Book of Evidences in deference to Caius' idiosyncratic and misleading choice of title.[78] The Lease Books never changed their character and remained exclusively a copy of leases granted by the college so long as they were maintained. In contrast, the Pandects lost its original purpose very soon after the book was started. Caius had started it immediately upon taking up the mastership, and at the time he envisaged it as a comprehensive chronological record of 'internal' actions and decisions taken by the college and

73 Statute 7.

74 *Pace B.H.* III, p. 266, n. 1.

75 Some of the first entries of the *Status Collegii* have been struck through in a way that suggests that they had been preparatory drafts for more formal documents and discarded once the latter had been made.

76 Caius specifically uses the term *liber rationalis* in Statute 59. For a statement by the registrary (Chr. Husband) that he had collated the whole record with the originals and transcribed them with his own hand, see *Lib. Rat.* (LD 1608).

77 See J. Venn, *The Annals of Gonville and Caius College* (Cambridge 1904) and *Biographical History of Gonville and Caius College*, vols. I–III (Cambridge 1897–1901).

78 Not surprisingly the later volumes were known as the Lease Books.

its officers similar to the chronological record of 'external' events affecting the college which was to be provided by the Annals.[79] He described it broadly in Statute 59 as a record of all things done corporately since the last audit (*omnia promiscue usque ad tempus computorum*), and elsewhere in his statutes he required the recording in the Pandects of various specific actions which necessarily took place in the treasury and not elsewhere, such as the sealing of all deeds (Statute 81) and the taking out of money, records and other articles stored there (Statute 84). The regularity with which such events occurred appears to have led to the Pandects itself being kept permanently in the "counting-house" or treasury, particularly during the numerous periods when Caius was absent in London.[80] It is possible, therefore, that the moving of the treasury to the oratory and loft above the ante-chapel in the 1560s and the consequent inconvenience of frequent access to the Pandects may explain why transactions occurring 'downstairs' elsewhere in the college ceased to be recorded in the book almost immediately and entries in it were thereafter confined almost completely to events that necessarily occurred 'upstairs' in the counting-house, *i.e.*, sealings and the taking out of items from the chest. Other events such as elections and choice of subject soon came to be recorded in the *Acta*.[81]

79 The first events recorded were the appointment of one fellow to be president and another to be steward of the manors. For an account of the Pandects in Caius' time, see Catherine Hall, "*Dr Caius' Counting House*", *The Caian* (1986–7), pp. 41–55.

80 The sealing of deeds – mostly for leases, presentations to a benefice and execution of obligations – would not have been particularly frequent, but in the middle and later years of Caius' time as Master the Pandects record the frequent drawing out of money to defray the cost of building in Caius and Tree Courts and the numerous occasions on which documents from the great chest (the hutch) were sent to Caius in London at his request: see, *e.g.*, the entries for 1570 in *Pandectae* (1559–1658). The Pandects were also used to record the audits of the chest by the key-keepers in the years before the *Status Collegii* records were begun (*ibid.* fols. 14v, 23v, 27, 28 and 29v), and, as a crucial record of the chest's contents, the book itself may well have been kept locked in it.

81 The last 'downstairs' event to be recorded in the Pandects appears to be the accord between Caius and the four resident fellows on 1 March 1573 for the mutual discharge of obligations between Caius and the college for financing the purchase of Bincombe (Plate XIII above). By that time two months had passed since the sacking of the Lodge, Caius was ill and was in Cambridge for a short return to the college; all the four fellows left in college were his staunch friends and supporters (Tracie, Perse, Churche and Hownd). The *Acta* were at first recorded on separate sheets and for some inexplicable reason were bound up in the *Exiit Books*. Both *Pandectae* and *Acta* eventually gave way to the *Gesta* during the Commonwealth period: cf. *B.H.* III, p. 264.

The steward and his staff: obsonator, promus, *cook and under-cook. [Statute 56]*

Senescallus was the Latin term which was used in the statutes of most other Cambridge colleges to denote their domestic steward, but in his statutes Caius deliberately opted instead for a term which emphasised the financial responsibilities of the officer (*oeconomus*), and he restricted his use of "*senescallus*" exclusively to the manorial steward. Although the term *oeconomus* was used thereafter for the domestic steward in the college's records while they were still written in Latin, the term was translated into the vernacular as "steward" on the rare occasions on which English was used in those records in Elizabethan times.[82]

In Statute 56 Caius envisaged that the steward would have under him a principal assistant, whom he designated as *obsonator* or *dispensator*, and specifically ranked him as a scholar on the foundation. His principal function seems to have been the purchase and provision of food, and his office to have been that of a purveyor. Bateman had provided in his statutes for such an official (*officiarius*), whom he termed *dispensator*, and he had directed that the *dispensator*, like the fellows, should receive a payment from the chest for stipend and robes. This official was included by Parker and his fellow commissioners in their report to Henry VIII in 1546 under the title of "manciple" (*mancipium*);[83] but it is doubtful whether Parker's term was ever used in Gonville Hall and, by Caius' time or soon after, the accepted English term for this member of the staff was "caterer".[84]

Earlier in his statutes Caius had included a second official, the *promus*, as a member of the foundation.[85] Unlike the *obsonator*, the *promus* had not been mentioned by Bateman, but he had been listed by Parker. There has been some confusion about the respective functions of these two members of the college's staff. On one occasion Venn translates *promus* as "working steward" and reserves the term "butler" for the *obsonator* or *dispensator*,[86] but this is clearly an unintentional slip on Venn's part, for elsewhere he correctly translates *promus* as "butler".[87] "Butler" would certainly seem the appropriate term for *promus*, as Statute 82 entrusts to him the care of silver vessels used at the common table.[88] Both *obsonator* and *promus* were included with the Master, fellows and scholars

82 *E.g., Status Collegii* (LD 1586).

83 *Documents*, I, p. 227.

84 "Cator" is the term mentioned in *Gerard's Case* (1582) and in *Allen's Case* (1617), Appendices D and F below. In his will Stephen Perse calls the *obsonator* the "caiter": Venn, *Annals*, p. 252.

85 Statute 2.

86 *B.H.* III, p. 240.

87 *E.g., B.H.* I, p. 38 *sub nom.* Denbye, M.

88 In Magdalene the *promus* was the gate-keeper: *Documents*, III, p. 356.

in the annual lists of members of the college who were 'on the foundation',[89] but the *obsonator* was the more senior and he was normally an academic who was a B.A.; in the early seventeenth century the *obsonator* occasionally stayed on in college after holding the office and became a fellow.[90]

It is clear from Statute 56 and elsewhere that the terms *dispensator* and *obsonator* were interchangeable in the sixteenth century and referred to a single office subordinate to that of the *oeconomus*. In the early seventeenth century a change in terminology occurred and a fellow might be appointed *oeconomus* under the title of *dispensator*: thus in 1611 a very senior fellow (Dr Welles) was appointed *dispensator*, and in 1613, when a bachelor scholar (Ds Edmonds) was appointed *obsonator*, another very senior fellow (Mr Stokys) was appointed "*senescallus sive dispensator*".[91] One suspects that the change in terminology may reflect a gradual transfer to the steward of the responsibilities of the *obsonator* for the purchase of provisions, perhaps beginning with function of purchasing the college's wine. The combined use of both the terms *seneschallus* and *dispensator* for this function did not last long, however, and the college soon reverted to using "*oeconomus*" in Latin and "steward" in English. By the middle of the seventeenth century the increase in the size of the college had made the appointment of an academic student to act as its purveyor quite inappropriate and the post of *obsonator* was finally discontinued in 1650.[92]

Bateman had also directed that two servants in the bakehouse and the kitchen should also receive a payment from the chest for stipend and robes, and in his statutes Caius continued the two servants on the foundation as members of the college, designating them as the cook and his assistant or under-cook.[93] They did not, however, continue to be members of the college for long and, unlike the *obsonator* and *promus*, they had already ceased to be members of the college by 1593.[94] Thereafter, like other townsfolk employed by the college, the cook and his assistant were free to marry and they lived outside college with their families.[95]

89 College Lists, *Acta* 1593, 1594, 1595.

90 *E.g.*, Ds Hearle (*B.H.* I, p. 141 *sub nom.* Harrell).

91 *Acta* Mich. 1611 and Mich. 1613. Edmonds' appointment as *obsonator* was conditional upon his resigning his scholarship.

92 MS 621/339, p. 320.

93 Statute 2.

94 They were not included in the earliest surviving list of members of the foundation in the *Acta* of 1593. In its set ways the bursary nevertheless continued into the nineteenth century to charge part of their salaries to the chest as if they were members.

95 On the occasion of the Great Plague in 1666, the cook and his family were received into the college "to provide commons for those few which venture to stay" and the college shut its gates and barred entry to everybody without exception: *Gesta*, 22 June 1666, cited *B.H.* III, p. 108.

The gifts of Geoffrey Knight and John Whitacre. [Statutes 60 and 61]

In his will Geoffrey Knight devised the Manor of Pattesley to the college in 1520 to enable it, *inter alia*, (i) to pay 40s. each year to a fellow to give a lecture in the hall of the college on humanity, logic or philosophy on four days a week in term time and in the great vacation, and (ii) to maintain two priests to serve at Pattesley, paying one of them a salary of 10 marks and the other 9 marks a year. Being only 20 marks a year, however, the annual income from the manor was insufficient to pay the two salaries and also pay 40s. (*i.e.*, 3 marks) to the lecturer. The manor was therefore exchanged in 1521 for that of D'Engaynes in Teversham and Stow-cum-Quy, which had a greater annual value (£21), the vendor receiving £96 from money given by another benefactor, Dr Bayley, to make up the difference in value.[96] The eventual outcome was that the lecturer was paid the full 40s. and the salaries of the two priests were equalised at 8 marks.

Geoffrey Knight had contemplated parish duties for the two priests which were more in the nature of chantries at Pattesley than of lecturing or administrative offices within the college, and the holders or "salarists" were given salaries (*subsidia*) which were in the nature of distinct fellowship stipends rather than payments to persons who already held a fellowship and stipend upon another foundation.[97] It is clear from the wording of his will that he had envisaged the appointment of two *additional* members of the college to discharge the duties he specified, one living in Gonville Hall and the other in Fishwick Hostel, rather than someone who was already a fellow, and each of the salaries provided by his gift was larger than the annual stipend of a fellow on Gonville's and Bateman's foundations. However, the Reformation and the loss of Fishwick Hostel in effect frustrated Knight's intention, and by the time of Caius' re-foundation his two *subsidia* were paid to persons who were already fellows, each of whom thus temporarily enjoyed a second full stipend.

When John Whitacre made a similar gift to the college in 1539 for a third salarist to provide divine services at Great St Mary's, the Reformation was already well advanced and the terms of the gift contemplated that the post would always be held by one who was already a fellow or other member of the college; nevertheless, the *subsidium* produced by his gift still amounted to £3. 14s. 8d., a sum which was not much less than a fellow's annual stipend.

96 *Annals*, pp. 21, 24–5, and *B.H.* III, pp. 244–5, 249, and IV(2), pp. 72–3.

97 For chantries, see Brooke, *History*, at pp. 7–8; essentially they were "funds to support the singing of masses for the souls of the founder, his family, friends and patrons", but "in practice the chantry often took a more substantial or material form, endowing specific priests in perpetuity, to celebrate at altars in parish churches or cathedrals".

By the time Caius was writing the final version of his statutes in 1572, the outlawing of prayers and services for the dead had rendered the duties of the three salarists markedly less onerous than the donors had contemplated, thereby producing a situation in which the holders of the posts enjoyed much greater remuneration than any other fellows, but for greatly diminished responsibilities. Not surprisingly, Caius added to their duties by imposing on all three an obligation to preach in person in all the rectories appropriated to the college, as well as at Great St Mary's and Barningham; in addition he directed that they should hold other offices at the same time only in exceptional circumstances.

The salarists were appointed on the nomination of the Master, who thus had a means of rewarding fellows for their earlier service in more demanding but less well-paid offices. Like other offices, the three salaries lost most of their value in the seventeenth century, but their usefulness as a reward for other service was preserved by the simple expedient of appointing one fellow to all three posts as "the salarist"; as a result it retained some small value (and duties) even into the early nineteenth century.[98]

Caius' use of the terms firma *and* firmarius. *[Statutes 86, 90, 93, 95 and 97]*

Caius used the terms *firma* and *firmarius* frequently in his statutes without consciously distinguishing between (i) the original, medieval use of the term *firma* to indicate the regular payment under contract of a fixed or 'firm' amount, usually of money and usually half-yearly, as a hiring-fee payable by a person (*firmarius*) in return for the occupation and use of property, whether or not he used it for agricultural and pastoral purposes, and (ii) the use of the terms *firmarius* and *firma* that was becoming popular by his time to indicate a 'farmer' who worked land for agricultural and pastoral purposes as a unit, a 'farm'.

The earlier sense of *firma* predominated in most of the statutes in which Caius used the word and it is usually quite clear from the context that he had in mind a payment of money, not an area of land, when he used the word. For example, in Statute 86 in which he specified in detail the requirements and restrictions which the college must observe when it was letting *any* of its land, whether urban property or rural, he described the act of leasing as being a letting of land 'to farm', that is, on hire (*in locandis ad firmam terris*); and in the same statute he prohibited the leasing of property in fee farm ("*ad feodi firmam*"), that is, he prohibited renting it out for a freehold interest as opposed to a contractual term of years. None of the provisions set out in that Statute 86 or in the three statutes

98 For an account of the three posts, see *B.H.* III, pp. 249–50; see also "*Stipends*", § V. 4, at p. 450 below.

which follow it was directed towards the obligations specifically appropriate to the leasing of a farm to a farmer in the modern sense, and the provisions of all those four statutes applied to the leasing of all the college's property, including town property or a mill.[99] Since the context can be relied upon to make it clear that Caius was referring to a payment, not to a unit of land, when he used the word *firma*, there will be little danger of misunderstanding if it is translated here with the English word which would have been used in his time, *i.e.* "farm".

On the other hand, Caius' use of *firmarius* was sometimes more ambiguous than his use of *firma* and reflected the gradual shift in meaning of 'farmer' in his time.[100] Thus, in Statute 90, which he entitled "*Conditiones firmariorum*", Caius set out obligations which would be appropriate only for a farmer in the modern sense, and it is clear that he had that concept in the forefront of his mind.[101] Even in Statute 90, however, Caius was concerned only with those farmers who held contractually under a lease from the college (*firmarii*) and whose obligations were specified in that lease, not with farmers who were copyholders and whose obligations were regulated by manorial custom: for Caius, both copyholders and leaseholders were "*tenentes*" (tenants), but only leaseholders were "*firmarii*". This assumption that "*firmarii*" were only those who held contractually and paid a *firma*, as distinct from those tenants who held in other ways, can be also detected in other statutes: (i) in Statutes 93 and 94 he resorted to the word *colonus*, not *firmarius*, to indicate a tenant who worked the land agriculturally or pastorally, *i.e.*, was a farmer in the modern sense; (ii) in Statute 95, where he dealt with entry fines payable on renewal of a tenancy, he carefully distinguished between those tenants who were copyholders and whose customary rents could not be increased and those tenants who were *firmarii* and whose rent could be increased when the contract came up for renewal since their right to hold the land derived solely from the payment of a contractual rent

[99] This appears to be the case, even in Statute 88, where Caius includes "*redditus firmae*" among the rights which the college must always reserve when granting land. It is tempting to translate the words as 'farm-rents' or 'rents of a farm', particularly as it follows immediately upon the rent of harvest works (*redditus operum autumnalium*), but in his use of *firma* here Caius has in his mind the rents arising from a lease, as contrasted with the rents of freehold and copyhold tenants and dry-rents, rather than the rents of a 'farm' in the modern sense.

[100] The lingering ambivalence in the use of the word *firmarius* long after Caius' death is well brought out in the first Bursar's Book (LD 1609). In this and subsequent books the payments of rents for the half-year to the college are classed as payments 'received from farmers' (*recepta a firmariis*) and the list of persons making such payments includes, *inter aliis*, tenants of houses in London and Norwich, other colleges for property in Cambridge (Jesus, Peterhouse and Trinity), and King James (*pro Hospito de Physwick*); but only the tenant of an agricultural property is individually described as "*firmarius*".

[101] Caius' concentration on farmers in the modern sense is understandable, since the great majority of the college's landholdings were agricultural or pastoral in character in his time.

(*firma*) for a fixed period;[102] and (iii) in Statute 97 it is clear from his equation of the term *firmarius* with *redemptor* that the form of payment was uppermost in his mind, not the nature of the intended use of the property.[103] In the light of Caius' identification of *firmarius* with one particular form of land-holding, *i.e.* a contractual tenancy, and given the automatic association today of the word 'farmer' with one particular use of land, *i.e.* use for agricultural or pastoral purposes, it would be misleading to translate Caius' "*firmarius*" as 'farmer', and for this reason the term 'lessee' has been preferred here.[104]

Caius' purchase of the Manors of Croxley, Runcton and Burnham Thorpe. [Statute 91]

When Caius was planning the re-foundation of the college, the particular aim which was foremost in his mind was the establishment of a permanent fund that could produce sufficient income regularly and reliably to support in perpetuity at least two new fellowships and twelve new scholarships and, eventually, three fellowships and no less than twenty scholarships. The only property which could provide such a fund was land, and to this end he achieved the purchase from the Crown of three manors which had passed to it on the dissolution of the greater monasteries in 1539: the manor of Croxley and Snellshall[105] in Hertfordshire from the abbey of St Albans, and the manors of Runcton Holme and Burnham Thorpe in Norfolk from the abbeys of St Edmund's Bury and Wymondham, respectively. The purchase price was assessed by the Crown at twenty years' purchase, that is, the usual rate of twenty times the currently assessed annual value of the manors; this amounted to £1,021. 12s. 6d., and in addition Caius paid £12 for the advowson of Runcton and Wallington churches.[106] He acquired the freehold title to these widely separated properties in a single grant from

[102] In both cases entry fines may be required when a tenancy is renewed, but in the case of *firmarii*, Caius directs that a fine should be levied only after the rent or *firma* has first been increased.

[103] Caius' interpretation of the term *redemptor* here to indicate a lessee is baffling, since the root meaning of the term was (and is) a person who makes a single payment in order to recover his property or to free himself or his property from an obligation to make future payments, *i.e.*, the opposite of a *firmarius* who undertakes to make periodic payments (*firmae*) in the future to obtain the use of another's property for a specific period.

[104] 'Tenant' would have suitable today, but it had a much wider meaning than *firmarius* in Caius' time, since it then included copyhold and freehold tenants of manors.

[105] In Mary's grant (and always thereafter) Croxley and Snellshall were treated as a single manor, but in the reign of her brother, Edward VI, they had been treated as two manors, as Mary's grant to Caius showed: for the grant see *Annals*, pp. 61–9.

[106] The advowson was bought at one year's purchase; this explains the apparent discrepancy of £12 between the statements in the Crown's grant of (i) the amount paid by Caius (£1,033. 12s. 6d.) and (ii) the 20-year purchase price of the manors (£1,021. 12s. 6d.): *Annals*, pp. 64, 67, 70.

Philip and Mary on 12 February 1558, six months after the re-foundation of the college by royal charter, and he conveyed them to the college on 1 March, in time for the formal inauguration of his new foundation on Lady Day later that month.[107] Surprisingly, on 20 April he took back to himself a 70-year lease of all three manors for the rest of his life:[108] whether he did this because he had begun to realise the problems that all three manors would present or because he already had doubts about the wisdom of entrusting their management to the then Master, Bacon, he does not tell us in the Annals. His election as Master the following year rendered the lease unnecessary.

As Caius shrewdly appreciated, the Crown's valuation of the properties was low and was based simply upon the amounts actually received from the properties at the time, and a great part of this came from lessees whose rents had been fixed many decades earlier. Caius recognised that those rents had been overtaken by inflation and that the true annual value of the three properties greatly exceeded the Crown's assessment.[109] He was therefore content to accept the low return on the properties until the existing leases would run out, at which time the rent from each of the three properties could be more than doubled. What he did not anticipate was the numerous troubles which they would give him for the rest of his life.

To understand those troubles one must keep in mind two complicating factors. First, by Queen Mary's time the owner of a manor wishing to lease his property had a choice between two different forms of lease, an 'old style' lease of the manor itself and a 'newer style' lease that was carefully restricted to the "scite of the manor" and the demesne lands, namely, those parcels of manorial land which by the custom of the manor were reserved to the lord's personal use and seisin and over which the manor's freeholders and copyholders had no claim.[110] By Mary's reign good conveyancing practice dictated that a sensible owner should always choose the latter form of lease, for it left in his hands the lordship rights over the manor, such as the quit-rents and other dues owed by

As explained below, the payment proved to be in vain as Edward VI had earlier granted the advowson to the Lord High Admiral, Lord Clinton and Saye.

107 Lady Day, 25 March, was the start of the Anglican calendar year.

108 BUR: DEEDS/ 25, 1, d. The lease was to be for the biblical term of "three score and ten years if the said John Caius so longe doe live" and the rent was to be one penny a year payable "yf yt be lawfullie demanded".

109 His valuation was £121 p.a., compared with the Crown's £51. 1s. 7½d.: see Statute 91.

110 The 'site' of the manor was that part of the physical land which was retained by the lord in his own seisin and not granted to freehold or copyhold tenants. It was contrasted with the lordship itself and the incorporeal rights (including the crucial right to hold a court) enjoyed by the lord over manorial lands held by such freehold and copyhold tenants. In effect the word indicated the manor-house itself (and its curtilage) and the demesne lands, the freehold of which would be retained by the lord. By Caius' time, the lord would normally lease these out for a term of years, but not the manor itself: cf. Sir Edward Coke, *The Compleat Copy-holder*, s. 31; J. Scriven, *A Treatise on the Law of Copyholds*, pp. 1–5.

the freehold and copyhold tenants, suit of court and, most importantly, the custody of the records of those dues; in contrast a lessee who had taken a lease of the manor itself could claim to be entitled to those rights during the continuance of his lease unless they had been expressly exempted from his grant.[111] All three manors purchased by Caius in 1558 were still subject to leases which had been drawn up in the old style before the dissolution of the monasteries, and the leases were still held by members of the original tenant's family; it would not be surprising therefore if the tenants had become accustomed by 1558 to claiming more than possession of the scite of the manor and its demesne lands, and, as will be seen later, it seems that they did so.

The second factor which contributed to Caius' later troubles lay in the letters patent containing the royal grant of the three manors to him. These were oddly drawn in a way which suggests that they were originally drafted to convey only Croxley to him and that the other two manors were added a little casually – and carelessly – as an afterthought. Only Croxley was indicated as the subject of the grant in the recitals and the whole of the purchase price was attributed to that manor alone; the other two manors appeared belatedly in the habendum and the annual values of the three manors stated there did not tally with the purchase price recorded in the recitals;[112] more importantly, it was only in respect of Croxley that the Crown's title was expressed to be subject to an existing lease and the interest conveyed to Caius was correctly described as being a reversion expectant upon the expiry of that lease, whereas there was no mention anywhere of the fact that Runcton and Burnham Thorpe were equally subject to prior leases and that the Crown's interest was merely reversionary in those two cases also.[113] Caius must have been aware of the existing leases when he purchased Runcton and Burnham Thorpe, but in both cases he seems to have been seriously mistaken on the question what property was included in the grant of the manors to him.

Caius had differing degrees of trouble with his three manors, the least with Croxley and the most with Burnham.

[111] As explained below, Caius himself made an 'old style' lease of the manor of Burnham Thorpe to Nicholas Mynne in 1571 and was careful to impose on the lessee an obligation to hand over the court rolls to the college every three years: *Liber Dimissionum 1551–1655*, fol. 81.

[112] The annual values of Croxley, Runcton and Burnham were assessed in the habendum at £23. 1s. 7½d., £22 and £6, respectively, giving a total of £51. 1s. 7½d. p.a. and thus would give a purchase price of £1,021. 12s. 6d. when multiplied twentyfold, not the amount recorded in the recitals as paid by Caius (£1,033. 12s. 6d.). As noted above, the discrepancy of £12 between the statements is explained by fruitless payment at one year's purchase for the advowson of Runcton and Wallington which Caius made: *Annals*, pp. 64, 67.

[113] The difference in treatment between Croxley and the other two manors may perhaps have been due to the fact that the prior leases of Croxley had been made by the Crown and copies were therefore readily available on the rolls to the Chancery clerks, whereas the leases of Runcton and Burnham had been made by abbeys before the dissolution of the monasteries and copies may have been less immediately accessible.

Croxley had been leased by the abbey of St Albans in its dying months to William Baldwin in 1538 for forty-three years and he had wisely surrendered the lease to Henry VIII and received from him in 1540 a shorter lease for twenty-one years but otherwise on the same terms and for the same rent as his lease from the abbey. By the time Caius came to purchase Croxley that lease had only three more years to run, but in 1551 Edward VI had granted to Robert Lee, one of the yeomen of his chamber, a reversionary lease to run for a further twenty-one years from the expiry of the lease to Baldwin. Unlike Henry VIII's old-style lease to Baldwin, Edward's lease confined the subject matter to the "scite of the manor", and Caius might therefore expect that the college would have a new-style tenant in the manor from 1561, when Henry's lease to Baldwin would run out. However, by 1561 Lee had already sold his lease to the Baldwin family, who therefore continued in possession of the manor for the further twenty-one years. Relations between the college and the Baldwin family appear to have been relatively uncontentious during Caius' life, but it seems that the Baldwins ignored any change to their status after 1561, and in 1577 their actions in respect of woodlands and copyholds led to the college's suing them in Chancery in the last years of their lease.[114]

Runcton had been leased for sixty years to one Conisby by the abbey of St Edmund's Bury, in 1522, long before the dissolution, and by 1558 it had passed to his widow and her second husband, Sir Thomas Ragland. It appears to have proved straightway more troublesome to Caius than Croxley and must have proved a distraction to him in the early years after his return to the college, just at a time when he was already heavily engaged in the reform of the college's finances and records and in dispute with some of the fellows. At the very outset he suffered an unexpected disappointment. He had purchased the advowsons and patronage of the churches of Runcton and Wallington as well as the manor and these had been expressly included in the royal grant to him in February 1558; he in turn had included them in his gift to the college the following month, but almost immediately he learned that they had earlier been sold by Edward VI to Lord Clinton and Saye, the Lord Admiral, and that neither he nor the college had acquired any right to them.[115] As regards the manor itself, he became rapidly embroiled in various minor disputes affecting tenants of the manor,[116] but also in a major dispute in 1561 with members of the Conisby family to whom the manor had been leased in 1522 and who had held it ever

114 BUR: DEEDS/ 30, 8. The college's complaint was principally that of most owners of manors, namely the taking of timber by the tenant, but it also related to the Baldwins' leasing of copyholds without the college's consent. For the later history of Croxley, which was "peculiarly productive of law-suits", see *B.H.* IV(2), pp. 73–7 at 74.

115 He sadly recorded a warning to the college in his Annals that the Admiral's title was unassailable and that it would be fruitless to contest it: *Annals*, p. 70.

116 BUR: DEEDS/ 25, 1 f, g.

since.[117] The basic issue in this dispute was, in essence, the same as the issue that underlay the college's litigation with the Baldwin family over Croxley, namely, how far were long-standing tenants of a manor holding under a lease drafted decades earlier entitled to exercise the rights of a lord over the whole manor as opposed merely to those parts of it to which a lord had a right to possession (*i.e.*, the scite of the manor and the demesne lands); but whereas the Croxley litigation did not arise until 1577, well after his death, Caius found himself embroiled with the Conisby family in a major Chancery suit over Runcton as early as 1561 – just at the time when he was heavily engaged in practice in London and with the government of both the College of Physicians in London and his own foundation in Cambridge.[118] Caius was successful in this litigation over Runcton, but it must have been an unwelcome addition to the remarkably heavy burden which he was already carrying and which may help to explain the irascibility and "overmuch rashness" that he displayed in his dealings with some of the fellows at that time.[119] He seems also to have had an acrimonious dispute of some mysterious sort with the owners of the neighbouring manor of Thorpeland at around this time.[120] We do not know when or why the dispute arose, but it caused Caius to include in Statute 93 a fierce injunction to the college never to allow Runcton to be leased to the owner of Thorpeland or any of his tenants and, in addition, a notable direction always to take a substantial conditional bond from its own tenants against their doing so whenever it leased Runcton.[121]

In the case of Burnham Thorpe uncertainty about the title and difficulty in obtaining the 'evidences' or title-deeds from the tenant plagued Caius to the end of his life. Before the dissolution the manor of Burnham Thorpe had

[117] BUR: DEEDS/ 25, 4. The college's successful suit was for the enclosure of demesne lands and commons and the detaining of court rolls, terriers and other evidences belonging to the manor; it was brought against Conisby's widow and her second husband, Sir Thomas Ragland, and also the well-known lawyer Sergeant Gawdy, to whom they had passed the lease.

[118] Caius had been President of the College of Physicians every year between 1555 and 1560, and again in 1562 and 1563, but had stepped down in 1561: *B.H.* III, p. 34.

[119] For Parker's very sensible assessment of the quarrels in the college at the time, see Appendix C text (A) below, and *B.H.* III, p. 45.

[120] Thorpeland is south of and adjacent to Runcton Holme, about 5 miles north of Downham Market. The lordship of the manor of Thorpeland came to be vested in the Hare family of nearby Stow Bardolf, and the college's records show that it had dealings in respect of Runcton with a Sir Ralph Hare at about that time (BUR: DEEDS/ 25, 1m). In Caius' time, however, the college's relations with the Hare family appear to have been amicable: Sir Nicholas Hare, M.R. (*ODNB sub nom.*), may have been at Gonville Hall and he had sent two of his sons there (*B.H.* I, p. 34).

[121] The injunction had not been included in Caius' draft statutes in 1558 and was presumably the result of some subsequent acrimonious dispute as yet untraced. Whatever the dispute, it clearly provoked very strong feelings in Caius. The prohibition was regularly included in leases of Runcton.

belonged to the abbey of Wyndham, which had also been entitled to a portion of the tithes out of the each of the rectories of Burnham Overy and Peterston,[122] and although the portions were not appurtenances of the manor they had been enjoyed *de facto* together with it. Upon the dissolution in 1539 the portions and the manor passed to the Crown along with the other property of the abbey. However, in the last months before its dissolution, the abbey had granted a lease of the manor – and perhaps the portions – for eighty years at a rent of just £6 a year and, surprisingly, Henry VIII does not seem to have required the lessee, Richard Southwell, to surrender the lease and take a shorter one as he had done in the case of Croxley. Southwell was thus still firmly in possession of the manor at the time of Queen Mary's grant to Caius, but his lease was not mentioned in her grant, nor was the grant to Caius made subject to it in the same way that the grant of Croxley had been.

The unqualified nature of the royal grant to Caius, coupled with his inability to track down the history of the lease to Southwell and his awareness that Wymondham abbey had in the past enjoyed a share of the tithes of Burnham Overy and Peterston, seems to have instilled in him a firm belief (i) that Southwell's lease was in some way defective as against the Crown and its successors and did not entitle him to exercise the lordship rights over the manor, and (ii) that Queen Mary's grant had had the effect of vesting in Caius, and through him in the college, not only the manor but also the two shares of tithes. In both matters he was mistaken, but he seems to have clung to his belief in both until 1572, when he was in the last year of his life. As late as 1571 he was pursuing Southwell for possession of title deeds to the manor and in the final version of his statutes he expressly coupled the share in the tithes of both Burnham Overy and Peterston with the college's ownership of the manor of Burnham Thorpe.[123] However, in 1572 he seems to have accepted that the share of the two tithes had not passed to him under Mary's grant, for he came to a quite extraordinary arrangement with Nicholas Mynne, a neighbour and opponent of Southwell, who had acquired a clear title to the share of the Burnham Overy tithes (by now quantified as 16 quarters of barley annually) through a grant from Queen Elizabeth in 1571. By this arrangement with Caius, Mynne conveyed his title to the tithes to the college in return for a twenty-one-year lease of the manor of Burnham Thorpe and the 16 quarters of barley at a rent of £8 p.a., and at the same time he undertook to sue Southwell and secure the complete annulment of the 1539 lease.[124] In making this arrangement Caius had to disregard the cardinal rule which his experience with the three manors

[122] The portion of the tithes of Burnham Overy had been fixed at a payment of 16 quarters of barley and was known as the "Garba" or sheath.

[123] Statute 91.

[124] BUR: DEEDS/ 27, 3b; *Annals*, p. 184. Southwell was to be thwarted and the 1539 lease invalidated once and for all ("*frustretur in aeternum*").

had taught him and which he had vehemently imposed upon the college in his statutes, namely that the college should *never* lease a manor, but only the scite of the manor and its demesne lands.[125] To give Mynne sufficient title to sue Southwell Caius gave him a 21-year lease of the manor itself and the manorial rights over its freehold and copyhold tenants, including the holding of courts.[126] Both Caius and Mynne must have felt passionately that right was on their side, but before a year had expired Mynne acknowledged that he was unable to dislodge Southwell; he abandoned the task and defaulted on his rent. Two years later the college re-entered on both the manor and the portion of tithes for non-payment of rent and so finally acquired title to the 16 quarters of barley, though not in the way Caius had believed.[127] The failure to dislodge Southwell meant that he and his later assign, Sir Charles Cornwallis, stayed in possession until his lease finally expired in 1619. Litigation inevitably followed and, sadly, though the college was successful in its action, the manor of Burnham Thorpe failed ever to produce for the college the returns for which Caius had hoped when he purchased it in 1558.[128]

Manorial stewards and bailiffs. [Statute 96]

In one of his very first acts as Master, Caius appointed a fellow, Henry Dethick, as steward of the college's lands (*seneschallus terrarium*),[129] but he soon ceased to appoint fellows to such a post and by the time he issued the final version of his statutes he had come to envisage exclusively the appointment of local stewards of individual manors (Statute 96). In the course of time the college

125 Statute 86.

126 *Liber dimissionum*, fol. 81. The lease required the lessee to hand over to the college every three years all court rolls, terriers and title deeds, and records of dues paid by freehold and copyhold tenants. It appears to be the only such lease the college ever granted after Caius' re-foundation.

127 BUR: DEEDS/ 27, 3e, f. Mynne's venture thus cost him the portion of Burnham Overy tithes that he had purchased from Queen Elizabeth, and Caius acquired it for nothing; but neither he nor the college ever succeeded in acquiring the Peterston tithes: *Registrum Magnum*, p. 429.

128 By 1619 the college's land had been so mixed with Cornwallis' own land that "a great suit in Chancery arose". In addition to its manorial rights in respect of the freehold and copyhold tenants, the college secured the return to it of the scite of the manor and 100 acres of demesne lands, which it thereafter let on 20-year leases for £8 p.a. until 1866. However, it failed to obtain the foldage which Caius had valued in Statute 91 as worth more than all the rest of the manor; furthermore, for some unfathomable reason the whole of the college's portion of the tithes of Burnham Overy was treated as corn money and divided among the Master and fellows. In addition the system of entry fines meant that until 1866 they also enjoyed the true return from the land and the college received no more than the £8 p.a. rent from the demesnes and just over £2 in quit rents from the freehold and copyhold tenants: see *B.H.* IV(2), pp. 15–17, and "*Stipends*", § VI. 4 below.

129 *Pandectae* (1558–1658), fol. 2: 24 January 1559.

came to appoint, as stewards for groups of properties, lawyers who did not live locally but practised elsewhere, either in the county town or, eventually, in London.[130] This appears to have been universally the college's practice by the beginning of the nineteenth century, but, curiously, the idea of appointing a fellow to be Steward of the Manors was revived in the course of that century, and the office was held in turn by fellows who were lawyers: John Tozer, who had a busy practice in land law in the Court of Common Bench and acted as bursar at the same time, Thomas Wiglesworth, who had an equity practice at the Bar in London, and finally William Buckland, who was a college lecturer in law and a distinguished academic lawyer.[131] The enfranchisement of all remaining copyhold tenure in 1922 brought the need for a steward to an end.[132]

Although Caius was careful to direct in Statute 96 that neither stewards nor bailiffs should hold their offices in perpetuity or for life, but should be appointed annually and during the college's good pleasure, the requirement for annual re-appointment seems to have been dropped very rapidly, and after first appointment both officers simply continued to hold their office during good pleasure. Unlike the steward, who was expressly barred from holding a tenancy,[133] the bailiff could be and generally was himself one of the tenants, and the office of bailiff might pass down in the same family for decades.[134] Typically a bailiff would be socially inferior to the steward, but that was not necessarily so in the case of those college manors where the demesne lands were leased to a single, substantial tenant: in such cases the lessee might be required under the terms of the lease to act as bailiff and collect the quit-rents and other dues from the freehold and copyhold tenants of the manor.[135]

130 *Gesta*, 5 October 1660 (Raphael Keneriche chosen steward for all courts in Norfolk and near Cambridge); 7 December 1663 (Richard Newman of the Temple appointed steward for courts at Croxley).

131 *B.H.* II, pp. 217, 268, 452; *Gesta*, C.O.3, 28 October 1847; *Annals*, p. xiii.

132 Law of Property Act 1922.

133 Statute 96.

134 Thomas Samways was appointed bailiff of Bincombe and Oborne in 1606 and held the office until 1642, when old age and the Civil War prevented him from journeying to Cambridge and he handed over the office to a second Samways (his son?). Another Samways was still discharging the office at the time of his death in 1697, and the Survey Book shows that a member of the Samways family was still a tenant in Bincombe in 1762.

135 When Caius gave a reversionary lease of the scite and demesne lands of Croxley and Snellshall as a single tenancy to his close and trusted friend, William Gerrard, esquire, in 1571, it was a term of the lease that Gerrard should act as bailiff and collect the quit rents and other dues from the free and copyhold tenants of the manor as well as pay the £40 rent for the scite and demesne lands leased to him: *Liber Dimissionum* (1551–1655), p. 75. Croxley and Snellshall were always leased as one tenancy in this way until 1878: *B.H.* IV(2), p. 74. Similarly, Thomas Wendy, gentleman, (the nephew of the benefactor of that name) undertook the same duties when he took a lease of Duxford in 1624: *Liber demissionum*, fol. 178v.

In the case of a distant estate the bailiff might be the college's only regular contact with its tenants there for many years, as it would fall to him to bring all their rents to Cambridge twice a year.[136] The college's two most remote manors, Bincombe and Oborne, provided a salutary demonstration in the course of 1606 of the value of having a reliable and trustworthy bailiff. The reversion to the two manors had been purchased by Caius in 1570, but they did not bring in any income to the college while the life tenant, Lady Allington, was alive;[137] when she died in 1592 and the college at last became entitled to the income from the estates, it continued John Allen, the existing bailiff, in office and only fourteen years later did it discover that it should have received £431 in rents and not the £327 which Allen had brought to it. Allen was summarily dismissed but it took several years for the college to recover the shortfall from him.[138]

[136] Even tenants in Cambridge might be expected to pay their rents through a bailiff: *Acta*, 11 July 1611.

[137] It is an intriguing question why Caius chose to purchase a reversionary interest in such remote property when it could not support for an indefinite period the scholarships for which the purchase money had been given to the college, but it is outside the scope of the present work to consider the likely explanation.

[138] The calculations are recorded in the *Liber Rationalis* (1606) following the Lady Day accounts. In theory the rents were due half-yearly, but as far as records go back the bailiff of Bincombe and Oborne appears rarely to have made the long journey more than once a year, and the Bursar's Book shows that the college was content to receive the whole year's rent at Michaelmas.

PART TWO

Background and Aftermath

V

Background

V. 1

Edmund Gonville and his Foundation

(BY CHRISTOPHER BROOKE)

The Gonville inheritance

Edmund Gonville was one of the remarkable characters of the fourteenth-century English church: a devout parish priest, a man of affairs, an entrepreneur, an expert conveyancer, a money lender[1] – a man in whose talents the service of God and the service of mammon were inextricably entwined. He came from a family of landowners formed – it seems – by the union of a modest landed inheritance near the borders of Norfolk and Suffolk with the family of a knight of French origin – a kinsman, apparently, of the earl of Lancaster.[2]

In 1252 William of Larling had lands in Norfolk in Larling, Foulden, Palgrave and Rushford – and he is also recorded in the Book of Fees as holding a knight's fee in Rushford and Shipdham in Norfolk in 1232–3, and in 1242–3 a third of a knight's fee of the earl Warenne in Rushford and Larling.[3] He seems to have

1 On Gonville see Brooke, *Churches and Churchmen in Medieval Europe* (London, 1999), ch. 16, esp. pp. 292–9 and references. Late in his life he was able to loan Edward III 300 marks (Brooke, *ibid.*, p. 292 and n. 12). Our knowledge of the Gonville family, and of Gonville's foundation of Rushford College, mainly depends on the deeds of the Buxton family – who acquired Rushford after the dissolution of the college in the sixteenth century – and whose relevant archives are now divided between the Cambridge University Library (from 1901) and the Library of Caius College (possibly about the same time). Many of them were calendared – with other documents from the Norwich bishops' registers and The National Archives – by the Reverend Dr E.K. Bennet in the 1880s: *Historical Memorials of the College of S. John Evangelist Rushworth or Rushford, Co. Norfolk* (Norwich, 1888), reprint from *Norfolk Archaeology* 10 (1888), 50–64, 77–382 – here cited from the book, hereafter referred to as Bennet). Bennet's work – and the archive – have long been known to Caius historians, but they still have some secrets to reveal. The Buxton deeds in the Cambridge University Library (henceforth CUL) have been calendared in full by Gotthelf Wiedermann (1998, typescript in CUL MSS Reading Room); those in the Caius library are calendared in M.R. James, *Supplement to the Catalogue of Manuscripts in the Library of Gonville and Caius College* (Cambridge, 1914), pp. 7–8.

2 See below, at n. 15.

3 Bennet, p. 82, nos 2–3; *Book of Fees* II (London, Public Record Office, 1923), pp. 1466, 906.

been still alive in 1280; but by 1295 William de Gonville – 'born a subject of the king of France living in England' – is recorded as holding a manor in Larling and property in Foulden and Palgrave.[4] Oddly, Rushford is not mentioned; but by 1315 Nicholas de Gonville is listed as lord of manors in Larling and Rushford. It seems clear that William de Gonville had settled in Norfolk and acquired the properties – or a major share in the properties – of the Larling family.

The most likely way in which this could have been accomplished would have been by marriage with an heiress. This possibility seems to gain some confirmation from the descent of the advowson of Rushford. In a document apparently of the 1290s it is assigned to Amicia, widow of William of Larling, of Larling.[5] On 30 June 1303 Edmund of Larling acolite was instituted as rector of Rushford, on the presentation of Matilda of Larling.[6] By 1320 the patron was Nicholas de Gonville, and the rector Edmund Gonville priest.[7] The simplest explanation of these details is that Matilda was daughter and heiress of William of Larling and wife of William de Gonville – keeping her maiden name in relation to her rights as patroness of Rushford. Nicholas de Gonville was presumably the son of this marriage, and the intimacy of Edmund with Nicholas' family makes it reasonable to assume – as has commonly been done in the past[8] – that Edmund Gonville was Nicholas' brother. It also seems clear that the Larling family retained their original name for a while after marrying into the Gonvilles, so that Larling and Gonville could be alternative surnames for the same person. Surnames were still fluid in the fourteenth century and it was not uncommon for a man to have two – William Bateman, for example, was commonly known to contemporaries as William of Norwich. There is an interesting parallel in a family of well-to-do peasants (sokemen) on Peterborough abbey estates in the late thirteenth century: Richard son of Mary of Peakirk was usually named after his mother, but occasionally from his father – Richard son of Geoffrey.[9] I conclude that

4 Bennet, p. 85, no. 13.

5 Bennet, pp. 85–6, nos 14, 17.

6 Bennet, p. 86, no. 17 = Norfolk Record Office Reg. 1/1 *sub anno* 1303 ('12' according to Bennet: the folio no. was not visible in the microfilm from which I read the entry). The previous rector, William of Shadwell, occurs in 1294–5 (23 Edward I: Bennet, p. 85, no. 12 = CUL Buxton Deed no. 7/19).

7 Bennet, p. 88, nos 23, 24 (= Caius MS 740/785 no. 1), 26. As Gonville was an acolite in 1303 and later a priest, it may well be that he was under the canonical age for priesthood, 25, in 1303. If he was about 20 in 1303, then he would have been born about 1283 and approaching 70 when he died in 1351. But there are many uncertainties in such calculations.

8 Apart from a misleading entry in an early version of the Caius Commemoration of Benefactors, which made Nicholas Edmund's father – which was the subject of severe animadversions by Bennet (pp. 64–7). Nicholas witnessed a deed on 4 February 1330 (Bennet, p. 89, no. 28 = CUL Buxton Deeds 8/21) and died *c.* 1333 (Bennet, p. 89, nos 30–31; cf. nos 28, 29). His widow, Alicia, was living in 1342 (Bennet, p. 91, no. 37 = CUL Buxton deeds no. 8/47).

9 *Carte Nativorum*, ed. C.N.L. Brooke and M.M. Postan, Northants Record Society 20 (1960), note to no. 289.

Edmund of Larling was an alternative name for Edmund Gonville, and that he was rector of Rushford from 1303 to 1320 – having been presented to the living by his mother, Matilda of Larling.[10] He was later rector of Thelnetham from 1320 to 1326, returning to Rushford from 1326 to 1343 – then rector of Terrington St Clement from 1343 to 1351.[11] He held only one benefice at a time. His wealth was acquired from his business dealings: he was never a pluralist.

Gonville Hall

Between 1347 and 1352 four tiny colleges were founded in Cambridge, each of them aimed primarily to provide a home and support for students towards the end of their arts courses, or heading into courses for higher degrees: Pembroke (1347), Gonville Hall (1348), Trinity Hall (1350) and Corpus Christi College (1352). In the conception of these mini-colleges it stands to reason that there is likely to have been some communication between the founders, and it is certain that, in the highly technical and very complex business of arranging the property conveyances in preparation for the founding of the first two, Edmund Gonville played a role.[12] In November 1351 Gonville died,[13] so that he could not participate in the founding of Corpus. But a crucial role of patron in the founding of Corpus was played by Henry earl of Lancaster in undertaking the office of alderman of the two guilds which merged to create the college.[14] In 1347–8, in a charter confirming the foundation of the Dominican priory in Thetford, Earl Henry had described Edmund Gonville as his "beloved clerk and kinsman".[15] We do not know precisely how they were related, but we can be confident that –

10 For a time from 1338 he held a life tenancy of Rushford manor from his nephew John – which was perhaps in lieu of payment of a debt (Bennet, p. 90, no. 34 = Gonville and Caius College Library MS 740/785 no. 4: *Supplement to the Catalogue of MSS in the Library of Gonville and Caius College* (Cambridge, 1914), p. 7) – converted to full tenure in 1342 (Bennet pp. 90–1, no. 37 = CUL Buxton Deed no. 8/47).

11 Brooke, *History*, p. 2 and references in n. 4. Gonville seems to have resigned Terrington shortly before his death: his successor was instituted on 17 October 1351 (Bennet, p. 94, no. 49).

12 For Pembroke, see J. Ringrose, 'The foundress and her college', in *Pembroke College Cambridge: a Celebration*, ed. A.V. Grimstone (Cambridge, 1997) pp. 1–12, esp. p. 5; for Gonville Hall, Gonville and Caius College Archives, BUR: DEEDS/ I passim. No evidence has been found linking Gonville to the founding of Trinity Hall, though it seems likely that he a played a role there too.

13 *The Caian* (1994), p. 67.

14 C.R. Cheney, 'The gilds of the Blessed Virgin Mary and of Corpus Christi', in *Letter of the Corpus Association* 63 (1984), pp. 24–35, esp. pp. 28–9; C.P. Hall, 'The gild of Corpus Christi and the foundation of Corpus Christi College …', in *Medieval Cambridge*, ed. P. Zutshi, pp. 65–91, esp. pp. 80–2.

15 *Calendar of Patent Rolls 1348–50*, p. 19. The royal letters patent confirming the earl's charter are dated 10 February 1348 – just a fortnight after the royal licence for the founding of Gonville Hall.

if Gonville had lived a few months longer – he would have played the technical role in the preliminary property conveyances for the founding of Corpus that he had played in preparing for Pembroke and Gonville Hall – especially as Corpus was founded in the same part of Cambridge in which he had helped to provide space for Pembroke and the original site of Gonville Hall. Friendship between the earl, from 1351 duke of Lancaster, and William Bateman, was to play an essential role in the complex arrangements by which Bateman moved Gonville Hall to the place which is now Gonville Court.[16]

The Dominican house at Thetford was the first of three religious institutions in whose foundation Gonville played a crucial role.[17] In 1337 he was John de Warenne's agent in its foundation – a process repeated in the charter of the earl of Lancaster of 1347–8, in which Gonville is again referred to as a major player. The smooth surface of these charters disguises a situation of extreme complexity.[18] Warenne and Lancaster were rival claimants for the lordship of Thetford; and in the 1330s – under an arrangement made in 1327 – Warenne had tenure for life of the lordship of Thetford, with reversion to the earl of Lancaster on his death. The elder Henry earl of Lancaster died in 1345, and Warenne died in 1347. The younger Henry earl of Lancaster was now in control and he and Gonville lost no time in confirming the foundation of 1335, but in language suggesting it was an original grant by the earl. These events presuppose careful diplomacy between Warenne and Lancaster in 1335, in which Gonville evidently played a key role.

The other complication in the founding of the Dominican house at Thetford was that it was founded on the site of a hospital, 'La Meisondieu'. This was one of several hospitals in Thetford and it appears that Gonville convinced Warenne and the earls that its functions could be better performed under the auspices of the friars – or, at least, that the real need in that region was for a team of trained preachers such as the Dominican Order could provide.[19]

The founder of the Dominican house may have been John de Warenne – succeeded by Henry of Lancaster – but the pastoral needs of that region of the see of Norwich were fairly remote from the concerns of these distant

16 See "*William Bateman and his Foundation*", § V. 2 below.

17 Venn suggests that he was also a benefactor to the hospital of St John at King's Lynn (*B.H.* III, p. 3). This was clearly based on Bennet, p. 17. No evidence for this has been found, and it seems that Bennet had confused the Dominican house at Thetford with the hospital at Lynn.

18 For what follows see C. Norton in Norton, Park and Binski [C. Norton, D. Park and P. Binski, *Dominican Painting in East Anglia* (Woodbridge, 1987)] pp. 88–9, n. 22 – correcting Brooke, *History*, pp. 4, 7: cf. *ibid*., repr. of 1996, p. 305.

19 It has been alleged that the Maison Dieu had been founded under William II, but there is no evidence for this – and it seems more likely that it effectively replaced the late eleventh-century cathedral, which had been briefly a Cluniac house from 1103–4 to 1114, after the monks moved north of the river Ouse in 1114.

potentates.[20] Gonville's personal interests have been seen to be reflected in the superb altar retable and frontal which has miraculously survived, in Thornham Parva and the Musée de Cluny in Paris.[21] Gonville's imaginative eye for the needs of his homeland is even more apparent in his two other foundations, at Rushford and Cambridge.

In 1342 the Thetford priory was followed by the foundation of a college for five chaplains (including the master) – a kind of group ministry to serve the parish and people of Rushford, near Thetford, and to celebrate masses and say prayers for Gonville himself and his family – and a wider circle. Rushford and Larling, nearby, were the homes of Gonville's family, and their churches provided the basis for the endowment and ministry of the chaplains of his college.[22] Early in his career Edmund had been rector of Rushford, of which Matilda of Larling (probably Edmund Gonville's mother) and Nicholas de Gonville (probably his brother) were successively patrons. In 1320, for some reason, he exchanged it for Thelnetham, returning to the rectory of Rushford in 1326. In 1342 he completed

20 Though Henry of Lancaster was personally interested in religious affairs (Brooke, *History*, p. 6 and n. 10, citing W.A. Pantin, *The English Church in the Fourteenth Century* (Cambridge, 1955), pp. 231–3).

21 On which see Norton, Park and Binski. Recent studies of the altarpiece include: *The Thornham Parva Retable: Technique, Conservation and Context of an English Medieval Painting*, ed. A. Massing (London and Whittlesford, 2003; Nicholas Rogers, 'The provenance of the Thornham Parva retable', in *The Friars in Medieval Britain*, ed. N. Rogers (Proceedings of the 2007 Harlaxton Symposium (2010), pp. 185–93; David King, 'John de Warenne, Edmund Gonville and the Thetford Dominican altar paintings', in *Tributes to Nigel Morgan: Contexts of Medieval Art, Image, Objects and Ideas*, ed. J.M. Luxford and M.A. Michael (London–Turnhout, 2010), pp. 293–306. Rogers mobilises some ingenious arguments in favour of the Norwich Dominican house as the original home of the frontal, and he and Binski (writing in *The Thornham Parva Retable*, p. 14), favour Norwich as the home of the artists. Norwich was a likely place for a major figure in the see of Norwich like Gonville to seek craftsmen, and is only 20 miles or so from Thetford. There is good evidence of a major fire in the Norwich convent in 1413 which wooden panels are unlikely to have escaped; that apart, effective argument must turn on evidence of patronage – and here Thetford still has the advantage, since St Edmund and two St Johns are prominent in the ensemble – patron saints of Gonville and Warenne – and David King (*art. cit.*) has found clear evidence in the background painting of the Warenne emblem. Rogers cites contrary evidence not quite so convincing.

22 The fullest account of the family is still that of E.K. Bennet, *Historical Memorials* (*op. cit.*). The chief sources are the Buxton family MSS, most of which are now in the Cambridge University Library. But about the time they were deposited in the Library (1901), most of the deeds relating to Gonville and his family were given to Caius and are now in a box labelled Gonville and Caius College Library MS 740/785. Many of the Buxton deeds, especially those relating to Rushford and the Gonvilles, were calendared by Bennet, pp. 82–119, and the whole collection was the subject of report by A. Jessopp in *Historical Manuscripts Commission, Report on Manuscripts in Various Collections* II, pp. xix–xxiii, 227–88. A complete catalogue of the Cambridge University Library's collection by Gotthelf Wiedermann is available in the MSS Reading Room in the Library.

the foundation of Rushford College and handed over the rectory to the college; from 1343 till 1351 he was rector of Terrington St Clement.[23]

Rushford was a pastoral chantry – founded to combine chantry masses and prayers for the founder and his family with pastoral care. Gonville Hall, as he himself called it, was an academic chantry: its name was a reminder that it too had a chantry function; but its purpose was equally academic, to provide support for young students. Letters patent of King Edward III licensed Gonville to found a college endowed with three messuages and a garden in 'Lurteburghlane' (Free School Lane),[24] Cambridge, named after him, for twenty scholars. In the event, Gonville died before he could provide effective endowment for the college, and the resources which were later provided by Bateman barely sufficed to support four or five fellows. What happened to the funds Gonville had accumulated to endow his college has been the occasion for much speculation, and opinion has varied between those who think Bateman failed to make proper use of his legacy and those who think the survival of the college owed everything to Bateman's tenacity and generosity.[25]

What is certain is that Bateman brushed Gonville aside after Gonville's death, claiming to himself the title of founder, renaming the college the hall of the Annunciation of the Blessed Virgin Mary. Bateman's statutes for Gonville Hall are closely based on those of Trinity Hall and owe virtually nothing to Gonville's own draft. Indeed, it is striking that the early statutes of the foundations of the 1340s and 1350s were markedly dissimilar. The vision of the needs of the people and clergy of the see of Norwich reflected in a Dominican house, a pastoral college of chantry priests and an academic chantry-college is partly at least Gonville's – he was a central figure in the process as well as a technical expert in the legal affairs involved. But he had no hand in the drafting of the statutes of any of the three new colleges in Cambridge apart from his own – and even in Gonville Hall Gonville's draft was wholly supplanted by Bateman's statutes. The countess of Pembroke planned a more elaborate constitution, with two rectors having a supervisory role, one a Franciscan friar the other a secular cleric; and her statutes were a great deal more elaborate than Gonville's.[26] And the statutes of Corpus were to be based on those of Michaelhouse, founded in the 1320s.[27] None the less, there is a characteristic mark of Gonville's influence in the clause concerning the seal and common chest "with three locks and keys of different

[23] An original charter of 29 January 1320 was issued by him as rector of Rushford: Caius Library MS 740/785, no. 1, calendared in Bennet, pp. 88, 92, with the record of his institutions in 1326 and 1343 from the bishop's registers.

[24] Now part of Corpus – following the exchange between the colleges described in "*William Bateman and his Foundation*", § V. 2 below.

[25] These possibilities are discussed in the following chapter.

[26] They are edited by Jayne Ringrose, 'The medieval statutes of Pembroke College', in *Medieval Cambridge*, ed. P. Zutshi (Woodbridge, 1993), pp. 93–127, at pp. 103–23.

[27] *H.U.C.*, p. 87.

pattern" – "*cum tribus seraris et clavibus diverse fabric*" as it is in the Rushford statutes of 1342, "*sub tribus clausuris seu serruris distinctis et totidem clavibus dissimilibus*" in Gonville's draft statutes for his Cambridge college, "*sub tribus clavibus diverse fabric*" in Bateman's statutes for both Trinity Hall and Gonville Hall, repeated in the Corpus statutes "*cum tribus clavibus diverse fabric*".[28]

Gonville's statutes for his Cambridge college are notably more elaborate than those for Rushford – just as the former in their turn are less full than Bateman's statutes for Trinity Hall and Gonville Hall. In the statutes for his academic college Gonville was much concerned with academic duties, and laid great emphasis on precise accounting. Both his sets of statutes reflect the prudent and experienced administrator, with advanced ideas of accounting – every year at Rushford a reckoning has to be made "whether their goods have been increased or diminished – *an eorum bona augmenta fuerint sive diminuta*".[29] This is significant, as profit and loss rarely entered medieval accounting systems, which were more designed to check the honesty and reliability of the accountant than his financial success.[30] Gonville's restriction on the alternative income a fellow might hold calculates it "according to the common estimate of true value – *secundum communem estimacionem veri valoris*" – a phrase which echoes the language of papal taxation records and reminds us that Gonville, as an expert in the handling of benefices, will have had ready and regular access to some version of the *Taxatio* of Pope Nicholas IV of 1291, which with some local modifications was the basis for clerical taxation till the advent of Thomas Cromwell and the *Valor ecclesiasticus* of 1535.[31]

Both sets of statutes have careful provision for discipline, tempered by a determination to avoid heavy punishment for minor faults. The sections on academic courses in the Gonville Hall statutes, especially cc. 15–17, naturally had no place in the Rushford statutes, and must have been the fruit of consultation with experienced academics. No doubt the clause at the end, in which the first Master, and the first fellows, testified that the statutes had been fully discussed with them, was literally true. But the most striking contrast between the two sets of statutes is in the provision for masses and prayers – for there is no such provision in Gonville's draft for Gonville Hall. At Rushford "all the

28 Bennet, p. 42, n. 10; Gonville draft statute 6, at p. 47 above; *Documents*, II, pp. 426–7, c. 12 (Trinity Hall); Bateman's statute 6, at p. 87 above (Gonville Hall); *Documents*, II, p. 459, c. 32 (Corpus). The equivalent clause in the Pembroke statutes (Zutschi, *Medieval Cambridge*, p. 114, c. 7) lacks the prescription for diversity in the keys.

29 Bennet, p. 42.

30 See, *e.g.*, *The Book of Wiliam Morton*, ed. W.T. Mellows, P.I. King and C.N.L. Brooke (Northants Record Society 16 (1954)) p. xli.

31 Pending the completion of the late Jeff Denton's great project for a new edition of the taxation records of 1291, we depend on the Record Commission edition, *Taxatio ecclesiastica Angliae et Walliae auctoritate P. Nicholai IV, c. A.D. 1291* (London, 1802). The reference to '*verus valor*' occurs both in Gonville's c. 19 and c. 20.

... priests shall celebrate daily *pro salubri statu me*" – by which he doubtless meant his spiritual as well as his temporal health – "during my lifetime and for my soul when I have left the light of day, and for the souls of my ancestors and heirs and all the faithful departed – unless they are excused on a reasonable ground".[32] Later on, after laying on the Master responsibility for the sacraments and sacramental,[33] he describes the arrangements for the daily chapter, noting that it follows the daily mass, at which prayers shall be said as aforesaid – "and for all other benefactors alive and dead – for the living with this prayer: *Deus qui caritatis*, for the dead with *Inclina Domine* and *Miserere quesumus*".[34] After briefly describing the chapter Gonville goes back to the beginning of the day, when the four *confratres* (who with the Master made up the whole college) recite the mattins of the Blessed Virgin, followed by "mattins and the canonical hours according to the use commonly observed in the diocese" – followed by four masses recited by the four *confratres*, partly in their house, partly in the church: masses of the Trinity, St Mary, for the departed, and the mass of the day. And every day the *confratres* recite or sing *Placebo* and *Dirige*. The master is not bound to attend all the services if he is too busy. "After my death let my anniversary day be solemnly observed every year."

Such provision would be normal – and fundamental indeed – in statutes for such institutions; and it is puzzling that Gonville's draft statutes for Gonville Hall make no provision for prayers and masses, even allowing that his memory would be amply celebrated at Rushford. In William Bateman's statutes for Trinity Hall (c. 8) there is a very general provision for priests to celebrate mass. But for Gonville Hall Bateman made elaborate provision of a very different character – mainly prescribing multiple *Aves* and other devotions to the Blessed Virgin;[35] and he promulgated a separate statute, dated 7 November 1352, for a yearly mass for Edmund Gonville, "first founder of this college".[36]

All that we know of Gonville's public career indicates a man deeply skilled in the affairs of mammon. In the cathena of references to him that one can collect from public and local records there is evidence of him acting as a judge on commissions of oyer and terminer, as a commissioner in Marshland, as a lawyer active in land transactions – and above all, in the handling of benefices and advowsons.[37] Yet, unlike so many leading churchmen of the thirteenth and fourteenth centuries, he was not a pluralist: he was successively rector of Thelnetham (Suffolk) from 1320 to 1326, of Rushford itself from 1326 to 1342,

32 Bennet, p. 39; for what follows, *ibid.*, p. 41.

33 *I.e.*, doubtless baptisms, marriages and requiems, etc.

34 '*Miserere quesumus*' is the only prayer in common between these and Bateman's prescriptions for the fellows of Gonville Hall.

35 Bateman 1353 and 1355, c. 1.

36 Gonville's exequy is preserved in the college cartulary, *Sheriffe's Evidences*, Gonville and Caius College MS 706/692, p. 26. See p. 7, n. 21 and p. 324, n. 7 for a different interpretation.

37 See references in Brooke, *Churches and Churchmen*, pp. 298–9, n. 44.

when he handed the living over to the Master of his college – and of Terrington St Clement in the Norfolk Marshland some distance further north from 1342 to 1351.[38] At the same time a man who could devote his best energies to founding three religious houses was evidently a person, in some sense, of exceptional piety. All that we know of Gonville's religious devotions is that the altar frontal devised, evidently under his patronage, for the Dominican church in Thetford has several panels depicting the life of the Virgin Mary – and the college seal he had made for Gonville Hall depicts the Annunciation. Thus it was evidently Gonville whose devotion to the Annunciation led to the College's dedication.[39] Mary also figured in the dedication of the Dominican house, to Holy Trinity, St Mary and All Saints – a surprising list, since Dominican houses were supposed to be dedicated to St Dominic.[40] But there were many exceptions, and it seems likely that it was dedicated to Mary as the old cathedral and Cluniac priory had been,[41] and to the Trinity as it was successor to the 'Meisondieu' – the Maison Dieu – evidently also dedicated to the Trinity. By the same token the dedication of Rushford college to St John the Evangelist very likely preserved the old dedication of the parish church – though mattins and mass of the Virgin Mary figure in the Rushford statutes. These details throw little light on Gonville – but his devotion to the Blessed Virgin, and especially the central moment of her life in the Annunciation, cannot be doubted.

Thus Gonville was a lawyer, an administrator, a man of affairs, an entrepreneur – and a devout country priest. That he achieved all this notable variety of tasks and was a central figure in the foundation of three religious houses reveals him as an exceptional personality. He was one of those men who could overcome immense obstacles and get things done. In this he resembles a notable character of the next generation to his, William of Wykeham (bishop of Winchester 1367–1404). Wykeham was a man, in this respect unlike Gonville, of humble origin, who made his way by impressing Edward III with his exceptional capacity for organising major building works and was richly endowed by the king. As well as building the monuments he provided for the king, he built his colleges in Oxford and Winchester, remodelled the nave of Winchester cathedral – in which he chose to be buried – and much else besides.[42] Wykeham was deeply involved in royal administration and worked on a much vaster scale than Gonville. But that is not the only difference: Wykeham lived to be eighty,

38 See n. 11 above.

39 The 'hall of the Annunciation' was Bateman's title for the College, and in regard to the dedication at least he evidently respected Gonville's intentions. For the altar frontal see Norton, Park and Binski, esp. plates 10–12.

40 W.A. Hinnebusch, *The Early English Friars Preachers* (Rome, 1951), pp. 153–5; Norton, Park and Binski, p. 90.

41 A. Binns, *Dedications of Monastic Houses in England and Wales 1066–1216* (Woodbridge, 1989), p. 117.

42 Virginia Davis, *William Wykeham* (London, 2007).

dying many years after the foundation of his colleges, which he was able to leave on a stable footing. Within four years of the founding of Gonville Hall the founder was dead.

Meanwhile, in the early months of 1348, all Edmund Gonville's major projects had come to a head. On 28 January 1348 authority was given for the licence for Gonville Hall and also for the same Edmund Gonville, royal clerk, to grant the advowson of Larling to Rushford college.[43] On 11 February there followed the royal confirmation of the charter of Henry earl of Lancaster "granting" the site of the Meisondieu at Thetford to the Order of Preachers – and instructing them to hold in daily memory the earl and "his dear clerk and kinsman" Edmund Gonville.[44] The charter for Gonville Hall records the assistance of a leading soldier in the royal service, Walter de Mauny, who also witnessed the earl's charter. Gonville had friends to help him in his approaches to the royal chancery – but it is clear that it was his own exceptional abilities which had won him the respect and support of a wide circle of notable men.

43 Calendar of Patent Rolls 1348–50, pp. 19–20.

44 *Ibid.*, p. 19.

V. 2

William Bateman and his Foundation

(BY CHRISTOPHER BROOKE)

The Background

In November 1351 and January 1355 Gonville Hall lost two founders in rapid succession – and yet survived. How this was achieved is a considerable puzzle, for which two recensions of Bateman's statutes, of 1353 and 1355, provide the most substantial clues.[1]

William Bateman was, like Dr Caius, a native of Norwich; he was also known as William of Norwich. As a young man he followed the full course for the doctorates of civil (Roman) and canon law; he was a lawyer and a diplomat.[2] In 1328 he was promoted to the archdeaconry of Norwich; in 1340 he became dean of Lincoln; but his career was really made in the papal curia in Avignon. By clever diplomacy in the service of both pope and king he won golden opinions from both, and in 1344 Pope Clement VI provided him to the see of his choice in his home country, at Norwich. Edward III made a show of protest against the papal initiative, but it seems clear that Bateman was acceptable both to the king and to the chapter of Norwich. To the pope he was very familiar as a former judge in the papal curia in Avignon; to the king he rapidly became a favourite envoy – ready at any moment to cross the channel to visit the French king or the papal curia at Avignon; a key figure in the endless, fruitless negotiations which maintained a show of peace in the Hundred Years' War between Edward's triumph at Crecy and Calais in 1346–47 and the great victory at Poitiers in 1356, the year after Bateman's death.[3] Medieval bishops were often

1 For these texts, and their complexities, see § I. 2 above. A third MS tradition seems to stem from *Sheriffe's Evidences* (*c.* 1471): on this see pp. 20–2 above.

2 The fullest account of Bateman is by A. Hamilton Thompson, 'William Bateman, bishop of Norwich, 1344–1355', *Norfolk Archaeology*, 25 (1935), 102–37 (henceforth Thompson); other useful accounts are A.B. Emden, *Biographical Register of the University of Cambridge to 1500* (Cambridge, 1963: henceforth Emden), p. 44; *ODNB*, s.v. Bateman.

3 Thompson, pp. 133–7, provides a useful itinerary based, however, solely on Bateman's register: for his diplomatic missions a narrative is provided on pp. 108–13. For the dates of his

peripatetic, commuting between their sees and Westminster; Bateman was a constant traveller – occasionally taking a summer holiday in Hoxne in Suffolk, his favourite manor house[4] – as we shall see – never, so far as we know, visiting Cambridge. Yet his heart was there.

His statutes for Gonville Hall prescribe, among many other devotions, that every fellow recite the *Ave Maria* and other prayers 150 times every Saturday morning. His provision of prayers and masses indicates religious devotion of a very formal and conventional kind. In theology he had apparently no interest. His career had been made in the study of Roman and canon law, and he planned that both his colleges – Trinity Hall and Gonville Hall – should provide trained lawyers to administer his own diocese and engage in like employment; and we do well to recall in his defence that pastoral theology in the medieval curriculum was a branch of canon law.

In 1350 he founded Trinity Hall, announcing the foundation on 15 January, gaining the first royal charter, a licence in mortmain making endowment a legal possibility, on 23 February.[5] Later in the year he arranged the appropriation to Trinity Hall of four rectories; two more followed in 1352. This gave the college the lion's share of the tithes of these six parishes and was a favourite form of endowment: by this means the founder provided a steady income to the college at minimum cost to himself – though it is fair to say that we do not know how much he paid to neutralize other interests in the parishes. On 1 June 1352 he attached his seal to the college statutes.[6] The preliminary work of donation was complete.

Meanwhile, as Hamilton Thompson acutely observed, the bishop's itinerary has a curious kink in it in September 1351, when he visited Rushford, Edmund Gonville's family home and seat of Gonville's other college – of chantry priests. It may well be that he went to receive Gonville's final instructions. On 17 November Gonville died, and Bateman lost no time in taking over the foundation: on 21 December he issued his charter declaring himself the founder of the Hall of the Annunciation.[7]

Thus Bateman was a man who knew how to act with despatch; but his plans for the Hall of the Annunciation went on more slowly than those for Trinity Hall. On 7 November 1352 he issued a statute for the celebration of Gonville's

appointments of vicars general for his visits overseas, see *The Register of William Bateman, bishop of Norwich 1344–1355*, ed. P.E. Pobst, 2 vols. (Canterbury and York Society 84, 90, 1996–2000 – henceforth *Register*), I, pp. xxviii–xxix.

4 His other favourite house seems to have been South Elmham, also in Suffolk.

5 C. Crawley, *Trinity Hall* (Cambridge, 1976 – henceforth Crawley), pp. 9–10; *Documents*, II, pp. 406–9; for the endowments, see Crawley, pp. 14–15 and p. 15, n. 1; *Documents*, II, pp. 409–13.

6 *Documents*, II, p. 435. Bateman's statutes for Trinity Hall are printed *ibid.*, II, pp. 417–35; his *Interpretatio*, *ibid.*, pp. 436–9 and in Appendix A below, pp. 557–8.

7 Brooke, *History* (1996 edn), p. 305, citing Brooke in *The Caian* (1994), p. 67. For what follows, see *B.H.* III, pp. 327–30. It seems likely that Gonville resigned as rector of Terrington St Clement in September, since his successor was instituted on 24 October 1351 (*Register*, II, no. 1555).

anniversary, a first indication that he could not altogether ignore Gonville's claims.[8] It was not until the summer of 1353 that Bateman took the next, decisive steps. It was a busy year. In February and March he was on a diplomatic mission to France; late April and early May were spent in Hoxne, then he travelled to London and Westminster.[9] There on 1 June 1353 he concluded an agreement with the Duke of Lancaster, patron and alderman of the guilds engaged in founding Corpus, for an exchange of land which established the Hall of the Annunciation in two stone houses on the north side of what is now Gonville Court – presumably aimed, as Dr Caius observed, to settle it as near to Trinity Hall as available land allowed.[10]

In August he was again at Hoxne, evidently engaged in drafting statutes for the Hall of the Annunciation: the first version was completed on 7 September. On the 17th, in Cambridge, the masters of Trinity Hall and the Hall of the Annunciation attached their seals to a 'treaty of perpetual amity'; on the 20th, at Newmarket, the bishop gave the treaty his formal approval, and passed on to London and Dover and yet another diplomatic visit to France.[11] The documents of June–September established what was evidently Bateman's immediate purpose: to forge the closest of links between the two colleges of which he claimed to be founder, and to make the Hall of the Annunciation a satellite of Trinity Hall.

The treaty of amity stipulated that all the fellows of both colleges – in perpetuity – should be "as it were very dear brothers" (*fratres amicissimi*), and promote the interests of their two foundations. "In public processions, the inceptions of masters, University masses, sermons and all other public acts of the university" all the fellows of both colleges who were present should process together – save that the master and fellows of Trinity Hall, "as first-born brothers and superior in honour", should have precedence – unless one of the Hall of the Annunciation had precedence under university statutes. The fellows of the two colleges were to be "very dear brothers" because they grew "from a single stem of foundation" (*ex uno fundacionis stipite prodeuntes*).[12]

Thus far Bateman pursued his aim, high-handedly. The natural implication is that he was paving the way for an amalgamation of the two colleges, and this is

8 Gonville and Caius College Library, MS 706/692 (cartulary of 1472, '*Sheriffe's Evidences*'), p. 26; cf. *The Caian* (1994), p. 67.

9 Thompson, pp. 113, 136–7.

10 *B.H.* III, p. 320; cf. J. Caius, *Annals of Gonville and Caius College*, ed. J. Venn (Cambridge, 1904), p. 4.

11 *B.H.* III, pp. 329–30; Thompson, pp. 113, 137.

12 *B.H.* III, pp. 329–30. The role of the colleges in processions implied in the treaty is puzzling, since the early statute (before 1390) on the order of processions makes no mention of the colleges at all (MS 706/692, fol. 20r – this part of the MS is of *c.* 1390–5; cf. M.B. Hackett, *The Original Statutes of Cambridge University* (Cambridge, 1970), p. 261; H.P. Stokes, *Ceremonies of the University of Cambridge* (Cambridge, 1927), p. 164).

strongly confirmed by the opening clause in the statutes of 7 September which stipulated that the fellows, having completed their arts course (as Gonville had intended) should go on to higher degrees; but where Gonville had stipulated theology – with a grudging permission for one or two fellows to seek other faculties – Bateman substituted civil or canon law or medicine.[13] As the first group of fellows (of whom we have knowledge) were in fact two lawyers and one physician, this may not have seemed unreasonable to him. But Bateman was above all a diplomat. The version of 1353 includes two insertions in a different hand, one brief, one lengthy – and the longer one specifically asserts that it was added in the bishop's own hand. The shorter one consists of a single word: 'theologie' has been interpolated between the laws and medicine (the bishop was perhaps in a hurry: he should probably have written 'theologiam'). This eloquent insertion is one of two remarkable indications that voices were raised among Bateman's closest disciples eager to preserve the memory of Edmund Gonville. The second will emerge in due course.[14] We may conjecture that the brave men who challenged the bishop included the first master, John Colton, who had been appointed by Gonville and came from Gonville's Terrington, and the two early fellows who are more than names, Richard Pulham, later Master from about 1360 to the 1390s, like Colton a lawyer, and William Rougham, the first medical fellow.[15] But it is clear that they found an ally in Bateman's faithful administrator, Walter of Elveden.

In 1354 Bateman was at last ready to help the Hall of the Annunciation to its first endowments.[16] As with Trinity Hall, they comprised rectories – three only in Bateman's time,[17] in contrast to Trinity Hall's six. In principle, they provided a steady income from the major tithes. But in practice such appropriations could involve complex and expensive negotiations with other interested parties, and

13 For Gonville's draft statutes, see above, pp. 40–57; *B.H.* III, pp. 341–5, esp. p. 344.

14 See below, pp. 327–32, on Walter of Elveden and the version of the statutes of 1355.

15 On Colton, see Brooke, *History*, pp. 18–19 and refs., esp. to J.A. Watt, 'John Colton, justiciar of Ireland (1382) and archbishop of Armagh (1383–1404)', in *England and Ireland in the late Middle Ages*, ed. J. Lydon (Dublin, 1981), pp. 196–213. On Pulham and Rougham, Brooke, *History*, pp. 30–1, 38, 309; C. Hall and C.N.L. Brooke, 'The masters of Gonville Hall', *The Caian* (1983), pp. 43–50, esp. pp. 43–6.

16 On 27 February 1354 Bateman issued letters of attorney for livery of seisin of the manor of Thriplow to the college; but there is no later evidence of the college's tenure (BUR: DEEDS/ I, 27; *B.H.* III, p. 12). Thriplow was an estate of the bishop of Ely, and presumably Bateman attempted to buy it from the bishop (cf. *Victoria County History of Cambridgeshire*, VIII, p. 239).

17 Three-quarters of the advowson of a fourth parish, Capel (Suffolk), were acquired in 1353–55 by a transaction of extreme complexity. The personnel and efforts of the early trustees of Capel are explained by Catherine Hall, 'The early fellows of Gonville Hall and their books', *Transactions of the Cambridge Bibliographical Society*, 13/3 (2006), 233–52 (henceforth Hall), at pp. 244–5; for its later history, see *B.H.* III, p. 315: in the long run it was reclaimed by the family of the lay patrons. This and the case of Thriplow (n. 16 above) illustrate some of the complexities and pitfalls in the efforts to endow a small and poor college.

if there was a sitting rector, his rights had to be respected. Thus the college had to wait till 1386 for the rector of Wilton to die.[18] None the less, a start was made, and the fellows of Gonville Hall paved the way by inducing the university to make a statute on 19 May for the exequies of William Bateman – 'nostre universitatis constantissimum zelatorem', whose many benefits had culminated in the construction of the Hall of the Annunciation.[19] The process of appropriating Mutford (in Suffolk, near Beccles) went forward in May and June 1354, to be followed by the appropriation of Foulden and Wilton (in south-western Norfolk) in September. On 28 September the bishop concluded his part in the process.[20] On 6 October he was at Dover, preparing to lead a major embassy to the papal curia at Avignon. And there he died, on 6 January 1355. His funeral in Avignon cathedral was attended by a galaxy of cardinals, and he is buried in the cathedral, in an unmarked grave.[21] It was little short of a miracle that both his colleges survived.

Thus far Bateman had been steering his two colleges closer together; but in diplomatic fashion he had not declared his final aim. Trinity Hall was his own foundation; but he showed respect to Gonville's memory – and to those who perhaps held it in greater esteem than he himself. He left the question unanswered: would the Hall of the Annunciation survive as an independent college with different aims from those of Trinity Hall?

The first version of the statutes of 7 September 1353, Gonville and Caius College BUR: DEEDS/ I, 15, is exceedingly brief for a set of college statutes, and in large measure consists of cross-references to the statutes of Trinity Hall. The earliest copy of those of 1355, BUR: DEEDS/ I, 16, is an act of the Official of the diocese of Norwich – whom we know from other evidence to have been Master Walter of Elveden.[22] It takes the form of a notarial copy dated 19 May 1355, reciting Bateman's foundation charter and its confirmations by the bishop of Ely

18 MS 706/697, pp. 45–6.

19 *B.H.* III, p. 330–1, dated "*die lune in festo ... sancti Dunstani ...*", *i.e.* Monday 19 May 1354 – not 21 October, as suggested by Venn, which was not in any case a Monday. There is no mention of Trinity Hall in the statute, which clearly indicates that it was inspired by the Master and fellows of the Hall of the Annunciation.

20 *B.H.* III, p. 7, without references: the documents relating to the three churches are conveniently gathered in MS 706/692, pp. 35–46; the originals are in Archives, BUR: DEEDS/ V, 1–3 (Mutford), VI, 1a–p (Foulden), VII, a–e (Wilton). The appropriation of Mutford is also in *Register*, I, no. 43, under a rubric which seems to indicate that the appropriations of Foulden and Wilton should accompany it – but their texts are not given. The difficulties encountered by Colton and his colleagues are illustrated by the re-institution by Colton of the sitting rector of Mutford on 8 July 1354 (*Register*, II, no. 1861; cf. *ibid.*, no. 995 – and see above on Capel and Wilton).

21 Thompson, pp. 129–30, partly based on the life of Bateman by Laurence, prior of Norwich (1352–7: ed. A.W.W. Dale, *Warren's Book* (Cambridge, 1911), pp. 3–7).

22 *Register*, II, no. 155. On Elveden, see A.B. Emden, *A Biographical Register of the University of Cambridge to 1500* (Cambridge, 1963), pp. 210–11; Hall, pp. 237–41, 244.

and the Chancellor and masters of the university, and the statutes, purporting to be an exact reproduction of an act of William Bateman dated 7 September 1353. The exactitude is confirmed by a galaxy of witnesses and the notary himself, and we must accept that the statutes comprise a copy of a lost 'original'. But the lost document was not that of 1353, which survives in BUR: DEEDS/ I, 15, evidently a genuine document of 1353, but very different from the version of 1355 – though that also purports to be of 7 September 1353.[23] Clearly, Walter of Elveden, acting on behalf of the fledgling Gonville Hall, expanded the genuine statutes of 1353 to make a more complete code – using Bateman's words as far as he reckoned possible, but omitting all reference to Trinity Hall.[24] The stated purpose of the Official's act is that the document needed to be exhibited in the papal curia, that is, at Avignon.

It is abundantly clear that the version of Bateman's statutes of 1355 was inspired by a serious crisis in the college's affairs: the reference to the curia implies it, and the desperate measure of rewriting the statutes in Bateman's name enforces it. The impressive list of witnesses collected by Walter of Elveden included a future archdeacon in the diocese of Norwich, at least two members of Bateman's household who had been with him at Avignon at the time of his death, a fellow of Gonville Hall, and the Master – or soon to be Master – of Trinity Hall.[25] It is evident from this list that the trouble in Avignon did not take the form of conflict between the colleges – nor would such struggling infant bodies have had the resources to litigate in the papal curia.[26]

Indeed, their finances are likely to have been severely straitened by Bateman's death. Since he died in the papal curia – though the cardinals might give him a splendid funeral – the curial officials sequestrated all his movable goods. His nephew Simon of Sudbury (future archbishop of Canterbury) was a curial official at the time and one of his executors, and he compounded with the papal camera for payment of 2,000 gold florins, the equivalent of approximately £340

23 See discussion in Brooke, *History*, pp. 14–17. Bateman's foundation charter and its confirmations are printed in *B.H.* III, pp. 327–8.

24 Independence from Trinity Hall was clearly of consequence in 1355; and this makes it all the more puzzling that the majority of copies of Bateman's statutes preserved in the college and copied from the fifteenth to the late seventeenth centuries comprise the version of 1353 with the Trinity Hall statutes spelt out in full. See "*Bateman's Statutes: The Manuscript Confusion*", § I. 2 above.

25 Master John de Cove, later archdeacon of Suffolk; John of Thetford, who had been with Bateman in Avignon, Master Adam of Wickmere, then or soon after Master of Trinity Hall; William de Lee, fellow of Gonville Hall, Thomas of Hempnall, also with Bateman in Avignon (for Cove, Wickmere and Lee see Emden, pp. 523–4, 638–9, 361; also *Warren's Book*, pp. 13, 152 for Wickmere and *B.H.* I, p. 1 for Lee. For Thetford and Hempnall, *Calendar of Papal Petitions*, I, 277).

26 No trace of references to Gonville Hall – or of any process which might explain the referral of the documents to the Curia – has been found among the (unprinted) Avignon registers of Pope Innocent VI (1352–61). The MS indexes in the Vatican Archives have been checked for us by the kindness of Patrick Zutshi.

sterling.[27] Sudbury paid 1,000 florins on 9 February 1355, and the other 1,000 florins on 7 September.[28] Although Sudbury seems to have made a composition with the camera which was far from crushing, it is clear that Bateman's infant colleges could hope for little in the way of cash from his executors.

Thus we may be sure that the trouble in the curia in May 1355 was not a dispute between the colleges. We must look elsewhere for the malefactor who threatened Gonville Hall in some way. There is a charming passage in Dr Caius' *Annals of Gonville and Caius College*[29] in which he interrupts the roll of benefactors: 'but these were benefactors. Malefactors were ...' – but the malefactors he names were all of the sixteenth century. No tradition survived in the college, evidently, of a malefactor of the 1350s. A possible clue lies in a mysterious document in the college Archives, a letter of attorney from Bateman for livery of seisin of 'our manor' in the vill of Thriplow (Cambs.) to John of Terrington – *i.e.*, John Colton, the Master, and four fellows of the Hall of the Annunciation.[30] This is extremely puzzling. The historical record seems to show that there was only one manor in Thriplow, and that it was part of the estates of the bishops of Ely from 1109 to 1600.[31]

Thomas de Lisle OP was bishop of Ely from 1345 to 1361: he had been promoted – very much like Bateman – by the pope against mild opposition from the king – mild because Edward III seems to have supposed that (like Bateman) he was a useful diplomat. His biographer, John Aberth, on the contrary describes him (in his later years at least) as 'the leader of a criminal gang'.[32] This may well give an exaggerated impression of Lisle's tendency to violence; but there is no doubt that he was very extravagant and in need of cash, which may well explain why he negotiated with Bateman for the sale of one

27 D. Williman, *The Right of Spoil of the Popes of Avignon 1316–1415 (Transactions of the American Philosophical Society* 78/6 (1988)), p. 127; H. Hoberg, *Die Einnahmen der apostolischen Kammer unter Innocenz VI* (Paderborn, 1953), pp. 88, 97. For the rate of exchange in the curia in 1355, see P. Spufford, *Handbook of Medieval Exchange* (London, 1986), p. 200, citing evidence of a rate of 3s. 5d. per florin in the Curia in 1355. We owe the references to Williman and Hoberg to the generous help of Patrick Zutshi.

28 On 17 September the pope instructed the archbishop of Canterbury, the bishop of London and the precentor of Hereford – that is, Walter of Elveden – to decide what was necessary about Bateman's will, owing to a dispute about some of his property, and naming his executors in England as Simon of Badingley, Ralph Urry, Robert of Walton and John of Winston. Winston was the notary who set his mark on Walter of Elvedon's version of the statutes in 1355. It is striking that there is no mention in any of this of any of Bateman's family apart from Sudbury – though he is known to have had at least seven nephews (Thompson, pp. 128–9).

29 Ed. J. Venn (Cambridge, 1904), p. 12.

30 BUR: DEEDS/ I, 27.

31 *Victoria County History of Cambridgeshire*, VIII, p. 239.

32 J. Aberth, *Criminal Churchmen of the Age of Edward III: the Case of Bishop Thomas de Lisle* (Pennsylvania, 1996).

of his manors.[33] It may well be that Bateman saw the opportunity of a quick purchase from a colleague in difficulties, and that Lisle used the confusion caused by Bateman's death to challenge the college's title by challenging its very existence – which seems to be the implication of Walter of Elveden's document. It may seem odd that Lisle was confirming the college's foundation in 1352 and licensing a future chapel in 1353[34] – and then turning on the college in 1355, at least to deprive it of its only solid endowment, at worst to destroy it. This is speculative; but it would fit Aberth's portrait of Thomas de Lisle as a mercurial and violent man. One can see that the loss of Thriplow and the extinction of the college were connected themes. Even allowing for the solid support he received from Elveden and the see of Norwich and some at least of the early fellows,[35] John Colton performed something like a miracle in preserving the college – and also, it seems, in reasserting its priority over Trinity Hall in the process.

John Colton was an ambitious young man who was later to be treasurer, chancellor and justiciar of Ireland and archbishop of Armagh (1383–1404); in the late 1350s at least he was content to live at Avignon while retaining the mastership of the college. His standing depended on early patronage from Bateman, his career was modelled on his patron's. Later in the 1350s he found in Avignon a new patron, Richard FitzRalph, archbishop of Armagh, who turned his attention to Ireland, where his later career was to flourish. But he was also John of Terrington, Gonville's Terrington, and evidently in origin a protégé of Gonville – and he had been chosen as first master by Gonville himself.[36] This helps to explain his obstinate loyalty to Gonville's memory.

At some moment very hard to determine the treaty of amity became null, at least to the extent that Gonville Hall (as it became once more after Bateman's death) successfully reclaimed the right of priority in processions and the like. This striking reversal seems likely to belong to the early days of the colleges, to a date when the facts of the two foundations could be clearly recalled. It looks as if John Colton won a notable victory at Avignon in 1355, and successfully asserted the independence of his college.

To do this he must have needed clear proof of Bateman's intention to give the Hall of the Annunciation a secure foundation of its own, and to this end his colleagues in Cambridge and Norwich provided a dossier comprising Bateman's

33 No central accounts for the bishopric survive to confirm his financial difficulties, but his early years undoubtedly involved heavy charges; and the pope gave him leave in 1345 to contract a loan for 12,000 florins, and subsequently licence for 'a charitable subsidy'. He was later accused of extortion and theft (Aberth, pp. 13–16, 114–15). But Ely was a rich diocese, and his executors were still able to produce 1,500 florins when he died in the Curia in 1361 after several years of exile and sequestration (Williman, *Right of Spoil*, p. 245, no, 1151; Hoberg, *Einnahmen*, pp. 358, 377, 410).

34 *B.H.* III, p. 328.

35 Notably Richard Pulham (see below) and William Rougham.

36 *B.H.* III, p. 326. On Colton see above, n. 15 and references.

foundation charter and its confirmations by the bishop of Ely and the archbishop of Canterbury – and a version of his statutes for the college, complete in itself without any mention of Trinity Hall. One of the college's friends was Walter of Elveden, who must in effect have forged the new version of the statutes; we may assume that he, like Colton, honoured Gonville's memory – they may well have been old friends.[37] We cannot tell who his helpers in the college were, but it is highly likely that Richard Pulham was one: he was to succeed Colton as Master and ruled the college from the 1360s to the 1390s, and was evidently very persistent and faithful in his efforts to preserve it.[38]

The treaty of amity provides strong evidence that the order of colleges in processions, seating at formal gatherings and so forth, was already established by the 1350s – surprisingly, granted the small number of colleges founded before 1350 and their modest place in the affairs of the university. But one has only to recall the Cistercian order, in which from an early date – so it seems – every abbot knew his exact place in the general chapter from the date of his house's foundation,[39] to appreciate how fundamental to a gathering of religious houses the status conferred by date of foundation could be. This was as true of the nineteenth century as it was of the fourteenth, and of every age in between; so it is tempting to argue that the transposition in the order of colleges between Trinity Hall and Gonville Hall was more easily accomplished in the 1350s than later – but also hazardous. We know so little of the process by which the order was established that it could (in the present state of knowledge) have happened much later.

None the less, the fate of Gonville Hall was in some way determined at Avignon in 1355. The masters of both colleges – Robert Stratton of Trinity Hall and John Colton of Terrington of the Hall of the Annunciation – were habitués of Avignon: like their patron, William Bateman, they made their careers in the papal law courts. The notary of 1355 observed that he had done his work at the request of the Master of the Hall of the Annunciation and that he was 'engaged in other business' (*aliis occupatus negotiis*). Grammatically this should refer to the notary; but this makes no sense – and it seems more likely that it originally referred to the Master of Gonville Hall – and a notary was not allowed to correct an error in his text. If so, it would be a clear hint that Colton was at Avignon in

[37] Not without reason Elveden has an honoured place in the first surviving list of benefactors – the catalogue of exequies in the cartulary of 1472, *Sheriffe's Evidences*, MS 706/692, pp. 26–7. He was a major donor to the Library: see Hall, pp. 237–41 – and perhaps a benefactor in other ways not recorded. Elveden is approximately 6 miles west of Rushford.

[38] On Pulham, see Brooke, *History*, pp. 24, 38 etc. His set of the Corpus Iuris Civilis, along with Elveden's – the whole or a major part of them – are probably still in the College library (see Hall, pp. 237–41, 247–8).

[39] See discussion in C. Brooke, *The Rise and Fall of the Medieval Monastery* (3rd edn of *The Monastic World*, London, 2006), pp. 252–5, 281–2.

the aftermath of the death of William Bateman there.[40] In any case, Elveden's preamble indicates that the documents were transcribed to be submitted to the papal curia, and the college must have had good representation in Avignon.

It may seem surprising that BUR: DEEDS/ I, 16 shows no sign of its travels to and from Avignon. But doubtless it was treated with the care it deserved by the college's messengers – and in Avignon itself by John Colton. This was an expensive notarial copy and was presumably used for the purpose for which it was intended.

From 1355 on, now one version of Bateman's statutes was copied, now another[41] – and between them they ruled the college until 1860.[42]

40 For Stratton and Colton at Avignon, see Brooke, *History*, pp. 16–19.

41 See § I. 2 above.

42 Supplemented from 1558–73 by Dr Caius' much more extensive statutes.

V. 3

John Caius and his Foundation

John Caius was born in Norwich on 10 October 1510 and we may assume that he was educated at school there.[1] He might appear at first sight to have been an only child, since he mentions no relatives in his will or elsewhere; but we know that he did have at least one sister who had several children,[2] and he included in his original draft statutes[3] the traditional preference for founder's kin in elections to the scholarships which he founded, although he omitted it thereafter. He entered Gonville Hall on 12 September 1529, less than a month before his nineteenth birthday, and thus a little later than was normal at the time. We do not know why this was or whether he came up straight from school; but he seems to have done so without a scholarship, and thus perhaps as a pensioner of the class that was admitted to the scholars' table.[4] It has been suggested that he may have grown up in relative poverty, but there is nothing

1 For full accounts of Caius' life, see *B.H.* III, pp. 30–63, reprinted with corrections in *The Works of John Caius, M.D.* (1912) and C.N.L. Brooke, *A History of Gonville & Caius College* (reprinted 1996), ch. 4. See also V. Nutton's article on 'Caius, John (1510–1573)', *ODNB* (Oxford University Press, 2004), and the Introduction to his *An Autobibliography by John Caius*, ed. V. Nutton (Routledge, forthcoming).

2 After his death his executors sought and obtained permission from Archbishop Parker and the college to make *ex gratia* payments to "his sister's sonne an old cloke and a hatt – vii^{s} iiii^{d}" and to "his poore sister dwelling in Norwiche for the relief of her and her poore children – x^{li}" (Lambeth MS 720, fol. 3); and the inventory of his estate records "a petticoat – v^{s}" and "viii olde neckerchers" as being "Apparell of his sister's daughter w[hi]ch died in his howse" in London (BUR: DEEDS/ I, 45): see *B.H.* III, p. 58. Why Caius ignored his relatives in his will is a mystery, for he left several expensive gifts to wealthy lawyers and ladies (*B.H.* III, pp. 391–2).

3 *Documents*, II, p. 341.

4 It was not uncommon for minor pensioners to be admitted to the scholars' table, or else the bachelors' table depending on their status (in the same way that major pensioners were admitted to the fellows' table). As Venn noted, students might be recorded in the matriculation book as "scholar", yet not appear in the accounts among the scholars who actually received a stipend until some years after their admission; such "scholars" no doubt had to wait for a vacancy in the few endowed scholarships: *Admissions*, p. xvi. For a short period during Legge's mastership minor pensioners were classified in three unexplained orders on admission, perhaps depending on the particular table at which they took their meals, *i.e.* at the bachelors' table, at the scholars' table or as sizars: see the matriculations for 1575–8 (*B.H.* I, pp. 83–97).

to indicate that he was admitted to Gonville Hall as one of its poor students (*pauperiores*) and he seems to have been in a position to travel widely and to acquire expensive books when he went to the continent ten years later.[5] Whatever his status was at admission, he revelled in the normal Arts course and rapidly acquired a mastery, not only of Greek and Latin, but also of Hebrew and through it of the Bible: by the beginning of his second year he had been elected into a scholarship, and he graduated B.A. in January 1533, being placed first of his year in the *ordo senioritatis*.[6] When he was of less than one year's standing as B.A. he was chosen as one of the two principals of Fishwick Hostel on 12 November 1533, shortly before he became a fellow on 6 December 1533.[7] We do not know what other offices he undertook in the five years during which he resided in the college as a fellow, but we do know that his interests turned entirely from theology to medicine and that he began to acquire a proficiency in the latter as swiftly as he had done in the former – sufficiently for the distinguished member of his college and royal physician, William Butts,[8] to arrange for him to go to Padua in 1539, no doubt with the further encouragement of the hall's other distinguished royal physician, Thomas Wendy.[9] He studied in Padua and elsewhere on the continent equally avidly for somewhat more than five years, returning to England in 1544 or 1545. He seems to have gone back to Cambridge only very briefly and he resigned his fellowship on 29 September 1545.

Caius later showed himself to be a keen antiquary and (somewhat blinkered) historian, and it is perhaps surprising that we know more of his doings in the five years that he spent abroad than we do of the seven years in which he resided in college. It is possible, as will be seen later, that he developed his interest in the history of the college in those seven years and he may indeed have prepared what later became the first volume of his Annals during them;[10] yet he seems to have paid no attention to the momentous events which coincided with his years in college. He had entered Gonville Hall as an undergraduate in the year in which Thomas Wolsey fell from power and the character of England's diplomatic relations with the continent of Europe changed radically, and he became a fellow in the year in which Thomas Cranmer became archbishop of Canterbury and the character of the Church of England changed irrevocably. He was one of the six fellows required with the Master to sign the college's Acknowledgment of the Royal Supremacy in the very same year, 1535, in which

5 By that time his father had died, in 1532, and probably his mother also, in 1537 (not 1547, the date given in an Italian document recording details clearly supplied by Caius before he returned to England in 1544: see *B.H.* III, p. 30, n. 1.).

6 *B.H.* III, p. 32.

7 *Ibid.*

8 *B.H.* I, p. 17.

9 *Ibid.*, p. 24.

10 See below at p. 337.

the Chancellor of the university, John Fisher, and the Chancellor of England, Thomas More, were beheaded for their refusal to make that acknowledgment. The following year saw the execution of the Queen, Anne Boleyn, and the election to the mastership of John Skipp, who had been her almoner until her death.[11] Caius had participated in Skipp's election and it is difficult to believe that these events were never mentioned at the common table or that Caius, as a fellow, remained unaware of them; yet he later made no mention of them. Similarly, he left England to take up medical studies in Padua in the year which saw the surrender of the greater monasteries, and he returned in the very year in which his older contemporary Matthew Parker and other Cambridge acquaintances succeeded in excluding Gonville Hall and the other Cambridge colleges from the Chantries Act and thus saved them from extinction; again, Caius made no mention of either of these events.

After he resigned his fellowship he gave his attention wholeheartedly to his medical practice, which appears to have taken him as far afield as Cumberland in 1548, Warwick in 1552 and to the coast at Selsey in 1555.[12] It no doubt also took him to his own town of Norwich and county of Norfolk, and he can hardly have been unaware of the savage consequences of Kett's Rebellion for both town and county, yet in later life he made no more mention of that event than he had of events which had occurred during his time in Cambridge.[13] Indeed, the only two events outside his own narrow world that he recorded later would seem to have been the successive debasements of the currency which followed relentlessly for two reigns after Henry VIII's war with France and the concomitant inflation which left prices three times higher than they had been in his time in Cambridge.[14]

He finally settled in London and was admitted Fellow of the College of Physicians on 22 December 1547, appointed an Elect on 30 March 1550 and to the Council in the same year. Thereafter, in the words of Venn, "for the next eight or ten years [he] seems to have led the life of a busy London practitioner. He was chosen President of that college in 1555, and annually re-elected until 1560 inclusive; again in 1562 and 1563, and for a ninth time in 1571."[15] In the light

[11] Another fellow, Nicholas Shaxton, had been her almoner before Skipp. Queen Anne's great grand-uncle, Thomas Boleyn, had been Master of Gonville Hall from 1454 to 1472, but it would be fanciful to assume that her choices of almoner were affected by that fact, even if she was aware of it.

[12] J. Caius, *History of Rarer Animals* (1570), pp. 34, 42, 55 and 57 (reprinted in *Works*); *B.H.* III, p. 34.

[13] He had at one time contemplated writing a history of Norwich: *B.H.* III, p. 62, but never in fact did so.

[14] *Annals*, pp. 81–3; Statute 39.

[15] *B.H.* III, p. 34. The office committed the holder to a busy round of London meetings (including the policing of apothecaries, surgeons and empirics). He did not hold the office in 1561, a year in which he was much pre-occupied with litigation over the manors he had given to the college:

of such a demanding practice it is not surprising that apparently he did not visit his old college until he returned as third founder in 1558. His absence did not mean, however, that the memory of his sixteen years as a pensioner, scholar and fellow grew dim: in fact the reverse occurred.

Venn believed that it was during those years of busy work in London that Caius formed the design of enlarging what he described in 1557 as "that poor house now called Gonville Hall", but it is not unlikely that he had, as a life-long bachelor, conceived the design much earlier. Certainly, by the time he first broached the possibility of a "well-minded and great benefactor"[16] with the Master and fellows in 1557 he had accumulated a remarkable hoard of money which he appears not to have invested in land but to have held ready for the venture he now proposed: for he was by that date able to lay out over £1,000 in the purchase of lands with which to endow his re-founded college.[17]

He obtained his charter of re-foundation on 4 September 1557 and returned to his old college in March 1558, perhaps for the first time since he had left in 1545. According to Venn, his visit was a disappointing one for him, and it is true that in later years he lamented the changes that had occurred in the college and university since his days as a student; but the solemnity of the formal inauguration of his new college on Lady Day, 25 March 1558, appears to have pleased him.[18] In addition to the other expensive symbolic objects that he gave to the college on this occasion, he gave to it a further gift which has attracted less attention, namely, an expensively and elaborately bound book of annals and statutes.[19] The book has not survived, but we can form a fairly clear picture of both parts of its contents, for we have the draft of the statutes which Caius made

see "*Supplementary Notes*" at pp. 302–8 above. In his final year as president in 1571, in view of his age, he was given leave of absence from all *comitia* except the regular quarterly meetings and others of special importance: Clark, *History of the Royal College of Physicians* (1964), I, p. 106. Even so, he was called upon in March 1572 to defend – successfully – the privileges of the college in its dispute with the barber-surgeons before the Queen's commissioners over the right to administer inward remedies: *ibid.*, p. 121; *B.H.* III, p. 35.

16 For the correspondence between Caius, the Master and the fellows, and the Queen and her officers, and the events leading to the re-foundation in 1557, see *B.H.* III, pp. 36–41.

17 £1,033. 12s. 6d.: *Annals*, p. 80. One suspects that he had lived an exceedingly frugal life for a long time and had developed something of an obsession with the hoarding of ready money, for there is no indication that he had ever invested his wealth in the purchase of land prior to his purchases of the manors of Croxley and Snellshall, Runcton Holme and Burnham Thorpe from the Crown in 1557–58; this would explain the long and detailed account of the successive debasements of the coinage which he gave in the *Annals*, pp. 81–3.

18 For the very full account of the proceedings which he gave in his Annals, see *B.H.* III, pp. 40–1.

19 "a book of Annals and statutes covered in untrimmed crimson silk and embellished with silver bosses, plates and corner-guards and having a silver chain" (*librum Annalium et statutorum holoserico villoso carmesino velatum, umbonibus, laminibusque argenteis angularibus, cathenaque argentea ornatem*): *Annals*, p. 57. He may have taken this book back to London, for his correction to the datum clause to the final version of his statutes states that his first statutes were completed in London on 30 March 1558. The College's surviving manuscript of the Annals

immediately after he obtained his Charter of Re-foundation[20] and we can be sure that the annals must have been what Caius later termed "the first book" of the Annals when he re-started them in 1563 after he had become Master.[21] If indeed the book which Caius presented to his new college on 25 March 1558 included Book I of the Annals, then he must have assembled the material for that book in the sixteen years 1529–45, when he was a student or fellow, for he would have needed access to the college's archives when he was assembling his material.

After the inauguration he returned to London content: but not for long. He seems to have had some misgivings about the then Master's ability to manage the three manors with which he had so generously endowed the college at the inauguration, for a month later he arranged with the college to take back to himself a lease of all three manors for seventy years if he should live so long.[22] This lease meant that he remained entitled to enforce the lessees' obligations, the rents came to him personally (apparently in London) and he provided for the stipends of his fellows and scholars personally. The lease proved to be an unnecessary precaution, as the Master, Thomas Bacon, died nine months later on 1 January 1559, and for his successor the fellows turned to their benefactor. Caius was elected on 24 January, three weeks later. By his own account he had been reluctant to accept the office, partly because he was not a theologian or cleric and

which Caius began in 1563 (MS 756/371) has an untrimmed chemise, but it does not have any silver embellishments or a copy of the statutes.

20 Cambridge University Library Mm.4.20, printed by the Commissioners in 1852 in *Documents*, II, pp. 321–65. For the dating of this document, see *B.H.* III, pp. 59–60. It was originally dated 20 April 1558, *i.e.* after the re-foundation, but that date was corrected to 7 May 1557 (which may possibly be an error for 7 March 1557/8). It may have been preserved and used by Caius for a short time after he became Master in January 1559, for a final folio (fol. 18b) makes provision for fellows elected after 25 November 1559. There can be little doubt that it represents the gist of the statutes given to Bacon at the re-foundation.

21 *I.e.*, pp. 2–17 of MS 756/371 (*Annals*, pp. 1–29). *Pace* Venn (*Annals*, p. vii), it is clear from the unvarying and uniform handwriting covering a period of many years from 1563 onwards that MS 756/371 was not taken down from Caius' lips, but is a copy transcribed by a professional scribe at a later date, almost certainly in Legge's time. When the scribe of MS 756/371 started making his copy of the book of Annals which Caius had begun in 1563 as "Book II", he included the earlier book and placed it before Book II, together with a copy of papal bulls and licences and exequies (MS pp. 18–30, *Annals*, pp. 30–42). The fact that the scribe preceded all the pages with a frontispiece dating the work as 1563 has led Venn and others to conclude that both the Books of Annals were started in that year; but it is clear from the distinct handwriting (and from the fact that, at page 30, the scribe for some reason restarted the numbering of Book II as page 25) that the first 30 pages of the manuscript were copies of what had been written earlier. The events recorded in Book I stop in the early 1540s and the handwriting suggests that later events were added subsequently both to it and to the list of exequies when it was being incorporated into MS 756/371.

22 See *Caius' purchase of Croxley, Runcton and Burnham* in "*Supplementary Notes to Caius' Statutes*", § IV. 3, at p. 303 above.

partly because his professional work would entail long absence from Cambridge, and he accepted only after pressure by fellows and by the Vice-Chancellor and other leading members of the university.[23] What may well have played an important part in his decision was the happy chance that he had included in his statutes a provision designed to accommodate the very situation in which he now found himself; for he had added medicine to theology, civil and canon law or arts as the disciplines in which Bateman required a Master to hold a degree, and he had expressly provided that a Master who was an egregious benefactor might be absent from college at his own discretion (for such a person could be trusted not to inconvenience or subvert it), provided only that he appointed a president or, in his absence, another fellow to act in his place.[24]

Caius and his relations with the fellows: the traditional view

The fourteen years in which Caius was Master have traditionally been regarded as an unhappy period throughout which the college was afflicted with constant quarrelling between an ageing, quick-tempered and authoritarian Master and a youthful fellowship which had little sympathy with his veneration for the past and which became increasingly intolerant of the religious views which he was widely thought to harbour. That view was expressed forcefully by Venn:

> The master … was prematurely aged, of somewhat feeble health, and apparently of gloomy and irritable constitution. He was a great admirer of the past, with little sympathy for new views, whether religious, political, or educational. In fact there is no reason to believe that he ever ceased to be at heart a decided Roman Catholic. The fellows, mostly if not entirely, were of the new way of thinking, Puritans; and apparently narrow-minded and bitter in spirit. Not one of them achieved any distinction in after life. They were also very young ….[25]

In fact, the college's surviving records of the time, particularly the Pandects,[26] present a rather different picture of his fourteen years as Master – one which

23 *Annals*, p. 78.

24 *Documents*, II, pp. 325, 350. This is not to suggest that he had had himself in mind when he was drafting his statutes. He would have been aware of the greater prominence played by professional men in Tudor administration since the Reformation, and if he had had examples in mind it would probably have been John Skipp (in whose election as Master he had participated in 1536), William Butts or Thomas Wendy.

25 *B.H.* III, p. 43.

26 References are to vol. I (1559–1658). Unpaginated after 1568, the *Pandectae* consist largely of brief notes of events occurring in the counting-house. They are frequently difficult to decipher,

differs from that depicted by Venn in many important respects. Caius may have been in poor health physically in his very last years, but for most of his mastership he was remarkably active, vigorous and successful in his efforts to recover money owed to the college and to restore its financial fortunes, at the same time combining his office in Cambridge with an exceptionally demanding life in London; moreover, he displayed to the end of his life a shrewd alertness to potential legal pitfalls when he was making purchases of land,[27] and in the year before he died he successfully defended the College of Physicians before the Queen's commissioners in its dispute with the barber-surgeons.[28] We may accept the view that he was of a gloomy and irritable constitution, but we should remember that he attached great importance to the practice of corporate dining and was generous in providing for it out of his own pocket.[29] He certainly admired the past and had little sympathy for new views, whether religious, political or educational; he regretted the passing of Catholic rituals and ceremonials, clung in his heart to doctrines which were anathema to extreme reformers – the spiritual efficacy of good works and prayers for the dead – and had a very un-Protestant devotion to the Virgin Mary; but, as Philip Grierson rightly pointed out, on the crucial question of acceptance of the papal bull excommunicating Elizabeth and releasing her subjects from their allegiance, Caius' allegiance to the Crown was never in doubt, any more than it had been in the reigns of her father, brother or sister.[30] His disputes with some of the fellows

but they give us the only surviving record of the payment of money into and from the chest during Caius' mastership, the identity of the person making those payments and the balance in the chest at the time of audits. They ceased after a few months to record any elections, appointments or college orders; they do not, therefore, perform the function which Caius envisaged for them and which the *Acta* and the *Gesta* later discharged.

27 *E.g.*, when he arranged the purchase from Trinity College of its four tenements in (what is now) Tree Court in return for an annual rent in 1564, it would have been normal practice for the vendor (Trinity) to retain a right to enter and retake the property sold in the event of any non-payment of the rent, but Caius took care to protect the courts of his college from any possibility of seizure by obtaining not only the normal royal licence in mortmain for Trinity to alienate the land, but a further licence in mortmain permitting him to substitute a right of entry upon the manor of Runcton in place of any right of entry upon the college courts. He carefully ensured that both licences were copied into the Annals, so that they would not be overlooked at some future date: *Annals*, pp. 90–111. He took the same care in 1570 to record the complex title to the manors of Bincombe and Oborne when he acquired them for the college, together with the advice he had obtained from the Attorney-General: *ibid.*, pp. 126–74.

28 See n. 15 above.

29 He paid for the feast following the re-foundation of his college (*B.H.* III, p. 40), and he instituted at the College of Physicians the custom of annual dinners, providing and paying for the first dinner, which was held in his London house (Clark, *History of the Royal College of Physicians* (1964), vol. 1, p. 123).

30 For a perceptive view of Caius' religious sympathies and an early warning that the disputes of the first seven years were not religious, see P. Grierson, "*John Caius' Library*", *B.H.* VII, pp. 523–5.

in his first years as Master may have been bitter, but they were bursarial in their nature, not doctrinal. We can readily accept that he was strongly hostile to Puritanism, but there is no evidence that any of the expelled fellows (or, indeed, any other fellows) were Puritans: indeed, the opposite appears to have been the case, for two of his three known disputes were with five fellows who had been elected in the reign of the Catholic Queen Mary and they had had no more difficulty in signing the Marian articles than they later had in accepting Elizabeth's Acts of Supremacy and Uniformity. Furthermore, those five fellows were no longer "very young" men by the time Caius quarrelled with them: at least two (Bateman and Sabine) were well into their forties, two (Clarke and Cowell) were well into their thirties and only one (Dethick) was under thirty. Admittedly, the third dispute did draw in two young fellows who were elected in Caius' own time as Master (Warner and Spenser): but that quarrel may have arisen over the way they performed the important office of key-holder rather than from any youthful disposition on their part; moreover, it seems to have been confined to a small faction within the Fellowship and appears to have been as much between two opposing groups of fellows as it was between fellows and Master. A religious element entered into it only at the bitter end.[31]

The traditional view of the expulsion of various fellows in Caius' early years as Master relies heavily upon the assertions made in 1566 by Warner and Spenser in a desperate attempt to persuade the Chancellor to reverse his decision not to hear their appeal against dismissal, and as a result the traditional view accepts too readily the appellants' insinuations that Caius alone was responsible for the expulsions, "he never being quiet since he came to the college, as may appear from the number of his expulsions which have been above twenty".[32] In fact, as will be seen later, on at least two of the three known occasions – the first and the third – the expulsions were made by "the Master and the more part of the company", that is, with the assent of a majority of the Fellowship.[33] The traditional view also assumes too readily that the quarrelling was predominantly between the Master personally on the one side and the Fellowship on the other, and implies that there would have been, in consequence, relative peace on the high table when Caius was away in London: in fact, the opposite may well have been the case, for Caius almost certainly spent far more time in London than he did in Cambridge during his mastership and the expelled fellows had at least as much ill-will against some of their colleagues as they had against the Master.[34]

31 For these quarrels, see below at pp. 347–59.

32 Appendix C, text (D) at p. 573 below; *B.H.* III, pp. 44–5.

33 Archbishop Parker' letter to Cecil, 29 December 1565, Appendix C, text (A) at p. 568 below. Similarly, Caius' earlier action in the Vice-Chancellor's court against Bateman, Cowell and Sabine (cf. below) was also taken "by the consent of the M[aster] and more part of the fellows": *Pandectae*, fol. 5.

34 By the time of Warner's and Spenser's assertions, the abrasive Francis Dorington, a particular bête noire of the expelled fellows, had been appointed president by Caius – over the head of

Caius' fourteen years as Master should in fact be seen as falling into two very different periods, each of which culminated in dramatic and memorable events. The first seven years culminated in the summary expulsion of three of the fellows and their unsuccessful appeal in December 1565 to the Chancellor of the university, Sir William Cecil, the secretary of Elizabeth's council and the most powerful layman in the realm. The second seven years culminated in the notorious invasion of the old Master's college rooms in December 1572, the ransacking of their contents and the triumphant burning in the college court of the popish trumpery which was found there. Each of those two dramatic events traumatised the college at the time, and they have thereafter coloured the 'accepted' view of Caius' relationship with his fellowship. Subsequent generations have assumed that the fundamental causes of the two dramatic events were the same, namely, a difference in temperament and an incompatibility in religious beliefs between Caius and his fellowship, and they have seen both events as manifestations of a continuing unhappy relationship which persisted between the two sides throughout the whole fourteen years of Caius' mastership. For two reasons that would be a mistake. *First*: the expulsions which culminated in December 1565 were the consequence of a series of disputes between Caius and a small number of identifiable fellows during his first seven years, and it would be wrong to assume that those disputes were the outcome of a rift between the Master and the whole body of fellows or to assume that such a rift persisted through the second seven years and brought about the outrage of December 1572: there is no evidence of any rift during the second period, and suspiciously little evidence that fellows played any active part in the outrage. *Second*: it would be equally wrong to attribute the cause of the disputes in the first seven years to the doctrinal controversies which brought about the outrage of 1572: that traumatic event arose from the sharp polarisation of religious views which occurred towards the end of the second seven years as a consequence of the Scottish Queen Mary's flight to England in 1568, the excommunication of Elizabeth in 1570 and the increasingly acrimonious theological disputes which had simmered in the two universities as much as elsewhere in the country, whereas the causes of the disputes within the college in the first seven years were essentially administrative and financial, and the expulsions had virtually no connection with any doctrinal differences.

Dethick, who was by then the most senior fellow. Caius had appointed Dorington president at least as early as 1564 (*Pandectae*, fol. 18v), only two years after his admission as a fellow; in doing so he was clearly anxious to forestall any repeat of the difficulties he had had with the preceding senior fellow, William Clarke, when there was no president.

The first seven years: 1559–66

When Caius returned as Master in January 1559 any contentment which he may have felt nine months earlier was soon replaced with anger and incredulity at the financial and physical state of his college. In the words of Venn, "he found everything in a terrible state of confusion: rents in arrear, buildings falling to pieces, title-deeds missing, chapel-ornaments misused and purloined by the fellows".[35] In Caius' own words, "you might say it had been an Augean stable".[36] Throughout the next two or three years he conducted a spring-cleaning of the college and a whirlwind of audits and inventories which must have exhausted (and irritated) Henry Dethick, the unfortunate fellow who had been appointed steward of the college's lands by Caius immediately upon his return and who appears to have acted as bursar in virtue of that office.[37] Without doubt the new Master conducted the spring-cleaning with a very new broom, and those who had been fellows of Gonville Hall experienced the sharpness of its bristles. We can be sure that he expressed his condemnation of their conduct to them orally and as frequently and strongly as he did in the Annals and, later, in his statutes, and it is not surprising that they resented his "never being quiet since he came to the college".[38] Given his later expulsions, it is important to remember that the energetic reforms which made Caius so unpopular with 'the old guard' arose from his passionately held conviction that the college was a corporate entity which served "not so much for our benefit as that of our posterity. For nothing belongs to any member either individually or collectively, apart from his stipend, livery, employments, distributions and offices."[39] He regarded the failure of Bacon and his fellows to safeguard the funds which had been entrusted to them as a betrayal of their most fundamental responsibility.

Caius was particularly upset by the parlous state in which he found the reserves in the chest.[40] The parsimonious style of life which had enabled him to

35 *Annals*, p. i; for Caius' protracted and unrestrained account of the state of the college, see *ibid.*, pp. 78–81.

36 *Augiae stabulum fuisse prius diceres*: *Annals*, p. 81.

37 Technically, as deputy-bursar: the Master had been the sole bursar under Bateman's statutes, and the indentures recording the accounts required by those statutes were always executed by the Master, not by a fellow. Caius, and later Legge, continued to sign them as Master until they were discontinued in the 1580s. Caius also appointed Dethick lecturer in the Humanities: *Pandectae* (1559–1658), fol. 2. For the details of Caius' audits and inventories in his first two years as Master, see Catherine Hall, "Dr Caius' Counting House", *The Caian* (1987), pp. 49–55.

38 Petition of Warner and Spenser to Cecil (Appendix C, text (D) below). They were no doubt relaying Dethick's views as they had not been fellows when Caius came back to the college.

39 Statute 63, discussed in "*Dividends*", § VI. 5, at p. 479 below.

40 For Caius the chest was a specific, tangible object, not an intangible financial concept termed "the Chest": see *The arca, cistae, thesaurus and aerarium* in "*Supplementary Notes to Caius' Statutes*", § IV. 3 at p. 288 above.

accumulate the wealth needed to re-found his old college seems to have led him to attach overweening importance to the accumulation of ready money in pure gold and silver as a protection against inflation and further debasement of the currency.[41] He angrily recorded in his Annals that only £4. 16s. of the £600 in pure gold which had been in the treasury when he left the college in September 1545 still remained in the chest when he returned to the college on 24 January 1559,[42] and for this he blamed the late Master and the fellows of Gonville Hall for this squandering of the college's seed corn.[43] In his anger he disregarded the fact that Bacon and his colleagues may have maintained twice as many senior and junior students in 1557 as their predecessors had done in 1545,[44] and that they were doing so on an income which was of much the same nominal value as it had been in 1545 but had shrunk in real value to a third as a result of debasement and inflation, factors of which he was very conscious.[45] Caius was in no mood to make allowances, however: he pursued Bacon's executor in

41 See Catherine Hall, *op. cit.*, for Caius' requirement that the form of the currency, and the amount in old (un-debased) gold, silver, foreign coin, must be checked and recorded and any base money returned to the bursar "to be restored upon the exchange". No doubt other professional men as well as merchants were equally prudent and mistrusted the coinage.

42 *Annals*, pp. 15, 79. One hesitates over the figure of £600 which Caius gives for 1545. £600 is a remarkable sum for one of the poorer colleges in Cambridge to have saved, given that Gonville Hall had had an expenditure of £155. 6s. 10d., as against a net income of £119. 19s. 5¼d., in that year, *i.e.* an excess expenditure of £35. 7s. 4¾d.: *Report of Henry VIII's Commissioners*, February 1546: *B.H.* III, pp. 338–9. (Parker and his fellow commissioners were anxious in1546 to present the colleges as poor as possible and not worth plundering, and carefully restricted their returns to each college's income, not its balances.) One suspects that the £600 included entry fines taken on long leases granted at low rents (The manor of Aynells had been let in this way the previous year: see *Beneficial Leases* in "*Dividends*", § VI. 5 below), and that the practice of treating such fines as dividends was adopted under Styrmin's and Bacon's oversight of the college.

43 His complaint against Bacon stemmed from his belief that Bacon had deliberately schemed to defraud the college and his other creditors by transferring his property to his brother Nicholas, a London merchant. Fraudulent transfers of this kind were certainly not unknown at that time, but the transfer by someone who was ill and was living at the time in his rectory at Chelsfield, Kent, at the time of his death might have been no more than a sensible step rather than hoarding it as ready money in the rectory as Caius might have done. (When he died in 1573 Caius left £428 in ready money, and over half of that, £241, in his London house.) It should also be said in Bacon's defence that by his time the greater part of the Hall's land had already been let on long or reversionary leases at rents which inexorably had lost their real value.

44 Thirty-one academics and servants in 1545 (*Documents*, II, p. 292); sixty-two academics and servants in 1557 (1 Master, 10 fellows, 10 scholars, 3 paupers, 33 pensioners and 5 servants: Caius, *Historiae*, p. 52). Gonville Hall was apparently larger in 1557 than Caius' new college was to be in 1564, *i.e.* forty-eight academics in 1564, just before the building of Caius Court (1 Master, 8 fellows, 11 major pensioners, 10 scholars, 18 other students: *B.H.* III, p. 63).

45 *Annals*, pp. 81–3; Statute 39. It is not surprising that Bacon had described the times as "stormye and evell" when he first welcomed the offer from an unknown benefactor in 1557: *B.H.* III, p. 36.

the Court of Requests and he prosecuted three of the delinquent fellows in the Vice-Chancellor's court.[46]

Caius' first and most pressing task was to remedy the parlous state of the chest. He could insist upon a better system of record-keeping and accounting, but there was little that he could do to achieve any immediate increase in the external or internal income of the college. As regards the external income, the greater part of the rents from Gonville Hall's endowments were frozen in long leases created by his two immediate predecessors, particularly Styrmin,[47] and even the rents from the three manors which he had just given to the college were similarly frozen and could not be raised to a realistic level for more than twenty years.[48] As regards the internal income, he seems at first to have toyed with the idea of introducing a charge of 10s. at admission for fellows elected after 25 November 1559 to be put towards the cost of utensils for the common table and the kitchen, and, even more contentiously, of discontinuing the recent practice of sharing out room rents as a dividend and accumulating those rents for repairs; but he then abandoned both ideas.[49] The fees paid by major pensioners, however, presented an immediate and less contentious source of income, and from his earliest days as Master he very deliberately encouraged the admission of such pensioners: there had been only one when he returned to the college, but within four months five new major pensioners had been admitted, and over the period to October 1564 the number admitted had risen to at least twenty-five.[50] It is not surprising that those major pensioners included many who had been members of another college and, being of Catholic persuasion or simply having a preference for ceremonial, had left their college as a result of the more puritanical atmosphere brought about in it by the enforced changes

46 *Annals*, pp. 79–80; John Bateman (*B.H.* I, p. 31), John Cowell (p. 43) and Sabine Smythe (p. 33) were the fellows sued: *Pandectae*, fol. 5. Later events suggest that he would probably have sued a fourth, William Clarke, if Clarke had not been overseas at the time. See pp. 348–51 below.

47 See *Beneficial Leases* in "*Dividends*", § VI. 5, at p. 520 below.

48 See *Caius' purchase of the Manors of Croxley, Runcton and Burnham Thorpe* in "*Supplementary Notes to Caius' Statutes*", § IV 3, at p. 302 above.

49 Cambridge University Library Ms Mm.4.20, fol. 18v. For his assertion that fellows had originally been obliged to contribute 20s. towards the cost of utensils, see *Annals*, p. 78. The proposal to discontinue the dividend cannot have made him popular with new young fellows, and in his statutes he subsequently modified his proposal so that it applied only to the rents from the new rooms in "our College", that is, the new court which he had himself provided: Statute 28. See *Room Rents* in "*Dividends*", § VI. 5, at p. 482 below.

50 See the university list of residents in July 1559 (*B.H.* I, p. 42) and the matriculation register to October 1564 (*ibid.*, pp. 43–55). It is difficult to estimate how many were in residence at any one time, for most were birds of passage and did not stay long; there were eleven in 1564 (see p. 205, n. 160 above). Of the six resident in July 1559 Henry Holland was the one major pensioner who had been admitted before Caius' return; he soon became a much-valued fellow and later president (*ibid.*, p. 39).

which followed the visitation by the new queen's commissioners.[51] Not surprisingly the migrants were attracted to Caius' college, for he was one of the few heads of house who had been chosen simply for his professional distinction and munificence to the college without regard for doctrinal considerations and he had consequently been "suffered to remain unmolested at the head of the society which he had himself reconstituted".[52]

Apart from the attracting of major pensioners to the college, there were few other ways in which the college's income could be increased, yet Caius straightaway began steadily to build up a comforting balance in the chest. On his return in January 1559 there had been no more than £4. 16s. in it, but the balance rose steadily year by year[53] and by the end of September 1563 it had risen to £186. 1s. 10d., even after £41 had been laid out in the purchase of lands in Cambridgeshire in order to make good a bequest that had been dissipated by Bacon and his colleagues.[54] The sums may seem small, but in the course of less than four years, virtually unaided and by his own industry and tenacity alone, Caius had managed to replenish the college's reserves sufficiently to meet any unforeseen repairs. He had done so simply by careful husbandry, by the welcoming of fee-paying major pensioners, by the unrelenting pursuit of the college's debtors and, as will be seen later, by the harrying of the college's officers; for, apart from waiving his stipend as Master, Caius had achieved his goal without the need to inject any of his own money.[55] What must have made

[51] Notably the Master of St Catharine's (E. Cousen, *B.H.* I, p. 48), and the Vice-Provost of King's (W. Whinke, *ibid.*, p. 43). For other former fellows of other colleges see William Kynge (p. 40), Richard Hall (p. 40), George Gardiner (p. 47), Thomas Barwick (p. 52) and Humphrey Busbey (p. 53).

[52] J.B. Mullinger, *The University of Cambridge from the Royal Injunctions of 1535 to the Accession of Charles I* (1884). Two of Caius' friends and colleagues, Parker and Wendy, were commissioners and would have recognised that he cared little for doctrinal controversies and was a conforming Christian who subscribed whole-heartedly to the supremacy of each of his sovereigns. For a thoughtful assessment of Caius' religious views, see Brooke, *History*, pp. 72–4.

[53] £14. 13s. 6d. by May 1559, though very little was in gold and silver and most was in base money (*Pandectae*, fol. 3); £47. 10s. 5d. by March 1560 (*ibid.*, fol. 6v.); and £117. 0s. 10d., by March 1562, now all in gold and silver (*ibid.*, fol. 13v). By March 1563 it had risen to £138. 4s. 2d. (*ibid.*, fol. 14v. The revaluation of English silver currency in 1560 and of foreign currency in 1561 caused the college some loss (*Annals*, pp. 81–2) and in subsequent accounts Caius carefully kept the old and new silver coinage separate (*Pandectae*, fols. 6v, 12, 13v, 14v).

[54] Shaxton had left £20 in 1556 for the purchase of land to provide for the warming of the hall but this had been completely dissipated by the time Bacon died three years later; the gift was now made good from the chest and a further £21 added in order to purchase lands in Steeple and Guilden Morden which could provide an income for the purchase of fuel for the new brazier which a major pensioner, Humphrey Busbye, donated to the college the following year: *Pandectae*, fol. 16v, *Annals*, p. 120.

[55] The summary of expenditure to September 1563 which he listed in the *Annals* (at p. 80) is reproduced by Venn (*B.H.* III, p. 42). He had spent over £1,000 in the purchase of the manors of Croxley, Runcton and Burnham Thorpe, but that generous gift did not contribute to the

the achievement the more galling for Caius is that his replenishment of the reserves could have been achieved in the same way by Bacon and his fellows. It is not surprising therefore that, as late as 1563, the need to make good the profligacy of his predecessor and the fellows of Gonville Hall still stirred him to anger.[56]

Shortage of money in the treasury was not his only challenge when he returned to the college: he was also faced with an acute shortage of fellows. Ten fellows had been named in the charter in September 1557, but in little over a year after Caius' return to the college in January 1559, death, departure or illness had reduced to two the number of those who were still fellows, and only one of these was available for office.[57] During the next three years he turned to three sources to supply the want of new fellows: the scholars of the college, its major pensioners and migrating members of other colleges. He looked first to the few graduate scholars of the college in residence in 1559, and in the period to 1562 five (and possibly more) scholars were elected into fellowships virtually as soon as they became bachelors and well before they qualified for the full degree of M.A.;[58] they acted as tutors straightaway, but their youthful election meant that

balance in the chest since the rents from the three manors were paid not directly to the college, but to Caius personally, and he paid out the stipends of his fellows and scholars to the college as they fell due: *Pandectae*, fol. 18v (payment by Caius to the college for Spenser's stipend). From 1564 onward he started to deposit very substantial amounts of his own money in the chest to provide for the purchase of the five tenements in Tree Court and to meet the cost of completing Caius Court, and thereafter the half-yearly balance in the chest was regularly over £250: *ibid.*, fols. 22v, 27. For his summary of expenditure from 1564 to his resignation of the mastership in June 1573, see *Annals*, pp. 186–7 and *B.H.* III, pp. 52–3.

56 The loss of Shaxton's gift clearly drew from him the angry comment that money had been dissipated by the incompetence of his predecessor and the senior fellows of that time: "*Quam pecuniam etsi exhaustam inutilitate praedecessoris nostri et sociorum seniorum ejus temporis*": *Annals*, p. 88. The expression of his anger would not have been confined to the Annals, and we can be sure that the two surviving fellows from Gonville Hall, Clarke and Dethick, would have been made aware of it.

57 Henry Dethick (*B.H.* I, p. 38). The second fellow, William Clarke (p. 43), had been abroad when Caius returned and although he was the most senior of the fellows, Caius pointedly omitted to appoint Clarke to any office on his return and eventually expelled him (cf. below). Of the other eight, Caius' old friend and contemporary William Barker (p. 27) had ceased to be a fellow but remained a generous benefactor to the college until his death in 1579; Vincent (p. 31) had died before Caius returned; Glyn (p. 42) had been made president by Caius, but left in October 1559; Burre (p. 32) and Kettilston (p. 43) were recorded as absent through illness in the return of resident members made to the Commissioners in July 1559 (p. 42) and, although they returned and briefly held office, they died early in 1560; the other three fellows, *i.e.* Bateman (p. 31), Cowell (p. 43) and Sabine (p. 33), had been sued by Caius in the Vice-Chancellor's court for malfeasance when Bacon was in office and had died, resigned or departed under a cloud.

58 Hugh Casselton (*B.H.* I, p. 37) and Robert Norton (*ibid.*, p. 43) appear to have been the first, becoming B.A.s in 1559 and fellows in 1561; Stephen Warner (p. 40) and William Lunt (p. 40) followed soon after they became B.A.s in 1560–61; and on graduating Robert Spenser (p. 42) became the first fellow on Caius' own foundation on 23 May 1562. In addition to these scholars,

they could hardly be deemed academically qualified for the lucrative offices of salarist or lecturer.[59] Caius turned next to the college's major pensioners, two of whom were elected fellows in 1561–62,[60] and finally, to supplement the still meagre fellowship, Caius brought in a significant number of ex-fellows and graduates of other colleges.[61] It was to the more senior of these newcomers that the lucrative posts of lecturer, salarist, tutor and even president tended to be given and, as will be seen later, this was resented by the 'home-grown' graduates and appears to have caused as much friction within the Fellowship as there was between fellows and the Master.[62]

Caius' exasperation with the state in which he found the college upon his return, coupled with his irascibility and inability to make allowances for any weakness, led to bitter disputes with those fellows whom he judged, rightly or wrongly, to be responsible, and during his first seven years he expelled or drove out of college a number of fellows whom he found wanting – "above twenty" by 1565 according to the petition of two expelled fellows to the Chancellor in that year.[63] The figure of twenty must have been a tendentious exaggeration, even though we know from Archbishop Parker that he had had "very much ado

a sizar, Thomas Smythe (p. 40), was elected a fellow in 1561 upon graduating B.A., but died in college the following year.

59 See Caius' apology for having "no auncienter man" than Norton to send to Pattesley as Knight's preacher in 1561: *B.H.* I, p. 43, *sub nom.* Norton. In January 1562 there were only four fellows in college, in addition to Dethick, to witness a transaction, one M.A. (Sherman) and three B.A.s (Norton, Warner and Smythe): *Pandectae*, fol. 12v.

60 One of them, Henry Holland (*B.H.* I, p. 39), was later to give valuable service to it as bursar and president at a critical time in the second half of Caius' mastership: see p. 360 below. The second major pensioner was Stephen Valenger (p. 49), who also gave long service to the college. In addition Caius called upon various major pensioners to act as tutors even though they were not fellows: see, *e.g.*, W. Kynge (p. 46), G. Gardiner (p. 47), T. Davys (p. 54) and particularly N. Cobbe (p. 55).

61 Richard Sherman (p. 44) was for some time the only one until Francis Dorington (p. 50), Matthew Trott (p. 50) and Francis Wiseman (p. 55) were admitted as fellows. It is not clear precisely how many were so admitted directly as fellows, since such persons did not have tutors or sureties and were not entered in the Matriculation Book.

62 The resentment was directed particularly against Francis Dorington, an abrasive and acquisitive individual whom Caius had brought into the college from Queens' in 1562 and had ill-advisedly made president in 1564. Dorington had accumulated a very large number of tutorial pupils, as well as teaching posts, and had shared responsibility for disbursements from the chest with Warner and Spenser as key-keepers in at least one year; see *Pandectae*, fols. 14v, 16v (1563) and pp. 354–6 below.

63 Stephen Warner (*B.H.* I, p. 40) and Robert Spenser (p. 42). Their petition is set out in Appendix C, text (D) below; for a careful appraisal see Brooke, *History*, p. 71, citing Public Record Office SP 12/39/11, pp. 262–4. They mention the figure of twenty expulsions and imply (but carefully do not state) that all the expelled were fellows; that can hardly be the case, even if one includes forced resignations, and the number, if anywhere near correct, must have included scholars and possibly pensioners as well.

with the quarrels of Gonville Hall from time to time".[64] It is difficult to untangle expulsions from the voluntary relinquishing of fellowships in the first seven years after Caius returned to the college, and impossible to identify anything near twenty expulsions or forced resignations; but we have some record or knowledge of the three distinct occasions on which friction between the Master and individual fellows led to the expulsion or forced resignation of more than one fellow at the same time, and this knowledge gives us some clues as to the nature of the friction which led Caius to the drastic step of expelling groups of fellows.

The first of these occasions arose within the first year of Caius' return as Master and was the inevitable outcome of his suing three senior fellows in the Vice-Chancellor's court for misappropriation of the college's funds in Bacon's time.[65] He appears to have brought separate actions against them individually over the course of 1559 as his examination of the records uncovered their apparent iniquity,[66] and by the end of the year all three had departed: Cowell resigned, and Bateman and Smythe may also have done so rather than await expulsion, but all three were doubtless included in the figure of "above twenty" expulsions later alleged against Caius.

The second occasion involved the expulsion of the only two fellows thereafter remaining from Bacon's time: William Clarke and Henry Dethick. The sole account that we have of this second incident is Archbishop Parker's brief reference to it in a later letter which he sent to Sir William Cecil on 29 December 1565 in connection with the well-known third incident in that year. In that letter the archbishop recalls that he and Edwin Sandys, the bishop of London, had been called upon to intervene in an earlier dispute and had "so compounded the matter, that we perceived it very needful to the quiet of that society to remove both Dethick and Clarke from their fellowships".[67] It seems clear that both were removed at the same time or in connection with the same offence; Parker does not say what that offence was or when the incident took place. The only pointer that he gives us in his letter in 1565 is to say that "after a year" he persuaded Caius to take Dethick back and that Caius did so; Parker was

64 Letter to Cecil, 29 December 1565, Appendix C, text (A) below.

65 *Annals*, pp. 79–80. John Bateman (*B.H.* I, p. 31), John Cowell (p. 43) and Sabine Smythe (p. 33) were the fellows sued; the actions appear to have been settled by the defendants' giving a bill obligatory acknowledging their indebtedness to the college: *Pandectae*, fol. 5. Later events suggest that Caius would probably have sued a fourth fellow, William Clarke, if he had not been overseas at the time.

66 The list of fellows who were resident in July 1559 (*B.H.* I, p. 42) omits Bateman, and it records that Cowell had been suspended by then; Bateman died during the autumn of that year (pp. 31–2), and Cowell resigned in November 1559 (*Pandectae*, fol. 4v); Smythe seems to have been the last to be sued, for Caius appointed him Knight's salarist as late as August 1559, *i.e. after* Cowell had been suspended (*Pandectae*, fol. 3v).

67 For Parker's letter, see Appendix C, text (A) below.

not intending to be precise, but if his estimate of a year is not wildly inaccurate we can be confident that Dethick's exile must have occurred between May 1563 and May 1564.[68]

Although we cannot say precisely when or why Clarke and Dethick were expelled, we can glean some idea of the underlying causes of the friction which developed between the Master and the college's two most senior fellows and led to their expulsion. So far as Dethick is concerned, it would seem to stem from Caius' complete loss of confidence in his bursar's stewardship of the college's finances. We know of three events which may have led to that loss of confidence after the initial three years during which Caius had relied on Dethick alone to manage the college's financial affairs while he was in London: the failure to discover the ruinous state of the Swan hostelry in Norwich before it was purchased in 1562, which forced Caius to sell it at a substantial loss the following year;[69] the retention of Spanish pistolets "and other not currant money" in the chest after the revaluation of English coinage in 1560 and foreign coinage in 1561, which involved Caius in charges for their disposal ("cariage") when he was sent them by Dethick;[70] and that fellow's protracted failure to settle his bursarial indebtedness to the college after the Michaelmas audit of 1561. This last was by far the most serious of Dethick's failings. He had been appointed steward of the college's lands by Caius on becoming Master in January 1559, and thereafter he had played a dominant and pervasive part in the management of the college's affairs, particularly during Caius' frequent and prolonged absences in London.[71] However, the Michaelmas audit in October 1561 revealed a deficit of £11. 1s. 10d. in the chest. A bursar would be expected to clear his account by the time of the following audit and Dethick continued to act as bursar until then; but his indebtedness to the college remained un-discharged at that Easter audit and was not finally settled for a further three months.[72] For Caius, striving tirelessly in London to replenish the college's finances and having necessarily to rely upon his deputy as bursar and the key-keepers in Cambridge for the safe-guarding of the chest, the failure by an officer to account for the funds entrusted

68 Dethick was still a fellow on 8 May 1563, when he was appointed one of the college's attorneys to convey to the purchaser the same Swan hostelry in Norwich that he had been partially responsible for buying; after that he disappears from the Pandects until 2 May 1564, when he was sent a title deed on college business: *Pandectae*, fols. 15, 18v. That deed, it was noted in the margin, was returned on September, so that he was presumably a fellow then. He is mentioned again in April 1565, when he was appointed salarist: *ibid.*, fol. 20v. If he was indeed a fellow when he returned the deed in September 1564, the only period remotely approaching a year during which he could have been without his fellowship must lie between May 1563 and May 1564.

69 *B.H.* IV(2), p. 70, and *Pandectae*, fol. 13v.

70 *Pandectae*, fol. 13v.

71 For the demands made upon Dethick and others, see Catherine Hall, "Dr Caius' Counting House", *The Caian* (1987), pp. 49–55.

72 *Pandectae*, fol. 12. It was not discharged until 23 June 1562.

to him was one of the gravest offences that a fellow could commit, and in his later statutes he provided the draconian sanction of automatic and immediate loss of fellowship if the debt remained unpaid for thirty days after it was first due.[73] On this occasion Caius was far more lenient and Dethick retained his fellowship.[74] After that audit, however, he was never subsequently appointed to the bursarship or to any other office which gave access to the chest.[75] For an ambitious man like Dethick who, according to Parker, harboured the ambition of becoming Master, the virtual ostracism must have rankled greatly. There is, however, no evidence of any further failing on his part that might have led to his dismissal from the college, and it seems likely that his colleague, Clarke, was the principal actor in whatever provoked Caius to expel both of them.

On the subject of Clarke the Pandects are unhelpful, for his name does not appear anywhere in that record until after he had ceased to be a fellow, even though he was the most senior fellow both by date of election as a fellow and by degree and standing in the university: he remains a shadowy and mysterious figure within the college.[76] He was abroad when Caius became Master, and, breaking with tradition,[77] Caius pointedly omitted appointing him president or to any office when he returned.[78] It is clear that Clarke was the person to whom Caius was referring in Statute 32 when he laid down that a senior fellow who arrogated any authority to himself or took certain prohibited actions should be expelled "because we have found by experience that a senior fellow who is not president will (if he is a bad man, rash and quarrelsome) be the instrument of all discord, all wrong and iniquity".[79] We do not know what Clarke's offence

73 Statute 55 ("... *ipso facto sint non socii.*").

74 See n. 68 above.

75 After the Easter audit 1562 his functions as *de facto* bursar and key keeper were taken over by Warner and Spenser for one year and they were then joined by Francis Dorington, one of the fellows whom Caius had brought into the college from outside: *Pandectae*, fols. 14–15v. Dorington's name then becomes as prominent in the Pandects as Dethick's had been. Dethick continued to be allocated one or two pupils as a tutor for few months, but not after October 1562: *B.H.* I, p. 49.

76 He is mentioned in the Pandects only after he had ceased to be a fellow. This was in connection with the settlement of an intriguing and apparently acrimonious action in the Vice-Chancellor's court between him and the college after he had left the college and become a fellow of Clare Hall (as Clare College was then called): *Pandectae*, fols. 21, 23, and see n. 78 below. He subsequently left Cambridge and had a successful career as a civil lawyer and ecclesiastical functionary.

77 According to a later commentator, when Caius appointed Dorington in 1564 to be president only two years after becoming a fellow, the Master "was observed to be the first that made the Innovation of preferring a Junior Fellow to be President, whereas before in that College the Senior Fellow was always President, and that always in the Master's Absence": Strype, *Life and Acts of Parker* (London, 1711).

78 He appears to have acted as tutor for one pupil only, his brother Edward Clerke: *B.H.* I, p. 49.

79 "*quod usu comperimus seniorem socium non existentem Presidentem, si vir malus sit, imprudens et factiosus, instrumentum esse dissentionis, omnis mali et iniquitatis*": Statute 32. No other senior fellow in Caius' time fits the bill.

was or when it was committed, and it may well have been one or more of the prohibited acts specified in Statute 32;[80] but whatever it was, he was doubtless associated very firmly in Caius' mind with the mismanagement of the college's affairs in Bacon's time. Even more than Dethick, Clarke must have resented his ostracism.

The resentment against the Master felt by the college's two most senior fellows, coupled with his distrust of them, culminated in their expulsion, apparently at some time between May 1563 and May 1564.[81] Clarke and Dethick sought to overturn their expulsion by appealing to the two most powerful churchmen in London, Matthew Parker, archbishop of Canterbury, and Edwin Sandys, bishop of London, both of whom had formerly been Masters of Cambridge colleges; but the two fellows did so without success.[82] Clarke was by this time Regius Professor of Civil Law and quickly found a fellowship elsewhere in Cambridge.[83] Dethick was initially far less fortunate, but after a year he successfully importuned Parker to prevail upon Caius to take him back. Rather surprisingly Caius did so, upon Parker's promising that "if by him any trouble should arise, I would take him from him again",[84] and Dethick's name reappeared in the Pandects in May 1564.[85]

Parker had to honour his promise rather sooner than he may have expected, for less than eighteen months later, in the summer of 1565, the third batch of expulsions occurred and Dethick was again expelled, this time with two younger fellows, Stephen Warner and Robert Spenser, both of whom had, in all probability, been Dethick's tutorial pupils.[86] The expulsion of no less than three fellows simultaneously must have been traumatic, and the incident

80 The prohibited acts were: renewing a deed, making a loan, entering into a bond, granting a lease or proposing a Grace in the university for anyone.

81 See n. 68 above.

82 The fact that Sandys, an ardent reformer, firmly rejected Clarke's appeal is a strong indication that the dispute with Caius was not religious.

83 He became a fellow of Clare College. He was a civil lawyer, and the mutual hostility between him and Caius immediately produced acrimonious litigation in the Vice-Chancellor's court. Clarke appears to have come off better than his former college: the claim and counterclaim were settled in July 1565 and the college obtained a bond for £14 from Clarke, but apparently only after paying him £34: BUR: DEEDS/ 4, 19; *B.H.* I, p. 43; *Pandectae*, fol. 21. The unexplained amount of £34 is intriguing.

84 Parker to Sir William Cecil, 29 December 1565, Appendix C, text (A) below.

85 He was appointed one of Dr Geoffrey Knight's salarists: *Pandectae*, fol. 20v.

86 For a full account of these expulsions and the consequent proceedings, see the introductory note to Appendix C below and the accompanying texts. Warner had certainly been one of Dethick's pupils (*Pandectae*, fol. 12), and Spenser had probably been one also, as he been admitted in November 1559, in Caius' first year as Master, at a time when Dethick had been the only fellow available to act as a tutor (see n. 57 above); Spenser was appointed by Caius as the first fellow on his own foundation on 25 May 1562, immediately upon graduation: *B.H.* I, pp. 40, 42; *Annals*, p. 60.

produced considerable comment in the university.[87] The immediate occasion which triggered the expulsions appears to have been the bringing of an action in the Vice-Chancellor's court by Warner contesting the Master's imposition of some punishment. In Caius' eyes this appeal to an external tribunal was a gross offence for which the culprit should be accursed (*execrabilis*) and deprived of all benefit from the college and excluded for ever from it (Statute 104). The offences of Dethick (who had been expelled once before and only recently been allowed to return) and Spenser appear to be that of aiding and abetting Warner and perhaps joining in his suit. Despite the notoriety which accompanied the subsequent appeals by the three fellows, there is little evidence to indicate precisely what lay behind the dispute and prompted Warner to challenge Caius' authority in the uncompromising way that he did: the three fellows presented themselves as blameless and we do not hear Caius' side of the dispute, but the suit must have been particularly galling to him, coming just at the time when he and the college had been worsted by Clarke in the same court.[88]

Later generations have accepted too readily the account presented by the two younger fellows in the petition against their expulsion which they submitted in vain to the Chancellor,[89] and, as will be seen later, they have tended to disregard the adverse opinion of the expelled fellows that was expressed by the only person who heard both sides in person, the eminently sensible Matthew Parker. For this reason it is important to bear in mind: (i) that Caius' "never being quiet since he came to the college"[90] may have been due directly to his on-going concern for the safeguarding of the college's finances; (ii) that the management of those finances was no longer the responsibility of one fellow during Caius'

[87] In a letter to Parker after the expulsions were confirmed, Andrew Perne, the Master of Peterhouse and Dean of Ely, wrote:

> "As I do well like Mr Doctor Caius' good zeal towards building up the walls of his college, so do I mislike his indiscreet severity against his fellows, … I do think no thing more requisite this day than prudent severity … But to use it as he doth in calling his fellows boys, knaves, beggars openly, and striving to put them into the stocks, expelling more fellows in one year than all colleges in Cambridge, making statutes daily upon private matters, which he will change shortly after, whereby he brings himself, his college and statutes in contempt." (Spelling modernised)

The original in Lambeth Library (MS 2002, fol. 119), is transcribed in P. Collinson, *Godly People* (Hambledon Press, 1983), pp. 331–2; cited Brooke, *History*, p. 74, n. 80. Perne may have obtained his view of Caius' conduct and statutes from William Clarke, who had originally been from Peterhouse.

[88] See n. 83 above.

[89] Cf. "This remarkable illustration of college life … from two of the older fellows, who represent themselves (probably with perfect truth) as reduced to the utmost distress and perplexity by their expulsion.": Mullinger, *The University of Cambridge from the Royal Injunctions 1535 to the Accession of Charles I* (Cambridge, 1884), p. 201, n. 1.

[90] The culminating complaint of the expelled fellows against Caius in their petition to Cecil, Appendix C, text (D) below.

absence, as it had been when Dethick had been in office, and it had become fragmented between the three key-holders appointed annually; (iii) that the rift may have been quite as much between fellows who were key-holders as it was between the expelled fellows and the Master; (iv) that the decision to expel was endorsed by the majority of the Fellowship; and (v) that the summary nature of the expulsions may represent not so much a hot-tempered reaction on Caius' part, but a blinkered application of the very singular and personal concept running through his statutes that a fundamental breach of obligations undertaken at admission triggers automatic and instant disqualification. These factors need examination.

(i) *Caius' concern for the college's finances.* It is clear from the Annals and the Pandects that Caius needed to spend much of his time – indeed, most of it – in London, where he was kept busy not only upon a professional practice and on the College of Physicians,[91] but also upon far more work there for his Cambridge college than is generally assumed: thus, litigation with sitting tenants in 1561,[92] the acquisition of licences in mortmain for the expansion of the site of the college in 1564,[93] the receipt of any rent and other payments made to the college in London,[94] and the raising of finance for the purchase of the manors of Bincombe and Oborne in 1570[95] all required his personal attention and presence in London. His prolonged absences from Cambridge meant that

[91] The amount of time and effort that he gave to the College of Physicians is well documented. There is, however, a temptation to assume that Caius had made his fortune by the time that he became Master and that he was accordingly able to reduce his medical practice in London substantially, if not completely. However, the fact that he continued to transmit relatively small amounts of money to Cambridge from time to time in order to reimburse the college for money which it had provided from the chest for the building of Caius Court (*Pandectae*, fols. 18v, 21v) suggests that he had expended much of his earlier savings on the purchase of the manors with which he had endowed the college in 1558 and that he needed to continue earning professional fees to restore his finances, and indeed to provide a substitute for the stipend which he generously waived on becoming Master. Cf. n. 95 below for his need to raise loans for the purchase of the manor of Oborne.

[92] For his litigation with the Conisby family who were the lessees of Runcton, see "*Supplementary Notes to Caius' Statutes*", § IV. 3, at p. 305 above.

[93] See *Annals*, pp. 90ff. For the acquisition from Trinity College of the four tenements in (what became) Tree Court, Caius enlisted the help of his powerful acquaintances in London, the Lord Keeper (Nicholas Bacon) and the Secretary of the Council (William Cecil).

[94] *Pandectae*, fol. 14. On 30 March 1563, when he came up for the Easter audit, Caius accounted for two years' back rent from the Crown for Physick Hostel, for other rents which he may also have received in London and for Spanish pistolets and "other not curant money exchanged which Mr Dethicke sent unto him in the college's behalf".

[95] *Pandectae*, 30 November 1570. Caius negotiated loans of £50 from the College of Physicians and £50 from his old friend William Barker (one of the fellows named in the charter of re-foundation) to finance the purchase; the college executed bonds to the lenders, but eventually they were not needed as "they were never accepted". Caius also acquired legal advice

he necessarily had to rely heavily upon those fellows to whom the management and safeguarding of the college's funds in the chest was entrusted while he was away and to whom he not infrequently had to transmit money,[96] *i.e.*, the three fellows who been elected key-keepers and in that capacity discharged the functions of a bursar and a steward:[97] Against that background Caius' insistence upon their scrupulous management of those funds and rigorous accounting during his absence is understandable.

(ii) *The fragmented management of the chest.* As virtually sole key-holder,[98] Dethick had until Easter 1562 discharged the duties later performed by two distinct officers, bursar and steward. In the three accounting years that followed those functions were shared between three fellows as key-holders, Warner, Spenser and Dorington,[99] and it is clear from the distinct differences in handwriting that key-holders acted quite independently of one another. This was particularly the case with Dorington,[100] and a bitter and acrimonious rift later developed between

in London from the Attorney-General in respect of the complicated conveyances of Bincombe and Oborne: *Annals*, p. 144.

96 He was careful to avoid the dangers inherent in transfers of money: on at least one occasion he made a (no doubt mutual) arrangement for a Cambridge merchant ("Mr Foxe, draper and burgess") to make payment on his behalf, and on two other occasions he relied on the friendly assistance of the Lord Chief Justice (Catlyn C.J.K.B.) to transfer money to the college: *Pandectae*, fols. 15, 22 and 30.

97 Although Caius had provided for offices of bursar and steward (*oeconomus*) in his draft statutes (*Documents*, II, p. 348), it is surprising to find that the offices do not appear in the Pandects in the early years of his mastership: instead, the Pandects reflect the provisions of Bateman's statutes, which did not contemplate such offices and entrusted the care of the chest to the key-keepers (Statutes 6 and 7). In fact, it is not clear that formal appointments to offices of bursar and steward were made in Caius' very early years as Master: thus Dethick is recorded as having been appointed steward (*senescallus*) of the college's lands by Caius on his arrival as Master, but not as bursar: *Pandectae*, fol. 2. Dorington would seem to be the first person specifically described as "bursar" in December 1562: *ibid.*, fol. 17v.

98 He had originally served with Kettilston and Sabine Smythe as key-keepers (*Pandectae*, fol. 2v), but after Kettilston's death and Smythe's disgrace, Dethick in effect acted alone.

99 *Pandectae*, fols. 13v, 14, 14v, 16v, 20. All three acted in 1562–63 and 1563–64, and Warner and Dorington continued to act in 1564–65, when Spenser was replaced by Holland. The years indicated here run from Easter 1562, when Dethick's tenure of office ceased abruptly, not the start of the academical year in October.

100 He seems to have become a key-holder very soon after he came to the college from Queens' in 1562 and, having rapidly taken over the purchase of provisions for fellows' and scholars' commons, he became responsible for much the greater part of the expenditure from the chest; he retained the function when he became president in 1564. He ultimately showed himself to be a profligate spender and when he finally departed in 1566–67 it took the Master and the bursar (Holland) repeated attempts to recoup from him the substantial sums that he owed to the college from his stewardship: *Pandectae*, fols. 26, 27v.

him and the other two key-holders.[101] Even before that happened, the sharing of management brought about a dramatic deterioration in the auditing of the chest and the recording of withdrawals from it. When one person, Dethick, had been in sole charge, the withdrawal and return of money and documents had been regularly and promptly recorded in the Pandects, and the audit of the half-yearly accounts by the Fellowship at Easter and Michaelmas had been followed by a report on the state of the chest recording the precise amount and currency of the money held in it and the resulting indebtedness of the bursar: after Easter 1562, when Dethick ceased to hold office, the recording becomes noticeably incomplete. The report on the chest on that occasion was sketchy and was recorded late,[102] no report on the chest was made six months later at Michaelmas audit that year, and none was made at Easter 1564.[103] It is not surprising that the new key-keepers reported after the next audit of the books, at Michaelmas 1564, "that after our books there remain £261. 19s. 1d. in the common hutches [*i.e.* chests] in gold and silver" but added "as we would guess, but how it shall fall certainly we know not till all be told over".[104] The uneven character of the entries made by the key-holders contrasts sharply with the clear and detailed accounts which Caius gave in the Pandects of his own dealings on behalf of the college.[105] It is unlikely that he remained silent about the way in which the chest was being overseen and, given his abiding memory of the state in which he had found the chest when he returned to the college, it would be understandable if his relations with the key-keepers became increasingly strained; no doubt they in turn resented his "never being quiet since he came to the college".[106] What bearing, if any, Warner's and Spenser's

[101] As their later petition to Cecil reveals: see Appendix C, text (D) below.

[102] *Pandectae*, fol. 13v.

[103] *Pandectae*, fols. 13v, 18v. It is clear from the chronological arrangement of the Pandects that no record of the auditing of the chest was made on these two occasions. This does not mean that there was no audit of the income and expenditure books at a college meeting; the checking of the money actually in the chest was a separate event which would normally take place in the counting-house at a later time after the college meeting: at Easter 1564, when there was no audit of the chest, there is an entry that Dorington brought up into the counting-house the £28. 12s. 6d. that he owed on the account books: *ibid.*, fol. 18v.

[104] *Pandectae*, fol. 19v, 20 October 1564; the word "told" is used in the sense of 'telling" or counting out money.

[105] *Pandectae*, fol. 14.

[106] See the petition of Warner and Spenser, Appendix C, text (D) at p. 571 below. One may sympathise with Spenser. During the summer of 1564 he had taken on responsibility for paying out of the chest for the necessary materials and equipment for the building of Caius Court, despite his youth and the fact that he had been a fellow for only two years, and he appears to have discharged that responsibility punctiliously, signing in the Pandects against each record of expenditure he made. His responsibilities for these purchases lasted only for one half-year,

performance as key-holders had on their expulsion the following year is tantalisingly unclear; but Caius' treatment of them should not be seen simply as the result of an old man's unwillingness to accept the changed life-style and manners exhibited by fellows who were young men, but more probably arose from impatience with two fellows holding key offices to whom he had entrusted the safe-keeping of the funds which he had been tirelessly striving to augment.

(iii) *Rifts within the Fellowship.* It is clear from their petition against expulsion that Warner and Spenser had come to nourish a festering resentment not only against Caius for his treatment of them, but also against "certain fellows of the College" whose expulsion for "the breach of diverse statutes" they urged in their turn.[107] The root cause of their resentment was two-fold. In part it may have stemmed from what they regarded as the undue financial favouring of those fellows who had been brought in from other colleges *after* they had themselves become fellows;[108] Caius' importation of those fellows to meet the pressing need for tutors and lecturers in his very early years had been understandable, but by 1565 the need was no longer pressing and Warner and Spenser had a justifiable complaint that they had undertaken the demanding office of key-keeper, but were not being allocated their fair share in the more rewarding positions of tutor and lecturer as they became more senior. Their animosity, however, seems to have been directed specifically against the two fellows who had been key-holders with them or had replaced them in that office rather than against other fellows – and more particularly against Francis Dorington, who had by that time become president[109] and appears to have been both acquisitive and abrasive.[110]

however, and he ceased abruptly to hold any office at Michaelmas 1564; *Pandectae*, fols. 18v, 19. His misfortune seems to have been to have lent his support to Warner in his ill-judged appeal to the Vice-Chancellor.

107 Petition of 7 January 1566, Appendix C, text (D). The petition hints that the breaches will continue "if they still there abide".

108 "Item that those fellows which shall remain in the house … may receive pupils (as other do) & have their chambers offices lectures & other preferments according to seniority which have been always the custom of the house …": *ibid.* Out of the twenty pupils admitted in the academical year 1563–64, eleven were allocated to Dorington as tutor, but only one to Spenser and none to Warner: *B.H.* I, pp. 52–5.

109 *Pandectae*, fols. 14v–22. Dorington was still a relatively junior fellow and his appointment as president over the head of the senior fellow (*i.e.* Dethick after Clarke's departure) appears to have been a break with tradition and, according to Strype, "the Cause of much Strife and Contention": *Life of Parker*, p. 201.

110 See n. 100 above. The petitioners charged Dorington with "contumacy towards Mr Vice-Chancellor" and with "the fighting with the fellows & bloodshed committed by Mr Dorington", Appendix C, text (D). They also urged that he and another fellow, Henry Holland, should be deprived of their fellowships on the grounds that they enjoyed more

It appears from the petition that the animosity was sufficiently bitter to result in fisticuffs at the high table – "fighting with the fellows and bloodshed committed". It was such incidents which prompted Caius' passionate outburst in Statute 47 and his lament that discords are the ruin of colleges and end in a Trojan war of evils,[111] and they may indeed have hastened the expulsion of the three fellows.[112]

(iv) *The attitude of the majority of the Fellowship.* The traditional picture is that of an isolated Master confronted by an almost wholly rebellious fellowship, but in fact the Fellowship was divided and, it was carefully noted by Parker, the expulsion of the three fellows was made jointly by the Master and the "more part of the company".[113]

(v) *The concept of instant disqualification.* The concept of instant disqualification had not featured in Caius' draft statutes of 1558, and it is not known when he introduced that penalty into the statutes, nor is it to be found at the time in other college's statutes so far as the present writer is aware; but it is clearly something which was very deep-rooted in his thinking. This draconian notion of punitive consequences following automatically and instantly upon a serious wrongdoing – without the need for action on anybody's part or formal dismissal, and certainly not for 'due process' – is found elsewhere in his statutes;[114] and it would seem to arise from a personal, quasi-theological conception that serious breaches of statutes were deadly sins which constituted a fundamental breach of the solemn undertakings given by a fellow at his admission (*periurium*) and terminated the fellowship "*ipso facto*".[115] It was this ingrained thinking rather than any quick temper which explains Caius' resort to expulsion so swiftly and evoked the criticism of moderate men like Parker who saw "overmuch rashness in the Master for expelling fellows so suddenly".[116]

benefices than Bateman's statutes allowed; it is significant that Dorington and Holland had served with Warner and Spenser as key-keepers in the years leading up to the expulsions: cf. n. 99 above. For Dorington's two livings, see *B.H.* I, p. 50.

111 "*demum Ilias malorum consequitur.*" His passionate outburst and appeal to both Homer and the Book of Proverbs in this statute is exceptional and is matched only by his execration in Statute 104 of those subverting the statutes.

112 In addition to Statute 47, see Statute 43 (for disturbance in the hall and the use of stocks, which was one of the actions Warner and Spenser complained of in their petition), Statute 49 (for immediate expulsion for striking the keeper *or president* even lightly) and Statute 104 (for seeking to overturn the founder's statutes).

113 See Parker's first letter to Cecil, 29 December 1565, Appendix C, text (A). The "more part" had also supported Caius in 1559 when he sued three senior fellows of Gonville Hall in the Vice-Chancellor's court: see p. 340, n. 33 above.

114 Cf. Statutes 43, 47, 48 and 56.

115 Cf. Statute 56 ("*ipso facto sint non socii*").

116 Parker to Cecil, 29 December 1565, Appendix C, text (A).

After their expulsion in the summer of 1565 the three fellows turned first to Archbishop Parker for help. No doubt they hoped that he would again persuade Caius to relent and restore them to their fellowships as he had done after Dethick's first expulsion, but although Parker was willing "to deal with the Master to obtain of him more commodity than I take them worthy to have", he flatly refused to press for restitution to their fellowships.[117] He was ready to persuade Caius to expunge the record of their expulsion and to allow them a year's stipend if they resigned their fellowships;[118] and he would have gone further and "bestowed Dethick in some benefice, and the other two in some other fellowships in other colleges".[119]

Parker's generous offer was acceptable to Caius, but it failed to satisfy the three fellows and they sought in the closing weeks of 1565 to appeal formally to the Chancellor of the university, Sir William Cecil. Before he agreed to hear their appeal Cecil sensibly consulted the archbishop. Parker responded on 29 December and, not surprisingly, he was tactful but emphatic in his advice. Although he took the view that both parties were to blame ("the truth is both parties are not excusable from folly"), the three fellows should not have their fellowships restored; their departure could be softened by other "commodities", but Cecil would be unwise even to hear their appeal, since he would "hear such cumbrous trifles and brabbles, that ye shall be weary"; moreover, to hear the appeal would set a dangerous precedent to other colleges.[120]

Cecil was well aware of what Caius had done for the college, for he had assisted him in the re-foundation in 1557 and in the acquisition of the greater part of Tree Court in 1564,[121] and he had no hesitation in accepting Parker's advice: he declined to give the appellants a hearing and on 4 January he issued his ruling. Like Parker, he realised that no peace would come to the college while the three fellows were there, and he directed that Warner should depart within the month and in the meantime should be deprived of "all voice or suffrage" within the college;[122] but he sensibly adopted Parker's suggestion that Dethick, Warner and Spenser "should appear willingly to depart from their fellowships,

117 *Ibid.*

118 On the analogy of the valedictory year which Bateman had allowed to fellows accepting a benefice.

119 Parker's *second* letter to Cecil, 4 January 1566, Appendix C, text (C) below. This second letter shows that Caius had already agreed to "commit the final end to [Parker's] disposition".

120 "If your honour will hear their challenges, ye shall hear such cumbrous trifles and brabbles, that ye shall be weary. And I would not wish particular Colleges (in these times) should learn to have, by forced appellations, a recourse to your authority as Chancellor, for the precedents' sake hereafter. And again, I would not have your time so drawn from better things in the weighty causes of the realm.": Appendix C, text (A) below.

121 *B.H.* III, p. 37; *Annals*, p. 90.

122 Appendix C, text (B) below. The order to leave applied specifically to Warner, but all three expulsions were upheld.

and yet to have one year's profits for their *ultimum vale*: to be borne for Spenser out of Caius' own purse, and for the other two to be borne by the college".[123] Despite this, Cecil's refusal to give them a hearing provoked from Warner and Spenser a petition in which they piteously rehearsed the complaints which they had doubtless put before Parker earlier.[124] They were no more successful with Cecil than they had been with Parker,[125] but, as we have seen, their allegations presented a one-sided picture of Caius' conduct which later centuries – unlike Parker and Cecil – have too readily accepted on trust.

It was during the appeal to Cecil that an ugly element was inserted into the dispute. In the articles which they laid before him the expelled fellows included a charge against Caius which they had carefully omitted to mention to Parker previously: that of "atheism", or in other words idolatrous papistry.[126] Parker only came to hear of this charge after he had sent his first letter to Cecil and he lost no time in responding to it in a way which removed its sting.[127] As the archbishop probably expected and perhaps hoped, Cecil remained unimpressed by the appellants' charge and took no further action on it. Unfortunately for Caius it was to return some years later in the febrile atmosphere of the early 1570s.

The second seven years: 1566–73

Cecil's rejection of the expelled fellows' appeal and his adoption of Parker's sensible advice that they be allowed to depart peaceably with a year's stipend, coupled with his direction that Dorington too should resign his fellowship, was swiftly followed by a prolonged and welcome period of calm in the college. The fact that the change from the turmoil of the first seven years happened so swiftly was clearly due to the insistence of the Chancellor that the expelled fellows should immediately be deprived of "all voice and suffrage" in the affairs of the college and should depart from it within a month; but why the calm lasted until the very last year of Caius' life is less obvious. The traditional explanation has been that the turmoil had been predominantly Caius' fault and that it ceased

123 Parker to Cecil, 4 January 1566, Appendix C, text (C) below. The *ultimum vale* was, in effect, the valedictory year which Bateman's statutes would have given them if they had relinquished their fellowships on obtaining benefices. The direction that Spenser's stipend should be paid out of Caius' own purse should not be taken as a criticism of the Master, as Caius had always paid Spenser's stipend in this way cf. *Pandectae*, fol. 18v.

124 Appendix C, text (D) below.

125 Appendix C, text (E) below. Cecil's order is reproduced in Plates IX and X above.

126 See Parker's second letter to Cecil on 4 January 1566, Appendix C, text (C) below. Warner and Spenser, however, made no mention of atheism in the petition to Cecil that they made immediately after he had refused to hear their appeal: *ibid.*, text (D).

127 For a full account see Appendix C below.

once his behaviour improved as a result of Parker's influence and Cecil's hint that he should be less hasty in future.[128] It would, however, be surprising that the calm lasted unbroken for nearly seven years, if the turmoil had all been due to the irascibility of one old man who suddenly and permanently mended his ways, and the Pandects suggest otherwise: the calm resulted from the removal of a divisive faction in the Fellowship and it was the Fellowship, not the Master, whose attitude changed. Unlike the 'old guard' from Gonville Hall, the remaining fellows appear to have understood and accepted their Master's anxiety to ensure that the college's financial stability was secured for future generations, and Caius found for the first time that he could safely depute the financial management of his re-founded college to fellows whom he could trust.[129] That he could do so would appear to have been due in large measure to one fellow whose contribution to the well-being of the college in those years has gone unnoticed: that fellow was Henry Holland.[130]

Holland came from an established Lincolnshire family and, having entered Gonville Hall as a major pensioner in 1556, he had experienced the squalor and disrepair into which it had fallen. Graduating shortly after Caius became Master, he had been one of the college's young B.A.s from whom Caius had supplemented his meagre fellowship and tutorship in 1561–62. In Michaelmas 1564 he became a key-keeper and, together with Francis Dorington,[131] he took over from Spenser the responsibility for the preliminary payments for the building of Caius Court.[132] In the fraught Michaelmas term 1565, which saw the expulsions of Dethick, Warner and Spenser, Holland was entrusted with responsibility for paying the builders and workmen during Caius' absence in London.[133]

[128] Cecil's principal direction to Caius was that any statute which he proposed to make should always be read and published to the whole fellowship on three separate days before it came into force: Appendix C, text (E) below.

[129] There appears to have been a striking change in Caius' practice after the expulsions. In earlier years he seems to have reimbursed the college for any expenditure *after* it had been paid out of the chest on his behalf (*Pandectae*, fol. 18v); in 1566, in what was clearly a surprising new development for the fellows then in college (who carefully attested the event), he started to transmit money to them in sealed bags with specific directions that it was to be held to be delivered or used at his future direction (*ibid.*, fols. 22, 23; see Plate XI); for a later letter in 1569 from Henry Holland to Caius in London, seeking urgent approval for use of such deposited money, see *B.H.* III, p. 50: "If you come not home quicklye we shall be driven to unseal some of the bags of gold sealed."

[130] *B.H.* I, p. 39.

[131] Then president and bursar.

[132] Caius had carefully arranged for the early acquisition of materials for the building of Caius Court in the spring and summer of 1564 and Spenser had been responsible as a key-keeper for the advances made from the chest for the purpose until Caius returned to Cambridge for the Queen's visit in August; but after the audit at Michaelmas that year Dorington and Holland had taken over the responsibility from Spenser: *Pandectae*, fols. 18v–19.

[133] *Pandectae*, fol. 21v. The payments made by the key-keepers recorded in the Pandects were advanced out of the college's money in the chest and were subsequently repaid to the college by

When Dorington had to resign in the latter part of 1566,[134] Holland became sole bursar and he continued to hold the office for a further four unbroken years. Throughout that time the Pandects show a striking improvement in the precision and detail with which a note was kept of payments into and from the chest, and they show, too, that the improvement was due to Holland's punctilious discharge of the bursarship.[135] In April 1570 he handed over responsibility for the expenditure on the next phase of Caius' plans for the expansion of the college – the building of the walls in what would become Tree Court – to Stephen Perse (an inspired choice by Caius, given the fact that Perse had only just become a fellow).[136] Holland finally relinquished office and returned to his native Lincolnshire in the course of the summer of 1570.[137] On his departure his work was shared between four fellows, two as bursars and two to oversee the remaining building work.[138]

The responsibility which Holland shouldered was exceptionally heavy, but the significance of his work lies not in its volume, but in the beneficial impact it had on the relations between the Master and the Fellowship. Caius now had a bursar (and eventually a president) in whom he could have complete confidence and to whom he was able to entrust responsibility for the management and preservation of the college's reserves, leaving him free to resume his professional

Caius out of money of his own which he sent or brought up from London; his reimbursements are noted in the margin of the Pandects.

134 Cecil's ruling had required Dorington to relinquish his fellowship before 26 March 1566 (Appendix C, texts (B) and (E)), but he was still in office as bursar in September that year, when he made a part payment of the very considerable debt he had incurred in that office (*Pandectae*, fol. 24v). The fact that he was unable to settle his debt for a further two years (*ibid.*, fol. 28v) justifies Caius' concern over the management of the college's finances by its officers during his first seven years as Master.

135 See the Pandects from Michaelmas 1565 to Michaelmas 1570 (fols. 21v onwards). For almost five years Holland carefully appended his signature to each withdrawal and to any extraordinary receipt (*e.g.*, fol. 28v: see Plate XII). After the completion of the west side and start of work on the east side of Caius Court in September 1565, Holland's attention and payments were principally directed to the building of the tower and turret staircase to the Master's rooms until Michaelmas 1567. Characteristically, when the work was complete Holland calculated the total of all the moneys that he had taken down from the chest for the work on the turret from April 1566 to Michaelmas 1567 (£141. 10s. 1d.), then the amount actually expended (£133. 4s. 7d.), and recorded "So he oweth the College £8. 5s. 6d." (*Pandectae*, fol. 26v). Neither Dethick nor Dorington ever took such care: both left office owing money to the college which remained unpaid for inordinate periods of time. See, too, the detailed account of the expenditure on the building of Caius Court which Holland sent to Caius in London on 16 May 1569: *B.H.* III, p. 50.

136 Perse had entered the college in 1565 and had graduated in 1568–69 (*B.H.* I, p. 57); Venn states that he became a fellow at Michaelmas 1571, but Perse had clearly done so by April 1570 when he took over responsibility for the building work from Holland: *Pandectae*, 2 April 1570 and ff.

137 He became vicar of Boston, his home town: *B.H.* I, p. 39.

138 Henry Hammond (*B.H.* I, p. 46) and John Staller (*ibid.*) became bursars, while John Tracie (p. 65) and Stephen Perse (p. 57) took over payments for the buildings.

practice and work for the college in London:[139] it is a mark of that confidence that Holland continued for four years to discharge the office of bursar alone and, apparently, made all withdrawals from the chest during that period. It would have been clear to Caius that Holland understood and sympathised with his conception of the college as a corporate entity which existed, not for the benefit of individual members or a particular generation, but for posterity.[140] The striking contrast between the calm which reigned after January 1566 and what preceded it is testimony to the friendly relations with the entire fellowship which Caius was now able to enjoy.

The outrage of 1572[141]

The calm in Caius' college appears to have lasted well into the year 1572. In contrast to the position within the college, however, the two universities had by that time begun to experience the rising strength of anti-Catholic feeling in the country; this intensified in the years which followed the flight of the Scottish Queen Mary to England in 1568, the Northern Rebellion the next year and the excommunication of Elizabeth in 1570.[142] Rumours of plots and

139 He appears to have negotiated the purchase of the manors of Bincombe and Oborne in London and to have raised the finance for it there (where he arranged for loans from the College of Physicians and his old friend William Barker: *Pandectae*, 30 November 1570). He became President of the College of Physicians for the ninth time in 1571 and in March 1572 he successfully represented that college before the Queen's commissioners in its dispute with the barber-surgeons.

140 This view of the college runs throughout Caius' statutes and is most clearly expressed in Statute 63: see "*Dividends*", § VI. 5, at p. 479 below. As Caius noted gratefully in his *Annals* (p. 89), Holland had shown his concern for the future of the college with the gift of an elegant window in his room in Gonville Court in 1563; he made a second gift in 1581, ten years after he left the college: *ibid.*, p. 191.

141 This was a humiliating affront to an elderly and widely respected physician, and it has been termed a catastrophe (Brooke, *History*, p. 75). The implication of disloyalty as well as the outrage to him personally must have been a terrible shock to him, but, apart from its traumatic effect on Caius individually, it had surprisingly little impact. In London, Burghley and Parker took no action upon it and Caius seems to have remained on friendly terms with them and other dignitaries such as the Chief Justice, Sir Robert Catlin C.J.K.B. In Cambridge, it led to no changes in the college, unlike similar events in King's three years earlier (cf. note following), and in the university it evoked no comment. It seems to have been generally accepted that his retention of the objectionable objects had no sinister implication. Is it fanciful to see a belated apology in the action of the same Vice-Chancellor and many other members of the university in meeting Caius' coffin at the town boundary six months later (*Annals*, pp. 187–8)?

142 In Oxford the Warden and fellows of All Souls had been ordered in 1567 to melt down their 'superstitious' plate and send up to London their books for mass and other services: *Correspondence of Matthew Parker*, ed. J. Bruce and T.T. Perowne (Parker Society, 1853), pp. 296–8. In Cambridge the Provost of King's, Philip Baker, had been expelled in June 1569

the fear of popery increased sharply in 1572 in the wake of the news of the St Bartholomew's massacre in Paris, and with that news the strident voice and power of Puritanism.[143] It was inevitable that a Master such as Caius, whose interest in the past, affection for ceremonial and very apparent delight in symbolism were as well-known in London as in Cambridge, should have become the target of puritanical attack, however amicable his relations with his fellows might be within his college. The character of that attack is well evidenced by the anonymous and undated "Articles concerning the preposterous government of Dr Caius, and his wicked abuses in Gonville and Caius College" which found its way to Lambeth Palace.[144] Venn ascribed the paper to the time of the earlier expulsions; but the puritanical (and virulent) character of its complaints against Caius' actions and its attack on his statutes as being "corrupt, contrary to God's true religion and repugnant to the laws of our sovereign lady the Queen" suggest that it was written much nearer 1572. Whatever its date, it is clear that attacks of this nature were becoming more vociferous in Caius' last year.[145]

The attacks culminated in a single, shocking event on 13 December 1572: the ransacking of the Master's rooms in college and the destruction of the "popish trumpery" found there. That event occurred in the last year of Caius' life and it has been viewed, by Venn and others, as the culmination of a protracted dispute between the Master on the one side and the Fellowship on the other that had run throughout his tenure of the office. It has already been argued that Venn's picture of a continuously fractious relationship between Master and fellows was incorrect, and it seems likely that his dramatic account of the outrage of December 1572 in turn presents a distorted picture of that shocking event. We should be cautious before we join with Venn and envisage the Fellowship on that December day as a united body at last rejoicing in its triumph over the Master and enjoying the fun of rummaging through his lodge.[146] In truth, participation in the event was almost certainly confined to a very small number of fellows, if indeed any, and the incident should be seen as one in which the principal perpetrators were ardent and vociferous reformers from outside the college who, being powerful and leading figures in the university, needed little assistance from the fellows.

upon suspicion of holding similar popish views as those charged against Caius: Cooper, *Annals*, II, pp. 244–7. He was accused of keeping "a great heap of Popish pelf" as well as ignoring his duties; he fled abroad rather than face a second visitation and was formally removed in 1570: *Oxford Dictionary of National Biography*, *sub nom.*

143 Ironically it was a Caian who was among the first to bring the news of the massacre to London: Nicholas Faunte (*B.H.* I, p. 69).

144 Lambeth MS 720 (among end papers); *B.H.* III, p. 46.

145 Caius' name was included in a list of papists in a protest in 1572 against the popish character of the College of Physicians: P. Grierson, *B.H.* VII, p. 524, n. 11, citing G.N. Clark, *History of the Royal College of Physicians of London*, I (Oxford, 1964), pp. 129–30.

146 *B.H.* III, p. 54; and see n. 158 below.

Caius had become Master just two months after the Catholic Queen Mary had died, and, given his reverence for the past and his love of such of its works as had survived, it is not surprising that he had carefully preserved the chapel vestments and ornaments which he found there when he returned; and when he converted the oratory into the counting-house and had in consequence to find a new home for its contents, it was only natural that he should find a home for them in his rooms. In truth it was no more a symbol of defiance that he did not destroy them than it was that he did not destroy the stained glass windows in the chapel and hall which asked for prayers for the donors' souls; but by 1572 the apparently secret preservation of "popish trumpery" and such objects "as might have furnished divers [celebrants of mass] at one instant"[147] had become more ominous, since any restoration of the mass now clearly implied the necessity for a change of monarch.

In the course of the Michaelmas term 1572 the unrelenting and increasingly powerful reformer Edwin Sandys, bishop of London,[148] became aware of Caius' retention of the objectionable objects and wrote to the Vice-Chancellor demanding that they be destroyed. The message was clear and the recipient, Dr Thomas Byng,[149] dared not ignore it. The events that followed during the afternoon of 13 December are best recounted in his letter to the Chancellor, now Lord Burghley, on the following day.

> I am further to give your honour advertisement of a great oversight of D. Caius, who hath so long kept superstitious monuments in his college, that the evil fame thereof caused my lord of London to write very earnestly to me to see them abolished. I could hardly have been persuaded that such things had been by him reserved. But causing his own company to make search in that college I received an inventory of much popish trumpery; as vestments, albs, tunicles, stoles, manacles, corporal-cloths, with the pyx and sindon,[150] and canopy, besides holy water stoups, with sprinklers, pax,[151] censers, superaltaries, tables of idols, mass books, portases,[152] and grails,[153] with other such stuff as might have furnished divers massers[154] at one instant. It was thought good by the whole consent

[147] See the letter of Dr Byng to Burghley below.

[148] As Master of St Catharine's Hall and Vice-Chancellor, Sandys had been a fervent supporter of the duke of Northumberland's attempt to exclude Mary Tudor from the throne, and after Elizabeth's accession and the rise of Northumberland's son, the earl of Leicester, Sandys' influence had grown as Parker's health deteriorated.

[149] Thomas Byng, Master of Clare 1571–99, Admiralty Advocate 1572, Regius Professor of Civil Law 1574–99, Dean of Arches 1595.

[150] A shroud for the pyx.

[151] An osculatory used at mass.

[152] A portable breviary.

[153] Chalices.

[154] Celebrants.

> of the heads of houses, to burn the books and such other things as served most for idolatrous abuses, and to cause the rest to be defaced; which was accomplished yesterday with the willing hearts, as appeared, of the whole company of that house.[155]

It is clear from Byng's account of the incident that the physical destruction of the books and the chapel ornaments was the work of the representatives of the university, rather than members of the college, and that he was the person primarily responsible as its principal officer in Cambridge. It is less clear precisely what part was in fact played by members of the college. A member of the college – or possibly a former member, for Caius' preservation of "much popish trumpery" can hardly have been a secret[156] – provided the inventory on the strength of which Byng felt justified in taking the extreme step of thrusting himself and a throng of other leading members of the university into a college uninvited by its governing body and blatantly, without the consent of its head and during his absence in London.[157] In his letter to the Chancellor Byng was careful to counter any possible rebuke by asserting that he had had "the whole consent of the heads of houses" and that it was done with the assent of "the whole company of that house"; and his assertion has led Venn and others to charge the whole fellowship, or at least the greater part of it, with complicity in the affair.[158] It must be remembered, however, that Byng was writing to justify his actions to the most influential man in the country less than six months after that person had been angered by the disturbances which had scarred the dispute between the Caput and the heads of houses on the one side and the young Regent Masters on the other – a dispute in which Caius had been one of the university's representatives who had been deputed to put the case on behalf of the Caput and heads of houses.[159] Byng was clearly anxious to assure Burghley that there had been no unwelcome intrusion and no disturbance – hence his assurance that all had been done with the willing hearts of the whole company of that house, a statement which he carefully qualified by adding that it appeared so to him. It may well be that none of the half-dozen or so fellows who were in college at the

[155] *Cambridge University Transactions during the Puritan Controversies*, ed. J. Heywood and T. Wright (1854), vol. I, pp. 124–5, transcribing Lansdowne MS, 15, art. 64; *B.H.* III, p. 53 (spelling modernised).

[156] Byng would have been a close acquaintance of William Clarke, for both were then at Clare and both were civil lawyers; Byng succeeded Clarke as Regius Professor of Civil Law two years later.

[157] As late as 2 December documents were sent to Caius in London, where he had been in June and throughout the Michaelmas Term: *Pandectae*, 2 December 1572.

[158] "Remembering what were the relations between most of the fellows and their master, we can well believe with what 'willing hearts' they set about the business, and how they must have enjoyed the fun of rummaging through the lodge in the hunt for the 'massing abominations' which they had so long denounced.": *B.H.* III, p. 54.

[159] The four heads were Whitgift, Perne, Mey and Caius; they had appeared finally before Parker, Grindal and Sandys: see "*The Master's Negative Voice*", § VI. 2 below.

time felt able to express opposition to the action of their Vice-Chancellor and the other heads of houses and university officers,[160] but we can be certain that there were some who would not have had willing hearts. In fact it is far easier to pick out fellows who would not have had any truck with the outrage than it is to identify any who would have done so. We can be sure that Caius' particular friends, Robert Churche and Edmund Hownd, would not have done so;[161] and we may be reasonably confident that the president, John Tracie, and the young Stephen Perse, to whom Caius had only recently entrusted the completion of his building projects, would not have done so either.[162]

In contrast, surviving records do not reveal which, if any, of the then fellows were zealous reformers either during their time in college or in later life. Our only clues are to be found in the account of the incident which is contained in the Annals. In it the writer (who presents himself as Caius but may not have been)[163] lays the blame for the actual work of destruction firmly upon Byng and the heads of the two royal colleges, John Whitgift of Trinity and William Goode of King's, but he also refers darkly to the part played by "certain disaffected fellows" (*quibusdam male affectis sociis*). Of these, he added, God had since carried off some by death and had removed others with ignominy; but only one fellow appears to have died before Caius himself,[164] and no others seem to have suffered ignominy during the remaining months of Caius' lifetime. Who these disaffected fellows were is unknown, but they cannot have been many;[165] moreover, Caius carefully limited his remark to "certain fellows", and it is only by conflating his account with Byng's that one can conclude with Venn that "most of the fellows" were ranged against the Master with willing hearts.[166] From what we know of the Fellowship at the time the opposite appears far more likely.

160 There were only four resident fellows the following term: cf. n. 172 below.

161 *B.H.* I, pp. 58, 62. Caius singled them out with legacies in his will, and they later proved staunch supporters of his successor, Legge. Hownd was a major pensioner at the time of the incident; he became a fellow soon after it.

162 *Ibid.*, pp. 65 and 57.

163 The characteristic style and sentiments expressed would suggest that the account in the Annals was written by Caius, but it includes a reflection on the subsequent fate of the evil-doers, whereas Caius survived the event by only seven months. *Pace* Venn, the uniform penmanship of the "original" manuscript of the Annals (MS 756/371) over many years suggests that it was a professional copy made in the later years of Legge's mastership; the passage about the sacking of the lodge may possibly, therefore, have been written after Caius' death.

164 Henry Raghet (*B.H.* I, p. 66).

165 In addition to Raghet and the four well-disposed fellows already mentioned, the only known fellows at the time seem to have been Richard Tompson (*ibid.*, p. 60) and just possibly Nicholas Edwards (p. 65) and John Clarke (p. 70). None of these was still in the college in the following term, when the only resident fellows were Tracie, Perse, Churche and Hownd: *Pandectae*, 1 March 1573. Staller, who had been bursar with Hammond in the previous year, 1571–72, had left to take a college living at Michaelmas; and Hammond seems to have left then too.

166 *B.H.* III, p. 54.

As we have seen, relations between Caius and the fellows had improved greatly in the years following the Chancellor's refusal in 1566 to reverse the expulsion of the last of the disaffected members of the society. During the five years from 1566 to 1571 Caius' energies had been absorbed in his work in London and he had had sufficient confidence in the fellows to entrust to them the physical implementation of his plans for the enlargement of the college – the completion of his new Caius Court, the building of the turret staircase to his lodge, the construction of the Gate of Virtue, the laying-out of the fellows' and other gardens in what was to become Tree Court, and the adapting of the houses there which he had just purchased from Trinity College. None of these projects was controversial and if we may judge from the correspondence that passed between Caius and the fellows when he was away from Cambridge it would seem that they co-operated very willingly in his enterprises.[167]

Against this background it would be surprising if the whole of the Fellowship was as united in animosity towards the Master as Venn would have us believe. The present argument that the animosity from outside the college displayed in the events of 13 December was not shared by most fellows is strengthened by the striking gesture of support which the Fellowship had made on 1 September 1572, just three months before the outrage. On that day a majority of the fellows voted to give Caius the authority to nominate his successor as Master. This was a power which Caius did not have, even though he was a founder; for, unlike Bateman, who had reserved to himself during his lifetime the power to appoint or remove the Master, Caius did not enjoy the same power, since Bateman's statutes (Statute 3) had provided that the election of a Master should be made by the fellows of the college and the 1557 charter prohibited Caius from making any conflicting provision. Given Caius' known affection for the past and his lack of sympathy with novel views, coupled with the certainty that he would not nominate a godly-minded reformer, it is highly unlikely that a majority of the fellows would have deputed the choice of new Master to him if they had been such fanatical Puritans as Venn depicted them.[168]

On 1 January 1573, three weeks after the outrage, Caius subscribed his name to the final edition of his statutes. When he did so, he gave vent to his indignation at the sacking of his rooms by striking out the appointment in Statute 25 of the Provost of King's College, one of the three principal perpetrators of the outrage, as one of the two superintendents of his fellows and scholars; but he made no similar alterations touching upon fellows or other members of his own

[167] *Ibid.*, p. 50.

[168] It seems likely that the decision to delegate was not undisputed (see Brooke, *History*, p. 87, n. 28); but that does not necessarily indicate animosity towards Caius, for three months earlier four fellows of whom two were his close friends (Hownd and Churche) and two were bursars at the time (Hammond and Staller) had opposed the new university statutes of which Caius was a leading exponent: Lamb, *Letters* (1838), p. 359.

college, and even as regards the Provost, he seems to have relented and directed the restoration of his appointment.[169] A few days later he left Cambridge and returned to his house in London. He was no doubt, in Brady's words, "much grieved and disturbed at the furious and rash zeal of those times",[170] but he did not waste time dwelling upon the outrage; instead, he immediately turned to what was for him the far more congenial subject of the history of the university and its colleges.[171] He continued to keep in mind the financial well-being of the college, however,[172] and despite the remarks in the Annals, he does not appear to have harboured any resentment against its fellows and other members either in his will or when he came back to the college for the last time in June 1573. Having resigned the mastership to Thomas Legge on 27 June he returned to London, where he died on 29 July 1573.[173]

[169] See *Caius and the Provost of King's* in "*Supplementary Notes to Caius' Statutes*", § IV. 3, at p. 290 above.

[170] Brady, *Extracts* (1), p. 23, in MS 617/549 fol. 12.

[171] He had Edward III's licence for the exchange properties with Corpus in 1353 sent to him in London on 21 January: *Pandectae*, 21 January 1573.

[172] On 1 March 1573, during a return visit to the college, he formally executed an acquittance discharging the college of "all suche money, as I have laid oute for the purchase of the Manors of Bincombe & Woborne" and received from the four resident fellows (Tracie, Perse, Churche and Hownd) a mutual discharge for any reimbursements made to him by the college: *Pandectae*, 1 March 1573 (Plate XIII). For Bincombe and Oborne, see Gross, *B.H.* IV(2), pp. 8–9.

The money which Caius advanced for the purchase of Bincombe and Oborne and for which he waived repayment shortly before his death would have brought to more than £3,500 the total amount of his financial generosity to his college. He spent £1,144. 4s. from 1557 to 1563, mainly spent on buying estates (*Annals*, p. 80; *B.H.* III, p. 42); this was followed by £1,834. 4s. 2d. from 1564 to 1573, again largely spent on building (*Annals*, p. 186; *B.H.* III, p. 52). Caius also contributed £66 for a staircase and other building work by foregoing his Master's stipend and allowances for seven years up to 1566 (*Annals*, p. 122). At his death, a further £240 (from the £400 entrusted to his executors) was given to provide cooking fuel for the kitchen, together with wages of the porter, and was invested in a manor at Caxton (*B.H.* IV(2), p. 31); and a further £175. 14s. 1d. was spent posthumously on building work (*Annals*, p. 187; *B.H.* III, p. 53). To the total recorded expenditure must be added the books he gave to the library.

[173] Sadly, he seems to have become estranged from his impoverished surviving sister, for she and her family were omitted from his will: cf. n. 2 above and *B.H.* III, pp. 391–2. Why this was so is a mystery, since one of his sister's daughters died at his London house.

VI

Aftermath

VI. 1

The Fellowship and the Governing Body

The establishment: twelve, thirteen or fourteen fellows?

In the years that followed the death of John Caius it became the undisputed belief of the college that nine fellowships had been founded prior to the re-foundation of the college in 1557 and that Caius had added three more, thereby producing an establishment of twelve, a number which prevailed ever afterwards. It comes as a surprise therefore to find two indisputable facts which appear at first sight to conflict with that unchallenged belief: first, there were *ten* fellows of Gonville Hall at the time of the re-foundation in 1557 and, second, Caius provided specifically in his statutes that there should be *thirteen* or more fellows in his new college.[1]

The ten fellows of Gonville Hall were identified by name in the charter and it expressly continued them as fellows of the new college. The charter also recorded Caius' intention at the time of providing funds for only two further fellowships, not three, thereby increasing the total complement to twelve. Caius himself was of course fully aware that the Hall had ten, not nine, fellows at the time when the charter was prepared and he assumed that there had been seven benefactors who had each established a fellowship, in addition to three original fellowships on the ancient foundation that had been envisaged by Gonville and funded by Bateman (for Caius, "the Reverend Father"). In the months following the grant of the charter he drafted statutes for his new college in that belief, and he provided in his draft of (what later became) Statute 2, *De Fundatione Collegii*, that there should be a Master and twelve fellows, of whom the Master and three fellows would be on the Reverend Father's ancient foundation, *two* on his own foundation and seven on those of other benefactors, together with any further fellowships that might later be established either out of his own generosity or

[1] Statute 2. When Henry VIII's Commissioners made their returns in 1546 they listed no fewer than eleven fellowships, by attributing two, not one, to John Bayly, but they may have been guilty of conscious inflation in their anxiety to protect the colleges from the same fate as chantries: *Documents*, I, pp. 229–30.

that of others.[2] He repeated the arithmetic (3+2+7=12) in the grant to his new college of the three manors of Croxley and Snellshall, Runcton and Burnham Thorpe on 1 March 1558.[3]

Within a year Bacon had died, and Caius became Master on 24 January 1559. He seems immediately to have busied himself with the affairs of the college and, in particular, with its history. By the time he had completed his first volume of Annals in the early 1560s he had come to the conclusion that fellowships had been created only by six benefactors in addition to the three by the Reverend Father and that a tenth fellow had been elected in error in recent times, hinting darkly, though opaquely, that this had been done reprehensibly ("*falso persuadentium, sed quo authore aut stipendio nescentium*") since Buckenham's mastership.[4] By the time he was writing his second volume of Annals, Caius had resolved to endow a third fellowship in addition to the two he had already specified in 1558, thereby expressly raising the establishment to thirteen in 1562.[5] By this time, however, a genuine seventh benefactor had appeared on the scene. This was Thomas Wendy, who had died in 1560 and had left the rectory of Haslingfield to the college after the death of his wife, but had done so on elaborate terms which would give his heirs both a perpetual right to possession of the rectory in fee farm and the advowson and thus would leave the college with no more than a fee farm rent of £10 to support a fellowship.[6] At the time of Wendy's death Caius recognised that this would bring the potential establishment up to fourteen fellows so long as the erroneous tenth fellowship survived, and to thirteen if it did not.[7] It is doubtful, indeed, whether Caius ever contemplated that the erroneous tenth fellowship would in fact survive beyond the duration of the fellowships of the ten individuals who had been

2 *Documents*, II p. 322. Caius would have been aware that Gonville had specified that there should be four fellowships; he was later to assert that Bateman had funded only three of them and that the fourth had withered away ("*evanuerat*") until *c.* 1395, when it had been funded by Sir Ralph Hemenhale and thereafter came to be called Lady Mary Pakenham's fellow: *Annals*, p. 16. It is clear from the 1546 returns cited in the previous note that Caius was transmitting a belief which was already established (*Documents*, I, p. 230). It was never disputed after Caius' time that only three fellowships were supported on the ancient foundation (*ex antiqua fundatione*): see *B.H.* III, pp. 213–14.

3 *Annals*, p. 73.

4 *Ibid.*, pp. 20, 86. One wonders whether this was yet another reflection on the shortcomings of his predecessor, Bacon.

5 *Ibid.*, pp. 60, 86–7. Earlier in the Annals he asserts that he had always intended to create three fellowships (*ibid.*, p. 42), but he does not mention that only two had been specified both in the charter in 1557 and also in the draft statutes and the conveyance of the manors in the following year.

6 *Annals*, pp. 83–4. Thomas Wendy [*B.H.* I, p. 24] was perhaps the most distinguished member of the college of the day, having been a former fellow and physician to four monarchs; for his benefaction see *B.H.* III, pp. 217–18. His widow, Margaret, died in 1570.

7 *Ibid.*, p. 87.

named in the charter and whose tenure he was constrained to honour by the terms of the third foundation.[8] Wendy's widow predeceased Caius, dying in 1570, and it became possible for him to contemplate a genuine seventh benefactor's fellowship: accordingly, in the final edition of his statutes Caius amended the arithmetic of Statute 2, *De fundatione Collegii*, to take account of the fact that he was now funding three fellowships of his own, but he was able to leave the number of fellowships furnished by benefactors at seven, thereby establishing, with the three on the ancient foundation, an establishment of thirteen. The precise size of the establishment, however, was not an issue during Caius' lifetime, for he appears to have made rather few elections to fellowships in the closing years of his mastership: only four fellows were available on 1 March 1573 to execute a discharge of liabilities between Caius and the college in respect of the purchase of Bincombe and Oborne,[9] and less than two years after his death there were only eight fellows to join his successor, Thomas Legge, in signing the college's acceptance of Archbishop Parker's *Interpretatio* in January 1575.[10] It was therefore not until the decade following Caius' death that the issue became a matter of dispute for the only time before the repeal of his statutes in 1860.

The issue arose in 1582 in relation to the fellowship for which Thomas Wendy had provided an annual income after the death of his widow.[11] The provisions of the will, however, soon provoked a long-drawn-out dispute with the benefactor's nephew and heir. Precisely what happened during the ten years following Margaret's death is unclear, but it would seem that at least one election to the fellowship was made and that Caius' own godson, Richard Gerrard, was elected to it.[12] If so, it did not last long, for the dispute led to Wendy's nephew ceasing to make the annual payment. As a result Gerrard appears in his correct order of seniority on the list of thirteen fellows in Michaelmas 1581 in the earliest surviving volume of commons accounts, but he does so without any stipend and with an unpaid commons debit of 43s. 3½d.;[13] he appears again in the accounts for the following Lady Day, 1582, still without a stipend and this time with an increased commons debit of 49s. 11½d. By now he had become the

8 *Ibid.*, p. 20. The *Libri Rationales* for the period before 1571 have not survived and it is not known at what rate the tenth fellow was paid his stipend; for these differences in stipend see below.

9 Tracie, Perse, Churche and Hownd: *Pandectae*, 1 March 1573; Plate XIII above.

10 See Matthew Parker's *Interpretatio*, § IV. 2, at p. 279 above; of the eight fellows, only Robert Churche, Stephen Perse, John Tracie and Edmund Hownd had been elected fellows in Caius' time. The paucity of fellows at the time of Caius' death helps to explain the well-known fact (not infrequently charged against him) that Thomas Legge brought in a number of members of his own and other colleges as fellows in the first years of his mastership.

11 Caius had originally envisaged this as becoming the college's fourteenth fellowship, but his later acceptance that there had been only nine funded fellowships in Gonville Hall and that the tenth had been an error meant that the Wendy's fellowship was now indisputably the thirteenth.

12 *B.H.* III, p. 61. In his complaint against Legge Gerrard claimed the credit for persuading the younger Thomas Wendy ever to make any payment: *Gerrard's Case* (1582), Appendix D below.

13 *Lib. Rat.*, Michaelmas 1581.

leading figure in a bitter dispute between the puritanical younger fellows on the one side and the tolerant Thomas Legge, who was in their eyes an excessively papistical Master, and the more senior of the fellows on the other.[14] By 1582 Legge's very great patience had finally run out and Gerrard was declared to be no longer a fellow: the main charge levelled against him was that he had held a disqualifying benefice for more than the permissible year and had thereby ceased to be a fellow. In his appeal to the Chancellor, Lord Burghley, Gerrard sought to answer the charge by claiming that he was a Wendy fellow and was not subject to the same provisions against holding benefices as applied to those on Caius' own foundation; but at the same time he claimed that the college was under an obligation under Caius' statutes to maintain thirteen fellowships and that the lapse of his Wendy fellowship from lack of funds required the college to furnish him with a replacement.[15] Gerrard was unsuccessful in his claim and departed from the college in 1583, still owing the college his unpaid commons bill. Thereafter the Wendy fellowship lapsed for thirty years[16] and the number twelve became the accepted establishment of fellows, notwithstanding Statute 2: three fellows on the ancient foundation of Gonville and Bateman; three upon Dr Caius' foundation; and six, not seven, on those of benefactors.[17] It was to retain the pattern of these three classes until the repeal of Caius' statutes in 1860.

No distinction between the three classes was made so far as seniority and the government of the college were concerned. Numerous provisions requiring action or agreement by the 'major part' of the Fellowship were contained in Caius' statutes, in some cases a majority of all the fellows and in others merely a majority of those present in the college or in this country;[18] but he did not distinguish in any way between different classes of fellow (apart from those in their first, probationary year)[19] any more than Gonville and Bateman had done. Consequently his statutes, like the charter under which they were made, have the same constitutional ring to them as our modern statutes: fellows might have different stipends, duties and tenure, but together they constituted the governing body of the college and they all enjoyed the same voting rights in that body.

14 See *Gerrard's Case* (1582), Appendix D below. See also Venn's account of Legge's mastership in *B.H.* III, pp. 64–9.

15 Even apart from his tenure of a benefice, Gerrard was on weak ground, for both Caius and Wendy had restricted their fellowships to Norfolkmen, and Gerrard appears to have been born at Harrow in Middlesex.

16 The dispute with Wendy's nephew and executor which caused the fellowship to lapse was not settled until 1610 and no further election to the Wendy fellowship could be made until after that date.

17 *Acta* 1594 (*Exiit Book* 1592–1618): see Plate XIV above.

18 Statutes 13, 43, 47, 56, 59, 80, 103; (present in college) 34, 48, 81, 92; (not overseas) 3; (*all* fellows) 54, 86.

19 Statute 13.

As is well known, however, the position was in fact very different for all but the first thirty years of the three centuries during which the college was governed by Caius' statutes. From 1592 onward the government of the college was conducted by the Master and the holders of the twelve fellowships created before that date – the twelve "senior fellows" – to the total exclusion of the holders of fellowships created later who were, in contrast, categorised as "junior fellows".

The decree on the Frankland fellows

The restriction of the government of the college to the Master and the twelve senior fellows flowed from the decision in December 1592 to deny to holders of the new fellowships endowed by Joyce Frankland any participation in the business of the college, thus treating them in effect as bye-fellows: "they are not to participate in College business with the other fellows, except in the [weekly] rendering of account by the steward each Saturday".[20] No reason for this dramatic decision was offered in the decree of 11 December 1592, and it is baffling to formulate any argument by which it could be justified however speciously. The charter and Caius' statutes had mentioned specific figures in relation to the number of fellows, but both documents expressly recognise and allow that the number might be increased by the provision of additional fellowships by future benefactors, and neither contemplates any distinction in the constitutional powers and position of separately funded fellowships: on the contrary, they clearly envisaged continued equality. However, if the justification for the exclusion of the Frankland fellows is obscure, the motivation is clear: the new foundation would have added no less than six additional votes and radically altered the constitutional structure of the college – with the prospect of unremitting pressure for an equal share in dividends, allowances and emoluments.

The decree left many questions unanswered. To what should any surplus in annual revenue from Mrs Frankland's property be directed, if not to the fellows and scholars on her foundation? Were the new fellows subject to all the obligations imposed on fellows by Bateman's and Caius' statutes in respect of, for example, attendance at prayers and lectures, residence, care of pupils, enjoyment of benefices and communal meals? And were they fellows for all the purposes of the university's and college's statutes? Their status was left unclear, and the college remained uncertain for nearly forty years whether they should even be admitted as fellows, and indeed whether the Master had any power to admit

20 "*Non intersint Collegii negotiis cum caeteris sociis, nisi in ratione reddenda per oeconomum singulis diebus sabbati.*" For the Frankland Decree, see Appendix E below.

them in chapel or administer the oath to them.[21] Notwithstanding this uncertainty there does not seem to have been any serious doubt that they were indeed fellows, for the terminology of "senior fellows" and "junior fellows" appears to have been adopted from the beginning, together with the practice of using the new fellowship as an initial step towards a fellowship on the older foundations.[22] The extent to which the senior fellows in later years derived dividends and other benefits from benefactors' funds such as that of Joyce Frankland is discussed elsewhere;[23] but one unforeseen consequence may be noted here. This was the impact that the arrival of the new fellowships came to have upon the Norfolk preference.[24] Joyce Frankland had not imposed any such preference on the choice of her fellows and the result was that there would now be more fellows from 'foreign' counties aspiring to senior fellowships. It is significant that the increasingly bitter arguments over the Norfolk preference in the following century seem often to have involved the competing claims of persons who were already Frankland (or similar) fellows and thus introduced the acrimony of personalities.[25]

The application of the decree to later fellowships

It was not until 1610 that the need to consider the foundation of further fellowships arose again. In that year the college finally reached a compromise with the younger Thomas Wendy, the benefactor's nephew and heir, and was in a position to make further elections to his fellowship. By that time Legge and all but two of those who had participated in the decision of 11 December 1592 had died or left the college, but Stephen Perse and John Gostlin were still fellows and we may conclude that it was they who ensured that the terms of the new agreement should provide that a fellow elected into the Wendy fellowship

> shall not have or expect from the said Colledge by reason of his said Fellowshipp anie dividencye or other profit peculiar or proper to the twelve senior places or Fellowshipps of the foundation of the same Colledge, but shall be in all things of the like order and sort as the Fellowes of Joyce Franklin's foundation within the said Colledge, and as it is set

21 *Cooke's Case* (1636), Appendix G below. The analogy of Statutes 13 and 14 and the probationary year and oath may have affected thinking on the matter.

22 Three of the first six elected became senior fellows within four years; a fourth, Henry Pratt, petitioned James I for a senior fellowship that fell vacant in 1604 and obtained an order in his favour, but apparently to no avail; the other two left the college, one for a living and the other for Rome.

23 See "*Dividends*", § VI. 5 below.

24 See "*The Norfolk Preference*", § VI. 3 below.

25 See, *e.g.*, *Allen's Case* (1617), Appendix F below.

> down and fully expressed in an order made by the executor of the last will and testament of the said Joyce Franklin and the Master or keeper and Fellowes of the said Colledge touching the ordering and direction of the Fellowes and fellowshipps of the foundation of the said Joyce Franklin.[26]

It would have been difficult to spell out more clearly the resolution to maintain the status quo – though it omitted to mention that the executor referred to had been the very same "Master or keeper" with whom the agreement had been made.[27] To make doubly sure, the college was at pains to warn the first Wendy fellow elected that he was being admitted on the very same terms as Frankland fellows, and to record the fact in the *Acta*.[28]

When in 1615 Stephen Perse himself came to provide in his will for the establishment of six fellowships he carefully directed that no Perse fellow "shall for or by reason of such their places have or claime any benefit of dividend or other priviledge but shall be contented with their stipend", though he added a proviso: "except it shall be hereafter thought fit by some supreme authoritie or by the said Colledge to incorporate my said fellows into the body of the said Colledge". It may be noted that he anticipated one question and provided expressly that his fellows should be subject to the statutes of the college and liable to the penalty of expulsion if they should be found by "the Master and most part of the twelve senior fellows of the ancient foundation of the said Colledge for the time being" "to be disobedient to the orders and statutes of the said Colledge".[29] An immutable pattern was set for the election of future fellows: Stokys fellows, Wortley fellows and finally the S.C. Smith fellow were all expressly warned that their admission was made on the same terms as the Frankland fellows and the fact that the warning had been given was carefully recorded in the *Gesta* until the repeal of Caius' statutes in 1860 and the replacement of all distinct and named junior fellowships with uniform unnamed fellowships and the consequent discontinuance of the warning.[30]

26 *Annals*, p. 222.

27 Thomas Legge. See *Annals*, p. 198.

28 See, *e.g.*, *Acta* 10 October 1611 (admission of Allen and Iken); *Annals*, p. 223. Venn (*B.H.* III, p. 209, n. 2) believed that the warning ("*in conditionibus quibus cautum est*") related to the requirement that the newly-elected fellow would not practise in the common law, but it was clearly stated that it related to the conditions that had been agreed between the college and Mrs Frankland's executor as to the status and emoluments of her fellowships, not the subject to be studied.

29 *Annals*, pp. 249–50.

30 See, *e.g.*, *Gesta*, 18 November and 15 December 1857. When the college accepted the Wortley benefaction it was carefully recorded in the *Gesta* and witnessed by the signatures of the Master and the fellows present that the acceptance was conditional upon the application to the new Wortley fellows of the same terms that applied to the Frankland fellows: *Gesta*, 12 October 1769. Such signing of the Gesta was rare.

The emergence of the present governing body

The first act of the statutory Commissioners, in 1858, was to remove from the mastership and from both junior and senior fellowships any restrictions or preference "in respect of such person's place of birth or of his having been a Scholar on any Foundation in the College, or of his being of any particular name, lineage, kindred, or of his being or having been a Scholar at any particular School". In 1860 they went further, on the grounds that the directions of the founders and other benefactors had become "impracticable or inexpedient" and that "it is advisable that the same should be repealed or altered, and that Statutes should be made for the government of the College more adapted to the practice of modern times, and better calculated to promote learning and religious education, and the main designs of the Founders and Benefactors".[31] The funds provided by the various benefactors to support the fellowships and other awards they had established were swept into a single anonymous account, the names of the benefactors were detached from the fellowships and awards and all distinguishing differences in stipend or qualification were eliminated. In their place there was to be a single uniform, anonymous class of thirty fellows to whose fellowships no name or differing characteristics were to be attached, and no restriction as to subject: they were to be the persons thought "to be of the greatest merit, and most fit to be a fellow of the College, as a place of religion, learning and education".

The 1860 statutes[32]

It might be expected that the distinction between senior and junior fellows would also have been swept away in the root-and-branch repeal of Caius' statutes. That did not happen: indeed, the reverse occurred. The resolution of 11 December 1592 excluding the Frankland fellows and giving to the twelve senior fellows the sole government of the college received statutory recognition in 1860 for the first time: "The Government of the College shall be in the hands of the Master and the twelve Senior Fellows, who shall be called the Master and Seniors" (Statute 4). The continuity with the past was emphasised, first, by continuing to restrict to the Master and Seniors the power of electing fellows and, secondly, by maintaining the requirement for any person elected a senior fellow to be re-admitted and make a further declaration in chapel even when he was already a junior fellow and had made one declaration in chapel. The fact that a fellow made a distinct declaration on becoming a Senior was an

31 Preamble, College Statutes 1860.

32 Appendix J below.

indication that participation in the government of the college was an essential part of his senior fellowship in exactly the same way that it had been from the first foundation of the college in 1348: it was neither a right which could be waived nor a duty from which exemption could be granted, and it was a function inherent in the holder's fellowship – as it still is in the mastership – and endured as long as the fellowship did. As will be seen later, the transition from this concept of inescapable membership of the governing body to membership by virtue of election or tenure of an office was not accomplished overnight: it took three complete revisions of the college's statutes (in 1882, 1904 and 1926) and ended only eighty-six years later on the death of the last life-member of the College Council in 1946.[33]

The 1860 statutes did, however, make two important changes that significantly diminished the role of the Seniors in the government of the college: (i) the election of a new Master was thereafter to be made by all the fellows; and (ii) the choice of person to be elected a Senior was for the first time to be confined to those who were already fellows of the college, and in that choice the electors were constrained to elect "the Fellow who may then be first on the Roll of Fellows … unless in the judgment of the Master and Seniors there shall be good cause to the contrary, and in that case, the Fellow next in order on the roll shall be so elected, and so on in succession". While this reflected a custom that had come to be normally adopted since at least the early seventeenth century, it did convert what had been merely an expectation into a statutory 'conditional entitlement' not far short of a right.

The 1882 statutes[34]

The election of Seniors under the 1860 statutes continued until those statutes were in their turn repealed twenty years later and replaced *in toto* in 1882 by new statutes made by the University Commissioners. These were far more radical. The distinct status of senior fellow was to be discontinued for the future, and the concept of government by the Master and twelve Seniors was replaced by that of a "Governing Body" consisting of the Master and twelve fellows which would have "control and management of all the affairs of the College", though subject to specific qualifications. This express vesting of the control and management in the Master and no more than twelve of the fellows made no change in the size of the body that had governed the college since the charter of Philip and Mary and Caius' statutes, but there was a substantial shift in three respects towards the right of the whole fellowship to participate in its government. For the first

33 W.W. Buckland; cf. below.

34 Appendix J below.

time since 1592 it became the right of all fellows to make any proposition "for the more efficient government of the College or the promotion of its interests" and thereby set in motion an entirely novel process by which two-thirds of the persons present at a General Meeting of the Master and all the fellows could adopt the proposition and render it binding on the governing body, subject only to the limitation that it did not contravene any of the college statutes. Secondly, for the first time up to four members of the governing body were to be elected by the General Meeting. The third change was contained in the Act of Parliament under which the new college statutes were made by the University Commissioners: by section 2 of the Universities of Oxford and Cambridge Act 1877 the power of those Commissioners to make statutes for the two universities and their colleges was to continue after they had completed their work and was thereafter to be exercised by a "governing body" comprising "the Master and all actual Fellows being graduates". Thereafter the college would have two different "governing bodies" until 1926: the governing body of the Master and twelve fellows constituted under the college's own statutes to govern it, and an opaquely-defined governing body designated by Act of Parliament for the one purpose of making changes to those statutes.

Under the 1882 statutes the possibility of any future fellows being elected Seniors was eliminated and the dominance of seniority in the government of the college would thus inevitably diminish in the course of time; but for two reasons it took a remarkably long time for that to happen.

(i) As has been explained, the 1860 statutes had converted a junior fellow's traditional expectation of being elected a Senior in due course into a statutory 'conditional entitlement' not far short of a right. As a consequence, when the 1882 statutes preserved existing rights as they were required to do by the enabling Act of Parliament, the relevant clause was framed to preserve not only the right of existing Seniors to membership of the governing body, but also the conditional entitlement of all other existing fellows to be elected Seniors in due course.[35] This meant that younger fellows were still becoming Seniors for several years after 1882 and thus life members of the governing body in addition to those who had already become Seniors before 1878.[36]

[35] Statute 47. The statute preserved the interests of Seniors and other fellows elected before 14 March 1878. The statute expressly provided that "with respect to all such Fellows as are not already Seniors elections to the Seniority shall continue to be made in the manner in which they would have been made if these Statutes had not come into operation." The long delay between the 'cut-off date' and the coming into force of the statutes in 1882 was in part due to a series of objections presented to the Privy Council by the governing body and four junior fellows.

[36] The last election of a Senior appears to have been that of Henry Milton in 1888: *B.H.* II, p. 402.

(ii) The 1882 statutes provided for (up to) four members of the governing body to be elected by the General Meeting, but Statute 3 did this in such a complicated way that it never proved possible for there to be as many as four elected members at any one time. Having specified that the governing body should consist of the Master and twelve fellows, the statute allocated the fellows' places to three classes: first, the Seniors; second, a completely new class of "resident members of the Governing Body by seniority"; and thirdly and lastly, such number of elected members (not exceeding four) as should make up the total to twelve. No rigid number was prescribed for the second class beyond a maximum number of eight, and within that limit the actual size of this new class in any particular year would vary with the number of Seniors: taken with the number of *resident* Seniors it was not to exceed eight, and taken with the number of both resident and non-resident Seniors it should not exceed twelve. The elaborate formula had two purposes: first, gradually to replace the diminishing class of Seniors with resident members by seniority, and, second, eventually to ensure that there would four places for elected members. It partially succeeded in its first purpose; but it could only achieve the second when there ceased to be any *non-resident* Seniors entitled to membership of the governing body.[37] To speed up the process, the statute introduced, for the first time in the history of the college, a right for a Senior – but no one else – to renounce his membership of the governing body and at the same time retain his fellowship;[38] but there continued to be at least one or more non-resident Seniors throughout the lifetime of the 1882 statutes.

The 1904 statutes[39]

The failure of the 1882 statutes to widen the representation of the whole fellowship in the governing body led to increasing pressure for further reform in the final years of Ferrers' mastership. In 1900 it was moved at a General Meeting of the Master and fellows "that the College be governed by a council

[37] The existence of any *non-resident* Seniors entitled to membership caused the combined numbers in classes 1 and 2 to rise above eight, and the existence of such non-resident Seniors meant that there were correspondingly fewer than four places left for elected members. Notable among the non-resident Seniors were Thomas Wiglesworth and Charles Monro: *B.H.* II, pp. 268, 310. Both were lawyers in practice in London and came up for college meetings; Wiglesworth served as Steward of the Manors for many years and Monro as college lecturer in law.

[38] Statute 3(1)(6).

[39] Appendix J below.

composed of the Master and certain Fellows elected by the whole body of the Fellows".[40] The motion was discussed but not pressed to a vote, and the meeting accepted instead the much narrower proposal that the senior tutor, the senior bursar and the senior dean should be members of the governing body *ex officio*. The discussion heralded the acceptance in the following term of proposals for a much more fundamental reform of the governing body: that it should continue to consist of the Master and twelve fellows, and that the latter should comprise (i) the senior tutor, the senior bursar and the senior dean *ex officio*, (ii) six elected members and (iii) three fellows in order of seniority provided they were both resident *and under the age of seventy*.[41] As thus formulated the proposals not only limited the third class to three, but also disregarded the existing rights of the surviving Seniors to membership of the governing body irrespective of age or residence: it was only subsequently accepted "that such Fellows as had rights to seats on the Governing Body before 1878 and are not included under the proposed new Statutes among the six members not subject to election should hold seats as additional members of the Body".[42]

By the time the revised statutes finally emerged in 1904, however, the provisions for the composition of the governing body had been modified very substantially. By then the last non-resident Senior on the governing body had agreed to resign his membership of it[43] and the number of Seniors in residence had fallen to three;[44] the number of resident members by seniority had consequently risen to five.[45] The original proposal mooted in 1900 would have meant that only the first three of the five would have continued to be entitled to membership, and the last two (Buckland and Swete) would not have done so. In the light of the requirement in the enabling Act for the saving of existing

[40] *Gesta*, 30 November 1900.

[41] *Gesta*, 21 January 1901.

[42] *Gesta*, 5 February 1901. This would have had the consequence of reducing the number of elected members to less than six.

[43] Wiglesworth renounced his membership of the governing body in 1904 expressly in order to facilitate the introduction of the 1904 Statutes. He had become a junior fellow in 1850 and was the last surviving senior fellow to have been elected (in 1859) before Dr Caius' statutes were repealed; by the time of his death in 1918 he had been a fellow for longer than anyone else before or after until Joseph Needham (fellow and Master 1924–95) and Philip Grierson (fellow 1935–2006).

[44] John Venn, Edward Gross and John Lock: *B.H.* II, pp. 313, 357, 383. Venn and Gross had become Seniors under the 1860 statutes shortly before 1878 and remained members of the governing body until their deaths in 1923. Lock had been a junior fellow at the time of the cut-off date, 1878, and thus was entitled to become a Senior in 1883 under the concession in the 1882 statutes; he subsequently served for many years as a member of the governing body and senior bursar and died in 1921. E.S. Roberts (*ibid.*, p. 370) had been a fourth Senior until his election as Master in 1903.

[45] Reid, Muir, Gallop, Buckland and Swete: *B.H.* II, pp. 432, 431, 504, 452 and 316 respectively.

interests[46] the college's statute was finally drafted in a way that preserved not only the entitlement of the three Seniors to membership but those of all "such Fellows elected before 9 October 1890 as under the Statutes repealed by these Statutes would have been entitled to be members of the Governing Body otherwise than by election".[47] The opaque reference to this particular date is still to be found in the college's statutes to the present day and has mystified successive generations of fellows; but the choice was in fact of no greater legal significance than its being the day immediately following the election as a fellow of the most junior of the five existing members by seniority, *i.e.*, Professor Swete.[48] In this way the statute ensured that all five of those who were already members of the governing body by seniority retained their right to do so; furthermore, they all did so without becoming subject to the new age-limit of seventy.[49]

In addition, the proposed ordering of the classes of membership of the governing body was reversed. The Seniors and the members by seniority now came first; the number of elected members would therefore rise to six only when the number in the first class dropped to six; and the *ex officio* members were demoted to last place and would become entitled only if and when the number by seniority dropped further to three. In fact six of the fellows entitled to membership for life proved to be very long-lived, and as a result the carefully planned scheme for the membership of the governing body in the 1904 statutes never came fully into effect before those statutes were repealed in 1926 following the passing of the Universities of Oxford and Cambridge Act 1923.

The 1926 statutes[50]

In 1926 the Commissioners were keen to complete the transformation of the governing body into an elected council, and they renamed it the "College Council" in the statutes that they made.[51] These provided that only the Master

46 Universities of Oxford and Cambridge Act 1877, s.34.

47 Statute 3(2).

48 Swete had originally been a senior fellow but had resigned in 1878 on becoming Rector of Ashdon. After a distinguished academic career in London he had been elected an honorary fellow; he was elected Regius Professor of Divinity in 1890 and was re-elected as a fellow on 8 October 1890: *Gesta*, 8 October 1890. He had become a member by seniority by 1904, but, unlike the other four existing members by seniority, Swete was close to seventy years of age by 1904 and would never have regained membership by seniority under the original proposals.

49 They were, however, given the same right as Seniors to resign their membership yet keep their fellowships: Statute 3(4).

50 Appendix J below.

51 It is not known whether the change of terminology was due to the then Master, Sir Hugh Anderson, who was one of the Commissioners, or to their secretary, Henry Holland, who undertook the actual drafting of new statutes for each of the colleges. The minutes of the

and two fellows, the senior bursar and the senior tutor, were to be members *ex officio* and that the other ten fellows were to be elected by the General Meeting for periods not exceeding four years; but in deference to the requirement in the enabling Act of Parliament, their statute included without alteration the existing right to membership of fellows elected before the mystifying date 9 October 1890.

At the end of the Great War in 1918 there had still been six such fellows: three Seniors (Venn, Gross and Lock) and three members by seniority (Reid, Gallop and Buckland), all of whom had been prominent and energetic participants in the government of the college. However, the last Seniors, Venn and Gross, died in quick succession in 1923 and Reid, the most senior of the remaining life members of the old governing body, did so in 1925.[52] This left Gallop and Buckland when the new statutes came into operation and it was their membership that required the continued reference to 9 October 1890.

Gallop died in 1936, and his death left Buckland, who had been elected president in 1923 on the deaths of Venn and Gross, as the last fellow who was a member of the governing council of the college *qua* fellow and not by reason of office or election. His death in 1946 finally brought to an end a concept that had been enshrined in the statutes drafted by Edmund Gonville six hundred years earlier and had been equally a cornerstone of those of Bateman and Caius: that participation in the government of the college was an essential function inherent in a fellowship and inseparable from it.

college's committee that negotiated with the Commissioners contains no comment on this point and remarkably little on any other. The college must have found the double meaning of "Governing Body" in its existing statutes very confusing and doubtless welcomed the change of terminology.

52 Venn and Gross remained members until their deaths in April and August 1923, respectively, the third Senior (Lock) having died two years earlier. Reid remained a member of the governing body until he resigned his membership in February 1925 on account of ill-health, shortly before his death in April. Gallop and Buckland were still members when the 1926 Statutes came into effect.

VI. 2

The Master's Negative Voice

Caius attached great importance to granting an overriding negative voice to the Master, that is, a right to override the vote of a majority of the fellows, and even a unanimous vote, simply by casting a negative vote. In Bateman's statutes the sole provision that could be construed as giving such a vote to the Master had been contained in the statute laying down the procedure in one matter only, that of the election of a fellow; this provision had merely provided that the election should be "agreed by the keeper and the majority of the fellows by way of scrutiny" within a month and that "otherwise the appointment and ordination of the fellow shall belong to the keeper alone on that occasion".[1] Since the vote was to be taken openly by scrutiny the provision was a little ambiguous, and it might be construed literally as the Keeper and a majority of the fellows or else as meaning a majority of the Keeper and fellows.

In contrast Caius accorded to the principle a specific statute of its own and extended it not just to the election of a fellow, but to all the affairs whatsoever of the college (*in rebus ejusdem quibuscunque*).[2] He made no mention, however, of Bateman's 'default provision' for an appointment to a vacant fellowship to be made by the Master alone if no election had been made within the one month, and he did not provide any default provision in his own statutes. His silence meant that, while Bateman's default provision would remain in force in the case of an election to a fellowship, the Master had no default power under either set of statutes in the case of all those other decisions which had, by statute, to be taken by the Master and fellows. The Master's refusal to go along with the majority of the Fellowship in those other cases would therefore not leave the ultimate decision to him:[3] instead it would result in a stalemate, a situation which Caius foresaw and which

1 Bateman's Statute 3: *Of the time and form of Election.*

2 Statute 5.

3 With one unforeseen exception which did not arise until the middle of the eighteenth century. Failure by the college to appoint to an advowson would cause the appointment to default to the bishop of the diocese and he might be the Master at the same time – as happened in the case of Sir Thomas Gooch, who was concurrently Master and bishop of Norwich at the time of an appointment to Mattishall in 1741: *B.H.* III, pp. 119–21.

he assumed would be settled by the pressure of outside opinion and, if necessary, by the Visitors. In the case of a fellowship election, however, a negative vote by a Master, if his concurrence was construed to be essential, would, under Bateman's statute, leave him free to impose his own choice after a month. Whether Caius considered this stark difference between fellowship elections and all other elections and decisions would seem doubtful, given his silence on the matter.

In view of the emphatic nature and wording of Caius' grant of a negative voice to the Master it is at first sight difficult to formulate an argument which could nullify his provision in law: yet we know that the arguments of the fellows prevailed in the only litigation which was later pursued, and we know also that the dispute lingered on for two centuries without ever being authoritatively settled. By what process of legal reasoning was it possible to mount such an effective (and successful) opposition to Caius' statute?

The explanation has to be sought in the oblique way in which Bateman had formulated his own statutes in 1353. He had not done so directly but had instead incorporated twelve of the statutes which he had provided for Trinity Hall, one being the ambiguously worded statute governing the election of fellows quoted above.[4] Bateman had provided for Trinity Hall an *Interpretatio* of this statute and in it he expressly directed that the statute should not be interpreted as giving the Master an overriding negative voice and that it merely required that the Master should have been present and able to express his vote when the election was made by the majority, whether or not that majority included him.[5] In other words, the election was to be made by a majority of the Master and fellows, not by the Master with the concurrence of a majority of the fellows. Bateman did not address one question which was implicitly posed by his *Interpretatio*: if the vote of a majority was sufficient whether or not the Master had concurred in it, what situation did he have in mind when he directed that the election should default to the Master alone after a month if it had not been made by then? Rather curiously, an answer to that question does not seem to have been expressly formulated until 1714, when it was suggested by counsel that Bateman had only intended his default provision to provide for the contingency that the Master and fellows had been unable to achieve *any* majority, whether or not it included the Master.[6]

Caius was well aware of Bateman's *Interpretatio*, as, indeed, others were.[7] He omitted the *Interpretatio* from his 'authoritative' edition of Bateman's statutes,

4 Statute 4 for Trinity Hall; this was Statute 3 for Gonville Hall.

5 See "*The Master's Vote: Bateman's Interpretation (1354)*", Appendix A below.

6 The suggestion was contained in the opinion given by Mr Cheshyre on 11 May 1714 on the occasion of Sir John Ellys's refusal to agree to the fellows' unanimous choice of Ds Morrant for election into a senior fellowship: MS 621/457. That occasion is discussed below and in *B.H.* III, pp. 111–13. It is surprising that this thesis was not advanced earlier by the fellows in *Allen's Case* (1617), but it appears not to have been: see Appendix F below.

7 The passage in Bateman's *Interpretatio* which Caius omitted from MS 711 was set out in full in the slightly later 'rival' manuscript, MS 760, and the fact that the relevant passage is highlighted

MS 711, and expressly provided in Statute 5 that Bateman's interpretation should have no application to Gonville Hall or to the newly re-founded Gonville and Caius College. He argued forcefully that Bateman's *Interpretatio* had had no application to Gonville Hall and therefore had none to his own re-foundation of the college; and he sought to give that argument the express force of a statute itself: "because the import of that passage is not about your College and you may not adopt that interpretation at any time, but it plainly concerns only his own [Hall of the] Holy Trinity".[8] He was clearly aware that the argument was crucial to his case; for he knew that the charter of 1557 expressly made his own power to make statutes subject by to the requirement that his statutes should not conflict with those of Bateman, and that any provision which did so would be invalid and null. He therefore sought the support of the University Statutes which had been made in the name of Elizabeth in 1570.[9]

Those statutes were primarily concerned with the constitution of the university and "effected a major shift in the basis of power within the university, from the regent masters to the heads of houses";[10] but it is not surprising that they involved a similar shift of power in the fourteen colleges, for colleges had experienced a rapid increase in the number of new, young fellows and those young puritanical fellows were prominent among the Regent Masters, who were a body confined to M.A.s of not more than three years' standing. The shift of power to the heads of houses was achieved within the colleges through the university's Statute 50, which set out ordinances for the colleges. Among those ordinances was a provision that the assent and consent of the Master or Provost should be necessarily required in each and every election of fellows, pupils, scholars, officers, lecturers and other members of the [particular] college, and also in every lease or grant whatsoever; and that, when they deemed necessary, the Masters or Provosts of colleges should have in their own colleges the power to impose all the penalties that another officer of the college had power to impose under the statutes of that [particular] college.[11]

in the margin there indicates an awareness of the importance of Bateman's direction in elections: see Plate XV above.

8 Statute 5.

9 Elizabeth's University Statutes 1570 were in fact issued by William Cecil as Chancellor of the University; they are commonly known today as 'Whitgift's Statutes' as he appears to have been principally responsible for their drafting, being at the time Master of Trinity College.

10 V. Morgan, *H.U.C.*, II, p. 71.

11 Ordinance 29: "*In omnibus et singulis electionibus tam sociorum discipulorum scholarium officiariorum lectorum reliquorumque membrorum cujusque collegii quam in omnibus et singulis locationibus et concessionibus quibuscunque necessario requirendus est magistri sive praepositi illius collegii assensus et consensus: et quod bene licebit magistris sive praepositis collegiorum in suis collegiis, si quando illis necessarium videbitur, omnes illas poenas exercere in delinquentes, quas aliquis officiariorum illius collegii per statuta ejusdem collegii imponere posit.*"

Caius was therefore not the only person in Cambridge to be pre-occupied with the question of a Master's negative voice during the reign of Elizabeth; and Bateman's two colleges (Trinity Hall and Caius) were not the only ones in which the question arose. It affected most colleges and it had already surfaced in another college in the first year of Caius' mastership. That college was Queens'.[12] The revised statutes made for Queens' College in the reign of Edward VI had provided for an election of fellows in which the greater part of the whole number, viz. President[13] and fellows both present and absent, had concurred;[14] but the wording was specifically altered by the college's royal commissioners in 1559 to require that the election be made by the President and the greater part of all the fellows both present and absent.[15] It is not known whether Caius was aware of this alteration, but there could not be a clearer illustration of the shift in the balance of power in the university from that which had prevailed in the time of Edward VI to that which was now introduced under the aegis of William Cecil in the reign of Elizabeth.

There had been no wide-reaching provision corresponding to Ordinance 29 in Elizabeth's earlier University Statutes of 1559,[16] for they had merely revived the statutes of Edward VI in place of those of Mary; so it is not surprising that the new ordinance was hotly opposed in 1570.[17] It was one of the points disputed between the fourteen heads of houses on the one side and the Proctors representing the Regents on the other. Not surprisingly, Caius appears to have taken an active part in the dispute, for he was one of the four heads deputed to argue the case before the archbishops of Canterbury and York and the bishop of Ely in May 1572.[18] The strength of feeling can be judged from the submissions of the Proctors and Regents to the hearing:[19]

[12] See *In the Matter of Queen's College, Cambridge* (1827) 5 Russ. 64.

[13] *I.e.*, Master.

[14] "*In quem major pars totius numeri, viz. praesidentis et sociorum omnium tam praesentium quam absentium consentierit.*"

[15] "*In quem praesidens et major pars sociorum omnium tam praesentium quam absentium consentierit.*"

[16] In the promulgation of which Matthew Parker probably played a leading role. He had not yet become archbishop of Canterbury at the time and was appointed as one of Elizabeth's Commissioners, together with Thomas Wendy (Gonville and Caius College) and others; he became archbishop in the course of the Commission's work.

[17] Together with other provisions which deliberately shifted authority and status in the University to the heads of houses.

[18] Matthew Parker, Edmund Grindal and Richard Cox, respectively; the four heads were Whitgift, Perne, Mey and Caius: Lamb, *Letters*, p. 357. According to Morgan (*H.U.C.*, II. p. 72) the cause was finally heard by Parker, Grindal and Sandys. John Mey, the Master of St Catharine's, was the brother of William Mey, who had been President of Queens' and had served so skilfully on the 1546 Commission with Parker, Wendy and Redman, the Warden of King's Hall, in saving the Cambridge colleges from dissolution with the chantries.

[19] Lamb, *Letters*, pp. 368–9.

1. These few words[20] overthrow all private statutes in most Colleges and is an intolerable injurie to establish the Master's tyrannie, to cause him to contemne all his fellows to foster and accustome students to servile flatterie yf they minde to obteyne such praefermentes in howses and abroade as fall to them by domesticall statutes. …
3. The greate inconveniences and shameful abuses of this negative voice hath already fallen owte both in leases and elections to the breach of statutes and discouragement all men …
7. This negative voice may wringe anie man oute of his fellowship at what time by private statutes he is bounde to take anye degree whereof attempte hath already been made.
8. And although some Masters before in some matters or all had negative voices yet the abuse thereof now sheweth ytself more playnelie by reason of there common and sole authoritie in all matters abroade wich causeth most men carelesslie to neglect there dewtie, or seeke to please them in their securitie or to consulte of leaving there place in the universitie.

The principal legal arguments put forward by the heads of houses in response were, first, that the statutes of "everie Colledge saving in one or two" gave the Master "an absolute negative voice in all things both at home and abrode privat and publique", and, second, that the statute 33 Henry VIII, c. 27 did likewise in respect of elections, leases and grants.[21]

The university statute stood, and so far as Caius College was concerned no challenge to the legality of the Master's negative voice surfaced in litigation during the remaining few months of Caius' mastership – a period in which doctrinal disputes no doubt left little time for legalistic ones and culminated in the notorious ransacking of Caius' rooms and the destruction of the religious artefacts he had preserved there.[22]

The university statute did not confer on a Master the unlimited negative voice that Caius' statute gave to him, but it was nonetheless far-reaching, since it applied to all elections and to the making of grants and leases, as well as conferring upon the Master all disciplinary powers given to other officers. It did not, however, give to the Master any default power of election to a fellowship in

[20] "*In omnibus et singulis electionibus tam sociorum discipulorum scholarium officiariorum lectorum reliquorumque membrorum cujusque collegii quam in omnibus et singulis locationibus et concessionibus quibuscunque necessario requirendus est magistri sive praepositi illius collegii assensus et consensus.*"

[21] Lamb, *Letters*, p. 384. For the Regents' reply to this, see *ibid.*, p. 396. As later legal opinion showed, the Henrician statute could equally be called in aid by those arguing in favour of a simple majority, whether or not it included the vote of any particular one person.

[22] Among those supervising the work of destruction was the same Dr Whitgift with whom Caius had appeared six months earlier on behalf of the heads of houses at the hearing into the University statutes.

the event that he and the majority of the Fellowship failed to agree, and it may be significant that Caius' immediate successor, Thomas Legge, does not seem ever to have resorted to Bateman's default power in respect of any fellowship election; for, if he had done so, we can be sure that Gerrard and his colleagues would have included the fact in the fifty charges of defaults in government that they listed in the complaint against Legge which they submitted to the Chancellor, Burghley, in 1582.[23] They did not include such a charge. Although they protested vigorously in their accompanying articles against the election of Depup as a fellow,[24] they did not assert that Legge had made the election on his own in defiance of a majority of the Fellowship, and their only specific complaint against Legge's exercise of the negative voice was directed to his failure to distribute college offices amongst the Fellowship.[25] As regards the actual elections made, their grievance was that he had used his chairmanship to propose the wrong persons and then "seekethe to compounde with the fellowes for ther voices", not that he had made elections and appointments in defiance of the majority of the Fellowship.[26] Given that the shift in power and responsibility to the heads of houses in the University Statutes of 1570 had been a response to the displeasure which Burghley, as Chancellor, had expressed over their failure to achieve "the ruling of inordinate youth, the observation of good order, and increase of learning and knowledge of God", it is not surprising that the complaint of Gerard and his colleagues to the very same Chancellor made no headway and that no lawsuit on the Master's negative voice arose during Legge's mastership. The constitutional position was neatly expressed by the standard form adopted in the *Gesta* to record decisions taken by the Master and fellows: that "it was so decreed by the majority of the Fellows of Gonville & Caius College with the assent and consent of Thomas Legge, LL.D., Keeper of the same College".[27]

A learned and distinguished civil lawyer like Legge would have been aware of the full significance of Bateman's statute governing the election of fellows, and the default clause that it contained; but he was a moderate and diplomatic person who was not given to passionate doctrinal views and the question whether a Master could, simply by withholding his assent or by casting a negative vote and then waiting a month, arrogate to himself alone the election

23 See *Gerrard's Case* (1582), Appendix D below.

24 *Articles concerning "certayne disorders for education of youthe"*: "[article] 6. … that immediately upon his cominge to the colledge, by his importunate labour he brought in one Depup to be a fellow of the howse, a man greatly suspected to be popishe, and otherwise well knowen to be notoriously vicious …": MS. Lansd. No. 33, art. 56, quoted *Cambridge University Transactions during the Puritan Controversies (1854)*, I, p. 317.

25 *Ibid.* "[article] 24. … that he hathe used his negative voyce against those that were chosen by the greater part of the company": *Gerrard's Case* (1582), Appendix D below. See also charges 21–26, *ibid.*

26 See art. 36: MS. Lansd. No. 33, art. 56, quoted *Cambridge University Transactions*, I, p. 321.

27 See, *e.g.*, the resolution of 11 December 1592 on the Frankland fellows, Appendix E below.

of a fellow did not arise in his time. His successor, William Branthwaite, was of a very different temperament; he was determined and puritanical in his views on both religious and lay issues, and his relations with the fellows were further impaired from the beginning by the fact that he had been brought in as Master from another, highly puritanical, college as a consequence of court intrigue and against the choice of an existing fellow by a majority of the Fellowship.

Even so, it was several years before the particular issue of the negative voice arose. It did so on the death of Stephen Perse, the college's most senior and respected fellow, on the last day of September 1615, and another senior fellow, Robert Welles, was unanimously 'translated' into his place. This resulted in a vacancy in the senior fellowship and in the ensuing election the majority of the fellows voted for an existing Frankland fellow, John Allen, who was a Devonian and not Norfolk-born. Branthwaite refused to agree and persisted in voting (three times) for the next junior Frankland fellow, Thomas Cooke, who was Norfolk-born. Branthwaite waited precisely a month and then nominated and admitted Cooke, "the majority of the fellows resisting this action by the Keeper in whatever ways they could". As the Annals continued vividly in Latin, at this point those sparks of discord which had lain dormant for a long time as if buried under ashes burst fiercely into flame and could not be extinguished save by a decision of the Chancellor as Visitor.[28] The fellows, it should be noted, did not seek to challenge the appointment of Cooke before the ordinary Visitors of the college, but took the drastic step of referring the question of Branthwaite's fitness to be Master to the Chancellor and seeking his removal from office.[29] Given the seriousness of the charge, it is not surprising that the matter dragged on throughout the year.

We are fortunate that the opinions of the civil lawyers consulted by the fellows have been preserved in the Annals.[30] Those opinions came down firmly on the side of the fellows, but, with neither side willing to give way, the Chancellor was

[28] "*Hinc illae discordiarum scintillae quae diu latuere quasi sub cineribus sepultae in ingentem flammam emicuere, quae non nisi sententia Cancellarii visitatoris extingui poterant*": *Annals*, p. 257. See *Allen's Case*, Appendix F below.

[29] In his Statute 44, Caius had specified the Masters of Corpus Christi College and Trinity Hall with the senior doctor of Medicine in the University as Visitors of his college, but subject to the exclusion of matters that Bateman had referred to the Chancellor; and by Bateman's Statute 5 one such matter was the removal of a Master for unfitness. This required the charge to be preferred by a two-thirds majority of the fellows. Because the issue was the Master's unfitness, not simply the disputed election of Allen, numerous other charges of breaches of statute were levelled against Branthwaite. These have been included in the Appendix together with his counter-charges and the fellows' response to them.

[30] They are reproduced in full in Appendix F below, as they illustrate the more diffuse civilian approach to the interpretation of a text in contrast to the more restricted common law approach to the interpretation of a parliamentary enactment. Any arguments of lawyers on Branthwaite's behalf have not been traced: they were not preserved in college and were not available to Moore in the last years of the Commonwealth when he undertook the work of writing up the Annals from 1603, the last year which Legge had covered.

finally forced to give judgment. He decided that Allen's election by a majority of the fellows was valid, notwithstanding Branthwaite's negative vote, which, the Chancellor ruled, had sprung not from any valid objection to Allen's election but "so that he might devolve it to himself and elect alone". In doing so he relied expressly, as the civilians had done, on the interpretation of the statute that had been expounded by Bateman for Trinity Hall. He did, however, diplomatically persuade the parties that Cooke should be elected to the next senior fellowship to fall vacant.[31]

Branthwaite's views on the Norfolk preference appear to have been very strong, and it took tactful persuasion from the Vice-Chancellor to induce him formally and publicly to accept the Chancellor's decision.[32] Even then he begged to be excused from admitting either Allen or Randolph (whose 'election' by the fellows to a senior fellowship in the course of the litigation had also been confirmed by the Chancellor). He pleaded that his oath would not allow him to do so and, there being no president, he requested that the Chancellor or Vice-Chancellor should admit him instead.[33]

Allen's Case appears to be the last in which a Master resorted to Bateman's default provision, and a hundred years passed before a dispute again arose in respect of the use of the Master's negative voice in fellowship elections. It did so during the mastership of Sir John Ellys.[34] Ellys had been a senior fellow for forty years and, in Venn's words, "during his long residence he had held all the usual college appointments" and was "unquestionably … the most distinguished and popular tutor of his day in Cambridge".[35] It is therefore difficult to understand why his relations with the fellows became so "inharmonious", to use Venn's very moderate term to describe his inexplicable non-cooperation with the Fellowship in so many aspects of college business, such as the passing of accounts, the presentation to a living and, finally, the election of fellows – inexplicable because he seems never to have offered any explanation or reason for his negative votes. Whatever his reasons, they did not prevent his acquiring the description of being "Com̄only called the divel of Keys".[36]

31 This had to be the next senior fellowship to fall vacant after the date of the judgment. The next senior fellowship to fall vacant after that filled by Allen had already been filled in the course of the litigation by the election of Thomas Randolph, against the negative vote of the Master, and it was also confirmed by the Chancellor. Cooke was subsequently elected to a senior fellowship in 1618 and many years later he caused great trouble to the college: see *Cooke's Case* (1636), Appendix G below.

32 Including the Chancellor's findings on the other charges.

33 Branthwaite left the office of president vacant throughout his mastership.

34 The dispute is recounted in full by Venn, together with that between the fellows and Ellys's successor, Sir Thomas Gooch: *B.H.* III, pp. 111–13, 120–1.

35 *B.H.* III, pp. 110–11.

36 Le Neve, cited by Venn, *B.H.* III, p. 111. Extreme old age and depression would seem the most likely explanation for his non-cooperation.

The dispute over fellowship elections first arose in 1712 over the election of Robert Sympson;[37] but in 1714, when Ellys again refused to accept John Morrant, the unanimous choice of the fellows, without giving any reason, they took legal advice.[38] That advice appears to have been taken from a common law practitioner,[39] not a civilian, but, like the earlier civilian opinions in *Allen's Case*, it was founded on the belief that it could not have been the intention that the Master, by the mere casting of a negative vote, should have the power to arrogate every fellowship election to himself; that Bateman's own interpretation avoided such an "absurdity"[40] and must therefore be binding on Gonville Hall as well as on Trinity Hall; that Caius' statute was consequently invalid in so far as it conflicted with Bateman's; and that it was not validated either by the University Statutes of 1570 or by the statute 33 Henry VIII, c. 27.[41]

On this occasion the fellows did not seek to charge Ellys before the Chancellor with unsuitability for office in accordance with Bateman's statute as had happened in *Allen's Case*.[42] Instead they appear to have sought a ruling from the college's Visitors under Caius' own Statute 5, and were successful: the Visitors ruled that the Master had been in error and that Morrant should be admitted without delay.[43] Like Branthwaite before him, Ellys absented himself from the admission and left the task for the president to perform in the presence of the Visitors. Venn tells us that the same process had to be gone through on a second occasion a few months afterwards, and then again in the following year.[44] Not surprisingly the fellows then considered proceeding against him under Bateman's statute for unfitness for office, but, in Venn's words, "nothing seems to have come of it" – perhaps because Ellys's failing health made it apparent that such action would soon be unnecessary.[45]

37 *B.H.* I, p. 516. It is recorded in the *Gesta* that "It was the unanimous desire of the fellows that the master would admit Sympson as fellow; but he refused to admit him, not excepting anything against him": quoted by Venn, *B.H.* III, p. 111. Sympson was a junior fellow at the time, and a new admission in chapel was necessary. He did in fact become a senior fellow in 1713, but it is not clear if and by whom he was admitted to his senior fellowship.

38 Morrant was a junior fellow (*B.H.* I, p. 516). Both Sympson and he were Norfolk-born.

39 Mr Cheshyre; his opinion is transcribed in MS 621/457, at pp. 13ff. (The term 'common law' when contrasted with civil law is used to include Equity.)

40 The word used both in *Allen's Case* and by Mr Cheshyre.

41 Both of which had been pressed by the heads of house in the dispute on the University statutes in 1572, described above.

42 Bateman's Statute 5.

43 Venn states that it was the Visitors to whom they referred the dispute (*B.H.* III, pp. 111–12) Under Statute 44 these would have been the Masters of Corpus and Trinity Hall together with the senior Doctor of Medicine in the University; but it should be noted that the proceedings appear to have been recorded for some reason in the University's records (MS, Univ. Reg. xi.38): see *B.H.* I, p. 517, *sub nom.* Morrant.

44 *B.H.* III, p. 112. The two fellows were William Selth (*B.H.* I, p. 512) and Peter Parham (*B.H.* I, p. 518). Both were Norfolk-born.

45 Venn does not indicate the source of his statement.

The question of the Master's negative voice arose twenty years later under his successor, Sir Thomas Gooch, who had been a fellow during the disputes with Ellys. It dragged on for five years;[46] for, on this occasion, there was a significant difference of opinion between the common lawyers' view and that of the civilians. The latter held to the opinion which their predecessors had given against both Branthwaite and Ellys, on the broad ground that it would be an "absurdity" to interpret the default clause in a way which would allow the Master to take advantage of his own dissent, and accordingly that Bateman's statute must be interpreted in the same way both for Trinity Hall and for Gonville Hall, thereby rendering Caius' statute invalid in so far as it directed otherwise.[47] The common lawyer consulted on this occasion, Mr Fazackerly, was of the contrary opinion: Bateman's interpretation was not binding on the Master and fellows of Caius' College, and there was therefore no inconsistency which would render Caius' statute invalid. As regards the devolution to the Master after a month, his view was severe: "It is most undoubtedly a most ridiculous Statute, but as the Founder might have placed the nomination of Fellows in the Master alone, I cannot say it is a void statute."[48] From a lawyer's point of view it is interesting to contrast the approach of civilians, accustomed to the interpretation of texts emanating from a single author whose intention might be ascertained from a broad spectrum of sources, with that of common lawyers, constrained to attributing a meaning to a parliamentary enactment made collectively by many authors whose composite intention must be gained from the text alone. It may be significant that the fellows of the two colleges whose dispute with their Master was heard in the university Chancellor's civil law court were successful and those of the two whose case was heard before the Lord Chancellor in the Court of Chancery as Visitor were unsuccessful.[49]

The dispute with Gooch was not pressed to litigation[50] and it proved to be the last occasion on which legal opinion was sought on the question of the Master's negative voice before its final demise in 1860 upon the abrogation of Caius' statutes.

46 See *B.H.* III, pp. 120–1.

47 Opinion of Dr Andrews, 26 November 1737, and Dr Edmunds, 17 March 1742: MS 621/457, at pp. 11ff and p. 21 respectively. Mr Cheshire, a common lawyer, had given a similar opinion in 1714: see above.

48 Opinion of Mr Fazakerly, 13 December 1737: MS 621/457, pp. 1ff at p. 7.

49 The fellows of Caius and St Catharine's were successful; those of Clare and Queens' were not: see *In the Matter of Queen's College, Cambridge* (1827) 5 Russ. 64. One must not exaggerate the significance of the contrasting decisions: each case turned upon the differing wording of the particular college's statutes.

50 Perhaps because Gooch had not made any default election and had carefully left the office of president vacant after it became vacant in 1738, so that there would be no one who could admit a new fellow and the only course open to the fellows would have been the doubtful one of charging Gooch (a member of the House of Lords) with unfitness for office before the Chancellor of the University as in *Allen's Case* in 1617.

VI. 3

The Norfolk Preference

Edmund Gonville and William Bateman did not include in their statutes any provision which restricted eligibility for election as Master, fellow or scholar to persons born in a specific diocese, county or locality;[1] in particular, neither founder's statutes contain any reference to a requirement or preference for a native of Norfolk or the diocese of Norwich.[2]

Such a reference first appeared in the version of Bateman's third statute that was contained in the fifteenth-century cartulary known as *Sheriffe's Evidences* (MS 707/692). That version incorporated in Statute 3 three substantial provisions which had not appeared in the certified copy of Bateman's statutes that Walter of Elveden had produced in 1355. The first and third of these provisions were (i) Bateman's requirement for prior study in the arts and logic, and (iii) his provision restricting the holding of benefices by fellows. These two provisions were not new and had previously appeared in Statute 12, where Walter of Elveden had placed them in 1355 (Statutes 14 and 15). Between these two transferred provisions, however, the scribe of the *Evidences* inserted an entirely new provision which had not been included anywhere by Walter of Elveden. This was (ii) the famous clause that has become known as the "Norfolk preference"

1 Gonville's draft statutes contained a brief statement in the third paragraph of the personal qualities that the fellows should seek in a Master (*quem scientia moribus industria conversacione et modestia magis credant necessarium utilem et idoneum pro adminstracione et regimine dicte domus*). Bateman included in his third statute an equally brief direction as to the degrees that a Master should possess, but he did so only in the (unlikely) event that it fell to the Chancellor to make the election, and he did not expressly impose any similar requirement in the more usual case when the election would be made by the fellows; he perhaps omitted to do so because he had made his foundation *inter vivos* and had reserved to himself the power of election to the mastership during his lifetime.

2 Although Gonville and Bateman were not concerned with the person's place of birth or upbringing before he came to the college, Bateman was keen to ensure the future services of a Master or fellow for the diocese of Norwich after he left the college. He required details of all those fellows who had departed from the college in the preceding year to be sent annually both to the bishop and to the chapter, and he imposed on Masters and fellows a life-long duty to act on the diocese's behalf in later life and not to be a party to any litigation against it: Statutes 12 and 16.

clause, though it was in fact a preference for the diocese of Norwich and thus extended to Suffolk as much as to Norfolk:[3]

> *Volumus insuper quod in omni electione prefectione et ordinatione custodis et sociorum imposterum faciend' omnis affectio singularis conspiratio et parcialitas excludatur, ut sic simpliciter melior et pro Collegio utilior, quantum eis Deus in conscientia ministraverit, elegatur. Proviso tamen semper quod in omnibus electionibus custodis collegii primo socius ejusdem Collegii, si ad hoc reperiatur idoneus, aut alius nostre dioc[esis] famosus, et in electione sociorum scholares nostre dioc[esis] non beneficiati beneficiatis, ac pauperiores ditioribus ceteris paribus aliis omnibus preferantur.*[4]

The reason for the transfer of the first provision remains unclear.[5] There does, however, seem to have been a very cogent reason for the insertion of the second, new, provision which followed it. The attractive suggestion has been made that this deliberate insertion of a preference for the diocese of Norwich was prompted by a desire to save the college from a member of a rapacious northern family, one Hamond Bothe, who had no known connection with the college or with the diocese but tried to infiltrate himself on the death of the Master, Thomas Boleyn, in 1472.[6] Caius had been aware that there had been "no slight disturbance" at the time of the election,[7] but it was not until 1983 that a connection between that "disturbance" and the introduction of the Norwich preference was made.[8] Unlike that of the first two, the insertion of the third provision appears to have been less deliberate and may simply be due to the fact that the new preference for the diocese of Norwich ended with an additional preference for those who did not hold a benefice over candidates who did, and this may have prompted the scribe to bring forward into Statute 3 the restriction on the holding of benefits that had originally been included in

3 In 1837 a large part of Suffolk (the archdeaconry of Sudbury) was hived off to the diocese of Ely, making the preference more restrictive. The rest of Suffolk was not hived off from Norwich (to the new diocese of Ipswich and St Edmundsbury) until 1914, long after the Norfolk preference had been swept away in 1858.

4 "It is our further wish that in every future election, choice or admission of a keeper and of fellows all personal affection, champerty and partiality shall be excluded, so that the person who is plainly better for, and more useful to, the college shall be chosen as God shall best guide [the electors] in [their] conscience: always provided however that in all elections of a keeper of the college a fellow of the college shall be [chosen] first, if one is found suitable for the office, or else another of distinction from our diocese, and in the election of fellows scholars from our diocese who are not beneficed shall be preferred to those who are beneficed and the poorer shall be preferred to those who are more wealthy, other things being equal."

5 It may have been intended to smooth the way to the introduction of the second provision.

6 See Brooke, *History*, pp. 16–17 and 39–40.

7 *B.H.* III, p. 19, citing the Annals.

8 C. Hall and C.N.L. Brooke, *The Caian* (1983), pp. 43–50.

Bateman's five final provisions and had correctly been positioned by Elveden after Statute 12.[9]

It is clear that the scribe carefully inserted into Statute 3 the first of the two transferred provisions (*i.e.*, the requirement for study in arts and logic) and followed this with the new Norfolk preference clause. He then passed on to Statute 4 and it was only after he had done so that he realised that he should also have transferred the provision restricting the holding of benefices. He was, however, able to insert no more than its first twelve words into the remaining space before the rubric of the following Statute 4, and he had to write the remaining fifty-eight words – almost the whole of the benefices provision – in the top margin. Whether he was prompted to transfer the benefices restriction simply because the new Norfolk preference clause had included a preference for those who did not hold a benefice before those who did, or whether the transfer of the two flanking provisions was intended to draw attention away from the novelty of the new provision inserted between them, remains a mystery; but the effect was to convert a procedural statute entitled "Of the time and form of election" into one on the requisite qualifications for election.

Sheriffe's Evidences is dated 1472, the year in which Edmund Sheriffe was elected Master, and the work was treated with veneration by Caius, who claimed to have found it in a parlous condition (*vetustate dissolutum et neglectum*) in the college archives and, as he recorded on its frontispiece, carefully had it repaired and rebound in 1564 in tribute to the past and for the edification of the future (*in vetustatis memoriam, et futuri temporis exemplum*).[10] It may have been Caius' veneration that led him to keep the preference provision in his own edition of Bateman's statutes, but it did not cause him to retain in Statute 3 the two other provisions that had been moved there in the *Evidences*: he returned them to the position in which Walter of Elveden had placed them in 1355, namely, after Statute 12.[11] It is clear from the fact that he did so that he had compared Sheriffe's version with the certified copy of Bateman's statutes which Walter of Elveden had produced in 1355 and which had been carefully preserved in the archives, folded and refolded time and again into a minute packet, and that he must have been well aware that the Norwich preference had not featured in that original version of Statute 3, nor indeed elsewhere in Bateman's statutes.

9 For these and other changes made in later versions of Bateman's statutes, see "*Bateman's Statutes: The Manuscript Confusion*", § I. 2 above.

10 Careful examination by Professor Brooke suggests that the cartulary is likely to include everything Sheriffe copied, as the arrangement of the quires does not suggest any substantial loss or dislocation. Caius' strictures should probably have been more properly directed to the binding than to the survival of the contents.

11 Statutes 14 and 15 in the present edition. Caius combined both provisions (and Statute 13) as a single paragraph at the end of Statute 12: see "*Bateman's Statutes: The Manuscript Confusion*", § I. 2 above.

Whatever the full story behind the introduction of the Norfolk preference, it was the formulation contained in *Sheriffe's Evidences* that was transmitted to later generations as the founder's enactment and was interpreted accordingly.[12] If we are to understand the bitter disputes which began in the seventeenth century and continued to fester thereafter until 1858 we must likewise approach the celebrated provision as if it had been included by the college's second founder in his statutes and expressed his intentions.[13]

In the course of time the provision came to present three questions.

(i) Was the injunction to "prefer" directed to the preferring of poor or un-beneficed persons within a rigidly exclusive class, namely, natives of the diocese? Or did it require merely that natives of the diocese should be preferred to persons from other dioceses and did not require that the latter should be wholly excluded? In other words, were the fellowships established by Bateman to be rigidly restricted to those born in the diocese of Norwich? (As a later Master, Dr Gooch, asked: if so, who were the "*aliis omnibus*" who were merely to be deferred in the order of preference but not totally excluded?)[14]

(ii) What were the "other things being equal" that brought into play the requirement that the preference was to be observed "*ceteris paribus*"? And how should the equality of "those other things" be assessed in the absence of any university or other formal examination?

(iii) Did the restriction or preference apply to fellowships endowed by a later benefactor or just to those that were established by Bateman in his statutes? And if so, did it apply notwithstanding a benefactor's express or implied intention to the contrary?

In the years between Bothe's unsuccessful attempt to infiltrate himself into the mastership in 1472 and John Caius' re-foundation of the college in 1557, five further fellowships were added by benefactors to the four that already existed. Of these, two were expressly restricted by the benefactor to natives of the diocese of Norwich, namely those of Elizabeth Clere in 1480 and Anne Scroop in 1503; but no specific qualification was required by the other three benefactors, Stephen Smith in 1478, Thomas Willowes in 1501 and John Bayley in 1525.[15]

12 It would seem, however, that Caius was not the only one to have realised that the preference had not been in the 1353 original or in Elveden's 1355 re-issue, for the author of the rival MS 760 must have done so also: see "*Bateman's Statutes: The Manuscript Confusion*", § I. 2 above.

13 It was not until 1852 that the absence of the provision from Statutes of 1355 was first acknowledged: see Brooke, *History*, p. 16, n. 35, citing D. Winstanley, *Early Victorian Cambridge*, 1940, p. 265.

14 "Who then are these *alii omnes*? Or to whom does, *ceteris paribus*, refer? If the Statute meant not a bare Preference of the Diocese, but an Exclusion of all others, the words *alii omnes*, are not only superfluous, but absurd": MS 621/457, pp. 57, 63.

15 For these fellowships see *B.H.* III, pp. 214–17.

Of these only Smith, rector of Blonorton, had an immediate association with Norfolk. Bayley had been rector of a parish in Ipswich in Suffolk, but Willowes was unconnected with either of the two counties that formed the diocese of Norwich, being a Cambridge tradesman and thus within the diocese of Ely, a fact which was not lost upon later critics of the Norfolk preference.

John Caius was himself a Norfolk man, born in the town of Norwich, and as a scholar (*bibliotista*) and then a fellow he must have been very conscious both of the strong Norfolk character which Gonville Hall had acquired by that time and also of the developing prominence in its affairs which the town of Norwich itself enjoyed by then.[16] As he later remarked in his statutes, all the founders were of Norfolk or Norwich, and the majority of benefactors likewise ("*omnes fundatores, Norfolkenses, aut Norwicenses erant, et maxima pars benefactorum item*").[17] When he made his statutes for his alma mater, it is not surprising that he should transmute the clerical preference for the diocese of Norwich which he found in Sheriffe's *Evidences* (*i.e.* for Norfolk *and* Suffolk) into a secular preference for the town of Norwich and the county of Norfolk. It cannot be said, however, that he was adept in the way in which he did this; he scattered his modification of the preference over three separate statutes, Statutes 4, 8 and 15, and he did so in a manner that added greatly to the complexity of the various statutory provisions governing the qualifications for election to the mastership, fellowships and even scholarships.

When he came to draft Statute 4 Caius took Bateman's third statute as his starting point. In the version of the statute that Walter of Elveden had faithfully transcribed for the college in 1355 the bishop had addressed the *procedure* for electing a future Master or fellow, but he had not spoken of the qualities that should be required of them beyond specifying that the Master must be a Doctor or Bachelor of Canon or Civil Law or a Master of Arts distinguished in letters, if it fell to the Chancellor to make the election. To that requirement the interpolated provision found in Sheriffe's *Evidences* had added a reference to the personal qualities and qualifications required, principally that the person elected should come from the diocese. Caius now formulated more elaborately the qualities and qualifications required in the case of a Master: he must be celibate and of the diocese of Norwich *if* at the time of the election he was or had been a fellow of the college, but if he had never been a fellow the requirement was replaced by the secular one of having been born in Norfolk or Suffolk. Statute 4 thus converted into a requirement what had been at most a preference; it did not, however, introduce a preference for Norfolk over Suffolk.

16 Gonville Hall had acquired the living of St Michael's Coslany in Norwich in 1441; when Caius entered the college as a scholar the living was held by the then Master, William Buckenham, and had been held by his two immediate predecessors, John Barley and Edmund Stubb, before him: *B.H.* III, p. 317; IV(2), p. 68.

17 Statute 8.

In Statute 8 Caius again referred to Bateman's provisions for elections; but whereas in Statute 4 he had confined himself to the election of a Master, he now extended his provisions to fellows. He proceeded to impose a sweeping preference for the county of Norfolk before Suffolk, both in the case of the Master and in those of a fellow or scholar: "in every election of a keeper preference shall be given to those who are born in the county of Norfolk, likewise in every election of fellows and scholars; [and] after those, natives of Suffolk". The saving words *ceteris paribus* were not included, and the silence after the mention of Suffolk left it unclear whether natives of other counties were ultimately eligible. The new county preference for Norfolk over Suffolk in the election of a Master was now extended to all mastership elections, whether or not the person elected had ever been a fellow. In the case of elections to fellowships the preference for Norfolk was expressed differently: in such elections scholars of the college from both counties were to be preferred, first from Norfolk then from Suffolk, before drawing upon scholars from other colleges. Finally, the (three) fellowships which he himself established were to be confined exclusively to natives of Norwich or Norfolk.

One is left with the impression that Caius had drafted Statutes 4 and 8 at different times,[18] and a similar – and more forceful – impression is created as regards the drafting of Statutes 8 and 15.[19] His sweeping directions in Statute 8 that preference should be given for Norfolk and then Suffolk in the election of scholars as well as in that of a Master or fellow, and that his own fellowships were confined to Norfolk-men alone, sit awkwardly with his elaborate scheme in Statute 15 for the election of scholars on his own foundation: eight of those were to be drawn from other, specific counties, and on any interpretation of Statute 8 those eight scholars from such other counties were wholly ineligible for subsequent election to one of his own fellowships (all three of which were confined to Norfolk-men) and they would stand a poor chance for any of the other fellowships in the College.

Caius' baffling provisions threw no light on the interpretation of Bateman's statutes and added instead a further question: were his own statutes in any way opposed or contrary ("*repugnantia seu contraria*") to those of the bishop and consequently *ultra vires* his powers under the charter of Philip and Mary?[20] Later disputes thus came to raise constitutional issues as well as questions of interpretation. Those issues were never very clearly recorded before the nineteenth century, but may be summarised as follows:

18 See Caius' alteration to the rubric of Statute 8 and the note thereto.

19 Both impressions are confirmed by a comparison with the draft statutes which he prepared in 1558 (*Documents*, II, pp. 324–8 and 341–2). In those statutes, what later became Statute 4 had been confined to Masters, and Statute 8 to fellows. In the forerunner to Statute 15 his twelve scholarships had been restricted to persons born in Norfolk. The alteration to the rubric to Statute 8 indicates that it had not originally been intended to deal with the election of Masters.

20 For the charter's requirement of compatibility see Appendix B below.

(i) Did the preference for natives of Norfolk in the election to fellowships that were not expressly limited to that county only arise as a last resort when the claims of candidates were otherwise equally strong, or did it arise as a first resort and, in effect, give to Norfolk-men a straight *priority* over other members of the college? In practical terms, when there was an election to any vacant senior fellowship that had not been expressly confined to natives of Norfolk, did the fact that there was an eligible Norfolk-born candidate automatically rule out the election of a candidate who had been born elsewhere, regardless of comparative merit or seniority?

(ii) If so, was that result compatible with the provision *ceteris paribus* in Bateman's statutes, particularly if the vacant fellowship was one that the bishop had founded, *i.e.* a fellowship *ex antiqua fundatione*?

(iii) Did the statutory preference or priority automatically apply to all fellowships founded by past and future benefactors irrespective of the express or presumed wishes of that benefactor?

The foundation of a large number of new, junior fellowships not specifically restricted to Norfolk following Mrs Frankland's benefaction inevitably introduced into those three questions a personal element that had the potential to cause acrimony. There would thereafter be a group of candidates who were already junior fellows of the college and it was from within that group that the choice of person to fill a vacant senior fellowship would naturally be made first: any automatic preference or priority might result in recently elected junior fellows from Norfolk leap-frogging their more senior colleagues. It would not be surprising if the instinctive reaction was to confine Norfolk requirement to the five fellowships that had been expressly restricted to that county or diocese (*i.e.*, those established by Elizabeth Clere, Anne Scroop and John Caius) and to make seniority a more important consideration than place of birth in the case of other fellowships. This seems to have become the practice by the time of Legge's death.

As a later Master, Robert Brady, was able to show, at least one fellow not born in Norfolk or Suffolk had been elected even in Caius' own time.[21] Thereafter

[21] Robert Churche [Gonville and Caius College 1566]. Churche had been born in Essex and been a sizar at St John's; he was admitted as a pensioner in October 1566 and was elected a fellow and tutor in February 1569 (*B.H.* I, p. 58). During his forty years as a fellow he became one of the two most senior and respected of the college's fellows; not being a Norfolkman, he remained Lady Pakenham fellow throughout and was never translated into a Caius fellowship as he might have been if he had been born in that county. Brady also included Francis Dorington (*B.H.* I, p. 50) and Henry Holland (*B.H.* I, p. 39), on the assumption that the first was from Staffordshire and the second from Lincolnshire; his list is preserved in MS 602/278. In addition, Edmond Hownd (*B.H.* I, p. 62) became a fellow shortly before Caius' death; he was born in London and was appointed by Caius to preach at his funeral service.

the story can be tracked through the pages of Volume I of Venn's *Biographical History*.[22] During Legge's mastership at least eight more from outside the diocese were elected into fellowships in the period before the new class of junior fellowships was introduced in 1592 following Mrs Frankland's benefaction.[23] In the further fifteen years of Legge's mastership at least seven Frankland fellows came from counties other than Norfolk or Suffolk, and three of them were later elected into senior fellowships.

After Legge's death it continued to be accepted without question both by his successor, William Branthwaite, and by the fellowship that 'foreigners' from counties other than Norfolk and Suffolk could be elected into Frankland fellowships, and several were so elected. In 1607 John Webbe, a Londoner, was elected into a Frankland fellowship; another Londoner, Thomas Wake, followed in 1610, and in 1611 two further scholars, John Allen from Devon and James Iken of London, likewise.[24] In 1613 a Lancastrian, Ralph Loude, was pre-elected into a Frankland fellowship; Loude had originally been at Branthwaite's old college, Emmanuel, and followed him to Caius in 1608 as his sizar.[25]

In his first few years as Master, Branthwaite also accepted without objection the careful procedure which the college appears to have adopted by then in respect of elections to fellowships. That procedure involved the artificial but effective practice of 'translating' fellows from one foundation to another in order to avoid any divisive 'leap-frogging' and to achieve instead an orderly progression from a junior to a senior fellowship. It thereby provided young fellows with a reasonable prospect of advancement in due course whatever their place of birth.

The system of translation worked in the following way. When a restricted senior fellowship (*i.e.*, one founded by Elizabeth Clere, Anne Scroop or John Caius) fell vacant and the most appropriate junior fellow was ineligible because

22 Brady's list (MS 602/278) also covers the period. He started it when he became Master at the Restoration. It is in two parts, one from 1660 onward, and the other from 1559 to 1659, but it contains only senior fellows. After Brady's mastership the list was later brought up to 1758 by Sir Thomas Gooch when he became Master. Writing in the middle of the eighteenth century Gooch argued strongly against any exclusive Norfolk preference: MS 621/427, pp. 57ff.

23 Richard Gerrard [Gonville and Caius College 1567], John Depup [1567], Thomas Temple [1573], Thomas Hinson [1574], Richard Swale [1576], George Estey [1577], John Fletcher [1578] and Christopher Grymston [1578]: *B.H.* I, pp. 61, 73, 81, 85, 90, 95 and 99. Many of the names featured in the dispute between the Master and the more puritanical fellows in *Gerrard's Case* (1582), Appendix D below. Swale, Fletcher and Grymston came from Yorkshire; Swale and Fletcher were both prominent in the affairs of the college; Swale was the president and Legge's principal ally in that dispute, and Fletcher was the author of the "Arithmetical Table" referred to in "*Dividends*", § VI. 5 below.

24 See *B.H.* I, pp. 169, 186, and 187; *Acta*, Michaelmas 1611; and College List 1613 (*Exiit Book* 1592–1618).

25 *B.H.* I, p. 200. Loude was later elected into a senior fellowship, but not until 1621, after Branthwaite's death.

he was not a Norfolkman, the college would, if need be, 'translate' into that vacant restricted fellowship the existing holder of one of the unrestricted senior fellowships who was a Norfolkman; this would thereby release the unrestricted fellowship for the desired election of the chosen Frankland fellow. If an unrestricted fellowship fell vacant, then the choice of successor would be unconstrained and no 'translation' would be necessary at that time. The system of translation enabled the college to avoid the necessity of having to promote a more junior Frankland fellow who happened to be a Norfolkman over the head of a more senior fellow when the latter had a stronger claim on any grounds other than his place of birth. The practice thus ensured that a fellow's prospects of promotion would not depend on the invidious expectation as to the order in which senior fellowships would fall vacant.

In this way, when the unrestricted Stephen Smith fellowship held by Edward Parker, who was himself a 'foreigner' from Ely, fell vacant in 1611, it was possible to elect the most senior Frankland fellow, Oliver Naylor of London, into it without the need for any translation.[26] A translation was also unnecessary when the unrestricted Willowes fellowship became vacant on the death of John Fletcher, a Yorkshireman, in 1613, and Thomas Kydman, the Frankland fellow next in line for promotion, was elected.[27] Thomas Kydman was in fact a Norfolkman and would have been eligible even if the Willowes fellowship had been restricted. In the following year, however, the restricted Scroop fellowship became vacant and, as the senior Frankland fellow was now a Londoner, Thomas Wake, who was not qualified for that fellowship, Kydman was translated into the restricted Scroop fellowship and the college was able to elect Wake into the unrestricted Willowes fellowship vacated by Kydman.[28] All these elections to senior fellowships were made with "the consent of the Keeper and the majority of the Fellows", as were also those to Frankland fellowships.

In the bitter dispute which was soon to disrupt the college, Branthwaite included in his complaints against the fellows their disregard of the statutory requirement that those born in Norfolk or Suffolk were to be preferred in elections to fellowships, but one is left with the impression from his participation in these elections to the Smith and Willowes fellowships that his objection may have been confined to Bateman's three fellowships *ex antiqua fundatione*. Moreover, the complaint would seem to have weighed far less with him than his principal contention, namely that the Master had a negative

26 *Acta*, 4 October 1611.

27 *Acta*, 12 November 1613; for Kydman, *B.H.* I, p. 174.

28 *Acta*, 25 February 1614. For some unexplained reason, the February proceedings are recorded retrospectively after Lady Day and are entered in a different hand. The fellowship would have gone to John Webbe, a Londoner, who was senior to Wake and had been pre-elected to the next Bateman fellowship; but Webbe was in the process of obtaining a benefice at the time and he never became a senior fellow: *B.H.* I, pp. 169 (Wake), 175 (Webbe).

voice that overrode the votes of any majority of the fellows. It was a contention which he held to with a tenacity that was rooted in his increasingly difficult relationship with a fellowship which would have preferred another to have been Master. The election of Branthwaite as Master had been forced on the fellows by the earl of Salisbury, the powerful royal minister, who had succeeded his father, Lord Burghley, as Chancellor of the university, and although Branthwaite was only moderately puritanical in his doctrinal beliefs he was severe in his personal judgements: "a man of excellent learning and good sense, but stiff and inflexible in his opinion of persons and things" in the words of one of his successors a century later.[29] It is not surprising therefore that his relations with the fellows were never cordial; but they seem to have remained sufficiently good for the conduct of business to be discharged amicably so long as the greatly respected senior fellow, Stephen Perse, remained the dominant figure in college.[30]

Perse died on the last day of September in 1615, and on 27 October Robert Welles, a Norfolkman,[31] was translated (with the unanimous consent of the Master and all the fellows) from one of Bateman's fellowships into the restricted medical fellowship on Dr Caius' foundation which Perse had held. Although Welles was by this date a very senior and respected fellow, it is clear that his translation was not simply a matter of promotion in the financial 'pecking order' of senior fellowships; for there was no system of promotion among senior fellows and they tended to stay with the fellowship to which they were first elected, despite small financial differences, unless there were a need to free their fellowship for someone else, and in any case there was an even more senior medical fellow who would have had a greater claim to promotion.[32] It is likely therefore that his translation into the restricted fellowship on Dr Caius' foundation was designed to render vacant the fellowship *ex antiqua fundatione* which he had been holding and by doing so to give effect to an important decision that had been agreed two years earlier, in Michaelmas 1613.

That decision two years earlier had arisen at a time when the college had been faced with the need to fill two senior fellowships; one was the restricted Clere fellowship and the other the unrestricted Willowes fellowship which had been held by a Yorkshireman, John Fletcher. As has been already mentioned it was agreed to elect the two most senior junior fellows into them: the most senior Frankland fellow, Thomas Kydman, into the Willowes fellowship and Thomas Weatherell, the first holder of the revived Wendy fellowship, into the

29 *Per* Dr Gooch: MS 621/427, p. 81.

30 As late as 1613 he was appointed bursar, as he had been very frequently in earlier years (*Acta* 29 October 1613). The precise hour at which he died and his place in the society thereupon became vacant is touchingly (and uniquely?) recorded in the *Acta* for 30 September 1615.

31 *B.H.* I, p. 122.

32 John Gostlin (*B.H.* I, p. 116), the Regius Professor of Physic, who had been chosen as Master on Legge's death but had been superseded by Branthwaite; he had held Dr Bayly's fellowship since 1592.

Clere fellowship.[33] As both were Norfolkmen, no problem arose. However, Kydman's election used up one of the unrestricted fellowships and, looking ahead, the next four Frankland fellows in order of seniority were not from Norfolk or Suffolk (Thomas Wake, John Webbe and James Iken from London, and John Allen from Devon)[34] and the only Norfolkman was the very junior fifth, Thomas Cooke, who had been elected just six months before.[35] In the light of this, when the meeting had elected Kydman and Weatherell to their senior fellowships at Michaelmas 1613, it had also pre-elected Webbe into the next fellowship *ex antiqua fundatione* that should become vacant in any way.[36] Before that happened, however, the restricted Scroop fellowship fell vacant three months later and it became possible to translate Kydman into it, thereby freeing Kydman's unrestricted Willowes fellowship, and, apparently with the consent of the Master as well as the fellows, Wake was elected into it.[37]

This left Allen as the senior Frankland fellow next in line for promotion to a senior fellowship, and the scene was set for the bitter dispute and lawsuit which followed Perse's death on 30 September 1615 and Welles' translation into his place the following month.[38] When the meeting on 27 October had unanimously translated Welles into his new fellowship it proceeded to the business of electing a successor to fill the fellowship *ex antiqua fundatione* thereby vacated. In line with the settled practice and the decision taken two years earlier the majority of the senior fellows cast their votes for Allen. However, Branthwaite refused to accept the choice of Allen as valid, on the grounds that he had a negative voice by virtue of the statutes and had not voted for him. Stalemate ensued: on three separate occasions the Master and the fellows remained immovable in their opinions and the month required by the statutes for an election passed. At 8 a.m. on the day after the month expired Branthwaite designated Thomas Cooke and proceeded to admit him to the vacant fellowship, "the majority of the fellows resisting this action by the Keeper in whatever ways they could".[39]

Although the question of the Norfolk preference was the immediate occasion of the dispute, at its heart lay the far more important question whether the Master had an overriding negative voice; for that would give him unfettered power over the choice of every new fellow. The fellows obtained supporting opinions

33 *Acta* 12 November 1613; *B.H.* I, p. 174 (Weatherell).

34 College List 1613 (*Exiit Book* 1592–1618); *B.H.* I, pp. 169, 175, 186 and 187.

35 Thomas Cooke (*B.H.* I, p. 183) had been elected on 28 April 1613 in the previous term.

36 *Acta* 12 November 1613.

37 *Acta* 26 February 1614. Webbe, who had been promised the next senior fellowship three months earlier, was in the process of obtaining a benefice and that left Wake as next in line. Very oddly and perhaps significantly, the events of February 1614 are not recorded where they should be, *i.e.* in the *Acta* for the six months from Michaelmas 1613 to Lady Day 1614, but are entered retrospectively in the *Acta* for the following six months; they are entered only after May 1614.

38 *Allen's Case* (1617) is related in full in Appendix F.

39 "*... sociorum majori parte quibus possit modis huic Custodis facto obsistente ...*": *Annals*, p. 257.

from civil lawyers, but Branthwaite was immovable. The dispute continued throughout the following year, 1616, and the refusal by either side to compromise finally led to the unprecedented step of Branthwaite's being charged before the Chancellor of the university with unfitness for office by two-thirds of the senior fellows under the provisions of Bateman's original statutes. In the (translated) words of the Annals, those sparks of discord which had lain dormant for a long time as if buried under ashes burst fiercely into flame and could not be extinguished save by a decision of the Chancellor as Visitor.[40]

The Annals for the period covering *Allen's Case* were not written until forty years later and unfortunately they do not contain the detailed arguments or any legal opinions that Branthwaite submitted to the Chancellor in response to the charges made against him. They do, however, include his unimpressive list of various "contradictions" between Bateman's statutes and those of Caius, and of "auncient practices" that had been adopted – by implication, adopted by the fellows and not by the Master – in breach of the college's statutes. The account in the Annals of the genesis of the list compiled by Branthwaite is confusing; but it would seem that the listed points had been submitted to the Chancellor and, if so, it is clear that Branthwaite did put to the Chancellor the question of the Norfolk preference as well as the hotly disputed issue of the Master's negative voice, for his list of statute contradictions concludes with the following assertion: "Touching the preferring of fellowes, Bishop Bateman decreeth thus, *In electione sociorum scholares nostrae Diocaesios non beneficiati beneficiatis etc.* But Dr Caius thus, *in socios vero ejusdem Collegii scholastici Norfolc. cum Suffolc. preferantur etc.*" It would seem to be Branthwaite's view that Caius' wording, and in particular his omission of the words *ceteris paribus*, overrode that of Bateman. In their reply the fellows readily conceded the preference for Norfolkmen, but they were careful to insist that the qualifying phrase *ceteris paribus* applied as much to Caius' directions (other than those for his own three fellowships) as to Bateman's: "Both the Founders agree that Norfolk men should be preferred in all elections, which cannot be understood in Dr Caius his statutes otherwise than in Bishop Bateman's, with this clause (*caeteris paribus*)[;] as for Dr Caius owne Foundation, as he hath made the places proper for Norfolke so they have been chosen still out of the Country."[41]

It would seem that Branthwaite was wholly unsuccessful in his argument that Statute 8 rendered Allen ineligible by reason of his place of birth, for the Chancellor dismissed it with the remark that the Master had not given "any just cause or reason of the Statute why Allen was not eligible". He accordingly upheld Allen's election by the major part of the fellows, notwithstanding the Master's refusal to vote for him.

[40] "*Hinc illae discordiarum scintillae quae diu latuere quasi sub cineribus sepultae in ingentem flammam emicuere, quae non nisi sententia Cancellarii visitatoris extingui poterant*": *Annals*, p. 257.

[41] "Country", *i.e.* county of Norfolk.

The Chancellor's rulings were communicated to the college on 17 July 1617 and Branthwaite was initially very reluctant to accept them. When they were published by the Vice-Chancellor twelve days later, he even went so far as to state publicly that he protested against them and would assent to them only "so far as they are agreeable to his oath, to Dr Caius' Statutes and the covenauntes between Dr Caius and the Colledge". He further desired that his protestation might be recorded.[42] Significantly he did not mention Bateman's statutes. After three weeks he was tactfully persuaded by the Vice-Chancellor to furnish to the Chancellor "further satisfaction" in the form of an unreserved and somewhat obsequious acceptance of all the rulings, including a concession that "he is willing for his parte that Mr Allein shall be fellow and have all right belonging thereunto". Even then he could not restrain himself from seeking to be excused from taking part in Allen's admission and requesting that the Chancellor or Vice-Chancellor should admit him instead, since "he verily thinketh he cannot doe it with safety of his oath".[43] Thereafter, in the carefully chosen words of a later historian of the college, "somewhat better accord seems to have been achieved" in the last two years of his life.[44] No doubt this was due to the shrewd direction of the Chancellor that the Master's protégé, the avaricious and aggressive Thomas Cooke, should have the next fellowship to become vacant.[45]

Branthwaite died two years later and in the same year (1619) the first elections were made to the six new fellowships which Perse had endowed in his will. This increased the number of junior fellowships from eight to fourteen, and only in the case of one of those fourteen did the benefactor, Thomas Wendy, impose a restriction to natives of Norfolk.[46] Indeed, Perse had directed that in elections to his fellowships a preference was to be given to those members of the college who had held his scholarships; and since his scholars were in turn, by preference, to be drawn from those who had been pupils at his new Free School for boys from Cambridge and its immediate neighbourhood, his direction ran counter to any preference for Norfolk or Suffolk.

42 *Annals*, pp. 264–6.

43 The "safety of his oath" may have referred to a regard for the Norfolk preference but it is more likely that he had in mind the Master's negative voice, since he also declined on the same grounds to admit a Norfolkman Thomas Randolph (Randell) at the same time.

44 Brooke, *History*, p. 109. Despite his earlier dispute with the fellows, Branthwaite left the lion's share of his remarkable library to the college, as well as founding four scholarships.

45 Cooke was elected the following year, thereby leap-frogging the more senior James Iken, who was a Londoner. Iken departed and became Rector of Stifford, Essex. Cooke stayed on in college and afterwards caused it much trouble before he was finally deprived of his fellowship in 1635: see *Cooke's Case* (1636), Appendix G.

46 Mrs Frankland had founded six unrestricted fellowships together with a chaplaincy that came to be treated as a fellowship; and to these had been added Thomas Wendy's restricted fellowship which had been re-established in 1610. Perse added six more.

It might therefore be thought that this increase in the number of junior fellowships would be reflected in the number of elections into senior fellowships of persons from outside the two counties in the years following Branthwaite's death. In fact the opposite occurred: in the twenty years from 1623 to the outbreak of the Civil War only two of those elected into senior fellowships were born outside Norfolk or Suffolk, and both of those were from the same Dorset family: the distinguished physician Francis Glisson in 1629 and his younger brother Henry, also a physician, in 1635.[47] As a result there was only one senior fellow at any time throughout the 1630s who had not been born in either of the two favoured counties, first Francis Glisson from 1629 to 1634 and then Henry from 1635 to 1640.[48]

The contrast with the first twenty years of the century is striking, and one's first reaction might be to attribute it to the adoption of a less liberal interpretation of the two founders' statutes than had prevailed in those earlier years; but it would be rash to do so in the absence of any continuous *Acta* that survive for the period.[49] A more likely cause is to be found in the subtle change in the perception of junior fellowships that was brought about by the virtual doubling of their number after 1619. Before that date there had been only seven such fellowships (if one puts aside the Frankland chaplaincy) and in appropriate cases the holders might reasonably look forward to a senior fellowship in time if they waited their turn. Junior fellowships could thus be perceived as first steps in an orderly process of promotion, and in that process seniority was naturally an important consideration. The doubling of the number of junior fellowships after 1619 altered that perception radically. Junior fellowships could no longer carry a realistic prospect of eventual promotion within the college for any but the most outstanding of their holders: for the great majority they now afforded no more than a few more years in Cambridge followed by a benefice, medical practice or other calling elsewhere.[50] Seniority inevitably became less significant

47 For the Glissons see *B.H.* I, pp. 236, 272. The next 'foreigner' to be elected was Ralph Philips from Yorkshire in 1642, by which time the Civil War had divided the country: *ibid.*, p. 288.

48 Naylor left in 1623, Allen in 1626 and Wake in 1630 (*B.H.* I, pp. 158, 169, 187). Aquila Cruso, whose election to a Frankland fellowship had been challenged by Branthwaite at the same time as he opposed Allen's election to a senior fellowship, was a senior fellow from 1622 until 1634; Cruso may have been born in Flanders, but as a boy he had been educated at Norwich School and Branthwaite's objections were probably not based on Cruso's place of birth, but on the fact that the Master had not participated in his election (*ibid.*, p. 209).

49 For the gap between 1619 and the earliest surviving *Gesta* in 1651 see *B.H.* III, p. 254.

50 Three promising scholars from outside Norfolk and Suffolk might have been expected to become senior fellows, but were drawn elsewhere: Eleazer Dunkon [Gonville and Caius College 1614], who went to Pembroke as a fellow and tutor as soon as he graduated (*B.H.* I, p. 224); Edmund Smith [1614], who was a junior fellow 1621–27 and left to pursue his medical practice in London with royal patronage (*ibid.*, p. 224); and, most famously, Jeremy Taylor [1626], who was a Perse fellow between 1633 and 1636 and would have undoubtedly become a senior fellow in time if he had not been drawn to All Souls in Oxford by Archbishop Laud (*ibid.*, p. 278).

in the selection of new senior fellows than it had been in the years leading up to *Allen's Case*, and perhaps with it a diminution in the practice of translating fellows between restricted and unrestricted fellowships.[51]

Even though there was never more than one senior fellow born elsewhere than in Norfolk or Suffolk at any time in the 1630s, the question of the correct interpretation of Bateman's and Caius' statutes in respect of the Norfolk preference nevertheless arose again in 1636. It did so, not in the form of any challenge to the election of the Glissons, but in the course of Thomas Cooke's attempts in that year to cling on to the senior fellowship to which he had eventually been elected in accordance with the Chancellor's diplomatic settlement of *Allen's Case* twenty years earlier. Branthwaite's erstwhile protégé had been presented to the living of Mutford-cum-Barnby in 1633 and had by various unscrupulous delays succeeded in holding on to his fellowship until 1635. His valedictory year having long expired, the Master and fellows finally declared his fellowship vacant. Cooke appealed to the king and put before the royal commissioners various charges of dereliction of duty against the Master, Batchcroft, including an assertion that he "contrary to his office and oath hath broken many statutes and caused of his owne accord many elections to be made of strangers of other Countryes [than Norfolk or Suffolk]". The assertion was disingenuous in the extreme; for Cooke was not only equating the election of senior fellows with that of junior fellows but also deliberately presenting the narrowest possible interpretation of the statutes as requiring the "Master and certain fellowes ever to be chosen out of the said Countries [of Norfolk and Suffolk]" and confining the statutory allusion to preference entirely to the "praeferring the poore before the rich if they be equally qualified with them in worth and parts". To this strained interpretation he added the unsustainable assertion that "all elections since the foundation have (for the most part) ever been made accordingly". Neither assertion impressed the three commissioners. They dismissed both of them peremptorily with the finding that:

> (Caius Stat. 8.) First touching the statute of election unto the said Colledge wee find that the same doth not absolutely require that Norfolke and Suffolke men and such as are of the Diocesse of Norwych bee onely chosen, but that first those of Norfolke then those of Suffolke and of the Diocesse of Norwych be preferred, and wee find that in all times there have beene some of other Countryes admitted, and that the present Master of the said Colledge hath so carefully pursued that statute as at this time of the twelve senior fellows of that house eleven are of Norfolke.[52]

51 In the absence of complete *Acta* it is unclear how far the practice of translation from unrestricted to restricted fellowships continued to prevail during the period; at some future date it may be possible to learn more from the *Liber Rationalis*.

52 *Annals*, p. 392; see *Cooke's Case* (1636), Appendix G. The three commissioners were the archbishop of Canterbury, the Chancellor of the University and the bishop of Norwich.

Although the commissioners accepted as valid some of Cooke's other allegations of breaches of statutes, they found them trivial and in the end all that Cooke got for his pains was a severe rebuke for wasting His Majesty's time. Cooke departed and ceased to trouble the college, and the question of the Norfolk preference did not arise again until after the Civil War.

The subsequent story is often presented as a steady process that proceeded inexorably towards the virtually total restriction of the whole fellowship to natives of Norfolk and Suffolk by the middle of the eighteenth century. It would seem, however, that the story was more complex: a sea-change appears to have occurred in the 1670s, largely as a consequence of the traumatic impact on the college of the Civil War and the Commonwealth.

So far as the composition of the Fellowship and the question of a Norfolk preference were concerned, the Civil War was indeed traumatic for the college. In April 1644 the earl of Manchester began in the college the work with which he had been charged by Parliament, the task of cleansing the university and ejecting from the colleges "such fellows as are scandalous". Within three months five of the senior fellows had been summarily ejected, and at least three more had suffered the same fate by 1651: in each of these eight cases the ejected fellows were replaced by graduates intruded from other colleges, none of whom were from either Norfolk or Suffolk. The culmination of the process came with the ejection of Batchcroft as Master in 1649 and the intrusion of William Dell from Emmanuel in his place, but the practice of intrusion continued thereafter. By 1652 no fewer than twelve senior fellows had been intruded from other colleges, notably Sidney Sussex and Emmanuel, in the eight years following 1644, and only one of the twelve had come from either of the two counties. The result was striking. At the start of the war all but one of the senior fellows had been born in Norfolk or Suffolk: by 1652 that proportion was reversed and only two of the senior fellows came from either of those two counties.

After 1652 fewer fellows were intruded from other colleges by the Parliamentary Committee for regulating the universities, and elections were again made by the Master and fellows primarily from within Caius' own college. As a result of the number of Norfolk scholarships the number of fellows elected from that county and from Suffolk (first to junior and subsequently to senior fellowships) began to rise again, but, given the preponderance of 'foreigners' among the electors, it is perhaps not surprising that the change was gradual: in the last year of the Commonwealth eight of the twelve were 'foreigners' and only four came from Norfolk or Suffolk.[53]

53 Linge [Gonville and Caius College 1642], Gelsthorp [1642] and Robinson [1651] came from Norfolk; Boult [1649] came from Suffolk (*B.H.* I, pp. 342, 349, 381 and 375). The eight 'foreigners' were Adamson [1644, Rutland], Naylor [1645, Devon], Felton [1647, Cambs], Wheeler [1649, Essex], Marsh [1651, Glos], Jenks [1653, Scotland], Thurston [1656, Somerset] and Mitteforde [1656, Northumberland] (*B.H.* I, pp. 352, 357, 371, 376, 383, 387, 393 and 393).

The Restoration swiftly brought about a change in the number of senior fellows from Norfolk and Suffolk, and with it a revival in the preponderance which those counties had enjoyed in the years leading up to the Civil War. The tenure of nine of the twelve who were holding senior fellowships at the Restoration was confirmed by Royal letter, but that of three fellows was not and their fellowships came to an abrupt end with the return of the monarch. Two of the three were 'foreigners' who had been brought in from other colleges and had been born elsewhere than in the two preferred counties.[54] In addition to the two 'foreigners' who were not confirmed, a third senior fellow (Marsh) whose fellowship had been confirmed resigned it soon after and was in turn replaced by a Norfolkman, John Gostlin. This meant that, by 1662, there were seven from Norfolk and five who were not from either of the two favoured counties.[55]

Although the Commonwealth practice of electing the great majority of senior fellows from outside the college and from 'foreign' counties was reversed at the Restoration, it left two legacies that had unfortunate consequences: (i) a burning sense of injustice which led to a fierce insistence upon an extreme view of the preference, and (ii) a loss of the Fellowship's collective memory of the practice of the college in the reign of the earlier Stuart kings. Those consequences came

54 Mitteforde and Wheeler; Boult, the third who lost his fellowship, was a native of Suffolk: see note following. It should be noticed that five of the nine senior fellows whose tenure was confirmed in 1661 had been elected during the period after William Bagge had become president in 1655 and the college had enjoyed a more settled administration as a result (Gelsthorp, Naylor, Thurston, Felton and Robinson); three of the other four had been elected in the two preceding years (Jenks, Linge and Adamson), and only Marsh had been elected earlier (in 1651). For the beneficial influence of William Bagge on the college, see Brooke, *History*, pp. 131–40.

55 It is baffling to trace the changes in the composition of the Fellowship in the months immediately preceding and following the Restoration; more work is needed to clarify Venn's account of the transition from the Commonwealth (*B.H.* III, p. 106). Mitteforde appears to have departed very early in 1660, if not before, and Boult had to accept the Stokys fellowship in place of his senior fellowship (*Gesta*, 5 October 1660). This made way for the immediate reinstatement of two senior fellows who had been ejected early in the course of Manchester's cleansing of the college (the elderly Blancks and Sheringham, both Norfolkmen). The Master, Dell, departed without waiting to be ejected, but the president, Wheeler, stayed until his fellowship was formally declared vacant by the Master and fellows "for just and sufficient cause for removal under the statutes", including "that he had been a great dishonour to the College, and is yet esteemed to be, and that he is judged no way able to promote the Credit, or advantage, of the College in any regard, which the Statutes make a sufficient cause of Removal upon consent of the Custos and major part of the Senior Fellows" (*Gesta*, 28 May 1661; Gostlin, *Historiola*, MS 621/457, pp. 85ff). Wheeler's expulsion allowed Boult to be re-elected to a senior fellowship, though he died in college of smallpox within a term and was replaced by a Norfolkman, John Ellys, the future Master (Gostlin, *Historiola*, p. 91). The fellowships of the remaining nine senior fellows were confirmed by Royal letter (*Gesta*, 9 March 1661). Marsh, however, resigned his fellowship in order to pursue a career in Ireland and this enabled the much respected John Gostlin, a Norfolkman, to be elected in his place (*Gesta*, 15 July 1661; Gostlin, *Historiola*, p. 91). The dominance of the two counties, and that of Norfolk in particular, was to be firmly maintained for another two hundred years.

to affect the college's approach to the Norfolk preference greatly during the twenty years following the Restoration.

The first consequence was immediately apparent. The confirmation in 1660 of all but three of the senior fellows and the reinstatement of the two surviving fellows from the reign of Charles I inevitably meant that the expectations of only one of the royalist sympathisers who returned to the college could be satisfied and, together with the younger members who had come up to the college after the Restoration, the other sympathisers had to remain content with the prospect of junior fellowships pending eventual vacancies in the senior fellowship. In Legge's or Branthwaite's day this might have been acceptable, for the financial difference between the two classes of fellowship had been relatively modest; but by the Restoration the gap had become considerable. In the intervening period the emoluments of a senior fellowship had been substantially increased: the stipend had been doubled (out of the income from the purchase of Great Shelford and Weeting) and then virtually doubled again by the dividend from corn money and entry fines, so that the combined stipend and dividend was now in excess of £40 a year.[56] In contrast the annual stipend of a junior fellow had remained unchanged at £10 since 1616, when it had been brought up to that figure in accordance with Stephen Perse's will; thereafter its value had been severely eroded by inflation and it was now barely sufficient to live on. While the half-yearly college account of a senior fellow would normally leave a small balance even without the distribution of corn money and entry fines, the accounts of a junior fellow might leave him with a debit balance and no dividend to settle it with, unless he was very frugal.[57] It is not surprising that the inability to live upon £10 a year featured prominently in the petitions to the king submitted by those who felt aggrieved by the frustration of their expectations.[58] The grievance of the Frankland fellows over the financial disparity can only have been intensified by a singularly ungenerous decision of the Master and senior fellows following the great Fire of London: "That the halfe year's rent which would have been due at our Lady['s day] last for the two houses which stood in Philip Lane, London, before the fire, be deducted out of the stipends of Mrs Frankland's fellows and scholars proportionately, the said

[56] See "*Dividends*", § VI. 5 below.

[57] In the nature of things fellows' bills differed. See, *e.g.*, the half-yearly accounts to Michaelmas 1662 (*Lib. Rat.* Michaelmas 1662): excluding the bursar and the steward (whose accounts included corporate revenue and expenditure), six senior fellows had a credit balance, and four had small debit balances that would be amply covered by the half-year's corn rent; the expenditure on commons of the junior fellows was markedly smaller, but it still left three of the seven Frankland fellows (and one of the four Perse fellows who was considerably less frugal than the other junior fellows) in debt on their accounts.

[58] See the petitions of Richard Watson [Gonville and Caius College 1628] in 1661 and Joshua Basset [Gonville and Caius College 1657] in 1669 (*B.H.* I, pp. 286,400).

houses being part of her gift."[59] Much of the frustration was inevitably directed towards the wholesale practice of importing members from other colleges into fellowships that had been practised successively by the earl of Manchester, the Parliamentary Committee and, finally, the college during Dell's mastership; and since the persons imported from other colleges had come from 'foreign' counties the resentment was eventually to find its expression in an aggressive assertion of the Norfolk preference. It was thus at this point that the smouldering question of the Norfolk preference became entangled with the acrimony that accompanied the return to the college of the Royalist sympathisers who had been forced out during the Interregnum and now had to be content with the award of junior fellowships – a result in their eyes of the confirmation of the elections that had been made to persons more junior and less deserving during the later years of the Commonwealth.

The second consequence became apparent only when the smouldering question became a burning issue in 1678. Although steps had been taken in the later years of the Commonwealth to revive the corporate memory of the college for the future,[60] the corporate memory of events before the Civil War had been kept alive after the Restoration only by Batchcroft and the two elderly fellows who had been restored to the fellowships which they had held before the Civil War, Blancks and Sheringham. The aged Batchcroft had returned to the college for only a few weeks in 1660 before resigning the mastership shortly before his death; Blancks died in 1676 and, although Sheringham was still alive when the issue finally arose in 1678, he died a few weeks later.[61] The death of Blancks in particular deprived the college of the first-hand memory of one who had been elected to a fellowship sixty years earlier – in the very year in which *Allen's Case* had been taken to the Chancellor.[62] Blancks' death seems to have obliterated that crucial case completely from the corporate memory of the college, for it was

59 *Gesta*, 17 April 1667; *B.H.* III, p. 108; Gostlin, *Historiola*, MS 621/457, p. 99.

60 The revival had been due mainly to the influence of the president, Bagge, who had started to "continue and endeavour to perfect the College Annals where they are defective" (*Gesta*, 16 May 1655); and Moore, one of the ejected fellows, had been asked to continue his work the following year. Following Bagge's lead, Adamson had undertaken the compilation of the *Registrum Magnum* shortly after that; he also started to make a new copy of the college's statutes (MS 727/754). Both Bagge and Moore had died before the Restoration.

61 *B.H.* I, pp. 204, 243. Sheringham, though very elderly, had attended the College Meeting on 19 February 1678 at which the issue was raised, but died in college in dramatic circumstances a few weeks later.

62 Even Blancks' exceptional sixty years as a fellow was outdone by Thomas Batchcroft who finally resigned the mastership sixty-five years after he had first become a fellow in 1595: *B.H.* I, p. 139. Like Blancks, Batchcroft had suffered the indignity of being expelled from his position during the Interregnum. In the context of the College's corporate memory it is significant that, in the years during the Interregnum after Batchcroft had been expelled as Master by Manchester in 1649, the complete break in the collegiate memory led to fellows having to be sent to Suffolk during the Interregnum to ask him questions about college precedents and property.

never referred to in the dispute in 1678, nor indeed was it mentioned for many years after. To a modern eye it is puzzling that such a crucial case was overlooked so completely, for the details of the case in the Annals are now readily available today; but it must be remembered that the account in the Annals of the years from 1603 to 1648 had only recently been compiled by Moore and transcribed by a clerk, and in 1678 copies may not yet have been readily accessible.[63]

Although the dispute over the Norfolk preference did not flare up until 1678 it had been smouldering since 1667. In that year George Thorpe, a Londoner, was elected into a senior fellowship. The son of a cook, Thorpe had been admitted as a sizar and had been elected into a Frankland fellowship in 1659 in the last years of the Commonwealth, when Dell was Master.[64] Like that of other Commonwealth junior fellows and scholars his status was considered not to require royal confirmation at the Restoration and he continued to hold his fellowship until 1663. In that year he was elected to a fellowship at Emmanuel and his departure automatically improved the prospects of the various Frankland fellows who were more junior to him. However, following a vacancy in the unrestricted Willowes senior fellowship, Thorpe returned to Caius in the summer of 1667 for some reason that is unrecorded.[65] On his return to Caius he was accorded his previous seniority among the Frankland fellows during the short period that elapsed before he was elected into the vacant Willowes fellowship.[66] The disappointment and discontent of three existing Frankland fellows who were more junior to him – all of whom were natives of Norfolk or Suffolk – at this abrupt setback to their expectations of a much sought-after senior fellowship must have been intensified by the fact that less than six months had passed since they had been required to accept the reduction in their inadequate half-year's stipend as a consequence of the Great Fire mentioned earlier.[67]

Joshua Basset, the most junior of the Frankland fellows, appears to have been particularly disgruntled; for he contrived to obtain a royal mandate that he should have the next senior fellowship on Caius' foundation to become vacant. Even that failed to satisfy him and the college assuaged his discontent by translating him into the Stokys fellowship which, though more junior than the

63 See Venn's Introduction (pp. ix–xi) to his edition of the *Annals* (1904). Translations of the completed Annals were made by Brady, but it is not clear whether they had been made by 1678. It may well be that Brady's work on the Annals and his compilation of a list of 'foreign' fellows was undertaken in the course of the dispute.

64 *B.H.* I, pp. 387–8.

65 It was perhaps because he had already been marked out to fill the office of dean; he became dean almost immediately after his return as a fellow. The vacancy in the senior fellowship had recently arisen as a result of the death of John Felton, another 'foreigner'.

66 *Gesta*, 6 September 1667. In the short period between his return and his election he incurred a charge for commons and his name was inserted into the accounts above three of the Frankland fellows: *Lib. Rat.*, Michaelmas 1667.

67 See n. 59 above.

Frankland, carried a greater stipend. He had to remain content with that until 1673, when he finally acquired the senior fellowship that he coveted so greatly. As his later conduct showed, he was as divisive a character as Thomas Cooke had been forty years earlier and one wonders how acrimonious meetings were in the five years during which both he and Thorpe were divinity senior fellows whose theological sympathies were very different.[68] Thorpe resigned his fellowship and left Cambridge in 1678, but he seems to have carried the memory with him; when he died forty years later in 1719, he was recorded by the then Master of Caius as saying that he would have given to Caius the handsome benefaction which he left to Emmanuel, had it not been for the Norfolk preference.[69]

Thorpe's resignation created a vacancy in the unrestricted Willowes fellowship. The strongest of the candidates was another Londoner, Ralph Barker, who was Stokys fellow and, in the words of a special memorandum included in the *Gesta*, was "senior to all the Fellows of Mrs Frankland's and Dr Wendy's foundations and a person acceptable to the Society, so that according to the Custome of the College hee was to be admitted into the next senior fellowship which should be vacant, had he been qualified as to his country but hee being born at London and the 8th statute of Dr Caius requiring a Norfolk or Suffolk man, his Majestie was pleased to dispense with that Statute, whereupon hee was elected and admitted."[70] As the writer of the memorandum dryly noted, the interpretation of the college's domestic statutes was properly a matter for the Visitor and no one else, but, as the writer added, no appeal was ever made to him in the case and no interpretation had of late been made that might raise any scruple that might hinder Barker's election: instead the Crown was approached.[71] The fact that it was felt prudent to record an explicit memorandum in the *Gesta* that, since he was a Londoner by birth, the election and admission was made in accordance with the king's mandate – even though the person to be elected had been chosen without any dispute *and* was a matriculated member of the college who had been successively a scholar, Frankland and Stokys fellow *and* the Willowes fellowship was not restricted by the benefactor – indicates a

68 For Bassett, see *B.H.* I, p. 400 (where Venn quotes a contemporary description: "He was such a mongrel papist, who had so many nostrums in his religion that no part of the Roman church could own him"). For Basset's theological sympathies, see Mark Goldie, 'Joshua Basset, popery and revolution', in *Sidney Sussex College Cambridge*, ed. D.E.D. Beales and H.B. Nisbet (Woodbridge, 1996), pp. 111–30, cited in *Emmanuel College*, p. 280.

69 According to Dr Gooch: MS 621/457, p. 79. Whether Thorpe ever contemplated leaving the benefaction to Caius may be doubted, but there is no reason to doubt that his experience of the Norfolk preference lingered sufficiently in his memory for him to make the remark recounted by Gooch, who may have been acquainted with Thorpe through their ecclesiastical connections. For Thorpe's benefaction to Emmanuel, see S. Bendall, *Emmanuel College*, pp. 334, 341–3, 366 and 612.

70 *Gesta*, 19 February 1678.

71 It would have been easy for the Master, Robert Brady, to approach the royal court, if he already had charge of public records.

total ignorance of the college's practice before the Civil War. The desirability for royal approval also suggests that the 'unconstitutional' practices of the Commonwealth may have tainted the election of 'foreigners' in Royalist eyes in the years following the Restoration. Furthermore, the perception of Caius' eighth statute as an absolute restriction to the two counties and not simply a preference *ceteris paribus* shows an unawareness of *Allen's Case* and implies that Moore's account of the case in his continuation of the Annals was not yet widely available in the college.

Barker's case marks a high-water mark of the Norfolk preference which went far beyond any previous ruling or assumption in two respects: first, in the absence of any reference to Bateman's statutes; and, second, in the novel interpretation of Caius' eighth statute as requiring a royal dispensation before any person not born in Norfolk or Suffolk might lawfully be elected into *any* of the twelve senior fellowships. Furthermore, by implication any discretion to prefer was to be confined to the preferring of poorer natives of the two counties before less indigent ones and perhaps to members of this college before those of other colleges.

Even that failed to satisfy the divisive Basset. Barker's election into the Willowes fellowship created a vacancy in the Stokys fellowship and, on 27 January 1679, this in turn was filled by the election of a Frankland fellow, John Lightwine.[72] This triggered the need to elect a scholar into the vacated Frankland fellowship. In the words of the *Gesta*, the Master thereupon "called to a Scrutiny for an election into Mr Lightwine's place, and the fellowes disagreeing, he pronounced *nulla est electio*".[73] The disagreement, it would seem, concerned the candidature of a scholar of the college, Amias Chichester, a Devonian.[74] On 7 March Brady again called for a vote, "but the Company not agreeing it devolved to the Master", and "hee pronounced Mr Chichester fellow of Mrs Frankland's foundation in Mr Lightwine's place, which Dr Gostlin Mr Halman and Mr Basset absolutely protested against as contrary to the 8th stat. of Dr Caius, Mr Chichester not being qualified as to his country; the rest of the fellowes seemed to suspend their opinions of the pronouncing him fellow and desired the Visitors might have notice of it, only Mr Topcliffe sayd that the Master had done very well, [w]hereupon Mr Chichester was not admitted".[75] Later the same month Brady again proposed his admission, "but after some

72 *Gesta*, 27 January 1679.

73 *Ibid.*

74 *B.H.* I, p. 437. Unlike Barker, who was already a junior fellow and a member of the Society at the time of his election to a senior fellowship the year earlier and was no doubt alert to the likelihood of opposition, Chichester was a scholar and would have had neither standing nor forewarning to obtain a royal mandate.

75 *Gesta*, 7 March 1679. The record there is, quite exceptionally, signed by Dr Gostlin as secretary: "*Ita testor J Gostlin Secr.*" Topcliffe, the most junior of the senior fellows, was himself a Norfolkman. Only one 'foreigner' (Jenks) was present.

debate, it was resolved that he should not be admitted till such time as the Visitors had determined whether his nomination were statutable or not and if they agreed it to be soe, that the sayd Mr Chichester should have the full profits of that fellowship, from the day of the Master's nomination of him to it, and also his seniority reserved".[76] Unlike Branthwaite, Brady had the good sense not to act unilaterally, but abided his time until Michaelmas. In the meantime another scholar was elected to a Frankland fellowship, but his admission "was defer'd, by consent of all the company, until the difference between the Master and some of the fellowes, concerning Mr Chichester's admission should be determined, if it could be done before Mich. next; otherwise, at that time, the Master by agreement might admit both of them when he pleased".[77] It is clear that Brady did not waste that summer, for he appears to have convinced all the fellows except the divisive Basset that an appeal to the Visitors was unnecessary. On 30 September Brady admitted Chichester, but, in the words of the *Gesta*, "Mr Basset protested against his admission as against the 8th statute of Caius, against the order when the first protestation was made and against the Master's promise to the contrary."[78] He protested to no avail.

Chichester's election appears to be the only occasion on which it was ever argued that the Norfolk preference applied to Frankland fellowships or to any other junior fellowships. In the case of senior fellowships, however, the extreme interpretation of Caius' eighth statute that had been formulated in Barker's case in the preceding year for *all* such fellowships prevailed unbroken until 1723, when an Essex man, James Husband, was elected. During those forty-four years

[76] *Gesta*, 24 March 1679.

[77] *Gesta*, 18 August 1679. The scholar whose admission was deferred was none other than Bartholomew Wortley (*B.H.* I, p. 444), who became one of the college's most generous benefactors and, though a Norfolkman, spent much of his later life in Chichester's native county, Devon.

[78] It seems highly likely that Brady had already compiled his list of past senior (but not junior) fellows born elsewhere than in Norfolk or Suffolk. The list is preserved in MS 602/278 and is referred to in a paper by a later Master, Sir Thomas Gooch, in which he also argued strongly against any exclusive Norfolk preference: MS 621/427, pp. 57ff. It may have been in connection with Chichester's election that Brady prepared his translation and edition of the Annals, which by then contained Moore's account of *Allen's Case* and *Cooke's Case*; see *Annals*, Introduction p. xi.

Basset was later to prove as divisive in Sidney Sussex as he seems to have been in Caius. During the reign of James II he managed to get himself appointed by royal mandate as Master of that Puritan college, where his Catholic opinions "brought him into constant struggles with the fellows" (*B.H.* I, p. 400). He was removed from the mastership there in December 1688 and his fellowship at Caius was declared void three months later. Chichester continued to hold his Frankland fellowship until 1695 before marrying and returning to Devon. During those years he held several college offices and would doubtless have gained a senior fellowship if he had been a Norfolkman. The unfairness of Chichester's case may well have prompted both Brady and the president, Lightwine, to make provision on Brady's death for a doubling of the stipends of the Frankland fellows (see MS 621/457, p. 255; *B.H.* IV(2), p. 36).

only two persons who had not been born in either of the two favoured counties were elected senior fellows, and in both cases the election was made in pursuance of a royal mandate: Christopher Green, the son of the college's cook, in 1682, and Edmund Scarburgh, the son of the king's physician, Sir Charles Scarburgh, in the same year.[79] Green's election illustrates very well the dominance which the extreme interpretation of Caius' eighth statute exercised in the thinking of the college at the time, for, as in the case of Barker four years earlier, the Master and fellows had been very ready to vote for Green and the only function of the royal mandate was to remove their scruples about his place of birth.[80] The royal mandate's function in Green's case contrasts sharply with the less reputable purpose it served in Scarburgh's case, namely, to force the election of the son of a royal favourite against the unanimous wishes and judgement of the college.[81] Christopher Green justified the royal mandate with a distinguished career in which he was finally Regius Professor of Physic for forty-one years: Scarburgh justified, with a singularly undistinguished career, the blank refusal of any senior fellow to vote for his election despite the royal mandate.

Forty-one years passed before the next occasion on which anyone not born in either of the two favoured counties was elected to a senior fellowship and it is significant that two important events had occurred shortly before that election was made in 1723.[82] First, in the preceding ten years before the election there had been a series of disputes between the aged Master, John Ellys, and the fellows over Ellys' refusal to admit into their fellowships no fewer than four persons who had been chosen by a majority of the fellows but in whose favour he had not cast a positive vote. Those disputes were unconnected with the Norfolk preference, for all four persons were Norfolk-born. The disputes concerned the question of the Master's negative voice, but they thereby brought into question the requirement in Philip and Mary's charter that no ordinances, rules or

[79] *B.H.* I, pp. 433, 458. Sir Charles was a former fellow and a professional colleague of Brady: *ibid.*, p. 308.

[80] Unlike the college's caterer (*obsonator*) and butler (*promus*), the college's cook was not a statutory member of the college, and Green's father was a Cambridge tradesman; as such, he could be married and he lived in the town with his family. During the Great Plague of 1666 the cook and his family were received into the college "to provide commons for those few which should venture to stay"; as a child Christopher would have come too. The college shut its gates to all outsiders, and all the bedmakers, except two, were "immediately turned out of the college" and a man was hired "for attending constantly at the Gate, to goe of errands into the town": *Gesta*, 22 June 1666 (cf. *B.H.* III, p. 108); Gostlin, *Historiola*, MS 621/457, p. 97.

[81] When the letters mandatory from the king requiring the college to elect Scarburgh were read by the Master to the senior fellows and he called them to scrutiny "not one of the fellows came up to give any vote". On the Monday following, Brady received a second letter from the king requiring him to admit Mr Scarburgh, which he diplomatically chose to do without seeking a further vote: *Gesta*, 15 June 1682.

[82] James Husband, the person elected, was an Essex man: *B.H.* I, p. 524. Husband was born in Essex but he went to school in Suffolk, first in Ipswich and then in Bury St Edmunds.

statutes made by John Caius should be opposed or contrary (*repugnantia seu contraria*) to those of Bishop Bateman. This in turn revived awareness, first, of *Allen's Case* and the Chancellor's rulings on the Norfolk preference as well as the Master's negative voice, and then of the royal affirmation of those rulings in *Cooke's Case*, neither of which appears to have been invoked in the course of Barker's or Chichester's elections. Those cases ensured recognition that any preference for Norfolk and Suffolk came into play only as a last resort *ceteris paribus* unless the terms of a particular fellowship prescribed a qualification as to place of birth.

The second event was the succession of Thomas Gooch to the mastership on the death of Sir John Ellys in 1716. Gooch had been a fellow when the dispute over the Master's negative voice had first arisen, and although he had resigned his fellowship in 1714 he was by that time well versed in the controversy. He later prepared a paper in which he argued cogently against any Norfolk exclusiveness and in favour only of a preference in the last resort, other things being equal. In the paper he was able to deploy not only the terms of the charter and the wording of Bateman's statutes but also Brady's collection of precedents proving that "in all this time, from Dr Caius to the year 1700, every Master was a Norfolk man ... yet under every one of them there was *one* or *more* elected who were not of the Diocese even tho' there were eligible persons of the Diocese resident in College". Finally, Moore's account of *Allen's Case* and *Cooke's Case* in the Annals enabled Gooch triumphantly to conclude: "having met with two cases, which may by lawyers be called *cases in point* I shall conclude with them, as I do verily think they are conclusive determiners of the Question before us".[83]

Thereafter there appears to have been no further suggestion of any Norfolk exclusiveness (as distinct from a preference) having been imposed by Caius' eighth statute on all twelve senior fellowships and not merely on those five for which the benefactor or benefactress had specified that the holder must be Norfolk-born.[84] In all other respects, however, Gooch's cogent argument had little effect. In the whole of the eighteenth century only one other person born outside the two favoured counties was elected into a senior fellowship in addition to James Husband in 1723, and that person's father was a resident Norfolk-man whose son happened to be born in London.[85] This overwhelming dominance of the two counties was not the result of any narrow interpretation of the college's statutes, but simply due to the fact that the first source to which the college looked for its replacement when a senior fellowship became vacant was the junior fellowship, and by then there were hardly any junior fellows from other counties. Like the senior fellowships these too had become very

[83] MS 621/457, pp. 57ff.

[84] The fellowships founded by Elizabeth Clere, Anne Scroop and John Caius.

[85] Benjamin Young, who was a senior fellow 1770–88 [*B.H.* II, p. 77]. For some purposes a person's county was determined by his or her father's residence, not place of birth.

largely confined by the eighteenth century to natives of Norfolk or Suffolk, even though there was not the same statutory preference for those two counties, and even though Perse had specified a preference for scholars from his school in Cambridge in the election of his fellows. As Venn dryly noted, in 1750 only one of the twenty-six senior and junior fellows did not come from either county, and he was the Master's stepson.[86] Even in other years the number of junior fellows who had not been born in either county did not rise above three at any one time during the century until the first elections to Mr Wortley's fellowships were made in 1771.[87] The dominance of the two counties in the election of junior fellows was not due to any rigid interpretation of the statutes but simply to the dearth of scholars and other suitable candidates from other counties. For this Venn laid the blame squarely on the electors of the time: "The fellows being disposed to elect none but Norfolk and Suffolk men, none but such men had much inducement to enter the college as students."[88] A more likely reason was, however, a financial one: the emolument of a junior fellow was by then so little that there was no inducement for a bright student to stay on in residence as a junior fellow in the hope of eventual election to a senior fellowship unless he was from the favoured counties.[89]

It was not until the nineteenth century that steps were at last taken to remedy a state of affairs which, in Venn's words, "had become seriously injurious to the college".[90] In 1805 the Master and five resident senior fellows recorded and signed in the *Gesta* a declaration of their sentiments on the power of electing into fellowships "young men not born in the diocese of Norwich". It is interesting that they saw no reason to address the question of junior fellowships; for they confined themselves exclusively to the twelve senior fellowships and

86 *B.H.* III, p. 210; the stepson was Charles Compton, a Londoner [*B.H.* II, p. 9]. Venn might have added, even more dryly, that when the number of one was doubled in the course of the year the second 'foreigner' was the Master's own son, John Gooch, who had been born in Cambridge [*B.H.* II, p. 58].

87 In his will Wortley had specifically required that one of his two fellowships was to be for a man from North Devon: *B.H.* III, pp. 218–19. Wortley's provision re-established the surprising flow of students that had come from the Barnstaple area in North Devon during the period between 1560 and 1680 after Caius' re-foundation of the college: see Venn, *B.H.* I, Introduction, p. xiii. (Both the principal *dramatis personae* in the leading cases, Allen and Chichester, were from the Barnstaple area.)

88 *B.H.* III, p. 210. The great preponderance of closed scholarships available only to natives of Norwich or Norfolk would also have played a part. See *H.U.C.*, II, pp. 199–206, for the numbers of Norfolk students at the college in the sixteenth and seventeenth centuries and for the particular influence of the City of Norwich.

89 For the stipends of junior fellows and the consequent tendency of junior fellows not to stay in residence but seek employment elsewhere, see *The augmentation of fellows' stipends: 1660–1825* in "*Stipends*", § VI. 4, at pp. 434ff below. The Stokys fellow was the only junior fellow who was paid at all adequately, and that fellowship was limited to divinity.

90 *B.H.* III, p. 211.

considered that the cause of the trouble lay entirely in the reading of Caius' statutes as exclusively limiting those fellowships to natives of Norfolk and Suffolk.

> We acknowledge most fully the general preference given by Bishop Bateman's Statutes, in cases of equality between candidates, to Natives of Norwich Diocese; and the absolute limitation of the two Fellowships of Lady Scroop's and Mrs Clere's foundation to persons so born, and also the restriction of the three Fellowships of Dr Caius' foundation to Natives of Norfolk only. But after a full consideration of our Statutes and a careful search into the Records of our College, we are of opinion, and do hereby declare, that the limiting of the remaining seven Senior Fellowships to the two Counties of Norfolk and Suffolk exclusively, is not enjoined by our Statutes, is contrary to the authority of the earliest practice, and in direct opposition to a determination of the Visitors of the College.[91]

They were clearly acquainted with Brady's research and Moore's recounting of Allen's and Cooke's cases, and presumably with Gooch's arguments as well; unlike Gooch however, they applied the limited preference not simply to the three fellowships founded by Bateman but to the four remaining fellowships, including that founded by the Cambridge tradesman Willowes.

Although this clear and firm declaration would seem to go much of the way towards settling the interpretation of the college's statutes and the primacy afforded to Bateman's statutes by the charter, it still left seeds of discontent: for it necessarily left untouched the express restriction to Norfolk or the diocese of Norwich which had been imposed on five senior fellowships by the donors. As three senior fellows later pointed out vigorously in a memorial which they submitted to the 1852 Royal Commission: "Of the twelve Senior Fellowships, three are confined to men born in the county of Norfolk, and two others to men born in the Norwich diocese, and these five Fellowships are still further restricted, three to divinity, and two to physic. The evils resulting from these restrictions are very great."[92] The three memorialists were not alone in their criticism of these restrictions. Two years earlier, in June 1850, all eleven senior fellows other than the president had signed a paper and entered a copy of it in the *Gesta* declaring that they bound themselves, "in electing College and

[91] *Gesta*, 9 January 1805. The full resolution is reproduced in *B.H.* III, p. 211.

[92] Memorial from Three Fellows of Gonville and Caius College, *Report of the Cambridge University Commissioners* 1852 (hereafter *Report*), Appendix, pp. 448–9. The three fellows came from Devon, Woolwich and Hertfordshire respectively: George Budd [Gonville and Caius College 1828], John Tozer [Gonville and Caius College 1831] and J.T. Walker [Gonville and Caius College 1833]: *B.H.* II, pp. 205, 217, 225. Tozer had clashed dramatically with the Master, Benedict Chapman, three years earlier: Venn, *Annals*, Introduction, pp. xii–xiii. By 1852 the provision had become even more restrictive after the transfer of the archdeaconry of Sudbury (and therefore most of West Suffolk) to the diocese of Ely in 1837.

University officers and in presenting to Livings not to consider that an election to a Senior Fellowship, confined to Norfolk or the diocese of Norwich, gives to the holder of such Fellowship any claim in preference to Fellows of prior standing as Fellows (whether Senior or Junior) in the College".[93] Six of the signatories, including the three later memorialists, signed unconditionally; the other five did so subject to the "presumed claims of all present Fellows". Not surprisingly, the six were not natives of Norfolk or the Norwich diocese: it is perhaps more surprising that only two of the other five signatories were from Norfolk and one from Suffolk – the balance on the governing body of the college had already swung strongly against the preference.

Although the memorialists' objection was fundamentally to *any* restrictions, their discontent was not so much directed against the restrictions to locality or subject taken separately, but rather to the combined effect of the two restrictions when taken together. In the case of Divinity it meant that young men from Norfolk or Suffolk were often advanced in seniority over the heads of men who had obtained higher university honours and were several years senior to them, and by reason of their earlier admission into the list of Seniors they had been considered to have a prior claim not only to college offices but to college livings also.[94] As regards Medicine the position was, the memorialists considered, even worse: "Few men now graduate in physic at Cambridge; the number of Norfolk men who so graduate is consequently very small, and it is seldom that one of these obtains a University distinction that would entitle him to an open Fellowship in the college."[95] In their view the overall consequence was that the college was sometimes compelled to elect as senior fellows "young men who otherwise would not be entitled to a Fellowship at all, while at the same time, men of other counties who have taken most distinguished honours have commonly to wait for ten or twelve years after their election as Fellows before they have any voice or authority whatever in College matters". Furthermore, those ten or twelve years would be years of hardship for "the Junior Fellowships are, with one exception, very poor".[96] The primary cause of these evils they

93 C.O.5 of 26 June 1850. See "*Submissions on the Norfolk Preference*", Appendix I below.

94 The virulence of feeling led two of the most recently elected senior fellows who were Norfolk-men formally to forego precedence in Hall, Chapel and the Combination Room over those who were of prior standing in the college but had been admitted to the seniority at a later date; however, they reserved their claims to offices and livings in accordance with date of election: see "*Submissions on the Norfolk Preference*", Appendix I below.

95 *Report*, p. 448. The picture drawn by the memorialists contrasts sharply with the reputation which the college had enjoyed in the early seventeenth century of being *the* medical college *par excellence* and which had attracted to the college such boys as William Harvey from Kent and Francis Glisson from Dorset and led Fuller to describe it as "such a little Montpelier is this College alone for eminent physicians!": Fuller, *Worthies* (1840 edn), p. 191.

96 The exception they had in mind was the Stokys fellowship, not the Wortley fellowships: see "*Stipends*", § VI. 4 below.

attributed directly to Dr Caius' statutes: "The restrictions and divisions of which we complain, and which we believe to be so injurious to the College, have been most of them introduced under Statutes supposed to have been given by Dr Caius in 1572."[97]

The memorial carried great weight with the Commissioners, who reproduced it verbatim and expressed their concurrence with its recommendations "that it would be a great benefit to the College if gradually, and without prejudice to the interests of existing Fellows, the different benefactions were incorporated and the Fellowships made more nearly equal".[98] The memorialists and their allies had to wait until the total repeal of Dr Caius' statutes in 1860 to see these aims fully achieved, but they had the satisfaction of seeing the Norfolk preference finally swept away two years earlier when, in 1858, an Order in Council confirmed a statute framed by the governing body and approved by the statutory Commissioners, by which it was enacted that

> No preference should thereafter be given to any person in elections to the Mastership, or to any Fellowship then existing in the College, in respect of such person's place of birth ... and that no preference should thereafter be given to any person in elections to any Scholarship, Exhibition or other Emolument then existing within the said College, in respect of such person's place of birth ... and that no person being a British subject should be ineligible by reason of his place of birth either to the Mastership of the said College, or to any Fellowship, Scholarship, or other Emolument then existing therein.[99]

By an ironic twist of fate, the memorialists did not have to wait even until 1858 for their greatest triumph. They had confined their complaint to the election of fellows, but the Commissioners went further in their Report in 1852 and applied their arguments to the one office that had, since Caius' day, been regarded as the preserve of Norfolk men: the mastership. Relying on the primacy afforded to the statutes of Bateman by the charter of 1557, the Commissioners challenged "the alteration introduced by Dr Caius, in the statutable regulations relating to the Mastership of Gonville and Caius College". They expressed the "opinion that the restriction should be removed; partly, as never having been of more than doubtful authority, and still more from the prejudicial consequences which are

97 In contrast their memorial lauded Bateman whom they praised (by a benign and slightly disingenuous reading of his statutes) as having founded a college "for a Master and four Fellows, who might be of any county or any profession".

98 *Report*, p. 168.

99 Order in Council, dated 6 April 1858. The commissioners who made the statute were not the 1852 Royal Commissioners (the "Cambridge University Commissioners") who had made the Report, but the statutory commissioners appointed under the Cambridge University Act 1856. The 1852 Commission is commonly called the "Graham Commission" after its chairman: see *H.U.C.*, III, pp. 522–3.

entailed upon the Society by so far narrowing the field of choice in the election of its most important officer".[100] On 30 August 1852 the Commissioners signed their report, and on 23 October in the same year the Master of the college, Benedict Chapman, died. Twelve days later, on 4 November, and doubtless aware of the Commissioners' view of Caius' restriction as "never having been of more than doubtful authority", the opponents of the Norfolk preference needed no further encouragement to force through the election as Master of Edwin Guest, who "came from Birmingham, and so was safely outside the statute".[101] Guest's rapid election was inevitably followed by vigorous protest, which, though ineffective, served as the final evidence of the bitterness that the Norfolk preference had provoked during the centuries since Dr Caius rewrote the college's statutes.[102]

100 *Report*, p. 153. The report was published in November, but there can be little doubt that the gist of its contents was widely known in Cambridge by the time of Guest's election on 4 November.

101 Brooke, *History*, p. 214. For the three scrutinies that were necessary, at the third of which Guest was induced to break the tie by voting for himself, see Venn, *B.H.* III, pp. 142–3, where he observed gravely "that, with the prospect of a complete change of statutes before long, it was hardly the time thus to sever the unbroken practice and tradition of five centuries". The need for three scrutinies was not mentioned in the *Gesta* for 4 November 1852. It was not considered to be in any way improper for a fellow to vote for himself: Chapman had done so at his own election (*B.H.* III, pp. 137–8).

102 For the protest of eight former fellows, including a distinguished judge of the Common Law courts (E.H. Alderson, at that time a Baron of the Court of Exchequer and previously Judge of the Court of Common Pleas) and two of the eleven fellows who had signed the declaration of 26 June 1850 in respect of Norfolk fellowships (G.E. Paget and J.R. Crowfoot), see "*Submissions on the Norfolk Preference*", Appendix I below.

VI. 4

Stipends

In the time since Caius' statutes were repealed in 1860 the college has come to use the term "stipend" to indicate the remuneration paid to college officers for the performance of their college office as distinct from any payment made in virtue of a fellowship. In sharp contrast to the present use of the term, we find that Caius never used it for payments to officers in his statutes, even though the term was already being used in that way in the statutes of nearby Tudor colleges which had been founded not long before his re-foundation of Gonville Hall.[1]

The fact that he did not employ the term "stipend" in relation to payments for the discharge of a college office is not in itself surprising, for he drew heavily upon the medieval statutes and language of his predecessor Bishop Bateman, when he was drafting his own statutes. For all three founders the overriding consideration in their planning was not the number of officers who would need to be remunerated, but the maximum number of fellows and scholars that the resources of their new foundations could support in their academic studies, in addition to a Master. That support took the form of a stipend and livery, and for all three founders the concept of a stipend was inseparable from the notion of a 'maintenance grant' which was intended to enable its holder to devote himself to his studies, not to be the payment of a wage or salary for administrative services: no member of the college could expect to receive more than one stipend, any more than he could expect more than one maintenance grant. As with the foundation of other medieval colleges, a fellow was expected to take his turn in performing, without any substantial additional remuneration, whatever tasks might be required for the running of the college.

1 Cf. Statute 43 of Trinity College. After Caius' death the term "stipend" was occasionally used in his college to denote a payment to a fellow for performance of an office (*e.g.*, *Bursar's Book*, Michaelmas 1609, *Exposita Extraordinaria*, payment of 50s. for a half-year's "stipend" for catechising): but such uses are rare until the nineteenth century: cf. *The change from salary to stipend*, at p. 477 below. For its use in St John's and Trinity Colleges by Caius' time, see the following note; see also its frequent use in the statutes of Emmanuel College 1585 (Statutes 14, 27, 30 and 39).

In planning his statutes in the 1550s Caius appears to have confined himself to studying Bateman's medieval statutes for Gonville Hall together with the statutes for the university that were current in Caius' own time. He seems not to have consulted the statutes which had been made relatively recently for the three other colleges founded earlier in the century, particularly the two royal colleges of St John's and Trinity, whose statutes had set out elaborate schemes of varying stipends for fellows and officers according to their responsibilities.[2] In contrast, Caius' statutes for his own college hardly address the question whether, apart from occasional fees for lectures,[3] any additional remuneration other than the stipend enjoyed by every fellow was due to those of them who undertook the many heavy obligations which his statutes imposed upon such college officers as the president, bursars, steward, deans, chaplain and librarian. The sole exception was the direction in Statute 59 that the registrary should be paid a salary of 20s. for his work.[4] Apart from that office, it is as if Caius assumed that fellows should be content to undertake all other administrative offices in their turn without additional emolument, in the same way that he expected that they should gratuitously teach students and take on the onerous responsibility for their pupils' financial obligations to the college. Whether he truly expected such important offices as the bursarship and stewardship to be wholly unremunerated may be doubted,[5] but whether he did so or not it is clear that he regarded offices to be transient appointments made annually and shared out among all fellows, and even if the holder might receive a fee during the limited period when he held a particular office, he should not expect a 'career wage' or stipend. Caius saw the stipend of a fellow as essentially different from a fee and, rather, as something akin to a modern maintenance grant to sustain the fellow through a period of study. The only continuing payment on which any fellow could rely was the stipend he received as a fellow.[6]

2 Statute 33 of St John's College and Statute 43 of Trinity College: *Documents*, III, pp. 299, 464.

3 Cf. Statute 34, allowing to the deans the fees from students for courses of lectures given by them.

4 Presumably 20s. for the year. Apart from this one specific provision, he referred to "salaries" occasionally, and in Statute 63 itself he allows to fellows "employments" (*servitia*) and offices. In Statute 60, he somewhat grudgingly allowed that fellows might keep the two salaries that had been provided by the earlier benefactions of Geoffrey Knight and John Whitacre. Only the registrary's fee and these two salaries were charged directly to the college (as *exposita ordinaria*) in the Bursar's Book; half-yearly fees of 5s were paid to the Master as first bursar and to the fellow who was second bursar, but, like fellows' stipends, these fees were set against charges for commons in the *Liber Rationalis*: see, *e.g.*, the accounts of Legge and Perse, *Lib. Rat.* (Michaelmas 1586).

5 See pp. 452ff below.

6 It is convenient to mention here the anomalous case of the Master. In the eyes of both Gonville and Bateman, he was the principal officer of the college who would discharge in person many of the functions that later became the immediate responsibility of other officers, but the emolument granted to him by Bateman in the preamble to his statutes hardly reflected that fact

FELLOWSHIPS

After the Wendy fellowship lapsed and the attempt by one fellow to persuade the college to replace it with a thirteenth fellowship failed in 1582,[7] the accepted establishment of fellows remained firmly fixed at twelve: three fellows on the ancient foundation of Gonville and Bateman; three upon Dr Caius' foundation; and six, not seven, on those of benefactors. These three classes were distinguished by small differences in the amount of their stipend and livery which finally became rigidly fixed in 1583 and were never again varied until Caius' statutes were repealed in 1860. In the long period before that repeal took place the stipends of all twelve fellows were gradually increased greatly, and since the increases were the same for all twelve fellows, the original differences between the classes became negligible long before they were abolished in 1860. Nevertheless, despite their increasing triviality the financial differences in stipend were rigidly observed, even though the three classes were regarded for other purposes as "being united to the others and formed with the Master into the Corporation".[8]

The tripartite pattern of the establishment

In his statutes Bateman had allowed fellows an annual stipend of 6 marks (£4) if they were M.A.s and 5 marks (£3. 6s. 8d.) if they were B.A.s., together with "sufficient robes of one livery a year", and this allowance had long been valued as one mark by Caius' time. In the period between Bateman and Caius the gifts from Willowes and the other intervening benefactors had specified

and was clearly a stipend or maintenance grant of the same character as that of a fellow, albeit a slightly larger one: 8 marks a year as compared with 6 marks for a fellow who was an M.A. and 5 marks for other fellows. It remained that sum (£5. 6s. 8d.) until Caius increased it to £10 in his statutes (Statute 37). The increase was conditional upon his taking an interest and residing in the college, and as such it might be regarded as a salary for performing an office rather than as a stipend, but in later years it was always reviewed in the same context as fellows' stipends: any increase in the one was linked arithmetically with that in the other, the principle being that the Master should receive twice the amount that a fellow was entitled to receive. That principle was adopted both in relation to the distribution of corn money and entry fines, the Master receiving two-fourteenths and each of the twelve fellows one-fourteenth of the total dividend, and whenever straight increases to fellows' stipends were made from 1614 onwards. It was also applied to various allowances, even if the allowance was not shared with all the twelve fellows (*e.g.*, Brady's portions and the sums paid to the managers of the Perse trust).

7 For the Wendy fellowship and Gerrard's claim that Caius' statutes required thirteen fellows, see "*The Fellowship and the Governing Body*", § VI. 1, and "*Gerrard's Case* (1582)", Appendix D. The dispute with Wendy's nephew and executor which had caused the fellowship to lapse was not settled until 1610 and no further election to the Wendy fellowship could be made until after that date.

8 MS 621/457.

(or been taken to specify) a stipend of 8 marks and a gown (or 1 mark) for their fellows, as in Thomas Willowes' gift in 1501.[9] Fellows on Gonville's and Bateman's foundations (*ex antiqua fundatione*) thus received a total of 7 marks a year if they were M.A.s, whereas those on the six other benefactions received 9 marks.[10] In 1558 Caius provided in his draft statutes that his own fellows should receive 8½ marks (£5. 13s. 4d.) after his death for both stipend and livery (*pro victu et veste*) from the rents and profits from Croxley, Runcton and Burnham Thorpe.[11] He also provided in the draft statutes that the payments to his fellows should be further increased to 10 marks (£6. 13s. 4d.) when those rents and profits came to be increased. By the time he formulated the final version of his statutes in 1572 an increased rent for Croxley had already been fixed, and he was able to make provision for at least part of the increases for his own fellows that he had envisaged in 1558. However, he now did that in a different way. Instead of giving a single figure for both stipend and livery, he split the payment between a (slightly smaller) stipend and a separate livery: in Statute 38 he gave his fellows immediate stipends of 8 marks (£5. 6s. 8d.) for M.A.s and 5 marks (£3. 6s. 8d.) for B.A.s, and in Statute 40 he provided that they should have liveries of 26s. 8d. (2 marks) if M.A.s and 20s. (1½ marks) if B.A.s, but not until the leases of his three properties had been renewed and the rents increased. In this way his fellows would ultimately receive the combined payment of 10 marks that he had originally envisaged when they became M.A.s. The wording of Statute 40, however, had the unfortunate and doubtless unintended consequence that *no* payment for livery would become payable until those leases were renewed and this meant, ironically, that, until then, the maximum paid to Caius' own fellows would be only 8 marks (for stipend), whereas that paid to the fellows of the other six benefactors would be 9 marks (for stipend and livery). Not surprisingly the operation of Statute 40 was one of the questions that were straightway submitted to Archbishop Parker for his interpretation. The archbishop was characteristically sensible and ruled that if the income from the property Caius had given to the college was sufficient to bear the cost of livery for his fellows, then the Master and bursars might meet it.[12] The college was quick to take advantage of the ruling, and during the interval before the leases were renewed Caius' fellows were paid the same additional amount for livery that the other

[9] In their returns in 1546 Henry VIII's Commissioners recorded 1 mark (13s. 4d.) as the amount allowed for livery for all the benefactors' fellows: *Documents*, I, p. 230.

[10] Prior to the re-foundation, it would seem from the Commissioners' returns cited in the preceding note that the Master would nominate fellows *ex antiqua fundatione* as Dr Knight's salarists, thereby augmenting their stipends very handsomely – in fact, doubling it: *op. cit.* p. 231. If this was in fact the practice, the restriction to those three fellows had clearly ceased by the time Caius wrote his statutes.

[11] *Documents*, II, pp. 342–4.

[12] See the *Interpretatio* of Matthew Parker above.

fellows received (1 mark if they were M.A.s).[13] As a result the payments to Caius' fellows became identical for a few years with those of the other six benefactors (9 marks); in contrast the three fellows *ex antiqua fundatione* received only 7 marks.

In 1582, the year in which the establishment finally settled at twelve fellowships, the leases of Croxley and Runcton Holme were renewed and the rents were raised to £40 p.a. in accordance with Caius' direction in Statute 91.[14] Without waiting a further thirty-seven years for the lease of Burnham Thorpe to be renewed, the college forthwith invoked Statute 40 and raised the payment for livery to the full 2 marks a year for the three fellows on Caius' foundation.[15] In every year thereafter, until 1860, Caius' fellows received 10 marks (£6. 13s. 4d.) in total annually, and consequently 1 mark (13s. 4d.) more than those on the foundations of the six intervening benefactors and 3 marks (£2) more than the fellows on Gonville's and Bateman's foundation. Caius' action had the result of creating financial differences between the twelve fellows. The differences were not inconsiderable in Caius' day, but they did not lead to any system of promotion, for fellows seem to have been content to retain their original fellowship unless a specific need arose for the holder of an unrestricted fellowship to be "translated" to another fellowship in order to enable the college to make another election to the unrestricted fellowship.[16] As mentioned already, the increases to the stipend made in later centuries were the same for all (senior) fellows and the differences in payments consequently became negligible, yet they continued to be observed meticulously until the reforms of 1860.[17]

[13] See the earliest surviving *Liber Rationalis*, Michaelmas 1581. In Statute 40 Caius had given a payment for livery to his scholars as well as his fellows, and Parker's ruling was sufficiently wide to apply to all the members on Caius' foundation, scholars as well as fellows, but in fact the college made no payment whatever for livery to the scholars until after the rents had been raised in 1582.

[14] Statutes 38 and 40.

[15] *Lib. Rat.* Lady Day 1583 (Paman, and the two most junior of the fellows, Grymstone and Robert: *B.H.* I, pp. 79, 115, 113). It was at this point that Caius' scholars also received for the first time the payment for livery that Caius had given them. Strictly speaking the words of the statute provided for all the increases to be delayed until the lease of the third property, Burnham Thorpe, had been renewed and the rent increased; but its rent was much smaller than that of the other two properties and as the lease still had thirty-six years to run the college did not wait.

[16] See "*The Norfolk Preference*", § VI. 3, at pp. 402–5, and *Allen's Case* (1617), Appendix F. Stephen Perse was translated between fellowships during Legge's mastership, more than once if Gerrard is to be believed. The practice of translating fellows from an unrestricted to a restricted fellowship continued until the restrictions were abolished by the University Commissioners' first statute in 1858: see, *e.g.*, *Gesta*, C.O.15, 25 October 1853.

[17] The differences are very convenient for historians of the college, for they make accounts such as the *Libri Rationales* much easier to analyse and more informative; it is curious that Venn did not draw attention anywhere to the differences even though he must have been aware of them.

1592–1615: the creation of junior fellowships

Joyce Frankland died in 1587 and in her will she founded six fellowships and twelve scholarships in the college in addition to a chaplaincy and a lectureship. She left to the college her principal house in London with an annual rental of £33. 6s. 8d. and the sum of £1,540 to purchase property to produce a further £70 annually. In her will she specified only that the holders of her fellowships should be paid an annual stipend of £7, a sum which was in fact greater than that of any of the three existing classes of fellow,[18] and consequently she did not give any direction about other emoluments such as liveries and distributions, even though the income of £103. 6s. 8d. she provided would have been amply sufficient to provide the holders with those additional emoluments.

According to the *Annals*, much of her property was laid out in loans and in many cases these had to be recovered by litigation which was in turn protracted by the deaths of two of the executors. As a result it would seem that it was not until 1599 that the Manor of D'Abernons with an annual rental of £70 was conveyed to the college by the surviving executor (Thomas Legge, the Master) and it fell into the college's possession only in 1611. Long before that happened the college had made its first decision to elect six fellows on the Frankland foundation at the Michaelmas audit in 1592,[19] and in the course of that term it had to face the question of how the bequest should be implemented, and in particular what further emoluments and allowances the new fellows should receive in addition to their specified stipend. The outcome was that on 11 December 1592 the Master and eight fellows solemnly ruled that the newcomers should have "nothing further", on the ground that "nothing more can be done without prejudice to the fellows and detriment to the college".[20] The only allowances that were grudgingly conceded were that for grain – which could hardly be withheld, given the wording of Sir Thomas Smith's Act[21] – and any hearth-money that might become available in the future, but not existing hearth-money.

At first sight this might seem curmudgeonly, but in fact the stipend of £7 was greater than that of any of the fellows on the existing foundations and their allowances did little more than bring them up to parity with Joyce Frankland's new fellows.[22] The yearly stipend and the livery paid to the existing fellows, together with the perquisites that they enjoyed, did not amount to much more

18 See above (£7 was 10½ marks).

19 Robert Welles (*B.H.* I, p. 122), Matthew Stokes (*B.H.* I, p. 124), Anthony Disberowe (*B.H.* I, p. 128), Henry Pratt (*B.H.* I, 131), Thomas Mallorie (*B.H.* I, 145), and William Barrett (*B.H.* I, 145) who was appointed to her chaplaincy.

20 See "*The Decree of 11 December 1592 on the Frankland fellows*", Appendix E.

21 For some reason corn-rent never became payable in respect of the Manor of D'Abernons: see "*Dividends*", § VI. 5 below. As a result Frankland fellows never received any corn money.

22 See "*Dividends*", § VI. 5.

than a maintenance grant which might reasonably support a young scholar in his early years but would leave him virtually nothing in his pocket after meeting his half-yearly college account. Whether the stipend and livery had been sufficient to meet the charges on a fellow's account in Caius' own day is unclear, but the accounts recorded in the earliest surviving *Liber Rationalis* show that by Legge's time the two statutory payments, stipends and livery, hardly sufficed to meet the charges and left many of the twelve fellows with a debit balance.

The fact that Mrs Frankland specifically provided that her fellows should receive a stipend (of £7) which was greater than that allowed by the college's statutes to the holders of earlier fellowships suggests a recognition by 1592 that the amounts specified in the college's statutes had become inadequate to provide a modest maintenance grant even for a young graduate scholar. By Legge's death in 1607, even Mrs Frankland's figure of £7 had ceased to be regarded as sufficient, for when the Wendy fellowship was revived in 1610 it was agreed with Dr Wendy's heir that the annual stipend should be £10; and when the most senior fellow of the college, Stephen Perse, established six new fellowships on his death in 1615 he not only fixed the stipend for his new fellows at £10 but also made generous provision in his will for raising the stipend of the Frankland fellows to £10 likewise. At the same time as these increases for junior fellows were taking place, however, the stipend of Caius' own fellows remained at £5. 6s. 8d. for an M.A. and £3. 6s. 8d. for a B.A., and that of the other nine senior fellows at less, and by the beginning of the seventeenth century that stipend had already become insufficient to meet the cost of a senior fellow's commons, even with the additional payments contemplated by the statutes (livery and distributions).

Given the discrepancy in stipend between junior and senior fellows, it is not surprising that the deed which re-established the Wendy fellowship in 1610 specifically provided that the holder of that fellowship was not to have or expect "anie profit or commoditie of the said Colledge more than the sum of ten pounds so to him allowed as aforesaid, and not anie divdencye or other profit peculiar or proper to the twelve senior places or Fellowships of the foundation of the same Colledge, but shall be in all things of the like order and sort as the Fellowes of Joyce Franklin's foundation".[23] Stephen Perse was likewise careful to include in his foundation a similar provision that none of his fellows should "have or claime any benefit of dividend or other priviledge but shall be contented with their stipend".[24]

23 *Annals*, p. 222. Thereafter the college was careful to record in the *Acta* that the provision was read out to each newly-elected junior fellow at his admission and expressly accepted by him: *e.g.*, *Acta*, 28 April 1613 (Cooke), *Exiit Book*, 1592–1618.

24 *Annals*, p. 249; he did concede "except it shall be hereafter thought fit by some supreame authoritie or by the said Colledge to incorporate my said fellowes into the body of the said Colledge", but that never happened.

1615–60: the emergence of a gulf between senior and junior fellows

By the Restoration in 1660 a dramatic reversal had occurred in the relative financial positions of senior and junior fellows: a resident senior fellow had by then come to enjoy a modest income rather than the bare subsistence grant which the statutes gave him, and a substantial financial gulf had developed between the twelve senior fellows and the fourteen junior fellows, as well as the constitutional gulf which excluded the latter from any participation in the government of the college.[25] Three factors had contributed to the creation of this financial gulf: corn money, entry fines and a virtual trebling of the statutory stipend of a senior fellow.[26]

At the beginning of the century the statutory stipend had been insufficient to meet the cost of a senior fellow's commons, even with the additional payments contemplated by the statutes (livery and distributions), and he would have needed to resort to his share of corn money to pay any debt to the college. By the time of the Restoration the statutory stipend had been twice augmented by increases of £5 p.a., and with the additional £10 the stipend was, for most senior fellows, sufficient by itself to meet their commons accounts and to leave them with a small credit balance.[27] The increments thus served to restore their stipends to the level which Caius had contemplated in his statutes, *i.e.*, a maintenance grant for frugal graduates that would meet their commons accounts in the years in which they studied for a further degree. In addition to that stipend a senior fellow could rely each year upon a share of corn money that would on average be between £15 and £20, and other small dividends and allowances would give him a further £5 p.a.: he was thus entitled to a regular gross income of roughly £40 p.a. His net income would vary depending upon the amount of his commons bills, but those bills would normally leave him every year with over £30 in his pocket even if he did not hold any college office.[28] In addition he would receive a share of the entry fines which a tenant paid whenever a beneficial lease was renewed,[29] and while the number and value of the fines would vary from year to year he could, on average, expect to receive a further

25 See *The Decree on the Frankland fellows* in "*The Fellowship and the Governing Body*", § VI. 1 above, and *The Frankland Decree* (1592), Appendix E below.

26 For corn money and entry fines, see "*Dividends*", § VI. 5.

27 The two increases in stipends had been made before the Civil War, the first as a result of the purchase of the manor and mills at Great Shelford in 1614 and the second from the purchase of Weeting Manor in 1632. For senior fellows *ex antiqua fundatione* these increases raised the stipend and livery from £4. 13s. 4d. to £14. 13s. 4d. p.a., and to slightly greater sums in the case of the six benefactors' fellows (£16) and the three Dr Caius' fellows (£16. 13s. 4d.).

28 See the *Lib. Rat.* and Gostlin's notebook for the half-year's payments at Michaelmas 1662 to, *e.g.*, Sheringham and Thurston.

29 See "*Dividends*", § VI. 5, at pp. 515ff below.

£10 p.a. from such fines. The gross emolument of a senior fellow, including dividends, was thus normally around £50 p.a. and this would leave him with not much less than £40 after he had paid his commons account.[30]

The Frankland, Wendy and Perse fellows, however, did not enjoy the benefit of any of the three factors which had combined to provide a senior fellow with a modest income by 1660: they were not entitled to corn money or to entry fees and their stipends remained at the £10 p.a. which had been judged sufficient by the most experienced fellow of the college, Stephen Perse, when he died in 1615. A stipend of £10 may have been considered sufficient in 1615, but twenty years later, in 1635, the stipend of the next junior fellowship to be established was set higher at £15, and 20s. for chamber-rent, by the donor, Matthew Stokys, another experienced fellow.[31] In the year 1639 the Master and fellows augmented the stipend of each of Perse's fellows by £4 a year out of his benefaction, but the Civil War brought the increase to an end three years later.[32] The Frankland fellows and the Wendy fellow did not enjoy a similar increase even for that brief period, for the benefactions which supported them had been treated as conditional gifts, not trusts, and no separate trust account was maintained for them.[33]

In 1660 the stipend of each of the thirteen Frankland, Wendy and Perse fellowships was still £10 p.a., as it had been in 1615,[34] but it was now barely sufficient to enable any but the most frugal and parsimonious of young fellows to meet his commons account.[35] In sharp contrast, the majority of senior fellows regularly had a credit balance after those charges were met, and the debit balances of the others were invariably less than their share of corn money: it

30 Compare his position with that at St John's, where £40 p.a. was thought to be a "favourable value for a fellowship" in the seventeenth century: *St John's College Cambridge: A History* (The Boydell Press, 2011), p. 110.

31 This was the last to be established until Bartholomew Wortley made provision for three further fellowships in 1749.

32 MS 621/457, p. 319.

33 After 1610 the Wendy gift consisted of an annual rent of 20 marks paid to the college and consequently it could not support an increase (*Annals*, pp. 217–22); Mrs Frankland's benefaction had been amply sufficient to fund increases in the stipends of her fellows and scholars, but no separate account for the benefaction was started until 1832 (*B.H.* IV(2), p. 42).

34 The holder of the fourteenth junior fellowship, which Stokys had founded in 1635, was only a little better off with £15 p.a.; the fellowship, which was restricted to divinity, seems to have been suspended during the Commonwealth, and elections were made only intermittently thereafter.

35 The *Liber Rationalis* for the period shows that the £10 stipend still met the charges for commons and absences of most junior fellows, but only if the charges for commons were very small or non-existent; the holder of the fourteenth junior fellowship, which Stokys had founded in 1635, was only a little better off. See the petition of Richard Watson [Gonville and Caius College 1628] who had been a junior fellow until he was ejected as a royalist in 1644 and was re-elected to his junior fellowship in 1660; being much older than the normal junior fellow, he petitioned the king saying that "his only income is £10"; the college was moved to make him some allowance: *B.H.* I, p. 286.

must have been apparent at the common meal that the Fellowship was now sharply divided into two halves, one of which enjoyed nearly five times the support that the other did.[36]

The augmentation of fellows' stipends: 1660–1825

The senior fellows

From 1614 onwards the stipends of senior fellows were increased through the purchase or gift of new lands, gradually at first during the seventeenth century and then more frequently in the earlier half of the eighteenth. Two substantial increases in their stipends had been made before the Civil War, the first as a result of the purchase of the manor and mills at Great Shelford in 1614 and the second from the purchase of Weeting Manor in 1632; these had together raised their stipends by £10 p.a. After the Restoration several further small increases (amounting in total to £12 p.a.) followed over the next one hundred years as a result of eleven more purchases of land, and by 1780 the stipend and livery of a senior fellow together stood at £29 p.a.[37]

In 1766 the college had begun to invest in government stocks as well as in land, and as a consequence came to enjoy a substantial increase in its annual revenue.[38] As explained later, much of the increase was employed to fund the introduction of salaries for college officers and also to improve the stipends of the junior fellows, albeit inadequately; nevertheless, some of the income from public funds was used to raise the annual stipend (and livery) of senior fellows to £47 in steps between 1781 and 1803.[39] Finally, in 1805 it was increased in a single step from £47 to £77 p.a. as a result of Mr Wortley's generosity to his old

[36] It was apparent to Robert Brady, the Master, and on his death he devoted the greater part of his estate to the improvement of the position of the Frankland fellows: see below.

[37] *Lib. Rat.* 1795–1815, p. 1. For the reasons already explained the precise amount of the stipend varied slightly between the three classes of senior fellow: see *The tripartite pattern of the establishment* at p. 427 above. The list of the properties purchased is conveniently reproduced by Gross: *B.H.* IV(2), p. viii. It must be remembered that the formal stipend and livery by 1780 constituted a relatively small and diminishing part of a senior fellow's income when compared with the amount received from corn money and entry fines: see "*Dividends*", § VI. 5 below.

[38] For details of the increase and its use, see *John Smith's reform of the college's finances*, pp. 467–71 below. Until the college started to purchase government stocks in 1766 it necessarily had to rely almost exclusively on the rent from land for its income, and the system of beneficial leases inevitably kept that rent artificially low, whether the land was agrarian or urban. The only form of investment other than land may have been loans to local merchants; there is some very slight but tantalising evidence that the college made such loans in the time of Legge in the form of pre-payments on the security of bonds for supplies of ale, bread and meat: see the *Status Collegii* for 1585 and following years for bonds given by John Nash, baker, Richard Bradley, brewer and John Goldsborrowe, butcher.

[39] By £5 in 1781, £3 in 1788 and £10 in 1803: *Lib. Rat.* 1795–1815, fly-leaf and p. 1.

college.[40] No further changes were made before 1816, but thereafter the regular introduction of rack rents in place of entry fines brought an immediate and steady increase in the annual stipends of a senior fellow: it rose to just over £100 in 1819, and to £130 in 1822.[41]

The junior fellows

When Stephen Perse endowed six additional fellowships in his will in 1615 he carefully ensured financial equality among the junior fellowships and made provision for the stipends of the Frankland fellows to be raised to the same level as that of his own and the Wendy fellows, namely £10 a year. An exception to that equality emerged before the Civil War when Matthew Stokys provided a stipend of £15 for the fellowship that he established by will in 1631;[42] but thereafter little change was made in the formal stipends of any of the four classes of junior fellowships until the last quarter of the eighteenth century.[43] From this it might appear that the financial equality between junior fellows which Perse had established had, broadly speaking, survived until it was fractured in 1771, when the first elections were made to the Wortley fellowships with their much enhanced stipends of £80 and £70.[44] In fact, however, the equality had already

40 *Ibid.* The increase to £77 in 1805 was far greater than ever before and it is an early illustration of the college's improving financial position by the beginning of the nineteenth century. The increase came not from government stock, but from the lands Wortley had left to the college.

41 *Lib. Rat.* 1816–1850. These and later increases in stipend, however, went in step with the discontinuance of beneficial leases and were accompanied by the loss to the recipient of the dividends which the entry fines would have produced: see "*Dividends*", § VI. 5. The rapidity of the changes is vividly and amusingly illustrated by the frustrations of the bursarial clerk in his attempts to maintain the traditional neatness of the *Liber Rationalis*. In that ledger only the total of each fellow's stipend was entered on the annual pages together with a printed cross-reference to page 1 ("*ut patet in Pag. 1ma*"), and it was on that first page that a chronological explanation of the stipend was neatly maintained. When a new volume was begun for the years 1816–50, the annual pages continued to carry the cross-reference to page 1 and the clerk at first strove to keep that page up to date, despite the frequent increases, but he then abandoned the task and struck through all his attempts in disgust. The next volume continued to include the printed cross-reference to page 1 but omitted that page completely – to the complete bafflement of later readers unless they consulted earlier volumes.

42 Very few elections to it, if any, appear to have been made until it was revived in 1665 in order to placate the complaints of the most vociferous of the discontented junior fellows, Joshua Bassett (*B.H.* I, p. 400), and temporarily satisfy his demands for a senior fellowship: see "*The Norfolk Preference*", § VI. 3 above. The stipend was later raised to £18.

43 The Frankland fellows had enjoyed additional "portions" from Dr Brady's estate since 1700, but the first change in the formal stipend of any of the three "£10 fellowships" was not made until 1778, when that of the Wendy fellowship was raised to £14 p.a.: cf. pp. 438–9 below.

44 For Wortley's fellowships, see *B.H.* III, pp. 218–19. Wortley had died in 1749, but the provisions of the will did not come into effect for twenty years and the first elections were not made till 1771.

been shattered long before that date. This, however, occurred for very different reasons in each of the four earlier classes of junior fellowship.

The Perse fellowship was the first to be affected, and the fortunes of the holders were changed far more dramatically than those of other junior fellows. Stephen Perse had left to the college a remarkable endowment which should have been amply sufficient to support, *inter alia*, the six fellowships that he established in his will, but the income of the fund fell greatly in the later years of the 1670s and did not recover until 1734.[45] As a result, for nearly sixty years thereafter stipends could not be paid to Perse fellows and those who were elected were required to accept at admission that they would receive no stipend but only the title and a right to rent-free rooms in the Perse building.[46] Not surprisingly, relatively few were elected and those that were tended to become wholly non-resident after a short stay in their first year or two.[47] Imperceptibly the character of the Perse fellowship changed: instead of being the support for a period of study in the university and potentially leading to a senior fellowship, it was in danger of becoming little more than a 'leaving prize'. After 1727 the fund began to recover and the Perse fellows started to receive some part of their stipends, but it was only in 1735 that they once again received the full £10 p.a.[48] Although the stipend was revived, the fellowship never recovered the character and status it had had in Jeremy Taylor's time before the Commonwealth: non-residence and non-participation in the life of the college remained the virtually invariable practice for Perse fellows. As a result, the stipend became in many cases little more than a small but pleasant payment made annually to a fortunate graduate of the college who was not beholden to the college and

[45] This appears to have been due initially to ill-judgement by Martin Perse in his purchases of land (particularly that in Bassingbourn) and later to mismanagement of the trust fund by college bursars. The income recovered only after the college re-organised its land-holdings in 1733 and the Perse land in Bassingbourn was exchanged for land in West Dereham which the president, John Lightwine, had left to the college shortly before. For the lands in Bassingbourn and West Dereham and their exchange, see *B.H.* IV(2), pp. 7 and 111; for the bursarial mismanagement during Sir John Ellys's mastership, see p. 463, n. 183 below and MS 621/457, pp. 335, 337.

[46] *Gesta*, 9 March 1681 (Hancock), 2 December 1681 (Hartstongue), 7 July 1691 (Barker and Coppin), 29 June 1697 (Leigh), 6 July 1698 (Hunt), 7 October 1702 (Inyon), 11 November 1713 (Fish). Hartstongue eventually had to be translated into the Wendy fellowship, which has usually been regarded as 'the poor relation': *Gesta*, 13 February 1684. The Perse accounts show that the Master and four senior fellows who were Perse managers had the good grace not to pay themselves their management fees; the Perse scholars continued to be paid their scholarships and the Frankland fellows to receive the £3 supplement to their stipends. For the trust's recovery after 1734, see pp. 437, 441 and 469 below.

[47] *E.g.*, there were only three Perse fellows in the years 1716, 1719 and 1721 and the *Liber Rationalis* shows that their half-yearly commons bills were less than £1.

[48] They were paid £3 from 1727 to 1730, £4 in 1731, £5 in 1733 and £7. 10s. in 1734.

made his living elsewhere and in other ways.[49] This explains why the stipend remained stubbornly at £10 p.a. throughout the eighteenth century, despite the striking recovery in the income of the Perse fund in the years between 1754 and 1778 as a result of the purchase of government stock. Even when a revaluation of the fund in 1786 prompted the managers to increase the stipends of various of the beneficiaries specified by Perse in his will and to double the £3 contribution which the fund made to the stipends of the Frankland fellows, no similar addition was made to the annual stipends of his own Perse fellows.[50] It was only in 1804 that a second revaluation led to their stipends at last being raised from the £10 p.a. which Stephen Perse had given them, and even then only to £13.[51] This still left the stipend far less than that of any of the other junior fellows and it was only in 1812, following a third revaluation, that the stipend was raised to £30 p.a. and brought up to that of the least well-paid of those others, the Wendy fellow.[52]

The stipend of the Stokys fellow was also paid out of a distinct trust fund, but, unlike the Perse trust, the income of Stokys' fund was generally sufficient to pay the emoluments of the one fellowship and three scholarships which he founded.[53] The leasehold nature of the trust property did, however, mean that it was not until the nineteenth century that the fellowship became significantly more valuable than any of the other junior fellowships. The income of the trust came from the rectories of Dilham and Honing in Norfolk, but what Stokys bequeathed to the college in 1634 was not a freehold interest, *i.e.*, lay rectories, but merely a beneficial lease from the bishop of Ely, and although the very modest rent paid each year to the bishop left sufficient income for the fellowship and scholarships,[54] the entry fines payable to him every seven years for the renewal of the (twenty-one-year) lease meant that it was the bishop rather than the college who took much of the gain from increases in the value

49 Some of the Perse fellows maintained very little contact with Cambridge and for them the fellowship was no more than continuing prize until they married or accepted a disqualifying benefice: *e.g.*, George Rhodes, who came from Devon, was a Perse fellow from 1798 to his death in 1842; he returned to his home county after his election, practised medicine in Exeter until he retired in 1806, and died there thirty-six years later, still a Perse fellow (*B.H.* II, p. 124).

50 *Gesta*, 20 December 1786. For the rise in the value of the Perse fund during Smith's mastership, see *John Smith's reform of the college's finances*, at p. 469 below.

51 *Gesta*, 12 January 1804. At the same time the £3 contribution which Perse had originally made to the stipends of the Frankland fellows was increased to £15 – more than the total stipend now paid to his fellows.

52 The 1812 decision was made at a meeting of the Perse managers and, unlike their previous decisions on stipends, it was not recorded in the *Gesta*. It was at this meeting that the managers started to give themselves the irresponsibly large increases in their own fees that finally led to the Chancery suit brought against the college in 1834.

53 The fellowship was limited to divinity and elections were made only irregularly.

54 The annual rent of £13. 6s. 8d. remained unchanged for 232 years until the lease was run out in 1867: *B.H.* IV(2), p. 40.

of the rectories. Fortunately for the trust, when the receipts from the rectories began to rise in the second half of the eighteenth century John Smith was the Master and he ensured that the surplus income was rolled up and invested in government stock, as he did with the Perse and other trust funds and the college's own surplus income.[55] Thereafter the income of the fund grew steeply from further purchases of stock and increasing receipts from the rectories, and with it the stipend of the Stokys fellow rapidly outstripped those of all other junior fellows. By 1794 the stipend had risen to £48 p.a., and then to £69 in 1803, £108 in 1814, £138 in 1818 and £200 in 1825;[56] apart from some fluctuation it remained at that figure till 1860 and provided the one junior fellowship, which did not leave the holder "very poor".[57]

Unlike Perse's and Stokys' foundations, however, the earlier benefactions made by Mrs Frankland and Dr Wendy's nephew were regarded as straight gifts to the college which were conditional on its fulfilment of the donor's directions to the letter, but no more;[58] accordingly no separate account books were started for those benefactions. It might be expected therefore that both the Frankland and Wendy fellows would fare worse, given Caius' categorical direction in Statute 36 that the college should not be burdened with supplementing the stipend of any fellow beyond what his benefactor provided. Indeed, in accordance with that statute, the college's contributions to their yearly stipends remained unchanged at what they had been when the fellowships were first created, namely, £7 for the Frankland fellows and £10 for the Wendy: despite this, however, the Wendy fellow in fact fared better than the Perse fellows throughout the eighteenth century and the Frankland fellows fared better than both of them.

In the early years of the eighteenth century the position of the Wendy fellow was substantially improved by the simple practice of appointing him Mrs Frankland's chaplain at the same time, thereby doubling his emolument to £20 p.a.[59] The practice did not last long, for the post of chaplain appears to have fallen into disuse in the middle of the eighteenth century and the Wendy fellow's stipend dropped again to its original £10 p.a. and fell back to parity with that of the Perse fellows;[60] but whereas the Perse fellows were largely non-resident and

55 See *John Smith's reform of the college's finances*, at p. 467 below.

56 *Lib. Rat.* (1795–1815), p. 1, (1815–50), p. 1.

57 In the words of the trenchant memorial of three senior fellows to the Royal Commission in 1852: see "*The Norfolk Preference*", § VI. 3, at p. 422, n. 96 above.

58 "The right of every allowance is due according to the donation of the Founder of it, and so it is to be employed as he hath ordered it, not otherwise": Fellows' Answer, no. 9, *Allen's Case* (1617), Appendix F; see Gross, *B.H.* IV(2), p. ix.

59 *Lib. Rat.* (1716, Green), (1719, Greenaway), (1721, Macro).

60 In 1677 the sinecure rectory of Pattisley had been assigned to the chaplain by college order as an addition to his stipend (*Gesta*, 23 July, cited *B.H.* III, p. 242), but appointments to the office had presumably ceased by 1743, when the rectory of Pattisley was consolidated with the vicarage of Mattishall (*B.H.* IV(2), p. 73). The chaplain's duty to 'conduct' chapel services passed

their stipend consequently remained at £10 until 1804, the Wendy fellow tended to reside and the obvious inadequacy of his stipend prompted first a fellow and then a Master to include bequests in their wills which brought it up to £14 p.a. in 1778 and £22 in 1794.[61]

The fact that the Frankland fellows fared rather better than either the Wendy or the Perse fellows in the eighteenth century was due to Robert Brady. He had become Master at the Restoration and had witnessed the discontent engendered by the inadequacy of a junior fellow's stipend, and had devised his estate in Denver to the college in 1700 for the payment of ten "portions", two to the Master and one each to the president, the six Frankland fellows and the college chest.[62] At first the portion simply brought the six fellows' income up to that of the Stokys fellow, but as the income from the estate which Brady had left to the college rose in the course of the eighteenth century, so did the annual additional payments to the Frankland fellows.[63] In addition, as beneficiaries under Stephen Perse's will they enjoyed further increases to the £3 supplement which he had given them in 1615;[64] all of these increases came from trust funds, however, and until 1831, when a separate Frankland trust account was finally established, they received nothing from the college itself except the £7 p.a. which Mrs Frankland had specified in 1587 – a striking testament to the rigidity with which Caius' injunction in Statute 36 was applied.[65]

to two fellows who were designated as "Conduct". The office of chaplain was not revived until 1851, following a report on the use of the Frankland Trust (*Gesta*, C.O.5, 4 April).

61 The fellow was Thomas Young (*B.H.* II, p. 49) and the Master was John Smith, whose reform of the college finances is assessed at pp. 467–71 below.

62 For Brady's estate, see *B.H.* IV(2), pp. 36ff. The value of the benefaction was greatly increased by the generosity of his executor, John Lightwine, an equally long-serving president (*ibid.*).

63 The portions from Brady's estate were gradually increased from £6 p.a. to £14 (1732), £17 (1791), £24 (1800) and £40 (1817): *B.H.* IV(2), pp. 36–7. One suspects that the portions were increased so readily only because they were payable to the Master and the president as well as the Frankland fellows.

64 Stephen Perse's £3 was increased to £6 in 1787, £15 in 1804, £20 in 1812 and, finally, £40 in 1825. The increases were recorded in the *Gesta* until 1804 (20 December 1786; 12 January 1804), but not thereafter, and the later decisions of the Perse managers can be traced only through the *Liber Rationalis* and the Perse accounts. The Chancery Master's scheme reduced the payment to £22. 10s., which restored the proportions between the Perse and Frankland fellows that Stephen Perse had specified in his will.

65 The Frankland fellows might have expected that they would at least benefit from corn money, given the wording of both the Act of Parliament and the college's decree of 11 December 1592, but, as will be seen later, the Duxford estate was never brought within the Act. Not only were the Frankland fellows denied corn money from Duxford, but the system of beneficial leases meant that the increased value of the Frankland lands manifested itself in the form of entry fines rather than increased income, and, as will be seen later, these fines were regarded as perquisites of the Master and senior fellows. It was not until 1832 that the eruption of the Perse scandal led the college to treat the Frankland benefaction as a separate trust and give it a separate account.

The first elections to the fellowships for which Bartholomew Wortley had provided in his will were made in 1771 and highlighted the inadequacy of all the four existing classes of junior fellowship; for the stipends of the two new Wortley fellows (£80 and £70 p.a.) were treble those of best paid of the other junior fellows and eight times those of the least well-paid.[66] The stark contrast prompted the benefactions for the Wendy fellowship mentioned above, and the position of the Frankland and Stokys fellows began to benefit from the steadily increasing value of the trust funds that resulted from the care given to the college's finances by the Master, John Smith,[67] and by the 1790s there were three distinct grades of junior fellowship: at the top were the Wortley fellows, then the Stokys and Frankland fellows, and finally the 'poor relations', the Wendy and Perse fellows.[68]

Thirty years later, by 1825, there were still three grades but the junior fellowships had changed places in the pecking order. The value of the property left to the college by Brady (Denver) and Stokys (Dilham and Honing) had continued to rise steadily, and with it the stipends of both the Frankland and the Stokys fellows; but since there were only one fellowship and three scholarships to be supported out of the Stokys fund, as compared with the ten portions provided by Brady, the stipend of the Stokys fellow had risen more sharply than that of the Frankland fellows.[69] By 1825 it was comparable with that of a senior fellow and was now substantially greater than that of the other junior fellows; in contrast, the combined stipend and portion of a Frankland fellow had merely brought his annual income up to that of a Wortley fellow. The less fortunate Wendy and Perse fellows remained the poor relations – or, rather, the even poorer relations.[70] Only the Stokys fellow received an amount which could be regarded as even moderately sufficient.[71]

66 At that date Frankland fellows received £24 annually, the Stokys fellows £18, the Perse and Wendy fellows £10.

67 For Smith's reform of the college's finances and the improvement in the Perse and Stokys funds see pp. 461–71 below.

68 In 1794 the relative positions were: (i) Wortley (£80 or £70); (ii) Stokys (£48) and Frankland (£30); (iii) Perse (£10) and Wendy (£14): *Lib. Rat.* (Michaelmas 1794).

69 From £48 in 1794 it had risen to £69 by 1803 and to £128 by 1818: *Lib. Rat.*

70 In 1825 the relative positions were: (i) Stokys (£138); (ii) Frankland (£47 and a £40 portion) and Wortley (£80 or £70); (iii) Perse (£30) and Wendy (£30): *Lib. Rat.* (Michaelmas 1820).

71 By 1840 the gap between the Stokys and the other junior fellows had widened yet further. The Stokys fellowship had finally risen to £200 by 1840 (*Lib. Rat.*); it was temporarily reduced to £184 in 1854 (*Gesta*, C.O.4, 31 October 1854), but it remained until the repeal of Dr Caius' statutes in 1860 as the one junior fellowship that did not leave the holder "very poor", in the words of the very forceful and bitter memorial submitted by three senior fellows to the Royal Commission in 1852: *Report of the Cambridge University Commissioners*, p. 449, discussed in "The Norfolk Preference", § VI. 3, at pp. 421–2 above. Although it was not limited by locality of birth, the Stokys fellowship was restricted to divinity and consequently was not open to many junior fellows and they could only wait for a non-divinity vacancy in the senior fellowship.

The disputed use of the Perse trust and the impact on stipends: 1825–60

The senior fellows

When Perse entrusted the management of his fund to the Master and the four most senior fellows, he had allowed £3 p.a. to the Master and 30s. p.a. to each of the four senior fellows as Perse managers, and this amount had remained unchanged until the later eighteenth century. After the college began to invest in government stocks from 1766 onward, surplus balances in the Perse fund were included in the purchases of stock and the fund thereafter enjoyed a regular and reliable income which produced a steady increase in both the capital value and the income of the fund.[72] On the revaluation of the fund in 1786 the distribution among the objects of Dr Perse's generosity was reviewed and, among others, the managers enjoyed a modest increase in their annual emolument to £2. 5s., and to £4. 10s. in the case of the Master.[73] A further revaluation in 1804 revealed that "the annual income from Dr Perse's Benefaction has very considerably exceeded the expenditure as adjusted in the year 1786", and the allowances to all the different objects of the benefaction were again re-adjusted.[74] In consequence, the annual additional payment to each of the four senior fellows was increased to £14, the Master again receiving double, and the emoluments of the beneficiaries of the trust were raised at the same time.[75] Up to that time, 1804, the decisions on increases in emoluments under the trust had not been unreasonable and were recorded in the college's *Gesta*, but after 1804 darkness descends on the Perse trust.[76] There are only occasional later references in the

72 By 1837 the trust had accumulated £23,100 Consols, £2,400 New South Sea Annuities and £5,000 Exchequer bills: per Ld Langdale, *A.G.* v. *Gonville & Caius College, Cambridge* (1837), cited in T. Duffus Hardy, *Memoir of Lord Langdale* (1852), vol. II, p. 419.

73 *Gesta*, 20 December 1786. The increase to each Frankland fellow was £3, the porter £1 and the college almswomen together £2. 8s.; the school and its master were not included.

74 *Gesta*, 12 January 1804.

75 The income amounted to £765. 17s. 4d. The relative distribution made to the different classes is of interest, given the opprobrium that the college later incurred. The number of recipients in each class and the total allocated annually to that *class* was as follows: the Master £28; four Seniors £56; six Frankland fellows £90; six Perse fellows £78; six Perse scholars £78; six Almswomen £96; three College women £9; (two) Deans £16; Steward £10; Bursar £32; Registrar £8; College Chest £125; School Master £50; (School) Usher £30; subsequent donation to the School "incorporated with this Fund" £4. 10s.; Cook £11. 10s.; Butler £5; Porter £5; Feast £6. 6s.; "Praestos" £1. 10s.; Preacher £5; Poor of three parishes £4. 16s.; Hobson's rivulet £8; the Hall Fire £2; charitable uses to be disposed of by the Master and four Seniors £6. 5s. 4d. No payments were made to the eight other senior fellows.

76 The later decisions in 1812 and 1825 which caused dissension, and ultimately scandal, do not appear in the college *Gesta*. The darkness obscured the position not just from later generations, but also from the other eight senior fellows: Bickersteth later wrote in his diary that "as I approached seniority, hints were frequently given to me of the advantages I should have when I became one of the four Seniors": Hardy, *Memoir of Lord Langdale* (1858), vol. I, p. 297.

Gesta to separate minutes (the "Perse *Gesta*"), but no such separate minutes have survived for the period before 1858, and as a consequence the controversial decisions which the Master and the other four managers took in 1812 and 1825 are shrouded in mist and we have to rely on secondary sources written considerably later.[77]

In 1812 the distribution of the income of the fund was further reviewed by the Master and the four most senior fellows, and they increased the additional payment to themselves to £60 a year, and double for the Master. This very sharp increase produced for the first time an appreciable difference in stipend between the four most senior fellows and the other eight senior fellows; for the additional payment of £60 from the Perse trust now nearly doubled the annual stipends of the four most senior of them, giving them each roughly £140, as contrasted with £80 for the other eight.[78] The relative difference lessened in the course of the following decade as the stipends of all twelve senior fellows were increased from time to time to compensate them for the loss of dividend whenever a beneficial lease was not renewed and a rack rent replaced the entry fine.[79] By 1825 the Perse fund had increased further in value and a fresh distribution was made by the managers to themselves; but this time the additional amount paid to the managers soared to no less than £220 a year for each of the four fellows and £440 for the Master.[80] The other senior fellows had not been alerted to the earlier increase in 1812, and it seems likely that they only learned of the 1825 increase because it was accompanied by a proposal to increase the salary of the bursar also and that needed the approval of a college meeting.[81] Not surprisingly, the managers' additional £220 "was not considered equitable"

(Printed as "Memoirs" on the title page, but correctly in the text.) The period of what amounts to secrecy from the ordinary meetings of the college coincides with Martin Davy's mastership, and he must bear much of the blame for the misappropriations that occurred during that period, since, as Master, he profited most from them.

77 Principally the account given by Hardy in his memoir of the life of Henry Bickersteth (see above) and statements in the judgment delivered in 1837 by Bickersteth (by then Lord Langdale, M.R.) in the suit in Chancery brought against the college for breach of trust in its administration of the Perse trust.

78 See, *e.g.*, *Lib. Rat.* (Lady Day 1814). In the absence of any *Gesta*, one is left to wonder what increases, if any, the other beneficiaries of the Perse trust received.

79 See *Dividends*", § VI. 5. By 1822 the stipends of senior fellows had risen from (roughly) £80 to £130 p.a.; the additional payment to the four most senior had remained at £60. The general increase in stipends, it should be noted, was not a net increase in income since it simply replaced the dividends from entry fines.

80 Hardy, *Memoir of Lord Langdale*, I, p. 295. The Perse *Gesta* have not survived, and no mention is made of the decision in the college *Gesta*; the *Liber Rationalis*, however, confirms that the payment was made for the half-year at Michaelmas 1825.

81 The bursar was the Perse Registrar and as such was an essential party to the decisions of the Perse managers.

by the other senior fellows when they learned of it,[82] and in the following term (Lent 1826) the additional payment was reduced to £140 a year.[83]

This did not quieten the other senior fellows, and discontent continued until the Lent Term 1830, when "it seems that two of the Junior fellows complained to the Master that they did not receive as much from the Perse Fund as they ought".[84] The following term Davy communicated the complaint to Henry Bickersteth K.C., a senior fellow who had become one of the four managers of the trust in 1823.[85] Bickersteth had practised at the Bar throughout his time as a fellow and, never being resident, had taken no part in the government of the college in the years since he had become a senior fellow in 1814. Bickersteth's well-known reaction is dramatically recounted by Hardy in his *Memoir of Lord Langdale*: the lawyer's insistence on examining both the will and the account books back to 1697; his conclusion that the Master and the four most senior fellows had been receiving money to which they were not entitled; his immediate setting-off for Cambridge; his failure to convince Davy and the other managers; his repayment of the money he had himself received; and his insistence on bringing the matter forward at the next college meeting of the Master and all the senior fellows.[86]

That meeting was held on 27 and 28 October 1830.[87] Not surprisingly, it did not reach a decision, and the only immediate result was to prompt the Master and the four most senior fellows to reduce their additional payments from the Perse fund to £50 and £25 a year respectively.[88] It took a further six months for Bickersteth to achieve the adoption of what Hardy later termed a "new and just

82 Hardy, *Memoir of Lord Langdale*, I, p. 295. Hardy describes the objectors as "Junior Fellows", but it is clear that he had in mind, both here and elsewhere, not the junior fellows but the eight less senior senior fellows: he follows Bickersteth in reserving the term "Senior Fellow" for the four most senior ones who were managers of the Perse trust.

83 The reduction to £140 p.a. went a long way to restoring the ratio between the four most senior and the other eight senior fellows to the ratio that had been established in 1812, *i.e.* double, since the stipend from the college to all twelve senior fellows had been raised to £130 a year by then.

84 Hardy, *Memoir of Lord Langdale*, I, pp. 295ff. It is clear that Hardy again had two of the other eight senior fellows in mind here rather than any of the junior fellows, and it is significant that the eventual outcome was far more favourable to those eight senior fellows than it was to the junior fellows. None of the events recounted by Hardy is mentioned in the college *Gesta*, and unfortunately no Perse *Gesta* for the period have survived.

85 For Bickersteth, see Brooke, *History*, pp. 196–201.

86 *Ibid.*

87 According to Hardy, Bickersteth "brought the matter forward and with much trouble got a new and just scale of payments adopted"; he also "immediately paid back every farthing of excess he had received, with interest at 4 per cent". (£748. 15s. + £25 after he had checked his arithmetic: *Memoir of Lord Langdale*, I, pp. 296–7. See also Brooke, *History*, p. 202.) No mention of the matter appears in the college *Gesta* until the following year.

88 As Perse had directed in his will, the Master received double the payment to the fellows. The reduced payments are recorded in the *Liber Rationalis* for Michaelmas 1830, but no decision by the full meeting of the Master and the twelve senior fellows is mentioned in the college

scale of payments": at the meeting of the Master and the twelve senior fellows on 21 May 1831 it was agreed "from the increase in the rents that £200 a year in addition be given to the Master and £100 a year in addition to each of the Senior Fellows to commence from Michaelmas 1830".[89] The meeting then proceeded to agree that a *further* addition of £100 a year should be added to the Master's stipend.[90] The College Order records the adoption of the new scale and the further addition to the Master, but it makes no mention of the background or of the Perse trust and presents an increase in the college's rents as the only reason for the increased stipends; the *Gesta* further omits any mention that the Master and the four most senior fellows continued to receive their respective payments of £50 and £25 p.a. from the Perse fund in addition to these generous payments.[91]

The new, generous increases in stipends to the Master and the twelve senior fellows fell, not on the Perse fund, but upon the college's corporate income from rents and other annual income. The charge upon the college's corporate funds was justified in the College Order as coming "from the increases in rents", and as a result the exceptionally large and generous increases which it sanctioned have been regarded simply as compensation for loss of entry fines,[92] whereas the order was in truth a hasty and over-generous response to the unprecedented inequality among senior fellows that had been brought about by the improper actions of the Master and the four most senior fellows as Perse managers in 1812 and 1825, and had been brought to light only by the actions of one upright fellow.[93] Being a knee-jerk reaction and not a carefully calculated compensation for the loss of entry fines, the abnormally large increases inevitably proved excessive and had to be reduced five years later.[94]

The new scale of stipends in 1831 increased the annual stipend of each of the twelve senior fellows by £100, taking it straight from £140 to £240.[95] Until

Gesta and it was presumably made by the Master and the four most senior fellows alone and contained in the Perse *Gesta*.

89 *Gesta*, 21 May 1831.

90 No reason is advanced for this increase. Davy had already received twice the increase given to the twelve senior fellows and this further increase presumably was intended to soften the loss of most of the £440 which he had enjoyed since 1825.

91 *Lib. Rat.* (Michaelmas 1831). The Perse accounts show that all payments to the managers stopped after three years, no doubt as a result of the filing of the bill in Chancery against the college in 1834. The Chancery Scheme made in 1841 in respect of the Perse trust authorised payments to £30 and £15 to the Master and other managers, respectively: Ord. 16, Cooper, *Annals*, iv, p. 643.

92 See Gross, *B.H.* IV(2), p. x.

93 The increases in stipend to the Master and the twelve senior fellows had amounted to an additional charge upon the Chest of £1,500 a year.

94 *Gesta*, 15 June 1836. The fellows' increase was reduced by only £20 a year (*i.e.*, to £80) and the Master's by £40 (*i.e.*, to £160): *Gesta*, 26 October 1836. As will be seen below, it was the poorest of the junior fellows, the Wendy fellow, who was hardest hit by this reduction: the increase was kept for the current holder of that fellowship but totally rescinded for future holders.

95 As mentioned in the preceding footnote, the stipend was reduced by £20 p.a. to £220 in 1836.

then corn money, entry fines and stipends had provided three roughly equal contributions to a senior fellow's income since the second half of the seventeenth century; but the position changed radically following the decision of 21 May 1831. The stipend now outstripped both fine and corn money in its importance to the fellow, and it continued to do so even after the college inevitably found it necessary in 1836 to reduce by £20 p.a. the over-generous addition made in 1831. In each of the two years 1840 and 1841 the annual stipend was £232, and, although corn money remained steady at around £70 p.a. on average (depending on the number of senior fellows in residence), the dividend from fines had by then begun to wither away: £44 in 1840, £91 in 1841, but only £17 in 1846.[96] The balance continued to tip inexorably in favour of stipends until the repeal of Dr Caius' statutes in 1860.[97]

The junior fellows

Bickersteth had not had junior fellows in mind when he made his dramatic intervention in 1830, but his action did bring some small benefit to them. Their position presented an embarrassing contrast to "the new and just scale of payments" which the College Order of 21 May 1831 gave to the Master and the twelve senior fellows as a result of Bickersteth's intervention in the management of the Perse fund. The contrast prompted the same meeting to "agree to grant as a donation to the Frankland and Wendy fellows so much as to make up their stipend to [£]100 a year subject to be withdrawn if an addition should be made to their income from any other source",[98] but the Master and senior fellows were not prompted by their embarrassment to make the donation retrospective to the previous year, even though they had just done this for themselves in the preceding College Order.[99]

The donation was in fact much less generous to the junior fellows than it might seem. It did not apply to the Stokys, Wortley and Perse fellowships, for which separate trust funds existed;[100] and, although the stipend of the senior fellows was raised *by* £100 p.a. (and that of the Master by £300), the stipend

96 *Fellows' Accounts* 1840–42, 1846–66. In 1840 the emolument of a senior fellow on Stephen Smith's foundation (Mr Stokes) amounted to £363. 10s. 6d., comprising a stipend of £231. 16s. 0d., corn money of £83. 5s. 7d., entry fines of £44. 9s. 5d., and £3. 19s. 6d. in small allowances for heating, commemorations and Tancred dividend: *Lib. Rat.* 1840–41; *Fellows' Accounts* 1840–42. Stokes also received £362. 13s. 4d. from his college offices as bursar, dean and conduct.

97 For the later history of the relationship between fellows' dividends and stipends and the curious reversal of terminology, see "*Dividends*", § VI. 5, at pp. 542ff below.

98 *Gesta*, 21 May 1831.

99 *Lib. Rat.* (Michaelmas 1831).

100 The Stokys was raised from £138 to £200, but not until 1835 (*Lib. Rat.* 1815–1850, p. 1); the Perse from £30 to £40 in 1825, and to £70 in October 1830, the month in which Bickersteth insisted on bringing the payments out of the Perse fund before the full college meeting (*ibid.*); the Wortley was not raised from £80 to £100 until the 1854 (*Gesta*, C.O.4, 31 October 1854).

of the Frankland and Wendy fellows was only raised *to* £100 p.a.; and since the stipend of Frankland fellows had already been augmented to £87 p.a. by increases in the "portions" provided for them by Dr Brady and by grants from the Perse fund, the amount of the increase agreed on 21 May 1831 merely resulted in an additional £11 a year for them.[101] The Wendy fellow alone benefitted, and then only for five years: his stipend of £30 p.a. was raised by £68 to £98, but the whole of the increase was rescinded in 1836 when the excessively generous increase to the Master and senior fellows had to be reviewed and reduced.[102]

The striking difference in the way the Master and the senior fellows treated the junior fellows in the wake of the Perse scandal, compared with the very generous treatment they accorded to themselves, explains the strength of feeling that was expressed to the University Commissioners twenty years later. The "new and just scale of payments" may have been just to the senior fellows, but it was far from being so to the junior fellows. It modified the contrast between the stipends of the junior and senior fellows which the decisions of 1812 and 1825 had brought about; but it did so only very slightly, and as the stipends of senior fellows continued to grow and the contrast re-emerged, so the discontent in the Fellowship grew during the following twenty years. Not only did junior fellows have to wait hopefully for a senior fellowship to become vacant, but the inadequacy of their stipends now meant that even small differences in stipend made one junior fellowship more desirable than another. A serious 'pecking order' developed, and for the first time it became the practice to promote junior fellows from one fellowship to a slightly less badly paid one when it became vacant;[103] that, however, was not always possible, for the only truly adequate

[101] This brought the Frankland fellows up to £98 p.a. As explained earlier, the stipend of £7 p.a. specified by Mrs Frankland for her fellows had been increased to £10 in 1616 by the gift of £3 p.a. by Dr Perse in his will, and by further grants from the Perse fund it had been raised to £13 in the course of the eighteenth century, and then to £27 by 1812. The annual stipend had thereafter been raised by further grants from the Perse fund to £37 and then to £47 in 1825. In addition to these formal increases in the "stipend" of a Frankland fellow, his position had been alleviated by the "portion" left to him by Dr Brady in his will and this portion had gradually risen to £40 p.a. in 1817, giving him in total £87 p.a. The decision of 21 May 1831 thus added only a further £11. Until that decision all the earlier increases had fallen on other donors' trust funds and not on the income of the college itself. The emolument of the Frankland fellowship fell back to £81 in the 1840s after the 1841 Chancery Scheme reduced the supplementation from the Perse fund from £40 to £22. 10s.; it was raised to £120 in 1852 (*Gesta*, C.O.13, 16 December 1852) and had finally reached £150 by the time the founders' statutes were repealed in 1860 (*Lib. Rat.* 1860).

[102] *Gesta*, 15 June 1836, cited above. The increases in the stipends of the Master and the senior fellows were "reviewed" and reduced slightly (by £20 p.a. for the fellows and £40 for the Master: *Gesta*, 26 October 1836), whereas the increase for the Wendy fellowship was totally rescinded and the next Wendy fellow received only £30 p.a. It was not raised to £70 until 1852 (*Gesta*, C.O.14, 16 December 1852).

[103] *E.g.*, C.O.6, 31 October 1854 (Mackenzie from Frankland to Stokys, Wiglesworth from Wortley to Frankland, and Ferrers from Wendy to Wortley).

junior fellowship, the Stokys, was limited to divinity.[104] In addition the gulf in stipends between senior and junior fellowships emphasised the increasing unfairness of the 'Norfolk preference', which enabled Norfolk-born junior fellows who were lower in the pecking order to leap-frog their colleagues in promotion to a senior fellowship.[105] In such an atmosphere it is not surprising that impatience engendered discontent, and discontent fostered bitterness and rancour. Much of that bitterness found expression only after Davy's death in 1839 and was directed against his successor, Benedict Chapman, but it would have been more appropriate to direct the bitterness to Chapman's predecessor, Martin Davy; for it was his actions that had brought about the gulf in stipends which had widened so greatly by the time the hapless Chapman succeeded him. Davy's actions in respect of stipends compare unfavourably with those of Robert Brady, who had been Master at the time of a similar depth of feeling over stipends almost two centuries earlier in the years following the Restoration. As we have seen, when Brady died, he made generous provision in his will for improving the stipends of the Frankland fellows, whereas when Davy died he left his equally valuable estate in trust exclusively for the Master.[106]

Chapman had been absent from Cambridge for twenty years before he returned in 1839 on Davy's death and, temperamentally averse to change, he was not the man to comprehend the depth of feeling in the Fellowship or to take steps to remedy the situation;[107] not surprisingly it was not until Guest succeeded him as Master that the junior fellows enjoyed some small but welcome improvement in their income. A long-overdue report into the use of the Frankland trust funds prompted the college to increase the emolument of the Frankland fellows to £120 p.a. in 1852 and at the same time the stipend of the Wendy fellowship was raised to £70;[108] and two years later those of the Wortley fellowships were raised to £100.[109] By 1860, the year in which the founders' statutes were finally repealed, the stipends of the junior fellows had finally reached a more acceptable level: £200 for the Stokys fellows, £150 for the Frankland fellows and £100 for both the Wortley and the Wendy fellows.[110]

[104] As were the second Wortley fellowship and the Wendy fellowship. The unrestricted nature of the Frankland fellowships made them particularly useful to the college and helps to explain why they overtook the Wortley in the pecking order in the 1850s.

[105] See the "*The Norfolk Preference*", § VI. 3 above. The restriction of many fellowships to divinity and medicine caused equal bitterness: *ibid.* The restrictions and preferences in respect of place of birth were abolished in 1858, but the restrictions to particular subjects survived until 1860, when the new statutes merged the individual benefactions into a single anonymous fund.

[106] For Brady's benefaction (Denver) see *B.H.* IV(2), pp. 36–9; Davy's (Heacham) *ibid.*, pp. 112–13.

[107] See *B.H.* III, pp. 137–40.

[108] *Gesta*, C.O.13 and 14, 16 December 1852.

[109] *Gesta*, C.O.4, 31 October 1854. The stipend of the Stokys fellow was temporarily lowered to £184 at the same time (*ibid.*), but it was back to £200 before 1860.

[110] *Lib. Rat.* Michaelmas 1860. No additions were made to the stipends of the Perse fellows, which had been fixed at £75 by the Chancery Scheme in 1841.

COLLEGE OFFICES[111]

The position before Caius' re-foundation

Both Gonville and Bateman saw their foundations as essentially a community of scholars, and their statutes laid upon all fellows an overriding obligation to devote themselves to study and the pursuit of learning and scholarship. Gonville's statutes made no mention of a fellow's undertaking any functions other than scholarship, and he appears to have envisaged that his modest foundation could be maintained by the Master through the employment of servants such as baker and laundress to provide such necessary services as the society required, without the need to distract any fellows from their studies.[112] Bateman apparently thought likewise, for he, too, judged it sufficient in his statutes to provide for the maintenance of the society by persons such as baker, purveyor, cook and menial servants, and required only one significant lay office of his fellows, that of key-keeper of the chest.[113] It is doubtful whether such a view as that of Gonville or of Bateman had ever been realistic, and by the time John Caius entered Gonville Hall as a pensioner in 1529 it had become usual for newly-founded colleges such as Christ's and St John's to make provision in their statutes for the annual or other election of fellows both to administrative offices such as those of bursar, steward and dean to share in the task of managing the college and its affairs, and to some form of lectureships.

[111] For the mastership, see p. 426, n. 6 above. One other 'office' is conspicuously absent from the account which follows. This is the tutorship. To the reader this will seem a glaring omission, since to the students and the outside world the tutors were the face of the college and its most important officers. Until the repeal of the founders' statutes in 1860, however, they were not regarded as holding a college office but as performing a function delegated to them by the Master as one of their fellowship duties. Their only 'appointment' took the form of the informal assignment of pupils to them by the Master and their only emolument flowed from their statutory responsibility as sureties for the debts of their pupils and the consequent channelling through them of all payments between pupil and college. Their 'appointment' was not recorded in the *Gesta*, and they did not feature anywhere in the bursar's half-yearly accounts. As a result it is not possible to assess with any accuracy how rewarding financially a tutorship was at any one time. It is possible to identify from the Matriculation Book which fellows acted as tutors and for how long: in the time of Caius and Legge the Master not infrequently took pupils himself and most fellows seem to have undertaken a short spell as tutor, but after the Restoration the spells became longer and the fellows undertaking them became fewer, and in the eighteenth century there were rarely more than two at a time and for some of the time only one (John Smith seems to have acted alone from 1747 until he became Master in 1763, even in the years when he was bursar and then president). For the tutorship, see *B.H.* III, pp. 25ff for this college; *H.U.C.*, III, pp. 300ff for the university; and C.N.L. Brooke in *Emmanuel College*, pp. 582–3 for the same difficulty of assessing tutorial emoluments in another college.

[112] Gonville's Statute 8.

[113] This laid upon the three fellows who were key-keepers the obligation to account yearly "for every item received, allowed, expended, performed and managed by them": Bateman's statutes, Preamble, §§ 4, and Statutes 6 and 7.

We can be confident that similar administrative offices existed *de facto* in Gonville Hall by then, and that one office, the bursarship, had already entitled the holders of the office to an allowance of 5s. a half-year against their commons account;[114] but we know from the returns made to Henry VIII by his Commissioners in 1546 that fellows elected to administrative offices in Gonville Hall could not expect any monetary remuneration from its straitened funds beyond their fellowship stipend.[115] This remained the stark fact throughout Caius' time as a fellow and it would have stayed in his recollection of the college when he resigned his fellowship in 1545 and left Cambridge to settle in London.

As regards teaching, his memories of Gonville Hall would have been different, for one paid lectureship had been established by the time he left and a second was in the process of being established. These two posts came to be known as the humanities lectureship and the Greek lectureship. The first had been envisaged by a generous benefactor, Geoffrey Knight, before Caius came up and, although it is unclear whether any lectures had in fact been given before Caius went abroad to Italy in 1539, they had started by the time he returned briefly to Cambridge in 1544.[116] Given his interest in the disputes over the pronunciation of Greek at the time, he would also have become aware during his short return to Cambridge that a lectureship in Greek was envisaged in response to Henry VIII's waiver of his right to the first-fruits due to the Crown from the college.[117] The two lecturers were paid out of the college's chest, but the payments did not involve any additional charge on the college's funds or furnish instances of a general practice to remunerate officers, for they had been established in pursuance of specific benefactions.[118]

[114] These allowances to the Master and to the second bursar are shown in the earliest surviving half-yearly account in the *Liber Rationalis* (to Legge and Paman in 1581: *Lib. Rat.* (1581)), and they always appear in subsequent accounts thereafter. The allowances were unique, for no similar sums were ever credited to any other officers. They appear in the earliest surviving commons account together with two allowances to fellows which go back to Bateman's time (distributions and commemorations), and it is likely that this modest allowance to the two bursars had also been an established practice in Gonville Hall before Caius' time. The fellow-bursar's allowance was increased to 25s. in 1620, but not the Master's (*Lib. Rat.* Lady Day 1620); no further increase was made thereafter. The allowances continued to be credited to the Master and the bursar until the repeal of the founders' statutes in 1860, even though they had long become quite worthless in comparison with the bursarial salary by then.

[115] In sharp contrast to their returns for King's College and St John's, the calculations for Gonville Hall made by Henry VIII's Commissioners in February 1546 did not include payments for any college offices other than the posts established by Geoffrey Knight and funded by him: *Documents*, I, pp. 227–35. Gonville Hall was ranked as the fourth poorest college in their returns: *B.H.* III, p. 339.

[116] The post, which became known as the Humanities lectureship (and later as the Rhetoric praelectorship), was finally established in October 1538 by deed between Geoffrey Knight's executrix and the college.

[117] 27 Hen. VIII, c. 42.

[118] The Humanities and Greek lecturers were paid £2 and £3 p.a., respectively.

Three further endowed posts had been established by the time Caius left Cambridge in 1545, two by the same Geoffrey Knight and a third by John Whitacre.[119] As explained in an earlier chapter,[120] Knight had contemplated the appointment of two *additional* members of the college to discharge the priestly duties he specified, one living in Gonville Hall and the other in Fishwick Hostel, rather than someone who was already a fellow, and each of the salaries provided by his gift (£5. 6s. 8d.) was larger than the annual stipend of a fellow on Gonville's and Bateman's foundations (£4. 13s. 4d.). However, the Reformation and the loss of Fishwick Hostel in effect frustrated Knight's intention, and by the time of Caius' re-foundation Knight's *subsidia* were being paid to persons who were already fellows, each of whom thus temporarily enjoyed a second full stipend.[121] When John Whitacre made his gift in 1539 the Reformation was already well advanced and the terms of the gift contemplated that the post would always be held by one who was already a fellow or other member of the college; nevertheless, the *subsidium* produced by his gift still amounted to £3. 14s. 8d., a sum which was not much less than a fellow's annual stipend.[122] In the time between Caius' departure from Cambridge in 1545 and the formulation of his statutes after his return to the college as Master in 1559, the outlawing of prayers and services for the dead rendered the duties of the three salarists markedly less onerous than the donors had contemplated, thereby producing a situation in which the three preaching offices carried diminishing responsibilities but greater remuneration than the two teaching offices, while the administrative offices carried little or no reward for the increasing responsibilities the holders shouldered.

The pattern set by Caius: annual rotation of offices without remuneration

The annual rotation of offices[123]

In his re-foundation of the college Caius shared the earlier founders' vision of a community of scholars, and, like them, he drafted his final statutes in the firm belief that study and the pursuit of learning was the primary and overriding

[119] See *The gifts of Geoffrey Knight and John Whitacre* in "*Supplementary Notes to Caius' Statutes*", § IV. 3, at pp. 299–300 above, and *B.H.* III, pp. 245, 249–50.

[120] See the preceding note.

[121] For the complications surrounding the establishment of Knight's two posts and his earlier humanities lectureship, see *The gifts of Geoffrey Knight and John Whitacre* in "*Supplementary Notes to Caius' Statutes*", § IV. 3, at p. 299 above.

[122] For Whitacre's gift see *B.H.* III, pp. 249–50. In this case too Caius extended the obligation to preach in his final statutes (in Statute 61): cf. the preceding note.

[123] For a list of bursars, stewards and registraries, see Catherine Hall, "College officers: the bursars, stewards and registraries of Gonville and Caius College", *The Caian* (1989–90), pp. 114–26. The list is incomplete for the years preceding 1608, but the Pandects provide a good idea of who acted as bursar during Caius' mastership (Henry Holland for the four years 1566–70) and a

obligation for which *all* fellows received their stipend. To ensure that no fellow should be unduly distracted from that duty, and that the task of managing the college's affairs should be regularly shared within the whole fellowship, he directed that no fellow should, as a general rule, hold more than one office at a time "so that they can be allocated among all fellows according to the fitness of each".[124] He imposed no restriction upon the period for which elections might be made to minor, less demanding offices, but he was careful to limit the period for which elections to the more onerous offices could be made. The registrary might be elected for one, two or three years "according as there is hope of better and fear of worse",[125] but the bursar and the deans were to be elected annually, and the steward for no more than three months.[126] Annual appointment did not, in itself, prevent a bursar from being re-appointed for a further term or terms, and during Caius' mastership this in fact occurred: after the quarrels of his first seven years Caius turned to one fellow, Henry Holland, to undertake the bursarship throughout the four years 1566–70 when he was away in London for much of the time, and it was only in his last two years that the practice of regular rotation was resumed.[127]

The scarcity of records earlier than 1581 and the fact that Caius' successor, Thomas Legge, occasionally undertook the office of bursar alone (and apparently that of steward at the same time)[128] in the early years of his mastership make it difficult to be certain for how long or how often a fellow might hold an office in the first ten years following Caius' death; but after 1581 it is clear that the pattern of annual tenure of office envisaged by Caius continued during Legge's mastership as regards the crucial offices of bursar and steward, if not others. Only on four occasions did a fellow hold the bursarship for a second year in

complete list of bursars and stewards can be constructed from the *Liber Rationalis* for the years from 1580, since a fellow was personally liable for receipts and disbursements while he was bursar or steward and this liability is reflected in his personal commons account. It should be remembered that appointments recorded in the *Liber Rationalis* and the Bursar's Book refer to the *preceding* six months' accounting period, whereas those in the *Gesta* indicate the date from which the election or appointment ran.

124 Statute 60.

125 Statute 39.

126 Statutes 24 and 56: the deans were to be elected at the Michaelmas audit, and the bursar either then or at the Lady Day audit. The very short tenure envisaged for the steward might seem strange, but it reflected the practice that had prevailed in Gonville Hall (*Documents*, II, p. 348) and it recognised the very onerous and time-consuming nature of the office at that time (see below): in his draft statutes Caius had provided that the function of steward should, as before, be undertaken for a period of three months by fellows in order of seniority unless they were profligate or in debt: *Documents*, II, p. 348. Stewards very soon came to be elected annually.

127 See "*John Caius and his Foundation*", § IV. 3, at p. 361 above.

128 *E.g.*, in 1580–81, when Legge acted alone as bursar, there was no separate steward: *Lib. Rat.* (Michaelmas 1581).

succession between 1581 and Legge's death in 1607,[129] and on no occasion was the stewardship held for more than a year. This meant that fellows might expect to be called back from time to time to offices which they had held earlier: during the period from 1581 to his death in 1615, Stephen Perse served as bursar on eleven separate occasions and was called back to act as bursar in 1613 in the penultimate year of his life;[130] another long-serving fellow, Robert Churche, who had first held the offices of registrary and bursar in the last year of Caius' mastership, was called upon to serve again as bursar as late as 1595–96 and 1598–99, and as registrary even after that.[131]

The absence of remuneration

On the subject of remuneration Caius was curiously ambivalent. The uncertainty stems from the fact that Caius was not drafting his statutes *de novo* but building upon those of Bateman, who had made virtually no provision for any payments to officers: as a result it is difficult to decide whether Caius, like Bateman, envisaged that fellows should take their turn to discharge the college's office without additional recompense when it came to their turn to undertake it or whether he assumed that officers should, as a general rule, be entitled to some salary from the college's funds for their labours. Caius' insistence that those enjoying the very generous payments (*subsidia*) provided by Geoffrey Knight and John Whitacre should not hold other offices appears to spring from a desire that others should have the chance to enjoy those other offices and this might imply an assumption on his part that all college offices would, as a general rule, carry a salary or other emolument.[132] On the other hand, he felt it necessary to make express provision in Statute 59 for a payment of 20s. p.a. to be made from the college's funds to the secretary or registrary as a "subsidy" (*subsidium*); yet he did not reward the bursar or steward with similar payments, even though he had just specified burdensome duties for them in Statute 56. Nor did he do so for other officers on whom he laid specific duties in his statutes – president,

[129] Thomas Grimston (1587–88 and six further months); Thomas Reve (1590–91–92); Stephen Perse (1603–4–5 and 1606–7–8). Perse's extended period covered the final years of Legge's mastership and the first of Branthwaite's; Reve's coincided with difficulty caused by Christopher Grimston's stewardship.

[130] Perse served as bursar in 1583–84, 1585–86, 1589–90, 1592–93, 1594–95, 1597–98, 1599–1600, 1601–2, 1603–4–5, 1606–7–8, 1613–14; he also served as steward for the summer half-year of 1582 and 1593 and for the year 1610–11: see *Lib. Rat.* He almost certainly served in those offices before 1581 (the year of the earliest surviving *Liber Rationalis*), as he had been called upon to undertake some bursarial responsibilities in 1570 in his first year as a fellow: see "*John Caius and his Foundation*", § IV. 3, at p. 361 above.

[131] Churche was registrary in 1571 and apparently for some years thereafter, and he was bursar with John Tracie in the traumatic year 1572–73: see Hall, "College officers", at p. 116, and *Lib. Rat.* (1582–83, 1595–96, 1598–99).

[132] See the direction in Statute 60.

chaplain or librarian[133] – and although he did allow a "salary" (*salarium*) to the deans in the form of fees for the lectures that he required them to give, those fees were not to come from the chest but from the students themselves or, in the case of scholars, from the funds that supported them.[134]

The absence of any provision for (i) the bursar and (ii) the steward is particularly striking to modern eyes.

(i) The bursar. At first sight the fact that Caius made no provision in his statutes for any payment to the bursars may seem distinctly odd, given that he placed upon them the responsibility for the safeguarding of the colleges' assets, and particularly its moneys, a matter on which he felt extremely strongly. It must be remembered, however, that he regarded the Master as the permanent and principal bursar who would be assisted by a succession of fellows elected just for one year; and like Bateman before him he granted to the Master a stipend and allowances commensurate with his position as principal (and virtually sole) executive officer of the college. Furthermore, the day-to-day duties of the college's bursar were less onerous than they became in the second half of the eighteenth century and thereafter. In those earlier years the regular supervision of the more important college estates would fall to the manorial stewards and bailiffs, and the principal function of the bursar would be the half-yearly receipt of the rents from the tenants[135] and the disbursement of those moneys in the period between audits. Even the responsibility for disbursements was less onerous than might be thought, for much of the money which the bursar paid out from the chest in the course of any half-year would simply be paid in substantial tranches to the steward to meet the bills for the college's catering and other domestic services, and it was the responsibility of the latter officer to account for his expenditure of those sums.[136]

[133] For specific duties laid on the president, see Statutes 42 (supervision of dissection), 52 (security at night); in addition Caius laid upon him most of the Master's functions during the latter's absence. For the chaplain and librarian, see Statutes 58 and 79, respectively. After 1587 the duties of the chaplain passed to Mrs Frankland's Chaplain, who received the equivalent of a fellow's stipend: *ibid.*, pp. 241–2. Caius did not envisage the care of the library as a separate office but a responsibility allocated to the Greek lecturer; the librarian became a distinct officer only in 1629, when he was granted an annual payment of £6 from the degree fees paid by B.A.s.: *B.H.* III, p. 191.

[134] Statute 24; and see below.

[135] Even the rents in Cambridge might be paid to a bailiff, not directly to the bursar: in 1611 Henry Boston was elected bailiff for collecting Cambridge rents at the pleasure of the Master and fellows (*Acta*, 17 July 1611).

[136] For the position in the sixteenth century, see pp. 454–5 and nn. 140, 141 below.

(ii) The steward. Caius does not explain why he kept the title "steward" (*senescallus*) exclusively for the steward of a manor in his statutes[137] and chose the esoteric title of *oeconomus* for the domestic steward of his re-founded college.[138] His action is curious, for the title was not in use then for that office in other Cambridge colleges and *seneschallus* had been the standard title used in the Tudor statutes of other foundations.[139] Caius frequently succumbed to the temptation to display his knowledge of Greek, but his deliberate choice of language here should, however, probably not be ascribed to vanity, but rather to his desire to stress the financial and accounting responsibilities of the officer. Because of the change in the relative status of the two offices in later centuries, we may be tempted to assume that the steward had always been a much more junior officer than the bursar, but Caius placed upon him responsibilities that could be almost as heavy as those shouldered by the bursars in the early years of the re-founded college. As explained earlier, accounting for the bursarial expenditure was considerably less onerous in the sixteenth century than it became later, for more than half of the bursar's annual expenditure consisted simply of three or four payments of substantial

[137] Statute 96. In one of his very first documents as Master, Caius appointed a fellow, Henry Dethick, as "*seneschallus terrarium*" (*Pandectae*, fol. 2, January 1559), but it is clear from Statute 96 that Caius had by 1572 come to envisage that the stewardship of a manor would not be a college office and that it would not be held by a fellow, but by a local official similar to the bailiff. Over the centuries, as travel became easier and quicker, the college came to appoint a single professional lawyer to act as steward for groups of manors, and stewards became increasingly remote from each individual manor: *Gesta*, 8 October 1660 (Mr Kerrick "chosen Steward for all our courts in Norfolk and near Cambridge"), *ibid.*, 25 November 1663 (that Richard Newman of the Temple Esq. be our Steward "for our courts at Croxley *durante bene placito nostro*"). Eventually, the college reverted to Caius' original practice of appointing a fellow to be steward of all its manors, but now a fellow who was a lawyer: John Tozer was so appointed in 1847 (*Gesta*, C.O.3, 28 October 1847) and he was followed by Thomas Wiglesworth and eventually by William Buckland (*Annals*, Introduction, p. xiii).

[138] Although Caius deliberately opted for the term *oeconomus* instead of *seneschallus*, the term was translated as "steward" on the rare occasions on which English was used in contemporary Elizabethan records: *e.g.*, *Status Collegii* (Lady Day 1586). In the early seventeenth century the college appears to have transferred to the steward some of the functions which had hitherto been performed by his assistant, the caterer (who had been described as "*obsonator sive dispensator*" by Caius in Statute 56). The office of *dispensator* was separated from that of caterer (*obsonator*) and transferred to the steward (or to another fellow), though it is not clear what duties were involved (perhaps the purchase of wine?). For a short time the term "*seneschallus sive dispensator*" was used in the *Acta* to designate the fellow elected *oeconomus* (Dr Welles: *Acta*, 30 October 1611; Mr Stokys: *Acta*, 8 October 1613). The use of "*seneschallus*" in the *Acta* for this purpose did not last long, however, and the college soon reverted to using "*oeconomus*" in Latin and "steward" in English.

[139] See the statutes of Jesus, Christ's, King's and Trinity Colleges.

tranches of money each quarter to the steward,[140] and it was the latter's obligation to supervise and account in detail for the expenditure of those sums by his assistants, the caterer and the butler.[141] It should not surprise us, therefore, to find that the most senior and respected of the fellows might be steward in the same year in which the most junior fellow was the bursar.[142]

Although Caius was silent on the question whether college officers generally should or should not be permitted any payment for discharging the duties laid upon them by the office, the principle underlying his approach to the question would seem to have been that the college had been endowed for the maintenance of its members, Master, fellows and scholars, for which they were paid an appropriate stipend, and that any further payment from the chest to those members could be justified only if money had been given specifically for such a payment by a benefactor (as in the case of the salarists and lecturers) or if it was expressly authorised by the founders' statutes.[143] Save in those few cases fellows should not look to the college's corporate funds for remuneration when they were discharging an office.

Payments from the chest

So long as appointments were made only for a year or other short period and the office circulated around the Fellowship as a matter of course, as Caius envisaged, the burden of unpaid office would be shared equitably. His successor, Thomas Legge, maintained this practice steadily throughout his mastership as regards the limitation of tenure to very limited periods and circulation of offices, but in his later years the college was faced with the need to ask fellows

[140] In the six months to Michaelmas 1610, the bursar paid £257 to the steward in six tranches (£60, £40, £40, £60 and £57), and expended a further £281 himself: *Bursar's Book* (Michaelmas 1610).

[141] The following figures (in £) from the *Liber Rationalis* for five half-years taken at random give (a) the bursar's receipts, (b) his total expenditure, (c) the amount within that expenditure which he simply disbursed to the steward, (d) the latter's expenditure, and the names of (e) the bursar and (f) the steward:

	(a)	(b)	(c)	(d)	(e)	(f)
1586 M.	288	296	161	173	Perse	Grimston
1598 LD.	367	417	311	312	Perse	Mallorie
1607 M.	534	484	290	254	Perse	Batchcroft
1610 LD	431	411	298	306	Parker	Browne
1611 LD	387	352	259	271	Browne	Perse

[142] See the *Liber Rationalis* (Lady Day 1611): the bursar was John Browne, and the steward was Stephen Perse, who had frequently been bursar in earlier years and was to become bursar again before his death in 1615.

[143] Caius' Statute 59 in the case of the registrary and Bateman's preamble to his statutes in the case of the cook and his assistant.

to undertake new duties not foreseen in Caius' statutes and to provide sufficient inducement to them to do so.

The last years of Legge's mastership saw the creation of three new posts: those of Mrs Frankland's chaplain, the Hebrew lecturer and the catechist. The first two had been created by Joyce Frankland in her will in 1587 and in both cases she had made specific provision for the remuneration of the holder: her chaplain was to receive £10 a year, a sum equivalent to the stipend and livery of one of Dr Caius' own fellows and substantially better than that of other fellows, including her own fellows, while the Hebrew lecturer was to be paid £4 a year, a sum twice that of Geoffrey Knight's humanities lecturer and more than that of the Greek lecturer. The post of catechist appeared shortly afterwards in 1592, not as the result of any benefaction but simply as a non-statutory task committed to a fellow who was suitably qualified and willing to discharge it and for which some inducement in the form of financial remuneration was needed even though the college had received no fund to provide this.[144]

Each of the three posts raised the question whether the holder should be added to the few college officers remunerated out of the college's corporate endowment, and in each case the answer was different. For the two posts founded by Mrs Frankland the answer was straightforward: her chaplaincy was regarded as being much the same as the fellowships she had also founded and the holder's stipend was credited to him not as payment for an office, but as an allowance against his commons account, like that of any fellow, while the Hebrew lectureship fell naturally into the category of college offices in the same way as the humanities and Greek lectureship had already done in Caius' statutes. The third post was less straightforward. The catechist appeared at virtually the same time as the Hebrew lecturer, and had very similar duties, but, unlike the latter, he was not added to the list of paid college officers and his remuneration was not included in the bursar's account of the quarterly payments made from the chest to those officers; instead the payment was included in the payments listed under the head of exceptional expenditure ("*exposita extraordinaria*"), along with miscellaneous payments such as those to carpenters, cleaners, joiners and plumbers and numerous others.[145]

On Legge's death, the recording of the bursar's accounts appears to have become more elaborate, and in 1609 a more systematic and detailed series of records was begun with the Bursar's Books. In these income and expenditure was arranged under various specific heads, and the payments of salaries to

[144] See *B.H.* III, pp. 247–8; the post remains one of the least well-documented offices in the history of the college.

[145] See, *e.g.*, *Bursar's Book* (Lady Day 1609), (Michaelmas 1611) and (Michaelmas 1620). The payment to the catechist was initially £5 a year, but after 1620, when catechising became mandatory by royal injunction, payment by the college was replaced by fees payable by pensioners and disappears from the Bursar's Book: *B.H.* III, p. 248, n. 1.

officers appear under a specific head of "Recurrent expenditure on Fellows and officials of the college" (*Exposita ordinaria sociis et officiariis collegii*).[146] Under that head the only payments regularly made out of the chest to college officers and debited to the endowment were:

(i) the *subsidium* to the registrary authorised by Caius' statute,
(ii) the three *subsidia* provided by Geoffrey Knight and John Whitacre for their preachers (later termed "salarists"),[147]
(iii) the payments to the three lecturers funded by the benefactors who had established the lectureships in the humanities, Greek and Hebrew,[148] and
(iv) the salaries of the cook and undercook.[149]

That list remained unchanged until 1783.[150] The long absence from it of all other officers is striking: Caius had required the appointment of other officers, notably president, bursar, steward and dean, yet for almost two hundred years none of them received a salary from the corporate endowment: no payments were debited to the chest in the Bursar's Book in respect of the demanding offices of bursar and steward until 1783 or to the deans until 1801.[151] If we took the Bursar's Book alone, we should have to conclude that the bursarship and the stewardship were undertaken entirely without any recompense until the last quarter of the eighteenth century, and that the deans could expect only fees from the students for any lectures that they gave.

This might be an acceptable conclusion if officers had continued to discharge their offices only for one year, but in fact the pattern changed over the course of the seventeenth and eighteenth centuries for the key administrative offices. In the seventeenth century most offices continued to rotate annually, but the

146 Unlike other bursarial accounts this particular head is made up quarterly, not half-yearly; this no doubt reflects the practice that had prevailed in the time of Gonville Hall. The terminology of the list is also informative. None of the payments was termed a "stipend" in the Bursar's Book; only the post of registrary was described as an "office"; neither the salarists nor the lecturers were ever described as holding an "office"; and the lecturers were paid simply "*pro lectione*".

147 The services of the three salarists were at first termed *servitia*, and the term "salary" (*salarium*) was applied only to the cook and his assistant, who were not members of the college; however, the use of the terms *servitium* and *salarium* was soon reversed and the term "salarist" was thereafter reserved exclusively for Knight's and Whitacre's preachers (cp. *Bursar's Book* 1609 and 1616).

148 For these posts see *B.H.* III, pp. 244–7.

149 It is curious that no similar payments to the butler (*promus*) and the caterer (*obsonator*) were recorded in the Bursar's Book, and presumably they were paid by the steward, not the bursar. Unlike the cook and his assistant, the *promus* and the *obsonator* were members of the college, and if they were scholars they had to resign their scholar's stipend before they could be appointed to those posts: *Acta* (Michaelmas 1613) (Ds Edmunds).

150 The amounts paid to the Greek and Hebrew lecturers changed in 1663 as a result of Dr Batchcroft's devise, but not the list of offices: see p. 461, n. 163 below.

151 *Bursar's Book* (Michaelmas 1783). See *The transition to salaries*, at p. 471 below.

practice changed twice in the case of the bursarship. That important office came to be held for prolonged periods until 1660,[152] and thereafter it tended to change hands after a spell of three or four years. By the eighteenth century the same practice of tenure for three or four years had spread to the other key administrative offices of steward and registrary.[153] Few fellows would be willing to serve for such periods without some remuneration and we shall not be surprised, therefore, to find that modest rewards had been devised for most college officers long before salaries were introduced in 1783.

The recourse to fees, fines, benefactions and the benefit of money in hand

Fees

In his statutes Caius provided for the payment of fees to an officer for his services in one specific case, namely, that of the two deans to whom he allowed a "salary" (*salarium*) of 16d. from each scholar and pensioner and 20d. from each bachelor-pensioner for the two courses of lectures that they were required to give each term; the charge fell not upon the chest, but upon the pensioners personally, and upon the particular scholarship fund in the case of scholars.[154] The deans did not remain long the sole recipients of fees. In the course of time they were joined by two groups of officer: (i) the bursar, the registrary and, we may presume, the steward, each of whom came in various ingenious ways to enjoy fees that were levied personally and not through the college; and (ii) the catechist, the librarian and, very probably, the humanities lecturer or *praelector rhetoricus* as he became known in the seventeenth century, all of whom came to receive, as a form of salary from the college, part of the fees which the college levied upon its members.

(i) The bursar, the registrary and the steward

If we were to consider only the payments that were made through the college's books half-yearly, we should be forced to conclude that bursars remained virtually unpaid until late in the eighteenth century. In fact, however, we find from other sources that the fellow-bursar very soon came to enjoy at least

152 Robert Welles was bursar from 1616 to 1632 with only two half-year breaks; Joseph Loveland for the seven years preceding the outbreak of the Civil War; William Banks for seven years during the Civil War itself; and William Dell, the Master, for the same period during the Commonwealth.

153 See Catherine Hall's list cited at n. 123 above. In the case of the registraryship there was one striking exception to the pattern: James Burrough acted as registrary for thirty-three years (from 1721 to 1754, when he became Master), with a break of two years (1727–29) while he was bursar. As Mrs Hall has noted, the stewardship seems to have been used as a trial run for the bursarship; the office of registrary appears to have been used similarly.

154 Statute 24.

one additional emolument in the form of fees which did not pass through the college's books. These arose in connexion with the distribution of corn money.[155] As explained in the next chapter, corn money was not regarded as income accruing to the college but was instead divided between the fortunate members of the college who shared in it. Since corn money came out of the corn-rents payable by the college's tenants, it was paid by the tenants to the bursar in addition to their money-rent and the bursar as the recipient of it was responsible for its half-yearly distribution to the Master and resident senior fellows, even though corn money never passed through the college's books. When it came to that distribution the first charge on corn money was always a fee of £1 to the bursar and at the end of the process he also took as a perquisite any fractional surplus remaining from the division; in addition, he took out of each fellow's share (whatever its size) a further fee of 5s. These amounts had become insignificant in value by the middle of the eighteenth century, but they would have been the equivalent of a senior fellow's stipend in the earlier half of the seventeenth century.[156] These fees which the bursar took from individual members were not, however, the only fees which he came to enjoy in later years. These took the form of fees from the college's trust funds for the management of any lands in which the funds were invested and since the fees were calculated as a percentage of the income from the college's trust funds, typically 4%, they did not lose their value, unlike the earlier fixed fees; when the practice started is at present uncertain, since the fees were paid from the trust funds and never appear in the college's own accounts.[157] How many other similar fees the bursar also enjoyed is unclear, but it will be seen later that he came to enjoy a remarkably generous fee from the college itself for providing coal to it and the fellows.[158]

[155] See "*Dividends*", § VI. 5 below. As explained there, our earliest knowledge of the bursar's involvement in the distribution comes from the personal notebook that John Gostlin kept in the years following the Restoration, but we can be sure that the practice had always been the same. In the eighteenth century, a record of the distribution came to be kept in the college's Grain Books, but the payment of corn money and the bursar's fee for its distribution never passed through the Bursar's Book.

[156] Since there would regularly be eleven other senior fellows entitled to corn money, the total amount taken by the bursar each half-year would have been not far short of £4, *i.e.* £8 p.a., which was the average amount of the stipend of a senior fellow before the purchase of Great Shelford manor and mills in 1614: for those stipends see above.

[157] The little evidence that has been uncovered so far derives from the 1840s: see *Gesta*, C.O.6, 17 May 1842 for the 4% fee on the Heacham estate left to the college on trust by Martin Davy. The practice may have originated in the 1841 Chancery scheme made by the Chancery Master in the Perse action; this allowed the bursar 4% on the gross rents of the Perse real estates: Ord. 10, Cooper, *Annals*, iv, p. 641. Cf. *Fellows' Accounts* 1840–42, for the bursar's calculation in 1842 of his 4% fee from the Perse trust as £82. 7s. 11d.; cf. p. 477, n. 227 below.

[158] For this emolument see p. 475, n. 220 below.

In precisely the same way that the bursar took fees from the Master and senior fellows for the distribution of corn money, so the registrary also took fees from them for the distribution of the entry fines paid by lessees on the grant or renewal of his lease, and, like the bursar, he too was entitled to any fractional surplus remaining from the division. He also enjoyed what might at first sight seem a trivial perquisite in that he was entitled to keep for himself any surplus remaining from the fees paid by lessees after he had discharged the expenses of engrossing their deeds. These fees were a steady and not inconsiderable privilege, since virtually all leases granted by the college were renewable every seven years and, in addition, every lease granted by the college contained a specific requirement that it had to be replaced on the occasion of death or assignment *inter vivos* with a new lease to the assignee: each fee taken by itself might seem insignificant, but the perquisite was sufficiently valued that the college agreed in 1785 to allow the registrary £6 a year extra to make up the lost profit caused to him by the raising of stamp duties on deeds, and further to allow to him "the clear Profits of his Fees which he would have received" from a lease which it did not renew.[159]

Very few of the steward's records have survived from before the nineteenth century and consequently, in contrast to the bursar and the registrary, it is not possible to know with certainty whether the steward enjoyed any fees similar to those that were devised for those other administrative officers, despite his responsibilities. It would not be surprising, however, if he did derive some perquisites from an office that entailed the regular purchase of food and other supplies from merchants and tradesmen in the town, and we find, very late on, a hint in 1773 that he had in fact derived some such hidden benefit from his office.[160] Apart from this late hint no other evidence of any earlier payments to the steward appears to have survived, though it would be remarkable if he had not enjoyed some perquisites similar to those enjoyed by the bursar and the registrary.

(ii) The catechist, the librarian and the *praelector rhetoricus*

In his statutes Caius had provided that the deans should give lectures to the scholars and pensioners of the college and should receive in return a salary in the form of fees charged to the junior members of the college, and it is curious that the college was surprisingly hesitant in extending this form of remuneration to other officers who provided similar services to its members. As has been seen, the college had begun to appoint a catechist annually during the

[159] *Gesta*, 26 October 1785.

[160] In 1773 the Master and fellows "agreed to give up the small dividends, due to the Master, Fellows, Steward & Butler from the Brewer and the Baker and to allow the Steward from Wortley's Benefaction, from Perse's & from the College Chest £4 p.a. [from] each, and for the Cook's salary £5 p.a. from the Coll. Chest & from the above Benefactions £5 p.a. [from] each": *Gesta*, 13 January 1773. This would suggest that the steward had enjoyed a larger dividend in virtue of his office than the other fellows, since he was the only fellow to be compensated.

mastership of Caius' successor, Thomas Legge, and had sought to make some payment out of its general funds to the fellow who undertook the function of catechising, yet it was only in 1620 that the payment finally took the form of fees levied on junior members.[161] The practice of paying a salary out of such fees was extended to the librarian soon after in 1629, when he was allowed £6 a year out of the degree fees ("commemoration money") payable to the steward by B.A.s.[162] Although there is no clear evidence that any other officer received any remuneration in the form of fees from junior members, it would seem very likely that a fourth officer was remunerated in this way by the seventeenth century. This was the humanities lecturer, or *praelector rhetoricus* as he was by then more usually termed; as the holder of the college's most senior teaching office he had acquired the responsibility of presenting the college's graduands and collecting their degree fees in addition to the lecturing duties envisaged by the founder, Geoffrey Knight; despite this additional responsibility his salary of £2 p.a. from the chest was not supplemented when those of the Greek and Hebrew lecturers were increased in 1661 and remained unchanged until the 1850s, unlike those of every other office: one is left with the impression that his meagre salary must have been supplemented out of the degree fees he collected.[163]

Fines

In addition to the lecture fees which Caius allowed to the deans in his statutes, we learn from other sources that they had in fact acquired an additional, non-statutory emolument during Legge's mastership: this was the fines imposed on scholars and pensioners by Caius for infringements of the various statutory obligations in respect of chapel which he laid upon them. We first learn of this exceptional perquisite enjoyed by the deans through the proceedings before the Chancellor in 1617 in the dispute between Branthwaite and the fellows, where it featured as one of charges made by the Master against the fellows: "The Mulcts have been appropriated to the Deans, contrarie to the 73 statute, *volumus ut omnes mulctae cedant Collegio*."[164] In their answer to the charge the fellows defended the practice of allowing the fines on scholars to the deans as one of

[161] 6d. a quarter from those below M.A., and 1s. on major pensioners – a form of payment that survived to Venn's time: see *B.H.* III, p. 248, n. 1, and also p. 456 above.

[162] *B.H.* III, p. 191. The duties of librarian had previously been imposed by Caius on the Greek lecturer (Statute 79). The librarian appears to have received other small payments, presumably in the form of fees, until 1853: *Gesta*, 13 December 1853, C.O.15(e).

[163] On his death in 1661 Dr Batchcroft left his lands in Milton to the college to increase the salaries of the Greek and Hebrew lectureships; the fact that he did not include the humanities lectureship, even though the salary of the older lectureship was smaller, suggests that its holder was by then augmenting it in other ways. The formal salary from the college chest was still £2 p.a. in 1853, when it was discontinued together with similar small payments to other officers: *Gesta*, 13 December 1853, C.O.15.

[164] *Allen's Case* (1617), Appendix F below.

long-standing practice: "As to the mulcts of schollers they have been from time to time allowed to the deans for their paines in their offices, and (as we have heard our predecessors say) were so allowed in Dr Caius time."[165] The deans continued to take these fines until the last years of the eighteenth century, when it was finally decided "that the Mulcts upon the Students for non-attendance in Chapel, Hall etc. be in future applied to the College Chest, & that the College in lieu thereof allow to each Dean as much as will make up the annual assessment in the Steward's book 30£".[166]

Benefactions

The first half of the seventeenth century saw a striking increase in the number of students admitted to the college and the lecturing required, and at the same time a continued fall in the value of fixed salaries and stipends.[167] The college responded with the building of further accommodation to meet the increase in numbers, but it provided no increase in the stipends of its teaching officers.[168] The deans who received fees for their lectures were protected by the increase in numbers against any fall in the value of each fee they received, but not so the lecturers, who continued to receive only salaries that had remained unchanged since the time of Henry VIII. Their protection came from two long-serving fellows, Stephen Perse and Thomas Batchcroft, each of whom had more experience than any other fellows of both the fall in the value of money and the increase in the size of the college.[169] The lecturers who benefitted were, in Perse's case, the morning lecturers, and in Batchcroft's the Greek and Hebrew lecturers.

165 *Ibid.* The practice was defended on the somewhat dubious ground that the only persons mentioned in the statute were the fellows and that the requirement that all fines should go to the college must therefore be read as referring only to fines imposed on fellows. The fines diverted to the deans appear to be those imposed on students for non-attendance at chapel and hall, and possibly at disputations and lectures (Statutes 17 and 45); but *quaere* other offences such as students' absence from their rooms at night (Statutes 24) or fouling the courts (Statute 78).

166 *Gesta*, 25 October 1797.

167 For Venn's analysis of the number of admissions to the college and bachelor degrees conferred by the university in the period, see *B.H.* III, p. 392; cf. the figures for the different colleges given by Twigg, in *A History of Queens' College, Cambridge 1448–1986* (Boydell Press, 1987), Appendix 6.

168 The period saw four major building projects undertaken in response to the increase: the Perse and Legge Buildings in 1617 and 1618 respectively; the brick building extending down Trinity Lane from the hall to the north-west corner of the college; and the enlargement of the chapel in 1637 (*B.H.* III, pp. 83, 93 and 161). Only the last two were undertaken by the college out of its own resources: the initiative for the first two came from the benefactors after whom the buildings were named. For the increases in the stipends of senior fellows through the purchase of property at Shelford in 1614 and Weeting in 1632, see p. 432, n. 27 above, and *B.H.* IV(2), pp. viii, 80, 91.

169 Perse was a fellow from 1571 to his death in 1615; Batchcroft was a fellow from 1595 to 1626, and then Master until he was ejected in 1649, returning very briefly as Master for six months in 1660, and dying in 1661: *B.H.* III, pp. 57, 139.

The morning lecturers were the first to benefit. In Statute 24 Caius had laid upon the two deans the duty of giving lectures, one on Aristotelian logic and the other on moral philosophy, but the giving of the lectures appears to have been delegated by the deans in the early years of the seventeenth century to deputies known as the "morning lecturers" (*lectores matutini*). The fees prescribed by Caius were presumably shared between the deans and the morning lecturers, but Perse clearly thought that the two morning lecturers received less than they should, for he left £2 p.a. for each of them in his will. Those payments ceased when the income of the Perse trust fell substantially in value in the 1678 and, according to Venn, all reference to the lecturers "seems to disappear" after 1687;[170] the payment of fees by the scholars and pensioners to the steward for the deans continued, however, until 1853.[171] Ironically, payments of £15 p.a. to "morning lecturers" unexpectedly reappear in the last years before Caius' statutes were abolished in 1860 – not from any decision by the college but in consequence of the requirement in the court order made by the Chancery Master in 1841 in the Perse litigation that they should each be paid that sum.[172]

The statutory Greek and Hebrew lecturers had to wait for any increase in their salaries until Batchcroft's death in 1661. In his will he left his lands in Milton to the college on trust to divide the rent equally between the two lecturers and thereby supplement the original salaries of £3 and £4 p.a. which they had respectively received since their offices had first been created in the sixteenth century: as a result of his generosity each holder enjoyed an additional £3 a year until 1850.[173]

The decline of college teaching in the eighteenth century turned the college's lectureships into sinecures and, not surprisingly, the holders enjoyed no further increase in their salaries until the 1850s, apart from these benefactions by Perse and Batchcroft.[174]

170 *B.H.* III, p. 246. The Perse trust fell into severe financial straits from 1678 until 1734 (MS 621/457, p. 287) and during that period many payments intended by Perse were suspended, including even the payment of a stipend to the Perse fellows, who were required to waive that stipend at admission and had to be content simply with free rooms in the Perse Building: cf. p. 436, nn. 45, 46 above.

171 *Gesta*, 25 October 1853, C.O.6.

172 For the Chancery Order see Cooper, *Annals*, iii, p. 642. The *Fellows' Accounts 1856–1870* shows payments of £15 p.a. to "morning lecturers" in the years 1856–60 (to Collett 1856, Du Pont 1858, Lamb 1857, 1859 and 1860). Lamb and Du Pont were deans at the time and presumably gave lectures on ethics and moral philosophy.

173 Despite Batchcroft's directions, they did not benefit from later increases in the Milton rent, since the lectureships had by then become sinecures: see *Registrum Magnum*, p. 639 and *B.H.* IV(2), p. 65. As noted earlier, Batchcroft did not provide for the humanities lectureship, even though the salary of that lectureship was smaller; this suggests that the *praelector rhetoricus*, as the humanities lecturer was by then known, was by then receiving some part of the degree fees paid by graduands.

174 After the seventeenth century, whenever there was a need for the teaching of Hebrew, the college relied, not on the Hebrew lecturer, but upon a competent teacher from outside the

The benefit of money in hand

In addition to the various fees, fines and small salaries that a college officer might receive as payment for his services, at least one officer had come to enjoy by the beginning of the nineteenth century a benefit which would have angered Caius and was directly contrary to his statutes.[175] The officer was the bursar, and the offending benefit was the entitlement to retain personally any interest or other benefit that might have accrued from the money which he had had in his hands on behalf of the college as bursar. The benefit may seem startling today, given the strict rule prohibiting the intermixing of trust and personal money and the requirement upon fiduciaries to account for any profit that they may have made from the management of trust property: but a bursar's responsibility, like that of other officers, was regarded at the time as an obligation similar to the contractual obligation of a debtor or, today, of a banker to its customer, and his obligation to account for those moneys was limited to the sum that he had received, not for any interest that might have been earned during the accounting period.[176]

How and when this benefit arose is something of a mystery, given the safeguards which Caius had provided. When he became Master in 1559 he had been dismayed to find that there remained in the treasury only £4. 16s. out of the £600 in pure gold that there had been when he had left the college in 1545,[177] and he made strict provision in his statutes to ensure the preservation and safekeeping of the college's money in the future. The moral to be drawn from his statutes was not that of the parable of the talents: all money paid to the bursars should be received by them in the hall in the presence of another fellow; they should immediately carry what they receive into the treasury and deposit it in the common chest in pure gold and silver; and they should never have more than £5 in their custody; furthermore, they should never convert that money to their own uses and should never lend it to anyone else.[178]

college who was normally a member of the Jewish community and so barred from membership of the college by the Test Act: see *B.H.* III, pp. 246–7.

175 Cf. the bursar's oath set out in Statute 57: "… you will not make personal use of the money of the College or convert it to your own uses; nor will you lend it to others …".

176 Statute 56: "All shall pay to the college what they owe on their own account or that of their pupils within 15 days next following the accounting and do so in full, even if they are owed that money by other debtors. Otherwise they will be compelled to make payment by process of law and distraint of their goods …". Cf. statute 65. Amounts owing between the college and the bursars, stewards and tutors arising out of their offices appeared as credits or debits on their commons accounts in the same way as their personal debits and credits: *Lib. Rat.* Stewards may well have enjoyed similar benefits from the college's money, and the tutors did so in respect of the money that they received on behalf of their pupils, particularly caution money; but the college's accounts shed even less light on those cases than they do on that of the bursar.

177 *Annals*, p. 79. See "*John Caius and his foundation*", § V. 3 at pp. 342–3 above.

178 Statute 56.

The half-yearly audit of the chest shortly after the Lady Day and Michaelmas audits of the accounts, coupled with the annual change of bursar, effectively excluded the possibility of a bursar's making long-term loans of the sort by which Stephen Perse appears to have made his own remarkable fortune.[179] In addition, the early practice of bursars was to take down money from the treasury in tranches only as it was needed, and so long as this practice and annual tenure of office remained the regime, Caius' aims were met. However, it became usual in the seventeenth century, if not earlier, for bursars to take down straightway in a single tranche enough to meet the expected bills for the whole half-year, notwithstanding Caius' injunction that they should never keep more than £5 in their custody.[180] Furthermore, as has been seen above, it also became usual in the seventeenth century for bursars to hold the office for more than a year at a time, and by the end of the century the office was normally held for a period of four or five years. It still remained the practice to the end of that century for the bursar to accumulate large surplus funds in sealed bags in the common chest in the treasury and for the Master and several fellows to conduct a half-yearly audit of the chest following each audit of the accounts,[181] but one wonders whether the practice of "taking down" a single large sum – often the whole balance in the chest – immediately after the audit and "bringing up" a single large sum prior to the next audit had not already become book entries of what should be debited or credited to the bursar rather than a record of any actual taking down and bringing up of money to the treasury. It is not unlikely that it was ceasing by the end of the century to be the practice for a bursar solemnly to bring up money into the treasury every half-year to be checked by the Master and fellows and then for him to take it straight down again, and that the audit was becoming a paper accounting exercise recording what was due to

179 On his death Perse's estate amounted to over £11,000, most of which was out on loan; for his practice of money-lending and his preference for relatively long-term loans, see Brooke, *History*, pp. 98–100. Perse was frequently bursar during the long tenure of his fellowship (cf. p. 452, n. 130 above), but it is clear from the half-yearly audits of the chest recorded in the *Status Collegii* that neither he nor other bursars in the sixteenth or seventeenth centuries employed the college's moneys in money-lending.

180 See the comment on the position prior to 1781 by the then Master, John Smith: "It was formerly the constant Practise at the great accounts to carry up to the Treasury the Balance due to the College, and at the same time for the Bursar to take down from thence 6 or 700[l] for the Provision of Fellows Commons & Fuell …" (MS 621/457, p. 353).

181 See, *e.g.*, the *Status Collegii* (Michaelmas 1690), recording the deposit in the treasury of £593 in sealed bags in six tranches between January and April 1691. The money deposited in the chest was safe against theft, but not against fluctuations in the rate of exchange: part of the money was in guineas, a fluctuating currency at that time; by the time the money was brought down from the treasury in 1729 (to meet the expenses of renovating the chapel) the value of the guinea had been fixed at 21s., in 1719, and the college suffered a loss of 6d. on each guinea: *Status Collegii* and *Bursar's Book* for Michaelmas 1729.

or from the bursar, who was expected to "bring up" physically what he owed only when he finally came to hand over the office to his successor.

The system appears to have broken down in the fractious years of Sir John Ellys' mastership. The record of the audit of the chest suddenly ceases in 1707 and was not resumed until it was revived when John Smith became bursar.[182] It seems that any half-yearly audit of the chest also ceased and gave way to a single accounting done by a retiring bursar when he finally handed over the office to his successor;[183] if so, the likely reason for the discontinuance of the audit was that Ellys' notorious unwillingness to co-operate with the fellows in the transaction of the college's business had made it impossible to hold an audit.[184] The breakdown of the system meant that moneys received by the bursar were no longer deposited in the chest in the course of the half-yearly period in which they were received and that substantial sums were left in his hands until he paid them over to his successor when he ceased to hold office.[185]

Given that the obligation of a bursar was simply to account at the audit for what he had received and not for any interest thereon, it is not surprising that it is impossible to tell from the college's accounts what financial benefit bursars derived from having college moneys left in their hands or when it first came to be enjoyed. In fact so little evidence survives, and the idea of a college officer's benefitting in this way is so alien to modern minds, that one might be tempted to conclude that there was no such benefit. That may have been the case before the eighteenth century, but it would seem from the *Gesta* that the holding of college moneys came in the course of that century to be accepted as a benefit or profit enjoyed by a bursar. It was grouped with "the present Profits of his place"

[182] Smith became bursar in 1750 and immediately set about reviving the audit: see pp. 467ff below. He laid the blame principally upon Brampton Gurdon, who had been bursar from 1707 to 1710: "In his Bursarship the account called the *Status Collegii* became perplext and was laid aside": MS 621/457, p. 337.

[183] This was not always done promptly. Smith noted acidly that Gurdon was over two years late in settling his accounts; that Richard Fuller, the bursar from 1711 to 1715, owed the college no less than £1,100. 1s. 4d. when he left office, did not pay anything to his successor and took four years to clear his account; that Robert Simpson, bursar from 1721 to 1726, made up his half-yearly accounts four years late and was three years late in closing his final account; and that an intervening bursar (Lewkenor Lestrange) had left the college and the Perse trust with permanent losses of £772.1 5s. 7½d. and £202. 12s. 5½d., respectively: MS 621/457, pp. 335, 337.

[184] Ellys' refusal to participate in the audit of the bursar's accounts was one of the complaints brought against him by the fellows in their abortive appeal to the Chancellor in 1715 (MS 621/457, p. 334; *B.H.* III, pp. 111–12).

[185] The moving of the treasury to the top floor of the Gate of Virtue in 1718 may have been one reason why the practice of regularly depositing moneys in the chest under the supervision of four key-holders ceased in the earlier part of the eighteenth century: it seems doubtful whether the "great hutch" (as the chest was termed) would have been transported to the new home of the treasury, if indeed it still existed then.

when the question of paying a salary to the bursar was first mooted in 1778;[186] and by the 1820s it had apparently come to be accepted that the college should compensate the bursar for loss of interest if it had occasion to call upon him for "advances" of money prior to audit.[187] The question of just how valuable this elusive profit was and precisely when it ceased remains a matter of conjecture, but it does not seem to have outlasted the founders' statutes.[188]

John Smith's reform of the college's finances

A transition from casual fees and fines to regular salaries for officers occurred very rapidly in the last quarter of the eighteenth century. It was made possible by two developments in the preceding quarter: a reform in the management of the college's finances and its accounting practices enabled it to keep a better track of surplus income, and the prompt investment of those surpluses in government funds produced a steady increase in the amount of "unappropriated" income that became available each year to the college after meeting its existing needs. Both of these developments were due very largely to the college's twenty-seventh Master, John Smith, who deserves far more credit than he has received for his contribution to the marked increase in the prosperity of the college which became apparent in the following century. He oversaw its finances throughout the second half of the eighteenth century, first as bursar (1750–54), then as president (1754–64) and finally as Master (1764–95).[189] His concern throughout that period for the financial well-being of the college shows a striking similarity with the concern for the college's finances that John Caius had shown two hundred years earlier, and he shared the third founder's

186 *Gesta*, 6 July 1778: "it was agreed that Eighty Pounds a year Additional Salary to the Bursar over and above the present Profits of his place, besides having a sum of a Thousand Pounds in money in his hands for the use and to carry on the Business of the College would not be too great an Augmentation for his Trouble & Labour in the Business of his Office." See *The transition to salaries*, at p. 471 below.

187 See *Gesta*, 13 January 1819 ("Agreed to allow the Bursar £60, being the Interest at 4 per cent on the money advanced by him for the purchase of the Rectory of Beechampton, and £101 being the Int[t] of what ought to have been left in his hands at the last audit"); and *Gesta*, 17 December 1825 ("Agreed to allow the Bursar £69. 5s. 0d., being Interest on advances made by him, namely, £17 Int. at 4 per Cent, on £2,300 advanced for Bincombe, … £36. 5s. 0d. Int, at 5 per Cent, on £1,450, suppose for six months, to Michaelmas 1825, £16. 0s. 0d., Int on £400, (the sum that should have been left in his hands) for 1 yr to Mich[mas]. 1826; and that he be allowed further Interest at 5 per Cent on £1,450, from Michaelmas 1825, till the time of repayment.").

188 The perquisites from fees and fines enjoyed by other officers were specifically discontinued at various times when their stipends were being increased; this occurred most noticeably in 1853, after Guest succeeded Chapman as Master; in that year the small payments to the deans, registrary, librarian and praelector were discontinued (*Gesta*, 25 October, C.O.6; 13 December, C.O.15).

189 He continued to maintain a detailed analysis of the state of the college's finances to the last years of his mastership: see MS 621/457, pp. 353–7.

insistence on strict accounting and the maintenance of a sufficient surplus to meet repairs and other necessary calls (*usus extraordinarios*) upon the college's finances.[190]

Smith became bursar in 1750 and, like Caius, he was shaken by what he found when he took charge of the college's finances. In Caius' case it had been the parlous state in which he found the treasury that had excited his choler: in Smith's case, what concerned him was the failure over the preceding forty years to maintain the half-yearly record of the state of the treasury, *i.e.*, the amount of 'ready money' available to meet any unforeseen expenses. As explained above, no entry had been made in that record, the *Status Collegii*, since 1707, and on taking office Smith painstakingly reconstructed the half-yearly record for each of the forty-three years from that date to the year when he became bursar. At first sight, his action might seem unnecessarily pedantic, since the Bursar's Book had been maintained during those years, and that constituted the college's principal set of accounts. However, the Bursar's Book was simply a record of the receipts and payments made by the bursar during each half-year, even when those receipts and payments did not represent genuine income and expenditure; for the receipts recorded in it included not only rents and other recurrent income, but also legacies and other 'one-off' donations and, crucially, monies drawn from the college's reserves in the chest, while, on the other side of the account, payments would include the amounts, if any, returned to the chest. When taken separately the half-yearly accounts in the Bursar's Book thus failed to show changes in the state of the college's reserves and accordingly it was a poor indicator of the college's financial health. The state of the reserves was particularly important to the college, for its property lay entirely in land and it derived virtually the whole of its recurrent income from the rents payable by its tenants. As Smith realised, the system of beneficial leases meant that those rents had been frozen at an unrealistic level for nearly two centuries and were barely sufficient to meet, even in nominal terms, the particular needs for which the land had originally been acquired, let alone contribute to a reserve which could be called upon for repairs, extraordinary expenses or new ventures.

Smith's concerns were well illustrated by the case of the manor and mills of Great Shelford, which had been the college's first major investment in land with its own funds since the purchases made in Caius' time. They had been purchased in 1614 at a time when the stipends of the senior fellows had fallen behind those of the junior fellows and they provided each of the twelve senior fellows with an additional £5 a year, and twice that for the Master, *i.e.* a total of £70 p.a. The system of beneficial leases meant that, a hundred and fifty years later, the yearly income from the manor and mills was still bringing to the college no more than

190 See, *inter alia*, Statutes 56, 57, 58 and 71 (accounts) and 28 and 36 (reserves).

£77. 1s. 10½d.[191] As Smith drily noted, this left a remainder for "extraordinary expenses" of precisely £7. 1s. 10½d.[192] What the college received, of course, in no way reflected the actual return on the estate, for, as Smith further noted, "the Master and Fellows moreover receive out of this Estate a Corn Rent and a Fine on every Renewal of the Lease of the demesnes".[193]

In 1751, the first year of Smith's bursarship, the issuing by the government of Consolidated Annuities provided the college for the first time with an alternative investment other than land and thus would enable it to escape from the financial straitjacket in which the system of beneficial leases had placed it.[194] The need to meet the expenses incurred in 1752–4 in the rebuilding of Gonville Court[195] delayed the purchase of stock for a few years and purchases began in earnest only after Smith became Master in 1764: £4,634 stock had been acquired by that date, and the figure rose to £30,634 by 1789.[196] The college could thereafter rely on a regular and predictable amount of unappropriated income, the ability to invest surpluses without delay and the steady acquisition of a fully sufficient reserve.

The college's trust funds shared in this benefit, just as much as the endowment. This was particularly valuable for the Perse trust, since the funds of that trust had fallen greatly in the years between 1678 and 1734 and the objects of the trust had suffered accordingly.[197] After 1734 the position of the trust improved, gradually at first but very rapidly after Smith's appointment as bursar and then Master. He was able to record with satisfaction that, although it had been possible to add only £249 to the benefaction in the twenty years between 1734 and 1754, it

191 MS 621/457, p. 253. This included not only the items that did not vary from year to year, *i.e.*, the rents from the leases of the demesnes and the mill and the quit-rents on the copyholds, but also the average receipts from the occasional copyhold fines.

192 *Ibid.*

193 The entry fines from Shelford in the years between 1659 and 1763 amounted to £2,081, all of which went to the Master and senior fellows: see "*Dividends*", § VI. 5 below, and the *Tables of Fines* which Smith's colleague and successor as bursar, John Davy, compiled when he took over the office.

194 For a striking instance of the imbalance between rents and entry fines which resulted from beneficial leases, see the *Bursar's Book* (Lady Day 1753): the total of the rents received from *all* the college's tenants (£654. 14s. 9d.) for the half-year to Lady Day 1753 was less than the single entry fine of £770 paid by Mr Benjamin Bastard for a reversionary lease of one property for three lives. The property being in Oborne and held by copyhold tenure, the fine in that particular case came to the college and appears in its accounts, but the fines on leases of all the college's other estates except Bincombe and Oborne were taken by the Master and senior fellows personally as dividends: see "*Dividends*", § VI. 5 below.

195 These totalled £3,390: MS 621/457, p. 341. Smith was justifiably pleased that they were completed without unduly depleting the college's reserves: *ibid.*, pp. 329–30.

196 *Rentale Redituum*, p. 105. The £26,000 stock added between 1764 and 1789 was bought for £18,094. Further purchases were made steadily thereafter.

197 So much so that Perse fellows were elected on condition that they would receive no stipend, merely rooms: see p. 436, n. 46 above.

had gained a further £1,991 between 1754 and 1778.[198] Thereafter the Perse fund grew steadily and was in a position by the early nineteenth century to make loans of four-figure sums to the college at commercial rates of interest.[199] The improvement in the Stokys fund was equally impressive. Until Smith became Master the sole asset of the fund had been a leasehold interest in the tithes of two rectories, which the college sub-let. For many years the sub-lease brought in £70 p.a.,[200] but from 1776 the income from the sub-lease increased to £105 and the surplus income was rolled up and invested in government stock, so that by 1791 the trust fund had £1,000 in Consols. This enabled the college to dispense with the intermediary sub-lessee and compound for the tithes directly with the occupiers of the two rectories, thereby doubling the income to the fund and enabling it to start increasing greatly the payments to the fellow and the scholars, buy further stock and at the same time contribute to the cost of the extensive repairs to the college buildings that were undertaken at the end of the century.[201]

The first development that was made possible by the increase in the college's surplus income was the rapid introduction of salaries for college officers, but before that transition is considered it should be noted that the introduction of such salaries was only one of several changes that were made possible by that increase in surplus income during Smith's mastership. The surplus also enabled the college to envisage, for the first time, various ventures which had not previously been possible. These not only included increases in the benefits to the objects of the Perse and other trusts and in the stipends of both senior and junior fellows, but also various far-sighted changes which became feasible

198 MS 621/457, p. 287. The "gain" of £2,240 noted by Smith was the increase in the accumulated surplus over the period. The increase allowed the college to purchase £1,200 New South Sea Annuities, and use the income from that stock to augment the value of each of the Perse scholarships by £6 p.a. in 1767. The college was able to purchase a further £2,000 stock for the trust between 1782 and 1785, and this enabled it in 1786 to increase the payments to the Master and the four senior fellows as managers of the trust, and to some of the objects of the trust, *i.e.*, the Frankland fellows, the porter and the almswomen, but not to the Perse fellows or to the school or its master.

199 See, *e.g.*, *Gesta*, 2 November 1812 (loan of £3,000 to the college at 4% interest). Unlike the college, the Perse and other trusts benefitted, not only from investments, but also from the increasingly valuable entry fines on the beneficial leases of the trusts' lands, since these went to the trust and, unlike the fines on the college's lands, they were not diverted to the Master and senior fellows as dividends. By the time of Lord Langdale's judgment in 1837, the fund had accumulated £32,500 in public funds in addition to valuable land holdings: Hardy, *Memoir of Lord Langdale*, II, p. 419.

200 The rent sufficed to pay the occasional fellow and the scholars and to meet the septennial entry fines payable to the Bishop of Ely on renewal of the lease to the college.

201 For the increases in the stipends paid to the Stokys fellow, see p. 438 above, and for the improvement to the fund see *B.H.* IV(2), p. 40 and the *Rentale Redituum*, pp. 39–40, 43–4, 49–54, 117–38. When the Stokys fellowship and scholarships came to an end with the 1860 statutes, the fund had £7,550 Consols, £500 Annuities and £2,047 cash.

only when the college had sufficient surplus income to be able to contemplate long-term investments in land which would not bring any immediate return: notably, it became possible in Smith's time to start on the gradual process of substituting rack-rents for beneficial leases, and also to make the far-seeing purchase of the reversion to the block of dwelling-houses in the south-east corner of Tree Court.[202] Furthermore, in the years following his death the stock which he had accumulated also provided the college with readily realisable capital and enabled it to acquire additional land whenever that would enhance the advantages of enclosure awards made on its existing lands.[203]

The transition to salaries

Against this background, and given that the number of senior fellows in residence for most of the academic year was falling and the burden of office had to be shared among fewer individuals, it is not surprising that the availability of surplus income prompted calls for college officers to be given salaries, particularly the bursar, whose responsibilities were growing with the increase in the college's income and reserves. In 1778 a decision to purchase £1,000 of government stock was followed by an agreement "that Eighty Pounds a year Additional Salary to the Bursar, over & above the present Profits of his place, besides having a sum of a Thousand Pounds in Money in his hands for the use & to carry on the Business of the College would not be too great an Augmentation for his Trouble & Labour in the Business of his Office".[204] Three years later, in 1781, the college resolved to purchase a further £1,000 of Consols for the chest and £5,000 for the various trust funds and agreed at the same time that the additional payment to the bursar should be not £80, but £100 p.a.: £30 from the college, £30 from each of the Perse and Wortley funds and the remaining £10 from various smaller funds.[205] As a consequence of this decision, the bursar

202 For the substitution of rack-rents and the need for surplus income in order to compensate for the entry fines sacrificed in the process, see "*Dividends*", § VI. 5 below. The dwelling-houses on the site of N, O and P staircases in Tree Court were purchased in 1791 with the help of Wortley's benefaction, sixty years before they came into the college's occupation in 1850: *B.H.* III, p. 131. Smith's scrupulous management and allocation of the increased income of the college and the trusts during the years 1750–95 contrasts sharply with Davy's self-indulgent conduct during the period of his mastership in 1803–39: see *The disputed use of the Perse trust and the impact on stipends: 1825–60*, pp. 441ff above.

203 See, *e.g.*, *B.H.* IV(2), pp. 11 (Bincombe) and 18 (Barnwell, Cambridge).

204 *Gesta*, 6 July 1778. Five years earlier, the college had agreed to give up the small "dividends" from its brewer and baker and allow the steward £12 p.a., and the cook £15 p.a., in lieu; the amounts were to be drawn equally from the college chest and the Wortley and Perse benefactions (*Gesta*, 13 January 1773), but no payments to the steward and cook or to the bursar were debited to the chest until 1783: *Bursar's Book* (Michaelmas 1783).

205 *Gesta*, 11 January 1781. For the next twenty years only the £30 is recorded in the Bursar's Book, which is consequently seriously misleading as regards the bursar's real salary.

starts to appear in the time-honoured list in the Bursar's Book in 1783, though only the college's £30 contribution is recorded there, not the full £100.

From 1783 onwards, the steward, the librarian and the fellow acting in lieu of a chaplain (the "Conduct") also start to appear in the list.[206] Two years later the steward and the registrary received small increases to the modest salaries they were paid.[207] Finally, in 1801 the deans were added to the list in the Bursar's Book and received a slightly more substantial salary in lieu of the fines which had been the subject of Branthwaite's protest in *Allen's Case* (1617).[208] Thereafter payment of a salary to college officers became the rule, no longer an exception.[209]

As each officer began to receive a salary for his services in that office the payment was recorded in the Bursar's Book and the officer was added to the traditional list of registrary, salarists, lecturers and the cook and his assistant. We might assume therefore that the Bursar's Book would furnish a convenient record of this transition to the payment of salaries to college officers; but until 1804 that book recorded only the expenditure charged to the endowment, *not payments that were debited to the separate trust funds*. By the 1780s a substantial part of the college's surplus income came from Consols and other government

206 *Bursar's Book* (Michaelmas 1783). The Book records, for the first time, the payment of £6 p.a. which had been made to the librarian since 1629 and the payment to the conduct of the £10 p.a. which would have been the stipend of Mrs Frankland's chaplain. As in the case of the bursar, the Book records only the £4 p.a. contribution from the chest towards the payment of the £18 p.a. allowed to the steward since 1773 in lieu of the dividends previously received from the brewer and baker mentioned in n. 160 at p. 460 above.

207 *Gesta*, 26 October 1785. Both were allowed an additional £6 p.a.; as in the bursar's case, only the £2 contribution from the chest was recorded in the Book. The decision to increase the registrary's salary by £6 was made expressly "on Account of the Increase of Stamp Duties"; that increase in duty had reduced the surplus from the fees he was permitted to charge for preparing a deed. The decision was followed by a further order that the college should pay to the registrary "the clear Profits of his Fees" on the renewal of a beneficial lease, if the college did not renew the lease.

208 For *Allen's Case* (1617) see Appendix F. For the decision to substitute a salary for the deans in place of fines, see *Gesta*, 26 October 1797: "Agreed that the Mulcts upon the Students for non-attendance in Chapel, Hall etc. shall be in future applied to the College Chest, and that the College in lieu thereof allow to each Dean as much as will make up the annual assessment in the Stewards book £30." For the first payment of £28 p.a. from the chest to each of the two deans, see *Bursar's Book* (Michaelmas 1801). The payments to the deans were substantially greater than those to the steward and the registrary, because the payments to the deans were *in lieu of* payments they had been receiving previously, whereas those to other officers were in addition to their existing perquisites. The deans continued to receive fees from B.A.s and undergraduates for lectures until 1853: *Gesta*, C.O.6 of 25 October 1853.

209 The tutors were, to modern eyes, the most striking exception, but they were not regarded as holding a college office but as performing a function delegated to them by the Master as one of their fellowship duties: see p. 448, n. 111 above. Their appointments were not included in the annual elections of officers and they were not ranked as college officers until 1860 (College Statutes, 1860, Statute 7).

stocks held in those trust funds, not from the chest,[210] and consequently the college resorted to those trust funds to provide roughly two-thirds of the officer's new salary. As a result, although the Bursar's Books before 1804 are a convenient and reliable guide from which one can ascertain the *date* at which an officer first received a salary for his services, they are seriously misleading as regards the *amount* of that salary, since the greater part of many salaries was normally charged to one or more trust funds. Thus, when the bursar was first added to the list in the Bursar's Book of officers paid a salary in 1783 (and for twenty years afterwards), his salary was shown as £30 p.a.; but, as we have seen, that sum was in fact less than one-third of his actual salary for the office (£100 p.a.), since a further £70 was drawn from seven different trust funds.[211]

As Smith was aware, the reliance on the trust funds to provide part of the new salaries for college officers raised an issue of principle, for college officers did not qualify as such to benefit under the terms of at least some of those trusts, and in particular they did not do so under the Perse trust. Smith, however, justified payments to the bursar on the ground that that officer's services were essential for the proper management of the trusts;[212] but the later payments from the trusts to the steward, registrary, deans and other officers could not be justified in the same way.[213]

Smith died in 1795, and by the beginning of the nineteenth century the college had lost sight of his caveat and had begun to think of the Perse funds as a part of its endowment – thereby starting on the slippery slope which led eventually to the Perse Scandal. In 1803 Martin Davy became Master and one

210 As Gross has explained, these benefactions usually had conditions as to how the receipts were to be employed – generally in fixed payments; so that, when the annual receipts increased, the balances in these funds rolled up considerably and formed part of the college's reserves: *B.H.* IV(2), pp. i, vii. These balances came to form the "Reserve Fund" after the repeal of Caius' statutes in 1860.

211 £30 (College Chest), £30 (Perse), £30 (Wortley), £2 (Halman), £2 (Stokys) and £1 from each of the Stockton, Peters and Mickleburgh trusts: *Gesta*, 11 January 1781. Subsequent increases were spread in the same way: *e.g.*, *Gesta*, 1 March 1826. Similarly, the chest contributed only one-third of the increased salaries paid to the registrary and steward in 1785: *ibid.*, 26 October 1785.

212 Justifying the decision in 1781 to pay £100 p.a. to the bursar and share the cost between the chest and the trust funds, he commented: "since none of the Benefactions will suffer by their share in the payment of the Annuity to the Bursar even at present, but will all in the future be great Gainers. Moreover by this Order, We shall be freed from the Breach of the 57 statute, from danger of losing by the Bursar, & from neglect of the smaller Benefactions": MS 621/457, p. 354.

213 The complainants to the Chancery singled out in 1835 the college's resort to Perse's trust fund to contribute to the salaries of officers who had nowhere been mentioned by Perse in his will: "Dr Perse in his will gives nothing to the Dean, the Steward, the Conduct, the college Registrar, or the Gardiner; but his faithful Trustees have no scruple in extending to these meritorious personages the benefit of his munificence": pamphlet cited in S.J.D. Mitchell, *A History of the Perse School 1615–1976* (Cambridge 1976), at p. 38.

year later the revaluation of the Perse fund mentioned earlier[214] led to a review of fellows' stipends and officers' salaries. Following that review the whole salary paid to every officer was thereafter recorded in the Bursar's Book as coming from the chest, even when the greater part of it came from the trust funds.

Salaries under Martin Davy's mastership

The 1804 review of salaries was prompted by a revaluation of the income of the Perse trust, and most of the increases made in the review were directed towards the beneficiaries specified by Dr Perse: only very minor adjustments were made to the annual salaries which officers were by then receiving. The result was that the bursar continued, as before, to be the only officer who received a substantial salary (£107 p.a.), while the other major officers trailed well behind (the two deans £36 each, the steward £30 and the registrary £24). Not surprisingly, given that their duties had become entirely nominal, the salaries of the lecturers and salarists remained what they had been in the later seventeenth century, and thus in most cases what they had been in the time of Gonville Hall.[215]

For all but two of the college's officers the pattern set in 1804 persisted throughout Davy's long mastership, and their salaries remained virtually unchanged until the 1840s and in some cases until the 1850s.[216] The two exceptions were the salaries of the deans and that of the bursar. The increase for the deans was relatively modest;[217] but the increase in the bursar's salary which occurred while Davy was Master was striking. It is easy to understand why the salaries of some of the minor officers remained unchanged; but it is less obvious why the gap between the bursarship and such offices as the stewardship and the registraryship should have widened so very greatly as it appears to have done in the first half of the nineteenth century. The sharp difference between the treatment of the bursar and that of other officers in respect of their salaries during Davy's mastership mirrors the equally sharp difference that developed under his watch between the increases in stipend enjoyed by Davy himself and the four most senior fellows as managers of the Perse trust and the increases enjoyed by the other senior fellows. The difference in stipends had leaped in two silent bounds

[214] See p. 441, n. 75 above.

[215] The payments to Knight's and Whitacre's salarists remained what they had been when they were first founded in Henry VIII's reign, but by the eighteenth century the three posts were always held together by one person and so they retained some slight value.

[216] The annual salary of the registrary remained at £24 and that of the librarian at £6 until 1853, when they were increased to £36 and £21, respectively, and the fees and other small payments they had enjoyed were discontinued. The steward was allowed a increase of £10 p.a. in 1826 – at the same meeting as the bursar was awarded his increase of £100 p.a.

[217] The deans fared better than the librarian, registrary and steward (cf. the preceding note) and by 1825 their salaries had risen from £36 p.a. to £46 p.a. each.

from a modest £14 p.a. in 1804 to an immoderate £220 p.a. in 1825,[218] and the following year saw a correspondingly generous increase of £100 – from £107 to £207 a year – in the salary paid to the bursar, who was *ex officio* registrar of the trust and directly responsible for its management.[219] The extra £100 was not, however, the only increase in his annual salary that the bursar had come to enjoy by 1826, for he was already enjoying a further increase which did not appear on the college's books but was in fact even greater: it came from the coal fund, which had been managed by the bursar and from which he had come to draw a fee of no less than £130 p.a. – for managing an account in which his fee amounted to approximately a fifth of the total expenditure.[220]

As was seen earlier,[221] the indefensible increases which Davy and the four most senior fellows had agreed to award to themselves as managers of the Perse trust in 1825 evoked an immediate protest when the other senior fellows came to hear of them the following year; but the very generous treatment of the bursar did not evoke the same protest from the rest of the fellows in 1826. Their silence should not be taken necessarily to mean that they regarded the great difference in salary as a fair reflection on the relative burden of the bursarship as compared with other offices: for although the bursar's responsibilities had grown with the wealth of the college his duties were still of a routine character and were not infrequently combined with other college offices, such as that of dean, conduct and catechist, or with a medical practice in the town – indeed, as Venn pointed out, the bursarship could even be combined with a busy legal practice in the common law courts in London after the railway reached Cambridge in 1845.[222] It was not the burden of the office which made the increases in the bursar's salary acceptable, but a change in the way the office had come to be viewed by the Fellowship. The bursarship was still an annual office, but it had come to be

218 See *The disputed use of the Perse trust and the impact on stipends: 1825–60*, at pp. 441–5 above. In the Master's case the increase was twice as large, *i.e.* £440 p.a.

219 *Gesta*, 1 March 1826; as in 1781 (cf. p. 471, n. 205 above), the increase to the bursar was spread across the chest and the trust funds: £30 (College chest), £30 (Perse), £30 (Wortley), £4 (Mickleburgh), £2 (Halman), £2 (Stokys) and £1 from each of the Stockton and Peters trusts. The increases to the managers fell entirely upon the Perse trust.

220 In 1833 the total expenditure including the £130 fee was £599. 7s. 4d., and in 1834 it was £693. 9s. 3d.: *Coal Book 1834–1869*. The fee almost certainly first arose during Davy's mastership; the only earlier coal book which records expenditure shows that no fee had been paid in Smith's time as bursar: *Coal Book 1751–54*.

221 See n. 218 above.

222 *B.H.* III, p. 240. Alexander Thurtell and William Stokes both held the office of dean while they were bursar (in 1832–24 and 1839–41, respectively); George Paget established a medical practice during his bursarship (1834–38) and John Tozer, the ardent reformer, similarly built up a thriving legal practice in London during the five years he was bursar (1855–60): *B.H.* II, pp. 197, 194, 202 and 217, respectively. It was only in Tozer's last year as bursar when he had already become a sergeant-at-law that the college appointed the steward (William Hutt) as junior bursar to assist him: *Gesta*, C.O.3 and 4 of 2 November 1859.

held for three or four years at a stretch and, with the number of resident senior fellows having fallen to little more than half-a-dozen, each of those resident fellows could be confident of holding the bursarship in his turn, and the expectation of holding it for three or four years continuously had come to be viewed as an entitlement for those resident fellows, and the one opportunity to acquire a modest competence towards the time when he might possibly wish to marry and exchange his fellowship for a college living.[223]

The protest by the fellows in 1826 against the excessive increase in stipend which the Master and the four most senior fellows proposed for themselves, coupled with Bickersteth's trenchant condemnation of the increase four years later, led to the uncomfortable realisation that the college had been guilty of considerable errors and irregularities in its management of the Perse trust.[224] Unlike the fellows' protest, Bickersteth's criticisms had been directed against the bursar personally as much as the managers, and since the payments to him had been partly funded from the Perse trust, the criticisms inevitably led to a reappraisal of those payments. Not surprisingly, the college decided in 1832 that the coal book should become a college account to be kept by the bursar and audited with his other accounts, and that the payment to him from the coal fund should in future be reduced to £100 a year.[225] Bickersteth's criticisms when he was a fellow were publicly re-affirmed in 1837 in the judgment which he – by then Lord Langdale – gave as Master of the Rolls in the action against the college for breach of trust in the matter of the Perse School; and when the action was finally concluded in 1842 and the college could no longer look to the Perse trust to help fund the salaries of its officers, it finally accepted the need "to make the necessary changes in the Bursar's Book consequent upon the decision of the Chancery in the Perse suit"[226] and, *inter alia*, to reduce the annual emoluments of the bursar quite severely: first the salary was reduced from £207 to £117

[223] Five of the nine fellows who held the bursarship during the period 1820–46 later exchanged their fellowship for a college living, most of them upon marriage: see *B.H.* II, pp. 132 (Okes), 158 (Turnbull), 197 (Thurtell), 194 (Stokes), 202 (Eyres). Of the other four, one married (Paget), two died young within a year of holding the bursarship very briefly (Rogers and Francis) and only one (Holditch) stayed on as a fellow till his death thirty-five years later: *B.H.* II, pp. 202, 155, 157, 170.

[224] See *The disputed use of the Perse trust and the impact on stipends: 1825–60*, at pp. 441–5 above. It also prompted the college to reconsider its conduct in respect of Mrs Frankland's benefaction and – very belatedly – to open a separate account book for it in 1832; for the complications that ensued in the division of the property between the new Frankland Account and the college's own funds, see *B.H.* IV(2), p. 42.

[225] *Gesta*, 22 December 1832. Even then the notion of entitlement led the college to delay the reduction until the then bursar finally relinquished the office "as Mr Thurtell has taken the Bursarship under a different arrangement": *ibid.*

[226] *Gesta*, C.O.4 of 17 May 1842.

and then the payment from the coal book from £100 to £75.[227] The payment to the bursar from the coal book was reduced further to £50 four years later, and finally withdrawn in 1847.[228] By the time that the founders' statutes were repealed in 1860 the reduction in the bursar's and deans' salaries in the 1840s, coupled with the modest increases in those of other officers in the 1850s, had produced a more equitable balance in the remuneration paid by the college to its officers.[229]

The change from "salary" to "stipend"

By the beginning of the nineteenth century the regime of casual fees and perquisites had given way relatively quickly to the acceptance that college officers should receive additional annual remuneration for their services; but it was some years before the annual payment was termed a "stipend". That term was still instinctively reserved for the statutory maintenance grant which a fellow received to support him in his studies and in return for which he should expect to undertake the performance of any administrative tasks that might be necessary: no fellow should expect more than one maintenance grant. When additional annual remuneration came to be paid to the bursar and officers in the last quarter of the eighteenth century it was termed a "salary" or a "payment in addition to the [Fellowship] stipend",[230] but by 1850 it had imperceptibly become a "stipend". The notion of a "stipend" was thus no longer confined to the founders' concept of a maintenance grant to a fellow or scholar: the term might represent also the emolument for the performance of an office, and a

[227] *Gesta*, C.O.5 of 17 May 1842. He was, however, compensated with an allowance of 4% of the gross income of the Heacham estate "for the management thereof": *ibid.*, C.O.6. The deans' salaries, which had also come partly from the Perse trust, were similarly reduced from £46 to £31 p.a. each. The reduction in the bursar's formal salary from £207 to £117 still left him far better paid than anyone other than the Master. In that transitional year 1842, the then bursar, William Stokes (*B.H.* III, p. 194), calculated his income as bursar from the college for the year as being £319. 1s. 1d. (salary £117, coal book £100, Perse 4% £82. 7s. 11d., Perse Registrar £15, Perse School Book £4. 13s. 2d.), from which he deducted £4. 14s. 6d. income tax; he also received £46 as dean and £9. 13s. 4d. as conduct: *Fellows' Accounts* 1840–42.

[228] *Coal Book 1834–69*. Responsibility for the coal book and the £50 payment was transferred to the steward, and the bursar was allowed instead the £30 which had been the steward's salary.

[229] In 1858 the annual salaries paid through the bursar's accounts to officers (other than the steward, praelector and deans, whose salaries were paid through the steward's accounts after 1853) were: bursar £172, registrary £36, librarian £21, Hebrew lecturer £14, Greek lecturer £7, morning lecturer £15, salarist £14. 6s. 8d., examiners of accounts and the Perse examiner £10 each.

[230] See *Gesta*, 6 July 1778 (bursar's "additional salary"); 1 March 1826 ("addition to the Bursar's salary"); 25 October 1826 ("Steward's salary"). It was often described as an addition to the officer's fellowship stipend: *Gesta*, 11 January 1781 (bursar); *ibid.*, 26 October 1785 (steward, registrary). For early references to it as a separate stipend, see *Gesta*, 24 April 1799 ("Conduct's stipend"); *ibid.*, C.O.3 of 28 October 1846 ("the Steward's present stipend").

fellow might now be entitled to more than one “stipend”. This dual use of the term “stipend” to denote both a maintenance grant and a payment for office survived the repeal of the founders’ statutes in 1860, but by an ironic twist it did not do so for long. As explained in the following chapter, the entitlement of fellows to corn money, entry fines and other dividends was gradually replaced by increases in their fellowship stipends. When dividends were finally absorbed into stipends one might have expected that the term “dividend” would be replaced by “stipend”, but after 1860 the reverse happened: in the statutes which replaced the founders’ statutes the annual maintenance grant to fellows came illogically to be termed a “dividend” and the notion of a “stipend” was restricted to the salaries that were paid to college officers.[231]

[231] See “*Dividends*”, § VI. 5, at p. 543 below.

VI. 5

Dividends

John Caius was profoundly affected by the state in which he found the college's finances when he became Master. In his Annals, looking back on the recent past of the college, he recorded his strictures on his predecessor, Thomas Bacon: in his statutes, he turned his attention to the future, making frequent references to the evils that financial maladministration could and would bring upon a college.[1] Whether he was fair in attributing so much of the blame for the state of the college to his immediate predecessor may be open to question, for it will be seen later that John Styrmin, Bacon's own predecessor, was far more at fault;[2] nevertheless, Caius cannot be criticised for his determination that the finances of the re-founded college on which he had lavished the greater part of his wealth should be tightly safeguarded. That determination runs throughout his statutes: in his very first statute he expressly indicated that it was his intention to include provisions which have regard for goods and lands as well as persons, in other words to establish a strict financial regime just as much as a constitutional one.[3]

He set out his guiding principle of that regime most clearly in Statute 63:

> When we say 'for the benefit of the college' in this and other places in the statutes, we do not mean for the benefit of the individual members of the college, but for the benefit of the college as a corporate entity (of whose wealth the counting-house is the guardian) to be held not so much for our benefit as that of our posterity. For nothing belongs to any member either individually or collectively, apart from his stipend, livery, employments, distributions [of largesse] and offices. Everything else shall be kept in common for the corporate uses of the college, for the collective needs of our own and future times, to be a provision for calamities that may occur, grave setbacks of chance, regrettable lawsuits, becoming decorations,

1 Cf. Statutes 2, 37, 44, 56, 83 and 92.

2 See *The Tudor beneficial lease* at p. 521 below.

3 Even before he succeeded Bacon as Master and became aware of the parlous financial state of the college, he had divided the draft statutes that he made in 1558 into the same two distinct parts that make his statutes so distinctive among those of contemporary Cambridge colleges: *Documents*, II, p. 352.

essential building repairs, purchases of income-producing properties, and other communal exigencies of this kind.

It would be difficult to find a clearer statement of the principle underlying the emerging concept of a charitable trust in the contemporary statutes of any other college, or indeed, anywhere else at that time. The Master and fellows were corporators to whom the government of the college was entrusted, but they were not concurrent owners, and unlike joint tenants or tenants in common or even life tenants they were not entitled to look upon the income of the college's property as their own any more than the capital.

For Caius, the crucial rule underpinning this principle was that neither the Master nor the fellows should have any right to any surplus income beyond the stipend and allowances expressly given to them in the statutes; nor indeed should any other members of the college. Thus, as regards income accruing internally from the rents of rooms, "we do not wish the rents of our college to be shared out among the fellows to the detriment of our college".[4] Likewise, as regards income accruing externally, "any surplus income from all foundations over and above the stipend of a fellow or scholar, fellows or scholars, shall accrue to the college for extraordinary uses such as repairs and any litigation in the necessary defence of the estates or their appurtenances, and for other incidentals of that kind".[5] In addition, penal fines were to go to the college "unless we have expressly directed otherwise".[6] Most importantly, entry and renewal fines should accrue to the college, not to the Master and the fellows.[7]

4 Statute 28. He disapproved strongly of the practice of sharing out room rents between the Master and fellows personally which had developed by the time he returned to the college: see *Room Rents* below.

5 Statute 36. In this statute Caius was not only concerned that surplus income from foundations should accrue to the college and not to any individuals. He was equally concerned that no shortfall in the income from a particular foundation should create a drain upon the finances of the college, and he was careful to direct that any such shortfall should fall upon the beneficiary, not the college: "We lay down categorically that the college shall not be burdened with maintaining any fellow or scholar, or with supplementing his stipend through the grant of free victuals, clothing and accommodation beyond the income of the property or estate provided by his founder or benefactor."

6 Statute 73. The only cases in which Caius did direct otherwise were those for non-attendance by scholars at dinner at their common table and non-attendance of members at the weekly presentation of accounts after dinner on Saturdays; in those two cases the fine was to go towards the commons of the rest of the diners: Statutes 68 and 71. For other fines which were not subject to any similar direction and consequently should go to the use of the college, see Statutes 45 (non-attendance at chapel), 62 (tutorial failure to enter pupils in the Matriculation Book), 76 (fires), 77 (damage to property), 78 (cleanliness of the courts), 79 (care of the library).

7 Statute 95. The fines of the manors of Runcton and Croxley were the subject of two apparently contradictory statutes. Statute 37 gave to the Master simply an increase of £4. 13s. 4d. in his stipend out of the perquisites from those manors (together with that of Burnham Thorpe) on condition that he resided in college. Statute 95 omitted Burnham Thorpe, perhaps because the manor there would not fall into possession until 1619 (see *B.H.* IV(2), p. 15), and it might be

Despite his severe temperament and the austere character of his statutes Caius was ready to accept that the Master and the fellows might enjoy small windfalls when they were resident, so long as those windfalls did not diminish the income from the property given to the college by its benefactors or impair that property in any way. Thus they might require from intending tenants "under the contract made with them and their successors, some sheep, fattened wethers and pigs and other fatted fowls towards the embellishment and increase of their common table at feasts and commemorations".[8] He was insistent, however, that a fellow given leave to study abroad should not be entitled to the various small benefits that might properly be enjoyed by a fellow while he was resident in college: a fellow given such leave might draw his stipend (minus 12d. a week), but not "distributions, exequy money and dividends, as people call them".[9]

What Caius precisely had in mind by "distributions" and "dividends" is frustratingly unclear today, just as it was equally unclear to the Master and the senior fellows in 1638.[10] We know from the *Libri Rationales*, the college's personal account books, that "distributions" were small in value,[11] and we may deduce from their value that they were the prest-money (*prestimonium*) that Bateman had specified in his statutes. As regards "dividends", Caius' language ("*ut vocant*") suggests that it had not been a term which was well-known to him in his earlier years in Gonville Hall, but we do know that at least one "dividend", room rents, had come into existence before 1559; and one of his first actions upon becoming Master was to commission the fellow acting as bursar, Henry Dethick, to collect "*dividenda*".[12] We cannot be sure what he had in mind when he spoke of "dividends"; however, as will be seen below, he was aware of the

read as giving to the Master the *total amount* of the fines and amercements from the other two manors on the same condition of residence; but that was probably not Caius' intention, and in the early seventeenth century the fines from Runcton and Croxley were treated as perquisites falling within Statute 37; they were credited to the college, not to the Master, and they were entered into the Bursar's Book as college income in the same way as other manorial fines without any corresponding entry of payment to the Master: see, *e.g.*, *Bursar's Book* (Lady Day 1610), (Michaelmas 1620) Extraordinary Receipts.

8 Statute 93.

9 Statute 54.

10 *London's Case* (1638), Appendix H.

11 Neither Caius nor the bursarial accounts offers any indication of the exact meaning of "distributions". However, the fact that the half-yearly amounts to each fellow were consistently 2s. greater at Lady Day (5s.) than at Michaelmas (3s.) suggests that they represent the prest-money (*prestimonium*) allowed by Bateman in his statutes to those fellows who were present on the Feast of the Annunciation (2s.) and the other feast-days of the Blessed Virgin (1s. on each). After the death of Queen Mary it ceased to be lawful to celebrate those other feasts (see Parker's *Interpretatio* of Statute 72); the payments continued, however, to be made: see, *e.g.*, *Lib. Rat.* (Michaelmas 1586), (Michaelmas 1662).

12 *Pandectae* (1559), fol. 2. This would suggest that, at that time, he expected the dividends to go into the college chest, but he later refers to "*dividenda*" in Statute 54 as one of emoluments of a fellow.

practice of sharing room rents (*summa cubiculorum*) between the Master and fellows as a dividend, much as he disapproved of it, and he may also have had in mind the sharing of "hearth money", the small sum made available half-yearly for heating (*pro foco*).[13] As we shall see, in neither case would the amount have been great in his day.

By the seventeenth century these two dividends *pro cubiculis* and *pro foco* had been joined by two far more valuable dividends which could not possibly be described as small benefits that might properly be enjoyed by a fellow while he was resident in college: these were corn money and entry fines. Unlike hearth money and room rents, we can be certain that Caius did not have in mind either of these dividends when he allowed dividends to fellows in his statutes: corn money came into existence only after his death and, as regards the second, he had emphatically directed that fines should accrue to the college, not to the Master and the fellows.[14] Despite that direction it was predominantly from corn money and entry fines that the concept of a very substantial dividend to be enjoyed by the Master and senior fellows came to be derived, notwithstanding all Caius' exhortations.

ROOM RENTS

No details of the practice of dividing among the Master and fellows personally the room rents that had been paid to the college by the occupants survive from the time of Gonville Hall, but we know from the strong disapproval expressed by Caius in the Annals that the practice had begun before his return to the college,[15] and his remarks and attitude suggest that this dividend *pro cubiculis* had come into existence in the period between his time as a fellow and his re-foundation of Gonville Hall in 1557.

A further indication of Caius' disapproval appears in the sharp distinction which he made in his statutes between the practice prevailing in respect of the rents from the buildings of what he termed "Gonville College" and the new regime which he envisaged for the payment into *his* chest of the rents arising from "Caius College", that is, the buildings which he had himself provided for his re-founded college.[16] So far as the older buildings were concerned he

[13] It was not increased and by the eighteenth century it had almost entirely lost its value; the half-yearly payment was £5, of which the porter received £1. 6s. 8d., the Master and the resident senior fellows sharing the remaining £3. 13s. 4d.

[14] See Statutes 93 and 95.

[15] *Annals*, p. 78. On his return as Master in 1559 he proposed to terminate the dividend for fellows elected after 25 November 1559, but abandoned the idea: Cambridge University Library MS. Mm.4.20, fol. 18v.

[16] Statute 28.

recognised with regret that a practice of sharing out the room rents had already come into existence and he was insistent that it must not be allowed to spread to any of the additional rooms which he had himself provided for the college. A justification of the practice does not seem ever to have been attempted by the recipients, and it remains the most difficult to explain today.[17]

Caius had very strong views on the subject of room rents, and he formulated them in Statutes 28 and 66. Those views were founded on two convictions: first, that the college should always be able to draw upon sufficient funds to enable it not only to maintain its buildings, but to meet the necessary costs of any repairs, renovation and renewal that might ever become necessary in the future,[18] and, second, that the principal source from which such reserve funds should be built up was the rents charged for those rooms and that they "are to be kept in our chest for that purpose": "for we do not wish the rents of our College to be shared out among the fellows to the detriment of our College": Statute 28. This emphatic direction raised two questions: (a) who was required to pay rent? (b) how was that rent to be divided between "our College" and the fellows?

The requirement to pay rent

Caius' answer to the first of these two questions was confused.

As regards pensioners, and especially major pensioners, he was emphatic that all must pay a quarterly rent or pension for the rooms that they occupied, whether the room rented was in "our College" or in "Gonville College", *i.e.* in the buildings he provided or in those of Gonville Hall;[19] and in addition to the quarterly rent they must maintain their rooms at their own expense if they were in his "College",[20] or make a contribution annually towards the maintenance of their rooms if they were in "Gonville College".[21] Furthermore, in order to build

[17] Richard Gerrard treated the dividend as a matter which needed no special comment in 1582 when he defended the retention of his fellowship on the ground that he did "offer of his owne accord to pay rent for his chamber as a divident amongst the rest of the felows, which he hath done ever since": "*Answer of Richard Gerrard*", *Gerrard's Case* (1582), Appendix D below. We know, too, that the only justification for the dividend offered by the fellows in 1617 was that it was "common practice": "*Answer to the Auncient practices against pretended against Statutes*", no. 5, *Allen's Case* (1617), Appendix F below.

[18] He was particularly concerned about the maintenance of the roofs, for they would not be covered by the obligation of the occupant of any room to keep that room in repair.

[19] In Statutes 28, 29 and 30, when speaking of his college in contrast to "Gonville College" or "the college as a whole", he was no doubt thinking primarily of the buildings he had recently erected in Caius Court, but, as will be seen below, they were not the only buildings that he provided for his re-founded college. He also provided the three houses in Trinity Street which became the Pensionary.

[20] As regards rooms in his own buildings, he imposed on every occupant a duty to decorate and maintain it at his own expense and make good any damage (Statute 28).

[21] The requirement upon pensioners who occupied rooms in the older buildings to pay an annual 'rent' towards maintenance in addition to their quarterly rent was decreed specifically by the

up funds for repairs, he decreed that all the rooms in "our College" should be reserved for ten years from Christmas 1570 for rent-paying pensioners, and that at least seven such rooms should thereafter be reserved in perpetuity for major pensioners.[22]

As regards scholars Caius was less clear. He propounded a general rule that scholars on any foundation (*ex aliqua fundatione*) must pay for their rooms, unless their benefactor had provided additional funds from which the rent could be paid; but he did not clarify what extra funds would exempt such scholars from the payment of room rent, though one imagines that he presumably would consider that he had himself done so and that his own scholars should not pay rent.[23] The fact that he specifically directs that Joan Trapps' scholars must pay rent reinforces the impression that he did not envisage that his own scholars had to pay rent;[24] but he then expressly limits the exemption of scholars from paying rent to "those scholars whose foundations were established before 1540 A.D."[25] Finally, he appears to direct that his scholars, like his fellows, should be free from rent, but only for ten years after his death.

As regards fellows, Caius' instructions were equally confusing. Neither of the two earlier founders had included any provision in their statutes for the payment of rent by a fellow and, so far as we can judge, the fellows of Gonville Hall had not

Master and fellows on 12 December 1569, not long after the building of Caius Court: cf. Statute 66. For the decree, see *Matriculation Book* (1569), fol. 206; this is the earliest precise wording of a College Order known to the present writer; it is printed in Venn, *Admissions*, 1558–1678, at p. xvii.

22 Seven might seem an excessive number, but Caius had attracted no fewer than six major pensioners by July 1559 and eleven in 1564 (*B.H.* I, p. 42, and III, p. 63); in the five years to 1564 at least twenty-five had been admitted: see "*John Caius and his Foundation*", § V. 3, at p. 344 above. He was keen to have major pensioners, since he shrewdly anticipated that they alone were likely to lavish money on the decoration and repair of their rooms. He specifically required that all improvements "whether the work be of iron, or wood, or glass, or lead, or mortar, or stone, or other material" should be left when the tenant departed: no scholar or minor pensioner, and few fellows, could be expected to incur such expenses. In 1562–63 Edward Parker, the future Lord Morley, paid £7 for the decoration of his room: *B.H.* I, p. 50. In 1564 Humphrey Busby, major pensioner, built a stone window in his room for £5: *ibid.*, p. 53. These events occurred in Caius' life-time, no doubt with his consent, for his prohibition on any alteration was intended to apply *after* his death.

23 Statute 28.

24 The Trapps scholars were at that time the only scholarships to have been created by a benefaction (other than his own) that was made after he had re-founded the college, as distinct from Gonville Hall.

25 1540 was the date of the death of Thomas Alkyn, who had created scholarships by deed the previous year. He was the last of four earlier benefactors who had endowed scholarships. A fifth, Peter Hewet, endowed scholarships in the months preceding the re-foundation, but his first scholars were not elected until later; consequently, Caius' reference to the year 1540 thus exempted the holders of all scholarships that had been endowed at Gonville Hall, but not his own scholars.

paid rent for their rooms before the re-foundation in 1557.[26] Caius now directed that those who held fellowships that had been established in the time of Gonville Hall – whom he termed "Fellows of Gonville College" – must pay a rent if they wished to have one of the rooms in the buildings that he had provided,[27] but he said nothing to alter the status quo as regards rooms in "Gonville College". His provisions for the fellows who were on his own foundation also left unanswered questions. The direction that fellows "of Gonville College" must pay rent if they occupied any rooms that he had provided suggests that he did not intend his own fellows to do so; but later in the same statute he appears to direct that his own fellows should only be excused rent for rooms in his buildings during the first ten years following his death,[28] and on the question whether they would have to pay rent if they occupied rooms in "Gonville College" he was silent.

Precisely how these confusing instructions about fellows and scholars were interpreted is only ascertainable from 1716 onwards.[29] A complex pattern emerges from that picture:

(i) the rents for rooms are still much the same in 1716 as they were when they had been set by Caius;[30]

(ii) the three fellows who hold their awards on Dr Caius' own foundation are not charged rent if they occupy rooms in Caius Court, but the question whether they have to pay rent if they occupy a room in

26 Evidence from the time of Gonville Hall is tantalisingly absent, but Caius' express requirement that fellows who were not on his own foundation must pay rent for a room in his buildings implies that rent had not been payable by fellows earlier.

27 He required them to pay 20s. for a ground-floor room or 26s. 8d. for an upstairs room in his buildings, the same rent as a pensioner.

28 As the Absence Books later showed, they continued to be excused rent even after the ten years had elapsed.

29 The Absence Books run from 1716. Until then nothing similar survives; the Bursar's Books run from 1609, but they record only the total sum paid into the chest in respect of Caius Court and the Pensionary, not the individual amounts paid by particular occupants. The Absence Books identified scholarships and junior fellowships by their foundation, but not senior fellowships. To ascertain whether a particular person held his senior fellowship on Caius' foundation or upon one of the older foundations, one has to turn to the *Liber Rationalis* to identify the category of his fellowship: for the three categories see "*Stipends*", § VI. 4, at p. 427 above. Rooms were not identified by staircase and number until 1797. In that year the staircases were lettered sequentially from A to E in Gonville Court and F to K (now H to M) in Caius Court; until then the rooms in Caius Court had been listed in reverse order, *i.e.* left to right, starting with those on what is now M staircase (and became K staircase in 1797) and working back to what is now H staircase. Salvin's addition of two staircases in Gonville Court in 1853–54 made necessary the present lettering of the staircases in Caius Court as H to M.

30 The annual rent for a single superior room was still only 28s., except in the later Perse and Legge buildings, where it appears to have been £2.

Gonville Court or elsewhere in the college seems not to have been answered;[31]

(iii) the other nine senior fellows (whose fellowships were funded before the re-foundation of the college) do not pay rent if they live in Gonville Court but are charged if they live elsewhere in the college;

(iv) as a result of this rigid observance of the provisions of Statute 28 there is a financial discrepancy between the holders of those nine fellowships depending on the location of their rooms;

(v) that embarrassing result is wholly or partly eliminated by the granting of an allowance to those senior fellows who are charged for their rooms;[32]

(vi) the allowance is met out of the rents from Gonville Court and, since the dividend *pro cubiculis* is thereby diminished *pro tanto*, the cost of the allowance is shared equally by the Master and all twelve senior fellows;

(vii) Frankland, Wendy and Stokys junior fellows have to pay rent for their rooms but receive no compensating allowance;

(viii) a Perse fellow who has his room in the Perse building (which had been built with money from Stephen Perse's benefaction) escapes paying rent;[33]

(ix) the twenty scholars who hold their awards on Dr Caius' own foundation are not charged rent if they are fortunate enough to occupy rooms in Caius Court, but they have to pay rent if they occupy a room elsewhere in the college;

(x) the embarrassing discrepancy between Caius scholars resident in Caius Court and those elsewhere in the college is modified (but not eliminated) by the allowance to the latter of part (but not all) of their rent, and in this case it is met out of the rents of Caius Court, and thus by the chest;

(xi) the six Perse scholars are entitled to free rooms in the Perse building, but *quaere* whether any allowance is made to those who live in other rooms;[34]

31 An allowance was given to Caius' scholars who lived elsewhere than in Caius Court and paid rent, but no such allowance to his fellows has been noticed. As there were only three fellows on Caius' foundation at any one time they could normally have had rooms in Caius Court.

32 The allowance was limited to the amount Caius had set for an upstairs room in Statute 28, *i.e.* 28s. p.a., and it was payable only to those senior fellows who were resident.

33 Free rooms were particularly valuable for Perse fellows in 1716, for at that time there was insufficient income from the Perse trust to pay them a stipend: see "*Stipends*", § VI. 4, at p. 436 above.

34 The Perse scholars were entitled to rooms rent-free in the Perse building until it was demolished in 1868 (*B.H.* III, p. 83); in the unlikely case that they had rooms in other buildings they did not get an allowance from the chest, and it is doubtful whether they got one from the Perse trust, given its parlous finances at the time.

(xii) one other scholar escapes the payment of rent, and he does so because his benefactor, Matthew Parker, expressly directed that his scholars should be free from rent;[35]

(xiii) despite Caius' direction in Statute 28, the scholars whose foundations were established before 1540 are charged for their rooms:

(xiv) in addition to the fellows and scholars living in the two courts or in the Perse and Legge buildings, there is a mysterious and unexplained list of eighteen persons "*incerti laris*", who are charged rent for unspecified rooms, and this goes to swell the dividend *pro cubiculis*.[36]

Despite the confusing details the salient features are clear. So far as senior fellows are concerned, the statutory distinctions between fellows of "Gonville College" and "Caius College" still affect book-keeping entries and clerical calculations, but the introduction of the allowance has, for all practical purposes, ironed out financial disparity between senior fellows in the matter of room rent: all twelve now have a *de facto* entitlement to reside in college free of rent.[37] As regards scholars, those of Caius' and Perse's scholars who live in their buildings still escape rent, but all (save one) of the scholars on other foundations pay rent and the amount of any allowance made to a scholar is only a partial one: the college is starting very gradually to move towards the position today where all junior members pay rent for rooms, scholars as well as pensioners. As regards junior fellows, however, the interplay of rent and allowances has had very different consequences. The growing financial gap between the stipends of junior and senior fellows has been cruelly widened: not only do junior fellows have to pay room rent out of their meagre stipends but, receiving no compensating allowance, they must have felt aggrieved that their rents went to swell the senior fellows' dividend. It is not surprising that the eighteenth century saw fewer and fewer junior fellows choosing to reside in college for any length of time as rents rose.

35 Parker provided that his scholar should be "*sine deductione cubiculi aut lectionum domesticarum*": *B.H.* III, p. 229. The scholarship was known as the Archbishop of Canterbury's scholarship. The fortunate holder in 1716 (Girault) had his room in Gonville Court.

36 The list *incerti laris* included fellows as well as scholars; some were resident, and some were absentees. The list became very much larger in later years, particularly as the number of non-residents increased markedly in the eighteenth century. The number varied from year to year and for some unexplained reason it 'spiked' very markedly for the whole of the academic year 1796–97. The term *incerti laris* might suggest "address unknown" or "of no fixed address", but the 1716 list includes one senior fellow who was resident through the half-year and whose address must have been known, together with several resident scholars. The precise significance of the term seems to have been forgotten by 1857, when it was agreed that the payment made under "the name of *Incerti Laris*" be discontinued: *Gesta*, C.O.12, 1 July 1857.

37 The allowance is limited to an "inferior" room, so fellows who opt for a "superior" room in the 'wrong College' and so pay rent will not recover the full amount of that rent.

The room rents were still very low in 1716, but a century later they had already begun to rise to a slightly more realistic level,[38] and, although the pattern which Statute 28 had created was still fundamentally the same, subtle changes had occurred by 1800. Fellows and scholars on particular foundations were no longer entitled to enjoy rent-free occupation of a room provided by their benefactor, and a rent was now charged, at least notionally, for all college rooms. The allowance to fellows had been increased, and although it had not kept pace with rents it continued to allow a (senior) fellow to enjoy the occupation of a room anywhere in college without a significant charge.[39] In contrast, the allowance to Caius' scholars had remained unchanged despite the increase in their rents, so that, like the scholars on other foundations, they felt the increased burden of their room rent. Junior fellows also felt the burden, and very few of them passed any time in residence.[40] Room rents continued to rise in the nineteenth century, and with them the allowance to the senior fellows,[41] but after 1836 the dividend *pro cubiculis* was finally discontinued and all room rents and allowances were thereafter paid into or out of the chest.[42]

The division of rents between the college and the Master and the fellows personally

Caius' answer to the second question posed by Statute 28 was clear and emphatic. He had had to abandon his initial proposal to discontinue the practice of diverting the room rents into the pockets of the Master and the fellows which had developed in Gonville Hall in the years before he returned to the college in 1559, but he was adamant that the rents from the rooms that *he* had provided

38 In 1716 the yearly rent for a first-floor room in Caius Court was still 26s. 8d., the amount specified by Caius in Statute 28. In 1718 it was raised to £3 p.a., and in 1725 an additional charge (between £3 and £6 p.a.) was made for wainscots in three sets. By 1751 the rent had risen to £5 p.a. and the additional £3–£6 was now charged for wainscots in six sets. By 1797 the additional charge had been subsumed into the rent, and this had become £8 p.a. These are the rents charged to fellows and scholars; the rents for pensioners were probably the same, at least for minor pensioners.

39 Whereas only resident fellows had enjoyed the allowance in 1716, a non-resident fellow who had a room for which he would previously not have been charged a rent now received an allowance towards the rent which he was charged.

40 In the twelve months from Lady Day 1825, only one of the nine junior fellows had a room and spent more than a few days in college: *Absence Book*, Michaelmas 1825, Lady Day 1826. During the summer half-year many (probably most) of the senior fellows and scholars also went out of residence; only the principal officers and two or three fellows remained in the college for the greater part of that half-year.

41 In 1826 room rents were increased substantially to £10 for a "single floor" and £15 for a "double floor" (in effect, a ground-floor room and a first-floor set of rooms, respectively) and the allowance to fellows was set at £12: *Gesta*, 17 December 1825. Subsequent increases in rents and allowances have not been tracked for the purposes of the present work.

42 *Gesta*, 26 October 1836. See *The end of the dividend pro cubiculis* at p. 492 below.

were to go to his chest and they were not to be shared out among the fellows to the detriment of "our College". In speaking of his college in contrast to "Gonville College" or "the College as a whole", he was no doubt thinking primarily of the buildings he had erected in Caius Court,[43] but they were not the only buildings that he provided for his re-founded college. At the same time as he started work on Caius Court he had also purchased from Trinity College the three tenements that were later replaced by the "Pensionary" in 1594,[44] and there is no reason to doubt that he intended his statute to apply to those three tenements as well as to Caius Court, for, as he explained elsewhere in his statutes, he used the terms "Gonville College" and "Caius College" not simply to indicate two courts but to distinguish different buildings by reference to the person who provided them.[45]

We should therefore not be surprised that we find this distinction between the two "Colleges" firmly established in the Bursar's Book when it began 1609, but the accounts show only the amounts which were paid into the college chest in pursuance of Caius' direction in Statute 28, not those which were shared out between the Master and senior fellows.[46] In the account for the half-year ending on Lady Day 1609 the rent for three groups of rooms is credited to the chest:

> £5.15s. "for rent for our founder Caius Chambers";
> 10s. "for the Pension of a chamber in Gonevile court";
> 48s. "for the rent of the Pensionary to make good the ould Rent of three tenements".[47]

Apart from the intriguing 10s. for the chamber in Gonville Court,[48] the payments credited to the chest were those from the rooms provided by its third founder: the rents for other rooms of the college were not paid into the chest

43 As Caius did in the two statutes that follow, *i.e.*, Statutes 29 and 30.

44 The "Pensionary" was the name later given (after they had been converted into college rooms) to the three tenements which Caius purchased from Trinity College in 1564 on the very same day as he started work on the building of Caius Court: see *B.H.* III, pp. 47, 68, n. 1. (The term "pensionary" did not imply that it was necessarily for pensioners.) The three tenements and the pensionary which replaced them were situated on Trinity Street, north of the Gate of Humility and facing St Michael's Church.

45 Statute 66. He deliberately uses "*authore*", not "*fundatore*". Elsewhere in his statutes he uses the term *atrium* to denote a court: *e.g.*, Statutes 52, 75, and the 1558 draft statute *De Atrio* (*Documents*, II, p. 358).

46 The Bursar's Books run continuously from 1609 to 1926. Only the rents paid into the chest in respect of rooms in Caius' buildings are recorded there. The first detailed record of the room rents for fellows and scholars in *all* the college's buildings appears in 1716 in the earliest surviving Absence Book.

47 *Bursar's Book* (Lady Day 1609).

48 The amount rarely changed from 10s. in later audits and the payment ceased in 1678. The chamber was identified as the room "by the parlour" (*Bursar's Book*, Michaelmas 1611). The "parlour" referred to was presumably the ground-floor room that served as a parlour for fellows until 1653 (*B.H.* I, p. 197), *not* the room above it lying between the Hall and the Library (*i.e.*, where the Senior Combination Room now is), which had been allocated by Caius for

and were shared out between the Master and senior fellows personally, as they had been in the time of Gonville Hall. The payment of *any* room rents to the chest seems to have been regarded at the time as the exception, not the rule: such payments were never classified as "ordinary income" (*recepta ordinaria*) along with the rents from the college's farms and estates and other recurrent receipts, but were listed instead as "exceptional income" (*recepta extraordinaria*) together with non-recurrent income.

We know the amount of rent credited to the college in 1609, and although we have no figures for the amount taken by the Master and fellows personally we can be confident that the two amounts would not have been very different in Caius' day – if anything, the college's share would probably have been slightly the larger, given the substantial increase in accommodation which Caius Court and the three tenements on Trinity Street had provided as a result of his generosity.[49] The wording of Statute 28, however, meant that the chest's share was permanently confined to the buildings that Caius had himself provided, and therefore the rent from any subsequent expansion in accommodation went exclusively toward the dividend enjoyed by the Master and the fellows. This meant that the balance would inevitably shift in time in their favour as the college grew.

The first modest increase in accommodation came in 1594 with the enlargement into the Pensionary of the three tenements which Caius had purchased from Trinity College; this provided a little more accommodation than the tenements had done, and in 1609 the chest was receiving only part of the rent from the Pensionary. The first big increases in accommodation came with the erection of the Perse building in 1618 and the larger Legge building the following year.[50] The Legge building replaced the Pensionary and this raised the question what part of the rents from the new rooms in the Legge building should be paid into the chest in place of the rents from the rooms they replaced, and it was formally agreed by the Master and senior fellows on 15 January 1619 that the old rent (*redditus antiquus*) should be paid into the chest and that the rest should accrue to the Master and senior fellows.[51] The payment to the chest

the Master's use until it was needed for communal use (Statute 28) and only became the Combination Room in 1653.

49 The half-yearly amount credited to the chest at Lady Day 1609 was £8. 13s.; the payment to the Master and the fellows from Gonville Court had not yet been augmented by the erection of the Perse and Legge buildings.

50 The two buildings substantially increased the amount of college accommodation. The Perse building had twelve chambers or sets and the Legge sixteen, and in both buildings each chamber had one, two or three studies in which undergraduates could be accommodated: see Willis and Clark, *The Architectural History of the University of Cambridge* (1886), vol. 1, pp. 204–8.

51 *Annals*, p. 278. The "old rent" refers to the rent of the tenements bought by Caius: cf. *Bursar's Book* (Lady Day 1609) cited in n. 47 above.

in respect of the Pensionary had been 48s., but it rose almost straightway to £4. 3s., and by the eighteenth century it had become one-third of the rents from the Legge building.[52] The rents from the Perse building and two-thirds of those from the Legge building thus increased the share taken by the Master and fellows and in addition they also took the rents that were charged to an increasing number of persons listed intriguingly as "*incerti laris*".[53] The erection in the north-west corner of the college of a third building adjacent to the hall in 1635 tilted the balance further and by 1662 the chest's share of the total room rents was falling towards one-third, with the Master and fellows taking personally the rest.[54] A few years later the chest's share dropped a little further when it ceased to receive any payment for the mysterious chamber in Gonville Court after 1677.[55]

From 1716 onward the detailed charges and allowances for fellows' and scholars' rooms are continuously recorded in the Absence Books, together with the names of the occupants and the net totals to be credited to the chest or apportioned as dividend, respectively; in that year the charges for a room were still broadly those that Caius had set in Statute 28, and the proportions taken by the college and the fellows, respectively, were still very much what they had been in Gostlin's time.[56] During the course of the eighteenth century, however, room rents rose appreciably. Although we might have expected that the shares taken by the chest and the Master and fellows would both have risen *pari passu*, the amount taken by the Master and senior fellows grew steadily, yet the chest's share hardly rose at all and even dropped in some years.[57] The payments to the chest were diminished by what must be described as 'creative accountancy' – only the original rent fixed by Caius was credited to the chest and any increases in the rents from Caius Court coupled with additional charges for wainscots in the rooms there were allocated to the dividend. Multiple occupancy of rooms

52 The Absence Books were still referring to it as the "Pensionary", not the "Legge Building", in 1860 when Caius' statutes were repealed.

53 For the *incerti laris* see n. 36 above.

54 In 1662 the chest received £20. 15s. 0d. and the Master and fellows shared £34. 10s. 4d.: *Bursar's Book* (Lady Day and Michaelmas 1662); Gostlin's Note Book. The Note Book gives us the size of the one-thirteenth share of the total dividend paid half-yearly to the Master and each of the twelve senior fellows by John Gostlin when he was bursar during the years 1662–65, and thus the total amount of the dividend *pro cubiculis* in each of those years. (The Master received the same one-thirteenth share as a fellow.) For Gostlin and his note book, see below in relation to corn rents.

55 *Bursar's Book* (Lady Day 1678).

56 For the half-year to Lady Day the chest took £16. 3s. 4d., while the Master and fellows divided £22. 7s. 4d.: *Absence Book* (Lady Day 1716). Each fellow's share of the dividend (£1. 14s. 0d.) was still very small compared with that from corn money and entry fines.

57 In the three *half-years* to Lady Day 1716, 1751 and 1800 the chest's share and the dividend, respectively, were: £16. 3s. 4d. as against £22. 7s. 4d. in 1716; £17. 8s. 4d. as against £67. 2s. 7d. in 1751; and £19. 3s. 4d. as against £101. 2s. 7d. in 1800.

diminished, and with it the number of rent-payers living in Caius Court, while the list of those *incerti laris* increased, and with it the dividend, so that the balance was tilted further in favour of the Master and senior fellows. By the end of the century the college was taking less than one-seventh of the net room rents:[58] as a result, Caius' aim of saving the room rents for repairs had been largely frustrated by 1800.

Thereafter there would seem to have been a growing disquiet that a disproportionate share of the college's room rents was being taken by the Master and senior fellows, many of whom spent only a few days a year in Cambridge. The balance gradually tilted back and by 1825 the share credited to the chest had climbed back above a quarter.[59] In the following year, 1826, the college finally took the step of increasing its room rents to a realistic level. Taken by itself this would have created a disproportionate increase in the dividend, as compared with the share paid into the chest, and it was agreed that the college was "to continue to receive the rent from Caius Court, and to be allowed £150, from the other rents".[60] At long last the college began to enjoy a greater share in its room rents than the Master and the senior fellows.[61]

The end of the dividend pro cubiculis

Ten years later the dividend *pro cubiculis* was finally discontinued. In 1836 it was agreed that "the rent of rooms and *Incerti Laris* be put to the Bursar's book [and that] each Fellowship be increased by £40 and the Master's stipend by £80 for the half-year".[62] These half-yearly increases were far greater than the ending of the dividend would have justified, and the Master (Martin Davy) fared particularly well, even though his share of the dividend *pro cubiculis* had been the same as that of each of the twelve senior fellows.[63] The ceasing of the dividend also meant that any allowance towards their rent which those fellows had enjoyed

58 At the Michaelmas audit, 1800, the chest received just £14. 2s. 8d., whereas the Master and fellows enjoyed a dividend of £98. 19s. 4d., each taking £7. 12s. 3d.

59 At the Lady Day audit, 1825, the chest's share was £42. 3s. 4d., and that of the Master and fellows £116. 11s. 0d. The increase in the chest's share was principally brought about by a change of accounting which ended the practice of allocating increases in the rents of Caius Court to the dividend instead of the chest.

60 *Gesta*, 17 December 1825. Room rents were increased to £10 for a "single floor" and £15 for a "double floor" (in effect a ground-floor room and a first-floor set of rooms, respectively.) The allowance to fellows was set at £12.

61 £162. 10s. 0d., as against the dividend of £149. 8s. 6d.

62 *Gesta*, 26 October 1836.

63 An individual's share of the half-yearly dividend *pro cubiculis* at the two preceding audits had been no more than £15. 2s. 2d. and £13. 13s. 2d., and the Master had never had larger share than a fellow (*Absence Book*, Michaelmas 1835, Lady Day 1836). The increases are typical of the indefensible attitude to stipends (particularly that of the Master) which characterised Martin Davy's mastership: see "*Stipends*", § VI. 4 above.

could no longer be met out of the dividend that the rents from "Gonville College" had previously provided. They did not suffer, however: the allowance was simply charged to the chest instead and senior fellows continued to enjoy *de facto* freedom from most of any room rent which they had notionally been obliged to pay in Statute 28.

When Caius' statutes were repealed in 1860 one might have expected that the question of charges for fellows' rooms would have featured in later college statutes, but in fact it did not do so until 1920. It was only in that year that the governing body (*i.e.*, what is now the College Council) was formally empowered to assign rooms to a fellow and to make such allowance for rent as they should think fit, provided the value of the allowance did not exceed that of the rent and rates.[64] That remains the position today.

HEARTH MONEY

Caius was himself responsible for the introduction of the dividend that survived longest: this was "hearth money" (*pro foco*), the sharing out of the sum of £10 each year for the purchase of fuel. It had begun soon after Caius' death, and more than three centuries later that same sum was still being solemnly shared out in 1887, the last year in which corn money was paid as a dividend to the five surviving senior fellows.[65]

In his will Caius directed that his executors should use any residuary money left in his estate to purchase and convey to the college so much land as that residuary money would buy at twenty years' purchase in reversion or twenty-five years in possession, and that the yearly rents and profits of the lands so purchased should be "yerelie employed and disbursed for the expenses and charges of the fyer in the kitchen within the said College for the necessarie dressinge of meate at lawfull tymes within the said kitchinge".[66] In this way the Master, fellows and scholars of the college were to be relieved of one specific burden, that of the expenses and charges for the kitchen fire. Despite his somewhat elaborate language, Caius does not mention and does not seem to have envisaged the sharing out of a fixed sum of £10 from the college's rents among any members of the college personally, a practice which was in principle anathema to him. Nevertheless, the subsequent practice of doing so had come into existence within twenty years and was attributed to this direction in Caius' will.[67]

64 College Statutes (1920), Statute 39(4).

65 *Absence Book*, Lady Day 1887. For the five surviving senior fellows, see the section on *Corn Rents* below.

66 *B.H.* III, p. 390.

67 See *ibid.* See also "*The Decree on the Frankland fellows, 11 December 1592*", Appendix E below ("*iuxta ultimam voluntatem doctoris Caiii fundatoris*").

What appears to have happened is (i) that the £241 in ready money which Caius had with him in his house in London in the last weeks of his life – not the whole of the ready money (£428) in his estate – was handed over to his executors before his death and used for the purchase of the demesne lands of Swannesley Manor in Caxton, which were then of the yearly value of £10,[68] and (ii) that this yearly sum was then allocated partly *pro foco* and partly to discharge the further direction in Caius' will that the college should maintain "a lustie and healthie honeste trewe and unmarried man of fortie yeres of age and upwards" as janitor and porter and should pay him yearly a stipend of 40s., with his chamber free. The upshot was that the porter received £2. 13s. 4d. each year out of the £10, and the remaining £7. 6s. 8d. was shared equally by the Master and the resident fellows (presumably for the provision of fuel for their rooms), with the kitchen fire and the scholars receiving nothing.[69] As in the case of other dividends, the bursar took as a perquisite any sum remaining from the division.[70]

In 1592 the college elected the first Frankland fellows. On 11 December in that year the Master and fellows decreed that the new Frankland fellows should have their stipend of £7 a year and nothing further: neither distributions, nor liveries, nor dividends (except for grain), nor commemorations, nor hearth money, since nothing more could be done without prejudice to the fellows and detriment to the college. The only concession was that, if other property should be bought to sustain the hearth in accordance with the last will of the founder, Dr Caius, they should be able to receive an equal share with other fellows.[71] The property at Caxton increased steadily in value over the centuries and could have accommodated a payment to the junior fellows, but in fact, since no *other* property was ever purchased for the purpose, they never came to enjoy hearth money: the increased value of Caxton was instead enjoyed by the Master and senior fellows in the form of corn money and entry fines.[72] The inexorable fall in the real value of what had originally been a small but appreciated emolument rendered the payment *pro foco* utterly negligible over the course of time, and although the size of each fellow's share of the dividend rose as the number of fellows in residence dropped in the course of the eighteenth century, the resulting 'increase' in the nominal size of each share, unlike that of corn money, did nothing to stem the erosion in value. In 1609 each of the thirteen shares of the Master and senior fellows for the half-year had been the not-inconsiderable amount of 5s. 11d.: in 1886 the share of the last six resident senior fellows was a

68 The purchase for a price of £241 was thus approximately at the valuation of "twentie yers purchase in revertion, or xxv yeres in possession" directed by Caius in his will: *B.H.* III, p. 389.

69 See, *e.g.*, *Exposita Custodii et sociis pro foco* for Lady Day 1609 in the earliest Bursar's Book.

70 The Master, it may be noted, received the same amount as a fellow, not a double share as he did in the case of corn money, so illustrating the fact that he was not then accorded a Lodge, but like a fellow, a set of rooms in the college's courts, albeit the best set.

71 "*The Decree on the Frankland fellows, 11 December 1592*", Appendix E below.

72 *B.H.* IV(2), pp. 31–3.

derisory 12s. 2d.[73] The fact that the bursary continued solemnly to make these payments for more than a quarter of a century after the repeal of Caius' statutes and their replacement by two sets of Commissioners' Statutes is testimony to the stubborn tenacity of the college's financial practices.

CORN MONEY

There is some evidence from the fifteenth century that Gonville Hall had on occasion received payment of rent in the form of grain long before the reign of Elizabeth, but the few surviving records note only that a named tenant "owed" corn,[74] and no obligation to pay rent in corn is formulated in any of the college's leases that survive from the period before 1576. In that year Parliament enacted the statute which has popularly come to be known as Sir Thomas Smith's Act.[75]

Sir Thomas Smith's Act

The Act directed that any subsequent lease granted by a college of the universities of Cambridge and Oxford for life, lives or years should include a provision that at least one-third part of "th'olde Rente"[76] should be reserved and paid in corn, the quantity to be calculated at a value of no more than 6s. 8d. a quarter for wheat and 5s. a quarter for malt, to be delivered yearly at the college on the specified days.[77]

73 *Bursar's Book* (1609, Lady Day); *Absence Book* (1887, Lady Day). By 1886 the Master no longer received hearth money. The following year the number of resident senior fellows had dropped from six to five; they received the last payment of corn money ever made, but no payment of hearth money is recorded.

74 *B.H.* IV(2), p. iii. The corn may have been owed under the custom of a manor, and not by a leasehold tenant holding for a term of years.

75 18 Eliz. c. 6 (*Statutes of the Realm*, III, p. 616). There seems no reason to doubt the tradition that Sir Thomas Smith was the draftsman of the Act. It seems probable that Andrew Perne, the Master of Peterhouse, had a hand with Smith in preparing the Bill and that it was managed through the Commons by Smith, and by Burghley in the Lords: see Collinson, in P. Collinson, David McKitterick and Elisabeth Leedham-Green, *Andrew Perne; Quatercentenary Studies*, Cambridge Bibliographic Society Monographs 11 (Cambridge, 1991), p. 19, citing Gerald E. Aylmer in *History of the University of Oxford* III, pp. 542–3.

76 The "olde rent" was not understood to be the rent that had prevailed immediately before the land was first leased under the Corn Act, but the rent that had been traditional before the dissolution of the monasteries. In the case of Runcton, discussed below, the "olde rent" was not taken to be the £22 rent that had been charged by the Abbey of St Edmundsbury since 1522, but the even older rent (£10) that had been levied before 1522. In a number of other cases the "olde rent" was no longer the current rent and for this reason the rent payable in money under the Act never represents precisely (the other) two-thirds of the old rent: see *B.H.* IV(2), pp. iv–v.

77 These statutory prices may be compared with average prices of wheat and malt in 1575 and 1576 quoted by Gross, namely, 15s. 11d. and 10s. 10d. a quarter, respectively, in 1575, and 22s. 2d. and 14s. 7d. in 1576: *B.H.* IV(2), p. iv.

In default the lessee was required to pay in ready money at his election the value of the corn, not at the statutory rate by which the quantity had been calculated but at the rate at which the best wheat and malt in the specified local market should be sold on the market-day immediately preceding the due date for payment.[78]

The Act had three aims: (i) protection against excessive annual fluctuations in the price of corn; (ii) repair of the damage done by the inflation which had occurred in the last years of Henry VIII and the reigns of Edward VI and Mary; and (iii) protection against similar inflation in the future. Prices for corn varied greatly according to the harvest, and the draftsman's first purpose was to ensure that colleges would be protected against the considerable and unpredictable variation in the price of corn from year to year and could be sure of a supply of corn or its market value despite the dangers of a bad harvest. As a perceptive writer on the causes of price changes,[79] Sir Thomas was also conscious of the inexorable rise in the price of the staple food, corn, which had occurred in the reigns of Edward VI and Mary and he deliberately fixed the statutory conversion rates at a very low level which had not prevailed since before the closing years of Henry VIII's reign; in this way the Act went some way to ameliorate the relentless fall in their wealth which colleges had experienced in the years that had followed Henry's death.[80] It is, however, the mechanism by which Sir Thomas achieved his third aim for which the Act is famous: by linking the rent automatically to future market prices he provided a safeguard against the danger of future depreciation or increased demand, and he thereby introduced what may be regarded as the earliest conscious protection against inflation.

It is clear from his statutes that Caius would have approved heartily of the three aims if he had still been alive; for he was very conscious both of the rise in prices which had occurred since his time as a fellow and of the future need to raise rents regularly in keeping with the market. Looking back, he recognised that "the cost of everything is three times what it was in past times" and that accordingly "the needs of our fellows cannot be met entirely out of the stipend

[78] It will be convenient to refer to the amount that the tenant was required by the terms of the lease to pay in money as the "money rent" and the payment that might be made by the tenant either in corn or in money in lieu of corn as the "corn rent". The term "corn money" will be reserved for that part of the corn rent which was not credited to the college as income but shared out as a dividend. As will be explained later, the college came to be credited only with the one-third part of "th'olde rente", thereby leaving the rest of the corn rent for distribution as corn money.

[79] Cf. R. Nield, *Riches and Responsibility: A Financial History of Trinity College, Cambridge* (Cambridge, 2008) (hereafter *Riches and Responsibility*), p. 20: "a remarkable man, Sir Thomas Smith of Queens' College, who not only held many high positions in the university and at court but also wrote such a perceptive analysis of the causes of price changes that he perhaps has claim to be the first Cambridge economist".

[80] *Ibid.*, p. 19; *B.H.* IV(2), p. iv; see also *Agrarian History of England and Wales*, vol. IV, ed. Thirsk, ch. ix (P. Bowden).

we provide";[81] and we can be sure that he had in mind the increase in the price of corn that had occurred since he was a fellow.[82] Looking forward, he forbade the creation of reversionary leases, the granting of the college's land in fee farm or its leasing for more than twenty years, three practices which had deprived colleges and other corporations of the power to raise rents and thereby protect themselves against inflation;[83] and he was insistent that, when a lease fell in, the rent should be raised "in the light of the fruitfulness and value of the property demised or leased and the needs of the college" and that the charge on the tenant "should remain within moderation and a little lower than those of nearby farms of the same quality".[84] In the same way, although entry fines might be levied in proportion to the fertility and fruitfulness of the lands, this should not be done before the rents had been raised to the appropriate level, "lest the fines eat up the rents".[85]

There was, however, a further provision in the Act which Caius would perhaps have been less ready to endorse. In his own statutes Caius had laid down categorically that the college should not be burdened with maintaining any fellow or scholar, or with supplementing his stipend through the grant of free victuals, clothing and accommodation beyond what was provided by the income of the property provided by his founder or benefactor, and in addition that all surplus income should accrue to the college for extraordinary uses such as repairs, necessary litigation "and other incidentals of that kind".[86] In contrast the Act directed that the corn or money paid in lieu (the "corn rent") was to be expended "to the use of the Relief of the Commons and Diett of the saide Colleges … onlie". Taken literally, the wording of the Act would actually *reduce*, by as much as one-third of the old rent, the amount of 'free' income received from its agrarian properties that the college could devote, if necessary, to the repairs and other extraordinary uses which its founder had been anxious to safeguard.[87] As will be seen later, the express requirement of the Act that the corn rent should be expended *only* in the way it specified, *i.e.*, the relief of the commons and diet of the college, inevitably raised questions for the colleges of both universities.

81 Statute 39.
82 Cf. *B.H.* IV(2), p. iv, and n. 77 above.
83 Statute 86.
84 Statute 93.
85 Statute 95.
86 Statute 36.
87 Being unaffected by the Act, the whole of the income from its urban properties would remain 'free' and available for repairs and incidental uses, but these properties were still relatively few and of small value. They were mostly in Cambridge and Norwich; the college had not yet received its London property from Mrs Frankland's bequest.

The application of the Act by the college

The Act did not take effect immediately or at a specified time, but in stages as each existing lease expired. As a result, the speed at which the impact of the Act was felt by the various colleges varied considerably, depending on the length of time its existing leases still had to run; this in turn depended not only on the date at which the lease had been granted but also on its length. Thus in the case of Trinity College, which had been founded by Henry VIII in 1546 and had acquired much of its northern property in the reign of Queen Mary, the practice had been to grant long leases and as a result the benefits of the Act were greatly delayed and dividends were not introduced until as late as 1630.[88] In contrast, in the case of Caius' college the Act took effect far more rapidly; for although much of its most valuable property had been granted on long leases in the years before Caius returned to the college in 1559,[89] its smaller properties had not been let for long periods and he had been insistent since his return on limiting the length of all leases to no more than twenty years. As a result the first occasion on which the college had to consider how the Act should be applied arose as early as 1579.[90] Two leases came up for renewal in that year, one at Cherry Hinton and the other at Barningham, and despite the peremptory language of the Act the college appears to have been initially uncertain how strictly it was to be applied, given the founder's competing injunction in Statute 93 that rents should be increased when leases were renewed. In the case of Cherry Hinton the Act was applied precisely in the way it directed; but in the other the Act was disregarded and no requirement for payment in corn was imposed, the rent being increased instead in compliance with Caius' own statute.[91] The question

[88] See *Riches and Responsibility*, p. 22.

[89] For the granting of long leases by Caius' immediate predecessors as Master, Styrmin and Bacon, see the discussion of entry fines below.

[90] It was in that same year that the college decided to construct its own oven and bake its bread instead of buying it in, a decision that was no doubt prompted by Sir Thomas Smith's Act three years earlier: *B.H.* IV(2), p. v. The Act must have rendered it difficult to comply with Caius' direction in Statute 87 that "the place of payment shall be the Hall of your College: its form genuine and lawful gold and silver", even if it had ever been practicable. The manorial barns at the college's two principal estates eventually leased under the 1576 Act have survived to the present time: the Great Barn at Croxley (photo 4, *B.H.* IV(2), p. 74); and the Red Barn at Runcton (*theredbarnnorfolk.co.uk*).

[91] In the case of lands in Cherry Hinton, the Act was applied: the "old rent" had been £2 a year, and in accordance with the Act the £2 rent was altered to £1. 6s. 8d. with 2 quarters of wheat in lieu of the remaining third of the old rent (13s. 4d.). In the other case, lands in Barningham in Suffolk had been granted in 1558 for twenty-one years at a yearly rent of £5, and on the expiry of that lease in 1579 it was leased for twenty years (by then the maximum length allowed by the college's statutes) at a rent of £10 a year; when that twenty-year lease expired in 1599 and the question again arose, the provisions of the Act were observed, and the money rent was re-set at £8. 6s. 8d. with 2½ quarters of wheat and 3 quarters and 3 bushels of malt, *i.e.*, one-third of the old £5 rent at the statutory conversion rate. It must be remembered that if prior increases had

arose again three years later in 1582 in relation to Runcton, one of the three manors given to the college by John Caius in 1557 at its re-foundation. Caius had purchased the manor subject to a lease of its demesne lands that had been granted by the abbey of St Edmund's Bury in 1522 for sixty years at a rent of £22, and in Statute 91 he had directed that the college should in due course raise the annual rent to £40. The first opportunity to do this arose in 1582 on the expiry of the sixty-year lease, and the college was therefore again faced with the need to reconcile obedience to its own statute with observance of the Act of Parliament. It implemented both: in compliance with the Corn Act the money rent was duly raised, not to £40, but to £36. 13s. 4d., the residue of £3. 6s. 8d. being taken in 5 quarters of wheat and 7 quarters of malt.[92]

Runcton appears to have been the last case in which the college sought to make any significant increase in the money rents of its agrarian property. Fifteen years later the lease of Croxley and Snellshall at Rickmansworth, the second property which Caius had conferred on the college at the re-foundation, came up for renewal in 1597.[93] In this case Caius himself had already raised the rent from the "old rent" of £15. 6s. 8d. to £40 in his own lifetime before the Act came into existence, and when the lease was renewed no further increase was made: instead, one-third of the "olde rente" (£5. 2s. 4d.) was taken in 7½ quarters of wheat and 10½ quarters of malt and the money-rent was *reduced* to £34. 17s. 8d.[94] Thereafter Caius' injunction in Statutes 89 and 95 to increase rents in the light of the fruitfulness and value of the property was disregarded and the injunction ceased to apply to any property. The rental burden of the college's tenants continued to increase with the inflationary increase in the price of corn, but the nominal amount of their money rents remained broadly static until the nineteenth century. As will be seen later, Caius' policy of seeking rent increases was displaced by the practice of granting 'beneficial leases' in return for fines.

By the time of Legge's death in 1607 most of the college's non-manorial agrarian properties had been brought within the Corn Act,[95] and an ingenious "Arithmetical Table" had been constructed by a fellow and one-time bursar,

already raised the rent above the old rent before the Act was applied, as occurred in the case of Barningham, then the total of the money rent from tenants shown in later Corn Rolls and Grain Books will be greater than two-thirds of the old rent, and accordingly the money rent rarely amounts precisely to twice the corn rent, *i.e.*, the one-third of the old rent payable in corn or money in lieu under the Act: see *B.H.* IV(2), p. v.

92 £3. 6. 8d. was not one-third of the £22 that had been the rent since the Abbey's grant in 1522, but was one-third of £10, a very "olde rente" that had been charged before the Abbey's grant in 1522.

93 The two manors were always leased together and treated as one property.

94 Making, with the one-third of the "old rent" taken in corn (£5. 2s. 4d.), the desired £40. The increased market value to which the required quantity of corn had risen by 1597 meant that the actual cost borne by the tenant immediately became substantially greater than £40.

95 The twenty-three tenancies brought under the Act by 1609 are listed in the Bursar's Book for that year.

John Fletcher,[96] in order to simplify the calculation and distribution of corn rent when prices of corn changed each year. That table was constructed in order to serve for much longer than a single year, but since it would work only so long as the total quantities of wheat and malt due from all tenants (and therefore the number of tenancies) remained unchanged, it is clear that Fletcher did not anticipate that further properties would be brought within the Act in the near future. That belief was shared by others in the college, for the Table was carefully preserved for future use in the new series of Bursar's Books which was started in 1609.

Legge was succeeded as Master by William Branthwaite and although two or three small properties were brought within the Corn Act in the first few years of his mastership, it is striking that no further properties were added thereafter until the 1630s, long after Branthwaite's death in 1619. It might be thought that this was due, in part at least, to the fact that he came from Emmanuel and would seem to have been imbued with the strongly puritanical attitude that was exhibited by that college. As at Sidney Sussex, the other puritanical college, less use of the Corn Act was made at Emmanuel than at other colleges, and Branthwaite may have brought with him to his new college the same disapproval of corn money as appears to have prevailed in those two colleges.[97]

A more significant reason, however, would appear to lie in the fact that most of the college's non-manorial lands and three of the college's seven important manors, Croxley, Runcton and Mortimer's, had already been brought within the Act by the time of Legge's death,[98] and no occasion to do so arose in Branthwaite's lifetime as regards the other four: these were Aynells at Westoning in Bedfordshire, Burnham Thorpe in Norfolk, and Bincombe and Oborne in Dorset. Long before Caius' statutes had restricted the granting of leases to twenty years, the manor of Aynells had been leased out by the college for ninety-nine years in 1544 and consequently it could not be brought within the

[96] *B.H.* III, p. 95: see the note on "*Mr Fletcher his arithmetical table*" appended to this chapter. Fletcher had been bursar in 1594 and 1601 and he may have constructed his table at one or other of those times.

[97] Bendall, *Emmanuel College*, p. 144. When he was at Caius, Branthwaite's puritanical disapproval of the enjoyment of "temporalities" by the fellowship was expressed vigorously in the concerns that he submitted to the Chancellor in his acrimonious dispute with the fellows in *Allen's Case* in 1617. In those submissions he did not advert expressly to corn money, but he did protest emphatically against the diversion from the college's corporate revenue of three other dividends, entry fines, mulcts and room rents, and there can be little doubt that he disapproved of corn money just as strongly: see his Protestation to the Chancellor against "Auncient practices against statutes": *Allen's Case* (1617), Appendix F.

[98] Croxley and Runcton had been re-let under the Act in 1582, and Mortimer's in Newnham in 1605. Mortimer's had been let to the corporation of Cambridge for ninety-nine years in 1507 and in order to avoid pressure from the corporation to renew that lease, the college granted a twenty-year reversionary lease (within the Corn Act) to a trustee for Legge shortly before the expiry of the lease in 1606: *B.H.* IV(2), p. 25.

Act before 1643.[99] The second manor, Burnham Thorpe, was also still subject to a long lease which would not expire until 1619.[100] The possibility of applying the Act to the third and fourth properties was even more remote, for the manors of Bincombe and Oborne, which the college had acquired in 1570 shortly before Caius' death, were situated in Dorset and the tenants of these two manors held their lands for three lives as customary tenants and, since they held by copy of the court roll and not by deed, their holdings never came within the Corn Act.[101]

While Branthwaite was Master the college acquired the freehold reversion to two further important manors: those of D'Abernoons at Duxford in 1611 and Buristead at Great Shelford in 1614. D'Abernoons had been bought by Mrs Frankland's trustees with the very substantial bequest which she had made to the college, and it was subject to an existing lease when it was eventually conveyed to the college in 1611;[102] Duxford's location and agricultural quality would seem to render the property ideally suitable for the application of the Corn Act, but for some unexplained reason it was not brought within the Act when the existing lease came to an end in 1625.[103] (As it happens, the Act had also not been applied when the eighty-year lease of Burnham Thorpe expired

99 A new lease with a corn rent was in fact agreed nine years earlier, in 1634: *B.H.* IV(2), p. 93.

100 *B.H.* IV(2), p. 15. An eighty-year lease of the manor had been granted by the Abbey of Wymondham in 1539 before it was seized by the Crown, from whom Caius purchased it in preparation for the re-foundation of the college. When the lease did eventually fall in, "a great suit in Chancery arose" and the Corn Act was not applied to the twenty-year lease that the college then granted. The manor was never brought within the Act. In Statute 91 Caius had directed that the rent should be raised from £6 p.a. to "not less than £13. 6s. 8d." on renewal, but when the lease was renewed in 1619 the rent was only marginally increased to £8 p.a. and it remained at that sum until 1866: *B.H.* IV(2), p. 16.

101 Although the Act applied to leases for lives as well as those for years, it applied only to leases by deed (into which the required provision as to payment in kind could be inserted) and therefore not to copyholds. It is difficult to explain, however, the apparently complete absence of any demesne lands in Bincombe or Oborne; such land would have been leased for a term of years by deed and the 1576 Act would have applied.

102 In 1599 Legge and her other trustees had bought the freehold reversion of the manor expectant on the death of a life tenant, Mrs Jane Middlemas. Four years after Legge's death, the manor was conveyed to the college by the surviving trustees in 1611, but although the life interest had ceased by that time, the property was still subject to an existing leasehold tenancy to which the Act did not apply (since the lease had not been granted by the college).

103 The rent under the existing lease had been substantial and virtually a rack-rent (£62 p.a.). The first chance to apply the Corn Act arose in April 1625 when the college granted a twenty-year lease of Duxford to Thomas Wendy (the nephew of the benefactor of that name): *Liber demissionum*, fol. 178v. Instead of applying the Act, the college re-let the manor at the same rack-rent, perhaps because giving the Frankland fellows corn money would have upset the equality of stipend at £10 p.a. which Perse had carefully engineered for all classes of junior fellows in his will. The manor was never brought within the Act and the rent remained at £62 p.a. until 1867; it was only when the rent had lost its value that the fines for Duxford began to rise steeply in the eighteenth century: for these fines see *B.H.* IV(2), pp. 42–3.

in 1619.)[104] Like Duxford, the Manor of Buristead at Great Shelford was also subject to an existing lease when the college bought it in 1614, and no opportunity to apply the Act had arisen in Branthwaite's lifetime either; but when the ancient lease granted by the bishop of Ely did eventually fall into possession in 1635 it was then leased under the Act.[105]

Great Shelford was in fact the last of the college's manors to be brought within the Act[106] and by the time of the Civil War all further application of the Act had ceased and the list of properties recorded in the Corn Rolls in the last years of the Commonwealth remained virtually unchanged for two hundred years thereafter.[107]

The beneficiaries of the corn rent

The express requirement in Sir Thomas Smith's Act that the corn rent should be expended exclusively in the way it specified, namely "to the use of the Relief of the Commons and Diett of the saide Colleges … onlie", inevitably raised questions for the colleges of both universities. As has been pointed out earlier, the wording of the Act would, if it was taken literally, actually *reduce*, by as much as one-third of the old rent, the amount of income received from its agrarian properties that any college would be free to devote to other needs, however pressing.

As early as 1582 All Souls' consulted its Visitor, the archbishop of Canterbury, on the matter, and it received from Grindall the ruling "That out of the increase of corn so much money be subtracted as maketh the full summe of the old

104 Like Duxford, Burnham Thorpe was never brought within the Act, but, for some curious reason, the share of the tithes at Burnham Overy (*i.e.*, the "Garba" to which Caius referred in Statute 91) was commuted into a money rent and treated as corn money even though the Act could by no stretch of the imagination be construed to extend to it; ironically, the Garba was the last surviving source of corn money left when the dividend was paid for the last time in 1887: *Corn Book*, 1878–87.

105 Like Great Shelford, Aynells had been let under the Act in the previous year.

106 Apart from advowsons, a few small urban properties in Cambridge and Norwich and a potentially more substantial one in London, the college endowment consisted at that time almost entirely of agricultural and pastoral land and after the lease of the manor of Buristead by far the greater part of the endowment was within Sir Thomas Smith's Act, with the notable exception of its manorial land in Duxford and in Dorset.

107 From the twenty-three listed in Fletcher's Table in 1609 the number had risen to thirty by 1658 as a result of sub-divisions and purchases, and to thirty-one by 1799. When a new Grain Book was needed in 1799 the application of the Act had become so rigid that the college could safely have the details of corn rents that did not change with the market (*i.e.*, those other than prices) pre-printed in the ledger for decades to come. The number had dropped to twenty-eight by 1832 when the college had to discard that ledger in order to cope with the alteration of the size of the bushel brought about by the introduction of the imperial measure; and it did not change again. The individual money rents also remained virtually unaltered, and with them the system of accounting set out in 1609.

rent, and *employed to the common use of the College besides commons*, and the residue of the same increase to be employ'd for the bettering and amending of the wardens masters fellows and probationers commons in such proportion as heretofore hath been used, and this order his Grace taketh to stand with the equity of the statute."[108] It is not clear whether or when this ruling became known to any Cambridge college, nor is it clear whether any similar ruling on the Act was obtained by them; but Grindall would certainly have consulted others and it is not unlikely that the influential Lord Burghley would have been among those consulted, as he had managed the Bill in its passage through the Lords and was Chancellor of the University of Cambridge. Moreover, the archbishop's ruling was expressly affirmed four years later by his successor, Whitgift, who had himself been Master of Trinity College in Cambridge and for many years a leading figure in that university, and it seems likely that the ruling would have become known in Cambridge very soon thereafter, if not earlier.

The ruling of the archbishop addressed two issues: (i) Must all of the part of the rent that the tenant was now required to pay in corn (or its value) be devoted solely to the commons and diet of those who were members of the college at the time or could any of it still be regarded as unrestricted corporate income available for general corporate purposes like other rent? (ii) In what manner should the part reserved for "the bettering and amending" of commons and diet be expended?

To the first question the ruling gave a clear and precise answer: in addition to the two-thirds of the old rent which was not affected by the Act, the college could still use for its general corporate uses so much from what the tenant now had to pay in corn as made up the full amount of the old rent, *i.e.*, the other one-third. The rest of the increasingly valuable corn rent was to be employed for the bettering and amending of the commons of the members of the college. As a result the college could still treat as its unrestricted corporate income the same amount of rent as it would have received if the Act had not been passed, though it might now receive some of it in corn; but it could increase the amount available for those unrestricted purposes only if it was able to agree an increased money rent with the tenant. The ruling thus meant that the automatic protection against past and future inflation which Sir Thomas Smith had constructed so ingeniously would be enjoyed only in respect of the provision of commons, not repairs or other pressing needs.

To the second question the archbishop gave a much less precise answer: merely that the rest of the corn rent should be employed for "the wardens masters fellows and probationers commons in such proportion as heretofore hath been used"; this might suffice in the unique case of All Souls, which had

108 C.R.L. Fletcher, *Collectanea* vol. I, 1st Series, pp. 243–4 (Oxford, 1885); the italicised words are as printed there. The 'equity of the statute' was a doctrine well-known to lawyers of the time.

only a Warden and fellows, but it would provide little guidance to other colleges, even if they were aware of it.

As regards the first question, Caius' college appears to have adopted from the beginning the practice of crediting to its corporate income the nominal amount that represented the one-third of the old rent. We do not know whether it was aware of Grindall's ruling for All Souls' when it did so, but the practice did no more than reflect an interpretation of the Act which would seem to have been accepted by other colleges in both universities.[109] The consequence was that the bursar recorded only the amount of the money rent and the one-third part of the old rent in his half-yearly accounts of the college's income and expenditure; and he solemnly certified with his signature the receipt of that sum, even though he had in fact received substantially more payment from the tenant (either in corn or in money) in discharge of his obligations under the lease.[110]

The practice had the further consequence that the bursar's half-yearly accounts, which have been carefully preserved from 1609, contain no record of the further payment which the tenant was required under the Act to make either in corn or in money in lieu – neither its payment by the tenant nor its distribution by the bursar.[111] In fact, we have to wait until as late as 1657 for our first record of the manner and proportions in which it was allocated by the college for "the bettering and amending" of its commons.

The absence from the college's accounts of any record of the full amount of the corn rent paid by the tenant has led to the belief, by both Venn and Gross, that the tenant paid only the money rent to the bursar, the corn rent being paid to those whose commons were to be bettered and amended, namely, the Master and the senior fellows, and they suggested that those persons probably took the corn initially and merely accounted to the bursar for the one-third part of the old rent that was due to the college.[112] It is now clear, however, that the reverse was in fact the case: the ingenious 'ready-reckoner' that was entitled "*Mr Fletcher his arithmetical table*" and preserved in the Bursar's Book shows that the tenant paid both money and corn to the bursar as the representative of his landlord – as indeed he was legally obliged to do – and the bursar was

109 Modern accounts of the various ways in which colleges shared out dividends as between college and members, and between different classes of members, tend not to distinguish between the various types of dividend. It is therefore difficult to be sure which other colleges besides Caius also adopted the practice of allocating to the college from its corn rents only the one-third part of the old rent. For details of the practice of colleges in respect of dividends generally, see the later discussion of fines below.

110 See, *e.g.*, the receipts for the rents from the lessee of Croxley signed by the bursar in the *Bursar's Book*, 1610 (Lady Day) (by Parker) and 1611 (Michaelmas) (by Browne).

111 Nor, unfortunately, did the Bursar's Book contain any record of grain prices, since the unvarying amount credited to the college did not depend on market prices.

112 See *B.H.* IV(2), p. v.

then responsible for the allocation of both money and corn.[113] From the total amount received from the tenant he deducted a sum representing the money rent and the one-third part of the old rent and credited that sum to the college in his account of the income and expenditure for the half-year; what remained was available for distribution ("*sic restat summa optata dividenda pro granis*", as Fletcher explained in his Arithmetical Table).

Fletcher's table answers the first question posed by Archbishop Grindall, but it does not indicate how or to whom this dividend was shared out and we have to wait until as late as 1657 for the first indication of the college's answer to the second question posed by the archbishop's ruling: that answer is contained in the only surviving file of the college's Corn Rolls.[114] This file of Corn Rolls for the ten years 1657–67 provides us with our earliest illustration of the way in which the corn money was divided between the fortunate members of the college who shared in it.[115] The first charge upon the fund was a fee of £1 to the bursar, followed by small payments to some (but apparently not all) of the scholars on Dr Caius' own foundation, leaving the bulk of the corn money to be divided into fourteen shares: two for the Master and twelve for the senior fellows; with the bursar taking as his perquisite any fractional surplus remaining from the division.[116] The junior fellows and the other scholars received nothing.

There is no reason to doubt that the system of division set out in 1657 had been the practice of the college from the beginning.[117] The small payment to some of the scholars may have been a concession to the direction in the Act that the corn rents should be used for the maintenance of the college and "the Fellowes and Scollers", but it is difficult to explain the restriction to scholars on

113 The instructions entitled "*Mr Fletcher his arithmetical table*" in the *Bursar's Book*, 1609 are mentioned above. Fletcher's table dates from the early seventeenth century, but there can be no doubt that the practice described there had been adopted by the college from the start. For the table see the note appended to this chapter.

114 *Corn Roll*, 1657 (Lady Day). This is the earliest of the eighteen half-yearly Corn Rolls (1657–67) that were gathered together in the one file which survives; the Corn Roll was audited by the Master (Dell in the case of the earliest rolls) as one of the two bursars *ex officio*. Since only the sums due to the college were carried to the college's permanent accounts, these fragile rolls remained as the earliest record of the distribution of surplus of the corn rent. This one surviving file of rolls has only recently come to notice and was not known to Gross when he included his account of corn rents in his *Chronicle of the Estates of Gonville and Caius College* in 1911: *B.H.* IV(2); the file appears to have been unknown also to Venn.

115 For this one surviving file of Corn Rolls, see p. 509 below.

116 In addition the bursar took out of each individual's share a further fee of 5s: Gostlin's Note Book (discussed below). Gostlin's Note Book shows us that the same entitlement to any small sum remaining from the division was also enjoyed by the registrary in his distribution of fines. No doubt other college officers enjoyed similar perquisites.

117 Caius' college seems never to have varied its practice in relation either to corn money or to entry fines. In contrast, many other colleges changed their practices from time to time in the seventeenth century (*H.U.C.*, II, ch. 8, p. 272).

one foundation alone, and even then only some of them.[118] The total exclusion of the junior fellows is a little easier to explain, though equally indefensible.

The Frankland fellows

In allocating a greater share to the Master, the college was reflecting the practice of many other colleges; as at St John's, the Master received twice as much as a fellow.[119] The division into fourteen shares gave effect to this practice by allocating one share to each of the fellows and two to the Master, but it reflected the assumption that there would be twelve fellows.[120] The acceptance of Joyce Frankland's bequest, however, immediately raised the number to eighteen and the college was faced with the question whether the new fellows should be equally entitled to share in the half-yearly dividend of corn money. As is well known, they were totally excluded from doing so. The exclusion again reflects the practice in some of the other colleges, though by no means all of them;[121] but it runs counter to the clear decree on the status of the Frankland fellowships which the college passed on 11 December 1592 and solemnly included in the 'authoritative' copy of the Statutes that had been signed by Caius. That decree expressly made an exception for corn money when it ruled that the new Frankland fellows should have only the annual stipend of £7 which Mrs Frankland had specified and that they should not enjoy dividends *other than corn money* ("*nisi pro granis*").[122] It is not known precisely why or when the

[118] The restriction to scholars on Caius' own foundation, and even then only some of them, is curious; but the restriction is later apparent in the Absence Books, which also show that these small payments varied slightly in amount from year to year and between different recipients. The reasons for the restrictions and the variations are obscure. The payment to scholars was discontinued in the nineteenth century. In St John's, scholars shared with fellows in the ratio of 2 to 1: *H.U.C.*, II, ch. 8, p. 272.

[119] The proportion allocated by colleges to their Masters differed considerably: *H.U.C.*, II, ch. 8, p. 272. The Provost of King's was allocated ten shares to every one share allocated to a fellow; whereas the Master of St John's, as in Caius, had two shares. In Pembroke the Master's share did not diverge from that of a fellow until 1646.

[120] There had been ten fellows when Caius obtained his charter of re-foundation, and in Statute 2 he envisaged that his college would have thirteen when he made provision for a further three fellows on his own foundation. By the time of his death (and thus by the time of the Corn Act) it had been accepted that there had been only nine funded fellowships before the re-foundation and that Caius' three fellowships took the number to twelve: see "*The Governing Body*", § VI. 1 above.

[121] Junior fellows enjoyed a dividend in both St John's and Trinity, though a much smaller proportion than senior fellows in both cases: *Riches and Responsibility*, pp. 48–9; *H.U.C.*, II, ch. 8, pp. 272–3. In Clare, fellows on the Exeter foundation were excluded: *ibid.*

[122] The ruling decreed that they should receive only the £7 a year that she had specified and should not enjoy distributions, liveries, dividends *other than for grain*, commemoration moneys or hearth money "since nothing is given under that heading, but only the stipend of £7, and nothing more can be done without prejudice to the fellows and detriment to the College": see "*The Frankland Decree (1592)*", Appendix E.

college decided to disregard that exception; but it is unlikely that the issue would have arisen immediately, for it would have been assumed, almost certainly, that the entitlement of a donor's new fellows should be restricted to a share in such corn money as arose out of land provided by that donor's benefaction, not corn money arising out of the college's own estates (since that would have entailed "prejudice of the fellows and the detriment to the College" and would have contravened Statute 36).[123] If so, no question of corn money would have arisen until Mrs Frankland's benefaction had brought agrarian land to the college, and this did not happen until the Manor of D'Abernoons at Duxford, purchased with her bequest, came into the college's possession in the early years of the seventeenth century.[124]

The decision to exclude the Frankland fellows and restrict the sharing of corn money to the holders of the twelve 'old' fellowships that had existed before 1592 had clearly been taken by the time that the Wendy fellowship was re-established in 1609: for it was carefully recorded that the holder of the Wendy fellowship was not to have or expect "anie profit or commoditie of the said Colledge more than the sum of ten pounds so to him allowed as aforesaid, and not anie divdencye or other profit peculiar or proper to the twelve senior places or Fellowships of the foundation of the same Colledge, but shall be in all things of the like order and sort as the Fellowes of Joyce Franklin's foundation".[125] It was equally carefully recorded at each subsequent admission of any junior fellow that the person elected had been informed of, and had agreed to, the ruling at his admission.[126]

123 "We lay down categorically that the College shall not be burdened with maintaining any fellow or scholar, or with supplementing his stipend through the grant of free victuals, clothing and accommodation, beyond what is provided by the income of the property or estate provided by his Founder or Benefactor."

124 The property had been bought with £1,540 left to the college by Joyce Frankland to buy lands of the annual value of £70. 10s. 0d. Her executors, of whom Legge was one, had been somewhat dilatory in completing the execution of her will and most of the land was still in the hands of the trustees under her will at the time of his death; following his death the trustees conveyed their (reversionary) freehold interest in the manor to the college in 1611: *B.H.* IV(2), p. 41. Duxford was a valuable agrarian property and, being situated conveniently close to Cambridge, might seem to have been an ideal subject for the application of the Corn Act. In fact, it was subject to an existing lease which had been granted at a substantial rent (£62 p.a.) before it came to the college and was not within the Corn Act; the lease was always renewed by the college at that rent until 1867 and was never brought within the Act.

125 *Annals*, p. 222.

126 The practice was extended to the Perse and Stokys fellowships when they were established. When the Wortley fellowships were established in the eighteenth century the full ruling was recorded afresh in the *Gesta* and it was subscribed to not only by the Master and seven senior fellows but also by the Masters of Trinity and St John's as the visitors of Wortley's foundation: *Gesta*, 12 October 1769. The practice of recording of a junior fellow's assent to the ruling at his admission was maintained until Dr Caius' statutes were repealed in 1860: *Gesta*, 20 November 1857 (the new S.C. Smith fellowship).

It has been generally assumed that the decision in December 1592 to limit the six new Frankland fellows to the stipend which their benefactress had mentioned and to allow them nothing further ("*ac praeterea nihil*") – specifically excluding them from the perquisites allowed to fellows by Caius in his statutes (distributions, liveries, dividends other than for grain, commemoration moneys and hearth moneys) and from the holding of any office unless it had been declined by each senior fellow – was a curmudgeonly act of pure self-interest which created, from the beginning, a festering financial gulf between senior and junior fellows as well as the great constitutional gulf created by the denial to the Frankland fellows of any part in the government of the college. In fact, the picture is a little different. Considerations of parity between fellows rather than greed seem to have prompted the decision; for the stipend of the new Frankland fellows was *greater*, not less, than that of the existing fellows, and the perquisites enjoyed by the latter merely restored the balance.[127]

The position by the time of the Restoration

Despite the total silence of the college's accounts and the absence of any continuous record of corn money in the sixteenth and seventeenth centuries, we are fortunate that two pieces of evidence have survived in addition to Fletcher's Arithmetical Table mentioned earlier: first, the Corn Rolls, a single file of very fragile annual rolls recording the full amount of the corn rent received from tenants for the ten years 1657 to 1667; and second, a personal account book kept by John Gostlin[128] in which he recorded his payments to the Master and

[127] See "*Stipends*", § VI. 4, at pp. 430–1 above.

[128] Gonville and Caius College 1647: *B.H.* I, p. 369. He was the fourth John Gostlin who was a fellow of the college during the seventeenth century. The first had been elected in 1592 and had been chosen as Master by the fellows on Legge's death in 1607, but the election had been summarily set aside in favour of Branthwaite at the instance of Robert Cecil, the Earl of Salisbury (Brooke, *History*, pp. 106–7; corrected in *H.U.C.*, II, pp. 406–7 and n. 89); on Branthwaite's death, he had again been elected Master: *B.H.* III, p. 74–85. The second, "John Gostlin the Younger", was a nephew of the Master and had been a junior fellow (1626–31) before he married: *B.H.* I, p. 244. The old Master had also had a great-nephew named John who was his godson, and that third John Gostlin was a fellow fleetingly, for a few months in 1649, before being ejected as a delinquent Royalist: *B.H.* I, p. 340.

Our John Gostlin (the fourth) was the son of John Gostlin the Younger, and thus a great-nephew of the former Master and a cousin of the ejected delinquent. A Royalist himself, he migrated to Peterhouse from Caius in 1653 during Dell's mastership, no doubt influenced by his cousin's ejection. He returned to Caius at the Restoration and became a senior fellow by royal mandate in 1661. He was made bursar immediately on his return and held that office from 1661 to 1664. He was steward in 1667–68, and the following year he became president until his death in 1704. Fortunately for us, he kept his personal account not only for the four years he was bursar and during the year he was steward, but also in the years when he acted as (or on behalf of) the registrary during his time as president; in those years he recorded in his note book the distribution of the entry fines paid on the renewal of beneficial leases. The approval of each

fellows of corn money during the four years 1661 to 1664 when he was bursar and, later, his distribution of entry fines on leases while he was president. These two sources enable us to draw a reasonably clear picture of the operation of the Corn Act in the college by the middle of the seventeenth century.

Like Fletcher's Table in 1609, the annual Corn Rolls include for each tenancy the details of the money-rent, the amounts of wheat and malt and their nominal statutory value; but they also include the current market value for the particular half-year and, significantly, the total sum of money that each particular tenant has to pay: they show clearly that payment is now entirely in money, not in kind. The fragile Corn Rolls record the information in the same ten columns that were used in the later Grain Books in the eighteenth and nineteenth centuries:[129] (1) the rent specified in the Act as payable in money;[130] (2) the amount of wheat; (3) its current market value (*Summa*); (4) the amount of malt; (5) its current market value (*Summa*); (6) the sum of these two values (*Summa Granorum*);[131] (7) the third part of the "olde rent" to be deducted from that sum (*Summa Deducenda*); (8) the amount remaining to be divided among the Master, senior fellows and scholars in the manner described above (*Summa Dividenda*);[132] (9) the sum to be entered in the Bursar's Book as income due to the college (*Sum' Lib' Bur'*);[133] (10) the total sum of money to be received from the tenant (*Summa Recipienda*).[134] In the Corn Rolls only a few of the columns include a total and occasionally a whole column is omitted,[135] but the column giving the *Summa Dividenda* is invariably included and added up.[136]

entry fine since 1651 is recorded in the surviving Gesta, but Gostlin's note book is the first, and apparently only, surviving record of the actual distribution to fellows of their shares before the eighteenth century.

The association of the Gostlin family with the college in the seventeenth century is further complicated by the fact that a further relative, Thomas Gostlin, was a fellow from 1613 to 1651, and so concurrently with each of the first three John Gostlins in turn; unlike his relatives, Thomas seems to have remained on good terms with the Puritan Master (Dell): *B.H.* I, p. 189.

129 The ten columns in the later Grain Books are admirably described by Gross: *B.H.* IV(2), p. v. In those books each of the ten columns is carefully totalled; in this way the totals of the rows and the columns produced a cross-check. In the later books the five columns and totals that do not vary from year to year (*i.e.*, columns 1, 2, 4, 7 and 9) are pre-printed in the book for decades in advance: the practice demonstrates vividly the deep-rooted assumption that rents will not be altered and that corn money will continue to be paid even if the property has not been let or the terms of the lease no longer required the payment of a corn rent.

130 *I.e.*, the money rent.

131 *I.e.*, the corn rent.

132 *I.e.*, the corn money.

133 *I.e.*, the money rent and the third part of the "olde rent".

134 *I.e.*, the money rent and the whole of the corn rent.

135 *E.g.*, in 1667.

136 The practice of recording the total amounts of wheat and malt introduced by Fletcher at the beginning of the century also appears in some rolls.

By a happy chance the ten-year period covered by the one surviving file of Corn Rolls overlaps the four years during which John Gostlin kept in a personal note book an account of all the payments he made to the Master and each of the senior fellows while he was bursar. The value of Gostlin's note book in the present context is that it records the final payment in cash made half-yearly by the bursar to the Master and each of the senior fellows and, as such, includes not only the stipends, liveries and other amounts payable through the college's half-yearly accounts (the *Liber Rationalis* and the Bursar's Book), but also the corn money which, as has been mentioned earlier, was always omitted from those accounts of the college's income and expenditure. From these four sources, the *Liber Rationalis*, the Bursar's Book, the Corn Rolls and Gostlin's note book, it is possible to piece together a picture of the half-yearly income that a senior fellow was receiving from the college each year by the middle of the seventeenth century and, in particular, the major contribution to the income of such fellows that was now made by the payment of corn money and the change in the structure and character of the fellowship that it had helped to bring about in the hundred years since Caius had formulated his Statutes.[137]

By the time of the Restoration the statutory stipend of a senior fellow had been twice augmented by increases and those increases, as a general rule, sufficed to meet his commons account and leave him with a small credit balance.[138] The augmentations thus served to restore the stipend to the level which Caius had contemplated in his statutes, *i.e.*, a very modest maintenance grant for a young graduate in the years in which he studied for a further degree. As a result, corn money was no longer needed to meet a deficit on a senior fellow's commons account and had now become a regular payment in ready money – literally, 'pocket-money' – made half-yearly to the fellow by the bursar after the Lady Day and Michaelmas audits. The exact amount of each payment inevitably varied with the market price of corn, which could fluctuate sharply, but corn money would on average bring to each senior fellow £15–20 a year, and in the quite exceptional year 1661–62 it rose to nearer £40.[139] Although it fell

[137] See "*Stipends*", § VI. 4, at pp. 432–4 above.

[138] *Ibid.* Two increases in stipends (each of £5 p.a.) had been made before the Civil War, the first out of the manor and mills at Great Shelford purchased in 1614 and the second out of Weeting Manor purchased in 1632; these brought the stipend to just under £16 p.a. By 1748 it had been possible to make further very modest increases from the purchase of new land. Until it started to purchase government stock in 1766, however, the college had necessarily had to rely almost exclusively on the rent from land for its income and the system of beneficial leases inevitably kept that rent artificially low, whether the land was agrarian or urban. After 1766 the college was able to make more substantial increases in stipends and in 1781 it started doing so. See MS 621/457 and *B.H.* IV(2), p. vii; *Lib. Rat. 1795–1815*, p. 1, and "*Stipends*", § VI. 4 above.

[139] The prices of wheat and malt rose very sharply after the harvest of 1661: from 4s. 0d. and 2s. 0d. a bushel in 1657 to 10s. 6d. and 4s. 6d. at Lady Day in 1662, before dropping to 2s. 8d. and 2s. 0d. by Michaelmas 1666. Prices continued to be low for one hundred years and reached the 1662 prices only twice (in 1709–10 and 1795–96) before 1800: *Corn Book 1732–98*.

during the remaining years of the seventeenth century, corn money normally provided at least half of the 'pocket-money' that a senior fellow enjoyed; and it could provide as much as seven-tenths of that pocket-money in a year when corn prices were high.[140] As will be seen later, he could also look forward to receiving periodically his share of the entry fines payable by tenants on the renewal of their leases. The fine on any particular property would be payable only on the occasion of the renewal of the lease and thus not more frequently than once in seven years;[141] but the number of properties and the differing dates for their renewal meant that a fellow could, over a period of years, expect to receive just over £10 annually from entry fines by the second half of the seventeenth century.[142]

These three factors, corn money, augmentation of stipends and entry fines, had combined to create a very sharp difference between senior and junior fellows.[143] That difference became more and more severe and led to increasingly bitter acrimony in the following two centuries.[144]

The eighteenth and nineteenth centuries

In contrast to the preceding two centuries we have three sets of full and continuous records for the eighteenth and nineteenth centuries: (i) the Corn Books, which set out the half-yearly amounts due under the 1576 Act on each Lady Day and Michaelmas in respect of the individual tenancies for every year from 1732 to the expiry in 1887 of the last lease granted under the Act; (ii) the Absence Books, which record the precise distribution of the shares of corn money half-yearly from 1716 onwards; and (iii) on the fly-leaves of the Corn Books a convenient list of the relevant prices of wheat and malt in the Cambridge market from 1694 to 1878. Accordingly, for the purposes of the present work, the story of the corn rents in the eighteenth and nineteenth centuries need be summarised only briefly here.

140 At Lady Day in the exceptional year 1662, in addition to his half-year's stipend and livery (£7. 6s. 8d. which was credited to him against his commons account), John Felton was paid, for the six months, £4. 1s. 10d. in dividends *pro foco* and *pro cubiculis* and distributions, £3. 10s. as Greek and Hebrew lecturer, and £19. 7s. in corn money; from this sum of £26. 18s. 10d. the bursar took a fee of 5s. for himself personally and also deducted £1. 5s. 5d. for Felton's debt on his commons account, leaving him with £25. 8s. 5d. pocket money: *Gostlin's Note Book* and the *Lib. Rat.* (1662, Lady Day).

141 For a period, the renewal of many leases very soon after the Restoration in 1660 led to a 'bunching' of renewal dates around 1667 and at seven-year intervals thereafter.

142 See the section on *Entry fines: Beneficial leases* later; see also "*Stipends*", § VI. 4 above.

143 See the petition of Richard Watson (Gonville and Caius College 1628), who had been a junior fellow until he was ejected as a Royalist in 1644 and was re-elected to his junior fellowship in 1660; being much older than the normal junior fellow, he petitioned the king saying that "his only income is £10"; the college was moved to make him some allowance: *B.H.* I, p. 286.

144 See "*The Norfolk Preference*", § VI. 3 and "*Stipends*", § VI. 4 above.

The price of corn in the eighteenth century naturally fluctuated from year to year, but overall it remained flat during the first three quarters of the century. In contrast, the other two factors which had contributed to the financial gulf between senior and junior fellows in the previous century, namely, stipends and entry fines, enjoyed a greater increase over the period. Consequently one might expect that corn money would have made a relatively smaller contribution to the annual income of senior fellows. In fact, however, the absence of any overall increase in corn rents did not reduce the relative importance of corn money as a source of income for senior fellows. This was due to two factors.

First, corn money was a payment for the relief of "commons and diet", and although the Master was entitled to his two shares whether or not he was resident, only *resident* senior fellows qualified for a share of the twelve remaining fourteenths. Since the practice of habitual non-residence (which had now became normal among the junior fellows) spread to the senior fellows in the course of the eighteenth century,[145] the share of corn money to which a resident fellow was entitled grew larger as the number who qualified dropped.[146] From the beginning of the nineteenth century the number in residence would rarely rise above half of the full complement of twelve in any accounting period and consequently the share paid to each resident fellow was regularly at least twice the one-fourteenth share to which he had originally been entitled: he now regularly enjoyed a share that equalled or exceeded the double share to which the Master was entitled.[147] Corn money in effect became an academic stipend for those senior fellows who chose to remain in Cambridge, and as such was not subject to the same degree of public criticism that was increasingly levelled against entry fines as a source of dividend.

The second factor that maintained the importance of corn money was the dramatic rise in the price of corn during the Revolutionary and Napoleonic Wars. This reached a peak as early as 1801. The autumn harvest of 1799 brought the Michaelmas price of wheat to double the price that had prevailed at Lady Day earlier that year;[148] and the consequent scarcity that inevitably resulted during

145 By the middle of the century there were frequently no more than half the senior fellows in residence. In the case of the junior fellows, only one or two would be regularly in residence; the Perse fellows were almost entirely non-resident. The remuneration of junior fellows had become so low that they could hardly afford to reside: "*Stipends*", § VI. 4 above.

146 As early as Michaelmas 1767 the number dropped as low as 3½ (one resident fellow having been admitted halfway through the qualifying period) and the share of a fellow was £50. 13s. od., whereas the Master's one-seventh was £29. 11s. od.

147 The Master was entitled to two-fourteenths, *i.e.*, a double-share, whatever the number of fellows in residence and whether or not he was in residence. The resident fellows, on the other hand, shared the remaining twelve-fourteenths between them: if, for example, only four fellows were resident, each of them would get three-fourteenths. For the ruling that the Master never took more than one-seventh, and for the qualifying length of residence for the fellows, see *Gesta*, 7 April 1671.

148 6s. 3¼d. (wheat) and 4s. 10¾d. (malt) a bushel at Lady Day; 12s. 6¾d. and 5s. 8¼d. at Michaelmas.

the winter forced the price of both wheat and malt even higher in the spring of 1800.[149] A second bad harvest followed that autumn and at Michaelmas the resulting rise in prices produced for the first time a half-yearly dividend of more than £100 for each of the five senior fellows in residence.[150] Scarcity over the winter again forced prices higher, and in the spring of 1801 prices and dividend reached peaks that were unrivalled before or later.[151] 1800–1 was indeed a 'good' year for the five resident senior fellows, if not for the rest of the country: never before or after did fellows enjoy even one half-yearly payment of corn money of £100, let alone two.[152]

Corn prices never again reached the heights of 1801 but, as is well-known, they remained high not only throughout the Napoleonic Wars but during the following decades until Sir Robert Peel's repeal of the import duties on corn took effect in 1849.[153] Corn rents accordingly also remained high, and since the number of the twelve senior fellows in residence during those decades rarely rose above half, corn money remained a substantial part of the stipends of those fellows who chose to remain in academic life in Cambridge.

In more and more cases in the course of the nineteenth century the name of the tenant is entered in college's Corn Books as being "*Collegium*". In some earlier instances this may reflect the fact that the holding was untenanted at the time and that the college was experiencing difficulty in leasing its farms in a time of agricultural depression, like other colleges,[154] and in such cases we may find that the name of a genuine tenant re-appears in later years.[155] In an increasing number of cases, however, no other name than "*Collegium*" is ever entered subsequently, and in those instances we may be confident that the entry does not reflect a failure to lease the property, but indicates that it is no longer held under a beneficial lease and that the tenant now pays a full rack-rent in place of the traditional rent to which

149 15s. 9¼d. and 9s. 7d. a bushel.

150 18s. 10d. and 11s. 2¼d. a bushel. The (Michaelmas 1800) dividend for each of the five fellows was £104. 19s. od., compared with £81. 9s. od. for the Master.

151 22s. 2d. and 11s. 2d. a bushel. This produced (at Lady Day 1801) a dividend of £116. 6s. od. for each fellow and £97. 18s. 6d. for the Master. This price of 177s. 4d. per quarter for wheat may be compared with the price of 6s. 8d. per quarter by which Sir Thomas Smith had calculated a tenant's obligation under his Act.

152 The payment of £220. 5s. od. for the twelve-month period from Lady Day 1800 to Lady Day 1801 (*i.e.*, £104. 19s. od. at Michaelmas 1800 and £116. 6s. od. at Lady 1801) may be compared with the payment of £16. 10s. for the corresponding period in 1664–65, and with the half-yearly sum of £4. 10s. in Fletcher's table in 1609.

153 9 & 10 Vic., c. xxii (1846), after a bad harvest in 1845. Another bad harvest and "the partial Failure of certain Crops" caused an emergency suspension of duty the following year: 10 & 11 Vic., cc. 1, 2, 3 (1847).

154 *E.g.*, St John's: Linehan, *St John's College Cambridge: A History* (2011), pp. 222, 233.

155 The college was temporarily named as the tenant of its land in Caxton during the years 1820–26, and in the next year a genuine tenant "Johnson" re-appears: *Corn Book 1799–1831*.

the 1576 Act had applied.[156] It is a striking tribute to the stubborn longevity of the notion of corn money as a right enjoyed by resident senior fellows that the college took over the tenant's obligation to pay corn rent in such cases and included the appropriate sum in the calculation of each half-year's corn money.[157] The fact that in many cases no corn rent was in fact being collected from the tenant meant that it became a futile exercise to calculate for each tenant his aliquot share of corn money and enter the figure in the Corn Book, and it is not surprising that the relevant columns were eventually left unfilled.[158] The only function of the Corn Book was now – as it had been of Mr Fletcher's Table in 1609 – to add up the total value of all the wheat and malt, deduct from it the (unchanging) total of the amount to be credited to the college and record the result as the amount to be divided as corn money. In 1878 only one property (Foulden) was still held under a beneficial lease and the college promptly discarded its expensive pre-printed Corn Book half-used; instead it substituted a smaller book in which the only details recorded were the quantities and value of the corn notionally due from two tenants: "*Collegium*" and the tenant of Foulden.[159] When the beneficial lease of Foulden was finally run out in 1887, the payment of corn money as a dividend finally ceased just three hundred years after the first payment had been made in 1579.[160]

[156] In some cases a tenant who was still paying a corn rent might no longer hold under a beneficial lease and might be paying a commercial rent that included the corn rent. In such a case the tenant will continue to appear as the 'tenant' until the lessee finally pays a full rack-rent and the college takes over the obligation to pay corn money to the Master and senior fellows: *e.g.*, Barningham, *B.H.* IV(2), p. 6.

[157] Although corn rent was no longer being paid by the lessee, it remained a straightforward task to calculate with certainty the precise amount of the corn rent and the corn money that would be payable under the Act; the college was thus able to regard the requirements of the statute as sufficiently satisfied by paying the amount of any corn money itself out of its general income. It was different as regards the fine that would have been payable on the renewal of a beneficial lease when it was being run out. When that was happening, the tenant would pay neither a fine nor a rack-rent while the beneficial lease was being run out (*i.e.*, in the seventh and fourteenth years), and the college itself would pay, as a dividend, the fine that the tenant no longer paid. When the beneficial lease had been completely run out and was replaced by a rack-rent, the fellows would be paid a fixed stipend in lieu of the fine: *e.g.*, Barningham and Burnham: *B.H.* IV(2), pp. 6, 16.

[158] *I.e.*, columns 6, 8 and 10 described by Gross: see n. 129 above. The practice started as early as 1840: *Corn Book 1832–1878*.

[159] The book also recorded the intermittent payment of the money value of the 16 quarters of barley to which the college was entitled from the Rectory of Burnham Overy (the *Garba* mentioned by Caius in Statute 91). Until 1847 the right to the 16 quarters had been rented out at £8 per annum for many years and for some reason the annual payment of the £8 and subsequently of the money value of the 16 quarters had always been included in the calculation of corn money even though the 1576 Act clearly did not apply to it. (As has been mentioned above, the Manor of Burnham Thorpe itself was never leased under the 1576 Act.) It is ironic that a payment to which the Act did not apply was the last to survive in respect of corn money.

[160] The instance in 1579 had been the lease of the college's land in Cherryhinton. A final payment of £30. 18s. 9d. was made in 1887 to each of the five remaining senior fellows who held their

ENTRY FINES

In his statutes Caius made frequent reference to the term "fine" in two of the three technical senses in which it was understood by lawyers in the sixteenth century. The meaning of these senses was different in each case and was so well understood at the time that Caius did not feel it necessary to distinguish them explicitly even when he used them in more than one sense in the same statute, despite his characteristic penchant for expounding his – often idiosyncratic – etymology for technical terms. The common factor in the different uses of the word was, as its Latin origin would suggest, the concept of a payment or other settlement that concluded some legal dispute or negotiation; apart from this, the three meanings were quite different from each other. These were (i) the penal fine or mulct, a money payment that brought an end to proceedings in lieu of any corporal or capital punishment.[161] Then there was (ii) the conveyancing fine or final concord, a transfer of property in settlement of an entirely collusive law suit that produced a particularly effective conveyance of freehold land and was much used by lawyers of the time for that reason; it is understandable that the term was not used here by Caius in this second sense, for he was concerned with the leasing of the college's lands, not their sale, and as a bachelor he would not have had occasion to become acquainted with its highly technical effects in barring descendants from disputing it. It is the third use of the term that is of interest in relation to dividends: (iii) the entry fine or payment made to the 'lord' by a would-be tenant to secure his admission to the estate or its grant to him, as in Statutes 93 and 95.

As Gross has explained,[162] these entry fines arise in relation to four categories of property so far as Caius' college was concerned: copyholds of inheritance, copyholds for lives, beneficial leases and building leases. It should be stressed that the law viewed the four as being of two very different kinds: (a) the fines customarily payable on entry into a copyhold estate, and (b) those paid on the conclusion of contractual negotiations between a would-be lessee and the landowner for the grant or renewal of a term of years or building lease.

Copyhold estates were "real property", interests which were, by the sixteenth century, fully recognised and protected both by the Courts of Equity and by the

fellowships under Dr Caius' statutes or those that had replaced them in 1860; the names of the five recipients are well-known to every student of the history of the college: Drosier, Venn, Gross, Roberts and Lock. Thereafter they received £50 annually in lieu. The archaic nature of the payment of corn money by 1887 was emphasised by the need for the bursar to write to the bursar of Trinity to ascertain the prices that wheat and malt had reached in the Cambridge market on the preceding market day (in a letter now loosely interleaved in the final Corn Book 1879–1887).

161 As in Statutes 18, 19, 20, 22, 23, 24, 27, 28, 45, 49, 55, 68, 71, 72, 73, 74, 76, 77, 78, 79. The multitude of references to penal fines brings out well the tone of Caius' statutes.

162 *B.H.* IV(2), pp. vi–vii.

Courts of Common Law as estates in land.[163] By Caius' time the copyhold tenant had come to be regarded not as holding "at the will of the lord" but "at the will of the lord and by copy of the court roll"; and what he held was an estate equivalent in duration and alienability to that of a freeholder.[164] It was now regarded as a "freehold estate" (for life or in fee simple, depending on the words of the grant), even though it was not held by free tenure but by the custom of the manor and was subject to the services and incidents countenanced by that custom. It was not open to a lord to alter the custom, and consequently the services and most of the incidents had long lost virtually all their value by the time of the abolition of copyhold tenure by the Law of Property Act 1922; but they were still valuable to the lord in Caius' day, and he attached great importance to the college's retaining the lordship of a manor, insisting that it should never lease more than the "scite of the manor" and the demesne lands.[165]

Terms of years, on the other hand, were regarded by the law as "personal property" which resulted entirely from a contract between the parties, and it was open to those parties to agree on such terms as they wished, unconstrained by any manorial custom. This left a lessee in a much weaker position than a copyhold tenant.

Copyholds of inheritance

The college's manorial properties were predominantly located in East Anglia and in them the copyhold tenants had come to hold estates of inheritance. Such tenants had originally held by villein tenure entirely at the will of the lord, and on the death of a tenant the payment of an entry fine had been intended as a real inducement to the lord to accept the dead tenant's heir in his place; but the customary expectation of the heir's acceptance by the lord had long hardened into a right of inheritance by virtue of the wording of the grant (*i.e.*, the "words of limitation") and the custom of the manor, and it had been recognised as such in the lord's manor court. By the sixteenth century the security of tenure of the

163 In Sir Edward Coke's quaint words: "But now copyholders stand upon a sure ground; now they weigh not their lord's displeasure, they shake not at every sudden blast of wind, they eat, drink and sleep securely; only having a special care of the main chance, (viz.) to perform carefully what duties and services soever their tenure doth exact, and custom doth require …. For if the lord's anger grow to expulsion, the law hath provided several weapons of remedy; for it is at his election either to sue a *sub-poena*, or an action of trespass against his lord. Time has dealt very favourably with copyholders in divers respects." (*The Compleat Copyholder*, section IX.)

164 *Ibid.*, sections XVI and XVII.

165 See *Caius' purchase of the Manors of Croxley, Runcton and Burnham Thorpe* in "*Supplementary Notes to Caius' Statutes*", § IV. 3, at pp. 303–4. The rents and services of the copyholders could still exceed the amount of rent from a manor's demesne lands in the middle of the seventeenth century, as in Great Shelford in 1624: *B.H.* IV(2), pp. 9, 80. The lord's right to timber and minerals as 'incidents' never ceased to be valuable and they were preserved by the Law of Property Act in 1922.

copyhold tenant and his right to alienate, coupled with the right of his heir to succeed, had been recognised as a freehold estate in fee simple by the law of the land. In addition to enforcing the customs of the manor and protecting the security of a copyhold tenant's tenure by writs of trespass[166] the common law courts had developed the rule that a manorial custom would be valid only if it were adjudged reasonable, and they had come to regard as unreasonable any custom which required an entry fine exceeding one (or, at most, two) year's annual value to be paid on the alienation or inheritance of a copyholder's fee simple.

The entry fines payable by an incoming heir or purchaser of a copyhold estate in these manors remained a payment made in the court of the manor on the occasion of the enrolment of the transfer on the court rolls. They were regarded as an integral part of the revenue of the lordship and as such were always credited to the college in the Bursar's Book as occasional income (*extraordinaria recepta*) in the same way as the tenant's rent was credited to it as annual income (*ordinaria recepta*); they never formed part of the dividends which came to be shared out among the Master and fellows.[167] As has been said earlier, it was a cardinal point with Caius that the college should always retain possession of the lordship of any manor it owned and he was emphatic that any lease of the manor should be expressly and rigidly restricted to the "scite of the manor" and its demesne lands, thereby ensuring that the college retained the right to the services and incidents due from its copyholders and the right to hold the manorial court and appoint and dismiss the steward.[168]

Copyholds for lives

This was the tenure by which copyhold lands were held in the college's two manors in Dorset, namely, Bincombe and Oborne. Tenancies for lives were a common form of copyhold tenure, particularly in the West Country, and they varied greatly from place to place: some were for as many as seven lives, with or without the right of widows to remain during their widowhood; in some the specified lives were those of grantees who might hold concurrently or successively; in others there was only one grantee and tenure was thereby limited to

[166] By the same writ of trespass *quare clausum fregit* as freeholders; in contrast, the lessee was restricted to the writ *de ejection firmae*.

[167] In his statutes Caius caused some confusion by combining provisions for entry fines on copyholds with entry fines on leases of Croxley, Runcton and Burnham Thorpe in a single statute: see Statute 95 and the note thereto. Despite that possible confusion, the fines from the *copyholds* of those manors were entered in the Bursar's Book as "extraordinary income" like all other copyhold fines; in contrast, the (far more valuable) fines on the *leases* there were always divided between the Master and senior fellows in the same way as the leasehold fines on other property.

[168] See Statute 86 above.

his life. In the case of the college's two manors in Dorset the tenancy was held for three lives with right of widowhood and the customary practice was for the tenant or tenants to apply, during his or their lives, to have a new life – usually the next generation – admitted to the tenancy in return for a fine. As Gross has noted, "the annual rent of each tenancy was exceedingly small and, not being affected by the Corn Act of 1576, remained so".[169] Furthermore, the amount of any fine was restricted by the custom of the realm.

The crucial feature of the tenure was that the grant was for life or lives and, in contrast to the fee simple interest enjoyed by the college's copyhold tenants in the eastern counties, there was no right of inheritance on death. Consequentially it was possible for the college to contemplate converting the tenure from copyhold to leasehold in the middle of the eighteenth century.[170] It was at first intended to substitute leases for ninety-nine years terminable on three lives (with widowhood) in place of the customary copyholds; but this caused alarm that the tenants would lose their parliamentary vote if they held only a term of years, since it would be merely personal property. The college's copyholds in Dorset were instead gradually replaced with leases for life; these, being created by deed and not by copy, destroyed the copyhold tenure and conferred a qualifying freehold estate upon the tenant, thereby preserving his entitlement to vote.

Despite any change in their legal status, the annual rents of the tenants in Bincombe and Oborne remained, in Gross' words, exceedingly small: the total of the rents from Bincombe had been £15. 9s. 0d. at the time of its purchase by the college in 1570, and it was still no more than £15. 12s. 8d. in 1794, even though the extended yearly value was £453. 9s. 5d.[171] It is not surprising therefore that the fines paid by the tenants on the admission of a new life formed "the real value of the Manor to the College".[172] Like the fines from the college's manors in the east of England, the fines for Bincombe and Oborne were carried to the Bursar's Book and were accumulated. As the Dorset fines increased in value the

169 *B.H.* IV(2), p. vii.

170 In 1752, following a survey of Bincombe and Oborne by the bursar and another fellow, the college resolved to grant terms of years as the copyhold estates expired. Having taken (somewhat unreliable) legal advice, its steward of the manor there proceeded to prepare leases for ninety-nine years determinable on three lives, notwithstanding Caius' absolute prohibition in Statute 86 against the granting of leases exceeding twenty years. What seems to have frustrated the exercise, however, was not a belated awareness of Statute 86, but a realisation that the grant of a mere leasehold interest might deprive the tenant of his parliamentary vote: the college abandoned its attempt and granted freehold estates for three lives absolute by deed instead. See MS 621/457, pp. 310–12, and *B.H.* IV(2), p. 9. For the unfortunate consequences for a tenant that might flow from the practice of converting copyhold to leasehold estates in Dorset, see Thomas Hardy's *The Woodlanders*.

171 *B.H.* IV(2), p. 10. Similarly, the total of the rents at Oborne was £14. 11s. 8d., whereas in 1753 one of the fines (which were calculated on the annual value) had been £770: *ibid.*, p. 70.

172 *B.H.* IV(2), p. vii.

accumulation provided the college with funds for the extensive alterations to the college buildings which were undertaken in the middle of the eighteenth century and later for the large repairs to them at the end of the century; finally, they helped to finance the purchase of beneficial leases in Bincombe and Oborne in the years following the enactment of an Enclosure Act for the parish in 1824. That Act led to the buying up or running out of the beneficial leases, and with it the practice of taking fines ceased and was replaced by rack-rents.[173]

For two reasons the copyhold fines from the college's two estates in Dorset eventually proved a more valuable source of income to it than the corresponding fines from its copyhold estates in the eastern counties. One reason lay in the fact that the Dorset manors were predominantly – almost exclusively – held by copyhold tenants,[174] whose fines accrued to the college, whereas in the case of the eastern manors much of the manorial estate comprised demesne lands held by leasehold tenants and their fines benefitted only the Master and senior fellows personally. The second reason lies in the difference in the nature of the transaction for which the fine was paid. As has been explained, fines on copyholds of inheritance were in the nature of conveyancing or court fees payable by an incoming owner who had a legal entitlement that was derived from inheritance or purchase from a third party, and, unlike fines on copyholds for lives, the fines on copyholds of inheritance were not the *quid pro quo* for a grant or extension of an interest by the college. Fines on copyholds for life, on the other hand, were just such a *quid pro quo*. This explains the difference between the formulas used to assess the amount of the fine in the two cases. On the change of tenant of a copyhold of inheritance, the college's practice in the eighteenth century was to take one year's purchase on a transfer *inter vivos* and one-and-a-half years' on an inheritance, "tho' in some other mannors I've been informed 'tis usual to take 1½ in case of Purchase [and] 2 in case of Descent".[175] In the case of the estates in Bincombe and Oborne, which were held only for lives, the tenant paid four years' purchase for the addition of one life, six years' purchase for two lives, and for three lives "(which is all one when the estate is run out)" twelve or fourteen years' purchase.[176] By the end of the eighteenth century the Bursar's Book reveals that the difference in income to the college could be substantial and that, on occasion, the fines from Dorset far outstripped those from the eastern counties. At Michaelmas 1792 the receipts in fines and

[173] *B.H.* IV(2), p. 70. The ending of the Dorset beneficial leases did not end the enduring relationship between the college and its tenants there: the Pashen family has provided a tenant in Bincombe for over 250 years and its tenancy was in its eighth generation when the tenancy passed to the female line in 2014 and the name "Pashen" itself ceased to appear on the lease.

[174] The complete absence of any demesne lands in the two manors is difficult to explain, but nevertheless it would seem to have been the case, since there is no record of any lease of demesne land or the payment of any fine on such a lease.

[175] *Epitome of Leases*, p. 77 (Archive MS).

[176] *Ibid.*, p. 75.

heriots from fourteen copyhold estates of inheritance in East Anglia amounted to just over £204, compared with £108 from a single fine (for three lives) in Dorset. In the eighteen months which followed the amounts from East Anglia and Dorset, respectively, were: £123 and £111 (Michaelmas 1793),[177] £50 and £305 (Lady Day 1794),[178] £28 and £300 (Michaelmas 1794);[179] and two years later the difference was even more striking: £19 and £420, respectively, at Michaelmas 1796.[180]

Beneficial leases

It is unfortunate that the same term 'entry fine' is used to mean not only the customary fine paid by copyholders but also the contractual down-payment by a leasehold tenant for the grant or renewal of his lease: the payments bear the same name, but they differ fundamentally in their legal character. Unlike the entry fines on copyholds, which reflected manorial custom, the fines arising upon the grant or renewal of a term of years were the outcome of the contractual bargaining that preceded final agreement. The interest conveyed by a lease was not real property in a lawyer's eyes, but personal property arising purely from a contract; likewise, the grant or renewal of the term did not result from obligations arising from any existing tenure between the landlord and tenant, but solely from the new contract that emerged out of negotiations between the parties.

As is well known, over the course of the sixteenth and early seventeenth centuries the fine on leases for terms of years granted by colleges and other corporate bodies came to supplement and then virtually to replace the annual money rents which the lessee paid to his landlord. As those rents remained unchanged for centuries and steadily lost their real value, the fine came to represent the true consideration paid by the lessee for the benefit which he would derive from land that was held under a 'beneficial lease' for which he paid very little rent.[181] The process by which this occurred has attracted the attention of numerous economic and social historians, and in this connection Caius' statutes deserve particular attention, for he re-founded the college at a critical time when the effect of twenty years' inflation was becoming apparent, and he was very conscious of the damage to a college's finances which the potential

177 Twelve estates at Croxley, Burnham, Teversham and Duxford; one fine and two heriots at Oborne.

178 One fine in each area.

179 Five fines in East Anglia; two in Dorset.

180 *Bursar's Book*, 1792–1810, fol. 81b. It must be borne in mind that the fines on copyholds varied considerably between holdings, both in frequency and in amount, even when the tenure was the same.

181 The term 'beneficial lease' does not imply that the lease is in some special way beneficial to the tenant.

misuse of fines on leases might cause. As a result, his statutes are exceptional in the inclusion of detailed provisions to ensure that his new college should not suffer the same damage from the grant of beneficial leases which he found had befallen Gonville Hall.

For reasons which will appear later we have to wait until the middle of the seventeenth century and the period of the Commonwealth and the Restoration before we are able to form a clear picture of the classic practice of the college in respect of the grant and renewal of a beneficial lease and the accompanying levying of a fine. That period is a watershed in our knowledge. From then onward we have a clear and detailed record of the unvarying practice of the college, but before the watershed virtually no mention of fines in relation to leases is to be found in any of the college's records that survive and we can draw only very tentative conclusions about the emergence of that practice.

So far as the earlier period is concerned the challenge is to explain how and when the curious and distinctly odd practice which we find firmly settled by the time of the Commonwealth ever came into existence. We shall find (i) that it has by then become the virtually invariable practice of the college to lease its lands to tenants for the maximum period permitted by its statutes, in most cases twenty years, and to do so at an unrealistically low rent, but (ii) that neither the grantor nor the grantee ever expect that the lease will last that long, and both assume that they will negotiate for the surrender of the lease after just seven years in return for a new grant for twenty more years – in effect, the grant of an extension in fourteen years' time for a further seven years at the same unrealistic rent – and (iii) that the tenant purchases the benefit of that further seven years' possession at the same unrealistic rent by paying a capital sum which is calculated fourteen years in advance and is paid, not to the corporate landlord to whom he pays his rent but to certain individual members of that corporation for the time being. How did such an artificial practice arise?

The Tudor beneficial lease

The beneficial lease has attracted much attention from economic and social historians over the years.[182] A number of factors contributed in their turn to its emergence in the sixteenth century and to the curious form which it took in the case of colleges and other corporations, but only four need be mentioned here.

The *first* was the practice of monastic and other ecclesiastical bodies to grant very long leases for moderate or low rents, a long-established practice that dated from well before the sixteenth century. The *second* was the use of such leases as a form of sale, particularly by the Crown and its favourites seeking

[182] In respect of the Cambridge colleges, it has been the subject of three valuable recent studies to which the writer is greatly indebted: *Emmanuel College* (1999); *H.U.C.*, II (2004); *Riches and Responsibility* (2008).

an immediate return on lands acquired as a consequence of the dissolution of the monasteries; here the fine, not the rent, served as the purchase price of an interest which amounted in duration almost to a freehold fee simple but allowed the grantor to retain a greater control over the land than could have been achieved easily if the tenant had been a freeholder. The *third* was the stimulus thereby given to corporate bodies to use the long lease as a form of sale, but for a rather different purpose: its use by Henry VIII had been to meet the urgent need to remedy the royal finances in the closing years of his reign, and its use by the Crown's favourites was to raise capital to finance building and other manifestations of power, whereas the use of the long lease by corporate bodies was open to the inevitable abuse that it could be used to benefit current members of the corporate body to the detriment of its future members in a time of rampant inflation. The *fourth* factor which fashioned the beneficial lease was the legislative response to the detriment caused to the permanent endowment of corporate bodies by that abuse. This led not only to the prohibition of long leases in Caius' statutes for his own college, but very soon thereafter to a series of Elizabethan Acts of Parliament in the 1570s which outlawed the grant of leases by colleges and ecclesiastical corporations for longer than twenty-one years or, in the case of urban property, forty years.[183]

The effect of these four factors can be tracked in the changing practice of the college. Until the last quarter of the fifteenth century Gonville Hall had very little lay land that it could lease, but it then received significant benefactions of land.[184] By the early sixteenth century it had started to adopt the monastic practice of granting long leases at moderate rents: in 1507 it leased its principal manor and most valuable lay property, the Manor of Mortimer's in Newnham, to the corporation of Cambridge for ninety-nine years at an annual rent of 20 marks (£13. 6s. 8d.); we do not know whether the Hall received a fine on leasing the manor, but there is no compelling reason to suppose that it did at that early date.[185] We may be fairly confident, however, that it would have received fines when it began to make a series of long leases in the years that followed the dissolution of the monasteries.[186] During the twenty years of the masterships of

183 For these Acts see below.

184 Principally lands in Barningham in Suffolk (in 1478 from Stephen Smith) and in Tuttington in Norfolk (in 1487 from Elizabeth Clere), and the Manor of Mortimer's in Newnham (in 1498 from Anne Scroope).

185 The town had sub-let the manor for £18 a year by 1515: *B.H.* IV(2), p. 25. Although there is nothing to suggest that a fine was taken at that early time, the practice seems to have become well established during the course of the century.

186 When a lease of Burnham Thorpe was made to Nicholas Mynne as part of an exchange in 1572 the fact that it was made without any fine being taken was thought worthy of comment ("*sine fine ut vocant*"): *B.H.* IV(2), p. 16. The absence of a fine on that occasion is understandable, since the lease constituted a *quid pro quo* in an exchange: it is the fact that the comment was made which is significant.

John Styrmin (1540–52) and Thomas Bacon (1552–59) all the manors and all but one of the more valuable other lands which Gonville Hall had acquired through the gifts of its recent benefactors were let on long or reversionary leases at rents which no longer represented the true value of the land. During Styrmin's tenure the Manor of Aynells in Westoning was leased in 1544 for ninety-nine years at the "olde rent";[187] then in 1550 the land at Worlingham for fifty years, and in 1551 the estate at Tuttington for sixty-one years, both also at the "olde rent".[188] As well as the grant of long leases, Styrmin's mastership saw another practice which John Caius also later outlawed: the grant of reversionary leases. In 1548 the college's land at Barningham was leased in reversion for a period of twenty-one years from 1558; and the Manor of D'Engaynes in Stow-cum-Quy was similarly leased in 1551 for a period of thirty-one years from 1559.[189] Even though the fault lay far more with Styrmin, it was his successor, Thomas Bacon, who particularly incurred the wrath of John Caius when he returned to the college, for during Bacon's mastership the college's two remaining manors were both leased for forty years: the Manor of Thornham at Titchwell in 1555, and the Manor of D'Engaynes in Teversham on 21 July 1557, the latter less than two months before the re-foundation.[190]

When Caius returned to the college as Master in January 1559 he found that the rents from all the college's manors (apart from the three manors which he had provided on its re-foundation) and much of its other land had been frozen for decades to come. He was determined to ensure that no similar fate should befall his newly re-founded college and his statutes are unique in Cambridge in the care and detail of the directions he included in them in order to safeguard the college's lands and other property. In an exceptionally strongly worded statute, Statute 86, he (i) decreed that no lease could be made without the express agreement of the Master and the majority of all the fellows at the time and in their presence; (ii) imposed an absolute limit of twenty years on the length of the term for which any of its lay lands could thereafter be leased; and

[187] The "olde rent" of £14 was not re-set under the Corn Act of 1576 until 1634, when the ninety-nine-year lease was finally surrendered and a new lease granted: *B.H.* IV(2), p. 93. Styrmin's predecessor, John Skipp, had been forced by the (later) Lord North to "sell" him the Manor of Bansteds in Cowlinge in 1540 and had purchased Aynells in its place: *ibid.*, p. 35.

[188] *B.H.* IV(2), pp. 90, 104. Tuttington had been given to the college by Elizabeth Clere in 1487 and Worlingham by T. Atkyn, the vicar of the college's living at Mutford, as late as 1539; Atkyn had also provided some of the property in Cowling which Skipp had been forced to sell to Lord North and he thus contributed also to the college's acquisition of Aynells: see the preceding note.

[189] *Liber dimissionum* (later bound as the *Liber evidentiarum*), fol. 68b (Barningham); fol. 7 (Stow-cum-Quy).

[190] *Liber dimissionum*, fol. 27 (Titchwell), fol. 53b (Teversham). "D'Engaynes" was the name of the manorial property at both Stow-cum-Quy and Teversham and later writers treat them as one manor; but leases of the two properties in 1551 and 1557, respectively, speak of them as if they were distinct manors: *ibid.*, fols. 7, 53b.

(iii) forbade the creation of reversionary leases intended to take effect at the end of an existing lease, requiring instead that the prior lease should first be surrendered.[191] In addition he took care to include further precautions in the same statute: no lease which did not comply with the statute should ever be sealed, and the Visitors should be alerted to any attempt to do so.[192]

The leasing of the manors particularly frustrated him; for the rents, fines and perquisites from the free and copyhold tenants as well as sub-lessees of the demesnes made manors especially valuable, yet all the manors had been leased in their entirety.[193] It is not surprising, therefore, that he was careful to direct that the college should never again lease its manors, but only the "scite of the manor" and the demesne lands, and that it should always retain the sole right to hold courts and appoint stewards.[194] The two ninety-nine-year leases of the Manors of Aynells and Mortimer's were also a special cause of discontent, in one case to Caius himself and in the other to the generation that succeeded him: both leases eventually ended in acrimony and litigation, for tenants holding for such a long period not unnaturally regarded themselves as little less than freeholders and behaved accordingly.[195]

Parliament very soon followed Caius' lead, and in 1571 the colleges of the two universities were included in the prohibition against ecclesiastical bodies' granting any lease other than for a term of twenty-one years or three lives from

[191] In the closing years of his life he broke two of his own rules in his anxiety to put the college's leases on a proper footing. In 1569, in order to ensure that the rent would be increased, he created a reversionary lease of Barningham to run for twenty-one years from 1579, when the existing (equally reversionary) lease granted by Styrmin in 1548 would expire; and in 1571 he substituted a new lease of Tuttington for the remaining forty years under the sixty-one-year lease granted by Styrmin in 1551: *Liber dimissionum*, fols. 72b, 70, respectively.

[192] Furthermore, to ensure strict compliance with the restrictions, the calendar year of the grant should always be written first in any lease and the regnal year after it: Statute 86.

[193] The Manor of Mortimer's had been let to the Cambridge corporation in 1507 at a rent of 20 marks (£13. 6s. 8d.). When the lease expired ninety-nine years later the rent to the Cambridge corporation from sub-leases appears to have totalled £90 a year: *B.H.* IV(2), p. 25.

[194] Statutes 86, 88. See *Caius' purchase of the Manors of Croxley, Runcton and Burnham Thorpe* in "*Supplementary Notes to Caius' Statutes*", § IV. 3, at pp. 303–4.

[195] Aynells had been let for ninety-nine years in 1544 and the tenant committed waste by cutting down the timber in the 1560s. Caius took steps towards forfeiting the lease, but reached a compromise with the tenant in 1572 shortly before his death, taking care to safeguard the college with a new indenture and obligations for the remaining seventy-odd years of the term: *Liber dimissionum*, fols. 1b, 85; *B.H.* IV(2), p. 93.

Mortimer's had been let to the Cambridge corporation for ninety-nine years in 1507, and in 1605 the corporation unsuccessfully sought to have the lease renewed by obtaining letters from King James commanding the college to renew the lease; the college succeeded in having the royal mandate withdrawn: *B.H.* IV(2), p. 25. It may be noted that similar acrimony ensued when an 80-year lease of the Manor of Burnham Thorpe finally expired in 1619 and the college endeavoured to recover the property, at which point "a great suit in Chancery arose": *ibid.*, p. 15. The lease had been granted by the abbey of Wymondham in 1539 shortly before the dissolution and Caius had bought the manor from the Crown subject to it.

the time the lease was made.[196] Caius' own statute had specifically extended the ban to reversionary leases unless any existing lease was first surrendered; but Parliament failed to do so and a further Act was needed to block the loophole in 1576: reversionary leases would thenceforth be valid only if they were made in the last three years before the expiry or surrender of the existing lease.[197]

It is interesting to note that the pressure to evade the 1571 Act and to lease land for more than twenty-one years seems to have been sufficient in the intervening five years to prompt corporate landowners not only to grant reversionary leases but also to execute bonds and covenants undertaking to do so, for the 1576 Act expressly provided that these were also to be void. Whether the pressure to circumvent the 1571 Act came from the corporate landlord seeking immediate fines or from the tenant seeking longer security of tenure is not clear; but the solution which was ultimately adopted by this and other colleges ingeniously satisfied both landlord and tenant. This was the practice of surrender and re-grant.

The practice of surrender and re-grant

At some point of time in the seventeenth century the practice developed whereby the college granted or renewed a beneficial lease for the full twenty-one years allowed by the Act of 1571,[198] and the tenant paid an appropriate fine as well as the traditional low rent; but it was fully understood by both parties that the tenant would surrender his lease after only a third of the tenancy had run and that he would be granted a new twenty-one-year lease at the same low rent in return for a fine which would reflect the benefit of the extra seven years that he would enjoy in fourteen years' time. In this way the college received more frequent, albeit smaller, fines and the tenant needed to set aside smaller and more manageable sums over no more than seven years.[199] In practice, as Gross

[196] 13 Eliz. I, c. 10, s. 2. Section 3 of the Act preserved the validity of any shorter restriction imposed by the private statutes of a college and as a consequence the limitation to twenty years imposed by Caius in Statute 86 continued to bind the college until the nineteenth century. St John's was also limited to twenty years, while Trinity was restricted to ten years until it obtained a change of statute from the Crown in 1595: *Emmanuel College*, p. 131, *Riches and Responsibility*, p. 21. As a temporary measure a college was allowed to grant a lease longer than twenty-one years in place of any long lease then existing, provided that the existing lease was surrendered and the new lease did not exceed the residue of the surrendered lease (s. 4); as has been mentioned in n. 191 above, Dr Caius had to make such a lease in the case of Tuttington and was no doubt aggrieved by the need to do so.

[197] 18 Eliz. I, c. 11.

[198] Twenty-one years in most colleges, but twenty years in the case of Caius' own college (Statute 86). The college adopted the same tripartite division into seven years that was a general rule in other colleges.

[199] As the college found out to its own disadvantage, every tenant needed to take care that he made adequate provision for the payment at the end of the seven years. In 1634 as a result of a bequest by a fellow, Matthew Stokys, the college became the tenant of a beneficial twenty-one-year lease of the rectories of Dilham and Honing. It duly paid a fine of £90 to the bishop

has put it, "it might then be said that the tenant paid a half-yearly rent due at the end of each half-year and a septennial rent paid at the beginning of each seven years".[200] The practice of surrender and re-grant after the first few years in the course of a lease had attractions for both a college and its tenants which made it more convenient for both parties than the taking of a single fine for renewal at the natural termination of the lease; but the practice also introduced two important factors which tended to reduce the monetary value of the fine.

The *first* factor was the need to introduce a rate of interest into the calculation of the appropriate sum to be paid in advance for the future enjoyment of a beneficial lease in (what would normally be) fourteen years' time, *i.e.*, the discounted purchase price of a future annuity. By the eighteenth century it was a widely voiced criticism that the fines taken by colleges on the surrender and re-grant of beneficial leases were very low by commercial standards, and a recent study has demonstrated that one reason why fines had long been so low had been the assumption of an unrealistically high rate of interest when calculating the present value of a future asset.[201] The *second* factor was the fact that the fine was now negotiated with a 'sitting tenant' who had a further fourteen years' security of tenure in the event of a failure to agree.[202] The college was now in a much less dominant position than it would be if the lease was on the point of expiring. Furthermore, the lands that a college received from its benefactors tended to be widely and haphazardly spread, and, as Caius recognised in Statute 93, it was in a college's interest to retain its tenants and to encourage their interest in the well-being of the land whenever possible, for the Master and fellows were not professional landlords and rarely had contact with their tenants more than twice a year: a more aggressive policy of always seeking the best commercial return from estates that were haphazardly scattered across East Anglia and beyond would have required far closer attention than was possible for them, or else undesirable delegation to local agents.[203]

of Ely in 1641 on the first occasion on which the twenty-one-year lease was renewed; but it then allowed the lease to run out in the confusion of the Civil War and found itself having to pay a fine of £500 for a renewal of the lease when the whole twenty-one years expired in 1661: *B.H.* IV(2), p. 40. (The annual rent of £13. 6s. 8d. to the bishop for the two rectories remained unchanged for 232 years.) The lesson was not forgotten: when in 1702 the then Master of the college, J. Halman, bequeathed to the college a beneficial lease at Mepal which was held from the Dean and Chapter of Ely, he took care to direct that the college should keep back and accumulate the greater part of the income from the property for five years to raise a fund to meet fines and other contingencies: *B.H.* IV(2), p. 63.

200 *B.H.* IV(2), p. vii.

201 See the detailed study by Sarah Bendall in *Emmanuel College*, pp. 170–2; see also the illuminating analysis by Nield, *Riches and Responsibility*, p. 33.

202 As will be seen below, the need to negotiate was regularly recognised in the authority given to the bursar in the *Gesta*.

203 The college appointed stewards to hold manorial courts and maintain the court records (cf. Statute 96), but they did not have responsibility for the management of the land; in time they

Given the importance of the practice of surrender and re-grant, it is regrettable that the absence of any surviving *Gesta* from before 1651 prevents us from pinpointing more precisely the date by which the practice had become general.[204] As will be seen shortly, we have to wait until the period of the Commonwealth and the Restoration in the middle of the seventeenth century before we are able to form a clear picture of the established practice of the college in its grant and renewal of beneficial leases; and by that time the practice of grant and surrender after seven years had become firmly established and virtually invariable. It remains, however, largely a matter of guess-work when the practice first developed.[205]

The lessee's fine

As in the case of corn money, we have to wait until the second half of the seventeenth century before we are able to obtain from the records of the college any indication of its practice in relation to the receipt and allocation of fines levied on the grant of a lease. The reason is the same for both corn money and fines on leases: neither was ever credited to the college as its income in the bursar's half-yearly accounts. In the same way that we have to await the surviving Commonwealth file of Corn Rolls in the case of corn money, so in the case of fines on leases we cannot safely go back beyond the earliest surviving record of the *Gesta*, which also comes from the Commonwealth period.

ceased to have any close connection with the land – if indeed they ever did have – and by the eighteenth century the college was appointing attorneys practising in London to act as steward for all the lands in a particular county. Eventually, the link became even more tenuous and the office of Steward of the Manors was finally held by a Law fellow of the college (for many years by Thomas Wiglesworth, the last surviving senior fellow elected before the repeal of Dr Caius' Statutes, and then by W.W. Buckland): *Annals*, p. xiii. In contrast, the bailiff was a valuable link between the college and its more distant properties. For a period of at least thirty-six years (from 1609 to 1645) the rent of all the tenants in Bincombe and Oborne was brought to the college every year by a single person, Thomas Samways, the bailiff, and it is doubtful whether the college had any direct contact with the tenants there except on the infrequent occasions of a visitation in pursuance of Statutes 97, 98, 102 and 103; Thomas was succeeded by another Samways, James, after 1645: *Bursar's Books*, 1609–34, 1634–61. In the absence of a bailiff as reliable as Samways, the rent might regularly remain in arrears for long periods, as appears to have been the position in the case of the Manor of Haglo and Pulton in the Forest of Dean, the demesne lands of which had been let by the benefactor for a term of 1,000 years in 1568 shortly before he left the manor to the college in his will: *B.H.* IV(2), p. 52.

204 The surviving *Acta* included in the first *Exiit Book* (1592–1618) do not include any reference to decisions on fines on the renewal of leases in the way that they were recorded in the later *Gesta*.

205 Early surrenders include two negotiated by Caius himself in return for a newly drafted lease, Tuttington in 1571 and Aynells the following year; neither was for longer than the remaining number of years under the earlier lease: cf. nn. 191, 195 above. The Manor of Mortimer's was surrendered in 1619 (when there were still six years to run on a twenty-year lease) and Shelford Manor in 1635 (when there were still eleven years to run on a sixty-year lease): *B.H.* IV(2), pp. 26, 82.

In the case of corn money we at least have the 1576 Act and Fletcher's Arithmetical Table of 1609 to guide us; but in the case of fines on leases we have nothing similar.[206] Instead, we have a sharp contrast between the fines from copyholds which are invariably credited to the college as non-recurrent income (*recepta extraordinaria*) in the Bursar's Book and the fines on leases which are never credited to the college anywhere, despite a statutory direction that they should be. In 1572 Caius carefully included in the college's statutes a direction that any fine levied on the grant or renewal of a lease should kept sufficiently modest to ensure that it did not inhibit the college from fixing the rent at a level that reflected the true annual value of the land, together with a clear and unambiguous direction that the benefit of all fines from its leases should in future accrue to the permanent endowment of the college and not to the members of the college for the time being personally.[207] Yet, we find that by 1672, a hundred years later, the practice of the college in respect of leaseholds goes diametrically against its statutes and no part of the fine is treated as income of the college; instead, the whole of the fine is divided up between the Master and the twelve senior fellows to the exclusion of both the college and all its other members at the time, the Master receiving twice as much as a fellow.

It might be thought that the practice does no more than reflect that of other Cambridge colleges and that Caius' college was merely following the herd. No other Cambridge college, however, had statutes that contained a specific provision which ran so completely contrary to the practice as that of Caius did. Moreover, far from following the herd, the college appears to have adopted its practice much earlier than colleges such as Trinity and St John's and even Emmanuel. Trinity and St John's did not distribute fines as dividends until 1629–30, and Emmanuel's practice appears to have varied uncertainly until the same time.[208] In contrast the practice in Caius had existed earlier than in Trinity or St John's and it had clearly become entrenched by Branthwaite's time. In *Allen's Case* in 1617 the first charge which Branthwaite preferred against the

[206] If Fletcher had produced an Arithmetical Table for entry fines in the way he did for corn rents it would have been invaluable in the answers it would have provided.

[207] Statutes 93 and 95. Caius' concern over fines on leases was shared by Mrs Frankland twenty years later. In the will in which she devised to the college her three houses in Philip Lane in London, she directed very firmly that the rent "I will not have abated, if so much may be made of the same, without any fine or income to be paid by any lessee or occupier of the same": *B.H.* IV(2), p. 57. She was a woman with a very shrewd financial sense and, having been one of the executors of the will of her mother (Joan Trapps), who had earlier left a benefaction to the college in 1563, she would have known John Caius and been aware of his concern.

[208] See *Riches and Responsibility*, p. 68; P. Linehan, *St John's College Cambridge: A History* (2011), p. 96; Bendall, *Emmanuel College*, p. 172–5. In the case of most colleges it is difficult to disentangle fines from corn money and other commons benefits which were not treated as income of the college but might be divided between its more privileged members; practices differed between colleges and in some only part of the fine was distributed and the rest was credited to the college: cf. *H.U.C.*, II, pp. 272–4, 279–82.

fellows in his submissions to the Chancellor was that "The fines upon leases which by statute are to goe to the Colledge, have been a long time divided amongst the company (statutes 93 and 95); *fines Collegii esse volumus non Magistri et sociorum*." To this the fellows could only reply a little disingenuously that "The Fellowes say that the fines of all copyholds have always been paid to the chest, the tenants benevolences for their leases have always been divided amongst the company, whereof the Custos have ever had a double part."[209] There is no evidence that the offending practice had ever been different.[210]

If the fines were modest in the period preceding Branthwaite's mastership that would explain why it is only during his term of office that the legitimacy of their division among the Master and senior fellows was first questioned. There are three reasons why it is likely that the levying of fines in respect of leases (as distinct from copyholds) and their division between the Master and senior fellows only gradually acquired sufficient financial importance to become an issue in the years following Legge's death, and not earlier: (i) some rents had been raised very substantially in Caius' lifetime, thereby reducing the amount of any fine which might otherwise have been required; (ii) additional rent resulting from the Corn Act three years after his death had increased the consideration paid by the tenant and reduced the amount of any fine as a consequence; and (iii) an opportunity to levy a fine on leases of the college's more valuable properties had arisen in only two cases during Legge's lifetime.

(i) Caius had had the opportunity late in his life to raise the rent of at least two of the college's estates. In both of these cases he broke his own rule and granted reversionary leases before the existing leases were due to run out. One of these was the estate at Barningham, where his eagerness to ensure that the rents should always reflect the true value of the land is shown by the fact that he broke his own rule in 1569 and granted a reversionary lease of the college's land there no less than ten years before the existing lease was due to run out.[211] The other was the college's most valuable property, the combined Manors of Croxley and Snellshall, where he granted a reversionary lease of them to his friend William Gerrard in 1571 eleven years before the existing lease would expire.[212] He

[209] "Auncient practices against statutes" (Branthwaite); "Answer to the Auncient practices against statutes" (Fellows): *Allen's Case* (1617), Appendix F, at pp. 598 and 600 below.

[210] No reference to leasehold fines is to be found in the earliest surviving Bursar's Book, which commenced in 1609, or among the *Acta* recorded between 1592 to 1618 in the earliest surviving *Exiit Book*.

[211] *Liber dimissionum*, fol. 72b. The yearly rent was raised from £5 to £10.

[212] *Liber dimissionum*, fol. 76. The property had been seized by the Crown on the dissolution of the monastery of St Albans, and when Caius bought it from Philip and Mary it was subject to leases which would not expire till 1582. When Caius leased it to Gerrard he raised the rent from £15. 6s. 8d. to £40 with the underwood (other than the timber, which Caius directed in Statute 88 should always be reserved) or £25 without the underwood. The inadequacy of the earlier

was anxious that his policy on rents should be maintained after his death and in Statutes 89 and 95 he directed that the Master and fellows should always raise the rent to a proper level (*ad iustum censum*) that reflected the prevailing rate for nearby farms of the same quality, when they were leasing, and that they should do so before they levied a fine "lest fines eat up the rents" (*ne fines consumant redditus*). Notwithstanding that direction, only one rent appears to have been raised after his death, and that was exceptional: the rent of Runcton, which was increased to £40 p.a. in 1582 in accordance with the express direction in Statute 91.[213]

(ii) A contributory cause for the college's failure thereafter to implement Caius' direction to raise rents would seem to lie in the enactment of the Corn Act three years after his death; for, as has been seen earlier, Sir Thomas Smith's ingenious provisions meant that the renewal of an agrarian lease produced for the tenant (though not for the college) an immediate and substantial increase in the burden of his half-yearly rent. In these circumstances he may well have been reluctant on the first renewal of his lease to pay a further increase in rent or any greater fine than had been payable in the past.

(iii) The third factor was the most important. No fine was payable until a lease came up for renewal, and only two of the college's six most valuable leases did so before Legge's death in 1607; as has been seen, those two were Croxley and Runcton and in both cases the rents had been substantially increased, thus reducing the amount of any fine that was taken.[214] The other four valuable leases fell in after his death: Tuttington in 1611, the Manor of Mortimer's (Newnham) in 1619,[215] the Manor of Aynells (Westoning) in 1634 and Shelford Manor[216] in the same year. It was only when the leases on these profitable properties came to be renewed that the enjoyment of entry fines would be sufficiently substantial to

rent is brought out by the fact that the free and customary rents of the manor alone amounted to £12. 6. 8d. without rent from any sub-leases: *B.H.* IV(2), pp. 72–3, and "*Supplementary Notes to Caius' Statutes*", § IV. 3, at p. 305 above.

213 Cf. p. 499 above.

214 The rents were increased twice, first by Caius himself (in the case of Croxley) or at his direction (in the case of Runcton), and a second time as a result of the Corn Act: see Statute 91.

215 The ninety-nine-year lease granted to the corporation of Cambridge in 1507 had finally expired in 1606, just before Legge's death, but a lease for twenty-one years had been granted by the college in somewhat mysterious circumstances to a trustee to the use of the Master, Legge, in the previous year. Although Legge had left his interest in the lease to the college on his death in 1607, the lease to the trustee was not surrendered to the college until 1619 and it was only when the manor was then leased to a genuine tenant that a new fine could become payable.

216 Shelford had been purchased by the college in 1614, but subject to a sixty-year lease that would not expire until 1646. In the event, that lease was surrendered eleven years early and the college was immediately able to grant a new twenty-year lease for a substantial fine ("*ob summam numerorum haud contemnendam*") in 1635.

provoke contention.[217] During Legge's mastership the fines would have been sufficiently modest to have been comparable with the perquisites which Caius himself had been happy to allow to the Master and fellows when granting of a lease. He had specifically allowed them to require from the tenants in the contract some sheep, fattened wethers and pigs and other fatted fowls towards the embellishment and increase of their common table at the more important feasts and commemorations of the founders; and, to encourage attendance to college business, he had further provided that a lessee, like other grantees, should pay a sum of 10s. which was to be shared between the Master and fellows who were present at the sealing of his lease.[218] It would not have been far-fetched for the fellows to have looked upon the relatively modest fines which tenants had paid in Legge's time as spontaneous gifts (or "tenant's benevolences" in the words they used in *Allen's Case* to defend the established practice) similar to the perquisites which Caius himself had sanctioned.[219] Such gifts were never mentioned in the lease and they could be regarded as distinct from the obligations which the tenant undertook in it.[220] If the fines were in fact modest in the period preceding Branthwaite's mastership, that may explain why it was only during his term of office that the legitimacy of their division among the

217 We do not have details of the entry fines that prospective tenants were willing to pay for a lease of any of the college's properties in the first half of the seventeenth century, but there is no reason to suppose that the *relative* values of the college's properties *inter se* at that time were significantly different from what they were in the hundred years from 1664 to 1763. Judging by the amount of the fines levied over those later hundred years (total given in brackets), the six most valuable properties were Croxley (£2,802), Shelford (£2,021), Westoning (£1,418), Tuttington (£1,000), Newnham (£925) and Runcton (£761). A seventh, Wilton (£1,069), also became as valuable, but only after 1681 when the Manor of Carles was bought. Apart from these only Titchwell (£649) and Teversham (£532) brought in more than £500 in fines over the hundred years.

N.B. This ranking indicates only the relative value judged by the amount lessees were willing to pay. It does not indicate the assessed annual value of the college's properties, as the following instances from the survey of 1751 show: (i) the annual values of Oborne (£420 p.a.) and Bincombe (£334 p.a.) were much greater even than that of Croxley (£284 p.a.), but their value derived from copyhold tenancies, not leases; (ii) the annual values of the college's ancient rectories of Foulden (£120 p.a.) and Mattishall (£110 p.a.) were greater than that of Tuttington (£90 p.a.), but fines were not levied on leases of those rectories (whenever they were leased to the college's vicars); (iii) similarly the annual value of the Manor of D'Abernoons at Duxford (£100 p.a.) was as great as Mortimer's (£102 p.a.), but the fines were very much less since the rent was much greater: see *Rental Book*, pp. 31–8.

218 Statutes 81, 93.

219 It is not inconceivable that some of the early smaller fines were paid in kind rather than in money in the case of agricultural tenancies.

220 In the eighteenth century the fine was mentioned in the epitome noting the heads of the lease, but never in the lease itself: see *Epitome of Leases 1715–35* (Archive MS).

Master and senior fellows was first questioned; but it remains a mystery how the one college whose statutes contained an emphatic direction that entry fines on its leases should belong exclusively to the college came to be one of the first colleges to accept so readily that no part of those fines should be regarded as its corporate income.

1660–1760: the classical period of the college's beneficial lease

From 1651 onward the record of the *Gesta* is unbroken and contains a continuous record of the decisions of the college meetings which approved the amount of the fine to be paid for the grant or renewal of all terms of years. From shortly after the Restoration we also have, in Dr Gostlin's Note Book, a record of the various payments that he made to his colleagues during the years in which he was bursar and subsequently when he was president. In the four years when he was bursar he recorded the payment of some entry fines, although he did not do so systematically, and he continued the practice in some of the years of his long presidency.[221] In addition to Gostlin's Note Book we have a valuable "Table of Fines" compiled by John Davy when he ceased to be registrary in 1763; this contains a virtually complete list of all the fines charged on the leases granted by the college in the years from 1658 to 1763.[222] From these three sources, *Gesta*, Note Book and Table, we can form a clear and complete picture of the settled practice of the college at that time.

(i) It had become the settled practice by the Restoration, and almost certainly from much earlier in the seventeenth century, to grant all leases for twenty years, the maximum duration which Caius had allowed to the college in his statutes.[223]

(ii) The obligations under the leases reflected almost word for word those which Caius had formulated in great detail in his statutes.

(iii) The rent which the tenant was required to pay half-yearly also remained unaltered and was not increased in successive leases to reflect the annual value of the land. Caius had in Statute 89 directed that rents

221 In those years he presumably acted either as registrary himself or else as the registrary's deputy.

222 John Davy was bursar 1754–56 and registrary 1757–63: *B.H.* II, p. 46. The table is stated to be in his handwriting.

223 The practice had become invariable by 1670. The only excepted properties were (a) the three rectories of Foulden, Matteshall and Mutford, which were regularly let for ten years in accordance with Caius' direction in Statute 86, (b) three properties which were let on rack-rents and (c) three urban properties which came to be let for forty years under the Act of 14 Eliz. c. 11 (1572) discussed below. In his Table John Davy listed four hunred leases by the college of its property in the years 1658–1763; apart from the nine excepted properties, only three leases of the other properties were not made for twenty years and those three were not new grants or renewals but merely substitute leases made without fine (*e.g.*, to other members of the same family as the tenant) and lasting only as long as the terms they replaced.

generally should be increased "in the light of the fruitfulness and value of the property", but, no doubt as a consequence of the Corn Act in 1576, the college ceased to review rents in the years following his death, and apart from the special case of Runcton few rents were thereafter increased.[224] Consequently, at the time of the Restoration, most rents still reflected the "olde" rents which had been charged before the dissolution of the monasteries, and they remained unchanged until rack-rents finally began to replace beneficial leases at the end of the eighteenth century.[225]

(iv) Although the lease was granted for a term of twenty years, it was the invariable practice for the college and the tenant to negotiate for the surrender of the lease after seven years in return for a new grant for twenty years – in effect an extension in thirteen years' time for a further seven years at the same unrealistic rent.

(v) For the reversionary benefit which the tenant obtained from the renewal – in effect a future annuity – he would in return be required to make a capital payment in the form of an 'entry' fine. Curiously, we have to wait until the middle of the eighteenth century for the first statement of the method by which the payment was calculated by this college. In a later appendix to Davy's "Table of Fines" that statement is couched in the somewhat obscure language of a surveyor rather than the mathematical formulation of a money-lender: the amount for the renewal of a twenty-year term after seven years had expired is stated to be "1¼ years" after deduction of the "reserved rent", together with one-fifth of "the last year's fine for every year afterwards".[226]

(vi) Although the formula has an appearance of precision, it presupposed the correctness of the initial valuation of the annual value of the land, and for this the college depended heavily upon an accurate survey and

224 Unless the area of the leased premises was altered. As explained above, the rent of Runcton was increased in 1582 in accordance with Statute 91.

225 Thus in the case of Tuttington, given to Gonville Hall by Elizabeth Clere in 1487, the "olde rent" of £4. 16s. 8d. was adjusted in 1611 under the Corn Act to £4. 8s. 10d. in money, 3 quarters 5 bushels 2 pecks in wheat, and 4 quarters of malt, and this remained the rent for 240 years. In the hundred years between 1663 and 1763, the fines for Tuttington amounted to over £1,000; its "true annual value" in 1767 was £90. 9s. 6d.: *Rentale Redituum*, p. 37.

226 Davy's "Table of Fines", fol. 18 (later note following the tables). For a forty-year (building) lease after fourteen years expired, the amount charged was 1¼ plus one-tenth for every year afterwards or one-fifth for every two years: for such leases see below.

Presumably "1¼ years" represented 1¼ times the estimated annual value or "true valew" (*Gesta*, 14 April 1653). The "reserved rent" that should first be deducted would properly mean the rent expressly reserved in the lease, *i.e.*, the money rent and the one-third of the old rent, and would not include the full amount of the corn rent; but it is difficult to believe that the calculation could have ignored the full burden on the tenant from the Corn Act: cf. *Riches and Responsibility*, p. 33, for a statement of the practice in Trinity in the early eighteenth century.

the competence of its local surveyor. In the middle of the seventeenth century the amount of the fine was still very much a matter of negotiation with the tenant. It is not surprising to find in the early *Gesta* that at their meeting on 14 April 1653 the Master and fellows agreed that a tenant might renew his lease for £20 "and what more the Bursar can get of him" and that another tenant might do so for £40 "at the least, more if it can be had".[227]

(vii) In addition to needing an accurate valuation of the present value of the land, the sale of a future interest required a formula for an accurate calculation of the proper amount that should be charged for the 'sale' of a further seven years' beneficial tenancy taking effect in fourteen years' time, and this in turn depended on the correctness of the assumed rate of interest that a pre-payment would earn over the fourteen years. The formula had been known to money-lenders for centuries, but there was widespread criticism in the early eighteenth century that colleges had assumed an unrealistically high rate of interest throughout the preceding century in the calculation of entry fines; as a consequence the fines that were being charged at the end of the seventeenth century were substantially smaller than the true annual value of the land warranted.[228] Although it had been recognised in professional literature by the early eighteenth century that entry fines ought to be higher, Davy's Table shows that they began to rise appreciably only towards the middle of that century, and even then the rise was noticeable only in the college's more valuable estates such as Croxley, Mortimer's and Aynells.[229]

(viii) Over the hundred years from 1664 to 1763 the total receipts from the entry fines from the leases recorded by Davy amounted to £16,000; the amounts received by the Master and senior fellows in any particular year varied considerably from year to year, of course, but over the period they produced an average of a little over £10 a year for each fellow and twice that for the Master.[230]

[227] *Gesta*, 14 April 1653. External factors might affect the calculation of the fine: thus in 1694, following the notorious Poll Tax, it was noted in the *Gesta* that the fines on six properties "were thus moderately sett in consideration of Taxes" now falling on the tenants: *Gesta*, 22 October 1694.

[228] Bendall, *Emmanuel College*, p. 171–3; *Riches and Responsibility*, p. 33; Kerridge "The Movement of Rent 1540–1640", *Economic History Review* (1953), pp. 16ff. In addition to any miscalculation of the rate of interest, prices of corn fell in the later years of the seventeenth century and with them the annual value of agricultural land: *Riches and Responsibility*, pp. 25–6, chart 1.1.

[229] The ten-year totals between 1664 and 1763 were: £1,041 (1664–73), £996 (1674–83), £1,369 (1684–93), £1,345 (1694–1703), £1,600 (1704–13), £1,870 (1714–23), £1,870 (1724–33), £2,427 (1734–43), £1,650 (1744–53), £2,319 (1754–63).

[230] The actual sums recorded amount to £15,983. 10s. 6d.; but, as we know from Gostlin's Note Book, a number of fines paid in the early 1660s were not included in Davy's lists. The total amount of the fines in any one year varied from nothing in eleven years, up to £634 in 1762. The

(ix) The bursar conducted the negotiations with the tenant, and no doubt the fine would have been paid to him by the tenant. He did not, however, credit it to the college as income in the Bursar's Book in the way he did with the entry fines on copyholds; instead it was the responsibility of the registrary to share it out between the Master and senior fellows, the Master's share being twice that of a fellow.[231] As its distribution by the registrary would suggest, the dividend was regarded as a payment for participating in the act of leasing by the Master and fellows rather than as a stipend. Unlike corn money, however, the entry fine was not viewed as a payment supplementing a resident's commons under the aegis of an Act of Parliament, and a one-fourteenth share of each fine was paid to all twelve senior fellows without regard to residence. The rationale would suggest that a fellow should be entitled only if he were present at the sealing and, if so, this may explain the apparent habit of non-resident fellows' returning to the college for the half-yearly audits and college meetings, since leases invariably ran from one or other of those two quarter-days.

(x) The registrary was responsible for the distribution of the fine and he was entitled to keep as a perquisite any small sum remaining after the division, in the same way that the bursar was entitled in respect of corn money.[232] Furthermore, the registrary also kept some part of the "Registrary's fee" which the tenant was required to pay for the execution of the new deed in addition to the fine.[233]

1760–1860: the transition from fines to rack-rents

It is relatively straightforward to obtain a clear picture of the practice in respect of entry fines during the hundred years from 1660 to 1760: in sharp contrast, it is extremely difficult to do so for the hundred years that follow, despite the survival of professional bursarial accounts recording the amounts paid as dividends.

The reason for the unexpected contrast is not difficult to find. In the earlier period the responsibility for the distribution of the dividend as each fine was

prospect of an imminent fine may help to explain the importance that continued to be attached in the eighteenth century to a fellow's right to a valedictory year after he accepted a disqualifying benefice, and arguably to three years in the case of the president.

231 In the same way in which the bursar was entitled to any small sum remaining after the division of corn money, the registrary kept any remainder after the division of entry fines; see, *e.g.*, the distribution on the lease of Aynells (Michaelmas 1680): Gostlin's Note Book.

232 In the nineteenth century the bursar took over the responsibility, and with it the perquisite; as a result his share of both corn money and entry fines was often a few shillings greater than that of other fellows.

233 See *Gesta*, 26 October 1785, allowing him the equivalent amount when the lease of Wilton was not renewed, and therefore a "Registrary's fee" was not paid by the departing tenant.

received fell upon the registrary and we are fortunate to have the record made personally by two exceptionally scrupulous registraries, John Gostlin and John Drury, without which we should know very little unless we choose to trawl through the *Gesta* (as Drury did) and assume that the fines approved there were in fact paid and distributed. In the course of the second half of the eighteenth century, however, *de facto* responsibility for the disbursement of entry fines on leases seems to have shifted entirely to the bursar and his professional clerk or clerks.[234] The disbursement of those fines was combined with the payment of all the other sums which the bursar credited half-yearly to the Master and each of the fellows, including stipends, allowances and dividends such as corn money; and as in the case of those other items, only his *total* share of any fines was carried to the summary statement of an individual's overall credit or debit balance in such bursarial accounts as survive. No details of the separate fines therefore appear in those Fellows' Accounts (or "Dividend Books" as they are now listed today).[235] None of the few surviving Fellows' Accounts are earlier in date than 1832, and, as they contain no cross-references to any record of the figures on which the entry fines were calculated, we are left to puzzle over the question from what other account those figures were taken.[236] The fines on leases were not considered to constitute income of the college, and they did not appear in the Bursar's Book and the *Libri Rationales*; yet no other series of college accounts from which the figures for entry fines must have been derived seems to have been preserved or even created. The contrast with the dividend from corn money is striking. Although only the total amount of the corn money is likewise carried to the Fellows' Accounts, there is no difficulty in identifying the source from which the total is derived, since the receipt of corn rent (and therefore of corn money) from each tenant was recorded annually in the Grain Books, and the identity of the persons entitled was recorded annually in the Absence Books along with the precise amount of his share. No such paper-trail survives for entry fines and there is no evidence that any similar set of books was ever compiled.[237] As a result, to obtain a detailed picture one would now need to

[234] A note book in the same style as Davy's *Table* continued his entries somewhat fragmentarily to the end of the eighteenth century before petering out: *Receipt Book 1763–1802*. This later note book is clearly the work of the bursar, not the registrary, for it contains the notes made by the bursar in his preliminary calculations and negotiation with the tenant: see, *e.g.*, *ibid.* Michaelmas 1797 and 1798.

[235] The title "Dividend Books" is misleading as dividends were only one head of the items they record. They are better designated "Fellows' Accounts".

[236] The only exception was that of the fellow's formal statutory stipend, where a reference was given to the *Libri Rationales*.

[237] As has been mentioned above, a note book in the same style as Davy's *Table* continued his entries somewhat fragmentarily to the end of the eighteenth century before petering out, and this would seem to be the most likely source; but even if subsequent books were ever maintained, they would have been too informal to serve as a source of the Fellows' Accounts.

trawl through the *Gesta*, as John Drury did, and then to cross-check against the records of the individual estates to be sure that the negotiations authorised in the *Gesta* had been implemented. In the present work it must suffice to mention the two salient features of the period 1760–1860: (i) the great increase in amount of the fine the tenant was required to pay, and (ii) the gradual abandonment of the beneficial lease and the transition from entry fines to rack-rents.

(i) The great increase in amount of the fine charged may have been due in part to the recognition in the eighteenth century that the rates of interest previously assumed in the arithmetical calculation of the annual value of the land had been unduly optimistic,[238] but it was also due to a real increase in the annual value of the college's estates as a result of improvements in agriculture, the sharp increase in the price of corn during and after the Napoleonic Wars,[239] and the financial benefits of parliamentary enclosures, particularly in the case of those manors where urban development was made possible by the commissioners' awards. The steady increase in the amount of the fines for each of the college estates has been fully documented in detail by Gross, and it is sufficient here to mention a few of the more striking instances. The increase in the agricultural value of the college's manors is well illustrated by the case of Duxford. The fines for Duxford for renewal for a further seven years rose from £14 in 1671 to £750 in 1812 and, after falling to £550 in 1819, climbed back to £726 in 1826.[240] Other agricultural properties, such as Mepal, Shelford and Tuttington, showed similar increases in annual value that reflect the rise in the price of corn during the Napoleonic Wars.[241] The wars appear to have had less effect on the fines for the college's few urban properties in Cambridge, Norwich and London. These fines also rose, but more slowly and less steeply than the agricultural ones, apparently even in the case

[238] This was clearly recognised in Emmanuel College, and no doubt other colleges: Bendall, *Emmanuel College*, p. 171–3.

[239] It is important to bear in mind that some of the fines levied in the first half of the nineteenth century were combined with an increase in the rent paid; the amounts of those fines were therefore less than they would have been if they had been intended to reflect the full annual value of the land.

[240] The fines for Duxford are set out very fully by Gross: *B.H.* IV(2), pp. 42–3. The dip in 1819 occurred also in Croxley. The sharp increases in the Duxford fines prompted a long-overdue recognition that the Frankland benefaction constituted a trust that required a separate trust account, and after 1832 only one-seventh of the fines were enjoyed by the Master and fellows: *ibid.*

[241] See *B.H.* IV(2) at pp. 64, 83 and 91 for Mepal, Shelford and Tuttington. The effect of the wars on the price of corn is well illustrated by the action of the college in respect of Croxley in 1812. At the College Meeting on 2 November it was "agreed that, by reason of the high price of corn, the Bursar be allowed to retain in his hands a Sum not exceeding £1,500": *Gesta*, 12 November 1812.

of the Frankland property in London.[242] What was, however, far more significant than the wars for the finances of the college in the long run was the effect of the Enclosure Acts on the development of Cambridge in the case of the Manor of Mortimer's, and the advent of the railways to Rickmansworth in the case of Croxley.[243] The effect of the awards on the development of Cambridge which followed the three enclosures has been fully recounted by Gross and it is unnecessary here to do more than refer to his monumental work on that development. In the case of Croxley the fine for renewal after seven years rose steadily from £140 in 1677 to £525 in 1805 and then sharply to £1,860 in 1812, and (after falling to £1,008 in 1819) to £1,865 in 1828.[244]

(ii) The second salient feature of the period, the gradual abandonment of the beneficial lease and the transition from entry fines to rack-rents, has been well described by Gross: "As soon as a lease had expired and the estate had been rack-rented and the [Bursar's] Book had in consequence been recouped, some addition was made to the stipends of the Master and seniors out of the rack-rent at which the tenancy had been re-let. Thus an increase of stipend was gradually substituted for the division of the fines by the Master and seniors. In this way during the first half of the nineteenth century most of the 20 years' leases were run out."[245]

The transition took over half a century to accomplish. The principal reason why it took so long lay in the long-established practice of surrender and re-grant of the lease as soon as seven years had elapsed. That practice meant that a decision by the college not to renew a beneficial lease but to seek a commercial rent instead of a fine had to be taken fourteen years before the existing lease expired. That decision would not only saddle the college for fourteen years with a tenant whose interest in the well-being of the land inevitably diminished over the years, but it also meant that no fine or increased rent would be receivable from the tenant during those fourteen years and the college would need to advance to the Master and senior fellows the amount of the two fines which would have accrued if the lease had been extended by re-grant.[246] Such advances

[242] See *B.H.* IV(2) for the fines on the Cambridge, London and Norwich properties.

[243] *B.H.* IV(2), pp. 17–29 (Cambridge) and pp. 73–7 (Rickmansworth). The three awards in Cambridge were in respect of the Pembroke Leys in 1801, St Giles' parish in 1804–5 and the Barnwell Estate in 1807–11. The Manor of Croxley benefitted a second time from the extension of the London underground line after the Great War.

[244] Davy's *Table* and *B.H.* IV(2), p. 74. The fine of £1,865 in 1828 was for nine years and was consequently a little greater than it would have been for seven years.

[245] *B.H.* IV(2), p. ix. For the increases in stipend see "*Stipends*", § VI. 4 above.

[246] The college had agreed in 1804 to make such advances on those occasions on which a tenant had been unable or unwilling to pay the fine when it became due, and it had then recouped the advance out of the increased fine it was finally paid: *Gesta*, 11 January 1804. In those cases the amount of the delayed fine would be greater, since the unexpired period of the lease would

required the existence of a reserve from which the fine could be advanced and it is noteworthy that the practice of systematically running out leases became a college policy only after the opportunity to build up such a reserve was provided by the possibility of investing in government securities as well as in land. Furthermore, the need to provide substantial advances to the Master and senior fellows meant that the practice of running out beneficial leases could be conveniently undertaken only gradually, a few leases at a time. It is not surprising therefore that the transition from fines to rack-rents which reflected the true annual value of the land leased took more than fifty years to complete.

The first instance in which the transition was completed occurred in 1816 in relation to the leasing of Runcton; no fines had been taken for that estate since 1796 and in consequence the twenty-year beneficial lease re-granted in that year finally ran out in 1816 and the annual rent of £40 p.a. which Caius had specified in Statute 91 was replaced by one of £600 p.a.[247] Thereafter the college gradually ran out the twenty-year beneficial leases on its other estates. As a result, while an individual fellow's corn money remained steady around £70 p.a. on average, depending on the number of senior fellows in residence, his dividend from fines began to wither away: £44 in 1840, £91 in 1841, but only £17 in 1846.[248] Fines were still taken and distributed in 1851 and 1854, but in 1855 the college took its last fines on twenty-year beneficial leases.[249] Only two twenty-year beneficial leases were renewed thereafter; in neither case was any fine taken, the rent being increased instead. After 1861 the college ceased entirely to renew

have been shortened by the delay and the eventual re-grant would consequently be *de facto* for a correspondingly longer period.

[247] *B.H.* IV(2), pp. 78–9; *Gesta*, 24 May 1816 ("Agreed to impower the Master & resident Fellows to take such steps about Letting the farm at Runcton as may appear necessary"). The lease of Wilton rectory had been run out even earlier (in 1791); but it had been re-let for a beneficial lease at an increased rent calculated to supply the college with the money for future fines as well as to reimburse it for the advances made during the period when the earlier beneficial lease was being run out. Payments to the Master and fellows in respect of Wilton continued to be made as fines and not as increases of stipend and they were discontinued in 1834 only in the light of a substantial increase in stipends that had been made in 1831: *B.H.* IV(2), pp. 100–1.

[248] *Fellows' Accounts*, 1840–42, 1846–66. In 1840 the emolument of a senior fellow on Stephen Smith's foundation (Mr Stokes) amounted to £363. 10s. 6d., comprising a stipend of £231. 16s. 0d., corn money of £83. 5s. 7d., entry fines of £44. 9s. 5d., and £3. 19s. 6d. in small allowances for heating, commemorations and Tancred dividend: *Lib. Rat.*, 1840–41; *Fellows' Accounts*, 1840–42. Stokes also received £362. 13s. 4d. from his college offices as bursar, dean and conduct.

[249] *B.H.* IV(2), p. x. The last fines were levied in 1855: *Gesta*, C.O.6 of 12 December 1855 (Shelford Mill £808, Haddenham £400 and houses in Norwich £80). A last dividend of £85. 17s. 4d. was paid to each senior fellow the following year: *Fellows' Accounts*, 1856. By this time the college had started to even out the payment to fellows by crediting the fine to the college and making increases in the *annual* stipend in lieu of dividing each fine separately (*Gesta*, C.O.6 of 16 December 1856); the practice of dividing fines was completely discontinued the following year and the stipend was substantially increased: see *The demise of dividends* at p. 542 below.

old-style twenty-year agricultural leases and the last such lease accordingly ran out in 1881.[250]

Building leases

The Act of 1571 restricted colleges to granting leases for no more than twenty-one years, but it was amended the following year to allow them to grant leases of "houses" and their grounds in "any Cytye Boroughe Town Corporate or Market Towne, or the Suburbes of any of them" for up to forty years, provided (i) that the lease was not reversionary, (ii) that the grounds did not exceed ten acres, (iii) that "the accustomed yearly Rent at the leaste" was reserved, and (iv) that the lessee was charged with "reparations".[251] The Act "opened up a considerable area for abuse, as the definition of a suburb was notoriously inexact",[252] but the only requirement that seems ever to have caused this college difficulty was the limitation to ten acres, when the Act came to be relied on for the development of its land in Cambridge in the nineteenth century.[253]

In the sixteenth century the college made no use of the 1572 Act, for it had very little urban property to which the Act could apply, just a group of eight houses in Norwich, one property on Peas Hill and then, at the end of the century, the three houses in Philip Lane, London, that Joyce Frankland left to it in 1586.[254] The college's first use of the Act appears to have occurred in 1621, when it granted a lease for forty years of part of the land in Free School Lane that Stephen Perse had left to it in 1615 for the foundation of his Free Grammar School. The purpose of the lease was the building of a house by the tenant so that the rent would provide for the repairs to the schoolhouse, and no fines appear to have been paid until 1722, and then not again until 1762.[255]

250 *B.H.* IV(2), p. x.

251 18 Eliz. c. 11, ss. 5, 7. The Act did not extend to the leasing of a dwelling house used for habitation by the college. Furthermore, it prohibited the *sale* of any house otherwise than by exchange.

252 *H.U.C.*, II, p. 278.

253 See *Gesta*, 24 May 1816, where the college wished to lease a field of 12 acres which had been allotted to it under the St Giles' Enclosure Act, and to require the tenant to expend not less than £2,000 on building "a substantial brick dwelling house and other back buildings". Given the substantial outlay required of the tenant, the lease should properly have been a building lease for forty years, but the college had to limit the lease of the 12 acres to twenty years and could only record that "the present Fellows do hereby recommend to the future Society, to renew the above lease at the end respectively of seven & fourteen years without taking any fine for the same".

254 For these properties see *B.H.* IV(2), pp. 21, 57–8 and 68–9.

255 *B.H.* IV(2), p. 108, and Davy's *Table*. A fine of £12 was paid in 1722 (for fourteen more years) and on the tenant's marriage three years later a new lease for forty years was granted to her and her husband without a further fine. By 1762, thirty-seven years of the lease had been allowed by the tenant to run out, and the fine for a further thirty-seven years thereupon rose steeply to £100.

Following the Great Fire of London, the college made further use of the 1572 Act in 1669 for the rebuilding of Joyce Frankland's houses in Philip Lane. The forty-year lease provided that the tenant "will within 5 years erect so many houses as he conveniently can, according to the Act for the rebuilding of the City" and that he should enter into a bond of £1,500 for the performance of the covenants of the lease. As might be expected, no fine is recorded until 1706, and the college does not seem to have become embroiled in the complications of the Act for the rebuilding in the way Emmanuel College did.[256] Following the example of its London property, the college started in 1693 to grant forty-year leases (in place of twenty-year ones) of one of its properties in Cambridge, the "Rose & Crown" in King's Parade; as in the case of the Philip Lane lease, this lease was a genuine building lease in which the tenant undertook to lay out £100 on the rebuilding, and no fine was taken when the lease was renewed in 1707 after fourteen years, "only Register's Fees".[257] However, the college appears never to have extended the practice of granting forty-year leases to its other houses in Cambridge and Norwich, all of which it had held from before Caius' time.[258]

After 1693 no forty-year lease appears to have been granted on any other property until 1799. In that year the college made its first genuine building lease in the modern sense, *i.e.*, leasing previously undeveloped land for the purpose of erecting urban buildings. A close belonging to the Manor of Mortimer's abutting the present Queen's Road, known as Butcher's Piece, was excepted from the lease of the manor when it was renewed in 1799 and the close was leased for forty years to Mr Wilkins, the father of William Wilkins, the architect and fellow, in order to build (what is now) Newnham Cottage. This marked the start of the successive enclosures which led to the dramatic rise during the nineteenth century in the value of the fines taken for the renewal of forty-year leases and in particular the development of the Manor of Mortimer's.[259] That rise must fall outside the scope of the present work and it is sufficient to say here that the gradual discontinuance of the dividing of the fines on forty-year leases between the Master and senior fellows appears to follow much the same pattern as that of the twenty-year leases described above. In 1858 the college acquired

[256] 19 Chas II, c. 3 (1667); *B.H.* IV(2), p. 58; Bendall, *Emmanuel College*, pp. 149–50.

[257] Davy's *Table*; *B.H.* IV(2), p. 22. The "Rose & Crown" had been devised to the college in 1626 by the Master, John Gostlin.

[258] The college did in fact grant a thirty-nine-year sub-lease of one other property in Cambridge. This was the land at the western end of Little St Mary's Lane known as Fairclough's Holt, which it held on a forty-year lease from the corporation of Cambridge. The lease of the holt or close had been bequeathed to the college in 1692 by a benefactor and, being inhibited from selling land in Cambridge by Statute 100, the college in effect sold the land by sub-leasing it with an undertaking to obtain a renewal of the lease from the corporation every fourteen years if the sub-lessee paid whatever reasonable fine the corporation might require.

[259] The successive statutory enclosures of St Thomas' Leys, St Giles' parish, the Barnwell Estate and Newnham are very fully documented by Gross in *B.H.* IV(2), pp. 17–21, 24–9.

power by Act of Parliament to grant leases for ninety-nine years and almost all its new building leases were granted upon this tenure thereafter.[260] It continued to take fines for the renewal of the older forty-year leases until 1880 and these were credited to the college in the Bursar's Book after 1857; but it ceased to take fines thereafter and substituted an increase in the ground rent instead.[261]

THE DEMISE OF DIVIDENDS

At the college meeting on 15 December 1857, it was agreed "That the practice of dividing Fines be altogether discontinued and that the Stipend of a Senior Fellow be fixed at £300 a year, to commence from Michaelmas last."[262] The other appreciable dividend, corn money, continued to be paid until 1887 to a dwindling number of senior fellows who had been elected under Dr Caius' statutes or the University Commissioners' statutes which replaced them in 1860, but the fact that after 1857 all entry fines were to be credited to the college and carried to the Bursar's Book might lead one to suppose that this would have sounded the death knell of dividends and that the principle enunciated so clearly by Caius in Statute 63 would have been recognised at long last. It comes as a surprise therefore to find that the reverse happened. In the 1860 Statutes the Commissioners extended the concept of dividend to the income from *all* the college's property, not merely from corn rents and entry fines. By the Commissioners' new Statute 28, the "clear annual balance" of "the income of all property belonging to the College, except that of the Davy Trust, the College Building Fund and the Endowment Fund", was to be ascertained and divided into 469 equal parts or shares, and a specified number of shares given to the Master and each of the twelve senior fellows, the eighteen junior fellows and the thirty-six scholars, leaving eight shares to be carried to the Endowment Fund.[263] One wonders what the reaction of Dr Caius would have been. It is not surprising that it took ten years before the college felt able to bring the provision into effect. Nor is it surprising that the provision lasted only for ten further years after that: the 1860 Statutes were repealed by the Statutes of 1882 and the

[260] Universities and College Estates Act 1858 (21 & 22 Vict. c. 44), s. 11.

[261] *B.H.* IV(2), p. vii.

[262] *Gesta*, C.O.11 of 15 December 1857. Fines were still paid on the renewal of forty-year leases until 1880; after the decision on 15 December 1857 these were carried to the Bursar's Book and credited to the college. At the same meeting on 15 December the college formally accepted the first of the statutes made by the University Commissioners in the process of dismantling Dr Caius' statutes: *ibid.*, C.O.8.

[263] Statute 28 (1860). The Master was to receive 5 shares, each senior fellow 15, each junior fellow 10, each of nine scholars 3, each of nine other scholars 2, each of six other scholars 1½, leaving 8 for the Endowment Fund. The first dividend under the statute was not paid until 1871: *Absence Book 1860–1961*, 1871 (Lady Day).

complicated system of division into 469 parts was replaced by the payment of fixed amounts specified in the statute.[264]

It might be expected that these fixed payments would be called "stipends" rather than "dividends", for the payments were no more than the culmination of the process of substituting increases in stipend for dividends from fines and corn rents which had been going on since the beginning of the nineteenth century.[265] Unlike the founders' original stipends, however, the annual payments which now replaced those dividends were notionally subject to a potential rateable reduction in the event of any insufficiency in the college's residuary income to provide them. As a consequence of this (entirely theoretical) liability to reduction, it was the term "dividend" that came to be adopted for the annual payments to fellows, and the use of the term "stipend" was confined to the salaries paid for the performance of college offices.[266]

The period between the wars

The system of "dividends" set up in 1882 remained unchanged in essence until 1926. Following the Great War the need of the two ancient universities for financial support from public funds led to the appointment of a Royal Commission. In its report in 1922 the Commission made far-reaching recommendations not only for the two universities but also for their constituent colleges. Those recommendations were translated into wholly new statutes for both university and colleges by the University Commissioners who were appointed under the Oxford and Cambridge Act 1923 to give effect to the Report of the Royal Commission. The new statutes which they made for each college contained two provisions that altered the character of dividend profoundly: the first provision established a relationship between fellowship and college office which had not previously existed under any of the three founders' statutes, while the second introduced a novel association between fellowship dividend and university office that had the effect of depriving the dividend of the greater part of its financial value.

(i) Under the founders' statutes the tenure of a fellowship had been completely independent of the holding of any office: college officers were elected from within the fellowship, and a fellow might be elected to one, or sometimes more than one, of the college's offices either for just one

264 £800 to the Master, £250 to each of the twenty-two fellows, an extra £50 to each of the eight surviving senior fellows who had opted to come under the new statutes, and amounts of £60, £40, £30 and £20 to each member of four categories of scholar: Statute 41 (1882).

265 The traditional terminology was used when the college resolved to discontinue the practice of dividing fines in 1857 in favour of an increase in the "stipend" of senior fellows: see C.O.11 of 15 December 1857 cited in n. 262 above.

266 See "*Stipends*", § VI. 4, at pp. 477–8 above.

year or successively for a number of years, and he might undertake the office on more than one occasion; but his fellowship was not dependent in any way on his holding that or some other office. Two comparatively minor deviations from that basic principle occurred in the years following the repeal of the third founder's statutes in 1860. The first was the establishment in 1860 of a class of professorial fellows who were elected into fellowships in virtue of their university office, received no dividend and held their fellowships for the period of their offices.[267] The second minor inroad on the principle occurred in 1882: the new statutes which came into force in that year introduced a limit (of six years) on the tenure of a fellowship for the first time in the history of the college and coupled with it a need for re-election at that point, unless the fellow was holding a qualifying office at the time.[268] No further erosion of the principle, however, occurred before 1926. In that year, however, the University Commissioners transformed the relationship between fellowship and office. Under the statutes which they made for each college, elections to fellowships would thereafter be made *in virtue of* a qualifying college or university office and tenure of the fellowship would be dependent on the holding of the office; the only regular exception was to be the relatively new class of junior research fellowships held for a strictly limited period of years and deliberately divorced from the distractions of office.[269] The unspoken effect of linking the election of a fellow directly to the appointment to an office was to alter fundamentally the character of the fellowship dividend; for all but research fellows the dividend was now regarded simply as an element in the stipend of the office to which the fellowship was attached, albeit an appreciable element, and the last vestige of its original character as a maintenance grant was erased for all but the (few) junior research fellows and, exceptionally, a person of outstanding academic distinction (whose fellowship was not dependent on the holding of an office).[270]

(ii) The second provision that ultimately came to alter the character of dividend was the requirement that half of the stipendiary fellowships[271]

[267] Statutes (1860), ss. 18, 28.

[268] Statutes (1882), s. 11. In addition to that of professor, the qualifying offices were those of tutor, assistant tutor, lecturer, bursar and dean; the list survives today as the college's "primary pensionable office".

[269] These had been introduced in 1890 as Drosier fellowships in accordance with the trusts of Dr Drosier's will: Statutes (1890), s. 1. There was also an exceptional power to elect a person of outstanding academic distinction into a fellowship without office: Statutes (1860), s. 18; (1882), s. 10(7) ("eminent for science or learning").

[270] Statute 14(4); see the preceding note.

[271] *I.e.*, fellowships carrying a dividend from the college, other than the junior research (Drosier) fellowships mentioned in n. 269.

should be reserved for two classes of university teaching officers, university lecturers and university demonstrators. The purpose of the Royal Commission in making this recommendation for "Reserved" fellowships had been academic rather than financial, namely, to integrate more closely the appointment of college and university teachers and thereby to distribute the load of tuition more equally.[272] The system did, however, have a marked financial effect. The dividend enjoyed by a university teaching officer who was elected to a reserved fellowship was regarded by the Royal Commission as his emolument for research, publishing and academic activities other than teaching. The stipend he received from the university was therefore not conceived as a full-time stipend but as a payment purely for (part-time) teaching and its amount was fixed accordingly. In the words of a later Syndicate, "In its financial effect, therefore, the system of Reserved Fellowships came to be a subvention of the University by the Colleges, additional to the monetary contributions they were required to make [by way of University Contribution]."[273] A further consequence was that a university teaching officer who was not fortunate enough to be elected to a reserved fellowship needed an additional payment from the university (the "fellowship allowance") to provide him with a sufficient stipend to live on.

The period after the Second World War

In its wake, the Second World War brought about a transformation in the financial relationship between the colleges and university. The system of reserved fellowships was no longer adequate for the rapidly increasing numbers of university teaching officers and the subvention to the university provided by the system no longer made a meaningful contribution towards the payment of their stipends. Furthermore, the balance of numbers between those university teaching officers who held fellowships and those who did not had shifted significantly, and the increasing number of university lecturers and demonstrators who did not hold fellowships meant that it was no longer sensible to maintain the Commissioners' notion that the stipends of university teaching officers should be regarded as being part-time stipends which would be supplemented by fellowship dividends or else, in a small number of cases, by a "fellowship allowance".

The rapidly expanding needs of the university required much greater reliance on public funds and in 1947 full-time university stipends for all grades

[272] *Report of the Royal Commission* (1922), § 101, rec. 27.

[273] *Report of the Syndicate on the Relationship between the University and the Colleges* (*University Reporter*, 13 March 1962), § 26.

of the academic staff were introduced, financed by the Treasury through the University Grants Committee. These full-time stipends were made subject to deduction (of all but £50 of the dividend)[274] if the recipients were fellows with dividend. This system of a full-time university stipend that was subject to a deduction on account of a fellowship dividend thus replaced the previous system of supplementation of a part-time salary by a "fellowship allowance" for those officers who were not fellows of colleges.[275] The system of reserved fellowships which the University Commissioners devised in 1926 was initially retained, but it was clearly inadequate by itself to meet the university's pressing need for the provision of fellowships for more members of its rapidly growing academic and administrative staff. The Commissioners' system of reserved stipendiary fellowships now acted as a brake upon the desired election of more university officers to fellowships, since the electing college would incur an obligation to contribute to the officer's university stipend if the fellowship carried a dividend. The obvious alternative would seem to be for colleges to elect into non-stipendiary fellowships, now that university stipends were full-time and fellowship dividends were no longer needed to supplement them; but although the Commissioners had included limited provision in colleges' statutes for the election of university officers into fellowships without dividend in 1926, they had imposed stringent restrictions upon the number of such non-stipendiary fellowships that a college was permitted to make.[276] Colleges were therefore encouraged to amend their statutes and remove the restriction on the number of non-stipendiary fellowships that they had power to elect or else to reduce drastically the size of the dividend. Gonville and Caius College amended its statutes in May 1949 and acquired a wide power to elect "any

[274] £50 had been the sum regarded by the Royal Commission in 1922 as the appropriate payment for the services expected of all fellows irrespective of any office or stipend (the "net dividend"): *Report of the Royal Commission* (1922), § 121 and rec. 42.

[275] For a clear and convenient summary of the relationship between dividends and university stipends in the forty years between 1922 and 1962, see the *Report of the Syndicate on the Relationship between the University and the Colleges* cited above, §§ 1–30.

[276] Caius College had been given power in 1926 to elect up to three such non-stipendiary ("Supernumerary") fellows: Statutes (1926), Statute 17(3). Since university stipends for university lecturers and demonstrators at that time were only part-time and presupposed that the lecturer or demonstrator either would be a fellow and receive a fellowship dividend or else would receive a fellowship allowance, this meant that non-stipendiary fellowships were not suitable for such officers but were intended principally for academic and administrative officers with a full-time stipend, including readers who did not have a professorial fellowship. The term "supernumerary" had originally been introduced into the college's statutes in 1882 to indicate fellows who chose to resign their right to a dividend and thereby ceased to count towards the number of fellowships that the college was required by its statutes to maintain (commonly called "fellowships on the foundation"): Statutes 1882, Statute 11(13). After 1926 it was used instead to denote those additional, non-stipendiary fellowships over and above the number of stipendiary reserved fellowships that the college was required by its statutes to elect.

person holding office in the College or in the University" into a non-stipendiary ("Supernumerary") fellowship.[277] Such changes of statute, however, left colleges with the financial burden of supplementing the university stipends of those who already held reserved fellowships and of making further elections in order to keep up the number of such fellowships to that required by the 1926 University Commissioners' statutes. This obligation, coupled with the rapid rise in prices at the time, imposed considerable financial difficulty on the poorer colleges.

In 1949 a Syndicate was appointed to consider the system of reserved fellowships and, more generally, the financial relations between the university and the colleges. It reported in 1951 and its recommendations were adopted with (retrospective) effect from 1 October 1950.[278] The eventual goal of its recommendations was the total abolition of the system of reserved fellowships and its replacement by non-stipendiary fellowships for as many university officers as the colleges could provide. Pending the eventual abolition of reserved fellowships the university would assume total responsibility for the full-time stipends of its officers and pay to the colleges sums equal to the amount of any deductions which it made from those stipends on account of a fellowship with dividend.[279] By themselves such repayments would benefit all colleges, rich and poor, at the expense of the university, and, since the aim of the Syndicate was specifically to assist the poorer colleges without unduly imposing a financial burden on the university that would have to be defrayed out of the public funds provided by the University Grants Committee, the colleges were called upon to make a compensatory increase in the University Contribution which they made to the university by way of taxation. That increase in taxation was borne mostly by the richer colleges, and the Syndicate's proposals achieved the double object of benefitting the poorer colleges and facilitating the offering of fellowships to more university teaching officers without unduly burdening the university.

Colleges were thus offered in 1951 two routes by which they might elect more university officers into fellowships: removal of statutory restrictions on their power to elect of non-stipendiary fellows, or reliance on the reimbursement of the dividends that they paid to university officers elected into reserved fellowships.

Gonville and Caius College chose both routes. It had already amended its statutes in May 1949 and acquired a wide power to elect into a non-stipendiary ("Supernumerary") fellowship "any person holding office in the College or in

277 Statute 17(3). This course was simpler and swifter than reducing the amount of the dividend, since that could affect the payment of pension contributions.

278 For the purpose and effect of the recommendations of the 1949 Syndicate, see paras. 28ff of the Report of the 1962 Syndicate cited above.

279 This would leave the fellow with a net dividend of £50 in recognition of his services *qua* fellow in accordance with the recommendations of the 1922 Royal Commission mentioned in n. 274 above.

the University".[280] Thereafter, as a matter of policy, whenever an intended fellow already held a university office, the college would take the route of electing him into a non-stipendiary fellowship rather than a stipendiary fellowship,[281] whether he was being elected in virtue of his university office or in virtue of some college office to which he was now being appointed. On the other hand, if he was being elected in virtue of a college office at a time when he did not yet hold any university post, the college would elect him into a stipendiary (official) fellowship,[282] as it had done between the wars, thus giving him a dividend as part of the remuneration for his college office.[283] If he later obtained a university office, then the college would continue to pay him his dividend and would recover from the university the amount which the university deducted from his university stipend.

The use of both routes produced in the college a complexity in the different classes of fellowship into which persons performing similar services might fall, and in time that complexity rendered the relationship between fellowship, office, dividend and stipend an arcane mystery understood by fewer and fewer fellows. In practical terms, the class of his fellowship made no financial difference whatsoever to the officer.[284] The only practical question was: which employer paid the employer's share on that part of his pension contributions?[285]

The two routes remained open to colleges until 1965. In that year, in the wake of the Report of the National Incomes Commission, the university undertook, through the General Board, a radical revision of university stipends and their relationship to college emoluments.[286] The underlying purpose of the Board's

[280] Statute 17(3).

[281] *I.e.*, into a supernumerary fellowship rather than an official fellowship.

[282] In many cases the college had no choice: if the person being elected to a college office was an unofficial fellow (*i.e.*, a research fellow) at the time, then he automatically became an official fellow with dividend by virtue of Statute 14(2).

[283] In the case of a teaching post the dividend would constitute the major part of the officer's stipend: the stipend of a college lecturer and director of studies in a major subject with twelve hours' supervision per week in 1950 was £500 p.a., of which £350 came from the dividend.

[284] A college lecturer who had no university post would normally be an official fellow with a dividend as part of his stipend, but he might be a supernumerary fellow with no dividend but an enhanced stipend in lieu. A college lecturer holding a university post as well as his college one would normally be a supernumerary fellow without a dividend, but he might be an official fellow and in that case he received both a dividend and a stipend from the college but suffered the deduction of all but £50 of the dividend from his university stipend; despite keeping that £50 net dividend, the official fellow would in fact end up no better off financially than if he had been a supernumerary fellow and not had any dividend, since his stipend as a college lecturer was reduced by £50 to ensure parity between college lecturers whichever class of fellowship they held.

[285] The employer's share on all the dividends was estimated to be about £10,000 p.a. in 1964: *15th Report of the General Board on Stipends* (*University Reporter*, 14 October 1964), § 35.

[286] The process was a long and much debated one, culminating in the 16th Report of the General Board on Stipends, which adopted the recommended revision. Although the Report was not

proposals was to ensure that Cambridge University could demonstrate clearly to the outside world (i) that any emoluments which a university officer received from his college in addition to his university stipend could not be regarded as an unjustified supplementation of that stipend for the performance of academic duties which similar officers in other universities would be expected to perform without supplementation; and (ii) that any college emoluments were demonstrably payments for additional responsibilities arising out of the tenure of a fellowship and were over and above what would be expected of corresponding officers in other universities.

In the view of the General Board, the essential step towards achieving that purpose was ensuring that any monetary payment to a university officer by a college for these additional collegiate responsibilities "should be in the form of a stipend, not in the form of Fellowship dividend" and that the full amount of any dividend paid should be deducted from his university stipend.[287] Only in this way, it was thought, would the university succeed in refuting any accusations that its academic stipends were being unduly supplemented in comparison with those in universities other than Oxford and Cambridge. The corollary was that colleges should therefore in these circumstances cease to pay a dividend to fellows not already enjoying a right and should take the necessary statutory power to avoid any further obligation to pay dividends and instead elect into non-stipendiary fellowships, if they had not already done that in the years following 1947. There would thereupon be no justification for the university to make any further repayments on account of dividend.[288]

It was recognised, first, that colleges would need time to effect a change of their statutes and might have to pay dividends until they had done this, and, second, that it would be necessary to safeguard the rights and reasonable expectations of university officers elected to fellowships before an appropriate 'cut-off' date, chosen to be 1 September 1965.[289] To meet the first point the university proposed a three-year period of grace, to 1 October 1968, during which it would repay to a college the amounts deducted from the university stipends in respect of dividends received by fellows elected *after* the cut-off date (*i.e.*, 1 September 1965), but not beyond 1 October 1968. To meet the second point it proposed, as a "temporary provision", that the existing arrangements for repayment to a

signed until 26 January in the following year, the revision took effect retrospectively from 1 September 1965. For the recommendations and the protracted negotiations, see the *15th and 16th Reports of the General Board on Stipends* and the documents referred to therein: *University Reporter*, 14 October 1964 and 16 February 1966 respectively.

287 *16th Report*, para. 3.

288 *Ibid.*, para. 9.

289 *Ibid.*, paras. 3, 9.

college in respect of a fellow appointed before the cut-off date should continue *sine die* if his or her college so desired.[290]

For Gonville and Caius College the first provision was unnecessary. The college had already acquired, since 1949, an unrestricted power to elect fellows to non-stipendiary (supernumerary) fellowships in virtue of college or university offices, and, instead of altering its statutes and abolishing dividends, it simply stopped making elections to stipendiary (official) fellowships.[291] Thereafter it ceased to make in the *Gesta* the traditional annual record of the dividend at the end of each calendar year.[292] The college did, however, take advantage of the "temporary provision", and it continued to pay dividends to official fellows elected *before* 1 September 1965 and to recover from the university the amount which the university deducted from the stipends of those who held university posts. This "temporary" arrangement lasted for no less than thirty years: in the course of time the payments inevitably dwindled in number and diminished in value, but it was not until the end of the academic year 1994–95 that the college's last dividends were finally paid to the four fellows still entitled to them.[293]

290 *Ibid.*, para. 9. The General Board proposed "that temporary provision be made for payments to Colleges to continue in respect of dividends received by those fellows, referred to above in paragraph 3, whose rights to 'net dividends' are to be preserved, but that payments in respect of fellows appointed on or after 1 September 1965 should be limited to the period up to 1 October 1968."

291 The college has continued on three occasions to elect into official fellowships under Statute 14(4) a person who did not hold any college or university post (and was therefore ineligible for a supernumerary fellowship) but could be considered to be a "person of exceptional distinction in science literature or art". The College Council, on one occasion, later made an election of a college officer to an official fellowship *per incuriam*, many years after any dividends had ceased to be made. It has taken care to avoid the automatic translation of a research fellow into an official fellowship under Statute 14(2) mentioned in n. 282 above.

292 The last record was that for the calendar year 1968: C.O.16 of 17 January 1969.

293 By a quirk of history, among the four was the great-grandson of the one of the last five recipients of corn money in 1887 (E.S. Roberts): cf. n. 160 above. In strict theory the stipends paid to research (unofficial) fellows continue to include an element of dividend (£300). This element has long been absorbed into the "special grant" which has, since the early 1950s, been paid to them annually under Statute 42(5) in order to bring the £300 up to a living wage. The hesitation of senior college officers on the Council in the early 1950s to raise the emoluments of research fellows above the statutory limit of £300 on their dividend was one of the more contentious issues in the disputes that have become known as "the Peasants' Revolt". It was solved only by recourse to Statute 42(5), which provided that "The College Council may make to any Fellows a special grant or grants out of the College income in view of the expenses which the special nature of his research work may involve." Today, almost 99% of a research fellow's stipend is provided by such a grant.

Note

"MR FLETCHER HIS ARITHMETICAL TABLE 1609"

This intriguing document is carefully preserved at the beginning of the first volume in a long series of half-yearly accounts known as the Bursar's Books[294] and was clearly regarded as being of lasting importance. It is set out in eight columns in a neat italic script and arabic notation on a single page,[295] and it was written by a fellow of the college, John Fletcher, who was a mathematician of some note in his younger days and became an astrologer of some celebrity in later life.[296] Although it is found at the start of the account for Lady Day 1609, it was almost certainly devised earlier, at a time when the author was bursar. Fletcher was not bursar in 1609 but he had previously served in that office on two occasions, in 1594 and again in 1601.

The purpose of the Arithmetical Table was to ease the task of the bursar at each half-year, when he had to assess the monetary value of all the corn rents received from the college's agrarian tenants under Sir Thomas Smith's Corn Act 1576 (*i.e.*, the part of their rent which they were required to pay in corn or its market value), and then calculate how much of it should be credited to the college as income and how much would remain to be divided between the Master, fellows and scholars – in theory for the "Relief of their Commons and Diett" but in reality to be divided between them. It is preceded by a list of the twenty-three properties which had been brought within the Corn Act[297] by the time it was written, and it is ingeniously designed as a convenient ready-reckoner for calculating the amount of corn money arising half-yearly from those twenty-three properties *in future years* as well as that in which it was written.

The table first lists in four columns (under the title "The tenants every half yeare do pay in Money, Wheat, Mault") what each of the twenty-three tenants has to pay half-yearly:

(i) the amount payable in money,
(ii) the quantity of wheat,

[294] The series of Bursar's Books was started in 1609 and continued unbroken until 1926.

[295] It came toward the end of a painfully long transition from the use of roman notation to arabic numerals. In their accounts the bursars or their clerks appear to have used Roman notation up to c. 1600, and even thereafter figures in an account might be entered in Arabic numerals but corrected – presumably by an older clerk – in Roman figures: *Lib. Rat.* (Michaelmas 1607). Roman numerals were still occasionally being used in the Bursar's Book in 1620: *Bursar's Book* (Michaelmas 1620). The use of two notations in a single account must have presented a challenge.

[296] *B.H.* I, p. 95.

[297] "A note of such farmers, as pay the third part in Corne".

(iii) the quantity of malt; and
(iv) the sum produced by combining (a) the amount payable in money with (b) the notional 'value' of the quantities of wheat and malt calculated at the statutory conversion rate fixed by Sir Thomas Smith in 1576, *i.e.*, a notional value which equals one-third of the "old rent", not the true value at the current market rate.[298]

Each of the four columns is added up, giving the total amounts due from all twenty-three tenants: money (£82. 15s. 5d.), wheat (39 quarters, 4 bushels) and malt (46 quarters, 2½ pecks), and the combined sum (£107. os. 6d.). This combined sum of £107. os. 6d. constitutes the amount to be credited to the college as the rent in the half-yearly accounts (what "the colledg hath in money"). The figures, it must be remembered, are *not* related to the actual market value of the wheat and malt and consequently do not vary from year to year: the four columns simply record the unchanging amount of money which the college corporately is entitled to from the twenty-three tenants under Archbishop Grindall's interpretation of the Act.[299]

It is, however, the four columns on the right-hand side of the page that are particularly illuminating. Two of the four columns list, separately for wheat and malt:

(v) the market value of the 39 quarters, 4 bushels of wheat and
(vi) the market value of the 46 quarters, 2½ pecks of malt.

Those values are calculated for a wide range of prices which are given in the final two columns:

(vii) for quarters and
(viii) for bushels.[300]

The bursar had only to read off the total value, first of wheat and then of malt, across the relevant line for the price prevailing in the Cambridge market and he could thereby ascertain at a glance the total monetary value of the wheat and malt due from all twenty-three tenants; he could then add to those two figures the amount required to be paid by the tenants in money (£82. 15s. 5d.). This gave him, in money terms, the total amount due from the twenty-three tenants in one form or the other. It then only remained for him to deduct the

298 The sum of (a) and (b) is what "The colledg hath in money".

299 These four columns, it may be noted, merely re-state conveniently in tabular form the information that is already contained in the preceding list of twenty-three properties brought under the Act. The fact that they merely reproduce the figures in the preceding list and are not the essential element in the Table is shown by the fact that figures in the left-hand columns have been wrongly copied (*e.g.*, for Runcton), yet the totals are the correct ones copied from the preceding list.

300 The prices are given in no less than fifty-three steps from 10s. up to £2. 4s. 8d. a quarter.

(unchanging) sum to be taken by the college as income (£107. os. 6d.), thereby ascertaining what remained to be divided as corn money ("*Sic restat optata dividenda pro granis*"). Lest subsequent clerks should fail to comprehend, Fletcher appended as an example the calculations for prices of 3s. 6d. a bushel for wheat and 2s. for malt.[301]

Fletcher's table appears to be the earliest surviving instance of the college's practice in relation to the apportioning of corn money between college and dividend. It shows that the whole of the increase brought about by the Corn Act was deducted as dividend and that the college corporately received no more than it would have done if the Act had never been passed, thereby undermining all of Caius' safeguards and frustrating each of Sir Thomas Smith's aims. The college's practice never differed in later years and there is no reason to doubt that the same practice had prevailed from the beginning. If so, the college would merely have been following the example of most Cambridge colleges, though each of them differed in its precise practice.

In constructing his table Fletcher, it should be noted, was interested only in the monetary value of *all* the corn due from the tenants, not that from each individual tenant, and, unlike the later Corn Rolls and Grain Books, his table does not involve the recording of the individual amounts of money which a tenant might choose to pay in lieu of corn.[302] It would seem from this that it was still expected in 1609 that tenants would normally make payment in corn and not tender money in lieu. In later years payment in money became the norm. Whether or not the payment was made in corn in 1609, it is clear that the payment was made to the bursar and that he made the necessary apportionment. Gross and Venn were mistaken, therefore, in their belief that the Master and fellows took the corn and accounted to the bursar for the one-third due to the college: the accounting was always the other way.[303]

The table was clearly constructed to serve for longer than the one year 1609 and the fact that it depended on a specific, unvarying quantity of wheat and malt due from all tenants would indicate that the college did not, in 1609, anticipate (i) bringing further properties within the Act in the near future, or (ii) raising the existing money rents.

301 £82. 15s. 5d. (money rent) + £55. 6s. od. (wheat) + £36. 17s. 3d. (malt) = £174. 18s. 8d.; "out of which always subtract due to the college" £107. os. 6d., leaving as dividend for corn money ("*sic restat summa optata dividend' pro granis*") £67. 18s. 2d. This would produce roughly £4. 10s. for each fellow. The illustrative prices are not necessarily those prevailing in 1609, but we may assume that they would not have differed greatly from those prevailing in the year when Fletcher constructed the table.

302 In the later rolls and books those amounts are entered in a separate column which is then totalled up to produce the amount of dividend.

303 Cf. *B.H.* IV(2), p. v. The £82. 15s. 5d. money rent is wrongly stated there as being for wheat.

VII

Appendices

VII. A

The Master's Vote: Bateman's Interpretation

[As transcribed in *Documents* (1852), II, 436–437]

[NOTE: The following extract is from Bishop Bateman's own interpretation of the corresponding statutes that he had earlier made for Trinity Hall. The Interpretation was given on 14 August 1354 in the period between the making of the 1353 and 1355 Statutes for Gonville Hall.]

Wilhelmus permissione Divina Norwicensis Episcopus, dilectis Filiis et alumnis, Custodi Collegii ac Collegio Scholarium Aulae Sanctae Trinitatis Cantabrigiensis et ejusdem Collegii et Aulae Sociis, et Scholaribus universis, praesentibus et futuris, Salutem, Gratiam, et Benedictionem:

Volentes nostram intentionem circa quaedam Statuta vestra per Nos facta, in his quas in dubium revocari poterunt declarare, ac Statutis addicere quaedam nova, quae utilia, imo vero necessaria Collegio reputamus, ad eam procedimus in hunc modum:

Imprimis, quia in Statuto, sub titulo *De tempore electionis et forma*,[1] circa finem taliter continetur: "Quod si locus alicujus Socii dicti Collegii quovis modo vacaverit in futurum, volumus, quod per Custodis et majoris partis Sociorum electionem concordem, per viam scrutinii, ut praemittitur, infra mensem alius subrogetur, alioquin ad solum Custodem provisio et ordinatio pertineat illa vice." Praefatum articulum taliter declaramus, Quod in electione Socii, Custodis praesentia necessario requiratur, si debite praemonitus, vel etiam expectatus, electioni voluerit interesse; non tamen quod votum suum necessario votis majoris partis conveniat Sociorum, imo volumus sufficere majoris partis Sociorum Collegii consensum, licet Custos majori parti non consenserit in electione Socii cujuscunque. Adjicientes insuper ad Statutum, Volumus quod in electione tam Custodis quam Sociorum dicti Collegii facienda, Socii praesentes in Collegio, per decem dierum spatium, a vacationis tempore computandum, si extra vacationum tempora, et per totum tempus vacationum, si infra vacationum tempora vacatio contigerit, et ultra per decem dierum spatium

1 The corresponding statute for Gonville Hall is Statute 3 *De tempore et electionis forma*.

post resumptionem Magistrorum, absentes cum licentia Custodis, Socios, si qui fuerint, expectare continue teneantur.

...

Data apud Southelmham, 14 die Augusti, anno Domini 1354, et Consecrationis nostrae undecimo.

[William by divine permission Bishop of Norwich to [his] beloved sons and wards, the Keeper of the College and the community of Scholars of the Hall of the Holy Trinity Cambridge and the all the Fellows and Scholars of that College and Hall, present and future, Greetings, Grace and Benediction:

Wishing to declare our intention in respect of certain statutes made for you by us, on those matters which require further consideration, and to add certain new statutes which we deem useful and indeed necessary for the college, we do this as follows:

First, since it is worded in the statute entitled *Of the Time and Form of Election*, at the end, as follows: "But if the place of any fellow of the said college becomes vacant in any way in the future, it is our will that another shall be chosen in his place within one month by an agreed election by the keeper and a majority of the fellowship by way of scrutiny as previously mentioned, otherwise the choice and appointment shall belong to the keeper alone on that occasion", we expound the aforesaid article in this way: That the presence of the keeper is a necessary requirement in the election of a fellow if he wishes to be present at the election and has been duly notified or is expected, but not that his vote must necessarily be in accord with that of the majority of the fellowship: rather, it is our will that the consensus of a majority of the fellowship is sufficient, even though the keeper has not agreed with the majority in the election of the particular person [chosen]. As an addition to the statute, moreover, it is our will that, in any election either of the keeper or of fellows of the said college, fellows who are present in college are required to await [the return of] any fellows who are absent with the leave of the keeper for a period of ten days running from the time of the vacancy, if it occurs outside a vacation, and, if it occurs during a vacation, for the whole period of the vacation together with a further ten days after the resumption of studies.

...

Given at South Elmham [Suffolk], on the 14th day of August, in the year of Our Lord 1354 and the 11th year of our Consecration.]

VII. B

The Requirement of Compatibility with Bateman's Statutes: Extracts from the Charter of 1557

[NOTE: Five provisions of the Charter of 4 September 1557 given to John Caius by King Philip and Queen Mary contained a reference to the statutes made by William Bateman for Gonville Hall: they are the provisions relating to

(i) the obligation of the Master and the fellows to obey and conduct themselves in accordance with the statutes and ordinances of William Bateman and John Caius;
(ii) the power to act on behalf of the college and to bind themselves and their successors in accordance with the statutes and ordinances of both founders;
(iii) the procedure for electing a Master, fellow or scholar;
(iv) the authority granted to John Caius thereafter to make and change statutes and ordinances for the college;
(v) the visitatorial power granted to John Caius to adjudicate on and settle all disputes arising within the college.

The relevant passages are italicised here.

Three of the five provisions, namely (i), (iv) and (v), included a precise and explicit requirement that any statutes and ordinances made by John Caius under the powers given to him in the charter should be valid only if and in so far as they were compatible with those made by William Bateman for Gonville Hall.]

(i) The obligation of the Master and fellows to conform to statutes and ordinances

… **Volentes insuper** et per presentes decernentes quod tam predicti Magister sive Custos et socii quam alii illis imposterum ut inferius exprimitur associandi et eligendi sive adiungendi in omnibus et per omnia se gerent exhibebunt conversabuntur et eligentur iuxta et secundum ordinaciones regulas et statuta

per predictum Willelmum quondam Episcopum Norwicensem in scriptis fact' habit' et redact' ac iuxta ordinaciones regulas et statuta per predictum Johannem Caius ad incrementum et communem utilitatem eiusdem Collegii imposterum authoritate subscripta fiend'. *Ita quod huiusmodi ordinaciones regule et statuta aut eorum aliquod per predictum Iohannem Caius sic imposterum fiend' non sint aut erunt repugnantia seu contraria predictis ordinacionibus regulis et statutis per predictum Willelmum nuper Episcopum Norwicensem ut prefertur factis aut habitis nec contraria prerogative nostre Regie.*

[WISHING MOREOVER and decreeing by these presents that both the aforesaid master or keeper and fellows and others to be associated and elected or joined to them in future, as is set forth below, shall in all things and in all ways conduct and comport themselves and conform to and be elected in accordance with the ordinances, rules and statutes made, held, and recorded in writing by the aforesaid William, at one time Bishop of Norwich, and according to the ordinances, rules and statutes hereafter to be made by the aforesaid John Caius for the increase and common good of the college by the authority hereinafter granted [to him]; [but] *so that such ordinances, rules, and statutes or any of them so made in the future by the aforesaid John Caius be not and shall not conflict with or be contrary to the aforesaid ordinances, rules, and statutes made or held by the aforesaid William, lately Bishop of Norwich, as previously mentioned, nor contrary to our royal prerogative.*]

(ii) The power to act on behalf of the college and to bind themselves and their successors

… Et quod predicti Magister sive Custos et Socii eiusdem Collegii et successores sui habeant et habebunt commune Sigillum ad omnia et omnimodas causas negocia evidentia res materias et cetera script' et fact' sive fiend' eos vel idem Collegium aliquo modo tangentia sive concernentia sigillanda per quod se et successores suos astringere et obligare possint et valeant ad tempus vel imperpetuum iuxta et secundum tenorem eiusdem scripti sic per illos sigillat' *ac iuxta predictas ordinaciones regulas et statuta per predictum Willelmum quondam Norwicensem Episcopum antehac habit' fact' edit' et usitat' Ac iuxta ordinaciones regulas et statuta per predictum Johannem Caius in forma subscripta imposterum fiend' et constituend'.*

[And that the aforesaid master or keeper and fellows of the college and their successors may and shall have a common seal for the sealing of all manner of causes, businesses, evidences, concerns and other writings made and to be made touching or concerning them or the college in any way, by which they

may be legally competent to bind and constrain themselves and their successors either for a period of time or in perpetuity in accordance with the tenor of the same writing so sealed by them and *according to the aforesaid ordinances, rules, and statutes formerly held, made, published, and used by the aforesaid William, at one time Bishop of Norwich, and according to the future ordinances, rules, and statutes to be made and constituted in the form hereinafter described by the aforesaid John Caius.*]

(iii) The procedure for electing a Master, fellow or scholar

… **Ac ulterius** volumus ac pro nobis heredibus et successoribus nostrum prefate Regine per presentes concedimus et ordinamus quod quandocunque et quotiescunque contigerit aliquem Magistrum sive Custodem aut aliquem socium sive scholarem predicti Collegii de Goneville et Caius fundat' in honorem Annunciacionis beate Marie[1] in universitate Cantabrigie pro tempore existentem obire recedere amoveri vel locum suum quocunque modo vacare quod extunc de tempore in tempus electio huiusmodi Magistri socii[2] et scholaris fiat et erit *iuxta predictas ordinaciones regulas et statuta predicti Willelmi nuper Episcopi Norwicensis Ac iuxta ordinaciones regulas et statuta per predictum Johannem Caius in forma subscripta imposterum fiend' et stabiliend'.*

[FURTHERMORE we wish and for ourselves and the heirs and successors of us the aforesaid Queen by these presents grant and decree that whensoever and as often as it shall happen that any master or keeper or any fellow or scholar of the aforesaid College of Gonville and Caius, founded in honour of the Annunciation of Blessed Mary in the University of Cambridge, then living die, depart, be removed, or in any manner vacate his place, that then on each occasion the election of such a master, fellow, and scholar may and shall [take place] *according to the aforesaid ordinances, rules, and statutes of the aforesaid William, lately Bishop of Norwich, and according to the rules and statutes in the future to be made and established in the form hereinafter mentioned by the aforesaid John Caius.*]

1 No *virginis*; probably because of a line-break after *Marie*.

2 Apparently lower-case for both *socii* and *scholaris*.

(iv) The authority granted to John Caius to make and change statutes and ordinances for the college

… **Ac eciam volumus** ac per presentes pro nobis heredibus et successoribus nostrum prefate Regine concedimus et ordinamus quod predictus Johannes Caius ulterius habeat et habebit liberam licitam et plenariam potestatem et facultatem de tempore in tempus durante vita sua naturali pro bono regimine ac communi utilitate et proficius eiusdem Collegii ac terrarum tenementorum hereditamentorum bonorum et catallorum eiusdem condendi et sanctiendi quecunque statuta ordinaciones regulas per Magistrum sive Custodem ac socios et scholares eiusdem Collegii et eorum quemlibet observand' et perimplend' ac eadem et eorum quodlibet in parte vel in toto tollend' mutand' augend' et alia de novo componend' prout eidem Johanni Caius de tempore in tempus durante vita sua videbuntur necessaria sive opportuna *dummodo et ita quod huiusmodi statuta ordinaciones et regule seu eorum aliquod sic per eundem Johannem Caius condend' et sanctiend' non sint aut erunt contraria sive repugnantia predictis statutis ordinacionibus et regulis aut eorum alicui in predicta nuper domo sive Aula ante hac vocata Goneville Halle per dictum Willelmum Norwicensem Episcopum antehac ut prefertur habitis factis seu editis nec contraria prerogative nostre regie.*

[AND WE ALSO WISH and by these presents for ourselves and heirs and successors of us the aforesaid Queen grant and decree that the aforesaid John Caius further have and shall have full, permissive, and plenary power and faculty from time to time during his natural life, for the good government and the common welfare and profit of the same college and of the lands, tenements, hereditaments, goods, and chattels of the same, of establishing and decreeing any statutes, ordinances, and rules to be observed and fulfilled by the master or keeper and fellows of the same college and any one of them, and of revoking, changing, or increasing the same and any one of them in part or in whole and of composing others anew, as shall seem necessary or opportune to the same John Caius from time to time during his natural life, *provided and so that such statutes, ordinances, and rules be not nor shall be contrary or in opposition to the aforesaid statutes, ordinances, and rules or any of them previously held, made, or set forth in the aforesaid former house or hall formerly called Gonville Hall by the said William, Bishop of Norwich, as is premised, nor contrary to our royal prerogative.*]

(v) The visitatorial power granted to John Caius to adjudicate on all disputes arising within the college

... **Volumus insuper** ac per presentes pro nobis heredibus successoribus nostrum prefate Regine constituimus et ordinamus quod quandocunque et quotiescunque contigerit aliqua dissidia divisiones lites seu controversias oriri seu moveri in predicto Collegio de Goneville et Caius fundat' in honorem Annunciacionis beate Marie virginis in universitate Cantabrigie in vel circa electionem nominacionem seu admissionem Magistri sive Custodis aut alicuius socii sive Scholaris eiusdem Collegii aut gubernacionem ordinacionem seu amocionem eorundem seu eorum alicuius aut in aliis causis materiis rebus seu negotiis quibuscunque idem Collegium aut terras tenementa hereditamenta possessiones bona vel catalla eiusdem Collegii quoquo modo tangentibus seu concernentibus. Ita quod predicti Magister sive custos et socii vel maior pars eorundem de huiusmodi dissidiis divisionibus litibus seu controversiis sic ortis seu motis inter se minime convenire poterint eademque infra duos menses finire et terminare, quod tunc et toties predictus Johannes Caius durante vita sua naturali habeat et habebit plenariam potestatem authoritatem et facultatem de tempore in tempus virtute harum litterarum nostrarum patencium huiusmodi dissidia divisiones lites et controversias audiend' et examinand' eademque *secundum ordinaciones regulas et statuta eiusdem Collegii per predictum Willelmum quondam Norwicensem Episcopum facta Ac per dictum Johannem Caius imposterum in forma predicta fienda, dummodo eadem ordinaciones regule et statuta per ipsum Johannem sic fiend' non sint contraria seu repugnantia dictis ordinacionibus regulis ac statutis seu eorum alicui sive aliquibus per predictum quondam Norwicen[se]m Episcopum ante hac fact'* componend' finiend' terminand' et penitus tollend'. Quibus quidem composicioni finicioni et terminacioni sic per eundem Johannem Caius fiend' et in scriptis pronunciandis predictos Magistrum sive Custodem socios et Scholares et eorum quemlibet firmiter stare et obedire volumus et ordinamus per presentes absque aliqua alia sive ulteriori calumpnia querela actione secta sive prosecucione quacunque proinde fiend' movend' seu prosequend'.

[WE WISH FURTHER and by these presents for ourselves and heirs and successors of us the aforesaid Queen appoint and decree that whenever and as often as it shall happen that any disagreements, divisions, suits, or controversies arise or are moved in the aforesaid College of Gonville and Caius founded in honour of the Annunciation of Blessed Mary the Virgin in the University of Cambridge in or about the election, nomination, or admission of master or keeper or any fellow or scholar of the same college or the governance, ordering, or removal of them or of any one of them, or on other causes, matters, things, or business whatsoever in any way touching or concerning the same college

or the lands, tenements, hereditaments, possessions, goods, or chattels, of the same college, in such a way that the aforesaid master or keeper and fellows or the greater part of the same can in no wise agree about such disagreements, divisions, suits, or controversies thus arisen or moved and finish and terminate the same within two months, that then and as often [as they arise] the said John Caius during his natural life have and shall have plenary power, authority, and faculty from time to time by virtue of these our letters patent to hear and examine such disagreements, divisions, suits, and controversies and of compounding, finishing, terminating, and fully disposing of the same *according to the ordinances, rules, and statutes of the same college made by the aforesaid William, at one time Bishop of Norwich, and by the aforesaid John Caius later to be made in the form aforesaid, provided that the same ordinances, rules, and statutes thus to be made by the same John be not contrary or in opposition to the said ordinances, rules, and statutes or any one or more of them made previously by the aforesaid former Bishop of Norwich*. We wish and decree by these presents that the aforesaid master or keeper, fellows, and scholars and each one of them shall abide strictly by and obey every such composition, conclusion and termination so made and pronounced in writing by the same John Caius without their making, moving, or prosecuting any other or further calumny, complaint, action, suit, or prosecution whatsoever.]

VII. C

The Expulsion of Dethick, Warner and Spenser (1565)

[NOTE: The spelling of the texts has been modernised here.

Dethick, Warner and Spenser were expelled at some time during the spring or summer of 1565. It is unclear whether the underlying causes of the expulsion arose in relation to some mismanagement of the college's finances or some misconduct in Hall which led to the use of the stocks; but the immediate occasion which triggered the expulsion appears to have been the bringing of an action in the Vice-Chancellor's court by Warner contesting Caius' actions in depriving him of some of the 'commodities' of his fellowship or imposing some other punishment (text E below). The choice of the Vice-Chancellor's court may have been prompted by a suit which an ex-fellow with a similar grudge, William Clarke, had just conducted successfully against Caius, but a Vice-Chancellor clearly had no jurisdiction in this internal college matter, and, in the later words of Archbishop Parker, "their appellation was not lawfully made, nor orderly prosecuted" (C below). In Caius' eyes this appeal to an external tribunal was a gross offence for which the culprit should be accursed (*execrabilis*) and deprived of all benefit from the college and excluded for ever from it (Statute 104). The offences of Dethick (who had been expelled once before and only recently been allowed to return) and Spenser appear to be that of aiding and abetting Warner and perhaps joining in his suit.

At the Michaelmas audit following their expulsion the three offenders were denied their stipends for the preceding half-year and fined for their absence from the college following their suit. In the Michaelmas term following the audit they appealed to Archbishop Parker, who had earlier persuaded Caius to take Dethick back after his first expulsion. Parker was ready to find a benefice for Dethick and fellowships in other colleges for Warner and Spenser, and he secured Caius' agreement to their being allowed to depart without the stigma of expulsion or perjury (breach of their oath at admission) and to have their stipend and allowances for the valedictory year which Bateman allowed to a fellow leaving to take up a benefice (texts A and C below). Parker distrusted their motives,

however, and flatly refused to persuade Caius to restore them to their fellowships; for he foresaw that "if they be there, there will ever trouble arise".[1]

Determined to regain their fellowships they sought to appeal to the Chancellor of the university, Sir William Cecil.[2] The cautious Cecil consulted Parker before taking any other step, and the archbishop replied on 29 December with the tactful but unequivocal advice (i) that the appellants did not deserve to have their fellowships restored, (ii) that it would be a waste of his time to give them a hearing and he might create an awkward precedent for himself if he did so, and (iii) that their departing might be made more palatable if it were tempered with some "commodities", *i.e.* financial compensation (text A below).

Cecil took Parker's advice: he declined to hear the parties, and on 4 January he ruled that Warner should be deprived forthwith of "all voice or suffrage" in the college and depart within one month, but should enjoy a valedictory year, and by implication upheld the expulsion of the other two appellants, though, rather oddly, he did not make an express ruling about them. He remitted the fines which had been imposed on the appellants for their understandable absence from college after they started to prosecute their appeal, and he expressly prohibited Caius from molesting or punishing any fellow for having testified on their behalf or "assented" to their appeal in any other way (text B below).[3]

On the same day that Cecil made his ruling, Parker learned that the appellants had included in their articles against Caius a charge which they had carefully omitted to mention to Parker: that of "atheism", or in other words idolatrous papistry. Parker and Caius had for some time been friendly acquaintances and fellow scholars,[4] and Parker would have been aware of Caius' antiquarian interests. So, when news of the charge of atheism came to him, he must have been tempted to dismiss it out of hand; but the retention of sacred vessels used in the Mass was now a matter for grave suspicion and he was himself becoming embroiled in controversy with the increasingly strident puritanical reformers over the subject of vestments. He immediately wrote a second time to Cecil to make clear that the advice which he had given the week before had been given

1 Parker to Cecil, 29 December 1565; text (A) below. He shrewdly added: "These fellows have diverse drifts they shoot at, which I think good to be disappointed. I see the faction hath laboured very much in this matter." In his second letter to Cecil (C below), Parker was more explicit: "… the drift was (as I judged) for Dethick to continue such stifflers in the College of his pupils, to win him in time, by hook or crook, the master's room &."

2 The submission which they made to him has not survived, but it clearly included some of the allegations made by Warner and Spenser in their later petition, including their complaint against Dorington (cf. text C below).

3 He also accepted the appellants' case against Francis Dorington, their particular *bête noir*, for holding two benefices with cure of souls for more than the year Bateman allowed to a fellow, and directed that Dorington should relinquish his fellowship before 26 March next. In fact, Dorington must have chosen to relinquish one of his benefices, for he was still a fellow in June 1566: *B.H.* III, p. 50.

4 Both came from Norwich and had had similar scholastic and linguistic interests when they had been together in Cambridge, Caius as a student at Gonville Hall and Parker as a young fellow and then Master of Corpus.

in ignorance of the charge and would not have been given if the charge proved true, at the same time hinting that he found the allegation unconvincing ("if I were credibly persuaded": text C below). He carefully suggested that Cecil might commission the Vice-Chancellor and "one other indifferent person" to investigate whether there was any truth in the allegation; but Parker also made it clear that unless the allegation were "well testified" he stood by the advice he had given and that although he had at first been disposed to lay much of the blame on Caius – understandably, having had to take Dethick back so soon after his first expulsion – he had come to a very different conclusion after he had found a readiness on Caius' part to leave "the final end" to his decision, as contrasted with a stubborn intransigence on the part of the expelled fellows to accept any compromise. Cecil remained unimpressed by the charge and took no further action on it.

On 7 January, having learned that they would not be heard and that Cecil had made an order, though apparently without knowing its precise contents, Warner and Spenser submitted a further petition to Cecil in the hope of regaining their fellowships and – by their final paragraph – reversing the reforms which Caius had introduced and returning to the laxer regime which had prevailed under the indolent Bacon. In their well-known petition (text D below), in addition to rehearsing the wrongs which they had suffered and the iniquities committed by other fellows as well as by Caius, they urged that "our master may be ruled by some good man's counsel hereafter" (that good man being Henry Dethick, Parker suspected). They were unsuccessful in their aim. On 10 January, with the assistance of Parker's Chancellor and Vicar-General,[5] Cecil made minor amendments clarifying his ruling, to which he had already added two further injunctions, first, that neither Dethick nor Spenser should in any way contend with Caius for the "title or possession" of their fellowships, and second, that Caius should publish any statutes he made to the whole fellowship on three separate days before they "be had or accounted for statutes" (text E below).[6]

The three appellants ceased to trouble the college and, significantly, no further expulsions appear to have taken place. Nothing more was heard of Warner or Spenser. Dethick – whom Parker had earlier promised to take into his clerical household in the event of his expulsion (cf. A) and who had not joined Warner and Spenser in their petition – appears to have been found a benefice, but eventually proved as troublesome to Parker as he had been to Caius: he was finally imprisoned by mandate of the archbishop and the High Commission and secured his release and a royal licence to go abroad only by making – at Parker's 'suggestion' – an unconditional gift of £40 to the college in 1571.[7] It no doubt gave Caius some satisfaction to record this typically kindly gesture by Parker.]

5 Dr Thomas Yale.

6 He also required that all the statutes should be read distinctly and openly before the Master and the company at the end of each quarter for the following two years.

7 *Annals*, p. 174.

(A) *Parker's first letter to Cecil, 29 December 1565* [SP 12/38 fol. 124]

Sir I have had very much ado with the quarrels of Gonvel Hall from time to time. The truth is both parties are not excusable from folly. At the first controversy betwixt the master and one Clarke and Dethick, my L[ord] of London and I so compounded the matter that we perceived it very needful to the quiet of that society to remove both Dethick and Clarke from their fellowships. Dethick after a year made suit to me to have ~~hi~~[8] a room again in the college. Upon his importunity I was importune upon the master to accept him, with the condition of my promise that if by him any trouble should arise I would take him from him again. Which promise made me to receive him into my house after this last expulsion by the master and more part of the company. From that they do appeal to your honour. I cannot see how rightly they can do it, or how your Vice-chancellor can deal in order with their college matters. The parties sued to me. I promised them to deal with the master to obtain of him more commodity than I take them worthy to have: only restitution to their fellowships I would not move. Wherein I see good cause; for if they be there[,] there will ever trouble arise. These fellows have divers drifts they shoot at which I think good to be disappointed. I see the faction hath laboured very much in this matter. Although I see overmuch rashness in the master for expelling fellows so suddenly etc. he hath been well told of it as well of my Lord of London as by myself; and surely the contemptuous behaviour of these fellows hath much provoked him. The truth is I do rather bear with the oversight of the master (being no greater than yet I see) in respect of his good done and like to be done in the college by him, than with the brag of a fond sort of troublous factious bodies. Founders and benefactors be very rare at these days; therefore I do bear the less with such as would (but in a mere triumph) deface him, and respect more that conquest than any quiet in the house; and the rather, for I think that if this matter be ended there will arise no more trouble in such kind there, for the master hath firmly assured me to do nothing in such innovations, but partly with my knowledge and approbation first, and other of his friends. But undoubtedly in my opinion, *computans omnibus circumstantiis*, I think it nothing meet to have them restored again, what other commodities so ever they may have of favourable departing. If your honour will hear their challenges, ye shall hear such cumbrous trifles and brabbles, that ye shall be weary. And I would not wish particular colleges (in these times) should learn to have by forced appellations a recourse to your authority as Chancellor, for the precedents' sake hereafter; and again, I would not have your time so drawn from better doings in the weighty causes of the realm. Scholars' controversies be now many and troublous; and their delight is

[8] Word started and deleted by Parker.

to come before men of authority to show their wits etc.; and I cannot tell how such busy sorts draw to them some of the graver personages to be doers, *an ex sinceritate et ex bona conscientia nescio*. My old experience there hath taught me to spy daylight at a small hole. Thus ye hear my fancy, which I pray your honour to take in good worth. To write much more my dull deaf head will not suffer me. I pray you if any offence be taken for my not oft attending, and to come (?) over the rheumatic Tempsis [Thames], answer for me.

Thus God be with your honour this 29 December, 1565.

Yours assuredly, Matth. Cant.

(B) *Order taken by Sir William Cecil, 4 January 1565/6* [SP 12/39 fol. 9]

London *iiii*^{to} *die mensis Januarii A*^{o} *Domini* 1565:

Order taken by Sir William Cecyll knight Principal Secretary unto the Queen's Majesty in certain contentions and suits depending betwixt Mr Doctor Caius M^{r} and Founder of Gonville and Caius College within the University of Cambridge and Stephen Warner M^{r} of arts with certain other fellows of the said College, and compromitted by the mutual consents of the said parties unto the order and end of the said Sir William Cecyll.

1. First it is ordered that henceforth the said Stephen Warner be [de]prived of all voice or suffrage within the said College, and that before the iiiith day of February next the said Stephen depart and remove his dwelling from the said College, no longer to continue in the same, nevertheless to enjoy the commodity of his fellowship without any defalcation for his absence until Michaelmas next coming.
2. Item it is ordered that such of the fellows by the M^{r} removed, be not mulcted with the defalcation of xii^{d} weekly for their absence, from the first prosecution of their appeal unto this day ~~only~~.[9]
3. Item it is ordered that the said M^{r} do not molest nor punish such of the fellows as assented in Testifying or other ways to their appeal that were removed, for their such assent or testimony.
4. It is further ordered that Mr Doryngton for that he hath had two cured benefices the space of one year and more, do before the xxvjth of March next relinquish his fellowship in the said College with all the commodities thereof.
5. It is also ordered that such decrees as my Lord of Canterbury his grace and my L. of London gave and published unto the said M^{r} and company

[9] Deleted by Cecil.

and by the said Lords not revoked, be observed so far forth as they be not repugnant nor derogate to these orders or any of them.

(C) *Parker's second letter to Cecil, 4 January 1565/6* [Lansd. MS VIII, 70]

[NOTE: The Tudor spelling has been modernised here, as elsewhere; but misplaced brackets, revealing the haste with which Parker wrote, have been left where he placed them. The document is printed with corrected punctuation in *Correspondence of Matthew Parker*, Parker Society (1853), pp. 251–3.]

Sir, no sooner than yesterday, I was informed of certain articles charged upon Dr Caius, not only sounding and savouring Atheism but plainly expressing the same, with further show of a perverse stomach to the professors of the gospel, of the which if I were credibly persuaded, I would take him *tanquam ethnicum et publicanum*, and would not vouchsafe him within my house; there is a difference betwixt the frailty of a man's mutability, and a professing of plain impiety. Sir, in my opinion it were good (if it could be indifferently testified)[10] before mr vice-chancellor, Dr Hutton, and one other indifferent man, so sent to by your letters, to know a truth so to suspend him, whatsoever order ye intend to take with the fellows of the house, and if it should fall out that they could be well testified, I would wish a better in his place to govern the house, and he to hold him in his foundership if he will. I like not the stones builded by such Impiety &c.

At the first stir of this matter betwixt them, hearing what then they alleged I saw good cause earnestly to blame the said Caius (blaming also the said fellows) but Caius was then so framed that he did commit the final end to my disposition. Whereupon I shall show your honour what I intended (if the fellows had not proceeded from me as trusting to win the conquest of their restitution)[11] which they perceived I would not grant. For I spied, so long as he was master there, and they fellows[,] there should be maintained but continual brawling; and the rather for that their appellation was not lawfully made, nor orderly prosecuted, and the drift was (as I judged) for Dethick to continue such stifflers[12] in the college of his pupils to win him in time by hook or crook the master's room &c.

For the ending of their controversies, I thought good to cause a writing indented to be made betwixt them, whereby the ~~fellowships~~ fellows should appear willingly to depart from their fellowships, but yet to have one year's profit; for their *ultimum vale*, to be borne for Spenser of Caius' own purse, for the other two of the college; and that the master should express to discharge them

10 Bracket clearly misplaced and intended to follow the words "your letters" later.

11 Bracket clearly misplaced and intended to follow the words "would not grant" later.

12 Sticklers, *i.e.*, vehement partisans.

of the note of expulsion, and the crime of perjury to their hindrance afterwards. And further, I meant within the compass of that year to have bestowed Dethick in some benefice, and the other two in some other fellowships in other colleges, but because they liked not of this, as trusting of further friendship otherwhere, I gave them over.

...

This ~~thr~~ [?] 4th of January, 1565

Your honour's always

MATTH. Cant.

To the right honourable Sir William Cecill, knight, principal Secretary to the Queen's Majesty.

(D) *Petition of Warner and Spenser, 7 January 1565/6* [SP 12/39 fols. 10–11]

To the right Honourable Sir William Cicill knight chief secretary to the Queen's Majesty and most worthy chancellor of the University of Cambridge.

In most lamentable & humble wise complaining beseecheth your honour your humble & daily orators Stephen Warner & Robert Spenser: that whereas your said orators do partly understand of certain orders appointed in the controversy betwixt our master and us, it may please you to consider our most miserable condition if that we (having always given ourselves to study) shall now be excluded the college not having elsewhere to abide: for that we shall not only hereby lose the favour of all our friends, whereby we shall be altogether undone but also utterly defaced in the whole University (not otherwise taken than[13] as expulsed persons) which shall be to our utter confusion. If it might have pleased your honour further to have expended the cause of our expulsion (which we were purposed to have showed you if we had been admitted before you with our master the last day) we are persuaded that you would have so judged of it as the whole University have heretofore diverse times judged. And not only our own case we had to show you of, but also as our oaths do bind us, of the breach of diverse statutes by certain fellows of the college which by no means can be observed if they abide still there, which thing in conscience we are moved to desire your honour to have consideration of. And last of all, concerning those orders which it shall please you to appoint for our quietness hereafter (which God forbid we should once repine at but only by humble petition to desire your honour's favour) our earnest request unto you is that it would please you in the appointing of them to have consideration of these few things subscribed. And

[13] Written "then", as commonly at the time.

thus only trusting to your honour's gentleness we conclude with earnest prayer to Almighty God for your good estate long to continue and prosper.

First that all such orders as for our quietness your honour shall appoint may plainly appear in writing to avoid all trouble hereafter, and that what allowance be made unto us of our fellowships it may be certain the value of Warner's fellowship being vii^{l} xii^{s} and Spenser's viii marks.[14]

Item that we may either be suffered to tarry in the college all the time of our allowance or else in our absence nothing be defaulted of our fellowships by Statute.[15]

Item that considering our great charges in this long suit our allowance may be considered accordingly and that nothing be defaulted by statute for our absence since our expulsion for that we would have been continually present if our master would have suffered us.[16]

Item that our stipends may not be defaulted for the last half year as our master have done in the last account.[17]

Item that those fellows which shall remain in the house be not oppressed or injured by our master for anything done heretofore in our behalf, but may receive pupils as other do, and have their chambers offices lectures and other preferments according to seniority which have been always the custom of the house, and that such mulcts as they have been heretofore unjustly punished with may be redressed, and that they may have licence of necessary absence according to statute as other[s] have.[18]

Item that Mr Dorington be not maintained in the college contrary to his founder's will and Mr Vice-Chancellor's order taken nor yet Mr Holland our statutes expressly against the same.[19]

Item that the contumacy towards Mr Vice-Chancellor the fighting with the fellows and bloodshed committed by Mr Dorington may be punished according to statute.

Item that no man's goods be confiscate for departing the college.

Item that no man hereafter be stocked or beaten for keeping his right until the matter be decided.

Item that my L[ords] of Canterbury and London their decrees may be observed.[20]

Item that Mr Vice-Chancellor or some other in the University whom it shall please your honour, may see your orders made, put in execution, and that our

14 Marginal note by Cecil: "to {~~be *socii*~~} have *ius socii* till Mich. without any suffrage".

15 Marginal note by Cecil: "*ad* 4 Feb.".

16 Marginal note by Cecil: "Allow this (?) for absence".

17 Marginal note by Cecil: "from the time they began to prosecute their cause".

18 Marginal note by Cecil: "that none of them be molested that did testify".

19 Marginal note by Cecil: "that Mr Dorington may depart the College ~~at~~ the 25th of March".

20 Marginal note by Cecil: "to be observed in all things not contrary to this order".

master may be ruled by some good man's counsel hereafter and not to drive the fellows to such chargeable suits and troubles wherein he delighteth to undo poor men, he never being quiet since he came to the college, as may appear in the number of {his}[21] expulsions which have been above twenty, with an infinite number of injuries to the old founders & benefactors & their fellows which is well known to the whole University.

Your honour's daily orators Stephen Warner & Robert Spenser fellows of Gonvill and Caius college in Cambridge.

[Endorsed]

7 January 1565. Stephen Warner and Robert Spensers petitions against Dr Caius etc.[22]

(E) *[Draft] Order taken by Sir William Cecil, 10 January 1565/6*[23] [SP/39 fol. 20]

[NOTE: Passages within braces which are italicised here were made by Cecil in italic hand and were inserted into a text which had been written in secretary hand. Other passages within braces are in the same secretary hand.]

[???] orders taken {*and pronounced the x of Januar. 1565*} by Sir William Cicill knight Principal Secretary unto the Queen's Majesty in certain contentions and suits depending betwixt Mr Doctor Caius M^r^ and founder of Gonvill and Caius college within the university of Cambridge and Stephen Warner M^r^ of arts {with} certain other fellows of the said college, and compromitted by the mutual consents of the said parties unto the order and end of the said Sir William Cicill {*in presence of Doctor Yale* [???] *of the* [*court of*] *audience of the Arch*[*bishop*] *of Cant*[*er*]*bury*}.

First it {*is*} ordered that {*from*} henceforth the said Stephen Warner be [de]prived of all voice or suffrage within the said college and that before the fourth day of February next the said Stephen depart and remove his dwelling from the said college {*and*} no longer to *continue* in the same, nevertheless {*he shall*} enjoy the commodity {*and profit*} of his fellowship without any defal[ca]tion for his absence ~~until~~ {*at any time from the beginning of his suit to the Vi*[*ce*]*-chancellor of Cambridge, by way of appeal until*} Michaelmas next coming.

Item it is ordered that such of the fellows as the M^r^ removed are not mulcted with the defalcation of xii^d^ weekly for their absence from the first ~~prosecution~~ {*begynning to prosecute*} ~~of~~ their appeal unto this day only.

21 Petitioners' own interlined insertion.

22 Query whether the date is that of writing or of receipt.

23 See Plates IX and X above.

Item it is ordered that the {said} master do not molest nor punish such of the fellows as assented {*by*} testifying or [in] other ways to their appeal that were removed, for their such assent or testimony.

[Item] it is further ordered that Mr Doryngton for that he hath had two cured benefices the space of one year and more {*contrary to the statutes of the College shall*} ~~do~~ also the 26 of March next relinquish his fellowship in the said college with all the commodities thereof {*or else to be by the Mr and the rest deprived thereof*}.

[Item] it is also ordered that such decrees as {*the most Reverend father the Archbishop*} of Canterbury his Grace and ~~my L~~ {*the rev father the B*} of London gave and published unto the said M^{r} and company and ~~by the said Lords not~~ {*be not at this day by them*} revoked {*shall*} be observed so far forth as they be not repugnant nor derogate{*ry*} to these orders or any of them.

Touching Mr Dethick and D^{s} Spenser it is ordered that after the 7th day of January nether of them both shall any ways contend {with} the said Mr Doctor Caius for the title or possession of their fellowships in the said college.

[Item] it is further ordered that such statutes as the said Doctor Caius shall give to the said college for the government of the same or the members thereof shall be first read and published by the said Doctor Caius {within the said college} in the presence of the greater part of the hole company {of the same} {~~*and by them agreed and allowed*~~} at three several days before they be had or accounted for statutes {*and that at iiii^{r} several times of the year during the space of two whole years* ~~*before the 25 of Dec*~~ *all the statutes of the house be read distinctly and openly before the M^{r} and the Company. that is to say the 24 of March the 23 of June the 28 of September and the 24 of December*}.[24]

[24] It may be doubted whether Cecil realised how long and elaborate the statutes already were and how tedious the task would be. Caius had already provided that his statutes should be read out twice a year, at Michaelmas and Easter when Bateman's statutes had to be read out (*Documents*, II, p. 365), and in his final statutes he added a little sourly "so that no one can plead ignorance": Statute 107.

VII. D

Gerrard's Case (1582)

[British Library, MSS Lansd. XXXIII, 47, 54. The spelling has been modernised here, and some punctuation supplied or amended.[1] The texts are also printed in *Cambridge University Transactions during the ... Puritan Controversies* (1854, reprinted Cambridge University Press, 2009) vol. I, pp. 321–6 and 334–7.]

[NOTE: Richard Gerrard[2] was the son of Caius' friend and executor, William Gerrard, and Caius was his godfather. He was admitted to the college as a scholar in 1567 and, after migrating to Trinity College, he was re-admitted in 1574 and became a fellow and tutor in that year. By the time he returned, if not earlier, he had become an ardent reformer. He became Rector of Stockport, Cheshire, in 1577 and, in addition, Prebend of Southwell in 1580; but he did not formally resign his Wendy fellowship, perhaps because there was uncertainty whether it had lapsed in any case following a dispute with the nephew and executor of the benefactor. His name is included in Michaelmas 1581 in the (earliest surviving) *Liber Rationalis* together with twelve other fellows; no stipend or other allowances are credited to him, merely an unpaid debit for commons (43s. 2½d.). He appears for the last time in the accounts for Lady Day 1582, again with nothing credited and an increased commons bill (49s. 11½d.).

The principal interest in his case centres on the increasingly bitter dispute with the Master, Thomas Legge, over the latter's alleged harbouring of papists in the college, especially among the pupils he had brought with him from Jesus College when he was appointed by Caius to succeed him in the mastership. That dispute, which is outside the scope of this work, became exceedingly bitter after Gerrard preached a sermon in Great St Mary's which was seen as a thinly veiled attack on Legge and his strong supporter Richard Swale, the president [*B.H.* I, p. 85]. Until that time (Whitsun 1579) Legge appears to have attempted to maintain the peace between the rival factions and to have turned a blind eye to the excesses of both sides. But thereafter even he found the position intolerable and, no doubt

[1] The Complaint against Legge illustrates the unpredictable variation of upper- and lower-case even in formal documents at the time.

[2] *B.H.* I, 61. Venn drew on the Lansdowne Papers and the Calendar of State Papers for a full account of the dispute in Volume III, at *B.H.* III, pp. 64–7. For an indication of what the printed texts omit from Lansdowne 33, see Brooke, *History*, p. 89, n. 40.

spurred on by the forthright and dominant Swale and others, he took steps to have Gerrard's fellowship declared invalid. The grounds for the declaration appear to be, first, that the tenure of a fellowship by Gerrard was, under both Bateman's and Caius' statutes, no longer valid since more than the permitted "valedictory year" had elapsed since he had obtained a disqualifying benefice; second, that he had never been properly re-admitted a fellow after his original fellowship had lapsed.

The interest of the case in the context of the present work is threefold: (i) the long list of fifty-one alleged breaches of Caius' statutes by Legge in the short period that had elapsed since Caius' death; (ii) Gerrard's arguments in his attempt to retain both a fellowship and at the same time his benefice and prebend on the ground that the restriction imposed by Bateman and Caius did not extend to Wendy's foundation; and (iii) the light shed upon the views of the time on the practice of "translation" and the procedure required for the restoration to a fellowship of an ex-fellow.[3]

The documents extracted here are: (A) the Articles alleging breaches of statutes by Legge, which accompanied and re-enforced the Complaint of seven fellows[4] respecting Legge's harbouring papists (not included here); (B) Gerrard's Answer to the charge that he was no longer a fellow.]

(A) *The Articles against Legge for breaches of statutes* [Lansd. XXXIII, 47]

Concerning the decay of revenues and defaults in government of the College during the time that Dr. Legge hath been Master.[5]

1. Imprimis: whereas the statute[6] (under pain of expulsion *ipso facto et restitutionis rei ablatae*) provideth that none of the said college (*sive custos sive socius*) shall impropriate or take to himself anything belonging thereunto: the Master, Dr. Legge (contrary also to his oaths both of Master and of Bursar) hath by the space of viij. years at the least taken yearly of the College treasure to the sum of iiij$^{li.}$ xiij$^{s.}$ iiij$^{d.}$ to his own proper use, amounting in the whole to xxxvij$^{li.}$ viij$^{s.}$ viij$^{d.}$ or therabout.[7]

[3] See "*The Fellowship and the Governing Body*", § VI. 1 above.

[4] It is significant that the Complaint signed by *seven* fellows included Gerrard: Lansd. XXXIII, 46. Since there were twelve fellows as well as Gerrard, the seven constituted a majority only if he could be numbered among them: John Paman [*B.H.* I, p. 79], Richard Gerrard [*B.H.* I, p. 61], Paul Gold [*B.H.* I, p. 78], Roger Browning [*B.H.* I, p. 80], Thomas Hawes [*B.H.* I, p. 96], Michael Rabbett [*B.H.* I, p. 104], and Thomas Howse [*B.H.* I, p. 75].

[5] The word "Master" is written as "Mr" or "mr" without distinction throughout.

[6] Statute 83.

[7] It should be xxxvij^{li} vj^{s} viij^{d}.

2. Item: whereas the statute[8] provideth that no man shall do his own business upon the college charge, the Master, being cast in the Fleet for contempt of her majesty's letters,[9] and that by his own default only, hath put the College to the charge of ten pounds, contrary to the said statute, as also to his oaths and statutes before mentioned.
3. Item: whereas the statute willeth for the bettering of the College real estate, either to raise rents or take fines to the College use, in letting our lands not lately improved, the Master never as yet (that we can remember) did either of both, but bestowed them, without any respect of the college commodity had, at his own pleasure.[10]
4. Item: the college houses are suffered by him to fall in decay, and some of our lands are in doubt to be lost for want of orderly and sufficient survey according to statute, as at Ronghton, Croxley, at Matsall, Hockhold [*sic*], and Wilton.
5. Item: contrary to his oath of Master taken he hath bestowed the College treasure otherwise than it ought to be bestowed; as, first, in that he hath given to his servant by the term of four years or thereabouts the porter's stipend, to the value of five marks yearly and that without consent of the fellows, his man being also incapable thereof, as under the age of xl. years, and not wearing any such livery as by statute is enjoined him.[11]
6. Item: contrary to his said oath he hath also bestowed on Fingley [*B.H.* I, p. 76], an arrant papist,[12] the office and stipend of the butler, and that of his own authority, without the consent of the fellows.
7. Item: contrary to the foresaid oath he kept Atkinson in the office of cator, by the space of half a year,[13] paying him the wages thereof, contrary to the minds of the fellows and refused to choose any other, although he were altogether unfit for the same.
8. Item: the foresaid Atkinson being dead, the Master, contrary to the same oath, placed in the same office of Cator one Harrison [*B.H.* I, p. 90] Mr. Swale's pupil without consent; which because that by statute he could

8 Statute 51.

9 Cf. *B.H.* I, p. 66.

10 Statute 95. The complaint was specious. In Statute 89 Caius had prohibited the raising of any rent he had himself increased (as in the case of Croxley) and the opportunity to do so in the case of his other manors had not arisen by 1581, since the leases on them had not fallen in by that date; very few other leases had come up for renewal since his death and in the two that had done so in 1579 (Barningham and Cherryhinton) the rent had been raised: see "*Dividends*", § VI. 4 above.

11 The age and livery requirements are to be found only in Caius' will, not the statutes: *Documents*, II, p. 311.

12 Beatified by the Roman Catholic Church in 1987.

13 Cf. Statute 56, limiting appointments to three months. The *obsonator* was reckoned as being 'on the foundation' and was listed annually with the scholars in the *Acta*. Atkinson, however, appears not to have been a matriculated member of the college.

not safely perform, he bore the fellows in hand,[14] that he could show an old decree permitting the same, which decree notwithstanding hitherto he hath not showed.

9. Item: whereas the statute[15] willeth that Stewards of our courts, and Bailiffs of our manors, should be yearly chosen, he wholly neglecteth the same, so that, by reason thereof, we never have any rules of courts or bills of extents sent unto us as the statute requireth, neither are our rents and such like gathered by any lawful officer, but himself dealeth as him liketh in all such matters.
10. Item: he constraineth not (as the statute[16] exacteth) the farmers to bring in or pay their rents in due time, bearing the fellows in hand,[17] that he would re-enter if they would permit him whereas the statute commandeth the same, by reason whereof our accounts are for the most part imperfect.
11. Item: at this present our accounts are not according to statute finished, and that by the Master's default for so much as he (for the most part) hath violated or neglected all things belonging to his oath of Bursar, as followeth.[18]
12. First, in that he hath not dealt faithfully with the college (*sic*) in the same his office, having withheld to his own use unlawfully such money as is before mentioned in the first article.
13. Secondly, in that he hath not left unto the College at every year's end his books of accounts fair written, but keepeth them to himself, dealing therein very suspiciously with the College contrary to his said oath.
14. Thirdly, in that he joyneth not the other Bursar with him in any of his dealings according to the statute.
15. Fourthly, he receiveth not the College rent in the place appointed, neither having his fellow Bursar with him.
16. Fifthly, in that he doth not presently carry up the foresaid money into the treasure house but keepeth it in his own hand so long as pleaseth him, his said oath enjoining him not to retain in his hand at once above the sum of five pounds.
17. Sixthly, in that he keepeth his fellow bursar ignorant, of all his dealings, not permitting him to have to do therewith (alleging for himself his continuance in such manner of dealing now by a long time, albeit against his said oath), so that the accounts are not rendered to the College by

[14] *I.e.*, insisted to the fellows.

[15] Statute 96.

[16] Statute 87.

[17] *I.e.*, insisting to the fellows.

[18] For this and Articles 12–17, see Statute 56.

them both jointly, neither is every particular sum subscribed with both their names set down with their own hands as the statute willeth.

18. Lastly, in that he causeth not indentures *de collegii statu, et de toto remanente residuo* to be drawn at the end of every account, refusing to make them after the form used, by the space of many years.[19]
19. Item: where there were three sales of timber made at our manor of Croxley to Mr. William Gerrard of Harrow upon the Hill[20] two payments whereof the Master hath received, we are desirous to be satisfied by the sight of the book of accounts, which the Master unjustly and suspiciously denieth unto us, whether the said money be answered unto the college or not.
20. Item: whereas the statute commandeth that our election of officers should be finished in Michaelmas account, the same hath been deferred by the Master from time to time contrary to the statute,[21] so that the house remaineth evil governed, and the youth not instructed as they ought, and this by the Master's default.
21. First, for that he hath not propounded all officers to the company.
22. Secondly, for that he hath not taken the voices of all the fellows for those officers which he hath mentioned.
23. Thirdly, for that he hath offered such men unto the company, as are either not eligible by statute, or such as are unmeet to be chosen to those offices, for which they were named.
24. Fourthly, for that he hath used his negative voice against those that were chosen by the greater part of the company.[22]
25. Fifthly, for that he taketh to himself the propounding of all matters not allowed him by statute, by the which he doth take unto himself a double negative voice.
26. Sixthly, for that he suffereth not an equal distribution of offices to be made amongst all the fellows (as the statute requireth)[23] according to every man's quality.

[19] See Bateman's Statutes, Statute 7. Bateman directed that the Master and the keepers of the keys to the chest should present an account of the balance remaining in it twice a year. In the medieval period this was done by indenture, and such indentures have survived for the years down to 1589. By the sixteenth century the accounts were prepared in draft on single sheets of paper which were then discarded. In 1589 the indenture was discontinued and the sheet of paper was instead signed by the key-keepers and preserved in a series that came to be entitled the "*Status Collegii*". This series survives from 1584 to 1926 and served as the college's 'Cash Reconciliation Statement' until the end of the nineteenth century.

[20] Richard Gerrard's father.

[21] For this and Articles 21–26, see Statutes 24, 56–60. Election at an audit was required only for the offices of dean and bursar.

[22] See "*The Master's Negative Voice*", § VI. 2 above.

[23] Statute 60.

27. Item: whereas the statute provideth that the College writings shall not be taken down from the treasury and kept in any chamber, he commonly useth to do the contrary.[24]
28. Item: whereas by statute the book of evidences should lie in the Treasure house, the Master continually keepeth it in his chamber, he keepeth also by him *librum annalium*, the statute not permitting the same.[25]
29. Item: whereas it is appointed by statute, that every scholar absent above one month in the year shall pay vi^d. weekly out of his scholarship to the college so long as he shall be so absent, he useth to remit the same at his pleasure.[26]
30. Item: the statute willing all College business should be talked of and handled *in loco capitulari* and that in matters of weight all the fellows should be present (the absent being warned to return within xv. days) he commonly observeth neither of both.[27]
31. Item: that divers scholars have been placed in their rooms by the Master, and others having not stood to be examined according to statute.[28]
32. Item: whereas the statute provideth that every pensioner and scholar shall have *socium collegii tutorem* [~~*et praesidem*~~[29]],[30] the Master taketh on him the tuition of both.
33. Item: Dr. Caius granting by his statute unto his own scholars chambers rent free in his new building, the Master so ordereth the matter that divers such scholars have no chambers at all, he having filled their Rooms with pensioners at his pleasure.[31]
34. Item: whereas it is by statute ordained that the Master shall not attempt any weighty matter without the consent of the greater part of the company, he hath often done the contrary.[32]
35. Item: whereas the statute (for the better government of the College) setteth down that there shall be yearly two Deans or Lecturers chosen,

24 See Statute 84.

25 See Statute 84. A very petty objection, given that Legge was scrupulous in writing up the Annals until 1603 and that they were wholly neglected thereafter until Charles I ordered their resumption in 1636: see *Cooke's Case* (1636), Appendix G below.

26 Statute 55.

27 Statute 3.

28 Statute 62.

29 Deleted by the scribe when he realised that he had mistaken Caius' *praes* (surety) for *praeses* (guardian).

30 Statute 65.

31 Statute 28. The complainants conveniently ignored Caius' direction that the rooms should be rented to major pensioners until 1580.

32 Statute 3.

the Master choose Mr. Depup [*B.H.* I, p. 61][33] (before named in the matters of education) for an whole year to be Lecturer and Dean alone.[34]

36. Item: Dr. Perse [*B.H.* I, p. 57] (being minister) and having, as the statute enjoineth,[35] set down his profession in divinity), was permitted and furthered by the Master to change both his said profession and his place to another fellowship whereby he professed physic,[36] since which time the said Dr. Perse hath twice changed his profession by the Master's permission.
37. Item: the Master suffered very great and continual disorder in Mr. Howndes' [*B.H.* I, p. 62] chamber, as black sanctus, and singing of lewd ballads, with heads out of the windows, and so loud voices, as that all the house wondered thereat to the very evil example of the youth.
38. Item: that the scholars at that time were suffered to live very licentiously, so that a great part of them were common drunkards, and great swearers, but no way punished or reformed by the Master.
39. Item: that Mr. Howse [*B.H.* I, p. 75] (fellow of our College) was earnestly moved by Mr. Hinson [*B.H.* I, p. 81], the Master's especial friend, and as it is to be presumed by the Master's procurement to enter into a bond of xx^{li} never to give his voice contrary to the Master.
40. Item: Mr. Barwick [*B.H.* I, p. 52] of St. Edmondes Burie a man well known to be popish, and the Master's old friend, threatened (now of late) to sue Mr. Browning's Brother upon a bond of an hundred pounds made (as he said) by his father, which bond he affirmeth to be forfeited, for that (the said Mr. Browning [*B.H.* I, p. 80] fellow of our College) will not be ordered in all matters by the Master.
41. Item: that the Master hath deferred the election of Scholars and fellows longer than by order they ought to be deferred.
42. Item: that be hath kept back good and toward scholars from preferment, by not suffering some to stand at elections, and by not propounding them that have been permitted to stand.
43. Item: that he hath given licence unto one of the fellows chosen Lecturer to substitute another for a time; and at the quarter's end he deprived the said Lecturer of his wages, for that he had dealt against a Papist.

33 Depup had particularly excited the wrath of Richard Gerrard and his co-complainants: "a man greatly suspected to be popish, and otherwise well known to be notoriously vicious; and such an one as of whom the founder had so great misliking, that he gave especial charge before his death that the said Depup should never be fellow.", *Cambs Trans*, I, p. 317 (*op. cit.* p. 575 above).

34 Statute 24.

35 Statute 28.

36 Perse was born in Norfolk, and therefore he might be (and perhaps was on several occasions) "translated" from an unrestricted fellowship to one restricted to Norfolk; it was only eventually that he held a fellowship on Dr Caius' own foundation. For the practice of "translation", see "*The Fellowship and the Governing Body*", § VI. 1 above.

44. Item: that the Master hath suffered certain of the fellows almost continually to absent themselves from the common table, punishing others being very seldom away.
45. Item: that Mr. Hinson, being Lecturer and dean, was permitted by the Master to be away from the College the greatest part of the whole year, to the great decay of learning and licentiousness of youth.
46. Item: that whereas the statute permitteth not small birds to be kept in the College, for troubling the students, the Master hath used continual and expressive loud singing, and noise of Organs, to the great disturbance of our studies.[37]
47. Item: that the Master keepeth one of the three keys of the common chest, where the College treasure lyeth; which is only permitted to three of the fellows yearly to be chosen as the other offices be.[38]
48. Item: that we having small room in the College, the Master very much anoyeth the house in letting out the College stable to such as keep hackney horses within the College walls, and taketh the commodity thereof to himself contrary to statute.
49. Item: whereas all contentious persons are by statute to be removed, whether it be Master or fellow,[39] both Master and President in many of their dealings have plainly shewed themselves to be both the authors and upholders of contentious quarrels in the house.
50. Item: whereas the founder Dr. Caius hath set down by statute,[40] that an Indenture with an obligation of xv^teen hundred pounds thereto annexed, between him and our College, binding us to the performance of certain covenants and conditions therein specified, ought to be kept together with our statutes by the Master and fellows of Benet College,[41] the Master hath been of counsel, or at the least wise privy, to the making away thereof.
51. Item: whereas an ancient statute of our house precisely commandeth that the Master of our College shall be presented shortly after his election to the Chancellor of our university,[42] the said Dr. Legge, now Master of our College, hath not as yet been so presented nor allowed.

MATTH. STOKYS[43]

1581.

[37] Statute 22. For the Reformers the true offence was not the loudness of the organ but its very existence.

[38] Bateman's Statutes, Statute 6.

[39] Statute 47; but it does not mention the Master.

[40] Statute 25.

[41] As Corpus Christi College was then styled under Puritan pressure.

[42] Bateman's Statutes, Statute 3.

[43] University Registrary 1558–91.

(B) *Gerrard's Answer to the charge that he was no longer a Fellow* [Lansd. XXXIII, 54][44]

The answer of Richard Gerrard unto certain pretended reasons alleged against him by Mr. Swale, to prove that he is not, neither hath been by the space of iiij. years last past almost, fellow of Gonville and Caius College.[45]

1. To the first, he answereth that the reason and the whole contents thereof is false and untrue, for that there was sometime a lawful and sufficient foundation of that fellowship, as may appear by the will of the benefactor yet remaining in the college,[46] and as is likewise evident by the second statute of D. Caius, where he maketh mention of xiii. fellowships, accounting this for one. And he further allegeth, that, whereas this fellowship was forfeited by breach of certain covenants, unto the heirs of the said benefactor, and thereupon the stipend thereof detained from the college by the space of certain years, this respondent, by the means of his friends, procured Mr. Wendy, heir to the said benefactor, to be contented to found the same anew, and to present this respondent thereunto, which presentation, for the more sufficiency in law, was penned by D. Legge, Master of the said college, and was read by him unto the fellows in the chapel, whereunto the Master and greater part gave their consent, viz. that this foundation should be good, during the time of this respondent, and that after his departure from the college, they should be to agree with the said Mr. Wendy upon new covenants, for that the conditions then offered, seemed to be somewhat unreasonable.
2. To the second he answereth, that he was chosen to this fellowship before he was lawfully cut off by statute from his former fellowship, and before he had enjoyed his personage[47] one whole year, and that he was again chosen to the fellowship he now hath, according to the manner commonly used in the college in the like case;[48] and that D. Perse and Mr. Hawes [*B.H.* I, p. 96] were chosen after the same manner to the fellowships they now have; and that Mr. D. Tracye [*B.H.* I, p. 65][49] and Mr. Canhan [*B.H.* I, p. 72] were no otherwise chosen unto the fellowships they lately had in that college; and if there were any oath, admission, or

44 On Gerrard's Answer, see "*The Fellowship and the Governing Body*", § VI. 1 above.

45 The reasons asserted by Swale have not been published, and their nature and content have to be deduced from Gerrard's answers.

46 The benefactor was Thomas Wendy [*B.H.* I, p. 24].

47 *I.e.*, benefice or parsonage.

48 No doubt deliberately, Gerrard conflates re-election of a former fellow after his fellowship has lapsed with the practice of "translation" from one foundation to another: see "*The Fellowship and the Governing Body*", § VI. 1 above.

49 John Tracy. (The "D" is for "Doctor"; he was a medical fellow).

other ceremony to be required in this case, the Master was in fault, who did not exact the same; notwithstanding for the oath, it was alleged by the Master himself that it was needless, for that this deponent was sworn to the college before.

3. To the third, as before to the second reason.
4. To the fourth, he answereth that it was objected by one of the fellows, at the time of this respondent's second election, according to the contents of this reason, and that then the Master alleged to the contrary, a parcel of one of D. Caius his statutes, viz. *cuique benefactorum licitum est, studii vitaeque genus suis sociis praescribere, quemadmodum et fundatori suis*:[50] and another parcel of one of D. Caius his statutes *de electione scholarium, videlicet, ad hunc modum proponantur, eligantur, etc., nisi aliter a benefactoribus constitutum sit*;[51] by the which the Master implied, that benefactors might dispense with the statutes of the founder, and that benefactors' fellows were no further bound to the statutes of the founders than should seem good to their benefactor. And he further affirmeth, that if benefactors might not in this case dispense, that then D. Caius could not have granted licence to his fellows to take a spiritual living of x$^{li.}$ value, being contrary to the statutes of the old founder.[52] And he believeth that if in respect of foundation, or other incapableness, this respondent had not been eligible by the statutes of the college, that then the Master, or the author of these reasons, and the rest of the fellows, being sworn to their statutes, would not have proceeded to the election. And that this respondent had been possessed of his living, either a year or more, it is untrue.
5. To the fifth he answereth, that the author of the reasons doth here speak contrary to his own knowledge, for that there was mention made of no such matter of countenance as is here pretended at the said election; but only that this respondent should have *jus socii*, taking no commodity of the house, even as he which is *canonicus*, hath by law, *vocem in capitulo, et stallum in choro*, though he have no living of the church. And further this respondent did at the same time offer of his own accord, to pay rent for his chamber as a dividend amongst the rest of the fellows, which he hath done ever since;[53] and he believeth that if his title to his fellowship

[50] Statute 108.

[51] Statute 15.

[52] Bateman's Statutes, Statute 12E. This limited the permissible value to 100 shillings, half the £10 allowed by Caius.

[53] Gerrard would seem to suggest that the payments that were divided were payments made by him voluntarily while he was absent from Cambridge during his valedictory year, but the practice was not restricted to such cases; as elsewhere he was probably indulging in special pleading. Cf. Branthwaite's 5th objection to "Auncient practices against statutes" and the fellows' opaque Answer in *Allen's Case* (1617), Appendix F below. The practice had been in

had not been good, that then Mr. Swale would never have been so importunate with this respondent for his voice at the election of Mr. Burton [*B.H.* I, p. 103], and at other times, as he hath been.

6. To the sixth he answereth, that this deprivation was unlawful, being without consent of the fellows, only mentioned in the hall at the table, and not in the chapel, no statute being alleged or fact proved, why this respondent should be deprived; and he affirmeth that there is nothing in the statutes why he may not enjoy his prebend with any fellowship, for that his prebend is not *beneficium curatum vel non curatum*; and if it were, he had a dispensation from his benefactor, before there was any proceeding against him, which was at that time judged to be sufficient in law, by the opinion of D. Binge;[54] and that he had enjoyed his prebend one year at the least, at the time of this pretended deprivation, it is untrue.
7. To the seventh he answereth, that there is no part of the reason true, and that he hath D. Perne's hand to shew to the contrary, in his letter written to the Master of the Rolls;[55] and that he, this respondent, had lately some conference with Mr. D. Howland concerning this matter, who affirmed, that he this respondent was restored according to the statutes of the college, and not otherwise; and whereas, at the time of the said restoring, Mr. Swale objected, that there was no foundation, and that this respondent was incapable of any fellowship, D. Perne and D. Howland replied that then they were perjured, which made choice of him to be fellow.
8. To the eighth he answereth, that he was lawfully maintained, whereat there needed no restitution at all, for that he was never removed by any lawful proceeding against him, neither any sentence pronounced, as is here pretended. What D. Perne, or D. Howland, did privately request of the Master, this respondent knoweth not; but he believeth they requested no such matter as is here pretended, for that he hath heard D. Howland speak to the contrary. As touching any promise that this respondent should behave himself quietly and friendly towards the Master, if the Master were an honest man, he might well do it, notwithstanding there

existence in Gonville Hall, and Caius directed in his Statute 28 that it should not apply to "our College" (Caius Court); the Absence Books show that it was never extended to that court. See the section on *Room Rents* in "*Dividends*", § VI. 5, at p. 482 above.

54 Thomas Byng, Master of Clare 1571–99, Admiralty Advocate 1572, Regius Professor of Civil Law 1574–99, Dean of Arches 1595. Byng had been Vice-Chancellor when Caius' rooms had been ransacked in 1572.

55 Dr Perne was Master of Peterhouse and was Vice-Chancellor in 1580. The Master of the Rolls was Sir Gilbert Gerrarde; his son, Thomas (*B.H.* I, p. 105), had recently been admitted to the college, in 1580. Like Richard Gerrard, Sir Gilbert also came from Harrow and was doubtless a relative.

was no such matter moved or assented unto; only D. Perne moved this respondent to make promise under his hand, to give his voice with the Master, or not against him, in all causes whatsoever, which this respondent refused utterly to do; but, at the motion of D. Howland, this respondent promised to confer with D. Perne and him whensoever there was any matter of weight in controversy, which promise he hath kept, and purposeth still so to do.[56]

9. To the ninth he answereth, that since the first time of his interest, his voice was taken and accounted of, as to make perfect or hinder elections, or else Mr. Burton [*B.H.* I, p. 103] was never perfectly chosen fellow; and he believeth, that if his voice had not been of account to perfect or hinder elections, since the time of his pretended deprivation, that then D. Legge would not so earnestly have craved his voice at Michaelmas last at the election of officers, and that the Master and fellows (being by statute and oath bound to make a true intimation of the number and names of their fellows yearly to the bishop and dean and chapter of Norwich) would not have certified this respondent's name in September last, in the said intimation, Mr. Swale himself being present at the sealing of the same under their college seal.
10. To the tenth he answereth, that till of late, his voice was never excepted against but only by Booth [*B.H.* I, p. 110], whom the Master and president make their instrument, to set abroad evil matters, which they are ashamed to begin themselves; and that his voice was not first excepted against, as prejudicial to any man's commodity, but for that he had preached a sermon, against corruptors of youth in St. Marys, which the Master and president interpreted to be spoken directly against them. Of late, he confesseth, that Mr Booth took exception to his voice, for that he denied to give his consent to the granting of a lease, which the Master and president did fraudulently seek to pass to one Homan Booth, his brother in law, to Booth his use, contrary to the meaning of the statutes of the house; and he further confesseth, that he was willed and commanded to depart, and threatened to be removed by force, if he would not depart, but only by the president, who commonly taketh upon him more than he hath to do, and with great words and brags, seeketh to make men afraid, who, being well acquainted with the same, make small account of it. That any other hath misliked of his presence, at any secret conference, saving Booth and Swale, he could in never any manner of way perceive.
11. To the eleventh he answereth, that until now of late his voice was asked, and accounted amongst the rest, by the Master, without any indirect

[56] The talks with Perne and the promise presumably arose out of Gerard's inflammatory sermon in Great St Mary's at Whitsun 1579.

means or motion; and that in two intimations, his name was inserted and placed among the rest of the fellows, the president himself being present at the sealing of the said intimations, and this respondent being then absent at his benefice; and that in all other intimations heretofore, this respondent's name hath been certified amongst the fellows, and that none have shewed their misliking of this respondent's being fellow, or giving his voice, saving the persons aforesaid, and for the causes aforesaid.

Rychard Gerrard.[57]

57 Gerrard subsequently abandoned his suit – albeit grudgingly – and shook the dust of Cambridge from his feet: *B.H.* III, p. 67. As a consequence of the hardening of attitudes many of those against whom Gerrard had campaigned also left Cambridge and sought refuge in Catholic countries on the continent. Thereafter Legge's relations with the fellowship appear to have been relatively harmonious.

VII. E

The Decree on the Frankland Fellows, 11 December 1592

[MS 711/756 pp. 110–11]

[NOTE: On the background and aftermath of this decree, see *The Decree on the Frankland fellows* in "*The Fellowship and the Governing Body*", and *The Frankland fellows* in "*Dividends*", §§ VI. 1 and 5 respectively above.

The Frankland property was regarded as corporate property which was not held on a trust but simply on a condition which could be interpreted strictly in favour of the grantee. Consequently any increase in the value of the property was not held for the Frankland fellows and scholars as the beneficiaries of a trust. Unlike later benefactions which were, from the time of Stephen Perse's will onward, treated as distinct trusts with separate trust accounts, and the beneficiaries – occasionally – benefitted accordingly, the Frankland bequest was not recognised as a separate trust until 1832: see "*Stipends*", § VI. 4, at p. 430 above, and Gross, *B.H.* IV(2) pp. 42–3.

The 1592 decree excluded the Frankland fellows from receiving dividends, but made a specific exception for corn money. This exception was no doubt made in deference to the wording of Sir Thomas Smith's Act 1576, but, despite the Act and this decree, Mrs Frankland's fellows never enjoyed corn money, since the Act was never applied to the only agrarian property acquired with her money (*i.e.*, the Manor of D'Abernoons at Duxford).[1] The exclusion of the Frankland fellows from other dividends was understandable: for they received an annual stipend (£7) which was substantially greater than that of senior fellows, and the value of dividends at the time hardly made up the difference. It is far more difficult to justify the exclusion of the Frankland fellows from any part in the government of the college, given the clear intention of both Bateman's and Caius' statutes. It is likely that it stemmed from alarm at the size of the increased number of participants if no less than seven junior fellows were added to the voters: the same attitude had not been adopted with regard to the single Wendy fellowship when it had been held by Richard Gerrard in the 1570s: cf. Appendix D above.]

1 See "*Dividends*", § VI. 5, at p. 501, n. 103 above.

Undecimo die Decembris A° 1592. Decretum est in loco Capitulari, per maiorem partem Sociorum Collegii de Gonvill & Caius, cum assentu et consensu Thomae Legge legum doctoris Custodis eiusdem Collegii, ut Sodalitia nuper ex donatione clarissimae faeminae Jocosae Franklande, ea lege tantum et conditione a Collegio reciperentur, et huiusmodi socii eligentur et admitterentur, quae sequitur. Viz. ut singuli huiusmodi socii habeant pro stipendio quotannis septem libras, ac praeterea nihil. Atque ut neque distributiones, neque liberaturas (ut vocant) neque divisiones nisi pro granis, neque commemorationum pecunias, aut pro foco habeant (cum eo nomine nihil a benefactrice sua Collegio donatum sit, sed tantum stipendium septem librarum, atque id[?][2] sine praeiudicio sociorum, et detrimento Collegii fieri non possint[)]. Ubi tamen alii fundi iuxta ultimam voluntatem doctoris Caii fundatoris ad focum alendum empti fuerint, parem cum caeteris sociis distributionem pro foco auferre poterunt. Non intersint Collegii negotiis cum caeteris sociis, nisi in ratione reddenda per oeconomum singulis diebus sabbati. Ut nullius officii sive publici sive privati; sive etiam servitii magistri Whitakres[3] sint capaces, nisi quod singuli socii prioris fundationis recusaverunt. Atque ut si quis aliter aut eligentur aut admitterentur, Electio eius sive Admissio pro nulla habeatur.

quod decretum ratum et firmum fore in posterum dicti Custos et Socii esse voluerunt. Die et anno supradictis.

Thomas Legge, Robert Church, Steph: Perse, Tho: Grimston, Rich: Stockdale, George Estey, Edw: Burton, Guil: Rant, John Gostlin.

[The 11th day of December 1592. It is decreed in the principal meeting-place, by the majority of the fellows of Gonville & Caius College, with the assent and consent of Thomas Legge, LL.D., keeper of the same college, that fellowships should be accepted from the recent gift of the most illustrious lady Joyce Frankland, and fellows of this kind be elected and admitted, only on the terms and condition that follow. Viz.:

– That each of the fellows of this kind shall have for a stipend £7 a year, and nothing further.

– That they shall have neither distributions, nor liveries (as they are called), nor dividends except for grain, nor commemoration-moneys or hearth-moneys, (since nothing is given by the benefactress under that heading, but only the stipend of £7, and nothing more can be done without prejudice to the fellows and detriment to the college). However, where other property shall have been bought to sustain the hearth in accordance with the last will [and

2 Perhaps *idem*.

3 John Whitacre. Cf. Statutes 60, 61.

testament] of the founder Dr Caius[4] they shall be able to receive an equal share with other fellows.

– [That] they are not to participate in college business with the other fellows, except in the [weekly] rendering of account by the steward each Saturday.

– That they are qualified for no office either public or private, or even Master Whitacre's service,[5] unless each of the fellows of the earlier foundation has refused them.

– And that if anyone should be elected or admitted otherwise, his election or admission shall be adjudged null and void.

It is the wish of the said keeper and fellows that this decree shall [be taken as] settled and binding for the future. The day and year aforesaid.

Thomas Legge (*B.H.* I, p. 73), Robert Churche (*B.H.* I, p. 58), Stephen Perse (*B.H.* I, p. 57), Thomas Grymstone (*sic B.H.* I, p. 115), Richard Stockdale (*B.H.* I, p. 130), George Estey (*B.H.* I, p. 90), Edward Burton (*B.H.* I, p. 103), William Rant (*B.H.* I, p. 111), John Gostlin (*B.H.* I, p. 116).]

4 A reference to Caius' testamentary gift of money to purchase lands to provide £10 p.a. for the maintenance of the kitchen fire, which was subsequently taken as authorising the distribution of the £10 as a dividend among the Master and senior fellows to the exclusion of junior fellows: see the section on *Hearth Money* in "*Dividends*", § VI. 5 above.

5 The holder had an obligation to preach and was paid a "salary" for the "service"; it was not regarded as an office, the fellow who held it being termed 'salarist': see Statute 60 and "*Supplementary Notes to Caius' Statutes*", § IV. 3, at p. 299 above.

VII. F

Allen's Case (1617)

[Venn, *Annals* (1904), pp. 257–70; *Acta*, 1617 (L.D.)[1]]

[NOTE: The spelling of the English texts has been modernised here and a translation appended to the Latin passages in the Annals. For this case, see "*The Norfolk Preference*", § VI. 3, and "*The Master's Negative Voice*", § VI. 2, above.

Stephen Perse died on the last day of September 1615 and another senior fellow, Robert Welles, was unanimously 'translated' into his place. This resulted in a vacancy in the senior fellowship and in the ensuing election the majority of the fellows voted for an existing Frankland fellow who was not Norfolk-born, John Allen, a Devonian. The Master, Branthwaite, refused to agree and persisted in voting for another Frankland fellow who was Norfolk-born, Thomas Cooke. Branthwaite proceeded to admit Cooke and the fellows, armed with opinions from Doctors' Commons, brought charges against the Master before the Chancellor, as provided by Bateman's statutes.[2] The Chancellor decided in favour of Allen, but diplomatically persuaded the parties that Cooke should be elected to the next senior fellowship to fall vacant. (Cooke was subsequently elected to that vacancy and some years later caused great trouble to the College.)[3]

Branthwaite's views on the Norfolk preference appear to have been very strong, and it took tactful persuasion from the Vice-Chancellor to bring him formally to accept publicly the Chancellor's decision. Even then he begged to be excused from admitting Allen and requested that the Chancellor or Vice-Chancellor should instead admit him.[4]

When forty years later the university librarian and former fellow, William Moore [*B.H.* III, p. 192] brought the Annals up to date from the year 1603 where Thomas Legge had left them, he drew upon a copy of the Chancellor's judgment and Branthwaite's ultimate acceptance of it which he found in the University Registry and which had been certified by the university registrary. As these two documents had been copied into the college's *Acta* immediately after one another on a single

1 *Exiit Book* (1592–1618).

2 Statute 5.

3 See *Cooke's Case* (1636), Appendix G below.

4 The office of president was vacant throughout Branthwaite's mastership.

page,[5] Moore presented them together in the Annals and only afterwards set out the protestation which Branthwaite had made to the Vice-Chancellor, the submissions which he had earlier made to the Chancellor and the fellows' answers. As a result the account in the Annals is confusing, since it is not presented there in chronological order. It has been re-arranged here as follows:

(A) the disputed election;
(B) the opinions of the civil lawyers;
(C) detailed arguments which Branthwaite submitted to the Chancellor; these set out four contradictions between Bateman's and Caius' statutes which had clearly been a matter of uncertainty to the college, together with nine alleged customary breaches of statutes;
(D) the fellows' answer to (C);
(E) the proceedings before the Chancellor and his judgment;
(F) Branthwaite's protestation when the Vice-Chancellor published the judgment;
(G) Branthwaite's final acceptance of the Chancellor's decision.

The principal interest in this case lies in:

(i) its ruling on the question of the effect of the Master's vote,[6]
(ii) its ruling in respect of the Norfolk preference,[7] and
(iii) the light which is thrown by the answer of the fellows on the reasoning justifying the introduction of dividends in respect of rents and on entry fines on leases, in defiance of Caius' strict instructions in his statutes.[8]]

(A) *The disputed election*

In locum Doctoris Perse ex fundatione Caii, Robertus Wells Norfolciensis Medicinae Doctor, unanimi Custodis et sociorum consensu per translationem (ut loquuntur) subrogatus est; et ad supplendum locum dicti Doctoris Wells ita vacantem, per viam scrutinii proceditur ad novam electionem. Major pars sociorum contulerunt sua suffragia in Johannem Allen Devoniensem, artium magistrum, et tunc temporis socium ex fundatione Jocosae Franclandae, sed Custos voce sua negativa sociorum electionem ratam habere noluit. Custode et sociis suis in sententiis immotis persistentibus, mensis (spatium per statutum electioni destinatum) elabitur, quo elapso Custos contendit provisionem de socio pro illa vice per devolutionem ad se solum spectare, et in locum vacantem nominavit et admisit Thomam Cooke Norfolciensem, artium magistrum, tunc

[5] *Acta*, Lady Day 1617: *Exiit Book* (1592–1618). The other documents were not copied into the *Acta*.
[6] See "*The Master's Negative Voice*", § VI. 2 above.
[7] See "*The Norfolk Preference*", § VI. 3 above.
[8] See "*Dividends*", § VI. 5 above.

quoque temporis socium ex fundatione Franclandiana, sociorum majori parte quibus possit modis huic Custodis facto obsistente. Hinc illae discordiarum scintillae quae diu latuere quasi sub cineribus sepultae in ingentem flammam emicuere, quae non nisi sententia Cancellarii visitatoris extingui poterant.

Anno 1616

Toto hoc anno litigatur de nupera facta electione, et ad jurisperitos utrinque concurritur, sed frustra, noluerunt enim socii Custodi cedere nec custos ad partes sociorum accedere, ante sententiam latam per Cancellarium Academiae, anno insequenti. Opportuna hic sese offert occasio enarrandi, quid utrinque a jurisconsultis in presenti lite assertum erat, sed (quod dolemus) ex utraque parte hoc prestare non possumus, quae enim fuerit sententia eorum qui a parte stabant Custodis, nos prorsus latet; at sane, si illius sententiae nobis unquam facta fuisset copia, nullo modo eam huc referre omitteremus, ne studio partium seduci, nec bona fide prout res transacta fuit enarrare videamur; interim, quamvis ex hac parte silere cogimur, tamen cum plurimum interesse Collegio et futurae ejus tranquillitati, optime prospici existimamus, si rationes hic adducantur jurisperitorum, a quorum partibus stetit victoria; has penitus omittere (quia alteras non possumus exhibere) haud aequum esse judicamus, proinde hic subjunximus sententias eorum qui ratam habuerunt electionem sociorum, in quibus non nuda sententia spectanda sed rationes quibus ad partes sociorum accedere moti sunt, ponderandae, eoque magis quod ex hac parte per Cancellarium facta erat decisio litis; scripta sequuntur jurisconsultorum proprias sententias subscriptis nominibus attestantium.

[In place of Dr Perse on Caius' foundation, Robert Welles M.D., a Norfolk man, was translated (as they call it) into his place with the unanimous agreement of the keeper and the fellows; and matters proceeded to a new election by ballot to fill the place of Dr Welles thereby vacated. The majority of the fellows cast their votes for John Allen M.A., a Devonshire man and at that time a fellow on Joyce Frankland's foundation; but the keeper was unwilling to recognise the election by the fellows as valid, on the grounds that his vote had been negative. The keeper and the fellows continued to be immovable in their opinions, and a month elapsed – the statutory period provided for an election – whereupon the keeper contended that the choice of fellow devolved on him alone, and he nominated and admitted Thomas Cooke M.A., a Norfolk man and also a fellow on the Frankland foundation at the time, the majority of the fellows resisting this action by the keeper in whatever ways they could. At this point those sparks of discord which had lain dormant for a long time as if buried under ashes burst fiercely into flame and could not be extinguished save by a decision of the Chancellor as visitor.

In the Year 1616

Throughout the whole year litigation proceeded over the election just made, and legal opinion was sought on both sides, but in vain, since the fellows were not willing to give way to the keeper nor the keeper to the fellows, until judgment was given by the Chancellor of the university the following year. An opportune occasion arises here to recount the legal opinion presented by lawyers on each side in the present dispute, but (to our regret) we are unable to present the arguments of both sides, for the arguments of those who took the keeper's side remain unavailable; truly, if the opinion of that side should have been accessible to us at any time, we should in no way have omitted to present them here, lest we should seem to favour one side and not recount faithfully the matter in the way it happened; in the meantime, although we are forced to remain silent as regards one side, nevertheless we think that the best interests of the college and its future tranquillity will be served if the arguments of the lawyers of the winning side are stated here; we deem it not right to omit them completely just because we are unable to present those of the other side; hence we append here the views of those who upheld the validity of the election made by the fellows in which there are not set down [merely] the bare conclusions but the reasons which, on consideration, moved them to come down on the fellows' side, and this all the more so because judgment was given for that side by the Chancellor; what follow are the individual opinions of the lawyers with their attesting names subscribed.]

(B) *The Opinions of the Civilians*

"I am of opinion that the election of Mr Allen by the greater part of the Fellows in the presence of the Master, though he dissented, was lawful, and ought to stand; for since the Founder whose statute in the letter is urged by the Master hath himself clearly interpreted the same as is afore expressed viz. *Quod in electione Socii, Custodis praesentia necessario requiritur, non tamen quod votum suum necessario conveniat votis majoris partis sociorum,*[9] there is no reason to press the Founder's words against his own interpretation, so evident; and if it be replied that the interpretation was upon an occasion fallen out in Trinity Hall not in this college, it must be remembered that the statute itself also was originally given to the same Trinity Hall and therefore if the statute itself by the pleasure of the Founder be made the Statute of Gonville and Caius College

[9] See Bateman's *Interpretatio*, Appendix A above.

of necessity it followeth that the interpretation thereof (which is the life of the statute) be the same there also."

Hen. Marten.[10]

"I am of the same opinion with Dr Marten, especially because the founder hath so interpreted the statute of Trinity Hall, (for seeing this statute of Caius College is made by relation to the statute of Trinity Hall), it is all one as if the founder had made this interpretation expressly to the Statute of Caius College, for a law or statute is not the bare words thereof, but the sense and meaning, and thereupon is grounded that rule of law, *Is committit in legem qui verba legis complectens contra legis nititur voluntatem*; and this interpretation is not a new statute nor addeth anything to the statute of Trinity Hall, but only declareth what the statute was from the beginning, and if by any other means it could have been known, that had been to be followed, as if the custom or practice of the house had so declared it without any interpretation at all, so that this relation to the statute of Trinity Hall is to be taken in that sense which Trinity Hall statute is interpreted to be, because he that made the law can best interpret it.

But suppose there had been no interpretation at all yet I am of opinion that in this case there should never have been any devolution to the Master, for that it were a great absurdity that in a College where it is intended that there should be a free election of fellows by the major part it should be in the power of the Master to bestow every fellowship where he liketh, and so frustrate the meaning of the founder.

Again, a devolution from one to another groweth ever for the supply of some negligence or fault in the electors, and as it were for a punishment of them who offend; but in this Cause the diligent persons who peradventure have chosen *dignissimum* should be punished, and he who peradventure would thrust in *indignum* should make gain of his own fraud, whereas *eligendo indignum* he looseth his voice, et *potestas eligendi in ejus poenam devolvitur in alium.*

Again, this may be likened to the case of a benefice, where generally if the benefice be litigious above 6 months, the ordinary may collate by lapse. Now if the true patron present his clerk to the bishop of the Diocese, who makes title himself to collate, whereby the benefice is now grown litigious, the bishop in this case shall never take benefice as by lapse.

Again the law generally was that *excommunicatus injudicio non erat audiendus*, but it must be thus understood *agendo non defendendo*, and the reason is for that it were an absurd thing that a man should be called in question and not permitted to defend himself.

[10] King's Advocate 1609; knighted 1617; Judge of the Court of Admiralty 1617–41; Dean of Arches 1624–33.

Query how the Master comes to be one of the scrutiny and how he gives his voice, for if he gives his voice but as an elector, he should have no negative voice."

Nyc. Styward.[11]

"In the cause propounded I am of the same opinion with Mr Doctor Martin, and Mr Doctor Styward, that the election of Mr Allen, made by the major part of the fellows, notwithstanding the Master consented not, is good, and available in law; for it is apparent in the words of the Statute, *Sed si locus alicujus dicti Collegii, &c.*, that the meaning of the Statute is that the Master, and greater part of the fellows, should consent to the election of a new fellow, in the roome that is void, *Et cum de contraria mente legis evidenter constare non potest a propria verborum significatione non receditur, et non aliter* (69 de Legatis 3). In the case propounded, the greater part of the fellows have given their uniform consent, the Master only refuseth to give his consent and objecteth three things; first because he did not consent there was not *concors electio Custodis et sociorum*; the second, and therefore the provision for this time to be devolved unto him; 3. that he the Master hath the grammatical sense of the statute to justify his proceedings.

To the first, by law one man's act cannot prejudice another, *Non debet aliquis alterius odio praegravari. c. cum non debet* (22 de Reg. Juris. in 6to etc.) *non debet* (74 Ff de Reg. Juris.) *et omnibus modis proconsul id agit ne cujus deterior fiat conditio ex alieno facto* etc. (Ff. de alienatione Judicii mutandi causa facta,) which laws I hold to be strong arguments; the Master his dissent may not abridge the fellows of the election and so prejudice them, much less gain unto himself a devolution. *Nemo enim ex suo delicto meliorem suam conditionem facere potest*, etc., non fraudantur 176 § nemo Ff de Reg. Juris. *et longe aequum est ex eo quod per fide gestum est actorem nihil consequi* (l. apud 4 § Marcellus Ff de doli exceptione gloss. l. finalis Ff de dolo). And the Law saith *si sine dolo malo stipulantis factum est: sub hac enim conditione committitur stipulatio ne quis doli sui praemium ferat* (l. ita demum 26 Ff de receptis: qui arbitrium *etc.). lex dans potestatem fratri majori dividendi bona intelligenda est voluisse excipere dolum, et captiosam divisionem* (Stephan. de Phedris (sic), De interpretatione legum parte 2da p. 162). And in the Case propounded because it was in the Master's power to perfect the election, and he did it not, I take it the election made by the greater part of the fellows standeth good in law, et in Jure Civili receptum est (122 Ff de reg. Juris. c. cum non 66 de Reg. Juris. in 6to).

To the third, to help the Master, admit further there be a statute in the College, that their statutes are to be understood literally, and according to the grammatical sense, and not otherwise, yet the Founder's meaning and motive

[11] Nicholas Steward, Admiralty Advocate 1573, LL.D. 1574.

must be observed (Baldus l. omnes populi 9 Ff de Justitia et Jure nu. 57), which was, that a fellow must be chosen cum consensu Custodis et majoris partis sociorum; ita est enim propria significatio per quam omnes casus in oratione contenti pariter determinantur, et quam major effectus sequitur, et quae plana et secundum litteram legis est (Stephan. de Phedris (sic) de interpretatione legum, parte 2[da] p. 113 et 114) et ille sensus legis recipiendus est, ex quo non sequitur aliquod repugnans cum antecedenti; Item ex quo non sequitur aliquod absurdum (idem eadem parte 2[da] p. 191). Againe si statutum dicat quod statuta intelligantur ad literam sine aliqua interpretatione finitiva, vel extensiva, non de interpretatione declarativa (Steph. de Phedris ubi supra parte 2[da] 115 et 264) ubi dicit doctores communiter tenere quod statuta poterunt interpretari, declarando et dis- tinguendo non autem restringendo vel ampliando.

As this case standeth all that I have said needeth not, for as it is set forth in the case propounded the founder himself hath resolved this doubt by an interpretation given in Trinity Hall, and (*dato sed non concesso*) that the Founder's interpretation concerns Trinity Hall only, *provisio testatoris facta, uno casu extenditur ad alium, quem testator verisimiliter providisset, si de eo fuisset interrogatus; et hoc prestat argumentum, quod statutum debet extendi ad casum de quo verisimiliter idem providissent statuentes, si interrogati fuissent* (Alex. l. Titius 25 § Lucius Ff. de liberis et posthumis; et ibi Castrensis et Jason, et Jason l. si extraneus 6. nu. 7 Ff. de Condictione causa data etc.; et l. sive apud 28 c. de transactionibus).

Again gloss l. tale pactum 40 § finalis, verbo exceptionem Ff. de pactis; et ibi Bartolus Castrensis Baldus et Jason. *Item nota id esse de jure servandum licet non sit statutum quod verisimile est statuendum fuisse si hoc quaesitum fuisset.* Now it is very likely that the founder having made his interpretation in Trinity Hall, that if this doubt had likewise fallen out in Caius College, and this resolution had been asked, in all likelihood he would have given the same interpretation in Caius College, *mutatio enim voluntatis non presumitur* l. Quingenta 14 et l. eum 22 Ff. de probationibus *maxime quando considerate loquutus est* autentica de conjectura ultimarum voluntatum c. 15 cum 4. by interpretation therefore of these Doctors the Founder's interpretation made in Trinity Hall upon the like Statute must be received in Caius College, though it be not part of the statute there."

Ita censeo, J. Hone.[12]

[12] John Hone, LL.D. 1579, Advocate 1589.

(c) *Branthwaite's submissions to the Chancellor*

Statute contradictions preferred to the Vice Chauncellour 1617.

1. Bishop Bateman saith, *Volumus in Medicinae scientia in dicto Collegio unicus tantum socius aut duo ad plus simul audire valeant et studere.* But Dr Caius appointed 2 besides of his own foundation, and giveth liberty for more; by occasion hereof there have been of the 12 seniors five physicians at one time.
2. Bishop Bateman maketh the cator an officer, habeant socii Collegii duos officiarios pistorem et dispensatorem: Dr Caius will have him a scholar, sit is scholasticus ex fundatione (statute 56).
3. Bishop Bateman saith, none can hold his place which hath 5^{li} yearly without cure in a benefice, or in a benefice with cure of what value so ever; *Ordinamus quod nullus curatum obtinens beneficium etc.* But Dr Caius alloweth to his fellows 10^{li} 6^{s} 8^{d} yearly, *Statuimus et ordinamus in uberiorem studiorum materiam etc.*[13]

   Upon these statutes it may be questioned whether a fellow may have temporalities there above the revenue expressed in the said statute, especially there being these words (sta. 8) *non excludimus indigorum generosorum etc.* and, if it be thought they may exceed, then how far they may exceed the proportion set down in statute, because the fellows think they may have lands of any value.
4. Touching the preferring of fellows, Bishop Bateman decreeth thus, *In electione sociorum scholares nostrae Diocaesios non beneficiati beneficiatis etc.* But Dr Caius thus, *in socios vero ejusdem Collegii scholastici Norfolc. cum Suffolc. preferantur etc.*

Ancient practices against statutes; whereas besides the statutes themselves we have this caution, *Constituimus ne quae consuetudo prevaleat adversus statutum aliquod.*

1. The fines upon leases which by statute are to go to the College, have been a long time divided amongst the company (statutes 93 and 95); *fines Collegii esse volumus non Magistri et sociorum.*[14]
2. The Mulcts have been appropriated to the Deans, contrary to the 73 statute, *volumus ut omnes mulctae cedant Collegio.*[15]

13 Bateman's Statute 12E; Caius' Statute 39.

14 See "*Dividends*", § VI. 5 above.

15 See "*Stipends*", § VI. 4 above.

3. The Fellows' problem hath been but once a week contrary to the old statute,[16] and new statute the 17, *non intermittatur problema sociorum et pensionariorum majorum etc.*
4. There have been but two problems of fellows in the Vacation contrary to the former statute, which saith they should continue *ad festum Bartholomei.*
5. Chamber rents have been divided which should go to the College (stat. 66), *constituimus ut pensiones cubiculorum utriusque Collegii etc.*[17]
6. The Fellows have often changed their professions against statute, *In scientia quam eligerint audiendum etc.*[18] It would therefore be ordered that every one be reduced to the profession he first took upon him and used to take his degree therein, and also that those who by their foundation were appointed to be divines should direct themselves to divinity and according to their foundation enter the Ministry.[19]
7. The Stewards are by Statute to be chosen quarterly (Stat. 56) *volumus … in tres menses eligatur*, but they have been anciently chosen for a year.
8. The Statute is there shall be two Indentures at every account of the State of the College whereof one to remain with the Master the other in the chest,[20] which have been omitted ever since Dr Caius' Statutes.
9. Lastly neither scholar nor fellow, by statute or practice of other houses, hath any right to any allowance before his admission or election, and therefore upon the vacation of places I have moved the stipend might go to the College, but it hath been denied. It would be therefore ordered if upon necessity scholarships be void, whether allowance shall be given from the vacation of the place, or their election.

16 Bateman's Statute 1.

17 Room rents were the first substantial subject of dividend to emerge in the college; it had become an accepted practice in Gonville Hall in the years between Caius' departure from the college in 1545 and his return as Master in 1559. Branthwaite cited Statute 66, but there Caius only directed that pensioners living in "either College" (*i.e.*, Caius Court and the older buildings in Gonville Court) should pay their rents quarterly, and in their answer to Branthwaite the fellows dismissively replied simply that the statute should be consulted. It is significant that Branthwaite did not cite Statute 15, where Caius prohibited the practice for rooms in his own Caius Court and appears to have accepted that the dividend applied to rooms in Gonville Court; in later years Caius Court was always excluded from the dividend: See "*Dividends*", § VI. 5 above.

18 Bateman's statutes, preamble § 3.

19 Gerrard complained in 1582 that Stephen Perse had been allowed to change his profession between theology and medicine several times: *Gerrard's Case* (1582), Appendix D above.

20 Bateman's Statute 7.

(D) *The Answers of the Fellows*

The answer to the Contradictions.

1. The Donations being by divers founders they do not conceive any contradiction, for that every benefactor is free to bestow his own gift as he judgeth it best. And so hath Dr Caius determined this matter (Sta. 107) *Si qua statuta nostra diversa etc.*
2. There is no contradiction that one Founder makes the cator an officer, the other a scholar, for that the same man may be both a scholar and cator for the College, as well as steward for the College and fellow.
3. Bishop Bateman alloweth but 5^{li} in spiritual living, and Dr Caius alloweth that his fellows may enjoy 10^{li} 6^{s} 8^{d}, is no contradiction, for that it is left to every benefactor to bestow his own with what conditions seem good to himself; neither of these statutes were ever questioned to concern temporalities of that value, but only spiritual preferments, neither can there be shown any practice, that ever any person was ever questioned for his temporal state, either in our College or Trinity Hall who have the same Statute made by Bishop Bateman, neither can a rule be made by deduction if it be not contained in the letter of the Law in a grammatical sense as the Founder speaks.
4. Both the Founders agree that Norfolk men should be preferred in all elections, which cannot be understood in Dr Caius his statutes otherwise then in Bishop Bateman's, with this clause (caeteris paribus)[;] as for Dr Caius' own Foundation, as he hath made the places proper for Norfolk so they have been chosen still out of the Country.

Answer to the Ancient practices pretended against Statutes.

1. The Fellows say that the fines of all copyholds have always been paid to the chest, the tenants' benevolences for their leases have always been divided amongst the company, whereof the Custos have ever had a double part.
2. The 75 Statute maketh mention of 10 persons but of fellows only,[21] and therefore the fellows suppose that (*omnes mulctae*) in that place cannot be intended of any mulcts but those that are imposed upon the fellows which ever have been paid to the College. As for the mulcts of scholars they have been from time to time allowed to the deans for their pains in their office,

[21] The statute cited should be Statute 73, not 75. The reference to "10 persons" is clearly a corrupt reading of "no persons". The sense of the argument is clear: that the reference to *omnes mulctae* in the final paragraph of the statute must refer to fellows' fines, since the paragraph envisages that the fellows might let each other off those fines and no persons other than fellows are mentioned.

and (as we have heard our predecessors say) were so allowed in Dr Caius' time.

3. The fellows' problems are so observed as Dr Caius left them, one kept by the fellows, another by the Bachelors, and the third by the interpretation of Archbishop Parker upon the 17 Statute cited is left with this query, *An sophistce possunt supplere vicem in problematibus ex utriusque statutis decernendum est.*
4. That there never were more than two Problems kept by fellows during the vacation between the Masters' commencement and Michaelmas not in Doctor Caius' time, so they have still been performed. In other Colleges (as far as we can learn) there are none kept by fellows during the vacation.
5. For answer to the 5th, consult the statute observed by the common practice.
6. The fellows never changed their professions but when they were removed into new places which gave them that liberty, and for urging any man to take the degree of Doctor which hath not means to maintain it the Society have ever held it unreasonable, seeing without the calling of them by the voice of the major part they cannot be compelled by any statute. As for those that by their foundation ought to enter into the Ministry it is always in the Custos' power to urge them to it, upon danger of their places.
7. The Stewards have been chosen annually with other officers, and so pass from quarter to quarter, *per tacitum consensum*, but if any doe not perform with that fidelity and care that is meet, the fellows have always been ready to join with the Master to remove such a steward at the quarter's end: if no just exceptions can be taken against him they desire not such an extraordinary trouble of removing and electing anew such officer every three months.
8. For the making of two Indentures our books of account do supply them, and perfect all reckonings at our audit.[22] But if the Custos require them, he well knoweth that no man will deny them.
9. The right of every allowance is due according to the donation of the Founder of it, and is so to be employed as he hath ordained it, not otherwise. The College chest hath a proper allowance to itself, which as it was ever sufficient for the common charge so the fellows never diminish it, therefore they have always thought that pensions designed for the maintenance of scholars or fellows are not to be converted to the filling of chests, unless the manifest necessity or want of the College were such as it needed to be relieved; neither do they understand how that which is given for personal maintenance should properly belong to any other then either the present possessor or future incumbent, as it is the practice both *de jure et de facto* in other livings in the land belonging to the maintenance of scholars; and

22 The "books of account" which replaced the indentures were the *Libri Rationales* and the *Status Collegii*, and also, from 1609, the Bursar's Books: see *Caius and the college's accounts and records* in "*Supplementary Notes to Caius' Statutes*", § IV. 3 above.

for this denial which Dr Branthwaite thinks an offence the fellows (*salvo superiorum judicio*) think they do God and the Commonwealth good service to urge a perpetual supply of students and prevent the danger that may ensue by keeping places void longer then they ought to be; they know no necessity of vacancy, the land having so great a number which want maintenance.

(E) *The Proceedings before the Chancellor*

Anno 1617

Hactenus praelusoriis telis dimicatur, hoc vero anno ad decretoria ventum est, sociorum enim duae partes admonuerunt Custodem Gulielmum Branthwayte statuti de inhabili Custode et de mala administratione officii sui, idque declararunt quibusdam articulis quibus inhabilitatem ejus ad regimen Collegii probare in se susceperunt; quos articulos una cum admonitione exhibuerunt simulque invitatur Custos ut officio suo sponte cedere voluerit, prout statutum monet faciendum; sed is renuens, Cancellarius Academiae, honoratissimus Dominus Thomas Howard, consulitur, qui in aedibus Audlianis adscitis sibi viris aliquot gravibus et prudentibus, Custode et sociis presentibus, plenariam habuit causae cognitionem, et sententiam suam certis quibusdam articulis declaravit; quos articulos scripto quodam authentico in registro Universitatis Cantebrigiae servando tradidit, eosque ad perpetuam rei memoriam tuto reponi et servari plurimum interest Collegio.

Hujus Decreti tenor hic est:

[Up to this time the dispute had been concerned with preliminary issues; in this year, however, it became a matter of judicial decree, for two-thirds of the fellows admonished the keeper William Branthwaite under the statute *de inhabili Custode et de mala administratione officii sui*, and set out their case in various articles in which they took it upon themselves to prove his unfitness to govern the college. They presented these articles [to him] with an admonition and at the same time invited the keeper to resign his office voluntarily as the statute requires. On his refusal to do so the Chancellor of the university Lord Thomas Howard was appealed to, and, in the company of various weighty and wise persons assembled with him in his house at Audley End, and in the presence of the keeper and fellows, he held a full hearing of the case and gave his judgment in various final articles. These he handed down to be preserved in certified form in the registry of the university and it is in the best interest of the college that they be set down and preserved as a permanent record of the matter.

The tenor of this decree is as follows:]

A Declaration of the order and decree of me Thomas Earl of Suffolk, Lord High Treasurer of England and Chancellor of the University of Cambridge, touching divers points of differences betwixt Mr Doctor Branthwaite Master of Gonville and Caius College within that University and the fellows there[23] upon a full hearing of both parties as followeth.

First that Doctor Harvey's 100^{li} be brought in by the Master into the College chest and employed with all convenience and speed to provide land for the maintenance of a scholar.

2. That the 30^{li} paid by the tenants of Caxton shall be brought into the College chest by the Master there to remain until the difference between the College and tenants be determined.
3. That the Master and fellows shall join to sue the tenant Mr Cradocke in an action of waste committed in the grounds.
4. That Allen shall have the place to which he was elected by the major part of the fellows, although the Master did deny him by his negative voice, three times and after the end of the month devolved it and elected Cooke; because he denied him as it seemed upon his own negative voice by the space of a month that so he might devolve it to himself and elect alone, not giving any just cause or reason of the Statute why Allen was not eligible; which I the rather determine thus because it agreeth with the exposition made by the Founder, Bishop Bateman, of the same Statute in Trinity Hall of his own foundation.

   And[24] because hereafter there may be peace and quietness between the Master and the fellows, I do further order that the Master and fellows shall consent by way of pre-nomination or pre-election that Mr Cooke shall have the next fellow's place that shall become void.
5. **That** the Master shall not keep courts without the consent of the major part of the fellows first had.
6. **That** it is fit the Master with the consent of the fellows do yearly according to statute renew the choice of their steward,[25] if they shall be found fit and sufficient for the places, yet notwithstanding to continue them that they may have the better knowledge, and experience to execute their places.
7. **That** there be yearly one of the fellows chosen Bursar with the Master according to the statute and that the Master's oath concerning the bursarship shall be taken once for all.
8. **That** the Master shall neither declare nor pronounce any place void, nor censure and punish any fellow with the loss of the rights and profits of his

[23] In the *Acta* the reference to "the fellows" is expanded to "at the instance of some fellows among [whom] were Dr Wells and Mr Stokys".

[24] In the *Acta*, this paragraph is numbered "5", paragraphs 5–8 are renumbered 6–9, and the final paragraph is left unnumbered.

[25] In the *Acta* the words "the steward and bailiffs" are substituted.

fellowship without the consent of the major part of the fellows according to the Statute.

9.[26] That the elections of Mr Randall[27] and Mr Cruso[28] shall be taken to be good and sufficient, because the Master did consent upon condition, which condition being *extra statutum* his consent was good.

Subscribed, T. Suffolk.

(F) *Branthwaite's protestation on publication of the Chancellor's decree*

The orders being published the nine and twentieth of July by the Vice Chancellor, the Master spoke publicly in the presence of those assembled; that he would assent unto them so far as they were agreeable to his oath, to Dr Caius' Statutes, and the covenants between Dr Caius and the College; otherwise as they might not stand with his oath or with Dr Caius statutes, or the Covenants between Dr Caius and the said College, he did there protest against them and desired also his said protestation might be recorded respective to his former protestation. Upon conference with the Vice Chancellor and some assistants, the 8 of August following, the Master to give further satisfaction to the Chancellor gave answer to the particulars in manner following which said answer is to be found upon the precedent page.[29]

(G) *Branthwaite's acceptance of the decree*

1. Docter Branthwaite Master of Gonville and Caius College in the University of Cambridge doth promise that he will bring the 100li into the College Chest at the next audit, or before the end of November next, so that he may be free from his Covenant made to Dr Gostling Dr Legg Executours.
2. **Item** he will deliver the 30li at the same time, so that he may be secured by the College from the tenants of Caxton.
3. **Item** he is content to give consent with the fellows to sue Cradocke in an action of Waste.
4. **Item** he is willing for his part that Mr Allein shall be fellow and have all right belonging thereunto; but for admission he humbly craveth pardon, because he verily thinketh he cannot do it with safety of his oath: yet having

26 Not numbered in the *Acta*.
27 Thomas Randolph (*B.H.* I, p. 182).
28 *B.H.* I, p. 209.
29 "upon the precedent page" in the Annals, but immediately following here.

a most affectionate desire to perform all offices of duty and respect to your Lordship, being so noble a Peer and Patron of our University, he doth yield that your Lordship as Chancellor, or Mr Vice Chancellor, shall admit him, as in causes of this nature is usual.

5. **Item** he is content courts shall be kept by consent of the Master and greater part of the fellows, neither did he ever as he saith keep any otherwise.
6. **Item** he consenteth that the Master with the consent of the fellows do yearly according to the statute renew the choice of their Steward and Bailiffs if they shall be found fit and sufficient for the places, yet notwithstanding to continue them that they may have the better knowledge and experience to execute their places.
7. **Item** he yieldeth that there be yearly one of the fellows chosen Bursar with the Master according to the statute, and that the Master's oath concerning the bursarship shall be taken once for all.
8. **Item** he neither will declare nor pronounce any fellows place void nor punish any fellows with the loss of the profits of his fellowship without consent of the major part, but in such causes where the statute saith *expellatur ipso facto*, and in those when the fact shall be made apparent in the presence of the Master, and the major part of the fellows, *aut ex concessione rei, aut per probationem duorum idoneorum testium.*
9. **Item** he acknowledgeth Cruso to be fellow, and so he is already admitted. And for Mr Randall his election shall be taken to be good and sufficient for his part and to be admitted as Mr Allein.[30]

And in all and every of these humbly submitteth himself in manner aforesaid so as he shall not be adjudged hereafter either to have incurred perjury or the College (by his fact) to forfeit a bond of 1500^{li}, and this is the only intent of all his former protestations, since the publication of the orders.

Wm Branthwaite.

Concordat cum originali in Registro Universitatis Cantabrigiae.
Ita testor, Jacobus Tabor, Universitatis Cantebrigiae Registrarius.

[This agrees with the original in the registry of the University of Cambridge: so witnessed: James Tabor, Registrary of Cambridge University.]

30 It is not clear whether Branthwaite's unwillingness to admit Randall was due to his place of birth (he had been at school in Norfolk but may not have been born there) or to the fact that he had been elected in the Master's absence. Cruso had been elected to a junior fellowship and the Norfolk objection would not have arisen.

VII. G

Cooke's Case (1636)

[Venn, *Annals* (1904), pp. 389–95]

[NOTE: The spelling of the English texts has been modernised here and a translation appended to the Latin passages in the Annals. For the background and aftermath of this case, see "*The Norfolk Preference*", § VI. 3 above.

The case arose out of Thomas Cooke's attempts in 1636 to cling on to his senior fellowship. He had been presented to the living of Mutford-cum-Barnaby in 1633 and had succeeded in holding on to his fellowship until 1635. His valedictory year having long expired the Master and fellows finally declared his fellowship vacant. Cooke appealed to the King and put before the royal commissioners various charges of dereliction of duty against the Master, Thomas Batchcroft.

The commissioners rejected peremptorily Cooke's main charges against Batchcroft, and, although they accepted as valid some of his other allegations of breaches of statutes, they found them trivial and in the end all that Cooke got for his pains was a severe rebuke for wasting His Majesty's time. Cooke departed and ceased thereafter to trouble the college.

The interest in this case lies principally in its rulings on (i) the Norfolk preference, and (ii) the status of junior fellows and the form of their admission.

The question of the Norfolk preference had arisen ten years earlier in *Allen's Case* (1617)[1] in connection with the same Thomas Cooke, and Cooke's election into a senior fellowship had followed as a consequence of the Chancellor's diplomatic settlement of that case. The two cases are recounted by Venn in the *Biographical History*.[2] Venn omits, however, to mention Cooke's assumption of magisterial powers on 30 May 1635 in the course of the later case – Cooke's conduct on that occasion would seem to justify Caius' very striking strictures in Statute 32 on the potentially disruptive tendencies of the person who was the most senior fellow.]

Thomas Cooke S. Theologiae baccalaureus et hujus Collegii socius tertio Augusti 1633 ad rectoriam Ecclesiae parochialis de Mutford cum Barnebie in comitatu Suffolciae praesentatus, ultra terminum per statuta praefixum manebat socius Collegii; partim dilatis institutione et inductione, partim nescio

1 Appendix F above.
2 *B.H.* III, pp. 71–2, 86–8.

quas lites sibi intentas comminiscendo; sed Custos et socii non ferentes vim ulterius inferri statutis, jubetur ad trigesimum Julii 1635 adesse in sacello ad reddendum rationem hujus facti, ubi Custode et duodecim sociis presentibus causam suam egit strenue, sed admonitus per Custodem de statuto Batemanni viz. *Item ordinamus quod nullus curatum obtinens beneficium etc.*, et de Statuto Fundatoris Caii de anno valedicendi *Reverendus Pater etc.*, interrogatusque ab eo, an juxta haec statuta Fundatorum ultra unius anni spatium a promotionis suae tempore jus ei esset ut socio manendi in Collegio, respondit, jus ei integrum esse, idque vi officii locum tenentis (quod officium olim sustinuit), tum etiam potestate senioris socii; sed custos una cum majore sociorum parte invalidas has ejus rationes judicans magistrum Cooke ulterius Collegii socium non esse debere pronuntiabat.

Hic memorandum, dictum Thomam Cooke constitutum locum tenentem in absentia Custodis, (scripto dato vicessimo secundo Maii 1625) secundum potestatem hanc sibi concessam 30mo Maii 1635, convocasse octo socios quotquot domi in Collegio tunc temporis reperti fuerunt, ut convenirent eum in sacello, qua conventione is nomine Custodis significabat supradictam rectoriam de Mutford cum Barneby vacare; et ut magister Robertus Sherringham Collegii socius dictae rectoriae praesentaretur proponebat, qui ipsius locumtenentis et majoris partis sociorum suffragiis, jus ad praesentationem obtinuit, idque postea communi sigillo confirmatum fuit; interim dictus Cooke nec resignaverat jus suum in manus Episcopi, nec postea cedere de jure suo in dicta rectoria voluit.

Pleniorem rerum in sacello gestarum in hoc negotio narrationem Custodis et sociorum nominibus testatam huc retulimus. [Blank page follows]

Mr Cooke sic sive amotus sive ejectus Custodis et Sociorum sententiis acquiescere noluit, sed Regiam Majestatem petitione compellit, Rexque serenissimus hujus causae cognitionem mandavit Reverendissimo in Christo Patri Domino Gulielmo Laud Archiepiscopo Cantuariensi, honoratissimo Henrico Comiti Hollandiae, Academiae Cancellario, et reverendissimo patri Matthaeo Wren, Episcopo Norwicensi, qui statim curant Custodem per literas accersiri Cancellarii quod sub hac forma protinus factum fuit.

[Thomas Cooke B.D., fellow of this college, was presented to the rectory of the parish church of Mutford cum Barnaby in the county of Suffolk on the 3rd August 1633, [but] stayed on as a fellow of the college beyond the period allowed by the statutes, partly as a result of delays in institution and induction and partly for I-know-not-what legal disputes contrived by him. However, the keeper and fellows would not suffer further infringement of the statutes and ordered him to appear in the chapel to explain his conduct. There he argued his case strenuously to the keeper and twelve fellows present, but was reminded by the keeper of Bateman's statute *Item ordinamus quod nullus curatum obtinens beneficium*

etc.,[3] and the statute of the founder Caius on the valedictory year, *Reverendus Pater etc.*,[4] and was asked by him whether he had any right under the statutes of the founder to remain as a fellow in the college beyond the period of one year from his promotion. He replied that he had an unqualified right by virtue of the office of deputy (an office he had held at one time) and also by virtue of his being the [most] senior fellow, but the keeper together with a majority of the fellows adjudged these reasons to be invalid and decreed that he was no longer a fellow of the college.

It must be recorded here that the said Thomas Cooke had been appointed deputy in the absence of the keeper (in writing dated 22nd May 1625), and on 30th May 1635, in virtue of that power granted to him, he summoned the eight fellows then found in college to meet with him in chapel, and at that meeting he intimated that the aforesaid rectory of Mutford cum Barneby was vacant and proposed that Robert Sheringham a fellow of the college should be presented to the said rectory; and [Robert] obtained the right to be presented by the votes of the same deputy and a majority of the fellows, and this was afterwards confirmed under the common seal; however, the said Cooke had not resigned his right to the bishop and was not willing afterwards to give up his right in the said rectory.

We have repeated here an account of the proceedings in the chapel witnessed with the names of the keeper and fellows. [Blank page follows.]

After he was either removed or ejected, Mr Cooke was unwilling to accept the decision of the keeper and fellows. Instead, he addressed a petition to His Royal Majesty, and His Serene Highness appointed the most Reverend Father in Christ Lord William Laud, Archbishop of Canterbury, the most honourable Henry, Earl of Holland, Chancellor of the university, and the most reverend Matthew Wren, Bishop of Norwich, to hear the case. They immediately ensured that the keeper should be summoned by letter from the Chancellor, which was done forthwith in the following manner.]

To Tho. Batchcroft Dr in Divinity at Cambridge these

After our very hearty commend[ation]s, Whereas his Majesty upon the complaint and petition of Thomas Cooke bachelor in Divinity, hath been pleased to refer to our hearing the matters in difference betwixt yourself and him, **These** are to let you know that we have appointed to hear this business in the Council Chamber at Whitehall upon Wednesday the second of the next month, in the afternoon, and do hereby require you by yourself or some other

3 Bateman's Statutes, Statute 15.

4 The passage cited is not in Caius' Statutes, but in his *Expositiones seu Interpretiones*, § *de anno valedicendi*.

sufficiently instructed and authorised by you, to attend accordingly: so not doubting of your care herein we bid you farewell, and rest

Your loving friend
Holland

Feb. 20, 1635.[5]

Quibus acceptis literis Custos statim se accingit itineri, comitatus magistris Moore, Dod, Loveland, et Pickarell, sociis consensu reliquorum deputatis, ut adessent Custodi eumque juvarent consiliis in praesenti negotio expediendo, insuper statutis Collegii, Annalibus, aliisque libris quibus in praesenti lite usus esset instruuntur.

Custos et socii comites, ad dictum diem praesto erant Londini, eo in loco ubi jussi erant expectare. Honoratissimi judices tempore praestituto aderant, adfuitque simul Mr Cooke stipatus et munitus duobus doctoribus juris ad ejus causam agendam, qui ex informatione dicti Cooke graviter accusant Custodem de non observatis statutis, quibus omnibus Custos per suos consiliarios (erant enim quoque duo doctores juris permissi) ita respondit ut calumniae adversarium facile arguerit, tandem post trium horarum disceptationem re exacte examinata et discussa, domini judices pro Custode sententiam ferunt, et magistrum Cooke juste per Custodem amotum statuunt, sententiamque suam Augustissimo Regi his verbis afferunt.

[On receipt of this letter the keeper immediately made ready for the journey, [and] a group consisting of Masters Moore, Dod, Loveland and Pickarell,[6] fellows deputed by the rest to attend on the keeper and assist him with advice in the dispatch of the present matter, also armed themselves with the statutes of the college, the Annals and other books which might be of use in the present litigation.

On the stated day the keeper and accompanying fellows presented themselves in London at the appointed place where they had been ordered to attend. The most honourable judges were present at the appointed time, and Mr Cooke appeared at that time accompanied and supported by two doctors of law as counsel in his action, and they formally charged the keeper on Cooke's information with not observing the statutes; to which the keeper through his counsel (who were also two doctors of law as permitted) made a reply such that he might straightforwardly refute the calumny of the other side, and at last, after three hours of legal argument, when the matter had been thoroughly examined and discussed, their lordships the judges gave judgment for the keeper and ruled that Master Cooke had rightly been removed by the keeper and submitted their decision to the Most August King in the following words.]

5 1636 (New Style).

6 *B.H.* I, pp. 192, 240, 243 and 265. It was William Moore who wrote this account of the case when he compiled the *Annals* twenty years later.

May it please your Majesty

According to your Majesty's gracious reference upon the petition of Thomas Cooke bachelor in Divinity shewing that whereas the said College is endowed with rich and great revenues by the founders and benefactors (being Norfolk and Suffolk men) for the maintenance of one Master and certain fellows ever to be chosen out of the said Countries,[7] with discretion of preferring the poor before the rich if they be equally qualified with them in worth and parts, and to that end have ordained statutes (enjoining the manner of election, and prescribed an oath for the due observation of the same), and that although all elections since the foundation have (for the most part) ever been made accordingly, and the present Master enjoys his preferment in right of both the countries and the statutes; yet contrary to his office and oath hath broke many statutes and caused of his own accord many elections to be made of strangers of other countries, and that being remembered thereof by the petitioner, and withall entreated either to redress the same at home or to be judged by certain visitors (to whom the power of interpreting statutes and impounding controversies is solely referred) hath not only refused so to do but still persists in his error and in uncharitable requital of the petitioner's discharge of his duty, hath of late endeavoured to make void his fellowship without any ground of statute or statutable proceeding.

Wee having heard the petitioner and his counsel and likewise Dr Batchcroft the present Master and divers of the senior fellows of the said College and their counsel, do in all duty hereby humbly declare to your Majesty what upon full hearing appeareth to us.

(Caius Statute 8.) First touching the statute of election unto the said College we find that the same doth not absolutely require that Norfolk and Suffolk men and such as are of the Diocese of Norwich bee only chosen, but that first those of Norfolk then those of Suffolk and of the Diocese of Norwich be preferred, and we find that in all times there have been some of other Countries admitted, and that the present Master of the said College hath so carefully pursued that statute as at this time of the twelve senior fellows of that house eleven are of Norfolk.

(Caius Statute 48.) Secondly concerning the said Master's refusing to be judged by visitors, it appeareth that the statute on that behalf requires that where the Master and the major part of the twelve senior fellows shall dissent in opinion touching the interpretation of any statute they shall repair to the visitors, but the Master and the major part being *capitulariter congregati* adjudged (as appears under the hands of the said Master and nine of the said fellows) that Mr Cooke's fellowship and benefice were incompatible by statute, which bound up the Master so as he could not without manifest breach of that statute repair to the visitors [as] Mr Cooke required.

7 *I.e.*, counties.

And thirdly where the said Master is charged to have wronged the petitioner in his own particular, we find his proceeding against the petitioner to have been with great equity and moderation, and that in all the said three particulars the Master hath been unjustly charged and is very innocent. And as we find just cause utterly to dislike the very frame of the said petition, and likewise the petitioner's ingratitude and boldness therein, laying heavy scandals on the Master of the said College who hath formerly been his tutor, and from whom the petitioner could not deny but to have received particular courtesies; so we were not well satisfied with the petitioner's carriage and behaviour at our hearing of this business, insomuch as if he had not been put out of his fellowship we should have enjoined him to have made a public submission to the Master in the said College.

But whereas the petitioner took occasion by the generality of the charge laid down in his petition to ravel into sundry particulars, accusing the said Master with the breach of divers statutes of that College, we cannot free the Master altogether, but find he hath been in some measure to blame in something, albeit not wilfully or singularly faulty in any material particular, but only where the steps of some of his latter predecessors misled him. And albeit we find many of the particular breaches of statute objected by Mr Cooke to be trivial; yet upon examination of them, we have made some observations which we have made it our humble duty to offer to your Majesty's consideration, to take such order for reforming of the same as in your Majesty's wisdom you shall think fit.

1. (Caius Statute 31.) That the Master may be enjoined yearly to appoint a president, albeit their statute doth not expressly so direct it.
2. That the junior fellows of the foundations of Frankland Perse or any other, present or that hereafter may be of the said College, may be sworn as well as the seniors, but not enjoy more profits or privilege of voice and suffrage, or any thing else by reason of that their oath than they do at this present, until they shall be chosen and admitted to be seniors. And for this purpose that your Majesty would be graciously pleased to give authority to the said Master to administer the said oath, which we doubt whether he hath now power to do.
3. That no lease *de futuro* be made by the said College, of any impropriation, for longer then five or ten yeares at the most, according to the Statute of Caius 86; and that the leases already made in that kind (however these stand good for the present yet) that they be not renewed hereafter for any estate above ten years.
4. (Caius Statute 93.) That the Master and fellows may be enjoined, after the expiration of the present leases made of their lands, not to renew the same or let any other to any person or persons contrary to the statute of the College so to do.
5. That they take good bonds of their tenants to whom they grant leases, obliging them or their under-tenants, (which are to be allowed by the

consent of the Master and fellows in writing) to reside on the land they hold of the said College; unless it be in cases where otherwise the statute gives way.[8]

6. That they may be enjoined to see that three several books be hereafter exactly kept; the one for accounts, containing the expenses of the house; a second a register of all the leases and grants, and other like acts made by the Master and fellows of their lands etc.; and a third containing the Annals of the most memorable acts and accidents of and in the said College; which two last books are to be written by the register there, as the statute on that behalf directs.[9] And whereas there hath been a neglect in keeping of the third book ever since 1603, that they see that due care be taken to draw down the Annals from that time to this present, as well as may be possible, and so to continue the same henceforth from time to time.

All which we humbly submit to your Majesty's Royal consideration.

Whitehall March 1. 1635.[10]

Signed: Lord Arch-Bpp of Cant., Earle of Holland, Lord Bpp of Norwych.

Concordat cum originali.

Ed. Nicholas.

Serenissimus Rex hac accepta informatione presentem litem finaliter diremit, ac in posterum summa cum gratia prospexit Collegii commodo regia hac sua infra scripta ordinatione.

[On receipt of this communication His Serene Majesty terminated the action and looked forward with pleasure to the good ordering of the College in the future in his words written below.][11]

8 The reference is presumably to Statute 90, though an obligation to reside on the land is not explicitly stated.

9 Statute 59.

10 According to Venn, *B.H.* III, p. 87, the committee reported on 11 March 1635/6, not 1 March. Despite the committee's animadversions on his conduct, Cooke appears to have sought a fresh enquiry from Archbishop Laud on the grounds that the president of the college had three valedictory years ('years of grace'), that as the actual senior fellow he was *ipso facto* the president, and that as such he had three years to enjoy his benefice rather than the statutory one year. All he received for his pains was an even more severe rebuke in the royal order that followed. (His claim that a president had three valedictory years was no doubt based on Elizabeth's 1570 University Statutes: c. 50, s. 26.)

11 The decree was copied in full into the "Book of Statutes", *i.e.* Dr Caius' original copy (MS 711/756, at p. 122). The fact that the royal order was transcribed into the "Book of Statutes" indicates the importance and binding effect accorded to it by the college. The royal order repeats in effect the recommendations of the commissioners above and adds a strong rebuke to Cooke for wasting His Majesty's time. It was also recorded in the *Acta* for 1636: *Acta* (1629–42).

VII. H

London's Case (1638)

[Venn, *Annals* (1904), pp. 399–405]

[NOTE: The spelling of the English texts has been modernised here and a translation appended to the Latin passages in the Annals. The case is principally of interest for the light it throws on the reasoning by which the Master and senior fellows justified the introduction of dividends in respect of fines on leases in defiance of Caius' strict direction in his Statutes. See "*Dividends*", § VI. 5 above.]

Anno 1638

Aprilis 14, 1638. Richardo London Norfolciensi artium magistro, collegio socio, et Medicinae studioso, concordi consensus Custodis et sociorum data est copia absentandi se, et studendi in transmarinis regionibus, sub iisdem conditionibus quibus per statuta cautum est, is, 26to Aprilis tactis evangeliis, juramentum suscepit, se studio tantum Medicinae alienas regiones velle invisere, reipublicae Brittanicae ac Collegii nostri honori consulere et consulturum. Quo juramento prestito, ut literas habeat testimoniales veniae absentandi se in regionibus transmarinis sub communi sigillo concessum erat. Insuper testimonio gradus, vitae, morum, et conversationis, eum honestavimus, scriptoque commune sigillum apponi fecimus; atque ex abundanti subscriptis Custodis et sociorum nominibus. His ita peractis, de emolumentis, tempore absentiae percipiendis ex sodalitio, coepit contendere, eaque de re Cancellarium Academiae petitione exhibita compellavit, cujus facti certiores nos fecit honoratissimus Dominus his infra scriptis literis.

[14 April 1638. The opportunity of absence and study overseas is given to Richard London, M.A., a Norfolkman, fellow of the college and student of medicine, with the agreed consent of the keeper and fellows on the conditions required by the statutes. On April 26th he took an oath with his hand on the Gospels that he wished to visit foreign lands solely for the study of medicine and that he was mindful of the honour of the British state and our college and would

continue to be so.[1] When he had taken the oath, he was granted certificates under the common seal excusing him from the offence of absenting himself overseas. We have further attested to his degree, character, morals and mode of life,[2] and have appended the common seal to this document; and for further assurance the names of the keeper and fellows have been subscribed. After this had been done, he started to claim emoluments from the society arising during the time of his absence, and urged the claim upon the Chancellor by submitting a petition, which the most honourable Lord brought to our attention in the letter below.]

After my very hearty commendations I understand by the petition of Mr Richard London one of the senior fellows of your Society, that according to the indulgence of your statutes to the study and professors of Physic, you have given him leave to travel, but withal refused him such allowances as by the same statute he conceiveth that he ought to have for his sustentation abroad. His address thereupon and request to me will best appear to you in his own papers, which I send you here enclosed for that purpose, desiring you if you find reason in them to make his contentment your own favour to him, especially in a case wherein his industry seemeth to deserve respect, or otherwise so to inform me in the business, as I may be able to make him such answer as is fitting, and so I rest

Your assured friend
Henr. Holland.

Greenwich
5 June 1638.

Inclusae chartae tales erant.

[The following documents were enclosed.]

To the Right Honourable Henry Earl of Holland one of his Majesty's most honourable privy council, and Chancellor of the University of Cambridge.

The humble petition of Richard London, master of arts, and one of the senior fellows of Gonvile and Caius College in the aforesaid University:

Humbly sheweth,

That whereas by a local statute of the said College, leave is given to the students of Physic only to travel beyond the seas for the study of Physic and the advancement of Learning in that profession, and whereto the petitioner by his fellowship (founded by Dr Caius) is bound by statute to apply himself and

[1] Cf. Statute 54.

[2] *Conversatio*: medieval meaning.

according to the statute hath lately obtained three years' leave of the said society with their joint consent under their College seal so to do, yet your petitioner is denied by the Master and many of the fellows such means and emoluments as by good advice upon statute he justly conceived to appertain to his fellowship in the said College, whereby he is made altogether unable to defray the charges of his journey and maintain himself in transmarine universities, as Padua, Bononia,[3] Montpelier, Paris, etc., mentioned in statute by our learned founder Dr Caius.

So that your Petitioner cannot fulfil that statute to his own benefit, the good of others, or the honour of the said College, as by oath he is obliged, and further it is the constant custom of all other Colleges (so far as he can learn) in Cambridge and Oxford to allow all dividends to travellers of this nature.

Your Petitioner therefore most humbly begs assistance from your honour herein, beseeching your Lordship of your honourable goodness and wisdom, to require of the said Master and fellows, in writing, or demand from them some sufficient reasons to the contrary, why all such dividends (not excepted by express statute whereunto your petitioner willingly submitteth himself) should not be allowed him towards his necessary expenses in travel as to any other actually present in the said College.

And your petitioner as in duty bound shall daily pray for your honours health etc.

To the Right Honourable Henry Earl of Holland, one of his Majesty's most honourable Privy Council and Chancellor of the University of Cambridge.

The humble petition of Richard London master of arts and fellow of Gonvile-Caius College in the University of Cambridge.

Having lately exhibited to your Lordship the ground of his complaint, with the inconveniences that must ensue to the students in Physic in that College, etc., and because some doubts may arise from these queries following, your petitioner most humbly prayeth your honour to desire the Master and fellows of the said College, to these and every of these to answer expressly to your honour in writing, that by this means your Lordship may truly judge how just the motives are of your petitioner's complaint, who desires no further favour from your Lordship herein then the justice and merits of his cause deserveth.

1. Whether by the word *dividendis* in the 54 statute of Dr Caius, bee meant that all dividends arising since the making thereof, as corn money, and many other dividends, should go to the use of the College or not.
2. Whether Richard London, fellow of Gonville and Caius Colledg, hath right to all dividends as any other fellow being present in the College.

[3] Bologna.

3. Whether they have any express statute (having given him leave to travel under the College Seal) to take away his corn rents and other dividends, or not.
4. Whether they have any custom against that particular statute, of Dr Caius 54, to deprive him of his dividends above mentioned.
5. Whether you have any convincing reasons to deny him those his rights and profits without which the statute is likely never to be put in execution.

Acceptis Cancellarii literis una cum inclusis chartis modo memoratis, protinus Custos et socii iis tale expediunt responsum.

[Having received the letter of the Chancellor with the accompanying documents set out above, the keeper and fellows forthwith sent the following reply.]

Right Honourable and our most Noble Lord.

In all humble obedience unto your Lordship's pleasure we here make tender of our answer unto the complaint of Mr London, and by these our particular replies unto his several queries (which is the way he desireth your Lordship to prescribe unto us) we hope not only to clear ourselves unto your Lordship's justice, but also to quiet him, if his aim be not more to molest us then to satisfy himself; if notwithstanding these our endeavours he shall still seem confident of his pretended right, it is our humble petition unto your Lordship to refer him (so soon as we shall actually detain whatever he may pretend herein due to him) and us to your Vice Chancellor's consistory, a court of justice and equity. And least he should pretend that therein we seek the advantage of his absence before he goeth (if his hast to foreign parts be such as that he cannot stay), he may sufficiently instruct his deputy and proctor. We are humbly bold to crave this at your Lordship's hands, because otherwise we fear the prosecution may prove both chargeable to the College and troublesome to our occasions. We were taught by late experience[4] how much disquiet one man's wilfulness may bring upon a whole society, the quieting of which puts us in mind of that never to be forgotten favour we then received from your Honour, which shall oblige us ever to remain

Your Lordship's most humble servants

Thomas Batchcroft[5]
Tho. Gostlin, Edw. Salter, Wm Moore, Hen. Glisson, Willm Blancks, Robt Pickarell, Jos. Loveland, Jo. Rant.[6]
From Gonvile-Caius College in Cambridge, June 19, 1638.

4 Clearly a reference to *Cooke's Case* two years earlier: see Appendix G above.

5 *B.H.* I, p. 139.

6 *Ibid.*, pp. 189, 249, 192, 272, 204, 265, 243 and 276.

To the Right Honourable the Earl of Holland the most careful Chauncellor of the University of Cambridge.

The reply and answer to Mr London's queries.

1. To the first, we answer that we conceive that the dividends specified in the 54 statute were only such as were in use in the time of Dr Caius, because he could not foresee what dividends might after arise, nor the reasons which might justly cause different proportion of division between the discontinuers and others that were resident.
2. To the second we answer that Mr Rich. London, while he is resident in the College, hath right to all dividends as other fellows have and always have received the same, and have moreover had his share with the present fellows of all those dividends which the absent lost, according to the custom of our College since corn money came in esse.
3. To the third we answer, the dividends in use in Dr Caius his time are debarred him by the express statute 54, and for the dividend of corn money which arose since, it being by the statute of the land ordered to be expended for the relief of the commons and diet in the College, whereof none absent can partake, we conceive that ground to have been sufficient for our predecessors at first to have founded that our custom upon, as also for us to continue the same, we being forbidden by statute of the College to alter the same manner of defraying of our diet and commons as was left us by Dr Caius, and before his time practised in our College.
4. To the fourth we answer that we have a custom to deprive all absent men, though upon as necessary occasions as he can pretend in this case of his travel, which custom is neither against that particular, or any other statute.

   And further for our parts we conceive no such absolute necessity of his travelling, which may be a privilege to him more than any other, and for the equity of the custom, it was lately approved by your Lordship and the rest of the Honourable referees deputed by his Majesty in Mr Cooke's case.
5. To the fifth we answer (1) that we conceive it as reasonable to deny him this dividend as to deprive others being absent upon as great if not greater necessity. Secondly we have reason to maintain this our custom so long practised, and lately approved by your Lordship. Thirdly we have enquired of the practice of some other Colleges, and do find that such as have leave to travel lose as much as other absent men, either in their corn-money or something equivalent to it according to their several customs. And for that clause [that without he may have his pretended dividend the statute is never like to be put in execution] we say that the statute is only permissive and not obligatory or commanding, and yet this indulgence of statute may very likely be put in execution by such as have both means and will to travel without desire of infringing our ancient customs or entrenching upon the rights and dues of such, as are necessarily constrained to attend upon the service and government of the College.

Huic nostrae responsioni nihil regerit Mr London, unde Magister Pickarell, quem constituimus causae nostrae actorem et sollicitatorem, domum dimittitur, Cancellario nostram responsionem approbante, sicut Henricus Lucas, qui ei a manu erat, hisce ad nos datis literis testabatur.

[Mr London did not respond to our reply, whereupon Master Pickarell,[7] whom we had appointed as our agent and solicitor, was sent home, since the Chancellor had approved our reply, as Henry Lucas who was his amanuensis testifies in this letter sent to us.]

Sir,

My Lord hath received and perused upon your answer to his Lordship's letters, and Mr London's petitions and queries. But he appearing not, to make any reply thereunto, Mr Pickarell is dismissed of any further attendance here, having received from my Lord his own expressions of accepting in very good part the respects and readiness of your answer. And for ought I can see in the business upon this issue you have driven it to, you are not likely to be any further troubled therein, unless Mr London think so well of his pretended right to pursue it in Mr Vice Chancellor's Court whither in that case you have invited him. Howsoever I pray believe I shall be always ready according to my weakness to serve the College and yourself as being

Your very affectionate and humble Servant

Henry Lucas St Martins Lane 21 June 1638.

To the Reverend and my much honoured friend Mr Dr Bachcroft Mr of Gonvile-Caius College in Cambridge.[8]

7 One of the senior fellows who had signed the college's response above.

8 London appears not to have pursued his claim further. It is not known whether he did in fact go abroad to study.

VII. I

Submissions on the Norfolk Preference

[NOTE: These resolutions recorded in the *Gesta* bear witness to the strength of feeling that the Norfolk preference engendered in the decade preceding the repeal of Dr Caius' statutes in 1860. The first paper shows how greatly the balance had turned against the preference by 1850: it was signed by all the members of the college's governing body except the aged Master (Benedict Chapman) and his president. The second reveals the strained relations between fellows which were engendered by the preference at precisely the time when the college elected the first Master who was not a Norfolkman (Edwin Guest). The third paper records the very strong reaction to that election among former fellows. See "*The Norfolk Preference*" and "*Stipends*", §§ VI. 3 and 4 above. Asterisks have been added here to indicate those signatories who were born in Norfolk.]

C.O.5 of 26 June 1850

To place in the Treasury a paper signed by all present, except the Master and President, and to enter a copy of it in the Gesta; the following is the copy.

"Gonville and Caius College, Cambridge, June 26, 1850.

We the undersigned Fellows bind ourselves in electing College and University officers and in presenting to Livings not to consider that an election to a Senior Fellowship, confined to the county of Norfolk or diocese of Norwich, gives to the holder of such Fellowship any claim in preference to Fellows of prior standing as Fellows (whether Senior or Junior) in the College.

G. Budd, E. Guest, C. Eyres, W.J. Johnson, John Tozer, J.T. Walker[1]

[1] *B.H.* II, pp. 205, 174, 202, 217, 217, 225.

And we the undersigned Fellows bind ourselves to the foregoing resolution, saving the presumed claims of all present Fellows of the College.

G.E. Paget,* W.H. Stokes, C. Clayton, J.R. Crowfoot, W.H. Drosier*[2]"

C.O.21 of 22 November 1852

To allow the following to be placed among the Gesta.

"We, the undersigned possessors of Senior Fellowships restricted to natives of Norfolk, voluntarily engage ourselves to forego precedence in Hall, Chapel & Combination Room over those of prior standing in the College, who shall have been admitted into the Seniority at a later period than ourselves: on the clear understanding that we reserve our supposed claims to offices and livings in the order of our election into the Seniority, and according to the heretofore established practice of the College.

Nov 22nd 1852 William R. Collett,* Alfred G. Day*[3]"

C.O.2 of 21 May 1853

To take into consideration at the next ordinary meeting the following Communication.

"The Undersigned desire to submit to the governing Body of Gonville and Caius College the following remonstrance and suggestion respecting the recent election to the Mastership and in so doing they consider that their former position as Fellows of the College, their knowledge of the Statutes and Customs, and their attachment to the College as well as desire for its welfare gives them a claim to attention.

They beg to state that their conviction has always been, and is, that the Mastership of the College is, by the plain grammatical sense of the Statutes, confined to the Norwich Diocese, so long as any properly qualified candidates born within that diocese are to be found. – In support of this opinion they refer particularly to Caius' Stat. (4) "*Qualis debet esse Custos*", and to his Statute (8), "*De electione Custodis*", which seem to be based on Bateman's Statute (3), "*De tempore et electionis forma*".

2 *Ibid.*, pp. 202, 194, 218, 234, 233.

3 *Ibid.*, pp. 254, 262. Unless it is restricted to presiding, this implies that the fellows sat in order of seniority in Hall at that time. In contrast to some other colleges, the practice had ceased in Caius by the Second World War (apart from presiding).

That this has been the contemporaneous interpretation, "*fortissima in lege*"[4] according to Lord Coke, and indeed the only interpretation hitherto given to the Statutes, is clear from the fact that although fourteen Masters have been appointed since Caius' time, all, with the exception of one only, Wm Dell, who was forced upon the College in the time of the Commonwealth, have been natives of Norwich Diocese.

That any doubt, if it can be said to exist, whether Dr Caius had the right to impose this restriction by his Statutes cannot affect this matter. For it is not open to those who have voluntarily undertaken upon oath to obey Statutes, to dispute the authority of those who made them, and this question, if it be a question of interpretation, is one proper only for the Visitor, both according to the Statute of Caius (107) "*De contradictione Statutorum Reverendi Patris et nostri*", which provides for it, and according to the general law and practice in all such cases. If it be sought upon this special occasion to dispense with the Statute itself, there is the alternative of applying to the Crown for a dispensation:–

That they are willing to allow it would have been for the interest of the College had the Statutes permitted an unrestricted choice, but they must submit that it is neither right, nor in any sense expedient, that the advantage should be attained in a manner subversive of correct principles, and bringing into hazard all the rights of Colleges and of the University itself, which depend on a sincere and true adherence to the Statutes and Customs by which they are governed:

That they disclaim any intention to disturb the choice of the majority of the Fellows, but having the honour & interests of the college deeply at heart, they suggest to the governing body that they should either refer to the Visitor,[5] the question or apply to the Crown for a dispensation thereby giving the sanction of law to the Election of a person not born in the Norwich diocese."

"The foregoing statement is affirmed and signed by

E.H. Alderson,* S.H. Alderson,* C. Porter, J.J. Smith, H.S. Pinder, G.E. Paget,* J.R. Crowfoot, H. Goodwin*[6]

May 1853"

4 Signatories' emphasis.

5 *Sic* MS.

6 *Ibid.*, pp. 144, 145,164, 189, 186, 202, 218, 234.

VII. J

The Government of the College: Statutes 1860–1926

1860 Statutes

C.—OF THE GOVERNMENT OF THE COLLEGE.

Statute 4.

The Government of the College shall be in the hands of the Master and the twelve Senior Fellows, who shall be called the Master and Seniors. A meeting of the Master and Seniors shall be called a College Meeting, and the orders of such a meeting shall be called College Orders. No business shall be transacted at any such meeting unless the Master and at least six Seniors are present. Voting shall begin with the Junior Fellow present, and go on in the inverse order of precedence. …

Statute 6.

The Election of Fellows shall take place on such day or days in every year as shall be appointed from time to time by the Master and Seniors.

All vacancies occurring in the Fellowships of the College shall be filled up at the latest within one year from the occurrence of the vacancy.

The Fellows shall be chosen from among Graduates of the College, or, if the Master and Seniors shall at any time think fit, of the University, who have distinguished themselves in the studies of the University, or in some department of science, learning, or art.

The Fellows shall be elected by the Master and Seniors at a College Meeting, and they shall choose that person (being otherwise duly qualified according to these Statutes) whom they shall think to be of the greatest merit, and most fit to be a Fellow of the College, as a place of religion, learning, and education.

The Master shall be always present at the election, unless prevented by urgent cause, …

Every Fellow so elected shall within thirty days after his election or appointment make in the College Chapel, and in the presence of the Master and the Registrary, the following declaration: "I, A.B. do solemnly declare, that I am *bona fide* a member of the Church of England, and I do sincerely promise that I will discharge the duties of a Fellow of Gonville & Caius College to the best of my judgment and ability;" on which he shall become a Fellow of the College.

On the occurrence of a vacancy in the Seniority, the place shall be filled up at the next College Meeting following such vacancy. The Fellow who may then be first on the Roll of Fellows shall be elected, unless in the judgment of the Master and Seniors there shall be good cause to the contrary, and in that case, the Fellow next in order on the Roll shall be so elected, and so on in succession. The election shall be decided by such votes as are required for a College Order.

Every Fellow on becoming a Senior shall, before proceeding to act in that capacity, make in the College Chapel, and in the presence of the Master and Registrary, the following declaration: "I, A.B. do solemnly declare, that I am *bona fide* a member of the Church of England, and I do sincerely promise that in addition to the duties of a Fellow of Gonville & Caius College, I will discharge the duties of a Senior to the best of my judgment and ability;" on which he shall become a Senior.

1882 Statutes

THE GOVERNING BODY.

Statute 3.

(1) The Governing Body shall consist of the Master and twelve Fellows and it shall (subject as herein-after provided) have the control and management of all the affairs of the College.

(2) The Fellows who shall be members of the Governing Body shall (subject to the provisions herein-after contained) be the Fellows comprised in the three following classes respectively; that is to say:

First. Such of the Fellows who shall be or become Seniors within the meaning of the previously existing Statutes of the College as shall not by writing under their or his hands or hand have at any time signified to the Master their or his renunciation of the office of membership of the Governing Body.

Secondly. The other resident Fellows (as herein-after defined) of the standing of Master of Arts or of some equivalent or higher degree in order (subject to the provisions hereinafter contained as to a Vice-Master) of their seniority as Fellows to a number not exceeding together with the

resident Fellows of the preceding class eight in all or together with the whole of that class twelve in all; provided that the number of members in this class shall never exceed eight.

Thirdly. So many other Fellows to be elected and to hold office as herein-after provided (herein-after called Elected Members) as shall be sufficient to make up together with the members of the preceding classes twelve members in all; provided however that no Elected Member shall during the period for which he shall have been elected be extruded from office by reason of any change in the resident Fellows; but in the event of any such change which would but for this provision have the effect of increasing the number of members of the second class the number of that class shall so long as necessary for giving effect to the foregoing provision remain correspondingly less than it otherwise would have been.

…

(6) It shall not be competent to any member of the Governing Body other than a member of the first class to resign his office except with the permission of the Governing Body.

…

1904 Statutes

B.—OF THE GOVERNMENT OF THE COLLEGE.

Statute 3.

3. *The Governing Body.*

(1.) The Governing Body shall consist of the Master and twelve Fellows of the standing of Master of Arts or Laws or some superior degree and it shall (subject as hereinafter provided) have the control and management of all the affairs of the College.

(2.) The Fellows who shall be members of the Governing Body shall (subject to the provisions hereinafter contained) be the Fellows comprised in the following classes respectively; that is to say:—

First. – Such Fellows elected before the ninth day of October eighteen hundred and ninety as under the Statutes repealed by these Statutes would have been entitled to be members of the Governing Body otherwise than by election.

Second. – The three Fellows other than the Senior Bursar, Senior Tutor and Senior Dean whose names stand first in order of seniority in a certain list called the Rota for membership of the Governing Body as herein-after defined.

Third. – Six Fellows not otherwise entitled to membership of the Governing Body to be elected from time to time as vacancies occur by a General Meeting under Statute 5 to hold office for any period not exceeding three and a half years provided that any elected member who having been qualified to attend all meetings of the Governing Body during the whole of one year ending the thirtieth day of September has not attended at least two-thirds of the ordinary meetings in that year shall then cease to be a member but may be re-elected.

Fourth. – The Senior Bursar the Senior Tutor the Dean taken in this order for the purpose of the proviso hereinafter stated. If one or more of these officers be not among the Fellows the place or places left vacant shall be filled up for the time being by appointment of the Governing Body.

Provided that a member of the fourth class shall be entitled by virtue of his office to membership of the Governing Body only if the number of twelve Fellows is not complete without him and that if the number of Fellows in the first and second classes taken together shall exceed six there shall be only so many elected members as shall be necessary to make the number of the Governing Body up to twelve without the Master.

(3.) If any elected Member of the Governing Body shall during his tenure of office as such become qualified to be a member of the Governing Body in any other way than by election he shall thereupon *ipso facto* cease to be an elected Member.

(4.) It shall not be competent to any member of the Governing Body other than a member by seniority to resign his place except with the permission of the Governing Body. Any member of the Governing Body by seniority may resign his place and thereupon his name shall be removed from the Rota for membership of the Governing Body by seniority, and it shall not at any time be replaced except by vote of a General Meeting.

…

1926 Statutes

STATUTE 3. THE COLLEGE COUNCIL

(1) The College Council (which expression shall when the context so demands be deemed to include the former Governing Body of the College as defined in any Statutes of the College previously in force) shall consist of the Master and twelve Fellows being members of the Senate of the University and it shall (subject as hereinafter provided) have the control and management of all the affairs of the College.

(2) The fellows who shall be members of the College Council shall (subject to the provisions hereinafter contained) be the Fellows comprised in the following classes respectively; that is to say:

First: – Each Fellow elected before the ninth day of October eighteen hundred and ninety who under the Statutes repealed by these Statutes would have been entitled to be a member of the College Council otherwise than by election and who has not signified by writing under his hand delivered to the Master his desire to resign his membership of the College Council.

Second: – The Senior Bursar and the Senior Tutor.

Third: – So many Fellows not otherwise entitled to membership of the College Council as shall be necessary to make a total number of Twelve to be elected as vacancies occur by a General Meeting summoned under Statute 5 and to hold office for some period not exceeding four years provided that any elected member who having been qualified to attend all meetings of the College Council during the whole of one year ending the thirtieth day of September has been absent from one-third of the ordinary meetings in that year shall then cease to be a member but may be re-elected. Provided that if an elected member shall cease to be a member otherwise than by expiration of the period for which he was elected the member elected to fill the vacancy shall hold office for the time only for which the member to whose place he succeeds would have held it if no such vacancy had taken place but so that he may be re-elected.

(3) If any elected member of the College Council shall during his tenure of office as such become qualified to be a member of the College Council in any other way than by election he shall thereupon ipso facto cease to be an elected Member.

(4) Except as hereinbefore in this Statute provided it shall not be competent for any member of the College Council to resign his place except with the permission of the College Council.

...

Index